INSTRUCTOR'S RESOURCE GUIDE

Leon Khalsa
Pierce College

to accompany

Psychology in Action

Fifth Edition

Karen Huffman
Palomar College

Mark Vernoy
Palomar College

Judith Vernoy

John Wiley & Sons, Inc.
New York • Chichester • Weinheim • Brisbane • Singapore • Toronto

Cover Image: "Human Achievement" by Tsing-Fran Chen, Lucia Gallery, NY/SuperStock, Inc.

To order books or for customer service call 1-800-CALL-WILEY (225-5945).

ISBN 0-471-35475-9

Printed in the United States of America

10 9 8 7 6 5 4 3 2 1

Printed and bound by Bradford & Bigelow, Inc.

CONTENTS

PREFACE

Dear Professor:

The purpose of this Instructor's Resource Guide is to powerfully support your teaching of **Psychology in Action**, 5th edition. We offer you a wide selection of tools closely coordinated with the unique features of the textbook. Since the field reviews of the 4th edition of this manual have been highly positive we retained most of its time proven tools. We did change the organization of the chapters to make them more immediately accessible for busy professors. The chapters are now visually organized by icons. New features are designed to reach students with diverse learning styles. We added an emphasis on brain based learning, the 7 *Intelligences* approach, and student success in the classroom and in life. The primary goal of promoting active learning has been retained.

If you review the preface to the text, you'll note a long list of special in-text learning aids (e.g., running glossary, learning checks, SQ4R format, "Try This Yourself" demonstrations, "Active Learning Exercises") and a wide array of ancillaries (e.g., Student Study Guide, Test Bank, Instructor's Manual, Video Modules, Videodisk, CD-ROM CyberPsych, Electronic Study Guide, Handbook for Non-Native Speakers, and so on). The text and its ancillaries were all carefully designed to meet the needs of BOTH student and instructor.

As one part of the ancillary package, this Instructor's Manual was designed to help generate student enthusiasm in the classroom, while also enhancing the effectiveness of the text. Based on our own classroom experience, and in coordination with the active learning focus and SQ4R method of the text, we chose to include the following features for each chapter (notations indicate which sections are new to the 5th edition):

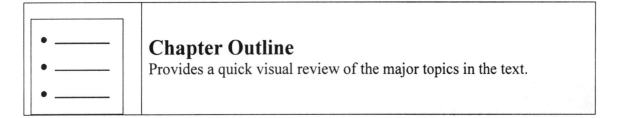

Chapter Outline
Provides a quick visual review of the major topics in the text.

Learning Objectives
Highlights the major concepts to be learned by the student.

Chapter Summary/Lecture Organizer

Presents a brief overview of the chapter, which helps to refresh your memory on specific details and to better organize your lectures.

Teaching Resources

This section organizes all the teaching tools offered by chapter section. It integrates learning objectives, activities, lecture lead-ins, lecture extenders, discussion questions, and so on.

Lecture Lead-Ins

Provide questions, topics, and brief exercises useful for introducing your lectures.

Lecture Extender

Presents an interesting, referenced summary of an important subject, extending or going into greater depth than the text.

Key Terms

Offers a chance to quickly check all boldfaced, page-referenced terms.

Discussion Questions
Help stimulate student participation and discussion.

Web Sites
New for the 5th edition, this section offers additional web-based resources for learning and teaching the material in this chapter.

Suggested Films and Videos
Award-winning, up-to-date films and videos are suggested as possible enhancements to lectures and discussions.

Books for Success
Helps students successfully apply psychology in their own lives. A *new* section for this edition.

Active Learning Section
Active learning exercises tied to specific chapter content. These activities include student self-tests, demonstrations, role-playing ideas, detailed suggestions for discussion, small-group exercises, and a variety of other activities.

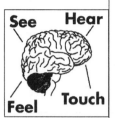

Brain-Based Learning

A *new* section for this edition. These are active learning exercises which engage the senses. Using an experiential learning approach they encourage students to see, feel, listen, move or draw.

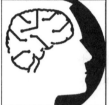

Critical Thinking Exercises

Help stimulate and develop critical thinking skills. Each chapter of the text, student study guide, and this instructor's manual offers specific critical thinking exercises that were developed to build skills related to the 21 elements of critical thinking.

Gender and Cultural Diversity Activity

Provides opportunities to build student awareness and increased sensitivity to gender and cultural diversity.

Writing Project

Helps improve student writing skills and responds to the call for increased "writing across the curriculum."

Circle Of Quality

A new section for this edition. It asks you, the reader, to help make the *next* edition of this Instructor's Resource Guide an even better tool based on your user tested feedback.

Mind Maps

A *new* section for this edition. The Mind Map offers a visual representation of the chapter content.

In addition to each of the chapter-specific features, we also have an appendix:

Appendix A: Teacher Resources
This section includes a list of film and video suppliers and resources for the instructor.

Due to space considerations the information contained in the previous edition's Appendix A – "Master Handouts" has been moved to the web. Should you misplace a handout from any chapter in this book you can now download the information from our publisher's website for this book at www.wiley.com/college/wave/huffman-vernoy5e.

NEW FEATURES OF THE 5TH EDITION

Here is a more detailed explanation of the purpose and scope of the newly added sections:

BRAIN-BASED LEARNING ACTIVITIES

The typical college classroom appeals primarily to only two of Dr. Howard Gardner's seven intelligences – the logical-mathematical and the linguistic. Given the much greater diversity of learners we find in our classrooms today, this section consciously aims at presenting abstract concepts in a sensory rich and attention engaging manner. Wherever possible I have tried to add activities that allow students to feel, see, move, or do. Our brains are not idea-based computing machines but emotion and meaning driven association networks. They thrive on rich, multi-sensory and context connected input. Too often our classroom activities violate what we know about optimum brain functioning as psychologists.

NOTE: Not all of these activities will fit into every classroom. Moreover, the sometimes unconventional quality of these activities may not be comfortable for every teacher or may seem too simplistic for a college or university setting. The web site associated with the textbook (http://www.wiley.com/college/huffman/ques5.html) refers to a frequently asked question "What if I'm used to lecturing and active learning feels awkward or different?" and offers the following answer, "Almost all college instructors are modeling the type of instruction we experienced during our college years. Active learning is different, but today's students, new research in educational methods and the rapidly increasing information explosion are requiring us to adapt our techniques. Two of the best tips to overcome the newness of active learning are:

- "Mix it up", alternate brief (2-3 minutes) activities with longer activities (10-50 minutes), and alternate traditional lecture style with "hands on" active learning exercises.
- Do what is comfortable for you. Start small and "shape" your new behavior. Remember: active learning exists on a continuum!
- Frequently remind yourself of the benefits of active learning:
1. Increased attendance and retention of students
2. Increased attentiveness, preparation, & participation of students
3. Improved class "climate" (e.g., friendlier, more interactive)
4. Increased critical thinking
5. Higher student evaluations of both teacher & class
6. More learning & retention of knowledge"

A lot of excellent resource material has now become available to educators interested in brain based learning. I especially recommend the following:

Caine, G. & Caine, R. (1997). **Unleashing the Power of Perceptual Change : The Potential of Brain-Based Teaching.** Alexandria: Association for Supervision and Curriculum Development.

Caine, G., Caine, R. & Crowell S. (1994). **Mindshifts: A Brain-Based Process for Restructuring Schools and Renewing Education.** Tuscon: Zephyr Press

Sylvester, R. (1995). **A Celebration of Neurons.** Alexandria: Association for Supervision and Curriculum Development.

MIND MAPS

Every chapter has a "Mind Map" which is aimed at presenting a visual overview of the content and structure of the chapter material. Mind maps are read from the inside out. The central theme, usually the title of the chapter, sits at the center of the map. Subordinate concepts attach on smaller branches. As you can see the mind maps present an entirely different way of organizing and summarizing the material. Initially, students will be unfamiliar with this approach. In a short time however, many will prefer this format for note taking or test preparation.

Each mind map can be used in a variety of ways:

The instructor can use mind maps
        As a transparency on the overhead - it can become the outline as you lecture on the chapter.
        To show how ideas relate to one another
        To divide tasks amongst groups of students
        To review the material for quizzes or exams

Students can use it to actively master the chapter concepts by
        Creating their own mind map of a chapter
        Adding notes, examples or smaller branches to the branches as they read the chapter
        Drawing arrows to relate concepts to one another
        Creating symbols for the main or sub branches
        Linking new key terms with the correct branch

To illustrate how mind maps can be used for review or test purposes, chapter 1 has two mind maps. One is a complete map, the other a partial map. You can create the same effect in subsequent chapters by copying the complete map and whiting out selected portions of the map which the students are then tasked to fill in. The key feature that makes mind maps so useful is that the material is not simply memorized it is integrated and learned. Active processing is the key to successful memorization and mind maps are the key to active processing.

Mind maps incorporate key principles of brain based learning. When they are created by the learner they are personal, spatial, and even kinesthetic products. They force the learner to distinguish the details from the main lessons and require critical thinking about the hierarchical organization of the chapter themes. Mind maps are idiosyncratic and reflect the eye of the beholder as well as the material. I encourage you and your students to re-arrange the maps so they work for you. Due to space and printing limitation all maps are arranged in a rectangular grid using black and white only. To see fully executed illustrations of mind maps and to understand the theory behind their effectiveness I recommend:
Buzan, Tony (1996). **The Mind Map Book.** New York: Plume/Penguin

The mind maps in this book were created using special mind mapping software called *The Mind Manager*. This product can be downloaded for free under a 30 day review policy. It can be found at http://www.mindmanager.com/english/download/index.html. With this software it is easy to customize the mind maps for your own best instructional use. I recommend this product because personally created mind maps are always much more powerful. The publisher of this expensive software product has agreed to donate fully functioning copies of the software **FOR FREE** to all users of this book. Please email him at the mindman.com web site requesting your free copy of this product. It will allow you to create you own customized mind map of any chapter in this book.

BOOKS FOR SUCCESS

Many students in our introductory courses are not psychology majors. They are often less interested in memorizing every new term or theorist. They are however interested in what knowledge or advice psychology can offer them to lead a better life. The old proverb about politicians applies equally to instructors. If we do not care for our students beyond the classroom why should they care about our field of interest? I have found it extremely impactful to bring to class my favorite how to books or resources. I let students look through these books during the breaks or will read to them an excerpt or two. The books in this section are not meant to be scholarly research references. They are meant to be accessible, practical and yet based on good science. The emphasis is on application, usefulness and an engaging writing style. Given the abundant supply of psychology/self-help books my selection is per force subjective and limited. If you have suggestions for other proven, useful books I would gratefully welcome your use of the Circle Of Quality form for submission.

The psychology I fell in love with is about healing and wisdom not just about hard scientific facts By bringing these books to the classroom we are making a powerful statement and modeling the many resources and qualities our discipline has to offer.

WEB SITES

Since the last edition of this book there has been a tremendous explosion of information available on the internet. Each chapter's web site listings presents a broad example of links. The Wiley web site associated with the text book has its own list of interactive links selected to get students involved in learning. It is at http://www.wiley.com/college/huffman/huff_ial.html . As always in cyberspace, links will go dead or become outdated faster than this print edition.

CIRCLE OF QUALITY

Quality is the result of doing, testing and improving. Quality teaching depends on regular feedback and so does quality writing. The measure of my success as a writer is the usefulness of this product to you, the end user. To help make this book even better in the next edition I am inviting all readers to provide feedback on the usefulness of these tools in your teaching environment. The one page form is designed for speed and convenience and can be e-mailed to the author at lkhalsa@pierce.ctc.edu or to Karen Huffman at KarnH@aol.com or it can be faxed to Palomar College, Behavioral Sciences Department at (760) 761-3516 or it can be mailed to Karen Huffman, Palomar College 1140 W Mission Road, San Marcos, CA 92069. Thank you for your kind attention to this request.

ACKNOWLEDGMENTS

I would like to thank the following individuals for their help in the preparation of this Instructor's Resource Guide:

- *Karen Huffman.* As a friend, mentor and colleague she has inspired me to continually improve my teaching and to put forth my ideas into this book. Throughout the writing of this manual her help, her knowledge and support have been immeasurable.

- *Wendy Hunter.* As colleague, friend and author of the accompanying Test Bank she has helped me in the difficult job of writing. She shared her excellent graphic and icon selection skills and encouraged me to persist in the face of frustrating computer problems. She also revised the learning objectives and selected the chapter heading icons.

- *J.R. Jones.* In the face of difficult deadlines he contributed to the improvement of the chapter summaries and the film/video lists.

- *Linda White.* As project coordinator, she put in countless hours of typing, revising and careful editing. She knows every one of the 1001 details that went into bringing this book to completion.

- *Linda Nelson.* For retyping the many revisions and grace for under pressure.

- *Drew Westen, Paul Wellman and Dean McKay.* Most of the website listings and descriptions are due to their diligent labor.

- *Katie Townsend-Merino* and *Sally Foster.* Both are experienced and accomplished teachers and shared their ideas for the section on Books for Success.

- *Parker Palmer.* His seminar (and excellent book) on *The Courage to Teach* was a timely influence during the writing of this book. Paradoxically, his focus on teaching beyond technique provided inspiration during the creation of many of the exercises new to this edition.

- *Michael Jetter.* As inventor of *The MindManager* software product he assisted me greatly in adjusting and transferring the chapter Mind Maps into the desk-top publishing software. A big Thank You for offering his superb product free to the readers of this book.

Thank you for adopting Psychology in Action, 5th edition. Best wishes for your teaching success!

Leon Khalsa
Pierce College, Washington

The First Day

As psychologists, we know (and teach) about the power of first impressions. Ironically, when it comes to our own teaching and the first day of class, we often find ourselves discussing reading requirements, grading policies, and college business--hardly material for a great first impression. While this information *is* important and must be discussed, the printed syllabus can be passed out at the first meeting and full discussion can be held at later meetings. For the first day, we strongly suggest the following activity:

Values Clarification--Introducing Introductory Psychology

Purpose:
- To set the stage for an interactive and critical thinking environment for the remainder of the term.
- To create a good first impression and a positive "set" toward your class and introductory psychology.
- To introduce the course and some of the major topics and chapters that you will be covering in Psychology in Action, 5th ed.
- To provide an opportunity for students to meet and interact with their peers.
- In conjunction with the text's emphasis on critical thinking, this exercise offers important practice in values clarification. To become critical thinkers, students must have insight into their personal biases, ideas, and beliefs, and the opportunity to practice expressing and defending these values.

Time: It will take approximately 50 minutes to complete this exercise.

Advance preparation:

- Before the first class meeting, you will need to make one copy for each student of the values clarification form shown at the end of this exercise.
- Make four poster size signs, printed horizontally, with the following words: *Agree, Disagree, Strongly Agree,* and *Strongly Disagree.* Before students arrive, post the four signs on the four walls of the classroom.

Instructions:

1. At the first class meeting, distribute your syllabus and tell students you will answer questions about the course at your next meeting. Then briefly introduce yourself and inform students that this session will be spent on what is known as a "values walk." Explain that introductory psychology includes numerous topics that touch on important personal values and beliefs. This exercise will help them explore their own values and will encourage a critical analysis of the reasoning behind their beliefs.

2. Begin the exercise by asking students to stand and move all desks away from the center of the room (just push them off to the sides). (If you have a large lecture hall with fixed seating or it is impractical to move the chairs, you can still ask people to move around the room—it is just a little "messier.") Once the chairs have been rearranged, ask students to stand in the middle of the room, and to leave their belongings at their desks.

3. Inform the students that this exercise has two main objectives—to get acquainted with one another and to get acquainted with the topics that they will cover in introductory psychology. If you assign active learning, critical thinking, or extra credit points in your grading, it helps to offer a few extra points for the one or two students who learn the most names while participating in this exercise.

4. Explain to students that the way this exercise is performed is as follows: You will allow them two minutes to walk around and meet (learn the names of) as many classmates as possible. At the end of the two minutes, you will call for their attention and read to them a simple, "values" statement. They should listen carefully to the statement, and then after deciding their position move to stand under the posted sign that best reflects their feelings or beliefs (e.g., strongly agree, disagree, etc.). You will then select individuals according to their raised hands and will ask them to explain to their fellow classmates why they hold their particular point of view. Ask them to begin by giving their names. (This also gives YOU a chance to learn names.)

5. Encourage students to be brief (one minute or so), and after their statement say "Thank you, _____." Then choose someone from a different position. It usually works best to choose different people to speak each time and select three or four individuals for each value statement. Once it seems that all the major points have been made, or the energy "runs down," or time runs out, stop and ask everyone to return to the center of the room.

6. At this point, instruct the students to spend another two minutes meeting others before you read the next statement. Once again, after reading the statement remind them to go to the appropriate area of the room. Repeat what you did in step 5. After approximately 30 minutes (three or four values statements), many students will have shared their opinions, most will have met most of the other students, and they will have gained an appreciation and enthusiasm for your course and topics you will be covering.

7. In the final 15 minutes, ask students to grab pens from their desks and then form a large circle. Ask them to sit on the floor, or lean against the wall, and fill out the "Values Clarification Form" (Handout 1.6). Remind them NOT to put their names on the paper—it is anonymous. Collect the forms and pass them around so that no student has his or her own paper. Starting with the statement "I learned that…," have each student read aloud what is written on the sheet. If that line is blank, the student should say "Pass." Repeat with each of the next three open-ended responses. You will find that any point you wanted to make regarding the purpose of this exercise is made by the students' written comments. In addition, you will discover that students consistently remark that they were "pleased" with the exercise and "disappointed" that the time was so short.

8. If time runs out and you can't finish step 7, have students complete the values clarification forms, collect them, and then redistribute and read from them at the next class meeting. The following meeting should also be a time for general reactions to the exercise, and a chance for students to ask questions of the instructor regarding topics in the discussion and the structure of the course.

9. In the last two minutes of the class, ask for one or two volunteers who think they have learned most or all of their classmates' names. Have them point to each student and give the name. Award the appropriate extra points.

References: This "values walk" was developed from similar exercises conducted at many Great Teachers' Seminars across the nation. It was adapted from an exercise created by Simon, Howe, and Kirschenbaum (1972). <u>Values clarification</u>, New York: Hart.

TIPS FOR SUCCESS

- Students may initially resist moving around the room. Tell them this is like a multiple-choice question—they must choose one of the four alternatives. If they say they don't like any of the choices or feel neutral, tell them they will probably encounter lots of test questions like this during the course and they must choose. It's important not to let the "neutral" or "uncooperative" students remain in their seats or in one spot.

- Set the stage for a safe, friendly learning environment where students are free to express their opinions. Encourage students to use "I" statements ("I feel," "I believe," "I think"). Remind the class that everyone comes from different backgrounds and that respect for everyone is expected. Encourage them to take turns and to listen to one another. Set specific rules, such as 1) raise one hand when you want to contribute, and 2) raise both hands if you notice a violation of the "put-down rule." The "put-down rule" is that verbal insults ("No way!" "Get Real") or nonverbal insults (rolling the eyes, hands on hips, etc.) are not allowed.

- To avoid turning this into a debate or argument, versus a values clarification and get-acquainted exercise, encourage students to move physically to another side of the room if they change their minds during the discussion. Remind them that one of the major goals of a college education and critical thinking is open-mindedness. Point out that willingness to listen to others and to change one's mind is a tremendous asset as a parent, friend, lover, etc.

- If students are repeating arguments or if one student is monopolizing the time, it helps to ask, "Does anyone have a point to make that has not yet been made?"

- Students may try to draw YOU into the debate. Resist. If they find that you have an opinion, many students will "shut down" and be less willing to participate. Explain that you will discuss many of the topics at various points in the course, and that this is a time for them to think about their own values. In addition, do not let students direct their statements or eye contact toward you. (Stand to the side of the room and look down or redirect their attention to their classmates.)

- On rare occasions, students have become upset and the debate has become uncomfortable. A great way to diffuse this problem is to tell everyone to stay where he or she is while you walk around and rearrange the signs that are posted on the wall. Reverse the positions by placing "Strongly Agree" above the group that was "Strongly disagree" and put the "Agree" sign above the group that was "Disagree." Tell them they must stay in the same position, and now they must present arguments from the opposing side. They may resist, but remind them that good debate and critical thinking requires everyone to be able to understand and articulate the opponent's position.

- Finally, be sure to go out of your way to be enthusiastic about your course, the material you will be presenting, and meeting the students. This class is perhaps your most important for the entire term. You are setting the tone and establishing the ground rules. Show your enthusiasm, and they will copy you. DO NOT be overly concerned about this list of possible problems. This exercise is GREAT! We use it every term and sometimes we repeat it three or four times in the same term, using different statements to introduce new chapters or to break up the lecture time.

SAMPLE VALUES STATEMENTS

1. Using animals for psychological research is inhumane and should be severely limited (Ch. 1).

2. Strong scientific evidence exists for extrasensory perception--ESP (Ch. 3).

3. The legal drinking age for alcohol should be 18 in all states (Ch. 4).

4. Spanking and other forms of physical punishment help develop "good" children and responsible adults (Chs. 5, 8, & 9).

5. "Only" children are more likely to have serious development problems (Chs. 8, 9, 14).

6. In almost all cases, divorce is bad for children (Chs. 8 & 9).

7. Drug-addicted mothers who give birth to drug-addicted infants are guilty of child abuse (Chs. 4, 8, & 9).

8. If I had my life to live over, I would come back as the other sex (Chs. 9 & 10).

9. Mothers of young children should not work outside the home (Chs. 9 & 10).

10. Abstinence education is the best sex education for teenagers (Chs. 9 & 10).

11. Condoms should be distributed in high schools (Chs. 9 and 10).

12. Lie detector tests can prove guilt or innocence in a criminal case (Ch. 11).

13. I would rather inherit a fortune than receive the Nobel Prize (Ch. 11).

14. I would rather have a high paying job with lots of stress than a low paying non-stressful job (Ch. 11 & 12).

15. A child's personality is generally set and unchangeable after age 5 (Ch. 13).

16. Insanity as a legal defense should be abolished (Ch. 14).

17. People who attempt suicide should be involuntarily committed to a locked psychiatric ward (Chs. 14 & 15).

18. Electroconvulsive shock therapy (ECT) should be illegal (Chs. 14 & 15).

19. Prejudice results from prejudiced parents (Chs. 5 & 16).

20. Viewing televised violence creates violent children (Chs. 5, 8, 9, & 16).

21. Most managers believe that workers are inherently lazy (Ch. 17).

SAMPLE "VALUES CLARIFICATION" FORM

--(cut here)--

I learned that ...

I was surprised that ...

I was disappointed that ...

I was pleased that ...

CHAPTER 1
INTRODUCING PSYCHOLOGY

TEXT ENHANCEMENT

DEMONSTRATIONS, EXERCISES, PROJECTS

Outline

Understanding Psychology

The Goals of Psychology
The Areas of Psychology
Psychology in Your Life

Psychological Research

Experimental Research

> **Research Highlight**
> Love on a Suspension Bridge

Non-experimental Research
Correlation versus Experimental Methods
Evaluating Research

> **Active Learning**
> Becoming a Better Consumer of
> Scientific Research

Ethics In Psychology

Research Ethics
Animals in Research
Clinical Practice Ethics

Schools of Psychology

Structuralism and Functionalism
The Psychoanalytic and Gestalt Schools
Behaviorism
Humanistic Psychology
Cognitive Psychology
Psychobiology
The Evolutionary Perspective
Cultural Psychology

> **Gender and Cultural Diversity**
> Universal and Culturally Specific
> Behaviors

Psychology Today

Tools for Student Success

GOAL

Learning Objectives

Upon completion of CHAPTER 1, the student should be able to:

1. Define psychology, and explain overt and covert behavior (pp. 4-5).
2. List and discuss the four goals of psychology, and explain the difference between basic and applied research (pp. 5-6). ·
3. List and describe the ten major areas of psychology (pp. 6-8).
4. Describe the difference between psychology and pseudopsychology (pp. 8-10).
5. Define or describe the following components related to scientific research in general: research methodology, data, variables, the study of cause and effect, theory, and hypothesis (pp. 10-13).
6. Define or describe the following components related to experimental research: independent and dependent variables, experimental and control conditions, and placebos and their effects (pp. 12-14).
7. List and describe the following possible sources of, and solutions for, bias in research: experimenter bias and the double-blind experiment; ethnocentrism and the need for multiple, culturally diverse researchers; and sample bias, including the difference between populations and samples, and the need for random assignment of participants to experimental and control conditions (pp. 14-15).
8. List and describe four possible explanations for the results of the Dutton and Aron "bridge study"(p. 16)
9. Discuss the merits and limitations of the following nonexperimental research techniques: naturalistic observation, survey, and case study (pp. 17-19).
10. Explain the difference between correlational (nonexperimental) and experimental methods of research, and describe the three ways two variables may be correlated (pp. 19-21).
11. Describe the four basic criteria used to ensure that research findings are accurate and legitimate. Define statistics, and describe the relevance of statistical significance and replication in determining the legitimacy of research results (pp. 22-23).
12. Discuss the issue of ethics in animal research, and describe the following ethical considerations for human research and clinical practice: informed consent, debriefing, deception, and client confidentiality (pp. 23-25).
13. Describe the similarities and differences between the following major schools of psychology: structuralism, functionalism, psychoanalytic, gestalt, behaviorism, humanistic, cognitive, psychobiology, and evolutionary (pp. 26-32).
14. Define culture, and describe cultural psychology and culture's influence on behavior; discuss how researchers determine whether behavior is culturally universal or culturally specific (pp. 32-34).
15. List the six perspectives in psychology today, and explain the eclectic approach which is prevalent in modern psychology (pp. 33).

Chapter Summary/Lecture Organizer

Introductory Vignette--Chapter 1 begins with a synopsis of a classic psychology experiment, by Dutton and Aron. Male subjects crossing a scary cable bridge hundreds of feet above the canyon were much more likely to call back the attractive female research assistant than subjects crossing a sturdy bridge low over the water. The experiment was designed to test the misattribution theory of emotional feelings. The results confirmed that subjects already aroused by the fear were much more likely to attribute their emotion to sexual attractiveness.
The study is one example of the type of questions psychologists ask and the methods of research they use to answer it.

I. **UNDERSTANDING PSYCHOLOGY** - Using the example of the Muller-Lyer illusion (Figure 1.1 text page 4), readers are cautioned regarding everyday misperceptions and the limits of common sense. Psychology, the scientific study of behavior, investigates overt, or observable, behaviors and covert behaviors, such as thoughts and feelings.

   A. **The Goals of Psychology** - The four goals of psychology are to (1) describe particular behaviors by careful scientific observation, (2) explain behaviors by conducting experiments to determine their causes, (3) predict when a behavior being studied will occur in the future, and (4) change inappropriate behavior or circumstances.
   Psychologists investigate behavior with basic research or applied research. Basic research is conducted to study theoretical questions without trying to solve a specific problem. It studies behavior for its own sake – simply for knowledge. Applied research, however, utilizes the principles and discoveries of psychology for practical purposes; finding solutions to real-world problems.

   B. **Areas of Psychology** - Psychologists can specialize in several areas, including clinical and counseling psychology, educational psychology, school psychology, industrial/organizational psychology, developmental psychology, social psychology, comparative psychology, neuropsychology, health psychology, and cognitive psychology. The percentage of doctorate degrees for each of these specialties is shown in Figure 1.2 (text page 8).

   C. **Psychology in Your Life** - Studying psychology offers practical solutions to everyday problems and develops an appreciation for scientific methods of research, as opposed to pseudopsychologies ("false psychologies") that pretend to discover psychological information through nonscientific or deliberately fraudulent methods.

II. **PSYCHOLOGICAL RESEARCH** - Research methodology includes experimental techniques designed to investigate cause-and-effect relationships and non-experimental techniques that provide descriptions of behavior.

A. Experimental Research - An experiment begins with a hypothesis, or possible explanation expressed as a prediction or statement of cause and effect. Independent variables are the factors the experimenter manipulates whereas the dependent variables are measurable behaviors of the participants. Experimental controls include a control condition, where participants are treated identically to participants in the experimental condition, except that the independent variable is not applied to them. In the experimental condition, all participants are exposed to the independent variable. Placebos, the placebo effect, experimenter bias, double-blind experiment, ethnocentrism, sample bias, sample population, and the problems of generalizability from college students and animals to the general population are all discussed as they relate to experimental controls. Stanley Milgram's classic study of obedience (1963, 1965, 1974) is used as an extensive example throughout this section.

B. Non-experimental Research Techniques - When it is not feasible for ethical or practical reasons to study behavior experimentally, psychologists use non-experimental techniques, such as (1) naturalistic observation - used to study behavior in its natural habitat (2) surveys - using tests, questionnaires, and interviews to sample a wide variety of behaviors and attitudes and (3) case study - an in-depth study of a single research participant.

> **Research Highlight: Love on a Suspension Bridge** – reviews 25 years of further research and theorizing on the Dutton and Aron bridge experiment.

C. Correlation versus Experimental Methods - While experiments are powerful tools for discovering the causes of behavior, non-experimental methods allow scientists to determine the correlation, or relationship, between variables. Positive, negative and zero correlations are discussed. Readers are strongly cautioned that correlation does not imply causation.

D. Evaluating Research - To judge whether research findings are significant, or due to chance, psychologists use statistics - data collected in a research study and the mathematical procedures used to analyze the data. A statistically significant relationship or difference is one that is believed to be true or real and not due merely to chance or coincidence. Replication, or re-conducting the same research study, is another way to evaluate whether research results are legitimate.

> **Active Learning/Critical Thinking: Becoming a Better Consumer of Scientific Research** - This exercise gives readers a chance to evaluate critically popular sources of information to see if they (1) confuse correlation with causation (2) lack a control group (3) display experimenter bias or (4) include sample bias.

III. **ETHICS IN PSYCHOLOGY** - Psychologists are expected to maintain high ethical standards, and the American Psychological Association (APA) has published specific guidelines detailing these standards.

A. Research Ethics - The problems of deception in experiments, such as Milgram's, and the limits of informed consent are discussed. Debriefing is discussed as a part of general research ethics and as a way of dealing with deception.

B. Animals in Research - To overcome misconceptions regarding unethical use of animals in research, readers are reminded that only 7 to 8 percent of all psychological research is done on animals, and 90 percent of that is done on rats or mice. Furthermore, most studies involve naturalistic observation or the use of rewards instead of punishment.

C. Clinical Practice Ethics - Successful psychotherapy often requires clients to reveal private thoughts and feelings, and therapists are required to uphold strict confidentiality standards and to conduct themselves in a moral and professional manner. Problems associated with radio and TV talk shows casually dispensing psychological advice are discussed.

IV. **SCHOOLS OF PSYCHOLOGY** - Psychologists have grouped together to form various schools of psychology with distinct approaches to the study of behavior.

A. Structuralism and Functionalism - Wilhelm Wundt is regarded as the founder of experimental psychology and is credited with establishing the first psychological laboratory in Leipzig, Germany in 1879. One of the chief methods of research was introspection, monitoring, and reporting on the contents of consciousness. Titchener brought Wundt's ideas to America and coined the term *structuralism*, which is now used to refer to the school of thought that focused on the sensations and feelings of perceptual experience. Feeling the need for practical applications of psychology, some psychologists turned to functionalism, the school that investigates the function of mental processes in adapting the individual to the environment. William James and John Dewey were prominent figures in this school of thought.

B. The Psychoanalytic and Gestalt Schools - Sigmund Freud's psychoanalytic theory examined psychological problems that were presumed to be caused by conflicts in the unconscious. The controversy surrounding Freud's theories is briefly discussed. Carl Jung is also a prominent figure. Gestalt psychology focuses on principles of perception, the interpretation of information from the senses. Gestaltists believe the whole experience (the gestalt) is qualitatively different from the sum of the distinct elements of that experience. The modern eclectic approach (looking at the whole person and utilizing techniques from various schools) is influenced by the gestalt school. Wertheimer, Kohler, and Koffka were prominent figures in early gestalt psychology.

C. Behaviorism - Believing that a truly scientific research method must be limited to objective, observable behaviors, the school of behaviorism was established. All behavior is viewed as a response to a stimulus. Watson, Skinner, and Thorndike were influential figures in behaviorism.

D. Humanistic Psychology - Proponents of humanistic psychology emphasize the importance of the inner, subjective self and stress the positive side of human nature. Rogers and Maslow are considered prominent figures.

E. Cognitive Psychology - A school of thought that focuses on reasoning and the mental processing of information is known as cognitive psychology. Proponents take what is called an information processing approach, that views people and computers in similar terms. Piaget, Ellis, Bandura, and Sternberg are important figures in cognitive psychology.

F. .Psychobiology - In the last few decades, psychobiology has become one of the most powerful schools of psychology. Proponents explain behavior as complex chemical and biological events within the brain. Muller, Lashley, Hubel, and Wiesel are considered prominent figures.

G. The Evolutionary Perspective - This perspective applies the theory of evolution by natural selection to human behavior. Ethology, sociobiology and evolutionary psychology are sub-disciplines of this perspective, which argues that evolutionary processes influence much of what we learn, feel, and think through interaction with environmental factors. Lorenz and Wilson are important figures in this area.

H. Cultural Psychology – It studies the influence of culture and ethnic practices on people's behavior. In a global community the search for human universals versus culture specific patterns is an increasingly important question. A leader in this field is Berry.

> **Gender and Cultural Diversity: Universal and Culturally Specific Behaviors** – Cultural psychologists conduct research to discover which behaviors are human universals and which are specific to individual cultures.

I. Psychology Today - The major "perspectives" that govern modern psychology are the psychoanalytic, behavioristic, humanistic, cognitive, biological, evolutionary, or cultural perspective. These perspectives will reappear throughout the text.

V. **TOOLS FOR SUCCESS** – This section offers well-documented tips, strategies and resources to assist students in becoming more efficient and successful.

A. Read Actively - The textbook is the major tool for success. Its special features include the Preface, Prologue, Table of Contents, Individual Chapters, Appendixes, Glossary, References, and Name/Subject Index. One of the best ways to read actively is to use the SQ4R method; the initials stand for six steps in effective reading: Survey, Question, Read, Recite, Review, and wRite.

B. Manage your Time - Set a balance between work, college and social life with four basic strategies: establish a baseline; set up a realistic activity schedule; reward yourself for good behavior; and maximize using the time you do have.

C. Improve your Grades - The four basic ways of getting better grades include: Improved Note Taking; Distributed Study Time; Overlearning; and Psyching Out the Instructor. Also, there are general test taking strategies.

D. Use Resources for Success – Don't overlook sources of support such as instructors, friends and family, and classmates and roommates.

E. Attitude - The final key to success.

Teaching Resources

SECTION I – UNDERSTANDING PSYCHOLOGY

Learning Objectives #'s 1, 2, 3, 4
Lecture Lead-Ins # 1
Lecture Extender # 1
Discussion Questions #'s 1, 4, 5, 8, 9, 10
Active Learning Activities #'s 1.1 & 1.2
Brain-Based Learning Activity #1.1
Critical Thinking Exercise #1.1
Writing Project #1.1

SECTION II – PSYCHOLOGICAL RESEARCH

Learning Objectives #'s 5, 6, 7, 8, 9, 10, 11, 12
Lecture Lead-Iins #'s 2 & 3
Discussion Questions # 3
Active Learning Activities #'s 1.3, 1.4, 1.5, 1.6, 1.7, 1.8
Brain-Based Learning Activities #'s1.2 & 1.3
Critical Thinking Exercises #'s1.2 & 1.3
Writing Project #1.1

SECTION III – ETHICS IN PSYCHOLOGY

Learning Objectives #'s 13 & 14
Discussion Questions #'s 2 & 6

SECTION IV – SCHOOLS OF PSYCHOLOGY

Learning Objectives #'s 15 & 16
Discussion Questions # 4
Active Learning Activities #'s 1.9 & 1.10
Brain-Based Learning Activities #'s 1.4 & 1.5
Gender and Cultural Diversity Activity #1.1
Writing Project #1.1

SECTION V – TOOLS FOR SUCCESS

Discussion Questions #7
Active Learning Activities # 1.11 & 1.12

Lecture Lead-Ins

1. Before you begin your lecture, ask students about their preconceived notions about psychology: Who do they think of when they hear the term "psychologist?" (They typically mention people like Frasier Crane from TV, Dr. Laura Schlessinger from radio or Sigmund Freud.) What do they think a psychologist does? (You will probably have a lot of comments centering on a clinical, counseling theme.) Use these two questions to frame your "introduction to introductory psychology." Put the following words on the board:

WHO?
WHAT?
WHEN?
WHERE?
WHY?
HOW?

You can then organize your entire lecture by answering these six questions.

WHO?   Discuss the common perception of all psychologists as being clinicians or counselors. List the *areas* of psychology (clinical and counseling, educational, school, industrial/organizational, etc.) and/or list the *schools* of psychology (structuralism, functionalism, psychoanalytic, etc.). You may want to emphasize that the MAJOR perspectives that are used today and found throughout this text are the psychoanalytic, behavioristic, humanistic, cognitive, biological, evolutionary, and cultural.

WHAT?   Define psychology - the *scientific* study of behavior (both overt and covert behavior). Emphasize the scientific foundation and how this differs from common sense. You may want to take time to ask them to complete Activity 1.1 "Myths and Misconceptions" at this point.

WHEN?   Mention 1879 as the founding of the first psychological laboratory in Leipzig, Germany by Wilhelm Wundt. It helps to mention how this laboratory was important because it established a break with philosophy, but our roots (like biology, history, and most academic subjects) are still reflected in the Ph.D. (If you like to display a little self-effacing humor, you can tell the old joke about how academics first get an A.A. degree, then a B.S., and then a Ph.D. The Ph.D. means "piled higher and deeper" while the B.S. is left to their imagination.)

WHERE?   You can mention that until recent times psychology has been focused on Western cultures. But with the increased attention to cultural psychology, we now have more interest and research being conducted on other cultures.

WHY?   Discuss the four goals of psychology - describe, explain, predict, and change behavior. If you want to break your lecture here, it works very well to have the class complete Activity 1.2 at this point. We usually save "HOW" for the next class.

HOW?   Discuss the various research methods - experimental and non-experimental.

2.   Ask students if anyone in the class smokes cigarettes; you will find someone who does. Ask this student why he/she smokes cigarettes. The answers will vary but will revolve around the theme of "because I want to," or "I am an adult, and I can make choices for myself." At this time point out that we are not allowed to use heroin, cocaine, LSD or PCP legally in the United States. Ask the question again. "Why can you smoke cigarettes?" You will now get some rather strange looks from the class. Ask the smoker to read the warning label on the back of the cigarette pack and ask the question again, "Why can you smoke cigarettes?" The suggestion on the label is that smoking causes lung cancer. Ask how the government can let a cancer causing substance be sold to the public. Use this discussion as a way to lead into your lecture on correlation and experimental methods. At the conclusion of the lecture, again ask the question. Most of the students will now understand that the research on cancer and cigarette smoking in HUMANS is only correlational. Discuss the merits and limitations of both experimental and nonexperimental (correlational) research. This leads to a natural discussion of the benefits of animal research and a tie in to the text's discussion of animal research ethics. You may want to add the latest data from the government on secondhand smoke and cancer. These data indicate that up to 17% of all cancer deaths in the United States can be attributed to secondhand smoke.

3.   To explain further the advantages and disadvantages of the experimental method, ask for volunteers for a smoking and lung cancer "experiment." Indicate that students will be randomly assigned to either the control group (no cigarettes) or the experimental group (three packs of cigarettes a day). Inform the students that the experiment will last twenty years and at the end of the experiment, you will count the number of participants who have developed lung cancer. If the incidence in the experimental group is statistically higher than in the control group, then we can say cigarette smoking causes lung cancer. Point out that TV cameras will be placed in working and living areas of both groups to determine if the experimental group smokes the three packs a day and if the control group does not smoke. Additionally, blood tests will be given daily to determine the level of nicotine in each individual's blood in order to monitor cigarette usage. Ask the students to form small groups and list all the problems associated with this hypothetical experiment. Use this list to lead into your lecture on experiments and research ethics. This is a good place to stop after your lecture and complete Activity 1.3.

Lecture Extenders

Naturalistic Observation

The naturalistic method has often been looked upon as a step-sibling to the more rigorous experimental design technique in which one can draw cause and effect conclusions. However, there are many situations in which participant-naturalistic observation reveals data that other methods are not able to tap. An excellent example of this type of research is Rosenhan's study, "On Being Sane in Insane Places." This study deals with the ability of mental health staff to accurately diagnose the presence of mental disorder in subjects who are asking for admittance to a psychiatric facility. The findings, which could serve as a plot for movie psychodramas where a "normal" person is unable to prove his/her sanity, do not make one feel confident about psychiatric expertise. The following material is based on Rosenhan's article:

Rosenhan, D. L. (1973). On Being Sane in Insane Places, Science, 179, 250-258.

In this classic study, Rosenhan's intent was to determine if it were possible to distinguish between those who "deserve" a psychiatric label and those who should be exempted from placement in a diagnostic category. He reasoned that the most logical way to measure this would be to take "normal" individuals, those who have never suffered from a serious psychiatric disorder, and have them request admittance to a mental hospital. If they were admitted, then the methods used for making this determination must be flawed.

Rosenhan recruited eight people (including himself) for this study. Their backgrounds included three psychologists, one homemaker, one pediatrician, one psychiatrist, one painter, and one graduate student. Their instructions were to call the hospital for an appointment and, upon arriving at the hospital, they were to report having heard vague voices that said "empty," "hollow," and "thud." Except for this one symptom (auditory hallucinations), they were told to act in a normal fashion, and after admission, to say the voices had disappeared. All questions relative to significant background events, such as family and important childhood events, were to be answered truthfully. The only information to be withheld was their true identity (to prevent the attachment of a permanent psychiatric label to their names), and if they were employed in the mental health profession, to give a false occupation to eliminate the possibility of special treatment. *All pseudopatients were admitted, seven with a diagnosis of schizophrenia.*

Many factors could have led to an error in diagnosis during admission. The pseudopatient indicated the presence of voices (looked upon by many as a first-rank symptom of schizophrenia), the pseudopatients were "nervous" during their initial contact with a psychiatric hospital, and the interaction between the admitting staff member and the pseudopatient was of limited duration. However, after a longer period on the ward, when the patient was engaging in normal behavior, one would expect the staff to recognize that the pseudopatients were not psychotic. This did not occur; the staff did not question the "insanity" of the pseudopatients. When they were released, after periods varying from 7 to 52 days (the average stay was 19 days), those who had been admitted with a diagnosis of schizophrenia were now diagnosed with the label of "schizophrenia in remission." The only persons who recognized that the pseudopatients were not "real" were other patients who asked them why they were there since they were not crazy. (35 out of 118 real patients voiced suspicions.) *The key point of this study was that not one of the pseudopatients was detected by anyone on the hospital staff.* According to Rosenhan, the fact that normal people cannot be distinguished from the mentally ill in a hospital setting points to the "stickiness of the diagnostic label." Once a patient is labeled as "schizophrenic," all of the individual's behavior is seen as stemming from that label.

Rosenhan speculated that part of the eagerness to diagnose might result from the admitting staffs' unwillingness to turn anyone away. Better to hospitalize someone who may be in need of treatment than to run the risk of suicide, etc. This premise was subsequently tested by informing the hospital staff of the earlier deception with the pseudopatients and by warning them of other pseudopatients who would try to enter within the next three months. Staff members were asked to rate all entering patients with regard to probability of faking on a 10-point scale in which a 1 or 2 indicated a high probability of a pseudopatient. Of the 193 patients who were admitted, forty-one received these low scores, indicating that they were perceived by the staff as pseudopatients. How accurate were the staff members in their perception? They were wrong 41 times--NO pseudopatient had tried to enter. This suggests that poor validity in assessment procedure does not result from being too cautious; rather, the error is in believing that sanity and insanity can be easily distinguished.

From Rosenhan's use of participant-observation we gained the opportunity to better understand the patient's point of view. One of the disconcerting things about becoming a mental patient is the loss of credibility as a person. It was easy for the pseudopatients to see how this would occur. Initiation of conversation between staff and patient was dependent on the staff member; if the patient tried to engage the staff in conversation, the staff member kept walking or failed to make eye contact. Staff members would discuss the patients as if they were not present. Physical examinations would be made in a semipublic room where other staff members casually entered. Personal belongings could be searched by staff and interview records could be perused by anyone remotely connected with the hospital.

Obviously, the staff members, if they were asked, would have asserted that they did care about the patients: they did not deliberately mistreat them. They simply lacked awareness of the "small" behaviors and daily routines that depersonalize patients and make them feel powerless. This type of information, from the participant point of view, is invaluable in illuminating many aspects of "truth" in the complex interactions that take place in human relationships, either in "real" life or in an institutional setting.

Adapted from Hock, R. (1992). <u>Forty studies that changed psychology</u>. Englewood Cliffs, New Jersey: Prentice Hall.

Key Terms

*Recognizing that many graduate programs and textbooks differ somewhat in their definitions for key terms, we provide the exact definitions found in the running glossary of **Psychology in Action, 5th ed.** for this first chapter. Due to issues of length for this manual, we will only provide text page references for the key terms in future chapters. We felt it might be helpful to include the exact terms for your first week in class, and as a reminder to alert your students to any differences between your presentation and the texts'.*

UNDERSTANDING PSYCHOLOGY

Applied Research - Research that utilizes the principles and discoveries of psychology for practical purposes, to solve real-world problems.

Basic Research - Research conducted to study theoretical questions without trying to solve a specific problem.

Behavior - Anything a person or animal does, feels, thinks, or experiences.

Covert - Hidden or unobservable.

Overt - Observable, not concealed.

Pseudopsychologies - "False psychologies"; popular systems that pretend to discover psychological information through nonscientific or deliberately fraudulent methods.

Psychology - The scientific study of behavior.

PSYCHOLOGICAL RESEARCH

Case Study - An in-depth study of a single research subject.

Control Condition - The part of an experiment in which certain participants are treated identically to participants in the experimental condition, except that the independent variable is not applied to them.

Correlation - The relationship between variables.

Data - Facts, statistics, pieces of information.

Dependent Variable - A measurable behavior that is exhibited by a participant and is affected by the independent variable.

Double-Blind Experiment - An experiment in which neither the participant nor the experimenter knows which treatment is being given to the participant or to which group the participant has been assigned.

Ethnocentrism - The feeling that one's own cultural group is superior to others, and its customs and ways of life are the standards by which other cultures should be judged.

Experiment - A carefully controlled scientific procedure conducted to determine whether certain variables manipulated by the experimenter have an effect on other variables.

Experimental Condition - The part of an experiment in which the independent variable is applied to the participants.

Experimenter Bias - The tendency of experimenters to influence the results of a research study in the expected direction.

Hypothesis - A possible explanation for a behavior being studied that can be answered or affirmed by an experiment or a series of observations.

Independent Variable - A variable that is controlled by the experimenter and is applied to the participant to determine its effect.

Naturalistic Observation - The systematic recording of behavior in the participant's natural state or habitat.

Placebo - A substance that would normally produce no physiological effect that is used as a control technique, usually in drug research.

Placebo Effect - A change in participants' behavior brought about because they believe they have received a drug that elicits that change when in reality they have received a placebo, an inert substance.

Population - The total of all possible cases from which a sample is selected.

Replicate - To conduct a research study again, following the same procedure.

Research Methodology - Standardized scientific procedures for conducting investigations.

Sample - A selected group of participants that is representative of a larger population.

Sample Bias - The tendency for the sample of participants in a research study to be atypical of a larger population.

Statistically Significant - A relationship believed not to be caused by chance.

Statistics - Data collected in a research study and the mathematical procedures used to analyze the data.

Surveys - Non-experimental research techniques that sample behaviors and attitudes of a population.

Theory - An interrelated set of concepts that is developed in an attempt to explain a body of data and generate testable hypotheses.

Variables - Factors that can be varied and can assume more than one value.

ETHICS IN PSYCHOLOGY

Debriefing - Explaining the research process to participants who participated.

Psychotherapy - Application of psychological principles and techniques to the treatment of mental disorders or to the problems of everyday adjustment.

SCHOOLS OF PSYCHOLOGY

Behaviorism - The school of psychology that focuses on objective or observable behaviors.

Cognitive Psychology - A school of psychology that focuses on reasoning and the mental processing of information.

Cultural Psychology - The school of psychology that studies the influence of culture and ethnic practices on people's behavior.

Culture - Values and assumptions about life and patterns of behavior that develop as a response to social and environmental factors and are passed on from generation to generation.

Eclectic Approach - An approach to psychology that considers the whole person and utilizes techniques appropriate for the specific circumstance.

Ethology - The study of animal behavior from an evolutionary perspective.

Evolutionary Perspective - The idea that certain behavioral characteristics have evolved through the process of natural selection.

Functionalism - The psychological school that investigates the function of mental processes in adapting the individual to the environment.

Gestalt - An organized whole or pattern of perception.

Gestalt Psychology - A school of psychology that focuses on principles of perception and believes the whole experience is qualitatively different from the sum of the distinct elements of that experience.

Humanistic Psychology - A school of psychology that emphasizes the importance of the inner, subjective self and stresses the positive side of human nature.

Information Processing Approach - An approach to studying mental processes that views people and computers in similar terms, as processors of information that has been gathered from the environment, then encoded for memory storage and retrieval.

Introspection - A technique for reporting the contents of consciousness.

Psychoanalytic Theory - Freud's theory of personality that emphasizes the influence of the unconscious mind.

Psychobiology - The study of the biology of behavior.

Sociobiology - The study of the evolutionary and biological bases of social behavior.

Stimulus - An object or event that causes an organism to respond.

Structuralism - An early psychological school that focused on the sensations and feelings of perceptual experience.

Unconscious - The part of the mind whose contents people actively resist bringing into awareness.

Discussion Questions

1. The goals of psychology (describe, explain, predict, and change) are a part of what we all do in our everyday lives. Ask students to generate specific examples. Then ask for suggestions where these goals might become unethical and unacceptable. They MAY remember the movie *Clockwork Orange*, which you could use as an extreme example.

2. PETA, *People for the Ethical Treatment of Animals*, is an animal rights organization that believes that it is wrong to use animals for experimental research. To what extremes should society go to protect the right of animals and at what point is all animal research unwarranted? Ask the students to think about their own feelings overnight and ask for volunteers to express their views at the beginning of the next class period. Would they side with PETA? Why or why not?

3. Is it really necessary to use the experimental method to study human behavior or is the correlational method sufficient? Ask students to write a short answer in class.

4. Ask students to describe how their ideas about psychology and psychologists have changed after reading this first chapter. Discuss how television and movie portrayals might negatively influence the viewer. Ask students to "vote" on the most interesting, most useful, and/or most appealing of the five major perspectives--psychoanalytic, behavioristic, humanistic, cognitive, or biological. We sometimes ask them to complete a 3 X 5 card with their name and vote and then compare their choices from the beginning of the term to the close of the term.

5. What motivates people to believe in pseudopsychologies and to spend millions of their hard earned dollars on psychic hotlines in the face of so much scientific evidence to the contrary? Discuss the problems.

6. When, if ever, should research ethics be violated? Does the data ever justify the means?

7. What specific skills can students learn from the study of psychology that will make them more attractive to employers? See http://research.apa.org/bac2.html for some answers.

8. Challenge students to come up with three or more areas of human endeavor to which psychology has nothing to contribute. Encourage other students to think of ways that these areas do use or could use the contributions of psychology.

9. What reasons are there for subjecting psychic claims to scientific examination? Do we have to know how psychic phenomena occur before we can test their validity?

10. How can the field of psychology help you become better, more successful learners?

 **Web Sites**

Demonstrations, Tutorials, & Class Materials
> http://www.uni.edu/walsh/tutor.html
> This site is maintained by Dr. Linda Walsh from the University of Northern Iowa. The site contains numerous links to web sites of interest for faculty and introductory psychology students.

Classics in the History of Psychology
> http://www.yorku.ca/dept/psych/classics/index.htm
> This York University site provides access to pages devoted to classic articles and books on psychology topics. Among the authors covered are Plato, Skinner, James, Wundt, and Watson.

Today in the History of Psychology
> http://www.cwu.edu/%7Ewarren/today.html
> This site provides access to over 3100 critical or key events in the history of psychology. The site is organized by date and allows a person to determine the events that occurred on that date in the history of psychology.

Graduate School and Careers in Psychology
> http://www1.rider.edu/~suler/gradschl.html
> This site contains information on the various careers of psychology and information on graduate training in psychology.

American Psychological Association
> http://www.apa.org

American Psychological Society
> http://www.hanover.edu/psych/APS/aps.html

The Psychology Hall of Fame
> http://www.angelfire.com/tx/jcr/Pschology.html
> This comprehensive web site provides students with access to short biographies of famous psychologists.

The University of Toronto Museum of Psychological Instruments
> http://psych.utoronto.ca/museum/
> One of the features that differentiated psychology as a science was its early use of physical instruments to study psychological function. This on-line museum provides access for students to view early research instruments such as a kymograph or a tuning fork.

Museum of the History of Psychological Instrumentation

http://www.chss.monclair.edu/psychology/museum/museum.html/

This comprehensive on-line museum contains hundreds of diagrams of early psychological instruments, an explanation of their purpose, and references for further study.

On-Line Psychology Experiments

http://www.yorku.ca/dept/psych/lab/links/online.htm

This site provides access to comprehensive sites that cover on-line psychology surveys or experiments.

Suggested Films and Videos

What Is Psychology?
Insight Media, 1990. 30 minutes. Leading psychologists discuss major approaches, subfields, and historical developments. A discussion of the goals of psychology as they apply to human behavior is presented.

Past, Present, and Promise
Annenberg/CPB, 1990. 30 minutes. The first in Zimbardo's "Discovering Psychology" series, this film discusses the relationship of psychology to other disciplines and the value of scientific methods for studying behavior.

Understanding Research
Annenberg/CPB, 1990. 28 minutes. The second in Zimbardo's "Discovering Psychology" series, this film explores various methodologies, data collection, and statistical analysis.

Career Encounters: Psychology
American Psychological Association, 1991. 28 minutes. A detailed examination of the field of psychology. Includes a discussion of private practice, science, public interest, and education.

Careers in Psychology: Your Options Are Open
American Psychological Association, 1990. 9 minutes. A brief presentation of career options including a sports psychologist, a research psychologist, and a clinical psychologist.

Psychology: Scientific Problem Solvers --- Careers for the 21st Century
American Psychological Association, 1995. 14 minutes. This short video is useful for introductory classes and career days. Interviews with psychologists in diverse fields and growth opportunities in the discipline are presented with a dynamic, MTV type interface. It complements the free booklet.

Scientific Method
Films for the Humanities & Sciences, 1997. 25 minutes. The video examines the basic elements of the scientific method. Shows applications, such as testing new medicines.

Beyond Science
Worth Publishers, Scientific American Frontiers, 1998. In this video, Alan Alda tests the claims of water dowsers or witchers through a double-blind procedure. It provides an excellent, non-technical and involving demonstration of the power of the scientific paradigm.

Psychology: Scientific Problem Solvers --- Careers for the 21st Century
American Psychological Association, 1995. 14 minutes. This short video is useful for introductory classes and career days. Interviews with psychologists in diverse fields and growth opportunities in the discipline are presented with a dynamic, MTV type interface. It complements the free booklet.

Success

Books for Success

Hock, Roger R. (1999). **Forty Studies That Changes Psychology (3ʳᵈ ed.)**. Prentice Hall
A new edition of this deservedly well known exploration of the history or research in psychology.

Myers, David G. (1992). **The Pursuit of Happiness**. Avon Books.
A classic book that illustrates psychology's contribution to man's striving for happiness.

Covey, Stephen R. (1989). **Seven Habits of Highly Successful People**. Simon & Schuster.
A proven, practical book on how to succeed in all areas of life.

Seligman, Martin, E. P. (1994). **What You Can Change…and What You Can't: The Complete Guide to Successful Self-Improvement: Learning to Accept Who You Are**. Knopf.
A practical review of what psychologists know about improving our lives.

Hettich, Paul I. (1992). **Learning Skills for College**. Brooks/Cole.
One of many books on how to succeed in college.

Moore, Roberta, Baker, Barbara & Packer, Arnold (1997). **College Success.** Prentice Hall
The first student success text to incorporate the SCANS basic skills and workplace competencies.

Bolles, Richard Nelson (1997). **What Color Is Your Parachute? A Practical Manual for Job-Hunters and Career-Changers**. Ten Speed Press.
The best known and ever improving resource guide to selecting careers and landing a job.

Active Learning

Active Learning Activity 1.1 - Myths and Misconceptions: Isn't Psychology Just Common Sense?

Purpose:

- To introduce your students to the many interesting topics that will be covered in an introductory psychology class.

- To provide students with research findings that they may find counterintuitive.

- To foster group interaction and help students get acquainted.

Instructions:

1. Make copies of Handout 1.1 – Active Learning.

2. Distribute the copies to your class. Tell students that although you want them to answer the questions honestly, the quiz will not be collected.

3. Discuss each statement and the relevant research. This is also a good time to discuss the difference between casual observation and scientific observation.

Answers to Handout 1.1- Active Learning: Myths and Misconceptions

1. Actions speak louder than words.

   True - When students watched videotapes of people whose self-descriptions conflicted with their actual behavior on characteristics such as "shy" and "friendly," their judgments were influenced much more strongly by what the people did than what they said.

2. Beauty is only skin deep.

   False - Attractive people turn out to have higher self-esteem and to be better treated than less attractive people. (We discuss the issue of physical attractiveness in detail in Chapter 16.)

3. Cry and you cry alone.

   True - Students who had talked on the phone to depressed people are not interested in spending time with these people, compared to students who had talked to non-depressed people.

4. Marry in haste, repent at leisure.

   True - People who marry young or after just a short courtship are more likely to seek a divorce later on, in comparison to those who marry after age 20 or after a long courtship.

5. Familiarity breeds contempt.

   False - In a variety of studies, people have indicated their preference for items (such as words, symbols, and photos) that they have seen frequently.

6. Opposites attract.

   False - Research shows that proximity, physical attractiveness, and similarity are the three most important factors in interpersonal attraction. (We discuss these factors in some detail in Chapter 16).

7. Misery loves company.

   True - Depressed people are more likely to seek emotional support from persons who are also depressed.

8. Spare the rod, spoil the child.

   False - Children who are severely punished when young are more likely to develop psychological problems in adulthood than are those whose parents "spared the rod."

9. The squeaky wheel gets the grease.

   True - When management students were asked to decide the salary levels of various job candidates, they awarded higher salaries to the applicants who had requested higher salaries.

10. Birds of a feather flock together.

   True - Similarity is the single, best predictor of long-term relationships (both friendships and love). (Use this item to point out the problems with "common sense" versus scientific studies. Note the contradictions between this item and #6, and even #5.)

*H*andout 1.1 – Active Learning

<u>Myths and Misconceptions</u>

Please answer true or false to the following questions:

_____1. Actions speak louder than words.

_____2. Beauty is only skin deep.

_____3. Cry and you cry alone.

_____4. Marry in haste, repent at leisure.

_____5. Familiarity breeds contempt.

_____6. Opposites attract.

_____7. Misery loves company.

_____8. Spare the rod, spoil the child.

_____9. The squeaky wheel gets the grease.

_____10. Birds of a feather flock together.

Active Learning Activity 1.2 - Identifying the Goals of Psychology

Purpose:

- To allow the students to practice identifying and explaining the goals of psychology.

- To develop the critical thinking skill of applying new concepts to real-world situations.

Instructions:

1. Following your presentation of the goals of psychology, distribute copies of Handout 1.2 – Active Learning. Students can do this exercise in groups or individually. We find that groups of three or four are most effective.

2. Instruct students first to complete the worksheet by themselves, and then to compare answers with the other students. If there is disagreement, they can refer to the text or to you.

<u>Answers</u> to Handout 1.2 – Active Learning: Identifying the Goals of Psychology

1. Researchers have recently identified a gene that predisposes certain individuals to become obese because their satiety mechanism doesn't turn on.

    Goal=Explain--This research answers the question of why people become obese.

2. Some developmental psychologists believe that a much larger number of playground accidents will occur this year among young children who watch Batman or Mighty Morphin Power Rangers.

    Goal=Predict--Psychologists' statement attempts to guess what will happen in the future.

3. Comprehensive sex education should be required in all high schools because studies demonstrate that such education has reduced the teenage pregnancy rate.

    Goal=Change--Statement suggests attempts to change (control) behavior leading to reduced pregnancy rates.

4. Surveys show that women who graduate from college earn as much money per year as men who graduate from high school.

    Goal=Describe--Survey results simply describe what exists in the world.

Handout 1.2 – Active Learning

Identifying and Explaining the Goals of Psychology

In the space to the left of each statement, identify which goal of psychology (describe, explain, predict, or control) is being met by each of these studies. In the space below each statement, briefly explain your choice of goal.

_____1. Researchers have recently identified a gene that predisposes certain individuals to become obese because their satiety mechanism doesn't "turn on."

_____2. Some developmental psychologists believe that a much larger number of playground accidents will occur this year among young children who watch Batman or Mighty Morphin Power Rangers.

_____3. Comprehensive sex education should be required in all high schools because studies demonstrate that such education has reduced the teenage pregnancy rate.

_____4. Surveys show that women who graduate from college earn as much money per year as men who graduate from high school.

Active Learning Activity 1.3 - Identifying Variables and Experimental vs. Control Groups

Purpose:

- To allow students to practice using the concepts they have learned. Our students often need lots of practice distinguishing between IVs and DVs.

- To develop the critical thinking skill of applying new concepts to real experimental situations.

Instructions:

1. Following your presentation of IVs, DVs, and experimental and control groups, distribute copies of Handout 1.3 – Active Learning.

2. Students can do this exercise individually; groups of 3 or 4 are the most effective.

3. Instruct students to do the worksheet first individually and then to check with the other students. If there is disagreement, they can refer to the text or to you. Review the correct answers before going on with new material.

Answers to Handout 1.3 - Active Learning: Labeling Variables and Groups

A. A researcher is interested in how the activity level of 3-year-olds is affected by viewing a 30 minute video of Teenage Mutant Ninja Turtles or a 30-minute video of Barney.

> IV=Type of video watched--Barney or Teenage Mutant Ninja Turtles
> DV=Activity level of children
> Experimental group=Kids watching Teenage Mutant Ninja Turtles
> Control group=Kids watching Barney

B. A therapist wants to test a new drug designed to increase the ability of teenagers with ADHD to take accurate notes in class.

> IV=Type of drug given--Ritalin or placebo
> DV=Accuracy of notes taken in class
> Experimental group=Ritalin
> Control Group=Placebo

C. A biopsychologist wants to know whether exposure to testosterone in adult female rats increases their aggressive behavior.

> IV=Type of drug given--Testosterone or placebo
> DV=Aggressive behavior
> Experimental group=Testosterone
> Control group=Placebo

D. An industrial psychologist believes that cooling the room temperature may have an impact on productivity of workers on the assembly line.
> IV=Temperature of the room--normal or cooler
> DV=Productivity
> Experimental group=Cooler room
> Control group=Normal temperature room

*H*andout 1.3 – Active Learning

<u>Labeling Variables and Groups</u>

Name the IV, DV, control group, and experimental group for each scenario.

A. A researcher is interested in how the activity level of four-year-olds is affected by viewing a 30-minute video of Teenage Mutant Ninja Turtles or a 30-minute video of Barney.

IV   _____

DV   _____

Experimental
Group(s)_____

Control Group   _____

B. A therapist wants to test a new drug designed to increase the ability of teenagers with ADHD to take accurate notes in class.

IV   _____

DV   _____

Experimental
Group(s)_____

Control Group   _____

C. A biopsychologist wants to know whether exposure to testosterone in adult female rats increases their aggressive behavior.

IV _____

DV _____

Experimental
Group(s)_____

Control Group _____

D. An industrial psychologist believes that cooling the room temperature may have an impact on productivity of workers on the assembly line.

IV _____

DV _____

Experimental
Group(s)_____

Control Group _____

Active Learning Activity 1.4 - Distinguishing Between Experimental and Correlational Studies

Purpose:

- To allow students to practice using the concepts they have learned.

- To develop the critical thinking skill of applying new concepts to real-world situations, using cases drawn from newspaper reports.

- To help students become better "consumers of information;" to remind them that methodology is rarely reported in the media.

Instructions:

1. Following your presentation of correlational and experimental studies, distribute Handout 1.4 – Active Learning.

2. Students can do this exercise in groups or individually; groups of 3 or 4 are the most effective.

3. Instruct students to do the worksheet first individually and then to check with the other students. If there is disagreement, they can refer to the text or to you. Review the correct answers.

Handout 1.4 – Active Learning

Correlational versus Experimental Studies

For each of the following reports:

1. Decide whether the study is correlational or experimental.

2. If the study is correlational, briefly describe how the variables are related and whether the correlation is positive or negative. List possible third variables or confounding causes that might also be influencing the results.

3. If the study is experimental, briefly describe how Variable A is causing Variable B.

Study I
A Dartmouth study found that overweight young women (age 23) earned 6.4% less than their non-overweight peers. Additionally, the study found that young men's earnings rose 2% for each 4-inch increase in height.

Study II
An Australian study reported that MSG does not cause people to be sick, as previously reported. The researcher told subjects that he was studying ingredients in a new soft drink and fed them either MSG or a placebo in the drink. The same number and type of symptoms were reported in both the MSG and the placebo groups.

Study III
USA Today reported that the stock market ends the year with a gain if the Super Bowl is won by one of the original NFL members--all the NFC teams and the three AFC teams (Indianapolis Colts, Pittsburgh Steelers, and Cleveland Browns).

Active Learning Activity 1.5 - Performing Naturalistic Observation

Naturalistic observation can easily be demonstrated either inside or outside your classroom. If your classroom has windows that will allow your students to observe on-campus activity, you can tell them to look out the window and objectively record a simple behavior, such as "How close do people stand to one another when they talk?" Give them ten to fifteen minutes to make their observations; then reassemble the class, list the results on the board, and incorporate the data into your discussion of naturalistic observation. If you do not have sufficient windows, you can send your students out of the room for a few minutes to record their observations or you can show a videotape of a television show or a movie and have students observe the actors as if they were actually conducting research. During your discussion of on-campus observations, ask if any of the participants noticed they were being observed and whether that changed their behavior. Ask students to think about times when they sing to themselves, such as while driving a car. Ask if they change their behavior if a car pulls up beside them. Ask why.

(Other possible hypotheses to test with naturalistic observation: Men tend to study and eat alone whereas women tend to study and eat in groups of two or more. People will generally return a smile with a smile.)

Active Learning Activity 1.6 - Illustrating Correlation

If you wish to discuss correlation in class, you can ask your students to write their height, shoe size, and the day of the month on which they were born on a slip of paper. Collect the slips and write the data on the board. (Make sure you start with your own data--this helps to make the students feel better about volunteering information about themselves. Also, some instructors have tried using height and weight, but some students [and teachers] are reluctant to volunteer their weight.) Plotting the height/shoe size data should give a reasonable positive correlation. To illustrate zero or near-zero correlation, plot the height data against the birthday data.

Active Learning Activity 1.7 - Experimental Controls

One way to illustrate the need for experimental control is to perform a "rigged" in-class mini-experiment on reaction time. For this demonstration, you will need either a device that measures simple reaction time or two stopwatches; the procedure is similar for both types of equipment. Here is the procedure for using two stopwatches.

First, explain that you want to see whether males or females are faster at stopping a stopwatch. Ask a male volunteer to come to the front of the room. Hand him a stopwatch and explain that he should start the watch at your first signal, then stop it as quickly as possible at your second signal. Explain that he will do this three times, and his score will be the total of the three trials, with the lowest score winning. Now allow your male volunteer to practice the procedure a few times and then proceed with the testing.

Now call up a female volunteer. Ask whether she understood the instructions; if not, demonstrate the procedure yourself, being sure not to let this second volunteer have a chance to practice. Now test the female volunteer. If all goes according to plan, the male subject who was able to practice will get the better score. At this time, you can then ask the class to analyze the procedure and point out any problems. (If you want to demonstrate obvious *experimenter bias* you can give outrageous encouragement to the first volunteer. Depending upon whether the volunteer is male or female, students will accuse you of favoring the males or females.)

Active Learning Activity 1.8 - "Which Design Would You Choose?"

Ask your students to quickly get into groups of three or four and pass out copies of Handouts 1.8 – Active Learning (2 pages). Remind the group leader to turn in a separate sheet that has been completed and has the names of all group members. You may want to assign active learning points (attendance, extra credit, or whatever method you've designed to encourage group WORK versus "chat time"). Instruct them that they are to "jot down" their group answers during a period of approximately ten minutes. If some of the groups are not finished in the time you have allotted, go ahead and discuss the correct answers--advising them to write down the answers on their own private copies as a separate study guide.

Remind students that the point of many active learning exercises is to ENCOURAGE critical thinking, and often there is no single correct answer. If the students have logical or even creative ways of providing alternative answers, you may want to praise and recognize the group and their answer. This will help create a more accepting and lively (active) atmosphere, while also encouraging the more inhibited students.

Active Learning Activity l.9 - Interviewing a Contemporary Psychologist

It might be possible to interview a contemporary psychologist associated with one of the major schools of psychology. You may know of a willing local psychologist or if not, the American Psychological Association has a list of prominent psychologists who have agreed to visit small colleges with low budgets and waive their normal lecture fees (although you will have to pay their room, board, and transportation).

It is sometimes possible to do these interviews via telephone and have students directly ask questions of the psychologist. If you do a telephone interview, have students submit questions in writing for approval before the interview to save time and prevent awkward silences over the phone. Also, call the psychologist beforehand to arrange a time for the call and send him/her a set of possible questions. Obviously, to make this work in class, you will need a telephone system that will put the phone conversation on a speaker so the entire class can participate.

Active Learning Activity 1.10 - Careers in Psychology
The American Psychological Association is a good source of information for students interested in discovering psychology as a profession and exploring the many types of careers that psychologists can choose from. Several resources can be brought into classroom for the beginning student:

1. Psychology: Scientific Problem Solvers -- Careers for the 21st Century
This FREE 37-page booklet presents psychology as a rich source of career opportunities. Included in the booklet is a broad overview of psychology, emerging growth opportunities in the field, and tips on how to go about making the choice to pursue a psychology career. Interviews with psychologists are featured in such diverse areas as memory research, organizational behavior and school counseling. Sections include: Sub-fields in Psychology, The Job Outlook, What Psychologists Do, and Educational Requirements.

2. The three APA videos describing career choices in psychology.

3. The APA student web site http://www.apa.org/students/ has much information for students interested in learning about graduate school programs, career choices, employment outlook and salary potentials. You can also bring in classified ads from the APA *Monitor* or the APS *Observer* to show how many positions and what kinds of specialties are sought after.

4. The APA bookstore has several good, book length guides about graduate program choices. These may be premature for the beginning student but can help define goals for future career development.

Active Learning Activity 1.11 - Student Success Web – Journey

Pass out the Handout 1.11 – Active Learning, on Student Success Web Sites. If your classroom is equipped for it, you may wish to demonstrate some of the master sites in class. Then ask the students to select 4 or 5 of the web sites from the list and to research them before the next class. Each student needs to select 5 specific skills or strategies as their favorite. During the next class they are to give a written or oral report on which skills they have selected as "most helpful" and why. The class discussion can then be guided to select strategies that the class can adopt as a group to help each other succeed.

Active Learning Activity 1.12 - Psychology and Job Success

Students who are taking PSYC101 because it is required and who are not majoring in psychology often see this course as irrelevant to their career or job prospects. They are quite surprised to discover that the opposite is true. Since 1991 the SCANS report *What Work Requires of Schools* has been one of the leading documents to guide educators in work force preparation. It presents a detailed list of five competencies based on a three part foundation.

Especially at the beginning of the semester it is useful to motivate students to take this course seriously. Use Handout 1.12 – Active Learning to challenge your students to discover how many of the 36 separate skills required for solid job performance are improved or developed through the study of psychology. Because our discipline covers so many aspects of human behavior many of the listed skills will be impacted positively through this course.

The SCANS report summary can be accessed at http://www.dcccd.edu/nlc/misc/scans/facts.htm. The associated web pages hold much added material of interest to educators.

Handout 1.8 – Active Learning

"Which Design Would You Choose?"

For each of the following research questions, decide which research design would be best and circle it. Then complete your selected design information. Be prepared to discuss the reasons for your selections.

Research Question: Is daycare or home care better for later success in elementary school?

Correlational Design	or	Experimental Design
Variable 1:		Independent Variable:
Variable 2:		Dependent Variable:
Limitations:		Limitations:

Research Question: Does schizophrenia run in families?

Correlational Design	or	Experimental Design
Variable 1:		Independent Variable:
Variable 2:		Dependent Variable:
Limitations:		Limitations:

Research Question: Does viewing television violence increase aggressive behaviors in children?

Correlational Design   or   Experimental Design

Variable 1:   Independent Variable:

Variable 2:   Dependent Variable:

Limitations: Limitations:

Research Question: Are boys better in math than girls?

Correlational Design   or   Experimental Design

Variable 1:   Independent Variable:

Variable 2:   Dependent Variable:

Limitations   Limitations:

Handout 1.11 – Active Learning

Student Success - A Web Journey

http://www.amazon.com/exec/obidos/ISBN%3D0030537932/collegepowerprepA/002-0158918-6759607
amazon.com example listing of books on student success.

http://www.lamission.cc.ca.us/ftproot/tovare/handbook/tips.htm
Center for Student Success at LA Mission College, useful review of several important skills

http://icpac.indiana.edu/index2.html
Master site on student success at the University of Indiana, many useful links including the top 10 study guides

http://www.powerstudents.com/college/index.shtml
The power students master site. Many college success tools as well as discussion groups and chat rooms for social support and motivational success stories

http://www.ee.calpoly.edu/~jbreiten/htbas.html
CalPoly's site on "How to be a student" with many recommendations and strategies

http://www.utulsa.edu/collegian/022597/increase-your-time-manag.html
How to increase your Time Management and Study Skills

http://www.howtostudy.com/topten.htm
Learn how to study with Howtostudy.com. A master site for student success. Many links.

http://www.yorku.ca/admin/cdc/lsp/lsphome.html
York University's Learning Skills Program site

http://snow.utoronto.ca/Learn2/introll.html
A very useful site on "Learning How To Learn". Broad range of topics and links

http://www.mindman.com/
Best site for learning about mind mapping on the web. Many links to mind mapping practitioners although few examples in education

http://www.apa.org/releases/positivepsy.html
Positive Psychology site at APA – based on Martin Seligman's approach to choosing the optimum explanatory style. Recommended for modeling successful thinking patterns.

http://www.mdcc.edu/vcollege/sls1535.html
An example syllabus for a semester long course on student success

Handout 1.11 - Continued

http://www.mdcc.edu/vcollege/sls1535.html
Maricopa College student success site

http://www.ece.msstate.edu/student/time.html
Taking control of your Life – Mississippi State counseling site

http://www.sheridanc.on.ca/career/study/time.htm
Study for success – Time management skills

http://snow.utoronto.ca/Learn2/studyskl.htm
Study skills and Memory Links – a master site with many useful listings

http://www.ttuhsc.edu/success/Survival.htm
Success strategies for medical students are applicable for most any college setting

http://quarles.unbc.edu/ideas/index.html
The ideas of a university – structured interviews with professors from multiple disciplines about their discipline and the university at large

http://www.cs.virginia.edu/helpnet/Time/time.html
Time management site integrates ideas from many leading thinkers

http://uac-server.stanford.edu/general/study_skills.html
Stanford University's Instant Study Skills site

Handout 1.12 – Active Learning

Psychology and Job Success

The United States Department of Labor –
Secretary's Commission on Achieving Necessary Skills (SCANS)

Three-Part Foundation

Basic Skills: Reads, writes, performs arithmetic and mathematical operations, listens and speaks.
A. Reading - locates, understands, and interprets written information in prose and in documents such as manuals, graphs, and schedules.
B. Writing- communicates thoughts, ideas, information, and messages in writing; and creates documents such as letters, directions, manuals, reports, graphs, and flow charts.
C. Arithmetic/Mathematics - performs basic computations and approaches practical problems by choosing appropriately from a variety of mathematical techniques.
D. Listening- receives, attends to, interprets, and responds to verbal messages and other cues.
E. Speaking - organizes ideas and communicates orally.

Thinking Skills: thinks creatively, makes decisions, solves problems, visualizes, knows how to learn, and reasons.
A. Creative Thinking - generates new ideas.
B. Decision Making - specific goals and constraints, generates alternatives, considers risks, and evaluates and chooses best option.
C. Problem Solving - recognizes problems and devises and implements plan of action.
D. Seeing Things in the Mind's Eye - organizes and processes symbols, pictures, objects, and other information.
E. Knowing How to Learn - uses efficient learning techniques to acquire and apply new knowledge and skills.
F. Reasoning - discovers a rule or principle underlying the relationship between two or more objects and applies it when solving a problem.

Personal Qualities: Displays responsibility, self-esteem, sociability, self-management, integrity and honesty.
A. Responsibility - exerts a high level of effort and perseveres towards goal attainment.
B. Self-esteem - believes in own self-worth and maintains a positive view of self.
C. Sociability - demonstrates understanding, friendliness, adaptability, empathy, and politeness in group settings.
D. Self Management - assesses self accurately, sets personal goals, monitors progress, and exhibits self-control.
E. Integrity/Honesty - chooses ethical courses of action.

Five Competencies

I. Resources: Identifies, organizes, plans, and allocates resources.

A. Time - selects goal -relevant activities, ranks them, allocates time, prepares and follows schedules.
B. Money - uses or prepares budgets, makes forecasts, keeps records, and makes adjustments to meet objectives.
C. Materials and Facilities - acquires, stores, allocates and uses materials or space efficiently.
D. Human Resources - assesses skills and distributes work accordingly, evaluates performance and provides feedback.

II. Interpersonal: Works with others.

A. Participates as a Member of a Team - contributes to group effort.
B. Teaches Others New Skills.
C. Serves Clients/Customers - works to satisfy customer's expectations.
D. Exercises Leadership - communicates ideas to justify position, persuade and convince others, responsibly challenges existing procedures and policies.
E. Negotiates - works toward agreements involving exchange of resources, resolves divergent interests.
F. Works with Diversity - works well with men and women from diverse backgrounds.

III. Information: Acquires and uses information.

A. Acquires and evaluates Information
B. Organizes and Maintains Information
C. Interprets and Communicates Information
D. Uses Computers to Process Information

IV. Systems: Understands complex inter-relationships.

A. Understands Systems - knows how social, organizational, and technological systems work and operates effectively with them.
B. Monitors and Corrects Performance - distinguishes trends, predicts impacts on system operations, diagnoses systems' performance and corrects malfunctions.
C. Improves or Designs Systems - suggests modifications to existing systems and develops new or alternative systems to improve performance.

V. Technology: Works with a variety of technologies.

A. Selects Technology - chooses procedures, tools, or equipment, including computers and related technologies.
B. Applies Technology to Tasks - understands overall intent and proper procedures for setup and operation of equipment.
C. Maintains and Troubleshoots Equipment - prevents, identifies, or solves problems with equipment, including, computers and other technologies.

Source: What Work Requires of Schools, A SCANS Report for America 2000, 1991, U.S. Department of Labor, 200 Constitution Avenue, N.W., Washington, D.C. 2021.

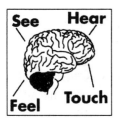

Brain-Based Learning

Brain-Based Learning Activity 1.1 - The Psychic Psychologist

Materials needed:

    One newspaper article with a large headline and one column of text.
    Scissors
    One envelope
    "Psychic" hat/turban/feather/blanket/crystal

Before class:

    Cut out the article with a large headline and one column of text attached.
    Cut the column of text close to the top underneath the headline and tape it back together **upside down** but aligned so it looks, from a few steps away, like an unbroken column. In actuality, most of the column is hanging upside down.
    Mark the envelope "Precognition", and in it write the first 5 to 8 words of the first sentence of the upside down hanging column, and seal it.
    Select three words or concepts from the first sentence that you will memorize.

In class:

    Students love this exercise, especially if you ham it up. It helps if you bring or wear special objects that are associated with psychics (such as the items listed above). They will help get you into the role. Then, you could state, "With my special _____, I have psychic powers that will allow me to read your minds and predict the future. In order for me to connect on the psychic plane, I need everyone to cooperate by being very quiet and calming your minds so that I can concentrate."

    As you are about to begin, you hand the envelope labeled "Precognition" to one of the students and ask that they keep it without opening it until you instruct them to do so. Next, hold the newspaper headline/clipping between the fingers of one hand with the tape splicing the column together facing away from the students, so the students can see the lettering. Be careful not to stand so close to them that they can read the letters and see that the column is actually upside down. In your other hand, you hold the scissors and move them up and down the column while you ask a specific student where you should cut…at the top, in the middle, at the bottom, or? Once the student tells you to make the cut, you put away the scissors and the rest of the article, and have one of the students pick up the piece of the article that fell to the floor.

Telepathy & Precognition:

    You tell the student who picked up the article piece that you can read his/her mind if s/he really concentrates on the article. You can close your eyes, hum, look at your crystal, demonstrate your focus power and then say something like, "I sense _____. (Pause).

Wait, wait, I also am getting _____. (Pause). Yes, it also has something to do with _____." The three things you mention should be the words or concepts from the first paragraph of the cut off piece that you memorized. For each phrase you pick, you ask the student for confirmation that the word or concept has something to do with the article fragment s/he has in front of him/her. Then continue with, "But, wait, that is not all. Not only can I read minds, but I can predict the future (="Precognition"). Before class, I tried to predict what the first 5 to 8 words were of the portion of the paragraph you asked me to cut off. I have written them down and sealed the envelope." Ask the student with much fanfare to open the envelope and pronounce the words, and then ask the student holding the column fragment to stand up and read the first few words of the fragment. Of course, they are the same, but make sure to look very pleased and take a bow.

The payoff:

Break the class into small groups of 4 or 5 students each and challenge them to come up with as many explanations as they can think of for what happened. They have 5 to 7 minutes, and the group with the most suggestions should win points or extra credit. It is not unusual to have groups come up with 10 to 20 suggestions. Encourage their creativity and their critical thinking by saying any hypothesis will be acceptable, including the one that you are really psychic.

Suggestions will range from use of a confederate, to mirrors, to fake ink, to spy cameras in the ceiling, to cutting where you wanted to not where the student told you to, to memorizing the entire article, etc. After writing them all down, challenge them to come up with ways to test their hypotheses. Ask, "What can we do to discover which is the correct explanation?" In a short class, make it their assignment for the next class. In a longer class, generate answers together.

This is a great opportunity for applying the concepts of experimental design, controlling variables, and replication. For each explanation/testing suggestion, ask the students to critique whether it would work or whether they would believe the answer. Challenge them to look at their logic by stating, "What if you had bet $1,000 on this explanation. Would you trust your procedure to produce accurate results?" Whenever possible, encourage students to use the terms hypothesis, design, reliability, replication, significance, and/or double-blind. With a little encouragement the students will get very involved and improve each other's suggestions.

In order for this to work, you must promise students that you will be truthful at all times by giving them honest data, as well as honest feedback. Usually, at the end of the demonstrations students will ask you to give them the "right" answer. Instead of revealing the trick I tell them that in science as in life we are never given the one "right" and final answer. The best we can do is to follow a carefully thought-out, scientific procedure and to accumulate the evidence.

Option 1: This can make a good writing or extra credit assignment. For example, each student could pick a suggested explanation from the chalkboard/whiteboard and write a one page paper on what kind of study or experiment s/he would conduct to test that explanation utilizing key research terms from the chapter.

Option 2: The video, "Beyond Science" (Worth Publishers, *Scientific American Frontiers,* Teaching Module, Episode #802), in which Alan Alda tests the claims of water dowsers or witchers through double-blind testing would make a very good companion to this exercise.

(Modeled after a presentation by R. Hyman at the 1997 Seattle WPA convention)

Brain-Based Learning Activity 1.2 - What's The Big Deal About Science?

One of the most difficult lessons for incoming students is to understand and appreciate the power of the scientific paradigm. The notion is abstract and seems far removed from their lives. The following two activities are designed to overcome this difficulty.

Materials needed: 2 - 9 x 12" or larger, boxes the height of 2 reams of paper (approximately 4 inches)
                          1 roll of toilet paper
                          1000 sheets (2 reams) of 8.5 x 11" paper

Instructions:
Divide the class into two groups:
        The first group (3 or 4 students) gets a box and the toilet paper roll
        The second group contains all remaining students. They get the other box and the 2 reams of paper.

Goal:
To fill both boxes so that the paper is even with the top of the carton across most of its surface area.
Group 1 (toilet paper) is allowed to wad up the paper and put it in the box.
Group 2 (1000 sheets) must deposit pages **one at a time** into their box.

Time:
From "START", time both groups to completion. The quickest time wins. Give both groups 3 minutes before the start to discuss strategy and divide labor. (Group 1 should be much faster, even though Group 2 is much larger.)

After the timed completion:
Pick a student of equal height from each group. Tell them to stand with one foot in their respective box and mark on a chalkboard/whiteboard a line at head height. The student from Group 1 will sink, the one from Group 2 will rise. Then, ask them to open the envelope pasted to the bottom of the boxes.
        The envelope for Group 1 will say "OPINIONS"
        The envelope for Group 2 will say "SCIENTIFIC FACTS"

Have them break into small groups and discuss:
        Why is Group 2's pile higher?
        Why did it take so much longer and involve so much more effort?
        Why does it take 1,000 pages to rise 4 inches?
        Why have we learned more in the last 100 years, than in the previous 10,000 years of human history? What central feature of science has made this explosion of knowledge possible?

Brain-Based Learning Activity 1.3 - What's in a Face?

Break students into small groups and give them 3 to 4 minutes to list the MAJOR emotions that human beings show in their faces. Each group should pick one or two emotions that they will model for the class. The other students should guess what emotion the face is demonstrating.

Ask them to come up with a list of interesting questions a researcher might ask about emotions and the face, and to predict how much time it would take to study these questions scientifically.

Then give them Handout 1.3 – Brain-based Learning, Paul Ekman – 30 Years of Research. Each group of 3-4 students is to find the major directions in which the research has branched out over the years. Sometimes the scientific language of the titles can be intimidating but every group can come up with some themes. To get their attention I will ask them to find which research theme the CIA is most interested in (How to catch a Liar?). Highlight how the research questions evolved from first devising an objective facial coding system to discovering how many basic emotions there are, to whether they are culture specific or universal, to understanding the underlying physiognomy of the face, to the connection between facial expressions and brain physiology and lateral specialization, to facial expressions in theater, to differences between fake emotions and genuine ones, to detecting liars, to modeling facial emotional expression through computer programs.

It is important to point out that Ekman and his colleagues were part of a larger community that tested their findings and challenged their explanations. In turn, Ekman's group was reacting to all the other advances that took place in the disciplines associated with measuring and explaining non-verbal behavior.

The lesson is to make science a process that can be accessible and meaningful to students, to show it as a powerful paradigm that takes a lot of effort, money and time; but that allows the accumulation of a very strong and ever expanding base that each successive generation inherits.

Brain-Based Learning Activity 1.4 - Role Playing an Early Psychologist

If you are a good actor, you might want to dress up like Wundt, Wertheimer, Freud or any of the other early psychologists, and give a lecture as if you were actually one of them. The drama people might be able to help you with costumes and makeup. If you are not a good actor, it might be possible to get a drama student to play the part while you interview him. If you do the interview, you should write a detailed script and rehearse the role-playing carefully before you and your assistant present the scene to your class.

Brain-Based Learning Activity 1.5 – Fields of Psychology

To enhance learning of the various fields of psychology, their names and their principal activities ask the students to complete Handout 1.5 – Brain-based Learning.

Handout 1.3 – Brain-Based Learning

Paul Ekman - 30 years of Research

- Ekman, P. & Friesen, W. V. (1969). The repertoire of nonverbal behavior: Categories, origins, usage, and coding. *Semiotica, 1*, 49- 98.
- Ekman, P. (1972). Universals and cultural differences in facial expressions of emotion. In J. Cole (Ed.), *Nebraska Symposium on Motivation 1971*, (Vol. 19, pp. 207-283). Lincoln, NE: University of Nebraska Press.
- Ekman, P., Friesen, W. V., & Ellsworth, P. (1972). *Emotion in the human face: Guidelines for research and an integration of findings*. New York: Pergamon Press.
- Ekman, P. (1973) *Darwin and facial expression; a century of research in review* New York: Academic Press.
- Ekman, P. & Friesen, W. V. (1975). *Unmasking the face. A guide to recognizing emotions from facial clues*. Englewood Cliffs, New Jersey: Prentice-Hall.
- Ekman, P. and Friesen, W.V. (1977) *Manual for the Facial Action Coding System*, Palo Alto: Consulting Psychologists Press
- Ekman, P. (1978). Facial signs: Facts, fantasies, and possibilities. In T. Sebeok (Ed.), *Sight, Sound and Sense*. Bloomington: Indiana University Press.
- Ekman, P. & Friesen, W. V. (1978). *Facial action coding system: A technique for the measurement of facial movement*. Palo Alto, Calif.: Consulting Psychologists Press.
- Ekman, P. (1979). About brows: Emotional and conversational signals. In J. Aschoff, M. von Carnach, K. Foppa, W. Lepenies, & D. Plog (Eds.), *Human ethology* (pp. 169-202). Cambridge: Cambridge University Press.
- Ekman, P. & Oster, H. (1979). Facial expressions of emotion. *Annual Review of Psychology, 20*, 527-554.
- Ekman, P. (1980) *The face of man: expressions of universal emotions in a New Guinea village* New York: Garland STPM Press.
- Ekman, P. (1982) *Emotion in the human face* New York: Cambridge University Press.
- Ekman, P. (1982). Methods for measuring facial action. In K.R. Scherer and P. Ekman (Eds.), *Handbook of methods in Nonverbal Behavior Research* (pp 45- 90). Cambridge: Cambridge University Press.
- Ekman, P., Levenson, R. W., & Friesen, W. V. (1983). Autonomic nervous system activity distinguishes among emotions. *Science, 221*, 1208-1210.
- Ekman, P. (1984). Expression and the nature of emotion. In K. Scherer and P. Ekman (Eds.), *Approaches to emotion* (pp. 319-343). Hillsdale, N.J.: Lawrence Erlbaum.
- Ekman, P. and Friesen, W.V. (1984) *Unmasking the Face* Palo Alto: Consulting Psychologists Press.
- Scherer, R. and Ekman, P. (1984) *Approaches to emotion* Hillsdale, N.J. : L. Erlbaum Associates
- Hager, J. C., & Ekman, P. (1985). The asymmetry of facial actions is inconsistent with models of hemispheric specialization. *Psychophysiology, 22(3)*, 307-318.
- Ekman, P. & Friesen, W. V. (1986). A new pan cultural facial expression of emotion. *Motivation and Emotion, 10(2)*, 1986.
- Ekman, P. & Fridlund, A. J. (1987). Assessment of facial behavior in affective disorders. In J. D. Maser (Ed.), *Depression and Expressive Behavior* (pp. 37-56). Hillsdale, NJ: Lawrence Erlbaum Associates.
- Friesen, W.V. & Ekman, P. (1987). *Dictionary - Interpretation of FACS Scoring*. Unpublished manuscript.

Handout 1.3 - continued

- Ekman, P., Friesen, W. V., & O'Sullivan, M. (1988). Smiles when lying. *Journal of Personality and Social Psychology, 54,* 414-420
- Ekman, P. & O'Sullivan, M. (1988). The role of context in interpreting facial expression: Comment of Russell and Fehr (1987). *Journal of Experimental Psychology, 117,* 86-88.
- Ekman, P. (1989). The argument and evidence about universals in facial expressions of emotion. In H. Wagner & A. Manstead (Eds.), *Handbook of social psychophysiology* (pp. 143-164). Chichester: Wiley.
- Davidson, R. J., Ekman, P., Saron, C., Senulis, J., & Friesen, W.V. (1990) Emotional expression and brain physiology I: Approach/withdrawal and cerebral asymmetry. *Journal of Personality and Social Psychology, 58,* 330-341.
- Ekman, P., Davidson, R. J., & Friesen, W. V. (1990). Duchenne's smile: Emotional expression and brain physiology II. *Journal of Personality and Social Psychology, 58,* 342-353.
- Chesney, M. A., Ekman, P., Friesen, W. V., Black, G. W., & Hecker, M. H. L. (1990). Type A behavior pattern: Facial behavior and speech components. *Psychosomatic Medicine, 53,* 307-319.
- Levenson, R. W., Ekman, P., & Friesen, W. V. (1990). Voluntary facial action generates emotion-specific autonomic nervous system activity. *Psychophysiology, 27,* 363-384.
- Ekman, P., O'Sullivan, M., & Matsumoto, D. (1991a). Confusions about content in the judgment of facial expression: A reply to Contempt and the Relativity Thesis. *Motivation and Emotion,* 15, 169-176.
- Ekman, P., O'Sullivan, M., & Matsumoto, D. (1991b). Contradictions in the study of contempt: What's it all about? Reply to Russell. *Motivation and Emotion, 15,* 293-296.
- Ekman, P. (1992) *Why kids lie : how parents can encourage truthfulness* New York: Scribner.
- Ekman, P. (1992) *Telling lies: clues to deceit in the marketplace, politics, and marriage* New York: Norton.
- Ekman, P. (1992). Facial expression of emotion: New findings, new questions. *Psychological Science, 3,* 34-38.
- Ekman, P. (1992). An argument for basic emotions. *Cognition and Emotion,* 6, 169-200.
- Ekman, P. (1992) Are there basic emotions?, *Psychological Review,* July
- Ekman, P. & Davidson, R. J. (1992). Voluntary smiling changes regional brain activity. Manuscript under review.
- Ekman, P., Frank, M., Friesen, W. (1993). Behavioral markers and recognizability of the smile of enjoyment; *Journal of Personality and Social Psychology,* January
- Ekman, P. (1993). Facial Expression and emotion. *The American Psychologogist,* April
- Ekman, P., Nickerson, C., Hammond, K., O Sullivan, M. (1993). Voluntary smiling changes regional brain activity; *Psychological Science,* September
- Ekman, P. (1994). Strong evidence for universals in facial expressions: A reply to Russell's mistaken critique; *Psychological Bulletin,* March
- Ekman, P. (1996). Why don't we catch liars?; *Social Research,* Fall

Handout 1.5 – Brain-Based Learning

MATCH DESCRIPTIONS TO FIELDS OF PSYCHOLOGY

Field of Psychology   **Principal Activity**

_____Clinical   1. Engages in laboratory testing of psychological theories.

_____Physiological   2. Studies thinking process and information processing.

_____Cognitive   3. Concerned with social, cognitive, personality growth in children and adults.

_____Social   4. Examines and treats patients in mental health settings.

_____Experimental   5. Assists educators to promote greater learning in students.

_____School   6. Discovers relation between emotions, behavior, stress, and illness.

_____Developmental   7. Interested in how individuals are influenced by other people or groups.

_____Industrial   8. Measures brain waves and function of nervous system.

_____Health   9. Compares universals and specifics of human behavior in diverse ethnic groups.

_____Cultural   10. Studies organizations, human factor design and employee training.

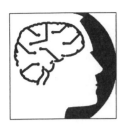

Critical Thinking

Critical Thinking Exercise 1.1 - Values Clarification: Introducing Introductory Psychology

Despite strong psychological evidence regarding first impressions and an intuitive recognition of the importance of the first few days in class, many instructors introduce their course with a distribution of the course syllabus and a predictable recitation of institutional rules regarding examination and attendance policies. With this type of introduction, students are unintentionally trained toward a passive rather than an active role in the classroom. In comparison, we have found that the "first day exercise" described in the preface of this manual is a wonderful way to start your class. It models active learning, critical thinking, and sets the stage for an exciting course. We strongly encourage you to try this exercise. It's a sure-fire winner!

This exercise also appears in the text, Chapter 1. We include it here for your convenience, and you may want to discuss it in class to reinforce reading of the text.

Critical Thinking Exercise 1.2 - Applying Abstract Terminology: Becoming a Better Consumer of Scientific Research

The news media, advertisers, politicians, teachers, close friends, and other individuals frequently use research findings in their attempts to change your attitudes and behavior. How can you tell whether such information is accurate and worthwhile?

The following exercise will improve your ability to critically evaluate sources of information. It is based on concepts you learned in the previous discussion on psychological research techniques. Read each "research" report and decide what is the primary problem or research limitation. In the space provided, make one of the following marks:

CC = The report is misleading because correlational data are used to suggest causation.
CG = The report is inconclusive since there was no control group.
EB = The results of the research were unfairly influenced by experimenter bias.
SB = The results of the research are questionable because of sample bias.

_____1. A clinical psychologist strongly believes that touching is an important adjunct to successful therapy. For two months he touches half his patients (Group A) and refrains from touching the other half (Group B). He then reports a noticeable improvement in Group A.

_____2. A newspaper reports that violent crime corresponds to phases of the moon. The reporter concludes that the gravitational pull of the moon controls human behavior.

_____3. A researcher interested in women's attitudes toward premarital sex sends out a lengthy survey to subscribers of *Playboy* and *Cosmopolitan* magazines.

_____4. An experimenter is interested in studying the effects of alcohol on driving ability. Prior to testing on an experimental driving course, Group A consumes 2 ounces of alcohol, Group B consumes 4 ounces of alcohol, and Group C consumes 6 ounces of alcohol. The researcher concludes that alcohol consumption adversely affects driving ability.

_____5. After reading a scientific journal that reports higher divorce levels among couples who lived together before marriage, a college student decides to move out of the apartment she shares with her boyfriend.

_____6. A theater owner reports increased beverage sales following the brief flashing of subliminal messages to "Drink Coca-Cola" during the movie.

Answers: 1. EB 2. CC 3. SB 4. CG 5. CC 6. CG

This exercise also appears in the Student Study Guide for __Psychology in Action__, 5th ed., Chapter 1. It is also a good follow-up to the Critical Thinking Exercise 1.2 in this manual. We include it here for your convenience, and you may want to discuss it in class to reinforce use of the Student Study Guide.

Critical Thinking Exercise 1.3 - Applying Abstract Terminology (A Cognitive Skill)

In Chapter 1 of your textbook, you learned research terminology that can be used to evaluate reports from politicians, advertisers, teachers, the news media, and even close friends. The following exercise will allow you to practice using some of those terms to critically evaluate several sources of information by asking you to assess the accuracy and worth of their reports. Read each "research" report and decide what is the primary problem or research limitation. In the space provided, make one of the following marks:

CC = The report is misleading because correlational data are used to suggest causation.
CG = The report is inconclusive since there was no control group.
EB = The results of the research were unfairly influenced by experimenter bias.
SB = The results of the research are questionable because of sample bias.

_____1. You have noticed that whenever it rains, you do poorly on exams. As a result, you have started to ask some of your instructors if you can take exams on sunny days.

_____2. A domestic auto manufacturer, concerned with slumping sales, conducts a survey in one of its auto plants to determine how people feel about purchasing a foreign auto.

_____3. At a major league baseball park, it has been noticed that beer and soft-drink sales are high when color advertising is used on the new billboard.

_____4. A researcher interested in how the public feels about Hollywood gossip publishes a survey in the *National Inquirer* and asks readers to mail in their responses.

_____5. A scientific report has been published that shows that aspirin can cause excessive perspiring. As a result, you stop taking aspirin.

_____6. After not doing well on an exam, you ask others who also did poorly how they feel about the professor.

Gender and Cultural Diversity

Gender and Cultural Activity 1.1

Objective: To introduce students to the concept that "culture is the shared way of life of a group of people" and that "in today's world, contact with people from other cultures is inevitable" and "getting along means not only understanding how they are different, but appreciating and respecting these differences." Berry et al. (1992).

Material: Gender-role Values Checklist

Procedure: Men and women students tend to hold somewhat stereotypical views of one another's expected behaviors. In this activity, the class is broken up into small groups composed of same-sex members. Using the Gender-role Values Checklist (Handout 1.1 – Gender and Cultural Diversity), the students develop a list of the top seven values they believe are most characteristic of their sex. The groups are then asked to indicate what they think the top seven values of the opposite sex would be. Results for the dual findings of each group may be tabulated on the board, allowing immediate discussion, or the groups can be assigned to bring to the next class their tabulated responses.

Conclusions: Unger and Sitter (1975) discovered a strong similarity between males and females on the values they considered important for themselves and for the opposite sex. Predicting the responses of the opposite sex resulted in stereotypic results along gender lines. Women tended to exaggerate men's culturally-defined responses and men tended to do the same for women. This exercise helps students' connections between stereotyping opposite-sex people in the same culture and developing erroneous conclusions about behaviors exhibited by people/groups in different cultures.

Handout 1.1 – Gender and Cultural Diversity

WOMEN ARE:	MEN ARE:
dependent	dependent
empathetic	empathetic
nurturing	nurturing
altruistic	altruistic
moral	moral
aggressive	aggressive
assertive	assertive
dominant	dominant
competitive	competitive
compliant	compliant
emotional	emotional
stoic	stoic
fearful	fearful

Writing Project

Given the need for improved writing skills in college students and to respond to the call for "writing across the curriculum," we offer writing projects for each chapter. In Chapter 1, we suggest a 2-3 page written response to one of the issues found on Handout 1.1- Writing Project. Recognizing the time involved in grading such writing projects, one alternative is to occasionally assign "peer grading." Collect the papers, remove student names, and assign each student a paper to grade. It helps to make their participation in peer grading part of the overall points for the writing project. This encourages a more thoughtful and responsible evaluation, as well as acknowledging and rewarding the additional work.

Handout 1.1 – Writing Project

Write a 2 to 3 page response to one of the following:

1. Psychologists are interested in a number of sensitive social issues such as AIDS, teen pregnancy, drug abuse and addiction, and sexual abuse of children. Describe a study that would improve our understanding of a similar problem that is of interest to you. Use specific terminology from Chapter 1 (independent variable, dependent variable, experimental method, nonexperimental method, survey, etc.). What steps would you take to ensure the fair and ethical treatment of your participants?

2. Cultural psychology is the newest branch or school of psychology. Locate 3 people from cultures different from yours (who have NOT taken introductory psychology). Ask them to describe their perception of psychology in general, what they think psychologists study, who do they think of when they think of famous psychologists, and whether they personally would consider a career in psychology. Why or why not? Also, ask which school of psychology is most interesting and acceptable to them. Ask what they think about the goals of psychology--to describe, explain, predict, and change behavior. Using your notes from these interviews, write your paper comparing and contrasting their answers. Describe how you think their cultures affect their responses. In your paper also discuss which of their cultural beliefs are most like yours, and which you find most surprising or different.

3. In western cultures, psychology is presented as a natural science, with great emphasis on the scientific method. Write a paper describing how psychology might be studied from a nonscientific approach. Include in your paper a brief description of a problem such as "teen pregnancy" or "televised violence" and how it might be studied from a nonscientific approach.

Circle of Quality – Chapter 1

Please give us your feedback. We thank you in advance for assisting us in improving the next edition. The contact information is listed in the preface.

What are the three most helpful teaching tools in this chapter?

1.

2.

3.

What are the three least useful teaching tools in this chapter?

1.

2.

3.

What are the three most difficult concepts to teach in this chapter?

1.

2.

3.

Additional Comments:

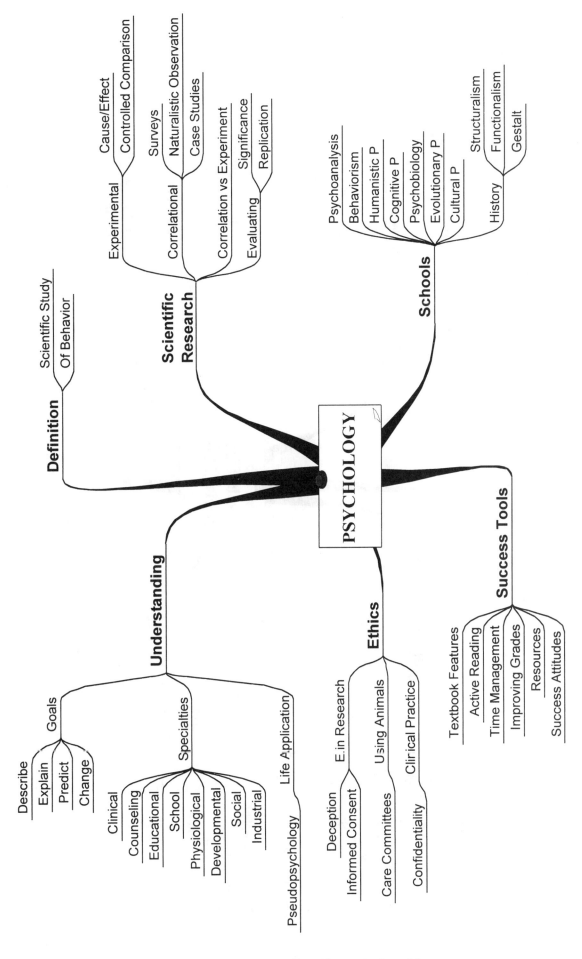

PSYCHOLOGY

Definition
- Scientific Study
- Of Behavior

Scientific Research
- Experimental
  - Cause/Effect
  - Controlled Comparison
- Correlational
  - Surveys
  - Naturalistic Observation
  - Case Studies
- Correlation vs Experiment
- Evaluating
  - Significance
  - Replication

Schools
- Psychoanalysis
- Behaviorism
- Humanistic P
- Cognitive P
- Psychobiology
- Evolutionary P
- Cultural P
- History
  - Structuralism
  - Functionalism
  - Gestalt

Understanding
- Goals
  - Describe
  - Explain
  - Predict
  - Change
- Specialties
  - Clinical
  - Counseling
  - Educational
  - School
  - Physiological
  - Developmental
  - Social
  - Industrial
- Life Application
  - Pseudopsychology

Ethics
- E. in Research
  - Deception
  - Informed Consent
- Using Animals
  - Care Committees
- Clinical Practice
  - Confidentiality

Success Tools
- Textbook Features
- Active Reading
- Time Management
- Improving Grades
- Resources
- Success Attitudes

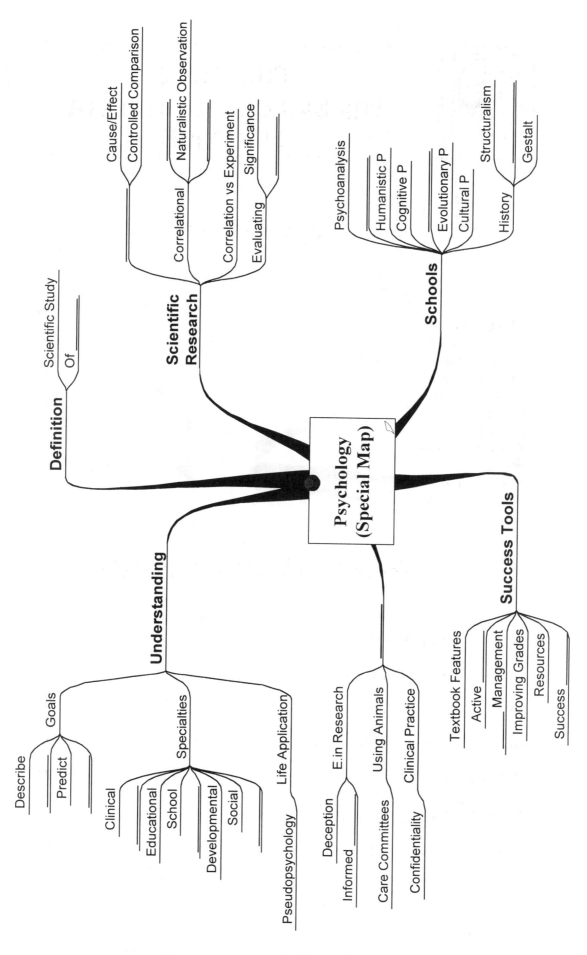

Psychology (Special Map)

Definition
- Scientific Study
  - Of

Scientific Research
- Correlational
  - Cause/Effect
  - Controlled Comparison
  - Naturalistic Observation
- Correlation vs Experiment
- Evaluating
  - Significance

Schools
- Psychoanalysis
- Humanistic P
- Cognitive P
- Evolutionary P
- Cultural P
- History
  - Structuralism
  - Gestalt

Understanding
- Goals
  - Describe
  - Predict
- Specialties
  - Clinical
  - Educational
  - School
  - Developmental
  - Social
- Life Application
  - Pseudopsychology
- E.in Research
  - Deception
  - Informed
  - Using Animals
    - Care Committees
  - Clinical Practice
    - Confidentiality

Success Tools
- Textbook Features
  - Active
  - Management
  - Improving Grades
  - Resources
  - Success

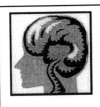

CHAPTER 2
THE BIOLOGICAL BASES OF BEHAVIOR

Outline

The Neuron

Structure of a Neuron
Resting Potential and Action Potential

Chemical Messengers

Nervous System Messengers

Research Highlight
The Search for Better Painkillers

Endocrine System Messengers
The Hypothalamus

The Peripheral Nervous System

The Somatic Nervous System
The Autonomic Nervous System

The Central Nervous System

The Spinal Cord
The Brain

Gender and Cultural Diversity
Sexual Orientation and the Hypothalamus

Gender and Cultural Diversity
Male and Female Differences in the Brain

Studying the Brain

Active Learning
Understanding Brain Anatomy and Function
Anatomical Studies

Lesion Techniques
Electrical Recording
Electrical Stimulation
Split-Brain Research
CAT, PET, and MRI

GOAL

Learning Objectives

Upon completion of CHAPTER 2, the student should be able to:

1. Define the two major divisions of the nervous system (p. 48).
2. Draw a neuron, label its parts, and describe the function of each part (pp. 48-49).
3. Describe the electrochemical process that changes a resting potential into an action potential, and explain the purpose of the sodium-potassium pump (pp. 49-53).
4. Define neurotransmitter and explain how neurotransmitters act to excite or inhibit action potentials (pp. 53-54).
5. Briefly explain how psychoactive drugs affect the synapse; describe the problems associated with morphine as a painkiller, and outline the scientific search for a new painkiller (pp. 55-56).
6. Describe the endocrine system and its major functions. Discuss the role of the hypothalamus within the endocrine system, and the concept of homeostasis (pp. 56-58).
7. List and describe the functions of the two major subdivisions of the peripheral nervous system (PNS); explain the differences between an afferent and efferent pathway; and describe the interactions between and functions of the parasympathetic and sympathetic nervous systems (pp. 59-62).
8. List the two major subdivisions of the central nervous system (CNS) and describe the functions of the spinal cord (pp. 63-65).
9. Describe the cerebral cortex; identify the location of the four cortical lobes, and describe the functions of each lobe; identify the location of, and describe the function of each of the following cortical areas: motor control, association, projection, Broca's, and Wernicke's (pp. 66-69).
10. Identify the location of the subcortical areas of the brain and describe the functions of each part (corpus callosum, thalamus, hypothalamus, limbic system); identify the parts of the limbic system involved with memory, aggression, and fear. Describe LeVay's research regarding the brain and sexual orientation (pp. 69-73).
11. Identify the location of the cerebellum and the parts of the brain stem (pons, medulla, reticular activating system); describe the functions of each of these parts of the brain (pp. 73-74).
12. Describe how male and female brains differ, including tasks that generally favor females and tasks that generally favor males (pp. 75-79).
13. Describe and explain the use of the following brain research techniques: anatomical dissection, lesion techniques, electrical recording, electrical stimulation, split-brain research, CAT, PET, and MRI (pp. 77-79, 81-83).
14. Describe the specialized and interdependent functions of the brain's left and right hemispheres (pp. 80-81).

Chapter Summary/Lecture Organizer

Introductory Vignette--Chapter two begins with the story of Phineas Gage and the blasting accident in which a tamping rod was driven through his frontal lobes. The resultant changes in behavior are used as an introduction to the chapter.

I.   **THE NEURON** - In reading this chapter, the students will learn that the brain and the rest of the nervous system are made up of billions of cells called neurons, which are responsible for transmitting information throughout the body.

A. Structure of a Neuron - The main parts of the neuron are the dendrites, the soma, or cell body, and the axon. The dendrites are small branching structures attached to the soma that receive information in the form of chemical messages from other nerve cells. The dendrites transmit the information received to the soma. The soma summarizes the information and, if enough stimulation is received through the dendrites, initiates an action potential that moves down the axon. The axon is a part of the neuron that is specialized for transmitting information to other nerve cells. It may be covered with an insulating substance called myelin. At the end of the axon are small structures called axon terminal buttons that form synapses with other nerve cells and secrete neurotransmitters. Nerves are bundles of axons from neurons having similar functions.

B. Resting Potential and Action Potential - When no information is being conducted by the axon, it is said to be at its resting potential. When the axon is transmitting information to other neurons, an action potential is being conducted. When an action potential reaches the end of the axon, which terminates in branching structures called axon terminal buttons, the terminal buttons secrete neurotransmitters that in turn pass information to other axons. The place where the axon terminal of one axon meets a dendrite of another axon is called the synapse. All action potentials in a given neuron are of the same intensity.

II.   **CHEMICAL MESSENGERS** - Chemical messages are directed by the nervous system, within and between neurons, and by the endocrine system which distributes hormones through the bloodstream

A. Nervous System Messengers - Information is transferred from one neuron to another at the synapse via chemicals called neurotransmitters. Neurotransmitters are released by axon terminal buttons when an action potential reaches the buttons. The transmitters can be excitatory or inhibitory. Most psychoactive drugs have their effect on the nervous system by affecting the amount of neurotransmitters that cross the synapse. When a neurotransmitter is released in to the synaptic gap, it binds to the receptor sites on the membrane of the receiving cell. With sufficient stimulation of this membrane an action potential will be generated. This action potential operates on the all-or-nothing principle; it either fires or it does not.

B. Endocrine System Messengers - The chemical messengers in the endocrine system are called hormones. Working with the nervous system the endocrine system effects changes in behavior as well as maintaining the body's "status quo." The primary function of the major glands of this system (pituitary, thyroid, adrenals and the pancreas) is to maintain homeostasis, the normal functioning of the bodily processes. A second major function of the endocrine system is to secrete hormones that regulate the reproductive system. The major link between the endocrine and nervous systems is the hypothalamus.

C. The Hypothalamus – This is the real "master endocrine gland" and the major link between the endocrine system and the nervous system, through its controls of the pituitary gland.

III.   **THE PERIPHERAL NERVOUS SYSTEM** - The two major parts of the nervous system are the peripheral nervous system and the central nervous system. The peripheral nervous system includes all nerves going to and from the brain and spinal cord. Its two major subdivisions are the somatic and the autonomic nervous systems.

A. The Somatic Nervous System - This system includes all nerves carrying afferent (incoming) sensory information and efferent (outgoing) motor information to and from the sense organs and skeletal muscles.

B. The Autonomic Nervous System - This system includes those nerves outside the brain and spinal cord that maintain normal functioning of glands, heart muscles, and the smooth muscles of the blood vessels and internal organs. The autonomic nervous system is divided into two branches, the parasympathetic and the sympathetic, which tend to work in opposition to one another. The parasympathetic branch of the autonomic nervous system is normally dominant when a person is relaxed and not under physical or mental stress. Its main function is to slow heart rate, lower blood pressure, and increase digestion and elimination. The sympathetic nervous system is normally dominant when a person is under physical or mental stress. It functions to increase heart rate and blood pressure and slow digestive processes, mobilizing the body for fight or flight.

IV.   **THE CENTRAL NERVOUS SYSTEM** - The central nervous system is composed of the brain and the spinal cord.

A. The Spinal Cord - The spinal cord, the communications link between the brain and the rest of the body below the neck, consists of the gray matter and the white matter. It is involved in all voluntary and reflex responses of the body below the neck. Gray matter contains cell bodies and synapses where information is transferred and processed in the spinal cord. The white matter is made up wholly of axons carrying information to and from the brain. Damage to the spinal cord can therefore cause differing amounts of paralysis, depending on the location of the spinal cord injury.

B. The Brain - The major divisions of the brain are the cerebral cortex, the subcortical areas, the cerebellum, and the brain stem. The cerebral cortex--the bumpy and convoluted area making up the outside surface of the brain--is divided into four lobes: frontal, parietal, occipital, and temporal. The frontal lobes control voluntary movement and speech. The speech area, which is found most often in the left frontal lobe, is called Broca's area. The frontal lobes are also involved with self-awareness, the ability to plan, and working memory. Working memory is located in the very front of the frontal lobes. The parietal lobes function as the receiving areas for sensory information from the limbs and skin. The occipital lobe is almost entirely involved with visual sensation and visual information processing. The major functions of the temporal lobes include hearing and language. The language area, which is found most often in the left temporal lobe, is called Wernicke's area.

The subcortex lies in the middle of the brain under the cerebral cortex and includes many different areas. The most important are the corpus callosum, the thalamus, the hypothalamus, and the limbic system. The corpus callosum is a connecting bridge of axons between the two cerebral hemispheres. The thalamus is the major incoming sensory relay center for the brain and may also be involved in working memory. The hypothalamus regulates functioning of the endocrine system and is the major brain center for the regulation of temperature, thirst, hunger, sex, and aggression. The limbic system is an interconnected system of several subcortical and cortical brain structures that is involved with memory and many types of emotional behaviors.

The cerebellum is located at the base of the brain behind the brain stem. It is responsible for the maintenance of smooth movement, postural adjustments, and coordinated motor activity. Recent research suggests it also plays a role in perception, cognition and motor learning. The brain stem lies below the subcortex and in front of the cerebellum. Its major areas are the pons, the medulla, and the reticular formation. The pons is involved with control of respiration, movement, facial expression, and sleep. The major function of the medulla is the control of respiration. The reticular formation is a diffuse set of neurons that are associated with attention and arousal.

> **Gender and Cultural Diversity: Sexual Orientation and the Hypothalamus** - Research shows relationships between the hypothalamus, gender, and sexual orientation. But we do not know what is cause and what is effect. This section includes the work by Allen et al. (1989) and LeVay (1991).

> **Gender and Cultural Diversity: Male and Female Differences in the Brain** - Recent research also seems to indicate that male and female differences may ultimately stem from biological factors. Early hormonal influence and anatomical differences in brain structure are being further investigated. This section contains the work of Kimura (1992), Reinisch et al. (1991), Collaer et al. (1995), and Diamond et al. (1996).

V.   **STUDYING THE BRAIN** - Students are introduced to several research techniques that have been used to study the brain and the nervous system. These techniques include lesions, electrical recording, electrical stimulation, split-brain surgery, and different types of brain scans such as CAT, PET, and MRI.

> **Active Learning/Critical Thinking: Understanding Brain Anatomy and Function** - Students are given two hypothetical cases regarding brain surgery and a car crash. They are asked to apply specific terms from the chapter to these two cases.

A. Anatomical Studies - Anatomical research techniques refer to studying the brain's structure through direct observation, such as examining the brains of cadavers, studying slices of brain tissue under a microscope, and most recently by compiling these slices into computerized views of actual human brains.

B. Lesion Techniques - Lesion research techniques involve destroying brain or nerve tissue and studying any resultant changes in the animal's behavior.

C. Electrical Recording - Electrical recording techniques allow researchers to monitor the electrical activity of the brain and nervous system. By inserting electrodes into the brain or on its surface, researchers can record and analyze large changes in brain activity and measure the electrical activity of the nervous system.

D. Electrical Stimulation - Electrodes can also be used to stimulate neurons to fire action potentials on command, which enables researchers to observe an animal to see what behavioral changes occur as a result of the stimulation.

E. Split-Brain Research - In split-brain research, patients who have had their corpus callosum severed to alleviate the symptoms of severe epilepsy are studied to determine the differences in functional abilities between the left and right cerebral hemispheres. Split-brain research suggests that the left hemisphere is specialized for language and analytical functions, whereas the right hemisphere is specialized for nonverbal abilities, including musical abilities and perceptual and spatiomanipulative skills.

F. CAT, PET, and MRI - These three techniques are used to study the structures and functions of intact, living brains without having to place electrodes in the brain or destroy brain tissue. Computerized Axial Tomography (CAT) allows brain researchers to use X-rays to view cross-sections of the brain. Positron Emission Tomography (PET) uses radioactive glucose to enable researchers to observe neural activity in an intact, living brain. Magnetic Resonance Imaging (MRI) produces images of the brain that are superior in quality and sharpness to CAT scans by sensing radio waves generated by different areas in the brain.

Teaching Resources

SECTION I – THE NEURON

Learning Objectives #'s 2 & 3
Lecture Lead-Ins # 2
Discussion Questions #'s1 & 5
Brain-Based Learning Activities #'s 2.1- 2.3

SECTION II – CHEMICAL MESSENGERS

Learning Objectives #'s 4-7
Lecture Lead-Ins #3
Brain-Based Learning Activity # 2.2

SECTION III – THE PERIPHERAL NERVOUS SYSTEM

Learning Objectives #'s 1 & 8
Active Learning Activity # 2.2

SECTION IV – THE CENTRAL NERVOUS SYSTEM

Learning Objectives #'s 9 - 13
Lecture Lead-Ins #'s 4 & 5
Lecture Extender # 2.1
Discussion Questions #'s 1 - 3, 4 & 6
Active Learning Activities #'s 2.3 – 2.7
Brain-Based Learning Activities #'s 2.3 – 2.7
Critical Thinking Exercises #'s 2.2 & 2.3
Gender and Cultural Diversity Activities #2.1
Writing Project #'s2.1 & 2.2.

SECTION V – STUDYING THE BRAIN

Learning Objectives #'s 14 & 15
Lecture Lead-Ins # 1
Discussion Questions # 4
Active Learning Activities # 2.8 & 2.9

Lecture Lead-Ins

1.   Ask students to bring in copies of *The National Inquirer*, *The Star*, and other "newspapers" that have articles related to brain and brain functioning. You'll often get stories about head transplants. Explain why this is impossible. You may want to ask, if it *were* possible, would they be willing to have a head or body transplant. This leads in to interesting discussions and emphasizes the point that we are truly "our brains."

2.   Take the extreme position that "all you are" is determined by the types and amount of neurotransmitters that ooze through your synaptic gaps. Ask students if they think that all their thoughts, hopes, dreams and aspirations are results of physiological process; their love, hate, anger and memories are only at the synaptic level. Take this extreme position and have the students debate this topic with you. You should meet with a great deal of disbelief that this is "all we are."

3.   Ask the students if they see any possibility for brain control through mechanical means. Are there methods available today that can be used to control behavior? Discuss the role of psychiatric drugs in modifying human abnormal behavior. Discuss the animal research on brain implants and lesioning, and drug infusion. Ask for student opinions on this topic and use their input for the lead-in to your lectures on brain and behavior.

4.   Ask the students if they know anyone in their lives with Alzheimer's, spinal cord injury, or Parkinson's Disease. If not, mention former President Ronald Reagan, former "Superman" Christopher Reeves or former boxing champion Muhammed Ali. Given a choice between a disease of the body or a disease of the brain, which would they choose and why? Explore what their reasons say about the importance of human brains in our culture.

5.   Your doctor informs you that your brain has grown too large for your skull. You will survive, as long as they operate right away. The doctor states that s/he must take out one part of the brain to make space. You must decide which part of the brain you could best live without. Which brain part would you give up and why?

Lecture Extenders

2.1 - Brain Disorders

Oliver Sacks, who has the training of a neurologist and the pen of a wordsmith, has chronicled his experiences with brain-damaged patients in a way that is unmatched by any current writer. The first selection from his book <u>The Man Who Mistook His Wife for a Hat and Other Clinical Tales</u> has become the basis for an opera. Sacks' writings on patients with encephalitis was the inspiration for the movie <u>Awakenings</u>. Sacks has the ability to recount these clinical sagas in such an engaging way that the reader can understand the world of the patient who, through a stroke of bad luck, has lost the ability to engage life from the usual parameters that most of us take for granted. Through Sacks, one is able to get a glimpse of how it must feel to have time stop, even though internally your mind continues to move forward. One enters the confused world of another patient who no longer understands his visual environment. The two following case histories are titled "The Man Who Mistook His Wife for a Hat" (the title of the book is taken from this case) and "The Lost Mariner."

In the case history "The Man Who Mistook His Wife for a Hat," Sacks describes Dr. P. (the patient) as a well-known musician who was a well-known singer and who is still on the faculty of a music school. Dr. P. had difficulty for some time in recognizing objects. He no longer recognized people by their faces, unless they had a characteristic mark such as a mustache, mole, etc. His primary cue for identification was sound, so he waited for people to speak before identifying them. This failure to understand what he was seeing had progressed so far that he made mistakes others found amusing: he mistook fire hydrants and parking meters for small children; he would speak to elaborate knobs on furniture, perceiving these inanimate objects as people.

At his initial examination with Sacks, Dr. P. was unable to finish dressing, forgetting which object was the shoe and what he should do with it. When Dr. P. was leaving the office, he confused his hat with his wife's head and tried to pick her up instead. When Sacks visited him at home, Dr. P. extended his hand to a grandfather clock in the room. It wasn't until he heard Sacks' voice that he distinguished between the clock and Sacks. Other observations indicated that Dr. P. could not recognize emotions on actors' and actresses' faces on television nor identify their genders. He did not recognize the photographs of relatives in his home--unless they had an unusual facial characteristic. When asked to name a rose, he called it a "convoluted red form with a linear green attachment." However, after smelling it, he immediately recognized it as a rose. He described a glove as a "continuous surface enfolded upon itself with five out-pouchings," but he had no inkling of the "real" name or what one did with it. In contrast, when shown complicated geometrical designs, such as a dodecahedron, he immediately gave the correct names. Interestingly, he no longer dreamed in visual images.

With such loss it was amazing that he could still function, but, according to his wife, he set everything to music. When he was dressing, bathing, or eating, he accompanied the activity by some melody. If he were interrupted in the sequence, he became confused and did not remember what he was doing. For example, if he were interrupted while eating a meal, he would stop and stare at the food in confusion-- until he got a whiff of it.

Dr. Sacks refers to this as a case of visual agnosia due to some type of degeneration in the occipital cortex. Dr. P. can still see, but the images have no meaning. The impaired process is a judgmental loss concerning the visual images. One can see objects, but one does not know what one should do relative to these objects. They have lost their visual meaning. One interesting aspect of this case is that Mr. P. does not even know that he has lost this ability. He does not remember an earlier time when he responded differently. According to Sacks, not to know that one has lost something can be looked at as either good or bad, depending upon one's perspective.

In the second case, "The Lost Mariner," Sacks discusses a case in which the patient's memory was unable to store any new material. Jimmie G., age 49, was brought to a house for the aging (in 1975) because he was showing signs of confusion and dementia. Interviews with Jimmie indicated that he still perceived himself as age 19. He talked of his job with the navy, a brother who planned to become an accountant, and identified Truman as the current president. His memory of the past had stopped at 1945. In what Sacks refers to as a thoughtless response on his own part, he showed Jimmie a mirror, asking him to identify the reflection. As expected, he did not recognize himself and accused Sacks of playing a nasty trick on him. Sacks, after leaving the room for two minutes, returned and reintroduced himself to Jimmie who had no recollection of the earlier encounter.

All tests of IQ indicated a person with high ability. Jimmie solved all problems very quickly, unless they involved several seconds delay in which case he forgot what he was doing. He was excellent in games such as checkers, but for games like chess, his memory could not retain information for a sufficient period to plan moves. During his length of stay at the home (several years) he never learned to consistently identify anyone, although he developed a sense of familiarity regarding the others. The only strong emotional tie he expressed was to his brother since his brother existed in the only time sphere that Jimmie could remember. However, he was constantly puzzled by his brother's premature aging and could not understand why he looked so old.

Sacks tried different strategies to reinstate a memory process so that Jimmie could begin to establish a memory for recent events. He was given a diary and asked to write down daily events. Jimmie however repeatedly lost the diary until it was attached to him. Even the diary, however, was not a solution. When he looked at what he had written the day before, there was no recollection of the event or of having made the entry. Despite recognizing his handwriting, he could not remember. Sacks referred to Jimmie's memory as a "bottom-less pit" into which all new experiences disappeared.

What caused this total failure to record new events in permanent memory? Sacks diagnosed this case as Kosakoff's syndrome, a disorder caused by heavy drinking in which the mamillary bodies of the brain atrophy.

Reference: Sacks, O. (1987). The man who mistook his wife for a hat and other clinical tales. (pp. 8-42). New York: Harper & Row.

Key Terms

THE NEURON

Action Potential (p. 48)
Axon (p. 48)
Axon Terminal Buttons (p. 48)
Dendrites (p. 48)
Ions (p. 49)
Myelin (p. 51)
Nerve (p. 49)
Neurons (p. 48)
Resting Potential (p. 50)
Sodium-Potassium Pump (p. 50)
Soma (p. 48)

CHEMICAL MESSENGERS

All-or-Nothing Principle (p. 54)
Endocrine System (p. 53)
Homeostasis (p. 57)
Hormones (p. 56)
Hypothalamus (p. 57)
Neurotransmitters (p. 53)
Psychoactive Drugs (p. 55)
Synapse (p. 53)

THE PERIPHERAL NERVOUS SYSTEM

Afferent (p. 59)
Autonomic Nervous System (p. 60)
Efferent (p. 59)
Parasympathetic Nervous System (p. 60)
Peripheral Nervous System (p. 59)
Somatic Nervous System (p. 59)
Sympathetic Nervous System (p. 60)

THE CENTRAL NERVOUS SYSTEM

Association Areas (p. 67)
Brain (p. 63)
Brain Stem (p. 74)
Broca's Area (p. 67)
Central Nervous System (p. 63)
Cerebellum (p. 73)
Cerebral Cortex (p. 66)
Corpus Callosum (p. 70)
Dyslexia (p. 69)
Frontal Lobes (p. 66)
Limbic System (p. 71)
Medulla (p. 74)
Motor Control Area (p. 67)
Occipital Lobes (p. 68)
Parietal Lobes (p. 67)
Pons (p. 74)
Projection Areas (p. 67)
Reflex Arc (p. 64)
Reflexes (p. 64)
Reticular Activating System (RAS) (p. 74)
Spinal Cord (p. 63)
Temporal Lobes (p. 69)
Thalamus (p. 70)
Wernicke's Area (p. 69)

STUDYING THE BRAIN

CAT (ComputerAxial Tomography) Scan (p.81)
Electrodes (p. 79)
Electroencephalogram - EEG (p. 79)
Lesion Technique (p. 79)
MRI (Magnetic Resonance Imageing) (p. 82)
PET (Positron Emission Tomography) Scan
(p. 81)

Discussion Questions

1. Students are often surprised (and sometimes dismayed) about the content of this chapter. They seem to feel that the material is more appropriate to a biology or anatomy class. It helps to discuss how the study of the brain and nervous system belongs within the domain of psychology. Mentioning the role of diminished dopamine in Parkinson's and excessive dopamine in schizophrenia helps make the study of neurons and neurotransmitters more interesting. Also, tying in the use of L-Dopa and antipsychotic drugs to treat these illnesses further illustrates "why we need to know this stuff!" Asking students to describe friends and family members who suffer from brain function deficits, stroke, or brain-crippling diseases such as Alzheimer's also demonstrates how understanding the pure science of brain anatomy and functioning supports the applied science of helping people with disorders.

2. In Chapter 1, the text explored issues related to the ethical treatment of human and animal subjects. Ask students to discuss whether the transplants of tissue from human fetuses, animals, or other available donors violates these standards. Help students to separate their own feelings about abortion and animal rights from the ethical standards of scientific psychology. If time allows, you may want to try, or repeat, the Values Clarification (Critical Thinking Exercise 1.1) with a statement related to this chapter. You might also want to invite a guest speaker from a local hospital to explain the process and value of organ donation. Students have many myths and misconceptions in this area.

3. Chapter 2 contains a bewildering number of specific terms and concepts. One way to increase student retention is to ask them to form small groups and list the five most essential structures of the brain and the five least essential. This always leads to a lively discussion. Although there are obviously no "right" answers, the struggle to prioritize the various structures seems to help bring meaning and organization to chapter contents.

4. Ask the students how the human race might be different if humans had evolved a dominant *right* hemisphere?

5. Assign students to design a better nervous system. What's good or bad about the existing electro-chemical signal propagation? One group could be tasked with defining the major capacities of the existing system and another group could invent a brand new signal system based on different principles. Challenge the students to see if there is a simpler way to set up such a system capable of handling millions of messages. How does it compare to a telephone system or a computer network?

6. A large percentage of brain development in humans occurs after birth. This plasticity means that the early childhood environment has great influence on the subsequent development of the dendritic patterns. (Illustration - "How the Brain Works, text p. xx). What differences in size, complexity or functioning might we expect in the brains of children from undernourished, violent, boring, abandoned, secure, or enriched environments? What are the implications of every human being we meet having a different wiring pattern?

WWW. Web Sites

Brain Imaging

http://128.231.106.172/DIRweb/NAB/coghill.htm

This site provides examples of how imaging techniques have been used to visualize the pattern of brain activation in human subjects who are experiencing either acute or chronic pain. It is no wonder that this site is brought to you courtesy of the National Institute of Dental Research...

Basic Neural Processes Tutorials

http://psych.hanover.edu/Krantz/neurotut.html

Dr. John Krantz of Hanover College has created a tutorial site on neuron function and neuroanatomy. Among the features of this site are an interactive tutorial on the structures of the human brain, a link to an extensive collection of brain images, a tutorial on the physical factors that produce the action potential, and a glossary of terms relating to biological psychology.

The Action Potential

http://fig.cox.miami.edu/Faculty/Tom/bil255/action_potential.html

This site provides the advanced student with a brief coverage of the physical factors in the axon membrane that interact to produce the action potential.

The Whole Brain Atlas

http://www.med.harvard.edu/AANLIB/home.html

This is the complete and comprehensive site for students interested in images of the human brain. This Harvard University site provides a primer on neuroimaging and access to an extensive collection of images of the normal brain. Also covered are movies and images of brains that have suffered accidental damage or that have been damaged through disease (e.g. Alzheimer's Disease).

The Human Brain: Dissections of the Brain

http://indy.radiology.uiowa.edu/Providers/Textbooks/BrainAnatomy/BrainAnatomy.html

This colorful site provides a series of images of the human brain with each image accompanied by a description and a labeled diagram. Warning: This site is not for the faint-hearted as these images are taken from actual human brain dissections.

Dr. D's Neuroanatomy Stuff

http://web.vet.cornell.edu/public/education/neuro/index.htm

Dr. DelaHunta offers a site containing labeled and unlabeled sections of dog brain. These sections show the anatomy of the spinal cord through the forebrain and can be used for learning and review of neuroanatomy. The site also provides a nice coverage of the anatomy and function of the 12 cranial nerves (see the Anatomic Diagnosis section for this feature).

Conversations with Neil's Brain

http://weber.u.washington.edu/~wcalvin/bk7/bk7.htm

Neil is a young man who has suffered a series of epileptic seizures and who requires brain surgery to eliminate the seizures. This site provides a running conversation with the surgeons and Neil on his brain. Topics include: how the brain handles memory, vision, mood, and language. This site will be of great interest to students as they study the mind-brain problem.

Timmons and Hamilton: Drugs, Brains, and Behaviors

http://www.rci.rutgers.edu/~lwh/drugs/

Drs. Timmons and Hamilton have written an on-line book covering drugs and behavior. The site offers a brief history of psychopharmacology and a drug resource link as well as coverage of topics ranging from pain to fear and schizophrenia. The book also offers an on-line glossary of psychopharmacology terms.

The Limbic System

http://thalamus.wustl.edu/course/limbic/.html

This site contains labeled figures and text explaining the anatomy and function of the olfactory cortex, the amygdala, and the hippocampus.

Suggested Films and Videos

The Physiology of Behavior

Films for the Humanities and Science, 1993. 60 minutes. This video (also available as a videodisk) includes segments covering recent research on addiction, development of the human brain, dreams, genetic testing, memory, and others. You can easily play only those segments you want.

Evolution

Discovery Channel, 1994. 45 minutes. This segment from "The Brain: Our Hidden Universe" explores the evolutionary development of the brain and provides wonderful graphics depicting neural transmission.

Nerves

Insight Media, 1992. 24 minutes. This BBC presentation uses animation to demonstrate the development and propagation of an action potential. Synaptic transmission, transmitters, agonists, and antagonists are also discussed. Disorders such as Alzheimer's disease, Parkinson's disease, depression, and anxiety are considered.

Inside Information: The Brain and How It Works

Films for Humanities and Science,1991. 58 minutes. This video explores the latest research about the brain's processes. It is visually memorable and packed with information.

The Responsive Brain

Annenberg/CPB, 1990. 30 minutes. From Zimbardo's "Discovering Psychology" series, this video examines how the brain analyzes environmental information and controls behavior. It explores the relationship between structure and function. There is good use of human (maternal and touch studies) and animal (enriched environment studies) research to support the contention that environment influences brain development.

The Behaving Brain

Annenberg/CPB, 1990. 30 minutes. This segment of Zimbardo's "Discovering Psychology" series explores the process of neural communication through the action of several neurotransmitters in the formation of an action potential. Additionally, the overall structure of the brain is discussed, and its specialization features are explained.

The Enlightened Machine

Annenberg/CPB, 1984. 58 minutes. This film from "The Brain, Mind and Behavior" series uses microphotography and interviews with neuroscience experts to explain the functions of the brain. The viewer is introduced to modern recording techniques: CAT, PET, and EEG. Problems with strokes, Huntington's disease, multiple sclerosis, and hydrocephalus are used to reveal information about the brain's function.

Brain and Nervous System: Your Information Superhighway

Films for the Humanities & Sciences, 1998. 25 minutes. This program explores the brain and nervous system using the analogy of computers and the Internet. Topics include: electrical impulses and how nerve messages travel; parts of the brain and their functions; how the brain and spinal cord are protected; the senses; and diseases, drugs, and their effect on the brain and nervous system.

The Universe Within: Our Brain

Made for the Discovery Channel/The Brain Store, xxxx. Trilogy with each video being 45 - 90 minutes. High tech graphics and astonishing insights into the workings of the brain, including: perception, memory, emotions, brain structure, aging, and renewal.

Alzheimer's: The Tangled Mind

Films for the Humanities & Sciences, 1997. 23 minutes. Researchers discuss how old drugs, such as anti-inflammatories, and new drugs, close to approval, are being used to alleviate symptoms. We also meet a doctor who uses an experimental form of CAT scanning to identify individuals at risk of developing the disease.

The Center of Her Storms: A Struggle With Epilepsy

TV Ontario/Filmmakers Library, 1999. 55 minutes. A first person perspective, from a 24 year old, on the experience of living with epilepsy from the age of nine and how corrective surgery on the left temporal lobe improves extraordinary explosions in brain activity.

Success

Books For Success

Sylwester, Robert (1995). **A Celebration of Neurons: An Educator's Guide to the Human Brain.** Association for Supervision and Curriculum Development.
A superb introduction to improving teaching and learning by building on new information in optimizing brain functioning.

Pert, Candace B. (1997). **Molecules of Emotion:Why You Feel the Way You Feel.** Scribner.
A fascinating mystery story on discovering the biochemical basis of feelings. An important description of the extended effort by which progress in science is accomplished.

Ramachandran, V. S. & Blakeslee, Sandra (1998). **Phantoms in the Brain: Probing the Mysteries of the Human Mind.** William Morrow & Company.
A funny and thought provoking investigation of neurological mysteries and what we can learn from them about the functioning of the human brain and the nature of human consciousness.

Gamon, David & Bragdon, Allen D. (1998). **Building Mental Muscle: Conditioning Exercise for the Six Intelligence Zones.** Allen D. Bragdon Pub.
How to improve mental abilities.

Howard, Pierce (1994). **The Owner's Manual for the Brain: Everyday Applications from Mind-Brain Research.** Leornian Press.
A rare blend of good science and practical tools. The most widely useful book in this section.

Gupta M.D., Kapil (1997). **Human Brain Coloring.** Princeton Review.
Understanding anatomy by drawing not just by reading. An interactive approach to understanding the brain's organization and functions. Features 125 striking illustrations.

Kotulak, Ronald (1997). **Inside the Brain : Revolutionary Discoveries of How the Mind Works.** Andrews McMeel Pub.
Strong sections on brain plasticity and responsiveness to environmental factors. Essential reading for parents concerned about the impact of timely education and the damage from violence/stress.

Tyler, Timothy J. (1992-1996). **The Graphic Brain.** Didactic Systems (Brooks/Cole Pub.) - CD Software

Active Learning

Active Learning Activity 2.1 - The Graphic Brain

To illustrate the dynamic processes involved in the firing of nerve cells *The Graphic Brain* - (Software CD, Timothy J. Tyler, Didactic Systems, Brooks/Cole Pub.) has excellent demonstrations in the modules on Resting Potential, Action Potential, Synaptic Transmission, and Neural Membrane. Although some of the modules contain details beyond the scope of an introductory psychology course it is very easy to show only parts of each module.

Active Learning Activity 2.2 - The Role of the ANS

Inform students that you need to find out their average heart rates. Instruct each student take his or her pulse for 15 seconds and multiply their pulse count by four. Next, without warning, make a very loud noise using a fog horn concealed in a paper bag or simply pounding on the lectern. Now immediately instruct the students to quickly take their pulse again. Compare the two pulse rates. Discuss the adaptive and maladaptive components of the automatic response to activation of the ANS.

Active Learning Activity 2.3 - "Draw-a-Brain"

Before you begin your lecture or discussion of Chapter 2, an easy (and surprisingly fun) way to motivate students is to bring in large sheets of poster paper and colored pens. Have students get into groups of 3 or 4, give them one large poster sheet per group, a set of pens, and ask them to draw a brain and label the major structures. List the various terms on the board (cerebral cortex, brain stem, cerebellum, four lobes, right and left hemisphere, etc.). Encourage them to share their ideas, notes, their own brains--but NO books. Walk around to the various groups and you'll be surprised how difficult this is for them. You'll also be surprised at how engaged they become in the activity. Choose the best two or three drawings and post them with masking tape to the front of the room. During your lecture, refer to the drawings. If time allows, you may also ask them to list the functions of the major structures and/or to draw a neuron with its major parts and functions.

Active Learning Activity 2.4- Reflex versus Voluntary Action

Ask a student volunteer to come to the front of the class and to sit on the edge of the laboratory table, a high stool, or a chair with pillows. (The student must be high enough to be seen from the back of the room and high enough so that his or her legs dangle freely.) Using your fingertips, locate the soft area just below the student's kneecap. Take a reflex hammer, or standard ruler, and gently strike the soft area to elicit the knee-jerk reflex. You'll know you've hit the right spot when the student's leg shoots forward instantaneously and involuntarily.

Now instruct the student to voluntarily kick his or her leg as quickly as possible after you touch it. After a brief delay and a little discussion of the reflex arc, lightly touch the student's knee in the same soft region. Note how much longer it takes to execute the voluntary versus the reflex movement. Ask students to explain why. (The message for the voluntary movement must travel to the brain, a decision must be made, and a message must be sent back to the leg muscle. On the other hand, the knee-jerk reflex is processed in the spinal cord. The fastest voluntary action takes up to five times as long as a reflex.)

Active Learning Activity 2.5 - Brain Structures and Functions--Stroop Effect

A good way to begin discussion on the various parts and functions of the brain is to use the Stroop Effect. You can present the effect as originally done by J. R. Stroop (Studies of interference in serial verbal reactions. Journal of Experimental Psychology, 18, 643-662.), or you can use the transparency provided with this text. If you use the transparency, you will want to point out that for most people recognition of different colors is probably processed in the right hemisphere while the names of the colors are processed in the left hemisphere. In our classes, we often begin this demonstration by asking a student to read the words as quickly as possible while we time him/her. Then we take out a few coins from our pockets or purses, and lay them on the table at the front of class. We then state that we will give the money to the first student who can match the volunteer's time without making a mistake. The only difference is that this time they must read the colors. (We try to have about 50 cents in our pockets--Teachers in California haven't had a raise in a long time!) After several students have tried, and usually have failed, we give the money to the student who was the closest to winning. The demonstration stimulates students to want to know why it works and serves as excellent motivation for the discussion of brain function, research techniques, etc.

Active Learning Activity 2.6 - Sheep Brain Dissection

In addition to drawing diagrams on the chalkboard and pointing to models when discussing parts of the brain, it adds a bit of intrigue to dissect a "real" brain. Preserved brains are available from biological supply houses. Although human brains are very expensive, sheep brains can be purchased for under $5 and, though smaller than a human brain (they are about the size of a fist), they have all the major structures you will be discussing in class. You may want to follow procedures outlined in a good lab manual, such as Norman Ferguson's Neuropsychology Laboratory Manual.

If you do not have access to such a manual, a basic procedure follows. Before dissecting the brain, point out major surface structures such as the cortical lobes, the cerebellum, and the cranial nerves. Show the difference between gray and white matter by cutting a one centimeter slice off the posterior pole of the surface of the cortex. Now cut the brain into two symmetrical halves; this will expose brain stem and midbrain structures including the corpus callosum, the thalamus, the pons, and the medulla.

Active Learning Activity 2.7 - Brain Anatomy and Brain Function

You can involve your entire class in a review of brain anatomy and brain function by using different groups of students in the classroom to represent various parts of the brain. First, split the entire class down the middle, the right half being the right hemisphere and the left half being the left hemisphere. Tell those students in the front rows they are to represent the frontal lobes; the students in the back rows, the occipital lobes; the students on the sides, the temporal lobes; and the students left in the center, the parietal lobes. You can then review the positions of the cortical lobes by asking all of the students within each area to raise their hands when you name their cortical area. To demonstrate brain function, ask the students to raise their hands only when you name a function that is processed in the cortical area and the hemisphere they represent. Possible suggestions include, Left-hand movement (right parietal lobe), smell (both temporal lobes), reading a book silently (right and left occipital lobes and left parietal lobe), reading out loud (right and left occipital lobes, left parietal lobe, and left frontal lobe), pain in the right hand (left parietal lobe).

Active Learning Activity 2.8 - Drawing on the Right Side of the Brain

(This activity was designed after Edward's Drawing on the Right Side of the Brain, Los Angeles: JP, Tarcher 1970.) Things do not look the same upside down and it is difficult to categorize them by matching what we see with our memories and concepts. We will attempt to use this gap in the abilities of our left hemisphere to allow the right hemisphere to dominate.

Procedure:
Hand out a reproduction of a line drawing (pick your favorite), placing it upside down on the student's desk. Emphasize the following points:
- Try to be quiet.
- Do not turn the figure right side up.
- Look at the figure and notice the angles, shapes and lines. Try to see how they all fit together.
- Draw your figure upside down--like the sample. Start at the top and copy each line, moving from line to adjacent line, putting it all together like a puzzle.
- Don't name things; instead just notice what the lines do, how they curve and flow together.

After all the students have finished, turn the drawing right side up. The students will probably be quite surprised at the sample. Encourage the students to move around and look at other drawings. Note differences (for example, size). Many students find the drawings very funny.

Discussion:
The left hemisphere, confused and blocked by the unfamiliar image and unable to name or symbolize as usual, allows the right hemisphere to take over. The right hemisphere mode of consciousness is different from the left mode. Ask the students the following questions:
- What does the right brain consciousness feel like?
- Did you notice that you were less aware of the passage of time?
- Were you aware of the people around you?
- Did you attend to any environmental inputs?

Active Learning Activity 2.9 – Methods of Studying the Brain

Ask students to complete the Question Map on the methods of studying the brain (Handout 2.9) and discuss any areas of uncertainty.

*H*andout 2.9 – Active Learning

<u>Question Map – Methods of Studying the Brain</u>

Methods	What is the method?	What type of data does it generate?	What are the advantages?	What are the disadvantages?	What questions are we able to answer?
Anatomy Studies					
Lesion Technique					
EEG					
Electrical Stimulation					
CAT					
PET					
MRI					

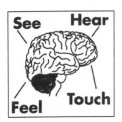

Brain-Based Learning

Brain-Based Learning Activity 2.1 - Neuronal Transmission

Make copies of the following paragraph and cut out a set of terms containing 8 separate slips of paper for each group of students. Be sure to mix them up for each group and task them to assemble these terms in the order in which information is received and transmitted through one neuron and onto the next.

Dendrite	**Soma**	**Axon**	**Axon Terminal Button**
Dendrite	**Synapse**	**Myelin**	**Neurotransmitter**

Brain-based Learning Activity 2.2 - Action Potential Propagation

Function: The following demonstration can be used to illustrate how an action potential moves down an axon. Choose about a dozen of your students to come to the front of the classroom. Have them stand in a line with each student facing the back of the student in front of them. Give the student in the front of the line a squirt gun. The student with the gun is the "axon terminal," while the rest of the students are parts of the axon. At the beginning of the exercise, all the students are at rest (resting potential) with their hands at their sides. Initiate an action potential by applying some stimulus to the last person in line, who taps the next person in line, who taps the next person, and so on. When the person with the squirt gun is tapped, s/he squirts the gun (neurotransmitter release).

Process: Arrange the class in groups around 4 or 5 student desks (or tables) aligned left to right with some spacing. Each desk has two parallel masking tape strips 25% in from front and back respectively. Each group has six pennies, six nickels and six dimes. The tape strips represent the axonic membrane. Place three nickels (sodium ions) in the top and 3 in the bottom area, representing the "outside" areas. Place six pennies (protein ions) and six dimes (potassium ions) in the "inside" of the membrane.

First, each group creates the ionic firing pattern by themselves.

Resting Phase: Each group keeps a tally of the electrical charge for each phase. For simplicity's sake all coins are considered to carry "one" charge. The silver coins are positive. The copper coins are negative. Have the group add up the charge on the outside, the charge on the inside and the charge differential between the two layers.

Action Phase: Get each group member involved in quickly moving the nickels into the membrane. Again add up the charges and calculate the differential. As the two positive ions repel each other the students now move the dimes out to reduce the charge differential. Again have them track the charge and show how the sodium potassium pump works to re-create the resting potential by having them slowly move nickels out and dimes in.

Second, the signal travels across the axon. Starting at the left desk the first group moves their nickels into the membrane. As soon as the charge is sufficient for the action potential, the group on the adjoining desk moves their nickels in, while the first group moves out their dimes (potassium ions) and so on down the line. When the action potential voltage arrives at the last desk in line, they tap the person with the squirt gun and s/he squirts the gun (neurotransmitter release).

Synaptic Calculus: After the action potential propagation has been understood you can add a desk to the left and explain this represents the incoming signals. Give them a non-transparent bag that contains a mix of coins. The students grab a handful of coins. Each coin represents a signal received by a dendrite. In each round eight coins are placed on the desk. The students must calculate the charge after each coin. Whenever the charge reaches 4 (or more) positive "units" the voltage activation threshold has been achieved and the nerve fires by tapping the desk to its right. Be sure to complete the full eight coin layout with each round to show that more positive charges will still result in the same signal being sent. Like a door bell the pressure is either sufficient to ring or not. The rule is that no coins can leave their respective desk. The signal propagates but the ions remain in place.

Psychoactive Drugs: You can add to the preceding set up by supplying each group with a group of foreign coins (pennies from Canada, Germany etc.) that have similar color and shape to American coins. These become the "drug" and are added to the eight coins of each turn. The students can see the powerful effect an excitatory or inhibitory drug can have on signal generation or prevention.

Brain-Based Learning Activity 2.3 - Draw-a-Neuron/Draw-a-Brain
Before you begin your lecture or discussion of Chapter 2, an easy (and surprisingly fun) way to motivate students is to bring in large sheets of poster paper and colored pens. Have students get into groups of 3 or 4, give them one large poster sheet per group, a set of pens, and ask them to draw the structure of a neuron including all of the major parts and functions.

Next ask them to draw a brain (a full view and a bisected view), and label the major structures. List the various terms on the board (cerebral cortex, brain stem, cerebellum, four lobes, right and left hemisphere, etc.). Encourage them to share their ideas, notes, their own brains - but, NO books. Walk around to the various groups and you'll be surprised how difficult this is for them. You'll also be surprised at how engaged they become in the activity. Choose the best two or three drawings and post them with masking tape to the front of the room. During your lecture, refer to the drawings. If time allows, you may also ask them to list the functions of the major structures and/or to draw a neuron with its major parts and functions.

Brain-Based Learning Activity 2.4 - Assemble the Central Nervous System

Make copies of the following paragraph and cut out a set of terms for each group of students. Be sure to mix them up for each group and task them to assemble these Central Nervous System elements in the proper sequence of major subdivisions and associated brain structures. Encourage students to pay particular attention to terms or placements that they are unsure of, and to concentrate on those for their next study group.

Spinal Cord	**Gray Matter**	**White Matter**	**Brain**	
Cortex	**Subcortex**	**Cerebellum**	**Brain Stem**	
Frontal Lobe	**Parietal Lobe**	**Occipital Lobe**	**Temporal Lobe**	
Thalamus	**Hypothalamus**	**Limbic System**	**Medulla**	**Fornix**
Pons	**Amygdala**	**Septum**	**Hippocampus**	

Brain-Based Learning Activity 2.5 -Shrink Wrapping the Brain

A simple demonstration of the evolution of the cortex is to take one of the large sheets of poster paper and hold it horizontally over your head. Walk around the room commenting how much simpler it is to have the cortex in one layer. Then ask, "Why does nature make it so complicated? Why can't we have larger sheets if we need larger brains?" If they are stumped, try walking through a doorway. That will usually get them laughing. After the students have come up with several reasons, simply wad up the paper until it is the size of your skull and hold that over your head, commenting on how much easier it is even though it looks more complex.

Brain-Based Learning Activity 2.6 - Clay Molding the Brain

For each group of students bring in squares of soft clay in 3 or 4 different colors. Their task is to mold the major elements of the brain (text figures 2.15, 2.17, 2.19) separately and then to assemble the pieces correctly. I allow them to look at the book and at the department's 3-D brain model. This exercise takes considerably more time than the Draw-a-Brain approach but produces a better spatial understanding in how the pieces of the brain fit together.

Brain-Based Learning Activity 2.7 - Hands on Your Head

When demonstrating the location of the major brain structures have the students place their hands on their own heads corresponding to the part under discussion. For the occipital lobe, have them grab the back of their head and say vision, for the temporal lobe they place their hands from the TMJ to the ear and say hearing, etc. During review have them pair up and hold hands in various locations while their partner has to identify the part indicated.

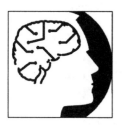

Critical Thinking

Critical Thinking Exercise 2.1 - Active Reading: Helping Students to Read - Critically

Chapter 2, the biological bases of behavior, is one of the most difficult units of an introductory course due to the large number of terms and concepts. For this reason, it is an ideal time for introducing critical reading skills. An important foundation of critical thinking is the ability to read and understand material well enough to interpret, analyze, and evaluate the information. Rather than actively questioning and thinking during their reading time, however, many students approach college texts by attempting to memorize isolated facts and long lists of terms and definitions. Instructors can help students resist this approach and become critical readers by providing specific training in proven study/reading techniques. This exercise will train students to use the SQ4R method (a general pedagogical tool of the text) and a lesser known, but highly effective, technique called "marginal marking."

Time: Depending on the level of detail you present and the amount of discussion you allow, the time will vary between 15 and 50 minutes.

Advance Preparation: You may want to remind students to bring their texts to class, and it helps to prepare an overhead transparency of the outline for Chapter 2, 2 or 3 sample pages of the chapter text, a page with the "learning checks," and the summary at the end of the chapter. You may want to review the SQ4R method ahead of time. It is explained in the preface of the book.

Instructions: Briefly discuss the basics of the SQ4R method of study. Use your overhead transparencies to point out how the text incorporates the various features of the SQ4R method. Once the SQ4R technique is clear, explain that you will demonstrate an alternative "writing" technique (the fourth "R") that will help with the Reading and Review steps. Point out that this "Marginal Marking" technique will save considerable study time, will improve critical reading/thinking skills, and can be used with any textbook. Using your overhead transparency of the 2 to 3 page section of Chapter 2, demonstrate how:

- Quote marks (" ") are written in the margin next to definitions or concepts which should be remembered verbatim.
- Double lines (‖) are placed in the margin next to important concepts and main ideas that should be remembered and reviewed.
- Single lines (|) are placed in the margin next to explanations and examples that help to explain important terms or concepts.
- Asterisks (*) are placed in the margin next to specific terms, names, or dates that should be remembered (not necessarily verbatim).
- Question marks (?) are placed in the margin next to items that are unclear and need future review or assistance from the instructor.

An important feature of marginal marking is that students are required to stay *active*, engaged, and critically evaluating while they're reading. Once the technique is mastered, reading time is more efficient and students often report an improvement in their comprehension and exam scores.

This exercise also appears in the text, Chapter 2. We include it here for your convenience, and you may want to discuss it in class to reinforce reading of the text.

Critical Thinking Exercise 2.2 - Clarifying Terms and Concepts: Understanding Brain Anatomy and Function

Being able to define a term or concept doesn't necessarily mean you fully comprehend it. Critical thinkers look at key terms from different angles. They not only ask, "What does this mean?"; they let their curiosity roam. They also ask, "What would happen if . . . ?" and "Suppose this were different, would . . .?" They explore key terms and concepts. Such free-wheeling exploration not only improves comprehension of the original term but also encourages the development of general critical thinking skills.

The following exercise will help to clarify your understanding of brain terminology and function. It also provides a model for the type of questions that lead to critical thinking.

Situation #1 - A neurosurgeon is about to perform brain surgery. The surgeon touches (stimulates with an electrode) a tiny portion of the patient's brain, and the patient's right finger moves. After noting the reaction, the surgeon stimulates a portion of the brain a short distance away and the patient's right thumb moves.

Questions to Answer

1. What section of the brain has been stimulated? What lobe is it in?

2. What hemisphere of the brain is being stimulated?

3. During the stimulation, would the patient experience feelings of pain? Why or why not?

4. Given that some parts of the brain are specialized for certain functions (e.g., receiving sensory information, controlling motor output), what would happen if the brain were disconnected from the rest of the body? Does brain functioning require feedback from the receptors in the body? If the brain could be kept alive outside the body, what could it do? Would a person be able to think without sensory input or motor output?

Situation #2 - The scene: An emergency room in a hospital. Two interns are talking about a car crash victim who has just been wheeled in.

First Intern: "Good grief! The whole cerebral cortex is severely damaged; we'll have to remove the entire area."

Second Intern: "We can't do that. If we remove all that tissue, the patient will die in a matter of minutes."

First Intern: "Where did you get your medical training--watching *General Hospital*?" The patient wouldn't die if we remove his whole cerebral cortex."

Second Intern: "I resent your tone and insinuation. I went to one of the finest medical schools, and I'm telling you the patient will die if we remove his whole cerebral cortex."

Questions to Answer

1. If the whole cerebral cortex is removed, will the patient die? Explain your answer.

2. If the patient is kept alive without a cerebral cortex, what kinds of behaviors or responses would be possible? What changes would you expect in personality, memories, and emotions?

3. What behaviors could be expected with only the subcortex, medulla, and spinal cord intact? What if only the medulla and spinal cord were functioning? Only the spinal cord?

4. If a patient could be kept alive without a cerebral cortex, would life be worth living? What parts of your brain could be removed before you would want to stop living?

This exercise also appears in the <u>Student Study Guide</u>, Chapter 2, and is a variation on the Critical Thinking Exercise presented in the text's Chapter 2 and in this manual--Critical Thinking Exercise 2.2. We include it here for your convenience, and you may want to discuss it in class to reinforce use of the Student Study Guide.

Critical Thinking Exercise 2.3 - Clarifying Terms and Concepts (A Cognitive Skill)

One of the most important elements of critical thinking is clarity of thought. A clear thinker understands that the simple ability to define a term is not evidence of true understanding. One must be able to extend basic definitions to higher, more complex applications. The clear, critical thinker allows his or her curiosity to roam to the "outer limits." They ask questions such as "What does this mean?" "What would happen if...?" "What if this were different?" They explore core terms and concepts from several different angles. This type of "free-wheeling" exploration not only improves comprehension of the original terms but also encourages the development of general critical thinking skills. The following exercise will help clarify your understanding of brain terminology and function. While so doing, it provides a model for the types of questions one asks that lead to critical thinking. By doing these "diagnoses," you will also be practicing another skill involved in critical thinking: employing inductive logic, or moving from the specific to the general.

The Setting: You are a famous neurosurgeon who specializes in brain damage involving the language system. In each of the following cases, make a "diagnosis" concerning where you believe brain damage has occurred.

Case 1: A 56-year-old female has suffered a recent stroke. She speaks in a curious manner resembling fluent English but the phrases make no sense. You find that she comprehends your verbal or written instructions perfectly and can even write them down, but cannot repeat them verbally. You quickly diagnose the problem as a lesion in the _____.

Case 2: A mother brings her 7-year-old son to you because he is having serious problems in learning to read. At age 5 his corpus callosum was sectioned in order to prevent epileptic seizures. She points out that he is a very intelligent child and she cannot understand why reading is so difficult for him. You explain that his reading difficulties are probably related to the fact that _____.

Case 3: An intelligent businessman comes to you and explains rather agitatedly that he awakened yesterday morning to find, much to his dismay, that he could no longer read. Your tests determine the following: a) He is totally blind in the right visual field. b) He speaks fluently and comprehends speech. c) He can write with his right hand but cannot read what he has written. d) He can copy written words but only with his left hand. You turn to your puzzled assistant and remark that this is indeed a tough one, but you are willing to bet that you will find brain damage in at least two areas, which are _____ and _____.

(**Answers**: Case 1: Left hemisphere, in the frontal and temporal lobes, probably Broca's area. Case 2: He had his corpus callosum severed, and his frontal, temporal, and occipital lobes are not integrating information. Case 3: Left occipital lobe, corpus callosum.)

Gender and Cultural Diversity

Gender and Cultural Diversity Activity 2.1 - Designing a Person

Materials: Handout 2.1- Gender and Cultural Diversity, describing "Designing a Person" activity.

Procedure: Students will be assigned to small groups and instructed to follow the directions on the handout.

Directions: Members of the group will decide which culture they are working with and develop the model individual(s) for this specific culture, beginning with brain function and development. During the construction process, students will need to be familiar with the rudiments of brain structure and function, as well as their physiological and cultural manifestations. During this activity, students will determine which brain structures are more important or less important to the full functioning of the individual they create and why. During large-group discussion, the instructor will pursue the question of why the small-group members felt a specific physical structure had a relevance to a specific social behavior (cultural relevancy).

Conclusion: This activity tends to expose various prejudices held by the students. In order for the activity to be effective, the instructor must remain sympathetic, yet detached, when exploring group reasoning behind the development of the small-group's individual. Discussion needs to remain on the plasticity of the brain. Any appearance of judgmental assessment needs to be avoided, since for many students this will be the first objective approach to understanding gender-based, racial and ethnic biases and prejudices they have considered inherent or natural.

Handout 2.1 – Gender and Cultural Diversity

Designing a Person

1. The members of your group will decide which culture they wish to select for this activity. (HINT: It is a good idea to select a culture which one of the group members has experienced.)

2. Your group will decide whether the individual you design is to be male or female. (HINT: you may design both male and female, as time permits.)

3. Your group will focus on known brain structures and functions obtained from reliable current scientific research (no artistic license will be tolerated here).

4. The group will determine appearance and overt behavior of your designer person, and your group members must be prepared to explain to the rest of the class their person and its behavior according to brain structures and cultural impact.

Writing Project

Given the need for improved writing skills in college students and to respond to the call for "writing across the curriculum, " we offer writing projects for each chapter. In Chapter 2, we suggest a 2-3 page written response to one of the issues found on Handout 2.1- Writing Project. Recognizing the time involved in grading such writing projects, one alternative is occasionally to collect the papers, remove student names, and assign "peer grading." It also helps to make their participation in peer grading a required part of the overall points for the writing project. This encourages a more thoughtful and responsible evaluation, as well as acknowledging and rewarding the additional work.

---(cut or copy from here)---

Handout 2.1 – Writing Project

Write a 2-3 page thoughtful response to one or both of the following:

1. The Case of Charles Whitman

    As a child and young man, Charles Whitman was kind, quiet, and known by all as a "good boy"-- serving as both an altar boy and an Eagle Scout. As a student at the University of Texas, however, he began to experience severe headaches, assaulted his wife, and became involved in numerous fights. He confided to his psychiatrist that he was fighting the urge toward even more extreme violent behavior. He lost the fight. Climbing to the top of the campus observation tower with a high-powered rifle, he shot wildly at his fellow students, ultimately killing 14 people and wounding more than 20 before the police finally killed him. An autopsy on Whitman's body revealed a large tumor pressing against his amygdala.

Recognizing that this area of the brain is known to regulate aggressive behaviors in animals (the research is less clear for humans), should Whitman be held fully responsible for his actions? Why or why not? If Whitman had lived, would you have been in favor of capital punishment or life imprisonment for his crimes?

2. What do you think about the possible use of brain stimulator implants to achieve control over mental patients? Under what circumstances would you believe such implant procedures should be considered? What about the idea of implanting electrodes in the pleasure centers of all newly born infants? If these electrodes could be used to soothe a crying baby, to replace drug effects in drug addicted teenagers and adults, would there be any disadvantages? Would you be willing to volunteer your own child or yourself for implantation if there was no possibility of physical harm?

Circle of Quality - Chapter 2

Please give us your feedback. We thank you in advance for assisting us in improving the next edition. The contact information is listed in the preface.

What are the three most helpful teaching tools in this chapter?

1.

2.

3.

What are the three least useful teaching tools in this chapter?

1.

2.

3.

What are the three most difficult concepts to teach in this chapter?

1.

2.

3.

Additional Comments:

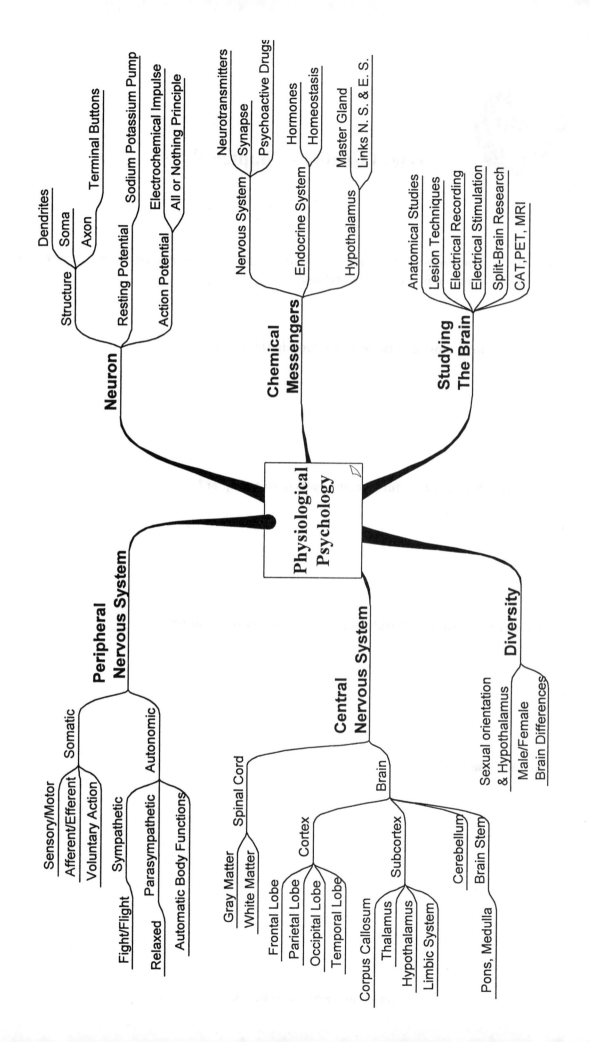

Physiological Psychology

Neuron
- Structure
  - Dendrites
  - Soma
  - Axon
  - Terminal Buttons
- Resting Potential
  - Sodium Potassium Pump
- Action Potential
  - Electrochemical Impulse
  - All or Nothing Principle

Chemical Messengers
- Nervous System
  - Neurotransmitters
  - Synapse
  - Psychoactive Drugs
- Endocrine System
  - Hormones
  - Homeostasis
- Hypothalamus
  - Master Gland
  - Links N. S. & E. S.

Studying The Brain
- Anatomical Studies
- Lesion Techniques
- Electrical Recording
- Electrical Stimulation
- Split-Brain Research
- CAT, PET, MRI

Peripheral Nervous System
- Somatic
  - Sensory/Motor
  - Afferent/Efferent
  - Voluntary Action
- Autonomic
  - Sympathetic
    - Fight/Flight
  - Parasympathetic
    - Relaxed
  - Automatic Body Functions

Central Nervous System
- Spinal Cord
  - Gray Matter
  - White Matter
- Brain
  - Cortex
    - Frontal Lobe
    - Parietal Lobe
    - Occipital Lobe
    - Temporal Lobe
  - Subcortex
    - Corpus Callosum
    - Thalamus
    - Hypothalamus
    - Limbic System
  - Cerebellum
  - Brain Stem
    - Pons, Medulla

Diversity
- Sexual orientation & Hypothalamus
- Male/Female Brain Differences

CHAPTER 3
SENSATION AND PERCEPTION

Outline

Experiencing Sensation

Sensory Thresholds
Sensory Adaptation

Vision

Light
The Eye

The Other Senses

Hearing

Research Highlight
Tracking Down the Gene for Deafness

Smell and Taste
Olfaction

Gender and Cultural Diversity
Do Some People Smell Better Than Others?

The Body Senses

Perception

Selection

Physiological Factors
Stimulus Factors
Psychological Factors

Organization

Form Perception

Gender and Cultural Diversity
Are the Gestalt Laws Universally True?

Perceptual Constancies
Depth Perception
Color Perception

Interpretation

Research Highlight
Early Life Experiences

Perceptual Expectancy
Other Influences on Interpretation
Extrasensory Perception
ESP Research

Active Learning
Problems with Believing in ESP

 **Learning Objectives**

Upon completion of CHAPTER 3, the student should be able to:

1. Define sensation and perception (p. 88).
2. Explain transduction, reduction, and coding in sensory processing (pp. 88-89).
3. Describe the absolute and difference thresholds and the importance of sensory adaptation (pp. 90-91).
4. Describe the physical properties of light and light waves (p. 92).
5. Draw a diagram of the eye, label the major parts, and explain how each part contributes to the visual process (pp. 93-95).
6. Explain dark and light adaptation (p. 96).
7. Describe the physical properties of sound and sound waves (pp. 96-97).
8. Draw a diagram of the ear, label the major parts, and explain how each part contributes to the auditory process (pp. 97-98).
9. Explain place and frequency theories with regard to the detection of pitch and loudness (pp. 98-99).
10. Describe the causes of nerve deafness and current research into genetically caused deafness; briefly describe three ways to prevent nerve deafness (p. 99).
11. Describe the sense of smell, including basic anatomy, the lock-and-key theory of olfaction, gender, developmental, and cultural differences in olfaction, and the role of pheromones in animals and humans (pp. 100-102).
12. Describe the sense of taste, including basic anatomy, how it works, and the causes of "picky" eating (pp. 102-103).
13. List and describe the general functions of the three body senses (p. 103).
14. Describe the skin senses and their functions. Explain the role of endorphins and the gate-control theory in the perception of pain (pp. 103-104).
15. Explain how the vestibular and kinesthetic senses provide information about the body (pp. 105-107).
16. Differentiate perception from sensation, and explain illusions (p. 107).
17. Describe the role of selection in the process of perception, and define selective attention. Describe the physiological, stimulus, and psychological factors that influence selection (pp. 108-110)
18. Discuss the research on subliminal perception (pp. 110-111).
19. List and discuss the Gestalt principles of perceptual organization. Describe cross-cultural research on the universality of these principles (pp. 111-114).
20. Explain the concept of perceptual constancy as it relates to size, shape, color, and brightness (pp. 114-116).
21. Explain how a person perceives depth, and describe both binocular and monocular depth cues (pp. 117-122).
22. Discuss how both the trichromatic and opponent-process theories are needed to explain how humans perceive color (pp. 122-124).
23. Describe how prior experience, personal motivations, and frames of reference influence perceptual interpretation (pp. 125-127).
24. Describe the different types of extrasensory perception; discuss the criticisms regarding ESP research; explain why people continue to believe in ESP; and discuss how four types of faulty reasoning perpetuate ESP beliefs (pp. 127-130).

Chapter Summary/Lecture Organizer

Introductory Vignette—The chapter opens with the story of Helen Keller. Although Helen Keller was both deaf and blind, she used her remaining senses (especially touch) to master the world around her. The problems and successes of Helen Keller's story serve as a dramatic illustration of the general processes underlying sensation and perception.

I. **EXPERIENCING SENSATION -** The beginning of this chapter introduces students to the processes involved in sensation, including reduction, transduction, coding, sensory thresholds, and sensory adaptation. Transduction, or the conversion of physical stimuli into neural impulses, occurs at the receptors in the sense organs. Each sensory modality is specialized to code its stimuli into unique sets of neural impulses that the brain interprets as light, touch, and so on. Since people receive much more information at the sensory receptors than can possibly ever be processed, it is necessary to select only the information that is important, a process known as sensory reduction. Reduction is performed chiefly by an area of the brain called the reticular activating system. Here, incoming sensory information is filtered and analyzed before going to the brain where the coded information will evoke a unique sensation.

    A. Sensory Thresholds - The absolute threshold is the smallest magnitude of a stimulus a subject can detect. The difference threshold is the smallest change in the magnitude of a stimulus that a subject can detect. Thresholds can be affected by the process of sensory adaptation.

    B. Sensory Adaptation - Sensory adaptation allows people to operate efficiently in a wide range of stimulus intensities by decreasing the sensitivity to constant, unchanging stimuli.

After reading about general sensory processes, students will be introduced to the structures and functions of the major sensory systems: vision, audition, gustation, olfaction, the skin senses, the vestibular sense, and the kinesthetic sense.

II. **VISION**

    A. Light - The physical stimulus for vision is light, a form of energy that is part of the electromagnetic spectrum. The wavelength of light determines its hue, or color; the amplitude, or height, of the light wave determines its intensity.

    B. The Eye - The function of the eye is to capture light and focus it on the visual receptors that convert light energy into neural impulses. The major parts of the eye include the cornea, the sclera, the pupil, the iris, the lens, and the retina. The cornea, the principal refracting surface of the eye, is the crystal clear bulge at the front of the eye, through which all light entering the eye must pass. The sclera is the tough, fibrous, outer covering of the eye that gives the eye its shape and protects the delicate inner structures of the eye. Light passes from the cornea through an opening, called the pupil, which is surrounded by a colored set of muscles known as the iris. These muscles can dilate or constrict to vary the amount of light entering the eye. Behind the pupil and iris is the lens, a clear elastic structure that can change its shape to focus an image on the retina at the back of the eye. The lens thins to focus light on the retina from distant objects and bulges to focus light from near objects. The retina is the back layer of the eye that contains the visual receptor cells. The visual receptors, called photoreceptors, are the rods and cones. The rods are very sensitive to light and enable individuals to see at night. The cones are specialized for bright light conditions and enable individuals to see close and fine detail.

III. **THE OTHER SENSES** - Hearing, taste, smell, and the body senses are also important for gathering information.

A. Hearing - The sense of hearing, known as audition, detects sound waves, which result from rapid changes in air pressure caused by vibrating objects. The frequency of sound waves is measured in cycles per second and is sensed as the pitch of the sound. The amplitude of the sound is measured in decibels and is sensed as the loudness of the sound. The ear is the sense organ specialized for receiving and converting sound information. The structures of the ear include the pinna, the external visible part of the ear; the eardrum, or tympanic membrane, that vibrates when hit by sound waves; the ossicles--the malleus, incus, and stapes—that transmit the sound vibrations through the middle ear; the oval window, the membrane separating the middle ear from the inner ear; and the cochlea, the structure that forms the inner ear. The major structures of the cochlea are the basilar membrane and the auditory receptor cells (hair cells).

> **Research Highlight: Tracking Down the Gene for Deafness** – further down the trail with recent advances in genetic research. There has been a lot of progress in locating these genes and in understanding the important role of *myosin*.

B. Smell and Taste - Olfaction (the sense of smell) and gustation (the sense of taste) are called the chemical senses and are closely interrelated. Taste receptors are located on the tongue and throat and are sensitive to the four major tastes: salty, sweet, sour, and bitter.

C. Olfaction - The receptors for olfaction are in the olfactory epithelium located at the top of the nasal cavity. According to the lock-and-key theory, humans can smell various odors because each three-dimensional odor molecule fits into only one type of receptor. The role of pheromones in attraction continues to be investigated.

> **Gender and Cultural Diversity: Do Some People Smell Better Than Others?** –A review of differences in olfactory sensitivity among Americans and Africans to androstenone.

D. The Body Senses - The body senses include the skin senses, the vestibular sense, and the kinesthetic sense. The skin senses, which include pressure, temperature, and pain, not only protect the internal organs but also provide basic survival information. The vestibular sense is the sense of balance. Located in the inner ear, the vestibular apparatus is composed of the semicircular canals and the vestibular sacs. The semicircular canals, three arching structures located above and attached to the entrance to the cochlea, provide the brain with balance information about the rotation of the head. The vestibular sacs, located at the end of the semicircular canals, provide the brain with information about the tilt of the head. The kinesthetic sense provides the brain with information about bodily posture and orientation, as well as bodily movement. The kinesthetic receptors are spread throughout the body in muscles, joints, and tendons.

IV.   **PERCEPTION** - The chapter continues with an overview of perception. Whereas sensation is the process of detecting and transducing raw sensory information, perception is the process of selecting, organizing, and interpreting sensory data into a usable mental representation of the world. Illusions have been used by psychologists to study the process of perception because illusions represent situations in which sensory information is interpreted improperly. This improper interpretation can give researchers insights into how perceptual systems process sensory information. The three basic processes of perception are selection, organization, and interpretation.

V.   **SELECTION** - The selection process allows people to choose which of the billions of separate sensory messages will eventually be processed. Thus, selective attention allows individuals to direct attention to the most important or critical aspect of the environment at any one time.

   A. Physiological Factors - During the selection process, feature detectors distinguish between various sensory inputs. Feature detectors are specialized cells in the brain that distinguish between different sensory inputs. Early deprivation may lead to problems with feature detectors.

   B. Stimulus Factors - The selection process is particularly sensitive to change in the environment. Stimuli that remain the same can cause perceptual habituation, in which the brain ignores the constant stimuli.

   C. Psychological Factors - Motivation and personal needs play a key role in selection. Attention is heightened when people are strongly interested in something or when they have been deprived of something they need.

VI.   **ORGANIZATION** - The process of perceptual organization was studied intensely by the Gestalt psychologists, who set forth several laws of perceptual organization explaining how people perceive form.

   A. Form Perception - One fundamental Gestalt principle is the distinction between figure and ground. Other Gestalt principles include proximity, continuity, closure, contiguity, similarity, and contrast.

      Gender and Cultural Diversity: Are the Gestalt Laws Universally True? - Using women from the former USSR as subjects, Luria (1976) concludes that the Gestalt principles are only valid for people who have been schooled in geometrical concepts, not for uneducated people who perceive shapes in an object-oriented world.

   B. Perceptual Constancies - The process of perceptual organization is also seen in the perceptual constancies—size constancy, shape constancy, color constancy, and brightness constancy. Size constancy is the process whereby the perceived size of an object remains the same even when the image of the object on the retina may change size due to changes in distance. Shape constancy occurs when an object is perceived to have the same shape even when the image of the object on the retina changes shape. Color constancy is the process whereby colors appear to have the same relative color in varying conditions of illumination. Brightness constancy is the process whereby colors appear to have the same relative brightness in varying conditions of illumination.

C. Depth Perception - Another part of the process of organization is the depth perception of size and distance, for which there are two major types of cues: binocular and monocular. Binocular cues, which require two eyes, include retinal disparity and convergence. Monocular cues, which require only one eye (but are, of course, available to people with two eyes), include linear perspective, aerial perspective, texture gradients, interposition, light and shadow, relative size, accommodation, and motion parallax.

D. Color Perception - The perception of color is another process of perceptual organization. Color perception is explained by a combination of two traditional color theories: the trichromatic theory and the opponent-process theory. The trichromatic theory proposes that three kinds of color systems are maximally sensitive to blue, green, and red. The opponent-process theory proposes that, indeed, three color systems exist, but that each is sensitive to two opposing colors—blue and yellow, red and green, and black and white. These systems work in an on-off fashion (for example, a person may see blue or yellow, but not both at the same time). It appears that the trichromatic system operates at the level of the retina while the opponent-process system occurs at the level of the brain. Some people cannot perceive color normally. Dichromats are missing only one type of cone system and cannot distinguish between red and green or blue and yellow. (Although it is not mentioned in the text, you may want to add that monochromats have only rods and no cones and see things only in black and white and shades of gray.)

VII.   INTERPRETATION - The final stage of perception is interpretation.

> **Research Highlight: Early Life Experiences: The Effects of Environmental Interaction** - Interpretation can be influenced by early life experiences, as seen in the research by Held and Hein. These researchers raised kittens in total darkness except for one hour a day when one "active" group was allowed to walk in a circular "kitty carousel" while the "passive" group rode in a gondola. Unlike the passive kittens, the active kittens developed normal visual perception.

A. Perceptual Expectancy - Interpretation is also affected by expectancies. Using special inverting lenses, psychologist George Stratton demonstrated how expectancies can be changed within a matter of days.

B. Other Influences on Interpretation - Cultural factors, needs and interests, and frames of reference also affect perception.

C. Extrasensory Perception - Extrasensory perception (ESP), another possible way of organizing sensory information, is the ability to perceive things through senses that go beyond the "known" senses. Although ESP research has led to impressive results in some cases, critics condemn its scientific validity because it lacks experimental control and replicability.

D. ESP Research – ESP has long been a subject of fascination. Rhine found corroborating evidence in the early 1900's. Recent, better controlled, studies report contradictory or "fragile" results lacking in stability and replicability. ESP's undiminished popularity can be attributed to our need to believe, and to people's difficulty with evaluating complex scientific information.

> **Active Learning: Problems With Believing in ESP** - Using so-called examples of ESP, students are given a chance to practice recognizing four types of faulty reasoning—fallacy of positive instances, innumeracy, willingness to suspend disbelief, and the "vividness" problem.

Teaching Resources

SECTION I – EXPERIENCING SENSATION

Learning Objectives #'s 1 - 4
Lecture Lead-ins #'s 1 - 3
Lecture Extender # 3.2
Discussion Questions #'s 1- 3
Active Learning Activities # 3.1
Brain-Based Learning Activities # 3.1
Gender and Cultural Diversity Activity # 3.1
Writing Project # 3.1

SECTION II - VISION

Learning Objectives #'s 5 - 7
Lecture Lead-ins #'s 1 & 3
Lecture Extender # 3.2
Discussion Questions #'s 1 - 4
Active Learning Activities #'s 3.1 – 3.6
Brain-Based Learning Activities #'s 3.2 & 3.3
Critical Thinking Exercise # 3.1
Gender and Cultural Diversity Activity # 3.1
Writing Project # 3.1

SECTION III – THE OTHER SENSES

Learning Objectives #'s 8 - 16
Lecture Lead-ins # 2
Lecture Extender # 3.1
Discussion Questions #'s 1 - 4
Active Learning Activities #'s 3.6 & 3.7
Brain-Based Learning Activities #'s 3.3 & 3.4
Gender and Cultural Diversity Activity # 3.1

Writing Project # 3.1

SECTION IV - PERCEPTION

Learning Objectives # 17
Lecture Lead-ins #'s 1 & 3
Active Learning Activities #'s 3.8 & 3.9

SECTION V – SELECTION

Learning Objectives #'s 18 & 19
Lecture Extender # 3.2
Gender and Cultural Diversity Activity # 3.1

SECTION VI - ORGANIZATION

Learning Objectives #'s 20 - 23
Active Learning Activities #'s 3.7, 3.10 & 3.11
Brain-Based Learning Activities # 3.5
Critical Thinking Exercise # 3.2
Gender and Cultural Diversity Activity # 3.1

SECTION VII - INTERPRETATION

Learning Objectives #'s 24 & 25
Lecture Extender #3.2
Discussion Questions # 5 - 7
Active Learning Activities #'s 3.1, 3.11 – 3.16
Brain-Based Learning Activities # 3.6
Critical Thinking Exercises #'s 3.2 & 3.3
Gender and Cultural Diversity Activity # 3.1

Lecture Lead-Ins

1. Ask students to explain this famous Zen Buddhism *koan*, or riddle, "Last night I dreamt I was a butterfly. How do I know today that I am not a butterfly dreaming I am a man?" Follow up with questions, such as "Does a tree falling in the forest make a sound if no one is there to hear it?" "Is there color if no one sees it?" "Does food have a taste if no one eats it?" Use their responses to lead in to your definition and distinction between sensation and perception.

2. Ask which of your senses would be the most devastating to lose? Have the students rank order sensory input in terms of most to least useful. Use this discussion as a lead-in for your first sensation lecture. If time allows, also ask what would be the most important senses for other animals.(e.g., dogs, cats, birds, fish, and chimpanzees). What are the evolutionary advantages for each of these dominant senses for each animal? What would have been the evolutionary fate of the animals if the dominant sense had been different?

3. A good way to start a lecture is to introduce the concept of what the sensory inputs are. Tell the class about what you see (colors of clothes, hair styles, background noises), and ask them how humans make sense of the marvelous jumble of raw data. What would mental health be like if no one could make sense of the jumble? Would we be "normal?" If not, what type of abnormality might humans have?

4. When anthropologists first contacted the pygmies in the jungle they brought with them photographs of animals in the wide open plains. When they showed these pictures to pygmies they could not make sense of what was in the picture. As hunters their eye sight was superb, but the pictures made no sense to them (see book illustration 3.12a). The close-in spaces of the jungle did not allow vision across long distances. Imagine you are the anthropologist with the pygmies in the jungle. How would you explain this "defect"? What tests would you arrange?

5. The early dot matrix computer printers had only a few dots per letter with lots of space in between. Reading their print output was especially difficult if the print head was misfiring. Imagine that you are seeing such a page for the first time. You find yourself having a very hard time reading the words. But, after some practice you are able to read almost as fast as if the characters were fully formed. What is your brain doing that allows you to read so fast? Are you aware of this process? Could it be said that you are reading information that is not actually there?

Lecture Extenders

3.1 - The Tactile Sense

The sense of touch is often looked upon as an "inferior" sense while hearing and vision are accorded more prominent roles in development. Actually, touch is indispensable: it is crucial in orienting a person to the environment and plays a special role in attachment to others. Ashley Montagu, in a third edition of his book <u>Touching</u>, has "touched" upon all aspects of the tactile sense, even extending the data to speculate upon the relationship between tactile deprivation and some forms of mental disorder. The material below is taken from his book.

The importance of touch was celebrated by writers long before psychologists were investigating this neglected sense modality. The literature abounds with examples of metaphors that attest to its importance: "rubbing people the wrong way," "abrasive personality," "the magic touch," "soft touch," "thick-skinned," "tactful," and "touchstone" are a few of the common phrases one sees. One industry that has capitalized on the tactile need has been AT&T which promotes long distance phone calls through the ad, "Reach out and touch someone."

Anatomically, what do psychologists know about the tactile sense and its development? Touch is the "mother" of all senses. It is the largest sense modality and the first to become functional in the developing embryo. When the embryo is less than one inch long and not yet six weeks of age, touching the upper lip elicits body movement away from the stimulation. By nine weeks, the fingers will close if the palm is touched. At twelve weeks, the mouth opens and the tongue moves about if the base of the thumb is touched.

The average adult has enough skin to cover the floor area of a "good-sized" room, approximately 19 square feet. Every four hours, the skin produces the equivalent of two new layers of skin. The skin varies in thickness; the thinnest layers are found on the eyelids, the thickest on the sole of the feet and the palm of the hand.

What does the skin do? Other than the obvious advantage of "gift-wrapping" the body to make it more presentable, it keeps out germs, bacteria, and other noxious agents, and also gives a waterproof covering. It also signals one's response to others. For example, humans blanch with fear and turn red with embarrassment. With regard to sensory stimulation, it provides information about the environment. In contrast to the hearing and seeing modalities which are referred to as distance sensors, the skin only picks up stimulation that is "close by." The infant is ready at birth to explore its nearby world with its tactile sense. One of the more obvious truths about infants of most species is their tendency to huddle against the mother or with their siblings. This craving for touch coincides with a body's need for touch. Much of family time togetherness is spent with the mother licking the infant. This phenomenon is true for dogs, cats, baboons, langurs, and many other species. In the case of dogs and cats, much of the time is spent in licking the perineal area. Without this stimulation, the genitourinary area would not function appropriately, and the offspring would die. Harlow's classic studies of surrogate mothers indicate that touch is more important than nourishment in providing the basis for an attachment in monkeys. Studies with rats that have varied types of sensory deprivation have shown that touch deprivation leads to an impaired immune system.

An impaired immune system may also be the explanation for infant marasmus, or infantile atrophy. This disorder is characterized by a failure to gain weight or thrive and the infant "wastes away". Observation in the 19th century of infants who had been placed in fondling homes indicated that close to 100% died before the age of two. Overworked staff seldom found the time to caress or touch the babies. After a systematic introduction of touch in which the babies were held several times each day, the mortality rate dropped to 10%. It wasn't until after World War II, however, that the medical profession noted that marasmus could also occur in middle-class homes if there was an absence of touching. More recent studies have concentrated on the premature infant who is often deprived of touch. Several excellent studies, using both control and experimental groups, have found that a premature baby who is touched has a higher IQ, better weight gain, less irritability, and more advanced central nervous system functioning. In one study, premature infants who were held went home six days earlier than those who were not. The difference in cost of hospital care per infant was $3,000. Current studies are looking at stimulation of both the tactile and kinesthetic aspects, assuming that the universal aspect of rocking a child to pacify him/her must have some physiologically beneficial effect. Special waterbeds are now being used to provide kinesthetic stimulation to infants.

Montagu, in trying to relate touch to mental disorder, does not make the mistake of assuming that all mental disorders can be linked to the "touching" practices within the family. However, he does indicate in some disorders (mainly autism) a more effective treatment may be to force the child into touching. Montagu cites the book Touching is Healing, by Older, which documents therapeutic successes with the use of touching. This is a provocative idea since two primary symptoms of childhood autism are the failure to enjoy cuddling and to draw away from human touch.

Although the practice of medicine is becoming more scientific, many lament the loss of the close contact with a physician and the trend towards impersonal contact. It is no wonder that throughout history, medicine has been referred to as "the laying on of the hands."

Reference: Montagu, A. (1986). Touching: The human significance of the skin (3rd ed.). New York: Harper & Row.

3.2 - Aging and Perception

Even though some general psychology textbooks discuss developmental factors in perception (mainly the development of depth perception in infants) they usually omit any reference to the changes that take place with aging. Yet this is an important factor in the coping ability of older persons. It is an established fact that the absolute threshold for all of the senses increases with aging. This means that a higher level of stimulation is needed. For example, older people like more salt on their food so it will taste "like it used to." They ask others to speak up and quit mumbling. They insist that their children need more light in order to read. Since sensation is the basis for perceptual activity, it follows that alterations in perception would naturally occur.

Older people have more trouble picking out embedded figures or separating figure from ground (Welford, 1980). What this means in terms of every day adjustment is that they will have more trouble finding their keys or any other missing object. This impaired ability involves more than short term memory loss or inability to recall where an object was placed. Older persons can be looking directly at the object they are seeking and not see it. When driving, they are more likely to overlook important information on a roadside, especially in a high speed environment. Another sensory change that relates to these difficulties is reduced visual acuity when events are out of central focus. Thus, the older person is less likely to see things out of the "corner" of his or her eye. These two changes, decreased sensitivity in peripheral vision and lessened ability to detect figure from ground, increases the difficulty of adjustment for the older person. The inability to screen out irrelevant material (separate figure from ground) increases their susceptibility to the Muller-Lyer illusion since they cannot abstract a part from the whole pattern.

Another well-known phenomenon is the increased amount of time that the older person needs for stimulus exposure (Welford, 1980). Visual images (iconic images) can build up for 0.5 seconds in the brain unless they are erased by a new incoming image. It is believed that this process continues for a longer period of time in the older person unless it is erased or masked. For the elderly, who need more time before making a perceptual judgment, it is easier to interfere with the earlier information. They may not be aware of incoming information before it is masked by new information. The more complex the judgment is, the greater the age related difference in response time. The older person can be overwhelmed by rapid presentation of visual stimuli. Another problem is that the increased need for more response time may lead to a reaction based on earlier information which is now faulty. For example, by the time the older person has established that it is safe to cross the street and acts upon this information, conditions may have changed.

Incomplete pictures are especially difficult for the older person (Welford, 1980). They are unable to integrate the separate parts into the whole picture. Thus, in their everyday environments, they will need more information before they can make perceptual judgments. They will have to see the entire stimulus—for example, the entire dog—before they can identify it (as a dog).

Surprisingly, binocular vision disintegrates with age (Welford, 1980). This decline is related to the slowed ability to integrate the information from the two separate images produced by binocular disparity. By age forty, depth perception has dropped for distances over one meter. The implication of this decline is that older persons will have trouble making decisions about distances. For example, they may have trouble gauging the distance of an oncoming car.

Another visual change that forces older people to modify their styles of living is the inability to see while driving at night. Night driving is especially difficult for older people because they need a higher level of illumination for sufficient visual acuity and their ability to dark-adapt is markedly impaired. It takes them much longer to regain dark adaptation after facing oncoming headlights.

One of the best indices of how well the nervous system can handle incoming visual stimulation is to measure critical flicker fusion. This is a measure of the perception of a flickering light; at about 40 cycles per second, it is perceived as a steady light source. Birren (1964) has shown that the ability to perceive the individual cycles peaks around age 20-25 and thereafter declines.

Although much of the knowledge on perception has come from research in the visual area, there is some data from other sensory modalities. The ability to perceive complex sounds, such as sentences, declines with age (Welford, 1980). The decline is slight as long as the conditions for listening are good, but if there are numerous interruptions, words are overlapped, or the normal rate of presentation is increased, there is a decline, beginning in the 30s, of the ability to understand what has been said. In everyday life, the older person is often confused by multiple conversations in different parts of the room and has more trouble screening out extraneous "noise."

The ability to make perceptual judgments about just noticeable difference thresholds is also altered (Birren, 1964). In one study, in which the subjects had to make judgments about lifted weights, the younger subjects performed better. Interestingly, the difference between the two age groups (18 to 32 years versus 58 to 85 years) was less when the two weights to be compared were placed successively in the same hand. The implication of this study is that older individuals' ability to detect difference between stimuli declines (e.g., detecting the difference in two weights or two colors that are similar).

Most older persons, consciously or unconsciously, make adjustments in their living to cope with their changing perceptual world. There are some artificial aids, such as spectacles and hearing devices, that make life easier, but not like it once was. Though many have tried, no one—not even Ponce de Leon—has yet found the panacea for aging perceptual equipment.

Sources: Birren, J. E. (1964). The psychology of aging. Englewood Cliffs, NJ: Prentice-Hall. Welford, A. T. (1980). Sensory, perceptual, and motor processes in older adults. In J.D.. Birren & R. B. Clone (Ed.), Handbook of mental health and aging (pp 192-213). Englewood Cliffs, NJ: Prentice-Hall.

Key Terms

Perception (p. 88)
Sensation (p. 88)

EXPERIENCING SENSATIONS

Absolute Threshold (p. 90)
Coding (p. 89)
Difference Threshold (p. 90)
Receptors (p. 88)
Sensory Adaptation (p. 91)
Transduction (p. 88)

VISION

Accommodation (p. 93)
Amplitude (p. 92)
Aqueous Humor (p. 93)
Blind Spot (p. 94)
Ciliary Muscles (p. 93)
Cones (p. 95)
Cornea (p. 93)
Dark Adaptation (p. 96)
Electromagnetic Spectrum (p. 92)
Fovea (p. 94)
Hue (p. 92)
Iris (p. 93)
Lens (p. 93)
Light Adaptation (p. 96)
Optic Nerve (p. 95)
Photoreceptors (p. 95)
Pupil (p. 93)
Retina (p. 93)
Rods (p. 95)
Sclera (p. 93)
Vitreous Humor (p. 93)
Wavelength (p. 92)

THE OTHER SENSES

Amplitude (p. 97)
Audition (p. 96)
Auditory Canal (p. 97)
Auditory Nerve (p. 98)
Basilar Membrane (p. 98)
Body Senses (p. 103)
Cochlea (p. 98)
Eardrum (Tympanic Membrane) (p. 97)
Endorphins (p. 104)
Frequency (p. 97)
Frequency Theory (p. 98)
Gate-Control Theory of Pain (p. 104)
Gustation (p. 101)
Hair Cells (p. 98)
Incus (p. 97)
Kinesthesis (p. 105)
Lock-and-Key Theory (p. 100)
Malleus (p. 97)
Olfaction (p. 100)
Oval Window (p. 97)
Papillae (p. 101)
Pheromones (p. 101)
Pinna (p. 97)
Pitch (p. 97)
Place Theory (p. 98)
Semicircular Canals (p. 105)
Skin Senses (p. 103)
Sound Waves (p. 97)
Stapes (p. 97)
Vestibular Sacs (p. 105)
Vestibular Sense (p. 105)

PERCEPTION

Illusion (p. 107)

SELECTION

Feature Detectors (p. 108)
Habituation (p. 109)
Selective Attention (p. 108)
Subliminal (p. 110)

ORGANIZATION

Aerial Perspective (p. 120)
Brightness Constancy (p. 116)
Closure (p. 112)
Color Aftereffects (p. 121)
Color Constancy (p. 116)
Constancy (p. 114)
Contiguity (p. 113)
Continuity (p. 111)
Convergence (p. 119)
Depth Perception (p. 117)
Empiricist (p. 117)
Figure and Ground (p. 111)
Gestalt (p. 111)
Interposition (p. 121)
Light and Shadow (p. 121)
Linear Perspective (p. 120)
Motion Parallax (p. 121)
Nativist (p. 117)
Opponent-Process Theory (p. 121)
Proximity (p. 111)
Relative Size (p. 121)
Retinal Disparity (p. 119)
Reversible Figure (p. 111)
Shape Constancy (p. 114)
Similarity (p. 113)
Size Constancy (p. 114)
Stereoscopic Vision (p. 119)
Texture Gradients (p. 121)
Trichromatic Theory (p. 121)

INTERPRETATION

Extrasensory Perception (ESP) (p. 127)

Discussion Questions

1. What would the world be like if the absolute thresholds for sensation were changed? If people could see X-rays and ultraviolet light or infrared rays and radar? If people were like bats and dolphins and could hear sounds up to 100,000 hertz?

2. What would happen if each sensory receptor (e.g., ears, eyes, skin) were receptive to every type of incoming stimuli? If a human's eyes were also sensitive to sound waves and odor molecules, could the brain distinguish and integrate this information?

3. William James, a famous early psychologist, suggested that, if a master surgeon were to cross the auditory and optic nerves, then humans would hear lightning and see thunder. How would this be explained?

4. What explains the fact that people who are blind tend to be better adjusted psychologically and less subject to emotional difficulties than people who are deaf?

5. A famous saying goes : "We don't see the world as it is but as we are". Consider the kitten experiments and what you have read about the importance of perceptual schemas to make sense of the data we receive. Is it possible that we all live in "illusion" since we don't see what we "see", but only what we interpret? Is reality nothing more than a joint social illusion? How else would you explain the fact that children from different tribes/environments perceive the world sometimes radically different?

6. Why do defense attorneys never want the jury to see their clients in prison clothes? Before most defendants enter the courtroom they change into nice looking attire, even though most jury members have seen enough TV to be aware of this arrangement. If you were a jury member and saw a person in prison clothes with a number stenciled on, with handcuffs and leg irons would it affect you? Suppose, after a "not guilty" verdict, you met up with the person in civilian clothes sharing the elevator with you. How would your feel? Why?

7. Ask students if they have heard of any of the following: telepathy, clairvoyance, precognition or psychokinesis. (Explain each in terms the students can understand.) You are sure to have some who have heard of these parapsychological phenomena and probably several students who have witnessed or taken part in one or more of the phenomena. There may also be someone who has studied these types of behaviors, through the informal network of astrology, the occult, or other parapsychological studies. If you have one of these individuals in class, engage him/her in a discussion of the validity of these phenomena. You could also have the students complete the Active Learning Exercise found in this chapter and in this manual (Active Learning—Critical Thinking Exercise 3.2) as a way of dealing with the inevitable "arguments" you will elicit from students who truly believe in ESP.

 **Web Sites**

Visual Demonstrations

http://psychlab1.hanover.edu/classes/Sensation/
Dr. Krantz offers a series of fifteen slides that illustrate major principles of sensation and perception. Among the slides are demonstrations of Gestalt principles of figure and ground as well as color afterimages.

Illusion Gallery

http://valley.uml.edu/psychology/illusion.html
The focus of this site (pun intended) is to offer on-line access to a series of twenty-one visual illusions. Students will enjoy classic illusion such as the Necker cube and impossible figures and will also appreciate Nik's mummy illusion. Faculty will find this site a good resource for in class demonstrations of common visual illusions.

The Joy of Visual Perception: A Web Book

http://www.yorku.ca/eye/
Dr. Peter Kaiser offers students an on-line book devoted to coverage of the visual system and perception. The book offers detailed explanation of the anatomy and function of the eye and the figures of this book are well done. Some of the material will be too advanced for introductory students but faculty will find the book useful as a source of images for in-class lectures.

IllusionWorks

http://www.illusionworks.com/
This advanced site offers students access to a large number of visual illusions as well as detailed explanations of each illusion. The major categories of illusions covered on this site include impossible figures and objects, ambiguous images, motion ambiguity, distortion illusions, afterimages, facial illusions, and color and shadow illusions. This site is worthy of a visit for students and faculty.

Tutorials in Sensation and Perception

http://psych.hanover.edu/Krantz/sen_tut.html
Dr. Krantz offers a tutorial on the concept of visual receptive fields and on the use of visual information in art.

Learning Studio: On-Line Exhibits

http://www.exploratorium.edu/learning_studio/lsxhibit.html

This on-line exploratorium exhibit profiles illusions and demonstrations that involve vision and audition. Many of these links require the prior installation of Shockwave on your computer in order to view these pages.

Demonstrations in Auditory Perception

http://www.music.mcgill.ca/auditory/Auditory.html

Dr. Welch offers a site containing basic information on audition, links to on-line experiments involving audition, and to other web sites that cover the field of audition. The site also offers an extensive glossary and bibliography.

Suggested Films and Videos

Perception
Discovery, 1994. 45 minutes. From the Discovery Channel's "The Brain: Our Hidden Universe Within," this video is an excellent (and current) presentation of the processes of sensation and perception. The computer graphics are superb and a number of fascinating case studies are presented.

Seeing Beyond the Obvious
NASA/Ames Research Center, 1990. 45 minutes. This is an interesting and informative video focusing primarily on visual perception. The first half is devoted to depth (demonstrating both binocular and monocular cues). The second half focuses on visual perception in novel situations (e.g., flying a jet).

Sensation and Perception
Annenberg/CPB, 1990. 30 minutes. From Zimbardo's "Discovering Psychology" series, this video demonstrates many sensory and perceptual phenomena and provides a nice overview of the chapter.

Smell
Films for the Humanities and Sciences, 1995. 23 minutes. This video tells students what is known about the complex sense of smell. The process of making scented products is also described.

Controlling Pain
Films for the Humanities and Sciences, 1995. 23 minutes. In this video the complex process of pain is described and ongoing research to find ways to alleviate it is discussed (including chemicals and electrical stimulation techniques).

Managing Pain
Films for the Humanities and Sciences, 1995. 18 minutes. This video looks at what can be done about pain besides taking aspirin. Some of the latest research on the nature of pain and its treatment is presented.

Secrets of the Psychics with James Randi
NOVA, 1993. 60 minutes. In this video, magician James Randi debunks paranormal phenomena and demonstrates the P.T. Barnum effect. There is also discussion about why humans want to believe in the supernatural. An educational and fun way to present psychic phenomena is discussed in Activity 3.11.

Perception: The Theories

Films for the Humanities & Sciences, xxxx. 48 minutes. In this program perceptual models such as those of Neisser and Marr are presented along with many examples of the perceptual theories. In addition the roles of Wundt, Wertheimer, Gregory, and Gibson are discussed along with key perceptual concepts.

The Study of Attention

Films for the Humanities & Sciences, xxxx. 43 minutes. The Selective Attention models of Broadbent and Triesman are described using real-life examples; Divided Attention theories are described; and the area of Visual Attention is illustrated with demonstrations.

Perception: The Art of Seeing

Learning Seed, xxxx. 24 minutes. This is a video about what it means to SEE. It's about bias, prejudice, credibility, and how we construct reality in that we don't so much "record" reality, as we create it, like directors.

 **Success**

Books For Success

Dowling, John E. (1998). **Creating Mind: How the Brain Works.** W.W. Norton & Co.
Award winning book on how the mind creates meaning in perception, memory and language.
Strong on neuro-science yet readable to the layperson.

Gregory, Richard L. (1997). **Eye and Brain: The Psychology of Seeing. 5th ed.**
Princeton University Press.
This newly updated classic text offers a comprehensive overview of the topic. Expensive.

Hoffman, Donald David. (1998). **Visual Intelligence : How We Create What We See.**
W.W.Norton.
Cognitive psychologist reviews how we construct an experience of objects out of colors, lines
and motions. We interpret what we see to fit our emotional well being and sense of place.
Very engaging and rewarding.

Weiner, David L. (1995). **Brain Tricks : Coping With Your Defective Brain.**
Prometheus Books
Describes how the innate assumptions of the mind can misinterpret reality in six basic areas
and influence our feelings and perceptions. highly readable and filled with practical
suggestions.

Active Learning

Active Learning Activity 3.1 - Demonstrating Movement Detectors in the Cerebral Cortex

This is a simple and quick demonstration that helps students experience firsthand the operation of visual movement detectors. It also helps students understand the difference between perception and sensation.

Materials:
- An 18-inch diameter, cardboard, black and white spiral pattern. You can make one by enlarging the example provided in this manual (Handout 3.1 – Active Learning).
- Drill a small hole in the center so you can mount it, like a record, on a small turntable.

Instructions:
- To get the best effect, the spiral should be viewed head on, so have your students move toward the center of the room.
- Rotate the spiral for about 60 seconds with the spiral turning clockwise (appearing to contract toward the center). Remind students to look straight forward and not let their eyes move.
- After 60 seconds, tell your students to look at you. You will look as if your head is expanding or exploding.

Explain to your students that when the over stimulated inward-movement detectors stopped firing, the outward-movement detectors began firing for a few seconds, creating the dramatic illusion that your head was expanding. If time allows, rotate the spiral in the opposite direction (so that the spiral appears to be expanding) for 60 seconds; the students will see your head shrinking. To demonstrate that this is a cortical and not a retinal phenomenon, have the students view the spinning spiral with only one eye, and then look at your head with the other. Because the retina that saw the spiral was not the same as the one that saw your head, the effect had to take place in the brain.

 Handout 3.1 – Active Learning

SPIRAL ILLUSION

Active Learning Activity 3.2 - The Difference Between Rods and Cones

In this simple demonstration of the differences between rods and cones, first have the class form groups of two individuals. Have one student become the subject and the other the experimenter. The experimenter stands behind the subject and chooses a brightly colored item (pen, pencil or ruler). The experimenter instructs the subject to fixate on a distant point. Then the experimenter moves the object slowly from behind the head into the peripheral vision. If this movement is slow enough, the students will detect the object before the subject can determine the color. Have the students switch their roles and repeat the demonstration.

Active Learning Activity 3.3 - Hole in the Hand

Retinal disparity can be demonstrated by the "hole in the hand" illusion. Ask each student to roll sheets of paper into tubes, and, while holding the tubes in their left hands, look through them with their left eyes. Then ask them to place their right hands to the right of the tube, next to the far end. When students look far away with both eyes, they will see a "hole" through their right hand. The brain, unable to reconcile the different views coming from the two eyes, chooses to see through the hand and out of the tube.

Active Learning Activity 3.4 - Ocular Dominance

Have each student in class raise their hands and point toward your head with his or her finger. Instruct them to shut one eye and then the other, while they continue pointing at you with their outstretched arm. Ask which eye "shifted" the most? Students who are right-eye dominant will experience little eye shifting when they shut their left eye, while those who are left-eye dominant will experience little shifting when they shut their right eye. Explain that both eyes are receiving the same stimulation and sending the same information to the brain, but the brain is only using the information for the dominant eye. Ask why. What is the evolutionary advantage? Further explain that about 65 % of the population is right-eye dominant while the remaining 35% is left-eye dominant.

Active Learning Activity 3.5 – The Graphic Brain

For an excellent illustration of both the structure and function of the sensory system, *The Graphic Brain,* (Software CD, Timothy J. Tyler, Didactic Systems, Brooks/Cole Pub.), has excellent demonstrations in the modules on Visual Sensation, Auditory Sensation and Mechanical/Chemical Sensation. Although some of the modules contain details beyond the scope of an introductory psychology course it is very easy to select only parts of each module.

Active Learning Activity 3.6 – Sensory System Grid

To help students learn both the similarity in structure and the differences in detail among the senses pass out Handout 3.16 (a) – Active Learning, to be used either singly or in groups. Have the students fill in the cells in the grid. Handout 3.16 (b) – Active Learning, can be distributed as a study guide.

Handout 3.6 (a) – Active Learning

The Sensory Table

Sense	Energy Source	Sense Organ	Receptor	Perception
Vision				
Hearing				
Taste				
Smell				
Vestibular				
Kinesthetic				
Skin Senses: Pressure				
Skin Senses: Temperature				
Skin Senses: Pain				

Handout 3.6 (b) – Active Learning

The Sensory Table

Sense	Energy Source	Sense Organ	Receptor	Perception
Vision	Light Waves	Eye	Rods, Cones	Sight, Color
Hearing	Sound Waves	Ear	Hair in Cochlea	Sound
Taste	Soluble chemicals	Tongue	Taste buds	Taste
Smell	Volatile chemicals	Nose	Olfactory Epithelium	Odor
Vestibular	Direction of Gravity	Fluid filled Semi-circular Canal	Hairs in Vestibular Sacs	Orientation, Balance
Kinesthetic	Body movement	Muscles, joints, tendons	Kinesthetic receptor	Movement
Skin Senses: Pressure	Light pressure	Skin	Mechano-receptors	Pressure
Skin Senses: Temperature	Hot/Cold	Skin	Thermo-receptors	Warmth/Cold
Skin Senses: Pain	Heavy pressure	Skin	Nociceptors	Pain

Active Learning Activity 3.7 - Effects of Color and Taste

Have the students prepare a meal for their friends or family using food coloring to make the food very different in color. Have the students record the reactions to the food. Good choices are black potatoes, green bread, blue butter, or purple milk. Have the students discuss in class their choices of colors and subjects' reactions. Why are the reactions so strong to these color changes?

Active Learning Activity 3.8 - Perceptual Expectancy

The text discusses George Stratton's experience with the inverted lenses. You can quickly demonstrate this in the class, by bringing in several hand held mirrors. Invite students to use the mirrors to write their names or copy simple geometric designs. Note the number of errors each student makes as he or she adapts to the new perceptual world.

Active Learning Activity 3.9 – Illusions in Action

A great website to use for in class demonstration is http://valley.uml.edu/psychology/illusion.html Allow the students to explore the various illusions and suggest explanations.

Active Learning Activity 3.10 - Shape Constancy

Shape constancy can be demonstrated by taking a familiar object such as a book or backpack and placing it on a table in the front of the classroom. Rotate the object and ask the class if it changes shape as it is rotated. Ask for a can of smokeless tobacco from the students and rotate the can. You can point out that even though the image of the object changes shape, humans do not perceive the object itself as changing shape.

Active Learning Activity 3.11 - The Moon Illusion

Size constancy and the moon illusion can be demonstrated very easily and also used as an ice breaker for the class. Consult a calendar for the full moon closest to your lectures on depth perception. After finding the appropriate day, plan your lecture on a date as close as possible to that date ending with the moon illusion. Most students will not believe that this explanation is correct. Tell the students to arrive at an appropriate viewing sight about moon rise (provide correct time) with a person or persons of their choice. Suggest to them that this is a good way to meet new people by telling them that they are helping with a psychology experiment. At moon rise have the students make a mental calculation as to the size of the moon. Then to disrupt the environmental depth cues, have the students STAND ON THEIR HEADS. This can often be best achieved with the help of the new friends helping to hold the feet up. Note the apparent size of the moon from this position. The moon will appear much smaller when the observer is upside down. Repeat the procedure as many times as combinations of individuals in the experiment permit. At the next class period, ask for volunteers to tell about the moon illusion.

Active Learning Activity 3.12 - A Critical Look at ESP

The text's discussion of extrasensory perception (ESP) is guaranteed to elicit strong student interest and resistance. One set of researchers found that 99% of their introductory psychology students believed in at least one form of paranormal experiences and over 65% reported personal experience with at least one phenomenon (Messer & Griggs, 1989). Researchers have also found a correlation between paranormal belief and reasoning deficiencies. Believers perform less well on syllogistic reasoning (Wierzbicki, 1985), probabilistic judgments (Blackmore & Troscianko, 1985), and evaluation of evidence (Alcock & Otis, 1980).

These data suggest that rather than spending valuable class time debating whether ESP exists, instruction should be directed toward the critical thinking deficiencies underlying belief in ESP. Each of the following suggested activities will address specific thinking skills. Try as many as your time allows:

1. Invite a magician to your class to perform psychic-like stunts (e.g., blindfolded reading, metal bending, etc.). Emphasize to your students how magicians capitalize on illusions, perceptual expectancies, and other topics discussed in Chapter 3. Also, remind your students that they will be seeing only tricks. Singer and Benassi (1981) found they needed to remind students six different times before occult belief reduced from 64% to 50%.

2. Make xerox copies of the text's critical thinking exercise for this chapter and in this manual (Active Learning—Critical Thinking Exercise 3.2). Have students discuss their answers in class.

3. To illustrate the pitfalls of ESP research, simulate the following experiment or simply read it aloud. Ask students to identify the research errors. Using a deck of 25 ESP cards (5 cards of each symbol), an experimenter sits at a table opposite the subject. The experimenter shuffles the cards, looks at the top card, and then asks the subject to guess what it is. After recording the guess, he/she tells the subject what the card was. The experimenter proceeds through the entire deck in this manner, then shuffles and repeats for a second trial. The subject gets five right in the first trial (chance level) and nine right on the second. Deciding that the first test was a "warm-up," the experimenter concludes that the second test demonstrates evidence of ESP. Possible student answers include: the experimenter gave unintentional signals to the subject (Clever Hans phenomenon); the subject saw the backs of the cards and may have read impressions from them; throwing out the first trial invalidates the results; the cards were not randomized by shuffling, etc.

As a large group or in small groups, discuss problems with the null hypothesis and the impossibility of proving that something does NOT exist. James Randi (a famous magician and debunker of psychics) tells a wonderful story about testing to see if reindeer really can fly. If 10,000 randomly selected reindeer were taken to the top of the Empire State building and one by one were pushed off (to test for "flying"), Randi suggests you would still lack conclusive proof since you may have missed the one flying reindeer or that these particular reindeer may have simply "chosen not to fly." Ask students how they could prove that reindeer do not fly, or that yellow elephants do not exist, etc.

References:

Alcock, J. E., & Otis, L. P. (1980). Critical thinking and belief in the paranormal. Psychological Reports, 46, 479-482.

Blackmore, S., & Troscianko, T. (1985). Belief in the paranormal: Probability judgments, illusory control, and the "change baseline shift." British Journal of Psychology, 76, 459-468.

Messer, W. S., & Griggs, R. A. (1989). Student belief and involvement in the paranormal and performance in introductory psychology. Teaching of Psychology, 16, 187-191.

Singer, R., & Benassi, V. A. (1981). Occult beliefs. American Scientist, 69(1), 49-55.

Wierzbicki, M. (1985). Reasoning errors and belief in the paranormal. Journal of Social Psychology, 125, 489-494.

Active Learning Activity 3.13 - Magic versus ESP

To demonstrate your own "magic" abilities (as an antidote to belief in ESP), ask the entire class to:

1. **SILENTLY CHOOSE A NUMBER BETWEEN 2 AND 9.**
2. **MULTIPLY THAT NUMBER BY 9.**
3. **ADD THE TWO DIGITS OF THE RESULTING NUMBER. (The result will always be "9.")**
4. **SUBTRACT 5 FROM THAT RESULT. (The result will always leave "4.")**
5. **THINK OF THE LETTER OF THE ALPHABET THAT CORRESPONDS TO THE NUMBER ARRIVED AT IN STEP 4. (This will always be "D," because 1=A, 2=B, 3=C, and 4=D.)**
6. **WRITE DOWN THE NAME OF A COUNTRY THAT BEGINS WITH THIS LETTER. (Most students will think of "Denmark." Also, remind students not to look at what others are writing. This helps to increase the impact of your final point.)**
7. **WRITE DOWN THE NAME OF AN ANIMAL THAT BEGINS WITH THE LAST LETTER OF THIS COUNTRY. (Most students will think of "kangaroo.")**
8. **WRITE DOWN THE NAME OF A COLOR THAT BEGINS WITH THE LAST LETTER OF THAT ANIMAL. (Most students will choose the color "orange.")**
9. **LOOK AT AND CONCENTRATE ON THE LISTED COUNTRY, ANIMAL, AND COLOR.**

At this point, you can "read the mind" of every student by simply saying something such as "There are no orange kangaroos in Denmark." Or better yet, you can write on an overhead transparency (WITH THE LIGHT OFF), the words ORANGE, KANGAROO, and DENMARK. Then ask a student to come to the front of the class and switch on the light. This seems to amaze the class. Ask the students to hold up their sheets of paper—almost everyone will have the words—orange, kangaroo, and Denmark.

SOURCE: "Sharing ideas on the Teaching of Psychology"—conference topic presented by Douglas A. Bernstein, University of Illinois. His source was a publishing company sales representative, who heard it at a party, who heard it from...? (Isn't this the way we get a lot of our best teaching ideas?)

Active Learning Activity 3.14 – The Psychic Psychologist

If you did not have time to do the psychic demonstration in Chapter 1 (The Scientific Method), Chapter 3's section on ESP provides another appropriate opportunity. You could add sensory specific language during the demonstration mentioning, "the delicate perception" and how "ESP arises from higher brain functions", and how "you need to concentrate on your (mystical) third eye point."

Active Learning Activity 3.15 – ESP at Work: Witching for Water

Ask students what they know about witching for water or dowsing? Have they heard about it? Have they used it? What "sense" do they think is involved in dowsing? Ask for a count on how many believe it could work. Break into small groups and give them 5 minutes to think up ways that they would test the ability of dowsers scientifically. Afterwards show them the video *Beyond Science*, (Worth Publishers, Episode #802) and ask for reactions.

If time allows you could place dowsing for water in a historical context by asking students how they could have located water 300 years ago and contrasting their answers with tools and techniques of today's engineers. What was reasonable in one age and condition may not be valid or useful in the world of today.

Active Learning Activity 3.16 – Seeing versus Feeling

To illustrate the interconnectedness of sensation and interpretation, present the following scenarios:

Situation 1: You have always enjoyed your favorite beach. One day you are swimming in the water when your skin starts burning fiercely. You are surrounded by a group of jellyfish and endure multiple stings before you can get out of the water. The next time you enter the water the waves look threatening and the darkness fearsome.

Situation 2: You have always enjoyed playing in the snow. One winter you and a friend are skiing on a hill when an avalanche carries your friend away. As you look at the snow, it no longer looks friendly and inviting, but menacing.

Situation 3: You have always enjoyed playing with animals. One day you are out walking when a dog runs up. You move to pet him but he bites your leg and won't let go. You require 27 stitches to stop the bleeding. The next time you are out in the park you no longer see man's best friend. You see dangerous, threatening animals.

Situation 4: You have a lovely, cozy back yard. One night you hear a crashing noise followed by a curse. You grab your flashlight and check out the yard. Everything looks strange, threatening and sinister. Familiar trees become dangerous objects.

Questions:
1. What do they have in common?
2. As you step into these scenarios can you separate the seeing from the feeling?
3. Do we see first and interpret second?
4. How does the brain's perceptual system interact with its feeling associations?

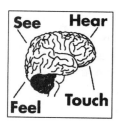

Brain-Based Learning

Brain-Based Learning Activity 3.1 - Cocktail Party

You can demonstrate the necessity of sensory reduction by creating a "cocktail party" situation in your classroom. Ask your students to pair up and get to know one another better by talking with one another about any topic for a few minutes. This should result in many different conversations. After a few minutes, ask the students to stop talking and engage them in a class discussion about sensory reduction by asking questions, such as: Could you easily attend to your partner? Could you understand any of the other conversations? What was it that you attended to? Why is sensory reduction necessary?

Brain-Based Learning Activity 3.2 - Locating the Blind Spot

The blind spot is created because there are no receptor cells where the optic nerve leaves the eye. This demonstration will allow the student to observe the location of his/her own blind spot. In a dimly lit room, hold up a small flashlight. Have the students close their left eyes and slowly shift their gaze toward their noses (with their right eyes) away from the light. When the blind spot is at the same angle as the incoming light, the flashlight will disappear. Encourage the students to move their gaze around slowly and try to identify the size and shape of the blind spot. After the demonstration, lead a short discussion on why humans do not attend to the blind spot.

Brain-Based Learning Activity 3.3 – Eye/Ear 3-D Model

If your department owns anatomical models for the eye or for the ear, disassemble the pieces and have small groups of students put them together. After they have been successfully assembled, have them take the model apart and explain the steps of the process by which the physical stimulus is converted into a physiological/neuronal impulse, demonstrating the role of each component.

Brain-Based Learning Activity 3.4 – Touch Mapping

Each pair of students gets a penny, a nickel, and a dime. The student who is guessing must close his/her eyes and guess the identity of the coin. The presenting student places the coins in mixed sequence on a) the inside forearm close by the elbow, b) the back of the hand, c) the center of the palm, and d) the flat of the thumb. For each location, the presenting student keeps track of how many guesses are needed on average before correct identification. Discuss the relation of detector density to function.

Brain-Based Learning Activity 3.5 – Distance Cues

Bring in a good quality copy of an Esher drawing or go on-line to pictures such as
http://users.skynet.be/sky70432/mcesher6.html or http://users.skynet.be/sky70432/mcesher3.html.
Applying the ideas from the section on "Monocular Cues", have the students detect through what
cues the artist is misleading the eye of the beholder into interpreting impossible shapes, such as stairs
that keep going up only to return to the same space. If this is difficult have the students look at the
picture from an unusual perspective (upside down, on edge, etc.) and again search the image for cues.

Brain-Based Learning Activity 3.6 – Camouflage Art

A great way to interest students in how the brain organizes unconnected dots into meaningful images
is to study the art of Bev Doolittle. Each of her paintings is a visual puzzle that unfolds as you spend
time looking past the "camouflage". The students really enjoy going on a visual "scavenger hunt".
After two or three examples they become aware of how pre-wired their brains are to seek and find
meaningful patterns.

Because of the details required to make the effect work, computer pictures are not ideal unless you
have a high quality computer set-up. Although her work is widely available on the web, many sites
do not show the pictures in sufficient detail. I recommend bringing in a book of her artwork or one
of her prints.

Pintos – Most people can see at least some of the horses. Have the students count how many they
spot. Chances are, not every one will detect all of the hidden horses without help.
http://fineart.artifactsgallery.com/detail.htf?title=Pintos+%2A+1979&picpath=pics/large/pintos.jpg&
id=843&artist_id=4&startpass=1

Doubled Back – The brain naturally follows the tracks in the snow up into the hills. Does everyone
see the bear hiding on the left?
http://fineart.artifactsgallery.com/detail.htf?title=Doubled+Back&picpath=pics/large/doubledback.jp
g&id=839&artist_id=4&startpass=6

Forest has Eyes – This is the most complicated picture of the three. Challenge the students to a
competition to find the many hidden faces in this picture.
http://fineart.artifactsgallery.com/detail.htf?title=The+Forest+Has+Eyes+%2A+1984&picpath=pics/l
arge/eyes.jpg&id=842&artist_id=4&startpass=6

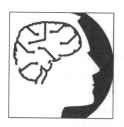

Critical Thinking

This exercise appears in the Student Study Guide, Chapter 3. It in included here for your convenience, and you may want to discuss it in class to reinforce use of the Student Study Guide.

Critical Thinking Exercise 3.1 - Empathizing (An Affective Skill)

In Chapter 3, you read about Helen Keller, an extraordinary woman who was blind from birth. The following exercise will improve your ability to empathize a bit with her and other visually handicapped people you might know. As you might read in the text, non-critical thinkers view everything and everyone else in relationship to themselves. They fail to understand or appreciate another's thoughts, feelings, or behaviors, as critical thinkers do.

Find a partner to take you on a blind walk for at least 20 to 30 minutes. Have the partner blindfold you and guide you on a walk filled with varied sensory experiences—up a hill, over a gravel driveway, across a dirt field full of potholes, past a bakery, through the school cafeteria, next to a rough wall, past an open freezer door, through a quiet library or the noisy student union, and so on—and see if you can tell where you are at any one time. Remind your partner not to give any hints as to what to expect so that it can be a truly sightless experience for you.

What happened when you were without your sense of sight? Did you find that you navigated better and could more easily determine where you were at the end of your walk—did you adapt? Did you compensate at all for your lack of sight—did you substitute another sense for your sense of sight? In what ways?

Critical Thinking Exercise 3.2 – Gathering Data and Developing Empathy: A Simulation of the Aging Process

Due to the highly technical and biological nature of the topic of sensation, this subject generally receives one of the lower ratings by many students (and some instructors). Despite the author's provision of many examples and applications, students have difficulty in relating this material to their everyday lives. One way to increase both their intrinsic interest and their intellectual understanding of the material is to provide learning experiences that require personal involvement (Evans, 1981).

This simulation exercise helps students experience some of the sensory changes that occur with the aging process. After participating in this exercise, students will have an increased understanding and compassion for the elderly (Wight, 1989). This ability to empathize or identify with differing populations is an important skill in critical thinking.

Time: One 50-minute class period.
Materials: A roll or two of plastic food wrap, cotton balls, rubber gloves, and masking tape.

Instructions: Inform students that they are being given a unique opportunity to experience a few of the sensory changes and problems that occur during the later stages of the aging process. To simulate blurred vision, have students tape a length of plastic wrap around their head to cover their eyes, being careful not to cover their noses. (This can also be accomplished by the removal or addition of eyeglasses.) Have them put cotton in their ears to simulate impaired hearing and wear rubber gloves to simulate reduced tactile sensations. (Although arthritis is not important to the topic of this chapter, student empathy for the elderly is further enhanced by asking them to wrap their knuckles and wrists with masking tape.)

Send students out into the hall or for a 10 minute walk to a protected area. Encourage them to pay close attention to all changes in their sensory processes and to note the difficulties in navigating small steps or drinking fountains. When students return, ask them to leave their "equipment" in place while you provide a 5 minute lecture. After students have removed the wrap, cotton, gloves, and masking tape, discuss their reactions.

Although this simulation does require 50 minutes, it has been an effective way to engage students in a difficult topic while also increasing their empathy for the elderly.

References:

Evans, J. D. (1981). Personal involvement projects in the psychology of aging: Some examples and an empirical assessment. Teaching of Psychology, 8, 230-233.

Wight, R. D. (1989). Fostering insight into personal conceptions of the elderly: A simulation exercise. Teaching of Psychology, 16, 216-218.

Critical Thinking Exercise 3.3 - Recognizing Faulty Reasoning: Problems with the Belief in ESP

The subject of ESP often generates great interest and emotional responses in people, and individuals who feel strongly about an issue sometimes fail to recognize the faulty reasoning underlying their beliefs. Belief in ESP is particularly susceptible to illogical, non-critical thinking.
In this exercise, you have a chance to examine common reports of ESP and to practice identifying possible examples of faulty reasoning. Begin by studying the following list of "common problems with ESP."

1. *Fallacy of Positive Instances* - Noting and remembering events that confirm personal expectations and beliefs (the "hits") and ignoring non-supportive evidence (the "misses").

2. *Innumeracy* - Failing to recognize chance occurrences for what they are due to, a lack of training in statistics and probabilities. Unusual events are misperceived as statistically impossible and extraordinary explanations, such as ESP, are seen as the logical alternative.

3. *Willingness to Suspend Disbelief* - Refusing to engage one's normal critical thinking skills because of a personal need for power and control. Although few people would attribute a foreign country's acquisition of top-secret information to ESP, some of these same individuals would willingly believe that a psychic could help them find their lost children.

4. *The "Vividness" Problem* - Human information processing and memory storage and retrieval are often based on the initial "vividness" of the information. Sincere personal testimonials, theatrical demonstrations, and detailed anecdotes easily capture attention and tend to be remembered better than rational, scientific descriptions of events.

Now read the following ESP reports and decide which type of faulty reasoning BEST describes each. More than one problem may be applicable, but try to limit your choice. Enter only one number beside each report, and then compare your answers with those of your classmates or friends. This comparison of results will help to sharpen critical thinking skills.

_____John hadn't thought of Paula, his old high school sweetheart, for years. Yet one morning he woke up thinking about her. He was wondering what she looked like and whether she was married now, when suddenly the phone rang. For some strange reason, he felt sure the call was from Paula. He was right. John now cites this call as evidence for his personal experience with extrasensory perception.

_____A psychic visits a class in introductory psychology. He predicts that, out of this class of 23 students, two individuals will have birthdays on the same day. When a tally of birthdays is taken, his prediction is supported and many students leave class believing the ESP has been supported.

_____A National League baseball player dreams of hitting a bases-loaded triple. Two months later, during the final game of the World Series, he gets this exact triple and wins the game. He informs the media of his earlier dream and the possibility of ESP.

_____A mother is sitting alone in her office at work and suddenly sees a vivid image of her home on fire. She immediately calls home and awakens the sitter who excitedly reports smoke coming under the door. The sitter successfully extinguishes the fire, and the mother later attributes her visual images to ESP.

Gender and Cultural Diversity

Gender and Cultural Diversity Activity 3.1 - Conducting Socratic Discussions: Thinking About Sensation and Perception

At the heart of critical thinking is critical questioning. The ability to delve beneath the superficial or to rise above mere appearances by considering logical consequences and possible boundaries is at the core of critical thinking. Socrates, an ancient Greek philosopher, modeled this type of thinking in his question-and-answer method of teaching. In a Socratic discussion, the questioner uses probing questions to learn what another thinks, to help the respondent develop his or her ideas, and to mutually explore the implications, consequences, and values of ideas. In turn, the respondent is comfortable and doesn't become offended, defensive, or intimidated because he or she knows the shared purpose is to clarify and evaluate a line of reasoning.

In this exercise, several discussion questions related to Chapter 3 are presented and they will help develop the method of Socratic discussions, while also reviewing important terms and concepts. Invite a colleague who is also interested in critical thinking skills to act as your partner as you demonstrate the basic Socratic Method--seeing instructors working/playing together with these questions will relax and inspire the students. They will recognize that we are all engaged in the critical thinking process--an important concept, making their own attempts more productive. Then allow students to practice. If the class is large, assign students to groups of 10. Two members of each group will conduct a Socratic discussion while the remaining students will observe, listen, and critique. One person should play Socrates and question the other for half the questions; then reverse roles for the remaining questions. We are providing sample questions (Handout 3.1 – Gender and Cultural Diversity) that Socrates might ask, and the respondent's answers should be followed up with questions such as "Why?" "How do you know?" "What is your reason for saying that?" "For example?" "Can I summarize your point as...?" Remind students to relax and enjoy their roles as both the questioner and respondent. Mention that Socratic questioners do not attempt to make another look stupid. This should be a fun "mind game" that stretches intellectual capacity and develops critical thinking skills. (A by-product of this exercise is that it also helps students master chapter material.)

If the class is composed of students of varying cultural backgrounds, it is possible to utilize their ethnic heritage by instructing them to respond to the Socratic questions according to the norms of their culture. This will help expose the cultural variations which exist in today's world. We live in a highly technologized Western society--loss of vision, hearing, or touch will have different meanings for us than for an individual living in a non-Western, pre-technological culture. Ask students for examples.

Handout 3.1 – Gender and Cultural Diversity

Sample Socratic Questions

1. Is there a sound if no one is there to hear it? Or, does a hamburger have a taste if no one is there to taste it?

2. What would the world be like if the absolute thresholds for sensation were changed? If humans could see X rays and ultraviolet light or infrared rays and radar? If people were like bats and dolphins and could hear sounds up to 100,000 hertz?

3. What would happen if each sensory receptor (e.g., eyes, ears, skin) was receptive to every type of incoming stimuli? If eyes were also sensitive to sound waves and odor molecules, could the brain distinguish and integrate this information?

4. William James, a famous early psychologist, suggested that, "If a master surgeon were to cross the auditory and optic nerves, then we would hear lightning and see thunder." How would you explain this statement?

5. How would you explain the fact that blind people tend to be better adjusted psychologically and less subject to emotional difficulties than deaf people?

6. If you had to choose between losing vision, hearing, or touch, which sense would you choose to lose? Why? What effect would it have on your life?

Writing Project

Given the need for improved writing skills in college students and to respond to the call for "writing across the curriculum", we offer writing projects for each chapter. In Chapter 3, we suggest a 2-3 page written response to the following activity. Recognizing the time involved in grading such writing projects, one alternative is occasionally to assign "peer grading." Collect the papers, remove student names, and assign each student a paper to grade. It helps to make their participation in peer grading a required part of the overall points for the writing project. This encourages a more thoughtful and responsible evaluation, as well as acknowledging and rewarding the additional work.

It is generally assumed that most people who are blind or deaf would prefer to be sighted or hearing. For this exercise, ask your students to imagine themselves as Helen Keller and to write a 2-3 page paper describing only the advantages of not having sight or hearing. This has been a very difficult, but effective writing project. By focusing on the advantages (and having to write two to three pages!), non-blind and non-deaf students are forced to reexamine their stereotypes and prejudices. Some students have come back many years after leaving college and commented on how this one writing project affected their lives.

Circle of Quality - Chapter 3

Please give us your feedback. We thank you in advance for assisting us in improving the next edition. The contact information is listed in the preface.

What are the three most helpful teaching tools in this chapter?

1.

2.

3.

What are the three least useful teaching tools in this chapter?

1.

2.

3.

What are the three most difficult concepts to teach in this chapter?

1.

2.

3.

Additional Comments:

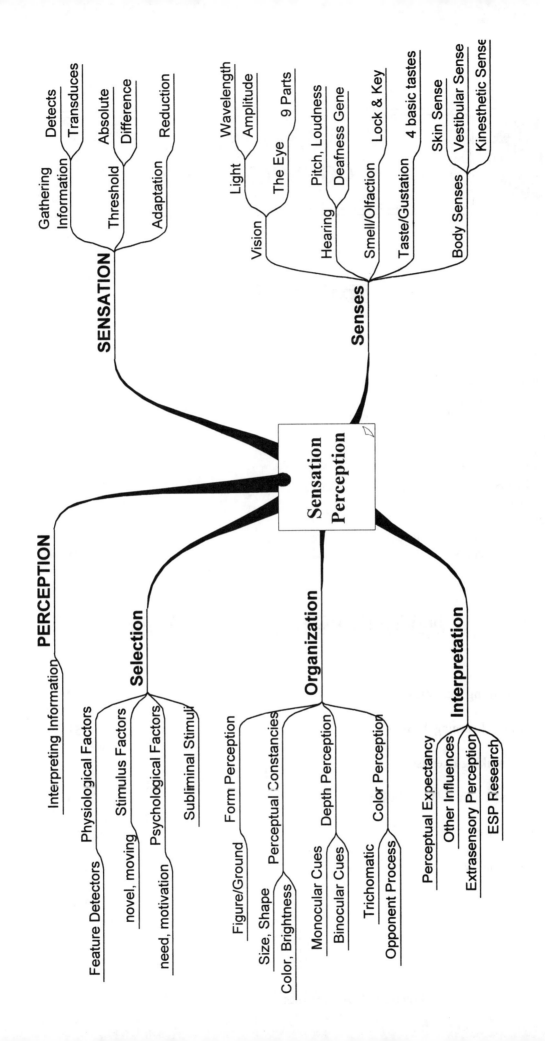

SENSATION

Gathering Information — Detects — Transduces

Threshold — Absolute / Difference

Adaptation — Reduction

Senses

Vision — Light — Wavelength / Amplitude

The Eye — 9 Parts

Hearing — Pitch, Loudness

Deafness Gene

Smell/Olfaction — Lock & Key

Taste/Gustation — 4 basic tastes

Body Senses — Skin Sense / Vestibular Sense / Kinesthetic Sense

Sensation Perception

PERCEPTION

Interpreting Information

Selection

Feature Detectors

Physiological Factors

Stimulus Factors — novel, moving

Psychological Factors — need, motivation

Subliminal Stimuli

Organization

Form Perception — Figure/Ground

Perceptual Constancies — Size, Shape / Color, Brightness

Depth Perception — Monocular Cues / Binocular Cues

Color Perception — Trichomatic / Opponent Process

Interpretation

Perceptual Expectancy

Other Influences

Extrasensory Perception

ESP Research

CHAPTER 4
CONSCIOUSNESS

Outline

Studying Consciousness

Levels of Awareness
Daydreams and Fantasies

Sleep and Dreams

Sleep as a Biological Rhythm
How Scientists Study Sleep
Sleep and Sleep Deprivation
Why We Dream
Sleep Disorders

Drugs and Consciousness

Understanding Drugs
Depressants

Stimulants
Narcotics
Hallucinogens
Explaining Drug Use

Research Highlight
Addictive Drugs as the Brain's "Evil Tutor"

Additional Routes to Alternate States

Hypnosis
Meditation

Gender and Cultural Diversity
Consciousness Across Cultures

Learning Objectives

Upon completion of CHAPTER 4, the student should be able to:

1. Define consciousness and alternate states of consciousness (ASCs); describe the various levels of awareness, including the difference between controlled and automatic processing, and the purpose of daydreaming and fantasies (pp. 136-139).
2. Identify common myths about sleep (p. 140).
3. Define circadian rhythms; discuss the effects of disruptions in circadian rhythms (pp. 141-142).
4. Explain how electroencephalograms (EEGs) are used to study sleep; and describe the various physical changes associated with each stage of sleep, including the REM stage and the non-REM Stages 1, 2, 3, and 4 (pp. 143-144).
5. Explain problems associated with sleep deprivation. Discuss possible biological causes of sleep; describe how the repair/restoration theory of sleep differs from the evolutionary/circadian theory (pp. 145-149).
6. Describe and differentiate between the psychoanalytic, biological, and cognitive views of dreaming (pp. 149-150).
7. Discuss the five major sleep disorders: insomnia, sleep apnea, narcolepsy, nightmares, and night terrors (pp. 151-153).
8. Define psychoactive drugs; compare and contrast drug abuse versus addiction, psychological versus physical dependence, and tolerance versus cross-tolerance (pp. 154-155).
9. Define depressants; describe the effects of alcohol on the nervous system and behavior, and discuss why alcohol is a growing social concern (pp. 156-158).
10. Define stimulants; and describe the effects of nicotine and cocaine (pp. 159-160).
11. Define narcotics; and describe their effects on the nervous system and behavior (pp. 156, 160).
12. Define hallucinogens; and describe the effects of LSD and marijuana on the nervous system and behavior (pp. 156, 160-162).
13. Briefly explain how drugs act as agonists and antagonists to neurotransmitters, and describe how psychoactive drugs can affect each of the four steps in neurotransmission (pp. 162-164).
14. Explain the four major reasons people use and abuse drugs, and describe recent research regarding the importance of dopamine and glutamate on drug addiction (pp. 164-166).
15. Define hypnosis, and discuss five myths and controversies regarding its use. State how hypnosis is used today in medical and psychotherapy settings (pp. 167-169).
16. Define meditation, and discuss its potential benefits (pp. 169-170).
17. Discuss why there has been such a strong interest in alternate states of consciousness throughout history and across cultures; and explain the three major functions of ASCs for all cultures (pp. 170-172).

Chapter Summary/Lecture Organizer

Introductory Vignette--Chapter 4 opens with non-fictional accounts of two individuals in drug related altered states of consciousness--one fully conscious and one not. Both, however, are unable to speak, move, or respond in any way to the people around them. Taken from the book The Frozen Addicts, George Carillo's story demonstrates how an illegal, tainted dose of heroin left him almost completely paralyzed while he remained fully awake and alert. Karen Ann Quinlan, on the other hand, lived for over ten years in a coma and a similar state of paralysis with a complete lack of awareness of her surroundings--"thanks" to a mixture of recreational and prescription drugs. These two cases are then compared to the sleep-deprived, altered state of Peter Tripp, a disc jockey who stayed awake for 200 hours. These case studies are used to illustrate the complexities associated with studying and defining consciousness.

I. **STUDYING CONSCIOUSNESS** - Consciousness is defined as the general state of being aware and responsive to stimuli and events in both the external and internal environments. Like most members of society, college students often expect psychologists to be interested in dreams, hypnosis, meditation, and other forms of ASCs. To explain the varying levels of scientific interest in this field, readers are taken through a brief history of the behavioristic and psychodynamic approach to the study of consciousness. The chapter concludes with an exploration of why humans seek these altered states of consciousness (ASCs).

    A. Levels of Awareness - Consciousness is not an all-or-nothing phenomenon. Instead, it exists on a continuum--with high awareness and *controlled processes* at the top, no awareness and coma at the bottom, and lower awareness and *automatic processes* somewhere in the middle. Our opening vignette has good examples of all three.

    B. Daydreams and Fantasies – These are a mid-ground level of awareness. Daydreaming is a personal form of reverie – a drifting off into a world of fantasy where we spend as much as one-third of our waking hours. Over 95% of both men and women have sexual fantasies. These provide excitement with safety and convenience.

II. **SLEEP AND DREAMING**

    A. Sleep as a Biological Rhythm - Biological rhythms affect many aspects of people's lives. Circadian rhythm affects not only the sleep and waking cycle, but fluctuations in blood pressure, pulse rate, body temperature, blood sugar level, and cell growth. Larks are more efficient in the morning, owls in the evening. Disruptions can cause problems, such as accidents or fatigue from shift work and jet lag. The breathtaking claims for melatonin supplements should be considered with caution.

B. How Scientists Study Sleep - Using the EEG, scientists have discovered important facts about the sleep process. A typical night's sleep consists of four to five 90-minute cycles. The cycle begins in Stage 1 and then moves through Stages 2, 3 and 4. After reaching the deepest level of sleep, the cycle reverses up to the REM (rapid eye movement) state. In REM sleep, the eyes dart about under the eyelids, the brain pattern of the sleeper is similar to the waking state and the person is often dreaming while the body is in muscle "paralysis".

C. Sleep and Sleep Deprivation – While some studies do not find significant negative effects, researchers have connected sleep deprivation to reduced immunity, mood alteration and increased stress and irritability. It can lead to serious accidents and diminished productivity. There are two theories of sleep. According to the *repair/restoration theory*, sleep is necessary to replenish our physical, emotional and intellectual energies. According to the *evolutionary/circadian theory*, sleep conserves energy and keeps us safe from predators. Both theories have merit. Sleep seems to be controlled by various areas of the brain and by several neurotransmitters.

D. Why We Dream - There are three major theories of why we dream. The psychoanalytic view (the *wish-fulfillment theory*) says that dreams are disguised symbols of repressed desires. It has received little scientific support. The biological perspective (the *activation-synthesis hypothesis*) argues that dreams are simply unimportant by-products of random stimulation of brain cells. The cognitive view sees dreams as information processing; they help us sort through everyday experiences, solve problems and think creatively. Dream content mirrors waking concerns.

E. Sleep Disorders - The text discusses five major sleep disorders: Insomnia (repeated difficulty in falling asleep), sleep apnea (temporarily stopping breathing during sleep, causing loud snoring and poor quality sleep), narcolepsy (excessive daytime sleepiness characterized by sudden sleep attacks), nightmares (bad dreams generally occurring during REM sleep), and night terrors (terrifying dreams usually experienced in Stage 4 of non-REM sleep)

III. **DRUGS AND CONSCIOUSNESS** - Psychoactive drugs are defined as chemicals that change conscious awareness or perception.

A. Understanding Drugs – People of all cultures have used and abused psychoactive drugs, which include everyday things such as caffeine, nicotine, and alcohol. Students are introduced to important drug terminology, including *drug abuse, addiction, psychological dependence, physical dependence, tolerance,* and *cross-tolerance.*

B. Depressants - Depressant drugs (sometimes called "downers"), like alcohol, barbiturates, and antianxiety drugs, depress the central nervous system, causing relaxation, sedation, or possible loss of consciousness. Next to tobacco, alcohol is one of the most widely used drugs in Western society. Alcohol abuse can lead to serious losses in cognitive functioning, as well as to major social problems such as drunk driving, spousal abuse, and death after binge drinking. It can encourage impulsive acts of aggression or sexual risk taking.

C. Stimulants - Caffeine, nicotine, amphetamines, and cocaine are all common stimulants (also known as "uppers"), which increase the overall activity and responsiveness of the central nervous system. Caffeine is now the world's most widely used drug. Nicotine not only affects the smoker, but bystanders who breathe it. Cocaine, which was once considered relatively harmless, is now known for its potential for physical damage, severe addiction and psychological dependence.

D. Narcotics - Narcotics, such as morphine and heroin, numb the senses and are used medically to relieve pain. They are also called opiates because they are derived from opium, the juice of the opium poppy. They are highly addictive. The recreational use of heroin has doubled since the mid 1980s.

E. Hallucinogens - Hallucinogens, like LSD or marijuana and commonly known as "psychedelics", produce sensory or perceptual distortions, including visual, auditory, or kinesthetic hallucinations. After years of research, researchers and the public continue to debate the possible ill effects and benefits of marijuana as it is a hard drug to classify as effects are dosage dependent. Years of research have not settled the ongoing hot debate. Some positive therapeutic results have been reported. Negative consequences include impaired memory, attention and learning, and an impact on the brain similar to highly addictive drugs.

F. Explaining Drug Use – After having explored the four major categories of drugs, two basic questions remain: "How do psychoactive drugs create alternate states of consciousness? And, why do so many people use and abuse them?" Psychoactive drugs change the effect of neurotransmitters in the brain in two ways: they enhance the effect and are called *agonists* or inhibit it (*antagonists).* People use these drugs for at least four major reasons: positive associations, addiction, withdrawal, and personal or social-cultural forces. Dopamine and glutamate are part of the brain's reward system.

> **Research Highlights: Addictive Drugs as the Brain's "Evil Tutor"** – Do addictive drugs "teach" the brain to be addicted?

IV. ADDITIONAL ROUTES TO ALTERNATE STATES

A. Hypnosis - Hypnosis is an alternate state of heightened suggestibility characterized by relaxation and intense focus. There are five common myths or controversies associated with it: forced hypnosis, unethical behavior, exceptional memory, superhuman strength, and fakery. It is employed as a respected clinical tool by physicians and dentists to reduce pain and increase concentration, and by therapists as an adjunct to psychotherapy.

B. Meditation - Meditation is a group of techniques designed to focus attention and produce a heightened awareness. Meditation can produce dramatic changes in physiological processes, including heart rate, oxygen consumption, brain waves, and respiration.

> **Gender and Cultural Diversity: Consciousness Across Cultures** - This section deals with the topic of alteration of consciousness across cultures. While the methods of induction vary, ASCs seem to serve the same three functions for all cultures--sacred rituals, social interactions, and individual rewards.

Teaching Resources

SECTION I – STUDYING CONSCIOUSNESS

Learning Objectives # 1
Lecture Lead-Ins # 1
Active Learning Activities #'s 4.1 & 4.5
Brain-Based Learning Activities # 4.1
Gender and Cultural Diversity Activity # 4.1

SECTION II – SLEEP AND DREAMING

Learning Objectives #'s 2 – 7
Lecture Lead-Ins # 4
Lecture Extender #4.1
Discussion Questions # 1 & 9
Active Learning Activities #'s 4.2 – 4.5
Brain-Based Learning Activities # 4.2
Critical Thinking Exercise # 4.1
Gender and Cultural Diversity Activity # 4.1
Writing Project # 4.1

SECTION III – DRUGS AND CONSCIOUSNESS

Learning Objectives #'s 8 - 14
Lecture Lead-Ins # 2 & 5
Discussion Questions #'s 2 – 5, 7 & 8, 10
Active Learning Activities #'s 4.4, 4.6 & 4.7
Brain-Based Learning Activities # 4.2
Critical Thinking Exercise #'s 4.2 & 4.3
Gender and Cultural Diversity Activity # 4.1
Writing Project # 4.1

SECTION IV – ADDITIONAL ROUTES TO ALTERNATE STATES

Learning Objectives #'s 15 - 17
Lecture Lead-Ins # 3
Discussion Questions #'s 6, 10 & 11
Active Learning Activities #'s 4.4 & 4.6
Brain-based Learning Activities #'s 4.3 – 4.6
Gender and Cultural Diversity Activity #4

Lecture Lead-Ins

1. Charles Tart, <u>Consciousness: Brain, states of awareness, and mysticism</u>, believes it may be impossible to study alternate states of consciousness scientifically--since science is a product of normal consciousness. Ask students to think about this assertion. Do they agree? Is science the best way to understand alternate states? What are the alternatives? Is a scientific description and measurement of ASCs like a blind man's description of a sunrise--gradually increasing warmth? These questions ALWAYS stimulate a great deal of discussion and provide a great lead-in to the topic of consciousness. They also serve as a model of critical thinking. Given that students have had a "heavy dose of science" in the preceding three chapters, this may be the first time they are given an opportunity to explore the limits of science. While the text's chapter focuses on the scientific contributions to the study of consciousness, you can demonstrate your willingness to explore and discuss other alternatives to studying ASCs.

2. As a lead-in to the topic of drugs, ask students, "Do you know the difference between drug use and drug abuse?" Many students will nod their heads. Ask everyone to quickly write a definition of each. Then form groups of three to four students, ask them to share their definitions and to develop a "consensual" definition for both drug use and drug abuse. Share these definitions with the class. If time allows, let leaders of each group write their definitions on the board or read them aloud to the class. (Whenever possible it helps generate class enthusiasm and active learning to "share the stage" with your students. You'll be surprised how much they enjoy writing on the board or coming to the front of the class. It also reinforces the point that group work is valued and not a chance to simply chat with classmates.)

3. Invite a trained hypnotherapist or other professional to talk to the class about alternate states achieved through hypnosis. Encourage students to ask the professionals questions regarding successes and failures with hypnosis, and their professional feelings and belief regarding controversial issues such as age regression, repressed memories, use of hypnosis for locating lost children, and so on.

4. As a lead-in to the topic of sleep, ask students, " How many hours of sleep should the average 19-30 year old get per night? How many (how few) can you get by with and still function well? How often do you dream during the night that you can remember?" Be sure to point out the wide individual differences in reported values. The book reports average values. Time permitting, you could mention how most human abilities or characteristics are distributed normally and how the students' sleep data relates to the normal curve.

5. In the past few years laws have been passed in some states allowing for the "medicinal use" of marijuana for pain control of chronically ill patients. If you were in charge of such a program, how would you determine who should be included under such an exception to the drug laws? Is pain control a legitimate reason to use marijuana? How does it differ from a prescription pain medication?

Lecture Extenders

4.1 - Dreams

Dreaming must be important to humans; otherwise, REM sleep would be shorter. Adults who sleep approximately eight hours per night spend about 22% of the time in REM. This means they are dreaming almost two hours each day, and almost one month each year. By age 60, one has accumulated five years in the dream state.

Studies have documented the cyclic nature of sleep and the changes in proportion of REM to NREM sleep as the night progresses (Van de Castle, 1971). The first dream of the night, which occurs within 90 minutes of the onset of NREM sleep, is typically the shortest dream of the night. With each successive cycle, the REM state becomes longer. The first dream may be as short as five minutes with the final one lasting up to an hour. This is contrary to the belief that dreams occur in a "split-second." Observations in sleep laboratories have shown that there is a close correlation between the reported dream and eye movements. The eye movements last for the period of time that the action in the dream would require for completion in the real world. Dreams not only become longer as the night progresses, they also become more intense and emotional. The first dream is likely to be a brief recounting to one's self of the day's events with each succeeding dream going further back in time. An interesting experimental confirmation of this was a study where participants were asked to wear red goggles during their waking hours (Van de Castle, 1971). The first dreams of the night contained many red images which did not appear in the later dreams of the night.

Many people believe that the onset of a dream is stimulated by environmental events such as the sound of an alarm or telephone. Studies indicate this is not so (Van de Castle, 1971). REM dreaming is caused by the initiation of the REM state which depends upon the sleep rhythms. External stimulations affect dream content only if one is already dreaming; then, the stimulus events may become part of the plot. If water is dripped on the forehead of a sleeper in both REM and NREM sleep, it has no effect on dream content unless the subject is in the REM period.

Dream content remains a fascinating area for most people. Today, as in earlier periods of civilization, people want to know what their dreams mean. They expect to uncover hidden parts of their personality or solutions to emotional problems. Thus, they are quite ready to believe that Freud' assertion that important, unconscious material surfaces through dreams. Others have suggested that dream content and interpretation rest upon personal preference.

What one dreams about has been fairly well documented through extensive surveys (Hall, 1974). Almost all dreams are based on visual images (excluding children who are blind from an early age), although sound and touch may be involved. The normal rules of logic do not apply. The dreamer may be in one location and then abruptly be translocated to another place. Most dreams occur in some sort of dwelling; the majority of the times this is not one's home. The most often reported room of the house for a dream is the living room. Work place is seldom mentioned. In many dreams, the dreamer is alone; however, the most frequent scenario is the dreamer plus two other people. Contrary to popular belief, famous people seldom appear in dreams. The vast majority of people dream about people who are significant to them, especially if there is an ongoing conflict.

Mundane or routine actions seldom occur--one does not brush one's teeth or wash dishes in a dream. Dreams tend not to be happy events. The three most common emotions are fear, anger, and sadness.

There are also male-female differences in the content of dreams (Van De Castle, 1971). Men dream more of the outdoors and of strangers. Women report dreams containing people with whom they have significant close relationships and the location tends to be indoors. Men dream more often of other men; women dream equally of both sexes. In other words, the male spends less time than the female dreaming of the opposite sex. Physical aggression appears more often in male dreams, and the aggressor is most often male for both male and female dreamers. Females are more often the victim during dreams of aggression.

Dream content has changed surprisingly little throughout recorded history, so many of these "modern-day" themes are not new. Additionally, some dreams are so common that they are found the world over (Gutheil, 1974). These universal themes include loss of a tooth, falling or flying, exhibition, examination, and arriving late for events. In ancient times, the loss of tooth dream was interpreted as an omen of an impending death, and even today, some primitive societies view it as such. Freud would link this type of dream to a death wish that has bubbled out of the unconscious; however, most contemporary dream theorists are more flexible in their assessment and consider the entire context of the dream. Flying and falling dreams are often referred to as kinesthetic dreams. The meaning probably relates more to the emotion that is experienced rather than the act per se. Many people who have flying dreams report feelings of mastery or being "above it all." Falling dreams appear to be associated with feelings of great anxiety. Indeed, one of the public myths about dreams is that one will die if the falling action is completed and one hits bottom. Most people do wake up because the anxiety is so great that the dreamer cannot tolerate it. Exhibition dreams usually deal with some private, hidden information one fears revealing. The most common exhibition dream is being nude or half-clothed in public. A similar dream involves "bathroom" behaviors and suddenly becoming aware of an audience. Freud attributes these dreams to wish-fulfillment. However, for those reporting these dreams, the most common emotion is one of great embarrassment and/or feelings of inferiority. The examination dream occurs most often when one is facing a test, hurdle, or new challenge. The plot often involves inability to handle the task. The final theme, arriving late, is associated with feelings of frustration; for example, one is unable to make a train, get to class, or run fast enough.

It would be interesting to speculate on the state of scientific knowledge and the world of dreaming in the year 5,000 A.D. Will people still want to understand, describe, and predict their dreams?

References:

Gutheil, E. (1974). Universal (typical) dreams. In R. W. Woods & H. B. Greenhouse (Eds.), The new world of dreams, (pp. 218-223). New York: MacMillan.

Hall, C. S. (1974). What we dream about. In R. W. Woods & H. B. Greenhouse (Eds.), The new world of dreams, (pp. 5-12). New York: MacMillan.

Staff (1981, July 13). The mystery of sleep. Newsweek, pp. 48- 53.

Van De Castle, B. (1971). The psychology of dreaming. New York: General Learning Press

Key Terms

Discussion Questions

1. Have you ever experienced extreme sleep deprivation or a situation that produced sensory deprivation (such as "flotation tanks")? How did you respond? Should bus drivers, airline pilots, and others who are responsible for public safety be required to wear monitors that would sound an alarm if they fell asleep? Why or why not?

2. With the increased emphasis on controlling illegal drugs, should the emphasis be on jail or education for individual drug users? If the answer was "education," at what age should this drug education begin and for how long should it last? If the answer was "jail," what should the jail terms be for various drug-related offenses? Be specific: LSD sales--10 years; Cocaine use--life; etc.

3. Aldous Huxley, in the novel <u>Brave New World</u>, wrote about an imaginary drug (soma) that made people feel extremely happy and cooperative. If such a drug existed, would you take it? What if it was as safe as aspirin? Should everyone be forced to take the drug? What would the world be like if everyone took the drug?

4. Are the risks (legal and health) worth the use of illegal drugs? Many students will have used, or known someone who has used, one or more illegal drugs. Ask the students to share their information or personal experiences, but remind them of privacy issues. Start this discussion with a list of famous people who have died from drug overdoses. Ask for suggestions from class.

5. Given the current evidence of dangers associated with nicotine, should American tobacco companies be allowed to continue promoting smoking in countries where there is less public awareness of the health hazards?

6. Hypnosis is sometimes used to enhance recall of crime details; should such evidence be admissible in court? What are the potential advantages and disadvantages? Mention to students that these issues appear in Chapter 6 of the text.

7. If brain surgeons could safely install an electrode in your pleasure center so that you could push a button anytime you want to flood your brain with pleasure, would you elect to have such an operation? How would it affect your life if you could control your pleasure centers directly? Would you connect with more people or less people than you are right now in your life? Would you produce more work or less? Would you relate to your family more or less?

8. In the movie *Total Recall*, Arnold Schwarzenegger goes on a "virtual vacation". If computers and virtual games advance to the point where you could get convincing sensory feedback by being hooked up to a real-as-life computer simulation, would you be interested in such a "game

machine"? If you owned one, on what basis would you decide how often and how long to use it? In what way would using such a machine be similar to or different from taking a drug?

9.   Other cultures, such as the American Indian tribes, place great value on going on a "dream quest". They believe that dreams can be a powerful tool for gaining visions and finding deep answers. Do you believe this is possible? What factors would entice you or prevent you from going on such a journey? How would your family or friends react to you if you went ahead with it?

10.   What is the difference between altering your consciousness through drugs versus using breathing, hypnosis, meditation, visualization, yoga or fasting? How does mainstream America value states of consciousness that differ from the alert, productive, focused state of working consciousness (controlled processes)?

11.   Monks, nuns or followers of long established religious paths (Christians, Moslems, Sufis, Jews, Sikhs, etc.) have used consciousness-altering tools throughout history to find God. When you consider fasting, operating on minimal sleep, dancing or kneeling for hours, repetitive prayers, singing or chanting, and other similar tools used in sacred rituals, does the end justify the means? Does it matter that these events are supervised in a religious group setting? How would you differentiate sincere striving for God-consciousness from brainwashing in cults?

 **Web Sites**

Psychopharmacology and Drug Resources
http://www.cmhc.com/guide/pro22.htm
This site provides an alphabetical index to drugs and drug information.

Institute for Brain Aging and Dementia
http://www.apa.uci.edu/dement.html
This is a fabulous site for medical and research related information on dementia. Information on the site includes coverage of the nature of dementia, its causes, and techniques for diagnosis. Don't miss the compelling MRI and SPECT images comparing the brains of persons with and without dementia.

The Self-Psychology Page
http://www.selfpsychology.org/
An outstanding site dedicated to a contemporary version of psychoanalytic theory that focuses more on consciousness and relationship issues, and less on sex and aggression. The site includes forums and discussion groups, the full text of scholarly papers, and much more.

National Institute of Drug Abuse
http://www.nida.nih.gov/
This is the homepage of the National Institute on Drug Abuse. It contains a very thorough and readable collection of pages about all of the major drugs of abuse. For each drug there is a "capsule" (interesting choice of words) that summarizes the drug, its effects, and abuse profile, and there is also a list of more scientific articles related to that substance.

Sleep Medicine Home Page
http://www.users.cloud9.net/~thorpy/
A comprehensive site for information on sleep and sleep disorders.

Web of Addictions
http://www.well.com/user/woa/
Another site that provides facts about alcohol and drug abuse, guides to treatment resources, and links to related sites. The section labeled "New" provides links to newly created web pages on alcohol and drug abuse.

Habitsmart Home Page
http://www.cts.com/crash/habtsmrt/
This site provides online assessment of alcohol consumption and provides details on the treatment and control of drug addiction.

Suggested Films and Videos

Wake Up, America

Films for the Humanities and Sciences, 1995. 24 minutes. This film covers many aspects of sleep: the functions of sleep, why there are differences in sleep needs, and disruption in circadian rhythms. A presentation of sleep disorders including sleep apnea, insomnia, and narcolepsy, as well as treatments in and out of a sleep laboratory, is included.

The Mind Awake and Asleep

Annenberg/CPB, 1990. 30 minutes. From Zimbardo's "Discovering Psychology" series, this video explores the nature of sleep, dreams, and altered states of consciousness. The importance of dreams in helping humans to understand their experiences is also discussed.

Sleep Disorders

Films for the Humanities and Sciences. 28 minutes. This program explores the world of sleep disorders with Dr. William Dement of Stanford University. It shows patients with a variety of sleep disorders being assessed and treated at a sleep laboratory.

A Good Night's Sleep

ABC'S *20/20*, 1990. 17 minutes. This segment features Dr. Richard Ferber, a children's sleep expert, demonstrating his behavior modification techniques for getting children to sleep through the night. This film follows one family's successful effort with Dr. Ferber. Classes really love this segment.

Dreams: Theater of the Night

Films for the Humanities and Sciences, 1990. 28 minutes. This film examines several theories of why people dream, including Freud's wish-fulfillment and the activation-synthesis hypothesis. PET scans are used to explore why humans dream and the dreams' possible functions. Additionally, an actual therapy session using dream analysis is presented.

The Mind Hidden and Divided

Annenberg/CPB, 1990. 30 minutes. From Zimbardo's "Discovering Psychology" series, this video discusses the unconscious aspects of the human mind and the effects of various states of consciousness on behavior. Anesthesia studies and drug studies are also mentioned in relation to the brain's ability to function. Hypnosis is demonstrated as one of Freud's primary techniques for studying the unconscious mind.

Addiction: The Family in Crisis

Films for the Humanities and Sciences, 1995. 28 minutes. This program tells the story of one man's addiction to alcohol. It explains the process of addiction in the brain and the role of the family in "enabling" the drinking behavior. The program follows the alcoholic through a treatment program as he learns the causes of his addiction and how to keep his alcoholism under control through abstinence.

The Addicted Brain

      Films for the Humanities and Sciences. 26 minutes. This documentary takes the viewer on a tour of the most prolific manufacturer and user of drugs--the human brain. This program also explores developments in the biochemistry of addiction and addictive behaviors.

Substance Misuse

      Films for the Humanities and Sciences, 1995. 30 minutes. This program nicely follows the text with a discussion of the most commonly misused substances including stimulants (amphetamines, caffeine, cocaine, nicotine, MDMA), depressants (alcohol, benzodiazapenes, barbiturates, solvents), hallucinogens (LSD, magic mushrooms), and narcotics (heroin, morphine).

Captive Minds: Hypnosis and Beyond

      Filmmakers Library, 1988. 55 minutes. This award-winning video explains how long-term conditioning takes place and shows that indoctrination methods used by disparate institutions are surprisingly similar. This film shows how the power of suggestion influences behavior and reminds everyone that all people are vulnerable to psychological manipulation.

Child Hypnosis with Dr. Perry London

      Psychological and Educational Films, 1990. 40 minutes. Dr. London asserts that hypnosis can be an effective treatment for stress-related disorders and is especially useful in children because of their trust and susceptibility. Actual demonstrations on a 10-year-old are shown. This is an excellent film to portray hypnosis and its use in psychotherapy.

Sleep and Its Secrets

      Resller and Holzinger for Prisma Filmproduktion/Filmakers Library, 1999. 56 minutes. This documentary, which interweaves informative interviews with internationally renowned researchers and vivid graphics, gives a clear explanation of what happens to us during those unconscious hours.

Addiction

      Films for the Humanities & Sciences, 1995. 24 minutes. Using sophisticated 3-D animation, this program, divided into two parts, takes viewers on a journey deep into the brain to study the effects of nicotine, cocaine, and marijuana.

B.F. Skinner: A Fresh Appraisal

      with Murray Sidman, Ph.D./Davidson Films, 1999. 30 minutes. Using both archival and new footage, this video takes a look at who the man was and what he really said. His terms are introduced in context so the student understands how they were intended to be used.

Chronobiology: The Time of Our Lives

      Films for the Humanities & Sciences, 1989. 58 minutes. This program examines the biological evolution of our internal timekeepers, examining the conflict between the time in our bodies and brains, and the time on our wrists.

Drugs: Profiles of Addiction and Recovery

      Films for the Humanities & Sciences, 1997. 25 minutes each. An informative three-part series, describes the miseries of substance abuse and methods of overcoming addiction.

Books For Success

Baars, Bernard J. (1997). <u>**In the Theater of Consciousness : The Workplace of the Mind.**</u> Oxford University Press.
Combining psychology with brain science, Baars shows how silent context operators shape conscious experience. Practical explanations of the structure of consciousness with many examples from daily life.

Csikszentmihalyi, Mihaly. (1998). <u>**Finding Flow : The Psychology of Engagement with Everyday Life.**</u> Basic Books.
A thorough analysis of how people enjoy their world, balancing science and self help. Offers tools to add stimulating, high skill / high commitment tasks into one's life. Research based advice on how to change one's state of consciousness from mundane to extraordinary.

Julien, Robert M. (1997 – 8th Ed.). <u>**A Primer of Drug Action : A Concise, Non-technical Guide to the Actions, Uses, and Side Effects of Psychoactive Drugs.**</u> W H Freeman & Co
Continuously improved since its first edition in 1975. The title says it all. The standard lay reference for students, parents or anyone concerned with the effect of drugs.

Ramachandran, V. S. & Blakeslee, Sandra (1998). <u>**Phantoms in the Brain: Probing the Mysteries of the Human Mind**</u>. William Morrow & Company.
A funny and thought provoking investigation of neurological mysteries and what we can learn from them about the functioning of the human brain and the nature of human consciousness.

Active Learning

Active Learning Activity 4.1 - Introducing States of Consciousness

Put the words *sleep, dreams, drugs, hypnosis, and meditation* on the board. Ask students to form groups and make a list of additional ASCs (e.g., daydreaming, dancing, chanting, etc.). You may want to offer extra points to the group with the longest list. Ask for examples from their lists and add them to the board. Use their lists of suggestions to differentiate the concepts of stream of consciousness, levels of awareness, and alternate states of consciousness. Ask which of these methods could be abused. Use their responses to lead-in to a discussion of abuse versus use, physical and psychological dependence, tolerance, and so on.

Active Learning Activity 4.2 - Field Trip to a Sleep Center

Try to arrange a field trip to a local sleep disorder clinic for a small group of students. For information on the nearest sleep center, contact Dr. William Dement, ASDC, Stanford University School of Medicine, Stanford, CA 94305. For on-line searches of the nearest sleep lab location, a good site to start at is: http://www.sleepnet.com/slplabs.htm.

Active Learning Activity 4.3 - Dream Diary

Ask students to keep a dream diary for several weeks. Encourage them to keep the materials next to the bed so they can immediately record their dreams upon awakening. Instruct them to record the time they went to bed, preceding events, physical and emotional state, food and drug consumption, number and relationship of the people in the dream, specific activities in the dream, and so on. Ask them to consider the various theories of dreaming (wish-fulfillment, activation-synthesis, etc.) and pick the ones most useful to their particular dreams. If you have time, it may be useful to share some of these journals during class time.

Active Learning Activity 4.4 - Personal Survey

Given the fact that students often enjoy structured activities that allow them to interact with other classmates, the following personal survey serves a "social" function for the students as well as an educational tool for introducing the topic of alternate states of consciousness. Inform the students that they will be sharing their responses with other students, allow them five to ten minutes to complete the form (Handout 4.5 – Active Learning), and then assign them to groups of four or five to discuss their responses.

Handout 4.4 – Active Learning

Personal Survey

1. Do you remember childhood experiences of whirling around in circles, mutual "choking," or other activities designed to create alternate states of consciousness? Please explain.

2. What is your favorite daydream? Under what conditions would daydreaming be helpful? Detrimental?

3. Are you a long or short sleeper? Do you enjoy sleeping or do you resist it? Explain.

4. Why are alcohol and cocaine such problem drugs for today's college students? What were the "drugs of choice" during your parents' college days?

5. Have you ever been hypnotized? Did you enjoy the experience?

6. Have you ever experienced an alternate state through meditation or peak experiences? What was it like?

Active Learning Activity 4.5 - Drug Interview or Speaker

Have students talk to friends or associates who have used drugs (this can include alcohol as one drug widely used and legal) and prepare a report on the various characteristics of ASCs. It can also be useful to invite speakers from local drug prevention agencies.

Active Learning Activity 4.6 – Methods of Altering Consciousness

Use Handout 4.7 – Active Learning, to focus students on learning the similarities and differences among methods of altering consciousness.

Handout 4.6 – Active Learning

Methods of Altering Consciousness

	Drugs	Hypnosis	Meditation
How aware are you of the external environment?			
How aware are you of the internal environment?			
Are you able to observe yourself consciously?			
How able are you to control your fine body movements?			
How alert are you to the passage of time?			
Who/What is directing the flow of your consciousness?			

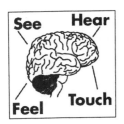

Brain-Based Learning

Brain-Based Learning Activity 4.1 – Levels of Consciousness

Keep your voice slow and low key as you read the following instructions.

"Close your eyes and remember driving to the campus. See yourself pulling away from your starting point, accelerating into traffic and navigating your way to school. Observe how much or how little effort it takes to make the correct turns, to notice traffic lights, to stop when the lights turn red, to start when they turn green. Notice the other cars on the road. Do they take a great deal of your attention or are you able to blend with them almost automatically? Are you engaging in any other activities while you are driving, such as being on the car phone, listening to music, talking to someone, or planning your day?

Now, just before you get to _____ (your campus), imagine you hear sirens and see those dreaded flashing blue lights and YES it is a police car pulling you over for a violation. Notice your reaction. What are you thinking, what are you feeling and where is your attention? Play out this scene for another minute; what the officer says and does, what you say, do, feel.

Now you pull up to campus ready for your class. The parking lot is unusually empty and quiet just now. Before you can get out of your car a classmate walks by and tells you that there is a note on the door that your class has been canceled. You now have two hours before your next class, and because the sun is shining and it is so pleasantly warm in your car, you lean back for a moment and close your eyes and soak in the warmth as you enjoy resting in your car seat. As you relax more and more under the gentle sun, you let go of your cares and allow your mind to just drift at ease. Again, you notice what it is like to have your mind that relaxed and carefree.

As you take a deep breath you can open your eyes and come back into this classroom, and write down some descriptions and details of what it was like to drive to school on a normal day, to then get pulled over by a police car, and finally to take a rest in the parking lot. How were you similar, how were you different in these three situations? Be sure to comment on the alertness of your body, the focus of your attention, and your breathing pattern."

After the students have had a chance to write down some of their observations, take down their comments in three separate columns, one for each setting. This provides an excellent opening for a discussion of levels of consciousness. You can use the student's comments to highlight important differences between the three situations and how they relate to *automatic processes, controlled processes,* and *daydreaming/lower levels of awareness.*

Time permitting, you can have the students reflect on how it is possible to manifest three very different states of consciousness while sitting in a chair with their eyes closed. What does it reveal about how consciousness functions?

Brain-Based Learning 4.2 - Spectacular Demos!

Invite an instructor from your campus chemistry department to your class to demonstrate what happens when chemicals are combined (colors change, liquids change colors, fires start, and explosions happen). Students enjoy these demonstrations--they are standard exercises done to catch the interest of chemistry students. You can also use the demos as a way of graphically illustrating the implications of mixing chemicals--or drugs! Ask your guest instructor to comment on the dangers. Although you may feel comfortable giving this presentation and demonstration yourself, it increases their learning (and bolsters your credibility) if other instructors make the point for you! Ask the students to give examples that they have heard from the media about musicians, athletes or other famous people dying because of unintended drug interactions.

Brain-Based Learning Activity 4.3 – Musical Relaxation/Meditation

Bring a musical meditation or relaxation tape or CD. Make sure the students are settled down and that no major classroom interruptions will take place for the next few minutes. It helps to lower the lights in the classroom. Have the students sit as comfortably as possible before you start the tape/CD and instruct them to keep their breathing long, deep and even. 5-10 minutes should be enough to experience the effect.

As they exit this state ask them to write down how they feel. Under what circumstances would this exercise be of use? Would they recommend such an experience to a friend? How effective are such approaches to dealing with stress, fatigue, study overload, finals week? You can connect this activity to the discussion on bio-feedback in Chapter 5 (Learning) and the material on stress reduction in Chapter 12 (Health Psychology).

Students who choose not to participate should be asked to stay quiet.

Note: This is not the best exercise for late evening classes as you could get unintended noise accompaniment.

Brain-Based Learning Activity 4.4 - Hypnosis--"Tricks of the Trade" #1

To demonstrate the dangers of stage hypnosis (as opposed to clinical hypnosis), it is often fun and interesting to simulate some of the basic "tricks of the trade." As demonstrated by the photo in the text on hypnotic suggestion, a well-motivated student (or instructor!) can easily stiffen enough to support his/her weight on two straight back chairs. Begin by having a student volunteer come to the front of the class and lie down on three straight back chairs--the two end chairs facing the head and feet of the subject and a center chair supporting the hips. Be sure the head and feet are as fully supported as possible by the two end chairs. Ask the subject to stiffen their entire body and lift their hips, while you slowly remove the third chair. The student will have no difficulty maintaining this position. You might even add a stack of books to the volunteer's abdomen, as a further demonstration of "superhuman strength." Discuss potential problems associated with stage shows of hypnosis. While they can be entertaining, they also reinforce common myths regarding hypnosis (superhuman strength, loss of personal control, etc.). Mention the famous magician, James Randi, who won the prestigious MacArthur Foundation award for his work in exposing unscrupulous use of magic. Randi crusades against "tricksters" who use legitimate magic tricks to mislead and exploit trusting audiences. Randi often cites the case of Jim Jones, the head of the People's Temple, who is known to have used standard magic tricks to convince his followers that he was "blessed by God." Remind students that in 1978, Jim Jones and 900 of his followers died in a mass murder/suicide in Jonestown, Guyana.

Brain-Based Learning Activity 4.5 - Hypnosis--"Tricks of the Trade" #2

As a follow-up to the above exercise, or as an alternative, ask your class if anyone has a needle or straight pin. Use this needle or pin for your demonstration. If you have no volunteers, take a standard paper clip and make a show of straightening it in front of the class. Announce that you will push the needle, pin, or straightened paper clip, under your thumbnail to demonstrate self-hypnosis. Explain that you have induced self-hypnosis prior to coming to class and that you need only to stroke your hand as a post-hypnotic suggestion for pain insensitivity. Make a show of gently stroking your left hand and pinching yourself as if testing for numbness. Ask the class to watch carefully as you slowly insert the needle. (The trick is that you have cut a thumbnail size piece of scotch tape and applied it to the nail of your "numb" hand before coming to class. During the presentation, you simply slide the needle between your nail and the piece of tape.) Explain to your class what you have done. Be sure to emphasize that your simple magic trick is to simulate tricks often used in *stage hypnosis*--NOT to discount the documented effects of pain relief through clinical hypnosis. Mention again the points made in the above exercise regarding James Randi and the possible manipulation and deception by unethical "tricksters."

Brain-Based Learning Activity 4.6 - Class Hypnosis/Guest Speaker

To offset the problems and stereotypes of stage hypnosis, it is also helpful to demonstrate a standard hypnosis technique. If you do not possess the requisite skills or feel comfortable with the demonstration, you might consider inviting a local hypnotherapist to class. Ask him or her to discuss the therapeutic effects of hypnosis and to demonstrate hypnosis to willing subjects in your class.

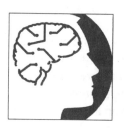

Critical Thinking

This exercise also appears in the text, Chapter 4. We include it here for your convenience, and you may want to discuss it in class to reinforce reading of the text.

Critical Thinking Exercise 4.1 - Tolerating Ambiguity: Exploring the Meaning of Your Dreams

Television, movies, and other popular media generally suggest that dreams are highly significant and easily interpreted, but scientists are deeply divided about the meaning of dreams and their relative importance. These differences in scientific opinion provide an excellent opportunity for you to practice the critical thinking skill of *tolerance for ambiguity*. A noncritical thinker often looks for the one "right" answer or one "right" theory, whereas the critical thinker recognizes the value in competing theories and accepts that each theory may be partially correct.

To improve your tolerance for ambiguity (and learn a little more about your own dreams), begin by briefly jotting down your most recent and vivid dream. This should be a minimum of three or four paragraphs in length. Now analyze your dream using the following perspectives:

1. According to the psychoanalytic view, or *wish-fulfillment theory*, what might be the forbidden, unconscious drives or desires represented by your dream? Can you identify the manifest content versus the latent content of your dream?

2. How would the biological view, the *activation-synthesis hypothesis*, explain your dream? Can you identify a specific thought that might have been stimulated and then led to this particular dream?

3. Psychologists from the cognitive perspective believe dream analysis provides important information processing, helps us make needed changes in our life, and even suggests solutions to real-life problems. Do you agree or disagree? Does your dream provide an insight that increases your self-understanding?

Now that you have analyzed your dream from each perspective, can you see how difficult it is to find the one right answer? Higher level, critical thinkers recognize that competing theories are akin to the story of the four blind men who are each exploring separate parts of an elephant. By listening to their descriptions of the trunk, tail, leg, and so on, critical thinkers can synthesize the information and develop a greater understanding of the larger picture.

Critical Thinking Exercise 4.2 - Recognizing Faulty Reasoning: Fallacies Regarding Drugs

The topic of drug use and abuse is of high interest to both students and the general public. It is also a topic which elicits numerous examples of lapses in critical thinking. The Student Study Guide's exercise for this chapter (Active Learning--Critical Thinking Exercise 4.3 in this manual) presents common statements regarding drugs and then asks the reader to identify whether the statements were based on "fact" or "opinion." As a natural follow up, you may want to examine common logical fallacies underlying such statements.

Time: Approximately 30 minutes.

Advance preparation: Make xerox copies of common logical fallacies (Handout 4.1 – Critical Thinking).

Instruction: Pass out the xerox copies and briefly discuss each fallacy. Then break the class into small groups and ask each group to examine the statements found in the Active Learning--Critical Thinking Exercise 4.3--you may also want to prepare xerox handouts of this exercise for those students who do not have access to the Student Study Guide. If time allows, you may want to expand your discussion to include other fallacies such as: "Straw Man," "Red Herring" (smoke screen), "Appeal to Belief," "Ad Hominem" (Personal Attack), and so on. Explanations and examples of these fallacies can be found in Chaffee, J. (1988). Thinking Critically (2nd ed.). Boston: Houghton Mifflin.

Handout 4.2 – Critical Thinking

<u>Common Logical Fallacies</u>

1. **False Dilemma** (also known as "False Alternatives") Reasonable alternatives between two polar extremes are ignored. (Example: "Since both interdiction and prohibition have failed, legalization is the only answer.")

2. **Slippery Slope** (also known as "the Domino Effect" or "the Camel's Nose") Occurs when one assumes that once the first step in a possible series of events occurs, the other steps will inevitably follow. (Example: "If you legalize marijuana, then you'd have to legalize cocaine, heroin, and all other dangerous drugs.")

3. **Sweeping Generalization** Occurs when a rule or statement is applied to inappropriate situations. (Example: "It's a free country, so people should be free to use whatever drug they please.")

4. **Fallacy of Positive Instances** Occurs when the speaker only remembers and quotes examples which confirm his or her personal beliefs and ignores nonconfirming instances. (Example: "Cocaine is a killer drug. Just look at what happened to basketball star Len Bias.")

5. **Appeal to Fear** Occurs when support for an argument is enlisted by warning of harmful or dire consequences. (Example: "Legalization would dramatically increase instances of welfare costs, auto accidents, domestic violence, child abuse, etc.")

Critical Thinking Exercise 4.3 - Distinguishing Fact From Opinion (A Cognitive Skill)

The topic of drugs often generates heated debate between people with different perspectives. When discussing controversial issues, it is helpful to make a distinction between statements of fact and statements of opinion. (A fact is a statement that can be proven true. An opinion is a statement that expresses how a person feels about an issue or what someone thinks is true.) Although it is also important to determine whether the facts are true or false, in this exercise simply mark "O" for opinion and "F" for fact to test your ability to distinguish between the two:

_____1. Marijuana is now one of America's principal cash crops.

_____2. Friends don't let friends drive drunk.

_____3. People who use drugs aren't hurting anyone but themselves.

_____4. Legalizing drugs such as cocaine, marijuana, and heroin would make them as big a problem as alcohol and tobacco.

_____5. The number of cocaine addicts is small compared with the number of alcoholics.

_____6. The American Medical Association considers alcohol to be the most dangerous of all psychoactive drugs.

_____7. Random drug tests are justified for personnel involved with public safety (e.g., air traffic controllers, police officers, etc.).

_____8. If parents use drugs, their children are more likely to use drugs.

_____9. Mothers who deliver cocaine-addicted babies are guilty of child abuse.

_____10. Alcohol abuse by pregnant mothers is one of the most important factors in mental retardation.

ANSWERS: Rather than offering specific answers to these questions, we suggest that you discuss your answers with your classmates and friends. Listening to the reasons others give for their answers often provides valuable insights in distinguishing between fact and opinion. (Adapted from Bach, 1988.)

Gender and Cultural Diversity

Gender and Cultural Diversity Activity 4.1 – Consciousness Across Cultures

Discuss the section in the text "Consciousness Across Cultures," especially the statement that "In a modern survey of 488 societies in all parts of the world, 90 percent were found to practice institutionally recognized methods of changing consciousness." Ask them if the United States is more likely to fall into the 90 percent or the other ten percent. Questioning followed by a lecture/discussion has been an effective approach to the gender and cultural diversity issues for this chapter. The following questions have generated enthusiasm for chapter material and considerable discussion:

1. Do you agree that seeking alternate states of consciousness is "natural" and world wide? What forms of ASCs are approved or disapproved of in our culture? How does this vary cross culturally? How did these differences develop?

2. Ask students to volunteer how long they typically sleep each night. If you have students from Asian cultures, ask them to describe cultural attitudes toward "long sleepers." Korean and Japanese students will often mention that sleeping more than five or six hours a night as a student is considered "lazy."

3. Ask how many students had a dream last night. Many students will raise their hands. Use their responses to lead into a lecture/discussion regarding dream content and dream theories. Ask the class to explain why some cultures (like Native-Americans) seem to have vivid dreams each night. (The answer is that these cultures value dreams more highly than typical Western peoples and they encourage their children to report their dreams.) Use the material in the accompanying lecture extender to go beyond the text's presentation.

4. In what ways are our legal drugs (nicotine and alcohol) an expression of mainstream values in North American culture? Why are certain drugs illegal? Does this also reflect our cultural values? How might other cultures differ in their choice of legal and illegal drugs? Meditation encourages a "passive, alert" state of consciousness. Is this in conflict with our mainstream values? Student responses to these questions often provide a great lead-in to the general topic of consciousness or to the more specific topics of drugs and meditation.

Writing Project

Writing Project 4.1

Given the need for improved writing skills in college students and to respond to the call for "writing across the curriculum," we offer writing projects for each chapter. In Chapter 4, we suggest a 2-3 page written response to the following activity. Recognizing the time involved in grading such writing projects, one alternative is occasionally to assign "peer grading." Collect the papers, remove student names, and assign each student a paper to grade. It also helps to make their participation in peer grading a required part of the overall points for the writing project. This encourages a more thoughtful and responsible evaluation, as well as acknowledging and rewarding the additional work.

This activity is a combination survey, interview, and write up. Ask students to administer the following questionnaire (Handout 4.1 – Writing Project) to ten friends or family members. Then ask students to explain the text's three major views on dreaming (the psychoanalytic, biological, and cognitive) to each participant and ask with which perspective they most agree. Encourage students to obtain "participant data" on their respondents (e.g., age, gender, ethnicity, college major, etc.) Using these data, have students interview participants regarding which dream theme was most common for them, least common, and their thoughts on how people might differ on their responses according to age, gender, culture and so on. Students should include any or all of this information in their 2-3 page write up. Our students have enjoyed this project, and we have enjoyed reading their papers. Also, by asking students to describe the three major views of dreaming to each of their participants, our students do very well on related quizzes and exams.

Once students have completed their surveys and write-ups, it is interesting to have students discuss their survey results in comparison to those of 250 other college students:

83%	_____ 1. Falling		56%	_____ 11. Finding money
77%	_____ 2. Being attacked or pursued		52%	_____ 12. Swimming
71%	_____ 3. Trying repeatedly to do something		49%	_____ 13. Snakes
71%	_____ 4. School, teachers, studying		46%	_____ 14. Being dressed inappropriately
66%	_____ 5. Sexual experiences		44%	_____ 15. Being smothered
64%	_____ 6. Arriving too late		43%	_____ 16. Being nude in public
62%	_____ 7. Eating		41%	_____ 17. Fire
58%	_____ 8. Being frozen with fright		39%	_____ 18. Failing an examination
57%	_____ 9. Death of a loved person		34%	_____ 19. Flying
56%	_____ 10. Being locked up		33%	_____ 20. Seeing yourself as dead

Reference: Griffith, R. M., Miyago, O., & Tago, A. (1958). The universality of typical dreams: Japanese vs. Americans. <u>American Anthropologist, 60</u>, 1173-1179.

Handout 4.1 – Writing Project

Dream Survey

Using the following list of common dream themes, please place a check mark next to each one you have ever dreamed about.

____1. Falling
____2. Being attacked or pursued
____3. Trying repeatedly to do something
____4. School, teachers, studying
____5. Sexual experiences
____6. Arriving too late
____7. Eating
____8. Being frozen with fright
____9. Death of a loved person
___10. Being locked up
___11. Finding money
___12. Swimming
___13. Snakes
___14. Being dressed inappropriately
___15. Being smothered
___16. Being nude in public
___17. Fire
___18. Failing an examination
___19. Flying
___20. Seeing yourself as dead

Circle of Quality - Chapter 4

Please give us your feedback. We thank you in advance for assisting us in improving the next edition. The contact information is listed in the preface.

What are the three most helpful teaching tools in this chapter?

1.

2.

3.

What are the three least useful teaching tools in this chapter?

1.

2.

3.

What are the three most difficult concepts to teach in this chapter?

1.

2.

3.

Additional Comments:

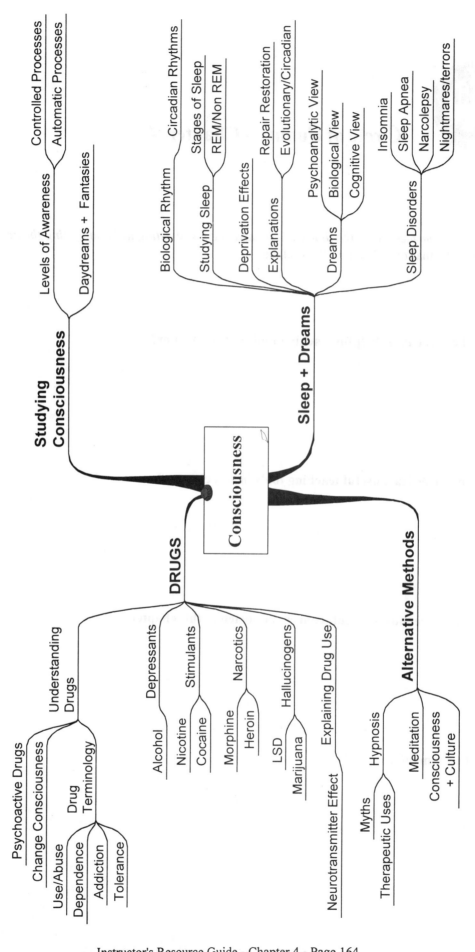

Studying Consciousness
- Levels of Awareness
  - Controlled Processes
  - Automatic Processes
- Daydreams + Fantasies

Sleep + Dreams
- Biological Rhythm
  - Circadian Rhythms
- Studying Sleep
  - Stages of Sleep
  - REM/Non REM
- Deprivation Effects
- Explanations
  - Repair Restoration
  - Evolutionary/Circadian
- Dreams
  - Psychoanalytic View
  - Biological View
  - Cognitive View
- Sleep Disorders
  - Insomnia
  - Sleep Apnea
  - Narcolepsy
  - Nightmares/terrors

Consciousness

DRUGS
- Psychoactive Drugs
- Change Consciousness
- Understanding Drugs
  - Use/Abuse
  - Dependence
  - Drug Terminology
    - Addiction
    - Tolerance
- Depressants
  - Alcohol
  - Nicotine
- Stimulants
  - Cocaine
- Narcotics
  - Morphine
  - Heroin
- Hallucinogens
  - LSD
  - Marijuana
- Explaining Drug Use
  - Neurotransmitter Effect

Alternative Methods
- Hypnosis
  - Myths
  - Therapeutic Uses
- Meditation
- Consciousness + Culture

CHAPTER 5
LEARNING

Outline

Learned and Innate Behaviors

Learned Behavior
How Do We Learn Things?

Conditioning

Classical Conditioning

Research Highlight
Scanning the Brain for Learning

Operant Conditioning
Conditioning in Action
Conditioning Yourself to Succeed

Active Learning
Operant Conditioning in the Real World

Cognitive Learning

The Study of Insight
Latent Learning

Observational Learning

Gender and Cultural Diversity
Scaffolding as a Teaching Technique in
Different Cultures

Learning Objectives

Upon completion of CHAPTER 5, the student should be able to:

1. Define learning; explain how learned and innate behaviors are different; and define the three major theories of learning: conditioning, cognitive, and observational (pp. 178-180).
2. Explain the process of classical conditioning, describing the differences between a neutral, a conditioned, and an unconditioned stimulus, and between a conditioned and an unconditioned response (pp. 180-182).
3. Describe how classical conditioning can explain emotional responses and higher order conditioning; describe recent PET and fMRI research on conditioning (pp. 182-184).
4. For classical conditioning: compare extinction with forgetting, describe spontaneous recovery, and compare generalization and discrimination (pp. 185-187).
5. Describe the three factors that distinguish operant from classical conditioning (pp. 187-188).
6. Define reinforcement and punishment, explaining how the terms positive and negative apply to each of these learning procedures (pp. 188-189).
7. Describe the differences between negative reinforcement and punishment, and state the negative consequences of using punishment (pp. 189-193).
8. For operant conditioning: describe extinction and spontaneous recovery (pp. 193-194).
9. Describe the different schedules of reinforcement, and state the effect each schedule will have on response rate and extinction (pp. 194-196).
10. Explain how unintentional reinforcement can lead to superstitious behavior (pp. 196-197).
11. For operant conditioning, define shaping and give an example of its use, and compare generalization and discrimination (pp. 197-198).
12. Explain the importance of feedback, timing, consistency, and order of presentation on the effective use of both reinforcement and punishment (pp. 198-199).
13. Describe the conditioning principles used in biofeedback therapy and programmed instruction (pp. 200-202).
14. Explain how insight and latent learning are examples of cognitive learning (pp. 203-204).
15. Define social cognitive theory (previously known as social learning theory), and describe the four processes involved in learning through observation (pp. 205-206).
16. Describe the cross-cultural use of scaffolding as a teaching technique, and explain how it combines the principles of shaping and modeling (pp. 206-208).

Chapter Summary/Lecture Organizer

Introductory Vignette--Chapter 5 begins with the story of Koko, the gorilla trained by Penny Patterson to communicate through American Sign Language. Koko's acquisition of language is used in the vignette and throughout the chapter as an example of the various terms and concepts involved in learning.

I. **LEARNED AND INNATE BEHAVIORS** - This chapter presents students with an overview of learning principles and techniques. It begins with a distinction between learned and innate behaviors. Innate behaviors are those that emerge during a predetermined period of an organism's life as a result of maturation only and not as a result of practice. While humans do exhibit reflexive (single response) behaviors, the text mentions that humans do not have instincts (a complex sequence of responses, such as elaborate mating rituals).

   A. Learned Behavior - Learning is defined as a relatively permanent change in behavior or behavior potential as a result of practice or experience.

   B. How Do We Learn Things? - Learning an association between a stimulus and a response is called conditioning. Classical conditioning involves learning reflexive, involuntary responses to stimuli that don't normally cause such responses. Operant conditioning involves learning voluntary responses to stimuli through the consequences of previous responses. Cognitive learning theory proposes that learning involves thought processes that may not be directly observed or objectively measured. Observational learning theory combines conditioning and cognitive learning theories, and suggests that we learn certain behaviors merely by watching someone else perform them.

II. **CONDITIONING** - The two major types of conditioning are classical conditioning and operant conditioning. Classical conditioning is a fundamental way that animals, including humans, learn new responses.

   A. Classical Conditioning - Using Pavlov's classic research studies of salivation in dogs, students are introduced to classical conditioning, where an initially neutral stimulus that does not normally cause any particular reflex or emotional response is paired with another stimulus that does cause such a response. After several pairings, this previously neutral stimulus (NS) will cause the response to occur. Each stimulus and response is named according to its cause or consequence. The neutral stimulus is paired with the unconditioned stimulus (UCS), the stimulus that causes the reflex or emotional response. The reflex or emotional response itself is known as the unconditioned response (UCR). When the neutral stimulus begins to cause the response on its own, it is then referred to as the conditioned stimulus (CS); the response caused by the conditioned stimulus is then referred to as the conditioned response (CR).
   Using the story of Little Albert, the students are shown how fears (and phobias) can be explained through classical conditioning. These fears would be called conditioned emotional

responses (CERs). Higher order conditioning, where a neutral stimulus is paired with a second conditioned stimulus (CS) that already causes a learned or conditioned response, explains many emotions and attitudes. Taste aversions are also used as examples of classical conditioning.

After introducing students to these terms, the chapter enters into a discussion of extinction, spontaneous recovery, generalization, and discrimination. When the UCS is repeatedly withheld and the previous association between the CS and the UCS is broken, extinction occurs. When a CR that had been extinguished spontaneously reappears, it is known as spontaneous recovery. Generalization occurs when stimuli similar to the original CS elicits the CR; discrimination occurs when only the CS elicits the CR.

> **Research Highlight: Scanning the Brain for Learning** – Researchers using PET and fMRI brain scans are now using computerized scanning to study learning.

B. Operant Conditioning - A second type of conditioning originally investigated by B. F. Skinner is operant conditioning, in which people or animals learn by the consequences of their responses. These consequences may consist of either reinforcement or punishment. Reinforcement is anything that is likely to cause an increase in the response. Punishment is anything that is likely to cause a decrease in the response. Positive reinforcement is being incurred when something desirable is added to increase the response rates. Negative reinforcement, which is different from punishment, occurs when something bad or aversive is removed in order to increase the response rate. Positive punishment occurs when something aversive is given to decrease the response rate. Negative punishment consists of removing something good to decrease the response rate. Punishment can lead to increased aggression as well as learned helplessness.

In operant conditioning, extinction occurs when the reinforcement is withheld until the subject stops responding to the stimulus. Spontaneous recovery occurs when a previously extinguished response spontaneously returns. The difficulty in extinguishing a response is directly related to the schedule of reinforcement being used to strengthen the response.

There are several schedules of reinforcement. Continuous schedules reinforce each response. Partial schedules reinforce some, not all, responses. The major types of partial reinforcement schedules are fixed ratio, variable ratio, fixed interval, and variable interval. Superstitious behaviors occur when people or animals make responses they think are connected to reinforcers; when, in reality, their responses have nothing to do with the reinforcers. Shaping is the process of teaching a person or an animal a complex task by reinforcing successive approximations to a desired response.

In order to use reinforcement and punishment effectively, it is advisable to keep the following principles in mind: (1) Provide clear and immediate feedback when the person or animal makes the desired response. (2) Apply reinforcers or punishers as soon as possible after the response is made. (3) Be consistent in applying both reinforcers and punishers. (4) Be sure to reinforce or punish after the behavior has been exhibited.

C. Conditioning in Action - After learning about "learning," students are shown that these principles have numerous real life applications. To treat migraine headaches, epilepsy, and high blood pressure, some researchers use biofeedback--a procedure in which people's biological functions are monitored and the results made known to them so they can learn to control these functions. Educational uses of conditioning are found in programmed instruction--a form of personalized instruction which allows students to learn at their own pace.

D. Conditioning Yourself to Succeed – One of the *Tools for Student Success,* this operant conditioning focuses on a critically important academic skill: meeting deadlines and avoiding procrastination.

Active Learning/Critical Thinking: Operant Conditioning in the Real World - To help students integrate the terms associated with classical and operant conditioning, students are given two problem situations and asked several questions that require them to apply text information.

III.   **COGNITIVE LEARNING** - Cognitive psychologists are interested in cognitive learning, the mental processes that lead to learned behavior.

A. The Study of Insight - Wolfgang Kohler, working with chimpanzees, demonstrated that learning can occur with a sudden flash of insight.

B. Latent Learning - Edward Tolman demonstrated latent learning--learning that occurs in the absence of reinforcement and remains hidden until it is needed.

IV.   **OBSERVATIONAL LEARNING** - Observational learning is the process of learning how to do something by merely reading about a behavior or watching someone else perform a behavior, rather than learning through doing. Social learning theory was proposed by Albert Bandura to explain how people learn by observing others who serve as models. In the 35 years since his original research, social cognitive theory has been applied to contexts such as social work, phobias and business management .

Gender and Cultural Diversity: Scaffolding as a Teaching Technique in Different Cultures - This section discusses the work of Wood et al. (1976) where scaffolding is used in informal situations between a master teacher and learner and involves a combination of shaping and modeling.

Teaching Resources

SECTION I - LEARNED AND INNATE BEHAVIORS

Learning Objectives #'s 1 & 2
Lecture Lead-ins # 1
Discussion Questions # 2
Gender and Cultural Diversity Activity #5.1

SECTION II - CONDITIONING

Learning Objectives #'s 2 - 13
Lecture Lead-ins #'s 3 - 5
Lecture Extender #5.1
Discussion Questions #'s 1 - 7
Active Learning Activities #'s 5.1 - 5.13
Brain-based Learning Activities #'s 5.1 – 5.4
Critical Thinking Exercises #'s 5.1 – 5.3
Gender and Cultural Diversity Activity #5.1
Writing Project #5.1

Transparencies Available from Wiley #'s

SECTION III – COGNITIVE LEARNING

Learning Objectives #'s 14 & 15
Lecture Lead-ins #'s 4 & 5
Discussion Questions # 3
Active Learning Activities #'s 5.14 & 5.15
Gender and Cultural Diversity Activity 5.1

SECTION IV – OBSERVATIONAL LEARNING

Learning Objectives #16
Lecture Lead-ins #5
Discussion Questions # 8
Active Learning Activities # 5.15
Brain-based Learning Activities #5.5

Lecture Lead-Ins

1.   Ask students to list all human instincts. They will volunteer things like "mothering," "fighting," "survival," and so on. Put their answers on the board and lead into a discussion of learned versus innate behaviors. Point out the advantages to NOT having instincts--more room in our brains for more complex behaviors, good behaviors can be acquired, and bad, unhealthy behaviors can be unlearned. While we are incredibly dependent on our caregivers as infants and other people throughout our lives, the lack of instincts allows humans an incredible level of freedom (we're not FORCED to swim upstream like the salmon to find our mate.)

2.   How does the information in this chapter apply to the typical classroom? Challenge the students to think up multiple ways in which the four kinds of learning take place. If at first they can't think of anything, mention bells for class signals, slips on the door for a canceled class, the announcement "Surprise EXAM!" or "Could I see you in my office please?" (said with a stern face). How do they react to "term-paper", "extra credit", etc.? Examples are endless and provide a good introduction to the topic. Are there non-verbal signals that you, the teacher, give off, that provoke an association or response from some of the students?

3.   Read the following quote to the class: "Give me a dozen healthy infants, well-formed, and my own specified world to bring them up in, and I'll guarantee to take any one at random and train him to become any type of specialist I might select---doctor, lawyer, artist, merchant-chief and yes even beggar-man and thief, regardless of his talents, penchants, tendencies, abilities, vocations and race of his ancestors." (Watson, 1924) Ask the class members if they believe this can be accomplished. Ask the class who made this statement. You should get some answers like the Nazis of World War II or some dictators of the third world. Explain that this quote of Watson's was a very important statement and changed the way psychology would be studied for 50 years. This is likely to generate a very lively discussion of free will vs. determinism. Use this discussion as a lead-in for your lectures on operant conditioning.

4.   Ask students to describe what information they thought this chapter would contain before they started reading, and how they feel after reading it. As instructors, we often forget (or are afraid) to ask such questions. We have found it particularly helpful to ask about student expectations and feelings regarding this chapter. Like the biological topics, the learning chapter contains a long list of new terms and concepts. Students often report feeling overwhelmed and fail to see "the forest for the trees." We find that the best way to lead-in to this lecture, and to maintain their interest throughout the chapter, is to emphasize the practical applications. Ask students to write about one successful learning experience they have had (learning to swim, drive a car, getting a good grade, etc.). Then, write down an unresolved, problem behavior they would like

to "unlearn." If time allows, have them form groups and share their papers. As an entire class, ask students to volunteer both successes and problems. Write these all on the board and use their suggestions as a lead-in to your lecture. Write a note to yourself so you can use these same examples for later lectures to the same class--they "perk up" when they see that you are taking their personal stories as examples.

5. Ask the students what they think might be the best way to learn to ski. If they have read the chapter, there should be some very interesting discussions including conditioning theories using positive reinforcement, the classical conditioning paradigm, and cognitive insight or observational learning. Students will have their own examples that always include interesting ideas. As you lecture on each section of learning, refer back to this discussion.

Lecture Extenders

5.1 - Social Engineering

The two men whose names are synonymous with behaviorism are B. F. Skinner and John B. Watson. They both share the belief that it is possible to improve the quality of living through the application of psychological principles. In many ways, their strategies are similar; however, Skinner extends his proposed design to change the structure of an entire community whereas Watson would limit his intervention to changes in child-care. Skinner's proposal for his utopian community is presented in his book Walden Two.

Skinner believes that all "important" behaviors, both human and infrahuman, are based upon the principle of operant conditioning. Behavior is controlled by its outcomes; the "amount" of the outcome is less important than the contingency relationship--if A occurs, then B is sure to follow. Through an experimental analysis of the outcomes that work best, a community can be set up that incorporates these relationships into its structure. One of Skinner's guiding principles is that reward is better than punishment, and he thinks that people can create communities which "naturally" allow desired behaviors to occur and be rewarded.

Skinner wrote the first edition of this book shortly after World War II, in the mid-1940s, but its publication generated very little interest. It was only after the decade of the 60s, when there was so much rebellion against the status quo in American society, that campus residents (both faculty and students) began to view communal ideas favorably. Interest in communal living peaked in the 1970s and has waned somewhat since that time.

If one is going to have a permanent community, it has to provide the correct environment for future generations, namely, the children. Skinner (in agreement with Watson) did not think that the family was an ideal place for child rearing. Most mothers did not have sufficient scientific knowledge for the task, and even if they did, the demands on their time from other areas was so great that they could not do a good job. He believed, as did Watson, that there is danger in a strong parent-child relationship which may interfere with the development of independence. Feelings of jealously and insecurity are more likely to occur in an intense relationship in which only one or two adults are trying to meet all the emotional needs of a child.

Child rearing is a shared communal task with infants segregated from the parents at birth and tended in groups by child care experts. The parents are free to come in as they please (if they don't come in too much), but they are asked not to overindulge their children or single them out for special favors. The children are shielded from both physical discomforts and the vagaries of "unplanned" interactions with less-knowledgeable adults. Training is regulated by one primary rule--a child has to learn to tolerate frustration. This is accomplished through the principle of shaping. In the typical upbringing by non-experts, children are exposed to frustration on a random basis; there is no effort to give it in graded doses. Undoubtedly, some children are able to survive this regime, but not all can do so. Adversity is a natural event in life, but when it occurs willy-nilly, children do not develop the necessary tolerance, and negative emotions such as anger, fear, and jealousy emerge.

From the earliest moment, a Walden Two child has programmed instruction in frustration tolerance. The best known example of this principle is the "lollipop training." Children are gradually trained to delay impulse gratification by having to wait for successively longer periods of time for a lollipop. For example, a child is expected to wait for one minute before licking the lollipop, then five minutes, and so forth. The eventual aim would be that the child could wait indefinitely with the lollipop hanging around his/her neck. This training involves more than just inhibiting the behavior; thought control is equally important. Skinner says that controlling the behavior is not sufficient if, while waiting, the child is simultaneously feeling rage or other negative emotions. Thus, one must learn ways to prevent these thoughts. Skinner equates this with the principle of "turning the other cheek." The ultimate hope would be that one is able to replace the negative emotion with positive feelings. It does no good to behave well if one is seething on the inside. Happiness cannot be achieved without the internal control of thinking, and this is brought about by scientifically administered shaping.

Skinner's anti-punishment stance is based on the observation that punishment creates hostility and other negative emotions, reducing the desire to cooperate with others. Children are not born with a natural ability to be part of a community. Self-interest is part of human nature, a part that one is able to submerge only through careful strategies. In a controlled environment where behaviors lead to the expected outcomes, it is possible to vary the reward system to increase a desired behavior. For example, in Walden Two, all adults are expected to work for labor credits. The number of labor credits for a given job depends upon the needs of the community. If enough people are not choosing kitchen chores, the number of labor credits for this job is increased. If there is an oversupply of kitchen help, the number of credits goes down.

One of Skinner's aims in writing the book was to develop a community that would free females from traditional roles of child-care and housework, leaving them available for occupational competition with men. In many ways, Walden Two has been a harbinger of today's society where many females are in the marketplace and seeking good child care facilities for their offspring while they work. However, most parents would be loathe to leave their children with child care experts for the entire day.

Source: Skinner, B. F. (1976). Walden Two (reissued). New York: Macmillan.

Key Terms

LEARNED AND INNATE BEHAVIORS

Classical Conditioning (p. 179)
Cognitive Learning Theory (p. 179)
Conditioning (p. 179)
Innate (p. 178)
Learning (p. 178)
Observational Learning Theory (p. 180)
Operant Conditioning (p. 179)

CONDITIONING

Avoidance Theory (p. 189)
Biofeedback (p. 200)
Conditioned Emotional Response (CER) (p. 182)
Conditioned Response (CR) (p. 182)
Conditioned Stimulus (CS) (p. 182)
Continuous Reinforcement (p. 194)
Discrimination (p. 186)
Escape Learning (p. 189)
Extinction (p. 185)
Feedback (p. 188)
Fixed Interval (p. 196)
Fixed Ratio (p. 195)
Forgetting (p. 185)
Generalization (p. 186)
Higher Order Conditioning (p. 183)
Learned Helplessness (p. 192)
Negative Punishment (p. 191)
Negative Reinforcement (p. 189)
Neutral Stimulus (NS) (p. 180)
Partial Reinforcement (p. 194)
Passive Aggressiveness (p. 191)
Phobia (p. 183)
Positive Punishment (p. 191)
Positive Reinforcement (p. 189)
Primary Reinforcers (p. 189)

Programmed Instruction (p.201)
Punishment (p. 188)
Reinforcement (p. 188)
Schedule of Reinforcement (p. 194)
Secondary Reinforcers (p. 189)
Shaping (p. 197)
Spontaneous Recovery (p. 186)
Superstitious Behavior (p. 196)
Unconditioned Response (UCR) (p. 181)
Unconditioned Stimulus (UCS) (p. 181)
Variable Interval (p. 196)
Variable Ratio (p. 195)

COGNITIVE LEARNING

Cognitive Map (p. 204)
Insight (p. 204)
Latent Learning (p. 204)

OBSERVATIONAL LEARNING

Modeling (p. 205)
Scaffolding (p. 206)
Social Learning Theory or Social Cognitive
  Theory (p. 205)
Vicarious Conditioning (p. 206)

Discussion Questions

1. How do advertisers use classical conditioning to get us to buy their products? How are politicians "marketed" to the voting public? Ask students for examples and point out that most advertisers and politicians are committed to creating a *positive* CER in the consumer/voter toward themselves or their product and a *negative* CER toward competitors/opponents.

2. Ask students to write down a superstitious behavior they have acquired or have noticed in a close friend. Encourage them to share their observation of this behavior with the class and to identify the reinforcers. Also ask them to design a method to change the behavior.

3. Ask for examples of latent learning. If they hesitate, ask where the closest water fountain is relative to your classroom. When it appears that most students know where it is, ask how many have not had a drink from the fountain. Then ask these students if they could find the fountain if they wanted a drink. They will say yes, an obvious case of learning (locations of fountain) without reinforcement (a drink). Now ask the students to think of examples overnight and be prepared to share their examples during the next class period.

4. Instruct the class to write a short paragraph on the following topic and be prepared to discuss the answer in class during the next session. "The concept of operant conditioning depends on the notion that the environment provides rewards and punishments for behaviors. Based on your own life, what are the chief rewards and punishments provided by your human environment? What rewards really make you feel good? Do they change your behavior or just make you feel good?"

5. Ask for students with unusual favorite food preferences. List them on the board. If you have a diverse student body probe for ethnic food idiosyncrasies. If you don't, supplement their list by adding the preferences of people from different countries, the stranger the better. Ask the students how they came by their preference paying careful attention to classically conditioned feelings as well as to the reinforcing sequences of their upbringing environments. Students will display strong reactions to food items such as snakes, worms, frogs, birds, dogs, horse, octopus, etc. and you can use these visceral reactions to again illustrate learned emotional reaction patterns.

5. Ask students what is the favorite music of their parents, their grandparents or any older generation they know. Again, you should get strong emotional reactions to these "antiquated" music preferences. Then ask them how their parents feel about the students' music preferences? Have them imagine 20 years into the future and how they will react if their favorite song of today is played then. You could also describe what happens to you when you hear a song of your youth. Students are often amazed to discover that the battle for

the car radio knob has to do more with memories and conditioned feelings than with music preferences.

6.   Alert students to pay attention to their emotional reactions and ask them to think of the face of their favorite friend. Then, ask students to imagine seeing a face of someone they really don't like across the room at a party. Have them remember the face of a baby they have known. In conditioning terms, what function do these faces play? Where do the reactions come from?

7.   Ask students to consider the role of observational learning and the heavy amount of TV that is watched each day by children in the United States. What are the children learning? How are we shaping our next generation? What might be the advantages and disadvantages of this type of shaping?

 **Web Sites**

Modern Models of Classical Conditioning
http://www.biozentrum.uni-wuerzberg.de/genetics/behavior/learning/classica.html
This site provides details of classical conditioning, including detailed elaboration of Rescorla and Wagner's model of learning. Also offers a summary of brain areas associated with classical conditioning

Learning History
http://psy1.clarion.edu/mm/general/Schools/Bschools.html
This site is more oriented to the history of conditioning, both classical and operant. Covers the major names and contributions to this area of psychology. Also provides key concepts of behaviorism in detail.

Boise State University Psychology Department Learning Lab
http://coehp.idbsu.edu/FACHTMLS/LROGIEN/Ch6ahtml/index.html
From Boise State University, this site covers the various types of behavioral concepts, with examples.

Behaviorism in Treating Psychological Disorders
http://pp1.nhmccd.edu/~bjdavis/learn.html
This site may also be used in covering the material for treating psychological disorders. The site is devoted to how behavioral theory has been applied to treat a variety of clinical disorders.

Memphis Zoo Home Page
http://www.memphiszoo.org/vet/opcond.htm
Illustrates clearly how behavior modification is used in applied settings, this time in the management of zoo animals. Provides fascinating examples including dolphins, primates, and other exotic animals.

Behaviorism Home Page
http://fccjvm.fccj.cc.fl.us/~jwisner/Irlm.html
Again, a source for key terms in behaviorism with illustrative examples of learning and theories of behaviorism.

Suggested Films and Videos

Learning

Insight Media, 1990. 30 minutes. This program explores the fundamental processes of classical and operant conditioning. It includes an interview with B. F Skinner, as well as a segment filmed at a child development center, which illustrates how the principles of operant conditioning are used to help hyperactive children with severe behavioral and learning problems.

Learning

Annenberg/CPB, 1990. 27 minutes. From Zimbardo's "Discovering Psychology" series, this video is an excellent introduction to both classical and operant conditioning with archival footage of Pavlov, Watson, and Skinner.

Pain of Shyness

ABC's "20/20,"1984. 17 minutes. Philip Zimbardo, author of <u>The Shy Child</u>, discusses the social and psychological problems with shyness and presents various treatments, including a demonstration of systematic desensitization.

Pavlov: The Conditioned Reflex

Films for the Humanities and Sciences, 1975. 23 minutes. This film presents Pavlov at work in his Leningrad laboratory, demonstrating the conditioned reflex.

Learning

CRM/McGraw-Hill, 1971. 30 minutes. Introduces the topic of learning with experiments, animation, and humor. This award-winning film covers a wide assortment of learning principles and key concepts. Although made in 1971, it is definitely worth showing.

A Good Night's Sleep

ABC'S "20/20," 1990. 17 minutes. This segment features Dr. Richard Ferber, a children's sleep expert, demonstrating his behavior modification techniques for getting children to sleep through the night. This film follows one family's successful effort with Dr. Ferber. Our classes really love this segment.

Behavior Modification: Teaching Language to Psychotic Children

Prentice-Hall (University of California Extension Media Center), 1969. 42 minutes. This superb film demonstrates the clinical and therapeutic uses of behavior modification. This program demonstrates the work of Lovaas (referred to in the text) with autistic and self-injurious children. This one is really worth showing!

The Compulsive Mind

Films for the Humanities and Sciences, 1995. 28 minutes. This program focuses on a woman with obsessive-compulsive disorder (OCD) who has a fear of contamination. This woman describes her cleaning routine, which includes 200 hand washings a day. This film discusses and illustrates the role of medication and behavior modification in the treatment of OCD.

Observational Learning

MTI. 25 minutes. This film shows a clip of the original Bobo doll experiment conducted by Bandura and Walters. Viewers watch young children imitating an aggressive adult model. A demonstration of vicarious emotional conditioning is also presented using the Papago Indian project. The detrimental effects of television and film violence are also discussed.

Classical and Operant Conditioning

The Psychology of Learning Series/Films for the Humanities & Sciences, 1996. 56 minutes. This program clearly explains, discusses and illustrates the complex classical and operant conditioning theories of Pavlov and Skinner. Features archival footage of laboratory work with dogs and present day work with rats in Skinner boxes.

Further Approaches to Learning

The Psychology of Learning Series/Films for the Humanities & Sciences, 1996. 57 minutes. The video explores alternative approaches and explanations of learning; and, emphasizes the recent move towards a cognitive theory of learning and examines the research in this area.

Faces of the Enemy

Insight Media, 1987. 58 minutes. For mature students, this documentary investigates how individuals and nations dehumanize their enemies. It analyzes the psychological roots of enmity and the universal images used in mass persuasion.

Scaffolding Self Directed Learning in the Primary Grades

Deborah Leong Ph.D. and Elena Bodrova, Ph.D./ Davidson Films, 1996. 35 minutes. This program shows the work of Vygotsky and provides examples of how learning can be structured so children are active learners, while teachers use their superior knowledge base to meaningfully guide learning. The three essential elements of scaffolding are explained and demonstrated.

Books for Success

Kohn, Alfie (1995). **Punished by Rewards: The Trouble With Gold Stars, Incentive Plans, "A's", and Other Bribes,** Houghton Mifflin Co.
Describes the destructive impact of overjustification, by which extrinsic incentives replace and diminish the intrinsic motivation of learners. Argues persuasively that students and workers are better motivated by collaboration, meaningful content and self-empowering choices.

Seligman, Martin E. P. (1990). **Learned Optimism: How To Change Your Mind and Your Life**, Pocket Books.
The most practical, positive book on the applied psychology of learning how to lead a better life. Eminently engaging with many practical exercises. Highly recommended for every student.

Active Learning

Active Learning Activity 5.1 - Classical Conditioning

Bring three or four volunteers to the front of the class. Demonstrate the knee jerk (patellar) reflex with a small rubber mallet, pupil dilation with a flashlight, and the eye blink with a turkey baster puffing air into the eye. Discuss the difference between reflexes, instincts, and learned behaviors. Demonstrate how the eye blink response can be conditioned to the sound of a bell.

Active Learning Activity 5.2 - Advertising

Ask students to tape their favorite commercial and to bring it to class. Play the various tapes and ask the class to identify type of conditioning, positive and negative reinforcers, vicarious conditioning, observational learning, etc.

Active Learning Activity 5.3 - Candy as a Reinforcer

Begin your standard lecture/discussion for this chapter. The first time a student asks a question, take a piece of candy out of your pocket, walk over and place the candy on their desk. While doing this, answer their question but do NOT explain or comment on your "candy dispensing behavior." Continue your lecture until the next question and then give the second piece of candy--again saying nothing about your own behavior. Continue answering and dispensing candy. Students will begin to laugh and their questions will immediately increase. Wait until someone asks you a direct question about the candy, and then ask them what they THINK you are trying to demonstrate. This is always effective and you can use the demonstration to teach several terms and concepts.

Active Learning Activity 5.4 - Candy as a Punisher

In a moment of inspiration, we once extended this candy demonstration (Activity 5.3) as a punisher to a troublesome group of students in the back corner who repeatedly ignored our requests to refrain from talking during our lectures. (Have you had this same group? They seem to come to many of our classes and appear on many campuses.) On the day we began giving out the candy, they started rolling their eyes and smugly giggling to one another (obviously thinking this was too childish for their level of "maturity"). In a moment of inspiration, we decided to try punishment. Each time they talked to one another, we quietly walked over and placed a piece of candy on their desk without comment. They were completely perplexed. They stopped talking for that day and for several subsequent sessions. We thought we had "won," but a few weeks later they returned to their initial behaviors (spontaneous recovery? or lack of reinforcers?). Since we didn't have candy with us on this day, we took our chances and decided to make the problem overt. (We had tried talking to them-individually and as a group--several times outside of class.) We described what we had done with the initial demonstration and the candy, how they had responded, and how they were now showing some of the problems associated with punishment. We talked in a calm, non-aggressive manner and listed several terms on the board. We talked about how candy was a reinforcer for some students and a punisher for the talkative group. We asked for suggestions to correct the problem using conditioning principles. The class decided that the best way might be to remove the reinforcers for talking within the group (i.e., spreading the group members out in the classroom). This was all done in a very gentle, "fun" manner. The offending students stayed after class that day, apologized, and "straightened-up" for the rest of the term. They remain friendly and in contact even years later. We mention this incident because we believe it sometimes helps to make our teaching strategies overt to our students and to use the class as a real life laboratory. If we can't "practice what we preach," our students lose respect for us and for the field of psychology. We also believe it may be helpful to someone reading this manual to see that we all have the same "talkative student" problems. Feel free to share this story with your class. It provides a good discussion of the problems associated with punishment.

Active Learning Activity 5.5 - Brainstorming

Speaking of problems with punishment (activity 5.2), have you noticed the incredible resistance to this topic? While psychologists generally accept the overwhelming evidence against the use of punishment, the general public (our students) remains committed to its value. One of the best ways we have found to "get around" this resistance is a very simple brainstorming session. Ask students to form small groups. Tell them you will give a prize (or points) to the one group with the longest list for the disadvantages of punishment. Give them about five minutes. Have the leaders of two or three groups with the highest number come to the front of the room and put their answers on the board. In one class we once had over 70 different problems! This activity really works. The board will be completely covered with various problems. Use their responses to build your lecture on the advantages of reinforcement over punishment.

Active Learning Activity 5.6 - Operant Conditioning--"Students as Rats"

If you have a Skinner box, there are several class demonstrations you can do. You can ask one of your students to come up to the front of the room and pretend to be a rat (or pigeon) by pressing the bar in the Skinner box. You can then reinforce the student "rat" on some unknown schedule and ask the student or the rest of the class to guess the schedule. If you have access to a rat (our department keeps two as pets), you can demonstrate shaping and various schedules of reinforcement with the rats in the classroom. (We have found it helpful to keep one of our pet rats naive, and to shape the other to bar press for a food reinforcement.)

Active Learning Activity 5.7 - Shaping Student Behavior

To demonstrate shaping, ask for a volunteer and tell him or her to go out of the room while classmates decide on a behavior they wish to shape. Make sure they choose a simple behavior that will not consume too much class time or embarrass the volunteer. Ask the volunteer to come back into the classroom. Explain that every time he or she performs the desired behavior, the class will clap. When the desired behavior is not being performed, the class will not clap. (If you know your volunteer and think that he or she can handle it, you might also try using punishment, where the class frowns or "boos" when the person performs a behavior the class members have previously decided they want to decrease. This should prove to be much more difficult, but it helps to point out the inherent difficulties in punishment.)

Active Learning Activity 5.8 - Shaping the Instructor's Behavior

An interesting activity is to mention to students that shaping has also been used by "dedicated" graduate students in psychology to shape professor's behavior. For example, pacing behaviors can be shaped if every time the professor paces to the left, students ask questions, stay awake, take notes, and look interested. If the professor moves to the right, students yawn, take no notes, talk to other students, and generally ignore the professor. Ask the class members if they think they can shape you. Remind them to pick a simple behavior and leave the room. Students really have fun with this activity. Even with this introduction and with the full awareness of the professor, they can be very successful. They have shaped us to write on the blackboard, to look out of the window, to touch our ear, and so on! One memorable class was particularly clever and discreet. Without our awareness, they gradually shaped us to let them out of class ten minutes early. It took us several sessions to catch on! We strongly encourage you to try this approach. Admittedly, it feels awkward at first, but students love you for allowing yourself to be the guinea pig and for being willing to look a little foolish. You can even point out that you're intentionally "modeling" for them to encourage their own willingness to volunteer.

Active Learning Activity 5.9 - Review and Practice of Classical and Operant Conditioning

After your presentation of operant conditioning, distribute copies of Handout 5.9 – Active Learning. Students can do this exercise in groups or by themselves.

Active Learning Activity 5.10 - - Learning in Everyday Life

Challenge the students to come up with at least ten examples of learned reaction patterns from their home. Initially this may be difficult, as students have not connected the chapter to their lives. You can give examples like the cat and the can opener, the dog and the leash (or walking stick), the alarm clock, the smell of cookies in the oven, the sound of the garage door opener (mom or dad are coming home). Another option is to take household objects and to examine their association patterns (TV remote control, beer bottle, toys, bills, textbooks, messy room, closed bathroom door, yelling, etc.). What makes some objects desirable and others hated? There are a lot of contingencies in every home. A survey of household objects and their meaning could also become a writing or extra credit assignment.

Active Learning Activity 5.11 - Culture and Symbols

Have students draw powerful political or religious symbols from cultures across the world i.e., flag, cross, Star of David, swastika, yin/yang, $. For each symbol have them identify what meaning or emotion that symbol holds for the host culture and/or for our culture. What different meaning would the American Flag hold for an Iranian vs. an American? How does this explain Iranians burning the American Flag? Encourage them to seek out other examples.

Active Learning Activity 5.12 - Schedules of Reinforcement

Challenge the students to come up with at least three examples of each type of schedule. If the response is limited try offering a list of examples and have them decide which type of schedule is being illustrated (Fixed/Variable, Ratio/Interval). Examples include: working by the hour, being paid on commission, being paid by the piece, buying a lottery ticket, holiday sobriety driving tests, DMV tailpipe emissions test, practicing in a baseball cage, using a radar tracking device, backing up your hard drive every time you leave work, the annual Christmas party, a graduation party, panhandling, purchasing with volume discounts, calling into a radio show for prizes, surprise locker inspections, logging into your e-mail account every evening, looking out the window repeatedly for your date to show up, playing Bingo, nervously clicking your pen again and again, playing the slot machines, and beach combing for perfect sea shells.

Active Learning Activity 5.13 - Conditioning in Nursing Homes

Volunteers in nursing homes report that too often family members and friends are uncomfortable when visiting their relatives. As a result of this association pattern, many people come less and less often.

For a few minutes have each group of students come up with a list of the events, sights, smells, noises, symbols that are in a nursing home that would affect visitors (or residents) negatively.

Then ask the students to come up with ideas that would make visiting a friend or relative a reinforcing experience they would want to repeat. For younger students this can be a difficult exercise. Challenge them to think like behavioral therapists searching to maximize reinforcement opportunities. Sharing music, memories, touch, poetry, favorite foods, or story telling are just a few of the avenues to be explored. The idea is not to endure suffering but to create mutually satisfying experiences for visitor and resident. Be sure to probe that the list of negative stimuli from the preceding paragraph has been addressed. How do the concepts of habituation, generalization or discrimination apply?

This exercise can also be expanded into a field visit, a diversity exercise or a writing project.

Active Learning Activity 5.14 - Cognitive Maps

The following mental imagery activity is a very effective demonstration of latent learning and cognitive maps. Start by asking students to close their eyes, sit comfortably in their seats, and rest one hand on their desktop. Tell them you are going to take them on an imaginary trip through "psychology land," and they should trace the route with a fingertip on the top of their desk. As you read the following passage, emphasize the words that are capitalized.

> *Place your fingertip in the lower left-hand corner of your desk. You are at the one and only gate to "psychology land." After you open the gate, move straight upward on your desktop. STOP at the upper left corner of your desk to visit Ivan Pavlov's laboratory where he is studying salivation in laboratory dogs. Picture in your mind a Russian physiologist rushing around testing his dogs. Note how the dogs salivate at the sound of the ringing bell. As you remember, this is because the bell (a previously NEUTRAL STIMULUS) has become a CONDITIONED STIMULUS. Through repeated pairings of the neutral stimulus with the*

UNCONDITIONED STIMULUS (meat powder), the dogs have LEARNED to salivate to the sound of the bell. We say this learning is a result of CLASSICAL CONDITIONING.

It is time to leave Pavlov's laboratory. Turn to your right and move your finger across the top of your desk--about the same distance as you traveled before. STOP. You have arrived at John B. Watson's laboratory where he is experimentally conditioning fear in a small infant boy named Little Albert. Note how Little Albert cries and tries to escape when he is presented with the white rat. This is because he has learned to fear the rat--it has been repeatedly paired with a loud noise. This fear is now known as a CONDITIONED EMOTIONAL RESPONSE (a CER). Recognizing that this type of research is no longer allowed in psychology, we wave good-bye to Little Albert and John B. Watson.

Again, turn to your right and travel the same distance down your desk. STOP. You have arrived at OPERANT CONDITIONING land. This time you are in the lab of the distinguished researcher, B. F. Skinner. Picture in your mind the long line of wire cages. In each cage you can see rats pressing levers to obtain the reward of food pellets. The rats are pressing at different speeds. Some are pressing all the time, while others seem to wait between presses. As you know, this is because the rats have been OPERANTLY CONDITIONED. They work at different speeds because they have been trained with different SCHEDULES OF REINFORCEMENT. The smell of all the rats in this one small room is getting to you. You decide to leave and go back to check on Little Albert. Using your finger, retrace your steps to Watson's laboratory. Now that you are there, you realize that psychology land is about to close. They will lock the gates in a matter of minutes. Move directly to the gate. Quick--before they close psychology land!

Now ask students to open their eyes and to raise their hands if they moved diagonally across their desks to get back to the gates. Most will raise their hands. Ask them why? Ask them what is the point of the demonstration? Some students will give the easy, obvious answer--you wanted to rehearse conditioning terminology with them. Admit that this is a side benefit, but press them for other possibilities. Eventually someone will volunteer the idea of cognitive maps. Although they had obviously never been to "psychology land," they did have a mental image or a cognitive map of the area--otherwise they would have had to return to the gate by way of Pavlov's lab. Mention that this type of cognitive learning also occurred with Tolman's rats. After the rats had been carefully taught a maze involving a complex series of right and left turns, it was not unusual for rats to jump out of the maze and head directly for the goal box where the food was located.

Active Learning Activity 5.15 - Observational Learning

To demonstrate observational learning, bring a student up to the blackboard at the front of the room and ask him or her to try to learn the rules for combining three symbols--a square, a circle, and a triangle--into four symbol words. Tell the other students that they are only to watch, not to speak to one another and not to ask questions. The rules are as follows: (1) a circle cannot follow a square and (2) triangles must be in pairs. Mark down how many tries it takes the first person to get four correct words in a row. Then ask another student, then another, and so on. If the students are paying attention, the second and third students should do better than the first. They will have learned by observation.

Handout 5.9 – Active Learning

Conditioning Worksheet

Read each of the following examples.

I. If you decide the situation seems to be an example of classical conditioning, you should label the UCS, UCR, CS, and CR.

II. If you decide the situation seems to be an example of operant conditioning, you should identify whether it is positive or negative reinforcement, or positive or negative punishment.

SITUATION 1

A very bright (mildly painful) light is turned on a rat. The rat has learned that he can turn off the light by pressing a lever on the other side of his cage. As soon as the light comes on, the rat runs across the room and presses the lever.

A. The behavior of pressing the lever is an example of _____ conditioning.

B. If you chose classical, follow part I of the instructions; if you chose operant, follow part II.

SITUATION 2

When a mother strokes her infant's skin, the stroking creates pleasure responses in the baby. After this goes on for many days, the baby begins to show pleasure responses simply at the sight of the mother (before even being touched).

A. The baby's pleasure response is an example of _____ conditioning.

B. If you chose classical, follow part I of the instructions; if you chose operant, follow part II.

SITUATION 3

A patient in a mental hospital is very disruptive at mealtimes. She grabs food from the plates of those sitting near her and tries to cram the food into her mouth. Because this behavior of stealing food is very undesirable, a plan is developed whereby every time the patient steals food from other plates, she is immediately taken to a room without food.

A. The mental health staff is attempting to change the behavior of stealing through _____ conditioning.

B. If you chose classical, follow part I of the instructions; if you chose operant, follow part II.

SITUATION 4

Johnny has developed a habit of yelling "Bye, Mom" and then slamming the door very loudly in his hurry to leave for school in the morning. The door slam causes his mother to flinch. After several days of the procedure, Johnny's mother begins to flinch at the sound of her son's words, "Bye, Mom."

A. The mother's flinching behavior can be explained through _____ conditioning.

B. If you chose classical, follow part I of the instructions; if you chose operant, follow part II.

SITUATION 5

Imagine you have a friend who keeps the temperature in her home so high that each occasion on which you visit her you find yourself perspiring. The last time you visited her, you noticed that you began to perspire and became uncomfortable as soon as you saw her house (before you even were inside).

A. Your perspiring behavior can be explained as _____ conditioning.

B. If you chose classical, follow part I of the instructions; if you chose operant, follow part II.

SITUATION 6

Mr. and Mrs. Jones are having a heated argument that both are finding very unpleasant. Mrs. Jones gets up and leaves the room, closing the door behind her. This has the effect of terminating the argument. From then on, every time Mr. Jones raises his voice, Mrs. Jones leaves the room. Mr. Jones stops raising his voice.

A. Mr. Jones stops raising his voice because of _____ conditioning.

B. If you chose classical, follow part I of the instructions; if you chose operant, follow part II.

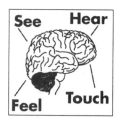

Brain-Based Learning

Brain-Based Learning Activity 5.1 - Positive Punishment / Negative Reinforcement

Students often have a great deal of difficulty understanding this distinction.

Step One:
Negative reinforcement

A. Make a tape recording of loud, distressed baby cries. Prepare a list of 50 words . About every 5th word is a word relating to fruits. Ask for a student volunteer. S/he agrees to listen to the tape through headphones at a strong volume. S/he slowly reads the list of words out loud. Every time the student reads a fruit word you turn down the volume of the headphones for the next two words.

Positive punishment
Prepare a list of 50 words. About every 5th word is a word relating to a color. Ask for another student volunteer. While wearing the headphones tell the student that they should slowly read the words out loud, one by one. Every time they read a color word you turn the volume on their headphones up high so they hear the vociferous crying. Towards the end of the list the student often shows a reaction before the color word is spoken out loud.

(If baby cries are hard to come by a police siren can be used, as long as the pattern is sufficiently varied to resist habituation.) If students are asked to sit very still during the exercise their reaction may be more pronounced.

Afterwards hand both students their list again and ask them to tell the class which words they liked to pronounce, which words they didn't. Have them describe their internal experience as the sound was added, or subtracted. Be sure to play the tape sound to the entire class for at least 30 seconds so every one can get the experience of its distressing quality.

Step Two:
Positive Reinforcement
Have a student read a list of 50 words wherein every 5th word is a word relating to beverages. Every time they read a word relating to beverages you give them a nickel. (Total gain 50 cents)

Negative Punishment
Give a volunteer three dollars worth of quarters. Ask the student to arrange his/her quarters on the desk in front. As they read a list of 50 words, in which every 5th word is related to clothing, you take away a quarter every time the student reads a word related to clothing. At the end, they should be left with just 2 quarters.

Afterwards ask both students to look at their list and state which words they liked and which they didn't like. How did their body react as they read the "special" words?

Another good example of Negative Reinforcement is the snooze button silencing the buzzing alarm clock. Ask students how many of them wake either just before the alarm goes off or as soon as the clock makes a click but before the buzzer can come on. How was this learned?

Application:
Following the above exercise, ask students about examples in their lives which fit each pattern. You can also offer a list of situations and ask the students to select which type of learning applies. Examples include: reduced allowance for bad grades, fining a hockey player who fights, putting a dollar into the coke machine, suspending a student who brings weapons to school, jailing convicted criminals, time out for small children, laughing at a friend's joke, grading students performance, praising the dog who sits at attention, getting your fifth massage free, yelling at the child who spilled juice all over the dining room table, winning at the races, waving your hand until a friend recognizes you in a crowd, setting off a car alarm in the parking lot, dropping your business card into the restaurant raffle, paying the yellow pages for advertising space, time off for good behavior in jail, earning a scholarship for making the Dean's list, being pulled over for speeding, kissing your lover after a nice date, filling a car out of gas at the station, and changing the oil every 5,000 miles.

Brain-Based Learning Activity 5.2 - Holiday Conditioning

Our culture and families often have very set expectations for the holidays. Christmas is supposed to be happy and filled with gifts; Thanksgiving a time of lots of food and warm family gatherings. Have the students explore what symbols, cues or expectations they learned from the culture and whether the learning history in their own family confirms or deviates from them. Can they remember how they learned these meanings?

Brain-Based Learning Activity 5.3 - Emotional Correctness

Make a list of emotions such as joy, anger, sadness, laughter, fear, love, passion, etc. Next to this label two columns as follows: allowed / forbidden. Then ask, what did you learn in your family about the expression of emotion? Which ones were safe, which were frowned upon? Depending on the size and openness of the class, you may wish to compile these answers anonymously.

In most classes every single emotion will be found to be allowed in some, and forbidden in other families. It always astounds the students that the emotional rules of expression they have learned to take for granted could be completely the opposite for another student.

Brain-Based Learning Activity 5.4 - Biofeedback Exercise

Ask for a couple of student volunteers. Apply one end of a stethoscope to a student's elbow or similar productive site. The hearing end of the stethoscope is rigged up to a microphone that amplifies the signal so the rest of the class can hear the heart beat. You can briefly guide the student through a relaxed and then a stressful situation to show the dramatic heartbeat difference. Following the guided example, ask the student to accelerate his/her own heartbeat above their normal level. Then ask them to lower it below their normal level. (Not everyone will be able to do this easily.)

After they have accomplished this on their own have them explain to the class what method they used to induce their heart rate to change.

Brain-Based Learning Activity 5.5 - Observational Learning

To illustrate the powerful time saving efficiency of observational learning, ask for a student volunteer to come to the front of the class. The other students must turn around so they cannot see him/her. The volunteer student then goes through the motions of a familiar operation such as making a peanut butter and jelly sandwich. S/he is not allowed to make specific noises or tell the other students words such as slicing, getting butter from the refrigerator, opening a jar etc., that would give the other students direct clues. S/he is allowed to describe in any detail the movements s/he is making. Encourage the other students to guess what is going on. After a few minutes ask the class what makes it so hard to follow the instructions. Then have the students turn around and observe the volunteer going through the motions of making a sandwich. Encourage the students to think back to their childhood memories to come up with examples of skills they learned largely from watching.

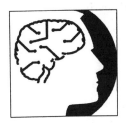 **Critical Thinking**

Critical Thinking Exercise 5.1 - Applying Knowledge to New Situations and Improving Student Creativity: Conditioning and Romantic Love

Students often have difficulty in mastering the terms and principles associated with classical and operant conditioning. One of the most entertaining ways to teach these concepts, (and to model the critical thinking skill of "Applying Knowledge to New Situations"), is to show how conditioning principles can be applied to specific behaviors and emotions associated with romantic love.

Time: Approximately 20 minutes.

Advance preparation: Obtain several country western records or tapes and a record player or tape player. If you send a self-addressed stamped envelope to the first author of the text (Karen Huffman), I will send you a copy of the tape I have created for my own classes. My address is: Karen Huffman, Palomar College, 1140 West Mission Road, San Marcos, CA 92069.

Instructions: After concluding your discussions of both classical and operant conditioning, describe the study by anthropologist James M. Schaefer who explored the relationship between alcohol consumption and listening to different styles of music. He found that country music led to more alcohol abuse than either pop or rock (cited in Stone, 1989).

After mentioning Schaefer's study to your class, play brief selections from Kenny Rogers's "Lucille," Crystal Gayle's "Don't It Make My Brown Eyes Blue," Willie Nelson's "Blue Eyes Cryin' in the Rain," and/or Hank Williams's "I'm So Lonesome I Could Cry." Ask your students to speculate on why these particular songs and country music in general are correlated with greater alcohol abuse. "What are the reinforcers?" "The punishers?" "How were the drinkers classically and operantly conditioned?" Ask students to bring in samples of their own favorite music and to explain the associated emotions.

As an alternative or adjunct to the record/tape exercise, you can encourage students to write poems or songs (outside of class) that incorporate any of the terms associated with classical or operant conditioning. This exercise not only improves their mastery of the material, but it also encourages creativity (an important component of critical thinking). As a starter, you may want to read the following student example (reprinted with author's permission):

References:
Stone, J. (1989, March). Lookin' for science in all the wrong places. <u>Discover</u>, pp. 96-99.

I Wish You Were A Neutral Stimulus Again!

Before I fell for you, life was peaceful as could be,
because you were then only a neutral stimulus to me.

You soon became a conditioned stimulus
and this is how I knew. Every time I saw you,
I blanked and didn't know what to do.

After you caused many problems,
I saw extinction should be quick.
But trying to unlearn my conditioned response
only made me sick.

Oh, how I wish I could make you a neutral stimulus again.
If it doesn't happen soon, I know for good I'll swear off men.

by Colleen Knudsen

This exercise also appears in the text, Chapter 5. We include it here for your convenience, and you may want to discuss it in class to reinforce reading of the text.

Critical Thinking Exercise 5.2 - Transferring Ideas to New Contexts: Operant Conditioning in the Real World

The major problem with "learning about learning" is that students don't integrate the new terminology and concepts into their everyday lives. They fail to appreciate the power of simple learning principles. But active learning requires that the learner rise above old, easy patterns of behavior and apply new knowledge to everyday situations. When you transfer an idea or concept from one situation to another your insight grows.

This exercise is designed to improve your basic understanding of operant conditioning while also developing your ability to apply new concepts to your life.

Situation #1

Suppose a large number of students regularly arrive late to one of your classes. The professor is obviously disturbed. How would you advise your professor to reduce tardiness? Consider the following four questions in developing your course of action.

1. Would you recommend that the professor punish students for being late or reinforce students for being on time? Why?

2. If the professor decides to use punishment, what type of positive punishment could he or she employ? What type of negative punishment?

3. What type of positive reinforcement or negative reinforcement would be effective for reinforcing timely attendance?

4. Once the goal of reduced tardiness is met, what type of reinforcement schedule would be best to avoid either the extinction of the behavior of coming on time or eventual ineffectiveness of the reinforcement?

Situation #2

Because of the rising crime rate in your city, you have decided that you want to condition your St. Bernard, Otto, to run to the door and bark every time someone knocks or rings your doorbell. Since this is a relatively complicated behavior, you decide to shape this behavior using positive reinforcement. To arrive at a plan for shaping Otto's behavior, consider the following questions.

1. What will you use as the positive reinforcement for Otto?

2. What is a likely list of successive approximations to the desired behavior?

3. Once you have shaped Otto to bark when someone is at your door, how will you keep this barking behavior from extinguishing when you are the only person to come to your door for several weeks?

4. How will you extinguish Otto's behavior if your neighbors complain about his barking?

This exercise also appears in the <u>Student Study Guide</u>, Chapter 5, and is a variation on the Critical Thinking Exercise presented in the text's Chapter 5 and in this manual--Critical Thinking Exercise 5.2. We include it here for your convenience, and you may want to discuss it in class to reinforce use of the Student Study Guide.

Critical Thinking Exercise 5.3 - Applying Knowledge to New Situations (A Cognitive Skill)

In Chapter 5, you learned about classical conditioning and that such learning can be applied to various situations in your own life. A critical thinker will be able to decipher the situations that are present during a learning experience. Such a thinker will also notice how often one stimulus situation is paired with another and that the two become associated with each other. However, identifying the neutral stimulus (NS), the unconditioned stimulus (UCS), the unconditioned response (UCR), the conditioned stimulus (CS), and the conditioned response (CR) can be difficult unless you have had some practice. The following paragraphs describe classical conditioning situations. Your task is to identify the NS, the UCS, the UCR, the CS, and the CR.

1. A researcher sounds a tone, then places a piece of meat into a dog's mouth, causing it to salivate. Eventually, the sound of the tone alone causes the dog to salivate.

NS: _____

UCS: _____

UCR: _____

CS: _____

CR: _____

2. You have a cat that always comes running when she hears the electric can opener.

NS: _____

UCS: _____

UCR: _____

CS: _____

CR: _____

3. While listening to a song on his car radio, a man accidentally bumped into a red car in front of him. Thereafter, whenever he saw red cars, he experienced a severe anxiety attack.

NS:_____

UCS:_____

UCR:_____

CS:_____

CR:_____

Gender and Cultural Diversity

Gender and Cultural Diversity Activity 5.1 - Testing Teacher Gender Bias

Procedure: Student groups will be assigned to observe either a preschool class, junior high school class, or a high school class. Remind students that someone in the group must obtain written permission from school administrators and classroom teachers to observe student/teacher interactions.

Materials: Handout 5.1- Gender and Cultural Diversity, a Behavioral Checklist.

Directions: Students will attempt to remain unobtrusive, objective observers. Their task is simply to record all teacher responses to student behaviors.

Conclusions: This activity often exposes a gender bias in teacher responses. Teachers at each level (preschool, junior high school, and high school) tend to respond more to boys (both positively and negatively) for the same behaviors. After student groups turn in their Behavioral Checklists (Handout 5.1 – Gender and Cultural Diversity), have them discuss their findings. If they found a gender bias, ask them to make lists on the board of which behaviors were most positively and negatively rewarded for boys and which were most rewarded for girls. Discuss how these differences in teacher treatment might affect the development of male and female students.

Handout 5.1 – Gender and Cultural Diversity

BEHAVIORAL CHECKLIST

MALES	FEMALES
1. ____HITTING	____HITTING
2. ____PUSHING	____PUSHING
3. ____SITTING QUIETLY	____SITTING QUIETLY
4. ____RAISES HAND TO SPEAK	____RAISES HAND TO SPEAK
5. ____YELLING OUT	____YELLING OUT
6. ____WANDERING IN CLASS	____WANDERING IN CLASS
7. ____WORKING ON TASK	____WORKING ON TASK
8. ____COMPLETING TASK	____COMPLETING TASK

Writing Project

Writing Project 5.1

Given the need for improved writing skills in college students and to respond to the call for "writing across the curriculum, " we offer writing projects for each chapter. In Chapter 5, we suggest a 2-3 page written response to the three areas discussed in Handout 5.1- Writing Project. Recognizing the time involved in grading such writing projects, one alternative is occasionally to assign "peer grading." Collect the papers, remove student names, and assign each student a paper to grade. It helps to make their participation in peer grading a required part of the overall points for the writing project. This encourages a more thoughtful and responsible evaluation, as well as acknowledging and rewarding the additional work.

Make xerox copies for the students of Handout 5.1 – Writing Project, the following material--it describes an interesting writing project that also has practical applications.

Handout 5.1 – Writing Project

Respond to each of the following points. Your paper should be typed, double-spaced, and a total length of 2-3 pages.

Learned Food Aversion

1. Describe a learned food aversion that you experienced. If you haven't experienced a food aversion, interview someone who has.
2. Show how the principles of classical conditioning (NS, UCS, UCR, CS, CR) apply to this food aversion.

Adolescent Emotional Experience

1. Describe an adolescent emotional experience that involves classical conditioning, such as being embarrassed in school or on a date.
2. Show how the principles of classical conditioning (NS, UCS, UCR, CS, CR) apply to this emotional experience.

Fear or Phobia

1. Describe a fear or phobia that you have that was classically conditioned.
2. Show how the principles of classical conditioning (NS, UCS, UCR, CS, CR) apply to your fear.

Please give us your feedback. We thank you in advance for assisting us in improving the next edition.
The contact information is listed in the preface.

What are the three most helpful teaching tools in this chapter?

1.

2.

3.

What are the three least useful teaching tools in this chapter?

1.

2.

3.

What are the three most difficult concepts to teach in this chapter?

1.

2.

3.

Additional Comments:

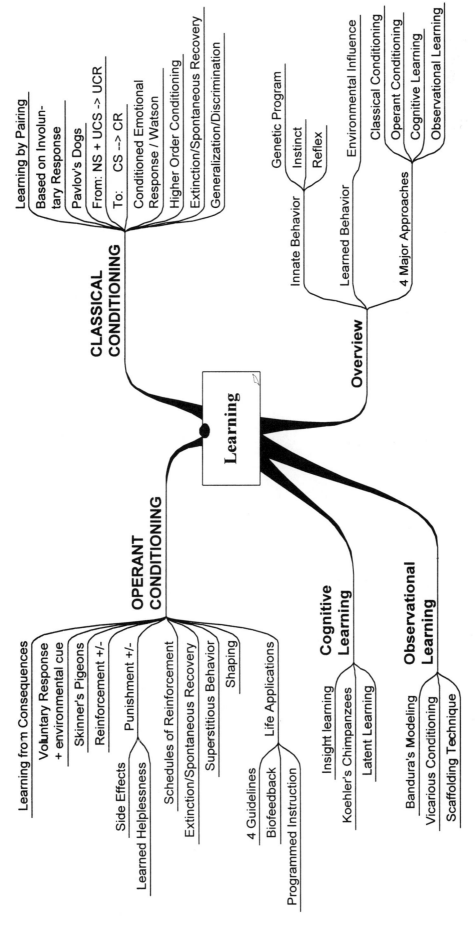

CLASSICAL CONDITIONING

Learning by Pairing
Based on Involun-
tary Response
Pavlov's Dogs
From: NS + UCS -> UCR
To: CS --> CR
Conditioned Emotional
Response / Watson
Higher Order Conditioning
Extinction/Spontaneous Recovery
Generalization/Discrimination

Overview

Genetic Program
Instinct
Reflex
Innate Behavior
Environmental Influence
Learned Behavior
Classical Conditioning
Operant Conditioning
Cognitive Learning
Observational Learning
4 Major Approaches

Learning

OPERANT CONDITIONING

Learning from Consequences
Voluntary Response
+ environmental cue
Skinner's Pigeons
Reinforcement +/-
Punishment +/-
Side Effects
Learned Helplessness
Schedules of Reinforcement
Extinction/Spontaneous Recovery
Superstitious Behavior
Shaping
4 Guidelines
Biofeedback
Programmed Instruction
Life Applications

Cognitive Learning

Insight learning
Koehler's Chimpanzees
Latent Learning

Observational Learning

Bandura's Modeling
Vicarious Conditioning
Scaffolding Technique

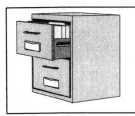

CHAPTER 6
MEMORY

Outline

The Traditional View of Memory

Sensory Memory
Short-Term Memory
Long-Term Memory
False Memories and Repressed Memories

Active Learning
Exploring your Memories

Gender and Cultural Diversity
Cultural Differences in Memory

The Problem of Forgetting

Research on Forgetting
Theories of Forgetting

Active Learning
Applying Theories of Forgetting

Exceptional Memories
Improving Memory

Learning Objectives

Upon completion of CHAPTER 6, the student should be able to:

1. Describe the three distinct storage systems in the traditional view of memory (pp. 214-215).
2. Describe the duration, capacity, and accuracy of sensory memory; discuss the process and purpose of automatic and deliberate selection at this stage (pp. 215-216).
3. Describe the duration, capacity, and accuracy of short-term memory; discuss the effects of chunking, dual-coding, levels of processing, maintenance rehearsal, and interference at this stage (pp. 216-221).
4. Describe the duration, capacity, and accuracy of long-term memory (pp.221-223)
5. Differentiate between semantic and episodic memory, and give an example of each (p. 223).
6. Discuss how long-term memory is organized, and differentiate between recognition, recall, and relearning (pp. 224-227).
7. Discuss the alteration of long-term memory, including the limitations regarding flashbulb memories and eyewitness events (pp. 227-228).
8. Differentiate between false and repressed memories, and discuss the research and controversy regarding the origins of these memories (pp.228-230).
9. Describe the impact of culture on short-term and long-term memory (pp.230-231).
10. Discuss forgetting and describe how each of the following factors affects remembering: serial position, distributed versus massed practice, and state-dependent memory (pp232-235).
11. Describe theories of forgetting: interference, decay, retrieval failure, and motivated forgetting. Differentiate between proactive and retroactive interference (pp.235-236).
12. Explain memory in terms of the following biological factors that occur in the brain: reverberating circuits, long-term potentiation, kinase enzymes, and specific brain areas (pp. 237-240)
13. Define amnesia, and differentiate between retrograde and anterograde amnesia (p. 240)
14. Describe the effects on memory of brain damage due to tumors, strokes, or surgery; discuss the causes, symptoms, and treatment for Alzheimer's disease, and compare this to the "normal" effects of aging on memory (pp. 240-243).
15. Describe eidetic imagery and discuss its benefits and drawbacks (p 243.).
16. Provide examples of the various mnemonic devices and describe how they help to improve memory (pp. 243-246).

Chapter Summary/Lecture Organizer

Introductory Vignette--This chapter begins with the story of Eileen Franklin, the adult who suddenly remembered, twenty years later, having seen her father murder her best friend when they were both eight years of age. The problems associated with the trial and conviction of her father, George Franklin, serve as an introduction to the topic of memory.

I.   **The Traditional View of Memory** - A flowchart for memory processes includes the three stages of sensory memory, short-term memory (STM), and long-term memory (LTM).

    A. Sensory Memory - Sensory memory occurs within the senses. Visual images last about 1/4 to 1/2 second and auditory images up to four seconds.

    B. Short-Term Memory - STM is our current attention span or working space in memory. It can hold about seven items in visual or verbal form and can store them for about thirty seconds; however, its capacity can be increased by chunking and its duration can be increased by maintenance rehearsal. Selection for STM can be done automatically or deliberately. Dual-coding refers to the visual and verbal input channels of STM. During the storage process between STM and LTM, the way information is processed affects its ability to be retrieved from LTM.

    C. Long-Term Memory - LTM is a more permanent form of memory where information and ideas are stored for future use. The type of LTM in which facts and their relations to another are stored is called semantic memory. Memories of specific events are stored in episodic memory. Semantic memory involves relating facts to each other. Episodic memory involves identifying specific events in a time sequence organized around landmark events such as getting married. Information in LTM is organized into categories and sub-categories that form a network. This network has been studied by analyzing the associations and linkages of redintegration and the tip-of-the-tongue (TOT) phenomenon.

Several pathways in the network lead to any particular piece of information, but, nonetheless, stored memories are not always retrievable. Retrieval is the process of getting information out of LTM. The two types of retrieval are recognition and recall. In recall, a general cue is used to retrieve information associated with the cue, as when we attempt to recall a name associated with a face or when we answer an essay question. In recognition, an item is matched to stored information, as when we recognize a face we have seen before or answer multiple-choice questions on a test. Measurements of relearning compare the amount of time it takes to relearn material after we can no longer recall or recognize it. This method was used by pioneer memory researcher Hermann Ebbinghaus to measure his relearning of nonsense syllables. When we are at first unsuccessful at remembering something, our brains sometimes continues the search unconsciously until an answer is obtained. This is called the Zeigarnik effect. Stored memories

are not always retrievable, and studies of eyewitness testimony show that memory can be modified and that the retrieval process is not always accurate.
Even when we have vivid "flashbulb memories" of surprising or strongly emotional events, we can be remembering altered versions of the original events.

D. False Memories and Repressed Memories - False memories are defined as memories that a person believes are real but are actually memories of events that never occurred. Repressed memories are defined as unconscious memories of a traumatic event. The controversy over repression and the recovery of stored childhood memories of abuse is discussed.

> **Active Learning: Exploring Your Memories** - The active learning exercise for this chapter allows students to practice reflective thinking--to "think about thinking"--and to use it to evaluate processes involved in recalling and storing memories.

> **Gender and Cultural Diversity: Cultural Differences In Memory** - The work of Ross and Millson (1970) used college students from the United States and Ghana and discovered that the Ghana students were better at memory testing for themes in stories presented aloud. Wagner (1982) found that previous experience plays a part in facilitating memory recognition. It appears that STM is not affected by cultural factors but that a person's culture provides background of experience and strategies for remembering factors specific to that culture.

II. THE PROBLEM OF FORGETTING

A. Research on Forgetting - Memory research indicates that more forgetting occurs for material in the middle of a list (the serial position effect) and when students use massed practice or "cramming" rather than distributed practice. Another important factor involved in forgetting is the state-dependent quality of memory. Retrieval is better when you are in an emotional state similar to that in which the original learning took place.

B. Theories of Forgetting - According to the interference theory of forgetting, proactive interference occurs when previously learned information interferes with newly learned information. Retroactive interference occurs when more recently learned information interferes with something we learned previously. The decay theory of forgetting states that memory, like all biological processes, deteriorates as time passes. The motivated forgetting theory states that retrieval can be blocked when memories are painful, threatening, or embarrassing. The retrieval failure theory of forgetting points out that information contained in LTM is never forgotten but may at times be inaccessible.

III.   THE BIOLOGY OF MEMORY

A. Theories of Memory - Biological changes during the processing of memory include temporary and permanent changes in the nervous system. During the time period of STM, reverberating circuits fire. If there is a disruption in this firing pattern such as occurs with brain trauma or electroconvulsive shock (ECS), the incoming information is not stored. Memory consolidation appears to depend on chemical and physical changes in the dendrites and synapses and in the genetic mechanisms of the neuron. Dendrites develop more sprouts and become more sensitive to neurotransmitters in enriched learning environments. The process whereby short-term memories become long-term memories is called long-term potentiation (LTP). Recent research shows that enzymes called kinases are involved in LTP.

> **Research Highlight: How Do Memories Get There in the First Place?** – Research shows that the prefrontal cortex and the parahippocampal cortex are most probably involved in the formation of new memories.

B. Amnesia - Retrograde amnesia (forgetting of events before a trauma) and anterograde amnesia (disruption of memory processing after a trauma) can be temporary or permanent.

C. Memory Impairment - In the case of H. M., surgical removal of portions of his temporal lobes resulted in his inability to store information from STM. Autopsies of brains of boxers reveal damage involved in memory impairment.

D. Alzheimer's Disease - In Alzheimer's disease, a progressive mental deterioration associated with shrinking of the cerebral hemispheres and neuron damage near the hippocampus results in decreased production of the neurotransmitter acetylcholine. The recommended treatment of Alzheimer's combines the prevention methods of exercise, diet changes an drugs that prevent neuro-degenerative changes with other drugs aimed at slowing the decline in mental functioning

IV.   EXCEPTIONAL MEMORIES - People with eidetic imagery or "photographic memory" are able to retain complete visual images seemingly unaffected by the usual limitations of STM.

A. Improving Memory - For people with exceptional memories, memory can be improved by using mnemonic strategies during learning or retrieval. The method of loci, peg-word, and substitute word strategies associate visual images with items to be learned. The method of word associations creates verbal associations for items to be learned.

Teaching Resources

SECTION I – THE TRADITIONAL VIEW OF MEMORY

Learning Objectives #'s 1 - 9
Lecture Lead-Ins #'s 1, 3
Discussion Questions #'s 2, 4, 5
Active Learning Activities #'s 6.1 - 6.8, 6.10
Brain-Based Learning Activities #'s 6.2 - 6.5
Critical Thinking Exercise # 6.2
Gender and Cultural Diversity Activity # 6.1
Writing Project # 6.1

SECTION II – THE PROBLEM OF FORGETTING

Learning Objectives #'s 10, 11
Lecture Extenders # 6.1
Discussion Questions #'s 2, 4, 5
Active Learning Activities #'s 6.5 - 6.10
Critical Thinking Exercise #6.1
Gender and Cultural Diversity Activity # 6.1

Writing Project # 6.1

SECTION III – THE BIOLOGY OF MEMORY

Learning Objectives #'s 12 - 14
Discussion Questions #'s 1, 6
Active Learning Activities # 6.5
Writing Project # 6.1

SECTION IV – EXCEPTIONAL MEMORIES

Lecture Lead-Ins #'s 15, 16
Discussion Questions # 3
Active Learning Activities #'s 6.5, 6.6, 6.10
Brain-Based Learning #'s 6.1, 6.4
Gender and Cultural Diversity Activity # 6.1
Writing Project # 6.1

Lecture Lead-Ins

1. Read the following words aloud at a rate of about one word per second:

    BED, QUILT, DARK, SILENCE, FATIGUE, CLOCK, SNORING, NIGHT, TOSS, TIRED, NIGHT, TOSS, TIRED, NIGHT, ARTICHOKE, TURN, NIGHT, REST, DREAM

    Wait 15 seconds and then ask students to write down as many words as they can recall. Now tell them to check their lists. Did they remember the word *sleep*? About one-third of the class will recall this word--even though it was NOT on the list (Deese, 1959). Point out that this demonstrates the constructive (distorting) nature of memory.

    Now, make a bar graph on the board with the frequency of recall of all 19 words along the X-axis and the number of students who recall that word on the Y-axis. (It helps to ask a couple of students to come to the front of the room to help with the drawing and counting.)

    The graph reliably shows
    *   Recall is better at the beginning and end--the primacy-recency effect.
    *   The highest recall frequency is generally for *artichoke*--distinctiveness.
    *   The word *night* is also high--repetition.
    *   The words *toss* and *turn* are also high--chunking and associations.

    Although this demonstration takes a little time (usually around 15 minutes), the final bar graph demonstrates several important concepts and provides a perfect lecture lead-in!

    Source: Deese. K. (1959). On the prediction of occurrence of particular verbal intrusions in immediate recall. <u>Journal of Experimental Psychology, 58</u>, 17-22.

2. As a lead-in to lecture/discussions on memory, ask students if they have known anyone with a memory problem (Alzheimer's, amnesia or brain damage). Many students will volunteer information and examples. Ask questions concerning the behaviors and problems presented by this loss. Use this discussion as a platform for lecture/discussions on problems with forgetting, and refer back to the examples in later lectures.

3. Ask the students to remember their first kiss. This should be easy for most of the students. Ask how they remember such a small event so long ago? Most will say it was pleasant or enjoyable. Point out other enjoyable events (birthdays are always good), and ask if the students remember all of their birthdays? Use these discussions as a lead-in for your lectures on long term memory.

Lecture Extenders

6.1 - Motivated Forgetting

The concept of motivated forgetting has been identified with the clinical branch of psychology because the concept has often been invoked to explain symptoms of clinical disorders. Freud, who had clients with emotional problems, found that something analogous to motivated forgetting was the simplest explanation for his observations. When Freud had a patient under hypnosis, the patient could recall emotionally laden material that was not available in the normal waking state. Freud felt that painful memories, which included emotions such as embarrassment and anxiety, were deliberately excluded from consciousness, a process he labeled repression. Although repression has generally been identified with conflicts from which one seeks treatment, Freud also maintained that it operated in all human beings in such phenomena as "slips of the tongue" or temporary forgetting of more trivial material. His book The Psychopathology of Everyday Life was an anecdotal account of these more common occurrences.

Dissociative amnesia, dissociative fugue, and dissociative identity disorder (previously known as multiple personality) are three of the diagnostic categories that place repression at the center of the problem. Dissociative amnesia is defined as an inability to recall the personal past as a result of psychological stress. It is not believed to be caused by organic factors. This type of amnesia appears to affect only episodic memory, not semantic memory and to be a reaction to severe emotional stress. For example, a person who views a friend's dying under violent circumstances may not remember the incident even though he tries to recall it later.

A dissociative fugue includes amnesia coupled with flight from the stress-producing situation. The person behaves normally in the new non-stressful situation that may be thousands of miles from the stressful situation, even though there is a section of life that has been forgotten. At the same time he or she may not remember having forgotten anything. For the normal person, the inability to recall any information from the week before would be stressful. The fugue disordered person does not appear to be bothered by loss of memory chunks. Some fugues have lasted for over 10 years, but in most cases they are over in less than a week. For those of short duration, a typical occurrence is for the person to appear at the hospital or police station complaining that he or she does not know who he or she is, the John or Jane Doe syndrome. With these individuals some ingenuous methods have been used to establish identification. In one case, electrodes were attached to the skin and changes in skin conductance were measured in response to the naming of months of the year: there was a greater change in response to the individual's birthday month. City of residence and other similar information was obtained in the same way. Information not available to the conscious system was still available in measures of autonomic nervous system functioning.

Dissociative identity disorder (still known to students as multiple personality) is the best known of these disorders, having received press through movies and talk shows, even though this disorder is still extremely rare. The etiologic factor of great importance is presumed to be emotional trauma (now speculated to be sexual abuse in childhood). The person has at least two personalities, sometimes 10 or more, and contrary to the two-way amnesia in the fugue state, there is only a one-way amnesia with alternation of control between the personalities. Quite often the personalities are contrasting ones, a schoolteacher and a prostitute, with one personality representing the "repressed" aspects of the other personality.

Although multiple personality is a popularly discussed disorder, there are some who feel it is created by the psychotherapist who encourages its appearance. Indeed, there are some experimental psychologists who do not feel that the concept of repression has been demonstrated. Freud, who did not feel that his concepts had to be verified in the laboratory, accepted his own clinical observations as sufficient for establishing the concept of repression. Recently, many of Freud's conclusions have been called into question based on the fact that his original sample of patients may or may not have benefited from his therapy. There have been attempts by others to verify the existence of this phenomenon. Zeller (cited in Gregg, 1986) had subjects learn a list of words which they later had to recall to demonstrate that the information "took." Then, they had to engage in a tapping task during which their performance was severely criticized as being well below average (an anxiety- inducing task). After the tapping, they were asked to recall the earlier syllables and, compared to a control group who did not have task-induced anxiety, their recall was worse. Recall was still impaired two days later. However, after being told that the earlier results on tapping had been rigged, their scores improved--presumably due to the lifting of anxiety. On the other hand, others have argued that this isn't the correct interpretation and suggest that response bias (one is hesitant to give the answers) rather than memory bias (repression) is the best answer.

Another research approach has been to use levels of emotionally laden material established by measuring the galvanic skin response (GSR) to stimulus words. In one experiment, subjects were asked to give associations to words that varied in ability to invoke emotion. Later, the subjects were asked to recall the earlier associations--the hypothesis being that the responses to the more emotional words had been repressed. The findings supported repression. Other investigators suggested that emotional words elicited more associations, so interference rather than repression was the better answer. To get around this argument, a later study measured the GSR response to a nonsense syllable paired with a digit. In an immediate recall test, those syllables with low arousal value were recalled best. This would seem a straightforward test of the effect of emotional arousal on recall of material; however, when these subjects tried to recall the material a week later, high-arousal pairs were remembered best as would be predicted in the verbal learning literature.

As with many of Freud's concepts, experimental testing is limited or impossible. It is a very difficult matter to verify the concept of repression in the laboratory. The anxiety induced is artificial, and there are always alternative explanations. But since many psychotherapists believe that it is the best explanation for many of the emotional problems they see in the clinic, repression will probably remain a popular explanation, no matter what is found in the laboratory.

Reference: Gregg, V.H. (1986). Introduction to human memory. Boston: Routledge & Kegan Paul.

Key Terms

Discussion Questions

(The writing project for Chapter 6--located at the end of this chapter section--also contains several questions that may be useful for class discussion.)

1. What are the chances that scientists will develop a safe, effective drug that dramatically improves memory? If such a drug were available, how would it affect education? Would you take the drug? Why or why not? What might be the advantages and disadvantages of such a drug?

2. Ask students if they have a "flashbulb memory" that is especially vivid. Invite them to share this memory. Note the role of emotion in the formation of the memory. Ask them to explain how these memories are formed and why they are so long lasting. Discuss inaccuracies and alterations of these memories. Many students have the misconception that "flashbulb" implies a perfect, photographic memory of the event.

3. Ask students who were born in another country to describe their culture's mnemonics (e.g., How do they remember the colors of the rainbow, or the number of days in the month?). Also, ask students who are from different states in the nation, to describe unusual mnemonics (e.g., people in Michigan use the back of their left hand to indicate locations of areas within the state, and people in California generally know that major highways running north and south have odd numbers, while highways running east and west have even numbers.)

4. What is the importance of the magic number 7 plus or minus 2? How does this apply to everyday life? Ask how this knowledge can be applied to help the students study for tests?

5. Describe a study routine that is supported by memory research. What could students do to increase the likelihood of studied material resulting in long-term storage and easy retrieval? Have students compare this routine with the way they now study. Ask if they will try this research-supported method or continue with their current method. Why or why not?

6. Discuss the long-term effects of Alzheimer's disease in terms of patient care and personal loss. Do the students think there will be a cure in the near future? If so, what will it involve and from what branch of science will it emerge?

 **Web Sites**

Shuffle Brain
www.indiana.edu/~pietsch/home.html
This site details brain and memory functions, with recent developments in these areas cited. The name of the site is derived from a salamander at the lab with that has successfully survived a brain transplant (from a frog).

NIH News Release: Human Memory Pinpointed
www.nih.gov/news/pr/feb98/nimh-26.htm
Details on where human memory is located moment to moment. Suggests that spatial memory is reliant upon highly specialized neural circuitry.

Research Index of Knowledge, Simulation of Human Memory
www.brainresearch.com/#1memory
This site provides links to other memory oriented sites, and associated brain areas involved.

Attention, Memory, and Language
www.fsw.leidenuniv.nl/www/w3_func/research.htm
Provides neural network explanations for memory from the Graduate Research Institute for Experimental Psychology.

Suggested Films and Videos

Memory--The Past Imperfect
Filmakers Library, 1994. 46 minutes. Part of "The Nature of Things" series, this film explores long- and short-term memory, the effectiveness of using hypnosis for recall, the phenomenon of amnesia, the memories of young children, and the problems with eyewitness testimony. This is a well-made video that is an excellent adjunct to chapter 6.

Remembering and Forgetting
Annenberg/CPB, 1990. 30 minutes. From Zimbardo's "Discovering Psychology" series, this video examines the complex processes involved in the creation of memory. Reasons for forgetting are discussed and several retrieval aids for improving memory are presented. This video provides a clear overview of the concepts involved in memory and has excellent graphics and commentary.

Memory
Insight Media, 1990. 30 minutes. Biological and cognitive research findings relating to encoding, storing, and retrieving of memories are presented in this film. The program also shows memory disturbances and how they are related to disease or injury. Our memory for dramatic events is examined and is applied to eyewitness testimony in criminal trials.

Learning and Memory
PBS Video, 1984. 55 minutes. From "The Brain" series, this video discusses the brain's role in the formation, storage, and retrieval of memory. The functions of specific brain areas, like the amygdala and the hippocampus, and their role in memory are also presented.

Thinking
PBS Video, 1990. 30 minutes. Part of "The Mind" series, this video focuses on the history and background of memory research. The prefrontal and frontal areas of the brain provide the springboard for memory discussion. Several interesting cases of brain damage and its impact on memory are presented.

Consciousness
PBS Video, 1990. 60 minutes. Also part of "The Mind" series, this video has a 13-minute sequence at the end that is superb for introducing the topic of memory. A symphony conductor, who suffered injury (through encephalitis) to his hippocampus and frontal lobes, is shown interacting with his wife and playing the piano. His loss of short-term memory is painfully clear. This short segment is definitely worth showing.

The Study of Memory
Films for the Humanities and Sciences, 1996. 74 minutes. This film covers a number of areas in the study of memory. Topics include the following: Basic terms such as encoding, storage, and retrieval. An explanation of modern theories of memory using diagrams and real-life examples. Reasons for forgetting, biological basis of memory, and methods of improving memory. The focus is on the recent shift in research from the laboratory to real life situations. Also presented are exercises the viewers can participate in, including memory tests and a test of recall based on eyewitness testimony research.

Memory
Films for the Humanities and Sciences, 1998. 57 minutes. This video examines how memory defines one's identity and provides a sense of personal continuity. The brain's fundamental processes and role in memory, why some things are remembered and others are not, the effects of normal aging and Alzheimer's disease, and how to preserve and improve retention are all discussed. Basic format is a panel discussion between authors and experts from Harvard Medical School and Howard Hughes Medical Center, among others.

Books For Success

Lorayne, Harry; Lucas, Jerry (1996). **The Memory Book.** Ballantine Books.
This book tells you how to find and utilize your mind's powers to remember .

Turkington, Carol A. (1996). **12 Steps to a Better Memory**. Arco Pub.
A user-friendly system of the most current techniques for remembering numbers, names, addresses, etc.

Higbee, Kenneth L. (1996). **Your Memory: How It Works & How to Improve It.** Marlowe & Co.
Tells how to use your mind as a "thought system", including special information on memory and aging and mnemonics.

Active Learning

Active Learning Activity 6.1 - "Dream Vacation"--With and Without Memories

Ask students to imagine for the moment that you (the instructor) are a "magic Genie," and you will grant each student an all-expenses-paid, two-week vacation anywhere in the world. The catch is that they must make a difficult decision. They can have the *actual* dream vacation with *no memory* of anything that happened. Or they can choose to have exquisite, vivid memories, but they won't experience the actual trip.

Now, ask them to stand up and to move to the right hand side of the room if they want the actual vacation--with no memories. If they want the memories, without the vacation, have them move to the left side of the room. (If your class is too large to move around like this, simply ask them to raise their hands for one or the other choice.) Now ask the students to explain their choice. This provides a wonderful lead-in to the topic (and value!) of our memories. You can refer to this activity throughout later lectures. Once students really think about what it would be like not to have any memory of an event, they appreciate the value of the memory process and increase their interest in chapter topics.

Active Learning Activity 6.2 - SQ4R and Memory

Given that the text is based on the SQ4R method, this chapter offers a perfect opportunity to point out the advantages of this method in improving memory. You can simply review the parts of the SQ4R method (detailed explanation available in the Preface of the text). In addition, you might want to use the following activity to further illustrate the SQ4R method:

Ask each student to find a partner. Tell Partner "A" (one-half the class) to shut their eyes while you write the phrases "flying a kite" on the board. Tell the other half of the class (Partner "B") to remember the phrase, and then erase the board. Ask the "blindfolded" students (Partner "A") to open their eyes. Read the following passage:

> *A newspaper is better than a magazine. A seashore is a better place than the street. It takes some skill, but it is easy to learn. Even young children can enjoy it. Once successful, complications are minimal. Birds seldom get too close. Rain, however, soaks in very fast. Too many people doing the same thing can also cause problems. One needs lots of room. If there are no complications it can be very peaceful. A rock will serve as an anchor. If things break loose from it, however, you will get no second chance.*

Ask all students to write down everything they can remember about the passage--reminding Partner B not to tell Partner A what you wrote on the board. Have the partners share what they wrote. There will be more detail in Partner B's responses. After disclosing what you wrote on the board, ask Partner As to explain why it was so difficult. Use their responses to point out the advantages of *context* and *encoding*. Since Partner B had access to the "secret words," the details in the passage made sense (they were "in context") and easily encoded. Explain that the *Surveying* and *Questioning* steps of the SQ4R method are important because they provide context for the chapter material and ensure encoding.

If time allows, have partners reverse roles and write on the board
  1. *christening a ship*
  2. *a broken parachute*
Erase the board, have the "blindfolded" partners open their eyes, and read
  1. *The voyage wasn't delayed because the bottle shattered.*
  2. *The haystack was important because the cloth ripped.*

Repeat the process described above--this time Partner A will have access to the "secret words" that simulate the Survey and Question stages of the SQ4R method.

Source: Klein, M. (1981). Context and memory. In L. T. Benjamin and K. D. Lowman (Eds.), Activities handbook for the teaching of psychology, p. 83. Washington, D.C. : American Psychological Association.

Active Learning Activity 6.3 - Rubber Pencil

Tell the class members they can use *sensory memory* to "turn a pen or pencil to rubber." Encourage them to find a partner. Have one student watch while the other holds his or her pencil in front of the viewer. Tell this student to grasp the pencil or pen with his or her thumb and forefinger about a third of the way from the end. Hold the pen or pencil horizontal to the viewer. Move it slowly up and down. The viewer will see what appears to be a blurred image of a "rubber pencil." This occurs because sensory memory briefly holds a trace of the various positions that the pencil occupies as it moves. Encourage students to reverse roles and repeat the demonstration. While many instructors perform this demonstration at the front of the class, we believe it is important to encourage "hands-on" active learning. It really doesn't take any more time in your class, and students remember the concept of sensory memory better when they have conducted the experiment for themselves.

Active Learning Activity 6.4 - Hand After Image

To demonstrate the *duration* of sensory memory, have students hold their hands up toward the light in the room and about six inches in front of their faces. "Stare at your hand for a few seconds and then shut your eyes. What do you see?" (Most will see a dark hand on a light background for a brief moment.) Remind students that this demonstrates the duration of sensory memory. Ask them to explain how they might use knowledge about sensory memory to improve their long-term memory.

Active Learning Activity 6.5 - Chunking

To demonstrate the *limits* of short-term memory (7, plus or minus 2) and the advantage of *chunking*, read the following letters individually at the rate of about one per second. Ask students to concentrate on trying to remember as many letters as possible.

N-F, L-C-B, S-U-S, A-V-C, R-F-B, I

Ask how many students remembered all 15 letters? Usually one or two students will raise their hands-- hopefully because they have read the chapter and understand the principle of chunking (or occasionally because they heard it at a party or in another class). Invite the "winning" students to the front of the room to explain their success. (They will have chunked these 15 letters into NFL, CBS, USA, VCR, FBI.) Giving winning students a chance to demonstrate, rather than keeping the spotlight on yourself, helps reinforce reading and preparation outside of class. It also helps make the class more visually stimulating--they get tired looking at just the instructor.

Active Learning Activity 6.6 - Penny Demonstration

Ask students to take out a sheet of paper and draw a sketch of the face (or "head") of a U.S. penny. Tell them to write down any words or numbers that are found on the penny. Encourage them to share their sketches with someone around them. Tell them NOT to get a penny out of their pockets or purses. Ask them to write down answers to the following questions:

1. Which way does Lincoln face (as you look at the penny)? To the left or right?
2. Is anything written above his head? If yes, write down what it is or add it to your drawing.
3. Is anything below his head? If so, what is it?
4. Is anything written to the left of his face? If so, what is it?
5. Is anything written to the right of his face? If so, what is it?

Now ask them to take out a penny and compare their results. Use their "lack of memory" as an example of problems with long-term memory. Point out that most of us have never "encoded" this particular information--despite having seen a penny thousands of times. Remind students that this helps explain poor exam scores--despite having read the chapters two or three times.

Active Learning Activity 6.7 - Rumor Transmission

This activity demonstrates several important terms and concepts for this chapter. It also elicits a great deal of laughter and enjoyment!

Method: Ask seven volunteers to step outside the class and inform them that you will call them in one at a time. They should use this time to decide who will go first, second, and so on. After they have left the room, inform the class that you will read a brief paragraph (Handout 6.7) to the first volunteer, while the others remain waiting outside. You will then bring in the second student and ask the first student to repeat the entire paragraph--with as much detail as possible. The second student will then repeat the story to the third student, the third to the fourth, and so on. Have the last student repeat the story to the entire class. Ask the class to watch for several examples of "memory in action." Tell them to take notes and look for the serial position effect, interference, constructive nature of memory, shortening of information, and so on.

Discussion: After thanking the student volunteers, have them return to their seats. Put the original paragraph (Handout 6.1) on an overhead projector and show it to the class. The seven volunteers, as well as the general class, will all be amazed at how the story changed. Ask for examples of serial position effect (they generally remember "the wild, sports shirt" at the beginning and "dismissing the class" at the end); the constructive nature of memory (they almost always turn the female dean into a male, they often have the students having sex vs. "making out" on the lawn, and they sometimes change "organism" into "orgasm"); interference; and, so on. Students will often come up with their own examples of terms from the book--so much the better. If time allows, you can ask someone from the general audience now to repeat the story. (Be sure the overhead for the Handout is turned off.) Even after hearing it many times, seeing it, and talking about it, he or she will have difficulty with a lot of the details. This can be used to point out that long-term memory is NOT a tape recorder and is not designed for precise memory of details. When they need this type of information, they must take extra steps to ensure a deeper level of processing.

Source: This exercise was *loosely* adapted from a similar "Rumor Transmission" exercise in The Activities Handbook for the Teaching of Psychology (Vol. 2). We changed the emphasis toward memory concepts versus "rumor transmission," we changed the English professor to a psychology professor (to make it more relevant to our classes), and changed the topic from Chaucer's poems to "motivation and emotion in single-celled organisms." (The change to "organisms" often leads to a substitution of the word "orgasm." This was not intentional, in the beginning, but it leads to lots of laughter, so we left it in the story. If you feel uncomfortable, simply change the topic to something like "motivation and emotion in primates.")

Handout 6.7 - Active Learning

Rumor Transmissions

A large, muscular, psychology professor who was dressed in his usual outfit of jeans and a wild sports shirt was walking across campus to teach his introduction to psychology course. As he passed the campus lake, he observed two students from his morning class passionately making out in the shade of a large elm tree. As he continued across campus, he met the dean of the graduate school who stopped to chat with him. She informed him that his application for a grant to study motivation and emotion in single-celled organisms was rejected because of a shortage of available funds. After debating somewhat violently the merits of his grant request, the professor continued walking to his class. Upon reaching the class, he discovered he had brought the wrong lecture notes and consequently dismissed class for the day.

Active Learning Activity 6.8 - Eyewitness Testimony

There are a number of staged incidents you could use to demonstrate the limits of eyewitness testimony. We use the following:

After you begin lecturing, have someone who appears to be another instructor enter the room to borrow something, such as a video monitor, podium, eraser, or the like. Have the person escalate their "request" until they reach the point of shouting. After the other "instructor" leaves, have your students write a description of the person's physical appearance, including face and clothing, and a detailed description of the dialogue.

After debriefing the students, have them share their "eyewitness" accounts. Now have the "instructor" walk in (wearing the same clothes). Have students compare their written descriptions of the person's appearance to the person's actual appearance. Discuss problems associated with eyewitness testimony and short-term and long-term memory. Point out how the slight emotions aroused by the "near shouting" may have affected their recall. Compare that to real life incidents where eyewitnesses are even more aroused and not asked immediately to record details. This will help emphasize the limits of eyewitness testimony discussed in the text.

Active Learning Activity 6.9 - Tip-of-the-Tongue Phenomenon

In order to elicit the tip-of-the-tongue phenomenon, read dictionary definitions of uncommon or vaguely familiar words and then ask students to produce the words. Have them describe what they can recall: the first letter, number of syllables, rhyming words, and so on.

Two references helpful in preparing this demonstration are

Brown, R., and McNeil, D. (1966). The "tip of the tongue" phenomenon. Journal of Verbal Learning and Verbal Behavior, 5, 325-337.

Eysenck, M. W. (1979). The feeling of knowing a word's meaning. British Journal of Psychology, 70, 234-251.

Active Learning Activity 6.10 - Memory Retrieval

Read each of the following sentences and have students write down their responses:

1. *What did you have for lunch today?*
2. *What did you have for lunch yesterday?*
3. *What did you have for lunch a week ago?*
4. *What did you have for lunch a month ago today?*
5. *Who, if anyone, were you with last Saturday at 1:30 a.m.?*
6. *What were you doing on Monday, May 6, 1992?*

Have students describe their retrieval processes for each example. The last one will require the use of landmark events and logical analysis.

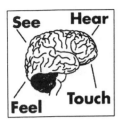

Brain-Based Learning

Brain-Based Learning Activity 6.1 - Comparing Memory Techniques

To increase students' appreciation of the strength and weaknesses of various memory techniques have them complete Handout 6.1 – Brain-Based Learning. The Handout has space to list each technique's advantages, disadvantages, the influence of other factors (e.g. the type of material to be memorized, situational factors, etc.) and it is a good example of how each technique could be used.

Brain-Based Learning Activity 6.2 - The Role of Cultural Scripts in Memorization

Group the class in teams of three students each.

> Student A is an exchange student from a culture without any experience with cars.
> (South American Jungle, Inuit Eskimo, Remote Pacific Island)

> Student B is part of his American Host Family who has been asked by the visitor to provide helpful instructions for buying a car. S/He has five minutes to do so and cannot use any terms or explanations that assume prior car knowledge.

> Student C is the observer who is to remind both people in case they forget that the exchange student has never driven a car and that there were no cars in the village were s/he grew up.

After the five minutes are up discuss what made it so hard for Student B to teach and what made it so hard for Student A to remember the instructions. How does this relate to the concepts of schemas and hierarchy of concepts discussed in the text?

Brain-Based Learning Activity 6.3 - Emotional Memory

Play some scenes from the movie *War of the Roses* which has some very dramatic fight scenes of a couple going through a divorce. Then ask, "Why do they haul out arguments and hurts from years and years in the past?" This video provides a dramatic introduction to the important role of emotions in forming and recalling memories.

Ask students why they remember all the wrongs from previous fights with a brother/sister or spouse when they are having a fight.

Ask the students to remember the happiest moment of their life.
Ask them to remember a painful episode of their life.

This can open a discussion on how we are able to search our memory not only by location (your childhood home) or year (What did you do for summer vacation two years ago?) or category (What do you know about stars?), but also by how we feel. Students usually do not appreciate how powerfully emotions are interwoven into the structure of our memories.

Brain-Based Learning Activity 6.4 – Deep Processing

Students often confuse deep processing with hours spent looking at the textbook. To emphasize the importance not only of the amount of encoding but also the variety of approaches, present the following exercise:

> Pick a concept from the chapter (chunking, 3 stage model) and write it on the board. Make sure that each student has a basic grasp of its meaning.

Then challenge the students to generate a list of ALL the ways that this concept could be taught or remembered. The more creative the suggestions the better.

> Examples include but are not limited to:

> Write it down; read it out loud; teach it to a buddy; draw it as a picture; make it into a song; create a mindmap; act it as a mime; generate three examples from your work; generate three examples from your home; create a symbol or series of symbols for it; invent a headline for a newspaper article about it, or a best selling book on the concept etc.

This is an excellent tie in to discuss multiple intelligences and diverse learning styles. The list illustrates that different students have different preferences and levels of familiarity with these approaches.

Brain-Based Learning Activity 6.5 – Movies and Memory

As a homework project students can rent videos such as: Total Recall, Rashomon, Dead Again, Groundhog Day, The Matrix, or similar movies which question the ability to remember or the ability to distinguish virtual reality (illusionary memory?) from actual reality.

After viewing one of these videos students would write a short reaction paper addressing the following issues:

> What did the movie teach about memory?
> What was the most important cognitive understanding you gained?
> What was the most important emotional understanding you gained?

Handout 6.1 – Brain-Based Learning

Comparing Memory Techniques

	Advantages	Disadvantages	Other Factors	Example
Peg Method				
Loci Method				
Substitute Word				
SQ4R				

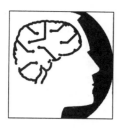

Critical Thinking

Critical Thinking Exercise 6.1 - Applying Knowledge to New Situations: Remembering Names

It is widely known that learning and remembering names is an important social asset, yet many students (and instructors) report that this is one of their poorest skills. Given the focus of this chapter, it would be appropriate to offer students specific help in remembering names. The ability to transfer new information to other concepts is also an important critical thinking skill.

Time: Approximately 20 minutes.

Part I: Invite seven students who don't know each other to the front of the room. Casually introduce the seven students to the class, or have each student introduce himself or herself. Announce that they will participate in a short-term memory experiment. Have the student volunteers take turns counting backwards from 100 by threes (the first student says "100," the second student says "97," the third "94," and so on). When the last student finishes, ask all seven students to write down the names of the other six. Also ask the class to write down each student's name. Tally the results of the seven volunteers and compare their scores to a show of hands from the rest of the class. Ask for specific "memory techniques" from those students who had the highest scores.

Discussion: Ask students why you had the student volunteers count backwards after they had introduced themselves? Once they offer the correct answer (to introduce a type of interference), offer other examples of interference and why they might want to improve their memory for names. For example, most people have great difficulty when they walk into an interview or a party where they are introduced to several people at one time. Remind them that with practice they can learn how to recognize and remember the names of a large number of people in a short period of time. This can even help them possibly land an important job or an important friendship or date!

Part II: With the seven students still remaining in front of the class, ask each student to restate his or her name, and this time provide specific suggestions for how to remember each student volunteer:

1. Make a visual, "bizarre" association. This forces one to pay attention to the name and tags it with a memorable association. If a student had the name *Brook Matthews*, for example, you could encourage students to visualize a flowing brook with a "mattress" (for Matthews) floating down the brook. Some names are easier than others (e.g., Richard Baker, Robin Barnard, etc.), but reassure students that it gets easier with practice. Ask students for suggestions of visual, bizarre associations for the names of the remaining six student volunteers.

2. Choose an outstanding facial feature. Every face has distinctive features. Point out flattering facial features of some of the volunteers. If possible, tie this feature in with the name. If Brook Matthews happens to have long, flowing hair, you could encourage the students to visualize her "flowing" hair flowing down the brook.

3. *Practice and repetition.* Encourage students to repeat immediately the person's name after they first hear it (either aloud or to themselves) and then to practice working it into the conversation whenever possible.

If time allows, ask for other volunteers from the class and show students that it is possible to learn 30 or 40 names within 15 or 20 minutes. Even if you are not adept at this yourself, you can "model" open mindedness and the willingness to practice the learning of a new skill. The more you practice this skill, the easier it becomes. One of our colleagues is so proficient that he learns the names of all students in his class (30-40) within the first ten or 15 minutes of the first class meeting. He uses this demonstration as a powerful introduction to the course and the benefits of taking psychology. While many of us may never reach this particular level of expertise, it does help to show students that we are willing to practice and work at learning new skills.

Discussion: This activity provides a good lead-in to a discussion of both short-term and long-term memory. After demonstrating the learning of names, you can discuss the seven-item capacity of short-term memory and relate it to the number of students chosen for the demonstration. Then proceed with your own lecture on this topic.

This exercise also appears in the text, Chapter 6. We include it here for your convenience, and you may want to discuss it in class to reinforce reading of the text.

Critical Thinking Exercise 6.2 - Practicing Reflective Thinking: Exploring Your Memories

Reflective thinking, also known as recursive thinking, is the ability to review and analyze your own mental processes--to "think about thinking." Reflective thinking is an important component of critical thinking. It allows you to examine your thoughts and cognitive strategies and to evaluate their appropriateness and accuracy. In the context of this chapter, we could employ reflective thinking to evaluate the processes used in recalling memories.

To practice reflective thinking,

1. Take out a clean sheet of paper and write down all you can remember about the first day of your introductory psychology course. What did you do from the minute you entered the room that day? What did the professor say or do? Write down only the things you can remember in vivid detail, not those you "think" you remember.

2. Now compare your memories with your classmates'. Are your memories exactly the same? Are some personal and some shared? Do you remember only the ordinary first-day happenings, or do you remember any unusual occurrences? Do you remember any feelings or emotions? What do you remember that your classmates do not? Do additional memories come flooding back when triggered by others' recollections?

3. By exploring your memories and those of your classmates, you can see how memories are stored and organized in your brain. Most people do not remember things in vivid detail. Most often memories are more general, allowing you to fill in the details according to how you "think" the memory should have been rather than providing all the details for you.

4. Finally, try to recall an older memory, a vivid memory from your childhood. Write down as much detail as you can and then try to evaluate which part of that memory is likely to be factual and which part of that memory is reconstructed. You may find it necessary to ask your parents or old friends to verify the accuracy of these memories. But it is unlikely that even your most vivid childhood memories are a perfectly accurate representation of the past.

This exercise also appears in the Student Study Guide, Chapter 6. We include it here for your convenience, and you may want to discuss it in class to reinforce use of the Student Study Guide.

Critical Thinking Exercise 6.3

Using the Substitute Word System for Remembering Names

Now that you have learned the substitute word system, it can help improve your memory for names. Try converting a person's name into a visual image that will act as a memory retrieval cue.

Some names, like Sandy Storm, are easily visualized. However, you can also use this system with more common names, like "Brewster." Ask yourself, "Are there any words I can visualize that sound like the name?" If not, break the name into parts and imagine substitutes for them. For example, for the name "Brewster," substitute the word "rooster" or divide it into "brew" and "stir." With "rooster," imagine a big rooster with the facial features of the person named "Brewster." For "brew" and "stir," you might visualize a large mug of beer being stirred by an oar. Each of the images you choose should be absurd, exaggerated, or as distinctive as possible. The idea is to form a lasting *image.*

For practice, use the substitute word system and create corresponding vivid images for the following names: George Washington, Plato, Pearl Bailey, Heather Locklear, and Ricky Martin.

Critical Exercise 6.4 - <u>Gathering Data</u> (A Behavioral Skill)

Collecting up-to-date, relevant information is an important component of critical thinking. To help build this skill, as well as to gain important insights into memory strategies, try the following:

a. Interview three classmates who do well on exams and that you believe have good memories. Ask about their study techniques and test taking strategies. Using the examples found in Appendix B of this study guide, ask which technique they find most useful? Now interview three classmates or friends who complain about their college grades and poor memories. Compare their study techniques and test taking strategies to those who remember well. What are the differences?

b. Interview three people who have taken a reading improvement or speed-reading course. What methods were taught that increased reading speed and comprehension? What changes have they noticed in their college grades or exam performances since taking the course? Did they use any of the techniques or mnemonics discussed in the text?

Gender and Cultural Diversity

Gender and Cultural Diversity Activity 6.1 - Oral Tradition and Narrative

Objective: To determine how oral-tradition cultures affect memory strategies as compared to memory strategies of cultures using written materials.

Materials: Invite an individual from Native American studies to speak of his or her oral tradition. (Audiotapes of such narratives may be substituted if you cannot arrange a speaker.)

Procedure: Inform your students that a guest speaker will be visiting the class. This speaker will be a storyteller, and they will have the opportunity to both listen to the stories and question the speaker on the memory strategies employed in the process of learning and reciting the narrative.

Conclusion: It is possible that many of your students will have had little or no experience with cultures that rely on narrative tradition rather than written material. This activity exposes these students to a new view of the world, via the storyteller's skills of memory and narrative. It also provides the students with the opportunity to recognize the value of these skills and to appreciate the narrative tradition as a valid, valuable method of cultural transmission.

Writing Project

Writing Project 6.1

Given the need for improved writing skills in college students and to respond to the call for "writing across the curriculum," we offer writing projects for each chapter. In Chapter 6, we suggest a 2-3 page written response to one of the issues found on Handout 6.2. Recognizing the time involved in grading such writing projects, one alternative is occasionally to assign "peer grading." Collect the papers, remove student names, and assign each student a paper to grade. It helps to make their participation in peer grading a required part of the overall points for the writing project. This encourages a more thoughtful and responsible evaluation, as well as acknowledging and rewarding the additional work.

The discussion questions for this chapter and the lecture lead-ins may also provide interesting topics for student writing projects.

Handout 6.1- Writing Project

You are to write a 2 to 3 page response to one or all of the following topics:

1. After completing Chapter 6, can you appreciate the connection between *chunking* and "academic jargon?" Do you see how giving a complex concept a technical term (academic jargon) helps facilitate storage and retrieval? What advantages can technical terms be expected to have on the ability to store information in short-term memory? Long-term memory?

2. Explain how "state-dependent memory" may lead to an escalation of conflicts. Can you see any advantages to this phenomenon? Describe the major advantages and disadvantages.

3. Write a brief "pro" and "con" argument for and against the use of hypnosis in retrieving blocked or repressed memories. Would you be willing to be hypnotized to explore possible forgotten memories? Why or why not?

4. Write a brief paper describing your current study habits and how you plan to change these habits to incorporate the information found in this chapter.

Circle of Quality – Chapter 6

Please give us your feedback. We thank you in advance for assisting us in improving the next edition. The contact information is listed in the preface.

What are the three most helpful teaching tools in this chapter?

1.

2.

3.

What are the three least useful teaching tools in this chapter?

1.

2.

3.

What are the three most difficult concepts to teach in this chapter?

1.

2.

3.

Additional Comments:

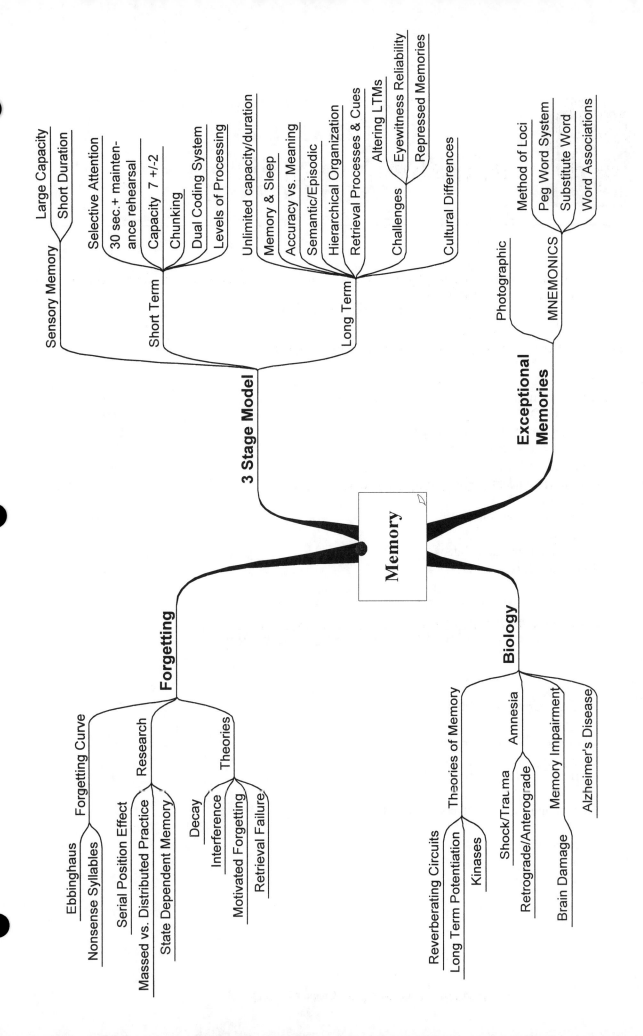

Memory

3 Stage Model

Sensory Memory
- Large Capacity
- Short Duration

Short Term
- Selective Attention
- 30 sec.+ mainten-ance rehearsal
- Capacity 7 +/-2
- Chunking
- Dual Coding System
- Levels of Processing

Long Term
- Unlimited capacity/duration
- Memory & Sleep
- Accuracy vs. Meaning
- Semantic/Episodic
- Hierarchical Organization
- Retrieval Processes & Cues
- Challenges
  - Altering LTMs
  - Eyewitness Reliability
  - Repressed Memories
- Cultural Differences

Exceptional Memories

Photographic

MNEMONICS
- Method of Loci
- Peg Word System
- Substitute Word
- Word Associations

Forgetting

Research
- Forgetting Curve
  - Ebbinghaus
  - Nonsense Syllables
- Serial Position Effect
- Massed vs. Distributed Practice
- State Dependent Memory

Theories
- Decay
- Interference
- Motivated Forgetting
- Retrieval Failure

Biology

Theories of Memory
- Reverberating Circuits
- Long Term Potentiation
- Kinases

Amnesia
- Shock/Trauma
- Retrograde/Anterograde

Memory Impairment
- Brain Damage
- Alzheimer's Disease

CHAPTER 7
THINKING, LANGUAGE, AND INTELLIGENCE

Outline

Thinking

How Do We Think?
Concepts
Problem Solving
Creativity

Research Highlight
Electronic Brainstorming

Active Learning
Solving Everyday Problems

Language

Language and Thought
Animals and Language

Intelligence and Intelligence Testing

Intelligence Defined
Measuring Intelligence
IQ Tests

Gender and Cultural Diversity
The Bell Curve Debate

Differences in Intelligence
Brain Efficiency
Heredity versus Environment

GOAL

Learning Objectives

Upon completion of CHAPTER 7, the student will be able to:

1. Define cognition and thinking (pp. 252-253).
2. Describe the dual-coding hypothesis for information processing; discuss the use of mental imagery and propositions in cognition (pp. 253-254).
3. Define concepts, and explain the hypothesis-testing theory and prototype theory for concept formation (pp. 254-256).
4. List and describe the three stages of problem-solving, including an explanation of the types of thinking that occur in each stage (pp. 257-259).
5. List and describe the two major barriers to problem-solving; discuss the role of incubation in overcoming these barriers (pp. 260-262).
6. Define creativity, and discuss how each of the following is related to the creative process: brainstorming, convergent and divergent thinking, and the investment theory of creativity (pp. 262-266).
7. Define human language and explain why it is different than other patterns of communication used by non-humans (p. 266).
8. Define and provide an example of each of the following building blocks of language: phonemes, morphemes, grammar, syntax, semantics, and pragmatics (pp. 267-268).
9. Describe the reference, definitional, and prototype theories for language comprehension (pp. 269).
10. Describe the research on teaching language to animals, and summarize each side of the "animal language" debate (pp. 269-271).
11. Explain why intelligence is difficult to define, and differentiate between Cattell's fluid and crystallized intelligence (pp. 271-273)
12. Describe Gardner's theory of multiple intelligences and Sternberg's triarchic theory of successful intelligence. State the textbook's definition of intelligence (pp. 273-275).
13. Define standardization, reliability, and validity, and explain why each is important for intelligence testing (pp. 275-277).
14. Explain how an intelligence quotient (IQ) is determined and differentiate between the Stanford-Binet Intelligence Test, the Wechsler intelligent tests, and group IQ tests (pp. 277-280).
15. Describe how IQ tests can be abused or misused, and discuss the factors that can influence IQ scores (pp. 280-281).
16. Describe the effects of age on intelligence, and discuss the extremes of mental retardation and mental giftedness (pp. 282-283).
17. Explain the concepts of brain efficiency and neural pruning in relationship to intelligence (pp. 284-285).
18. Discuss the effects of heredity and the environment on intellectual development, including a summary of the Minnesota Study of Twins Reared Apart and its impact on the nature versus nurture debate regarding IQ (pp. 285-286).

Chapter Summary/Lecture Organizer

Introductory Vignette--The chapter begins with selected journal entries from a young lady traveling abroad in Italy. She goes from being excited by the challenge of learning a new language to becoming bewildered, confused and frustrated in trying to meet that challenge. The story is used to introduce the student to a large repertoire of behaviors, which include feelings, motivations, attitudes, social interactions, learning strategies, and thinking processes.

I.   **THINKING** - Thinking is a component of cognition, which is the process of coming to know. Cognition involves the gathering and processing of information and includes sensation, perception, learning, and memory, which have been discussed in previous chapters; and thinking, language, and problem solving, which are discussed in this chapter. Thinking involves using knowledge that has been gathered and processed; mentally manipulating concepts and images to perform such mental activities as reasoning, solving problems, producing and understanding language, and making decisions.

   A. How Do We Think? - Controversy exists regarding how we think, but the latest evidence supports the dual-coding hypothesis. According to this theory, information is encoded into two separate but interacting systems: a mental imagery system for concrete items and pictures and a verbal system for abstract ideas and spoken and written words. Mental images are mental representations of objects and events. Research in the areas of mental rotation and relative size and shape of objects demonstrates the similarity of real objects and mental representations of them.

   B. Concepts - A concept is a mental structure used to categorize things that share similar characteristics (or attributes), including such things as color, shape, and size that can change from one stimulus to another. According to the hypothesis-testing theory, we learn new things by focusing on some attribute and formulating a hypothesis, which we then go on to test. If the hypothesis is wrong, we try other hypotheses focusing on different attributes. A second explanation for how we learn is the prototype theory, which suggests that when confronted with a new item, we compare it to a prototype of that concept.

   C. Problem Solving - Problem solving is defined as a series of thinking processes we use to reach a goal that is not readily attainable. The three major steps in problem solving are preparation, production, and evaluation:

      1. Preparation - As the first step, preparation involves identifying given facts, distinguishing relevant from irrelevant facts, and defining the ultimate goal.

      2. Production - During the production stage, possible solutions, called hypotheses, are generated. There are two major procedures for generating hypotheses--by using algorithms and heuristics. Algorithms are problem-solving strategies that always eventually lead to a solution. They often involve trying out random solutions to a problem in a systematic manner (e.g., 2 x 10 = 2 + 2 + 2...all the way to 10). Heuristics are rules of thumb or educated guesses developed from previous experience that involve selective searches for appropriate solutions to problems. Heuristics generally, but not always, leads to a solution. The three most valuable heuristics are means-end analysis, working backward, and creating sub-goals.

    3. Evaluation - The final step in problem solving, evaluation, involves appraising hypotheses to see whether they satisfy the conditions of the goal as it was defined in the preparation stage.

Barriers to problem solving include problem-solving set (only using methods that have worked in the past rather than trying new ones) and functional fixedness (the tendency to see only familiar uses for well-known objects). Setting aside a "time out," or incubation period, sometimes allows facts and possibilities to come into better focus, and leads to successful solutions to problems.

D. Creativity - Creativity is the ability to originate new or unique solutions to a problem that are also practical and useful. Guilford has identified two distinct types of creative thinking: convergent, where the person works toward a single solution to a problem; and divergent, in which the person tries to generate as many solutions as possible. Brainstorming is an example of divergent thinking.

    Research Highlight: Electronic Brainstorming – a short review on advantages of anonymous electronic brainstorming over the normal face to face group brainstorming.

    Active Learning: Solving Everyday Problems - The critical thinking exercise allows students to practice the three major problem solving strategies (algorithms and heuristics) and three specific heuristics (means-end analysis, working backward, and creating sub-goals).

II.   LANGUAGE

A. Language and Thought - Human language is a creative form of expression whereby people share ideas, information, and feelings with others by putting together sounds and symbols according to specialized rules. Phonemes are the basic speech sounds; they are combined to form morphemes, the smallest meaningful units of language. Phonemes, morphemes, words, and phrases are put together by rules of grammar (syntax and semantics). Syntax refers to the grammatical rules for ordering words in sentences; semantics refers to meaning in language. Whenever we use language, we take pragmatics into account--the appropriateness of the message, the vocabulary, sentence structure, and delivery to the intended audience and situation. Noam Chomsky believes that humans are born with an ability to put words together in a meaningful way. He also believes that every sentence has both a surface structure (the words themselves) and a deep structure (the actual meaning).

B. Animals and Language - Researchers have investigated animals' ability to learn human or human like language. The most successful of these studies have been done with apes using American Sign Language. In another successful study, dolphins were taught to comprehend sentences that varied in syntax and meaning. Although many psychologists believe that animals can truly learn a human language, skeptics suggest that the animals are being trained merely to respond for rewards.

III.   INTELLIGENCE

A. Intelligence Defined - There are numerous definitions for intelligence. Charles Spearman viewed intelligence as "g," a general cognitive ability; L. L. Thurstone viewed it as seven distinct mental abilities; J. P. Guilford viewed it as 120 or more separate abilities; and, Raymond Cattell viewed it as two types of "g"--fluid intelligence and crystallized intelligence. Contemporary theorist, Howard Gardner, identified eight different types of intelligence and suggested that teaching and assessing should take into account people's learning styles and cognitive strengths. Robert Sternberg, another contemporary theorist, developed a triarchic theory, which emphasizes the thinking process rather than the end product (the answer). Triarchic theory suggests there are three separate but related aspects of intelligence--the internal components, the use of these components to adapt to environmental changes, and the application of past experience to real-life situations. The text defines intelligence as the cognitive abilities employed in acquiring, remembering, and using knowledge of one's culture to solve everyday problems and readily to adapt to and function in both changing and stable environments.

B. Measuring Intelligence - In order for any test, including an IQ test, to be useful, it is necessary for the test to be standardized, reliable, and valid. Standardization is the process of giving a test to a large number of people in order for the norms for the test to be developed. Standardization also refers to the requirement that procedures for administering the test must be formalized so that all people who administer the test do so in exactly the same way. Reliability is a measure of the stability of test scores over time. Good tests will return similar scores when given to the same person at different times. Validity refers to how well the test measures what it is intended to measure. An IQ test is considered valid if it predicts grades in school.

C. IQ Tests - IQ tests do not, and are not intended to, measure overall intelligence; rather, they are designed to measure verbal and quantitative abilities needed for school success. There are several individual IQ tests, the major ones being the Stanford-Binet, and the Wechsler. The Stanford-Binet measures primarily verbal abilities of children aged three to sixteen. Although the Stanford-Binet also has sub-scales that can measure adults, most often adult IQ scores are measured using the Wechsler Adult Intelligence Scale. There are actually three separate Wechsler intelligence scales, each designed to test distinct age levels, and each designed to measure both verbal and nonverbal abilities. There are also many group IQ tests. The group IQ tests with which your students are probably most familiar are the SAT and the ACT. Both of these tests are given to incoming college freshmen in hopes of predicting grades in college.

> **Gender and Cultural Diversity: The Bell Curve Debate -** Many things can influence a score on an IQ test, including environment and heredity. The gender and cultural diversity section explores the controversial book--The Bell Curve by Hernstein and Murray. The problem of African-Americans and other minorities scoring lower than whites on IQ tests is discussed. Lowered school success for many children can be traced to lack of school readiness and language barriers. Governmental programs such as Head Start combat these problems by providing early education for low-income children.

D. Differences in Intelligence - As we age, there is no overall decline in intellectual abilities except for the speed in which we perform these abilities and the speed required to acquire new knowledge. The concepts of giftedness and retardation are discussed. People with IQs of 70 and below are identified as mentally retarded, while people with IQs of 140 and above are identified as gifted.

E. Brain Efficiency - Brain efficiency refers to the amount of energy used by the brain to solve problems. The more efficient brain uses less energy to solve the same problem than the less efficient brain. Brain efficiency may be due to neural pruning--the decrease in the number of synapses after age five.

F. Heredity versus Environment - According to the largest twin study ever done, the Minnesota Study of Twins Reared Apart, heredity and environment appear to be equally important factors in intellectual development. Heredity equips each of us with innate capacities, but environment significantly influences whether an individual will reach full potential.

Teaching Resources

SECTION I - THINKING

Learning Objectives #'s 1 - 6
Lecture Lead-Ins # 1
Discussion Questions # 1
Active Learning Activities #'s 7.1-7.7
Brain-Based Learning #'s 7.1, 7.2

SECTION II - LANGUAGE

Learning Objectives #'s 7 - 10
Lecture Lead-Ins #'s 2,3
Lecture Extenders # 7.1
Discussion Questions # 1

Active Learning Activities #'s 7.2, 7.8

SECTION III - INTELLIGENCE AND INTELLIGENCE TESTING

Learning Objectives #'s 11- 18
Lecture Lead-Ins # 4
Discussion Questions #'s 3, 4, 5
Active Learning Activities #'s 7.9 - 7.11
Brain-Based Learning #7.3
Critical Thinking Exercise # 7.1
Gender and Cultural Diversity Activity # 7.1
Writing Project #7.1

Lecture Lead-Ins

1.   Students are often familiar with the problem of *functional fixedness*, the inability to see unusual uses for objects. To illustrate what might be called "functional flexibility," read the following edited version of a letter written to Dear Abby:

Following the eruption of Mt. St. Helens in 1980, many automobile engines were stalled due to obstruction of the air filter by the fine volcanic ash. One ["functionally flexible"] motorist removed the clogged filter, covered the air intake with a pair of pantyhose and continued on. A highway patrolman stopped the driver asking how he could keep going when all other cars were stalled. He explained what he had done and how he shook the ashes from the pantyhose each time the engine stopped. The highway patrol quickly added pantyhose to all squad cars.

Ask students for examples from their own lives of both functional fixedness and "functional flexibility." This usually generates a great deal of discussion and enthusiasm and provides a nice lead-in to the chapter.

2.   In the Writing Project for Chapter 6, we mentioned that one of the advantages of learning technical terms ("academic jargon") was that it allowed *chunking,* which in turn facilitates storage and retrieval of memories. As a lead-in to this chapter, ask students if learning a second language might affect *chunking* or other processes involved in the storage and retrieval of memories? What effect might it have on the way we think and solve problems? Ask students who are bilingual to volunteer their experiences and thoughts.

3.   Most colleges and universities have a foreign language requirement for graduation. Is this a good idea? Why or why not? What are the advantages to bilingualism or multilingualism? In what ways might bilingualism or multilingualism increase thinking and creativity? Are there any disadvantages?

4.   Read the following quote:

"...the borderline feeble minded...(are) very common among the Spanish-Indian and Mexican families of the Southwest and also among the Negroes. Their dullness seems to be racial...Children of this group should be segregated in special classes...They cannot master abstractions, but they can often be made efficient workers. There is no possibility at the present of convincing society that they should not be allowed to reproduce, although from a eugenic point of view they constitute a grave problem because of their unusual prolific breeding"
                    Lewis B. Terman, creator of the Stanford-Binet IQ Test

Ask students to discuss this quote. It surprises many students (and instructors) to find that the originator of one of the major IQ tests had such a belief. How might these beliefs have affected the development of the Stanford-Binet and its results? Use their responses as a lead-in to intelligence lectures or the general chapter topics.

Lecture Extenders

7.1 - Intelligence

The textbook refers to Gardner's theory of multiple intelligences, naming the various components proposed by Gardner. Since Gardner has a well-developed rationale for his identification of these different abilities, it seems that a more in-depth discussion is merited. The material for this discussion is taken from Gardner's book, Frames of Mind: The Theory of Multiple Intelligences (1983).

Gardner feels that the present psychometric approach to intelligence does not do justice to the broad array of competencies that characterize human beings. Part of the reason for this omission is the context in which the original IQ test was developed--in the educational domain. In contrast, Gardner, who has had a strong interest in neurological functioning, has tried to incorporate data from those who have brain damage, those who are diagnosed as autistic, and those who have been pronounced as geniuses in selected areas. He also acknowledges the contribution of Piaget's approach to intelligence along with some of the ideas from other cognitive theorists.

Gardner lists one prerequisite for an ability to be labeled as sufficiently important to qualify as an intelligence: It must be essential for the solving of important problems and it must allow a person to gain new knowledge. If an ability survives this prerequisite, then there are several criteria he imposes. The most important criterion is the independence of this ability; it has to be autonomous of other abilities in terms of a specific location in the brain. Thus, one can have brain damage that interferes with several abilities, leaving this one intact, or one ability can be lost without any effect on the others. A second criterion is that this ability is normally distributed in a population. There will be those who possess an inordinate amount of this ability and others who are deficient. Also, one would expect with independent abilities that most people would show an uneven distribution of these various abilities. It would be a rare individual who would be equally proficient in all areas. There should also be an identifiable core operation or set of operations that identify an ability. For example, two important operations in musical intelligence is the ability to hear pitch and rhythm. Another criterion is an identifiable developmental history for all normal individuals. For example, in linguistic ability, the developmental sequence is from babbling to one-word sentences, and so forth; yet, there are differences in the level of expertise at the end of development. A fifth criterion, which Gardner admits is more difficult to establish, is an evolutionary history: songbirds show some components of musical ability; chimpanzees have fairly well developed bodily-kinesthetic ability as shown by their ability to forage for termites with a stick. Three final criteria are support from experimental psychology and psychometric data and susceptibility to encoding in a symbol system. The last criterion is important since culture cannot utilize knowledge or intelligence that is not shared through a common symbol system.

Linguistic intelligence is one of the intelligences that has received attention from all psychometricians. It plays a prominent role in both the Stanford-Binet and the Wechsler tests. Gardner identifies four functions of the linguistic system: rhetorical, mnemonic (encodes memories), explanatory (as in books), and metalinguistic (allows one to think about language itself). The two most basic properties are syntax and phonology which for most persons are processed by the left temporal lobe. It has been well documented that this ability can be destroyed, as in aphasia, and yet a person can retain other abilities. The literature on the developmental history is extensive, probably the best known of any of the intelligences.

Musical intelligence is based mainly on pitch and rhythm. This is an ability primarily ascribed to the right hemisphere although there is some alteration of processing as one becomes more musically sophisticated. However, it remains relatively independent of language since damage to one system will leave the other system intact. For example, after becoming aphasic, Maurice Ravel still retained his musical ability. Gardner maintains that of all of the intelligences, this is the one in which precocious ability is the most apt to express itself at a very early age.

Logical-mathematical ability emerges when a person confronts the objects in the world. Although many feel that this ability is related to linguistic ability, Gardner maintains that the auditory-oral route is not the source of this ability (as it is in the linguistic system). Part of his rationale for a separate system is derived from Piagetian descriptions of the development of the principle of conservation in children. Briefly described, a child realizes there is order in objects, that one can perform operations on these objects, predict relationships, and, ultimately, arrive at abstractions about the physical world.

The spatial intelligence is essentially the ability to create mental images. This serves many purposes such as orienting one's self to the environment, reading maps and diagrams, manipulating geometrical forms, and making artistic productions. This is a static manipulation of objects relative to their location rather than an active manipulation as is found in logistic-mathematical ability. This ability, located in the right cerebral hemisphere, is "immune" to accidents that may happen in the linguistic areas and, as is well known, can be developed to an extraordinary degree in individuals who are "poor" in other areas.

The bodily-kinesthetic ability has been downgraded in our society through the tradition of separating mental and physical abilities, but Gardner feels it should be recognized as equal to the other abilities. It provides the basis for skilled movements of the entire body (as in dance and athletics) and for the movement of the hands in working with small objects (as in constructing a radio set).

Social intelligence involves two aspects: self-perception or the ability to access one's own feelings, and social sensitivity, the ability to notice distinctions among others with regard to motivations, attitudes, and other subjective indices. This ability is molded by society since norms for social behavior are embedded in cultural learning. Gardner believes that the most likely physical location for this ability is in the prefrontal lobes since damage in these areas changes personality.

One interesting speculation by Gardner is the way in which the educational system would be changed if the agenda of developing all the intelligences was adopted. While he sees this as desirable, educational leaders may lament further erosion of the time spent on "reading and writing" if the school system is expected to develop the other abilities such as bodily kinesthetic and social intelligence.

Source: Gardner, H. (1983). Frames of mind: The theory of multiple intelligences. New York: Basic Books.

Key Terms

Discussion Questions

1. Infantile amnesia refers to the finding that most of us have few memories prior to acquisition of verbal abilities. Does this suggest that thought is determined by language capabilities? What about the preverbal infant who smiles at the sight of the mother or father? What is he or she thinking?

2. Children of today have far less free time (after-school structured activities, organized sports, and part-time jobs during high school) and far more access to television, computers, and video games. How might the lack of free, unstructured time affect the development and expression of creativity and intelligence? Do computers increase or decrease creativity and intelligence? Do computers affect the way we think and process information?

3. Computer simulations and artificial intelligence (AI) are major research fields in cognition. Can computers think? What differences are there (if any) between what humans call thinking and what computers do? What questions could you ask if you wanted to determine whether you were talking to a computer or a human? Do computers have language capability? Why or why not? Can computers be creative? Why or why not? And the biggest question of all, are computers *intelligent*? Why or why not?

4. Is intelligence testing a useful method of measuring a person's potential for academic achievement? Ask the students if they were an employer would they prefer a highly motivated worker of average intelligence or a worker with average motivation and high intelligence? Ask which they would prefer for a romantic partner? Which would they themselves prefer to be-- highly motivated or highly intelligent? Now, ask whether colleges and universities should base admissions more on SAT and ACT scores or high school grades and activities? Discuss the relative effects of motivation and intelligence on achievement.

5. Should intelligence testing be used to "track" high school students (placing them in college prep versus vocational education courses)? Ask education majors for their opinion on this subject. Ask students who were placed in vocational education courses in high school, but are now in college, how they feel about "tracking." Does this approach damage education as a whole or simply make it more efficient?

 **Web Sites**

Chimpanzee-Human Communication Institute
http://www.cwu.edu/~cwuchci/main.html
Discussions on the efforts that have been made to study language processes in primates. This site provides coverage of the chimp Washoe.

Experiments in Cognition
http://kahuna.psych.uiuc.edu/ipl/cog/level_2_cog.html
This cognitive site offers students the opportunity to take part in several online experiments. Students can assess their own reaction time (simple or complex), can learn about the Stroop effect, and can study the perception of chimeric faces.

Creativity Web
http://www.ozemail.com.au/~caveman/Creative/index.html
This home page focuses on resources and research related to the study of creativity.

Language Sites
http://rampage ss.onramp.net/~world/langlinks.html
This page offers access to lists of sites dealing with language and language study.

Intelligence: Spearman
http://Galton.psych.nwu/GreatIdeas/intelligence/spearman.html
Provides a detailed overview of the science and methods that drove the psychometric view of intelligence. Also details the foundations of the two-factor theory developed by Spearman.

Intelligence: Binet
http://Galton.psych.nwu/GreatIdeas/intelligence/binet.html
Provides information regarding the original Binet intelligence scale, and later derivations up to and including the current version, the Stanford-Binet 4th Edition.

Multiple Intelligences: The Theory
http://208.161.180.245/lSk12mac/gsh/harness/_lib/_reform/edweb/edref_m3.htm
Gives details regarding the origins, current research, and status of the theory of multiple intelligences. Separate pages describe each of the 7 intelligences described by Gardner.

Center for Research on Concepts and Cognition
http://www.cogsci.indiana.edu
A site devoted to cognitive science, it provides links to other sites related to intelligence, as well as offering a contemporary perspective related to experimental findings.

Dolphin Intelligence and the Captivity Issue
http://whales.magna.com.au/POLICIES/levasseur/
It has been suggested that Dolphins are highly intelligent, and some believe that this is compromised when they are in captivity. This site offers information regarding this issue, as well as information regarding the research on Dolphin Intelligence.

Traditional Intelligence in Education
http://edweb.gsn.org/edref.mi.histschl.html
The history of intelligence in academic settings has been consistently associated with increased learned material. This site details the history of this tradition, and where it is heading in the future.

Suggested Films and Videos

The Creative Spirit

Ambrose Video, 1991. 59 minutes. Each program in this four part series blends humor, animation, original music, and on-location action to capture the spirit of emerging innovation and creativity.

Dyslexia: Diagnosis and Therapy

Films for the Humanities and Sciences, 1995. 52 minutes. This program features eight children and adults of different ages who have had their lives severely affected by dyslexia. The video stresses the importance of early recognition and alerts viewers to the signs of dyslexia and possibilities for therapy.

Dyslexia: Diagnosis and Treatment

International University Consortium, 1995. 52 minutes. Video explains exactly what dyslexia is, the many ways it is manifested, the extensive testing needed to make a diagnosis, and the role of heredity. The treatments presented include neurological, psychological, individual adapted language, auditory, reading, and spelling training programs.

Language

Films for the Humanities and Sciences, 1995. 23 minutes. This new video explores the relationship of language abilities and specific areas of the brain. This program examines, from an evolutionary perspective, both human and nonhuman animal language development. New work on communication between humans and animals is presented.

Language and Thinking

Insight Media, 1990. 30 minutes. This program investigates the role of the brain in facilitating and processing language during early childhood. The beginnings of language in infancy and the role of grammar in language development are also discussed. The relationship between language and certain cognitive skills is examined.

Signs of the Apes, Songs of the Whales

PBS Video, 1983. 57 minutes. For your students who are already familiar with Washoe, here is the sequel: Washoe is visited 10 years later. In this excellent NOVA film, language experiments with chimps, gorillas, dolphins, and sea lions are demonstrated. In addition, the complex signals that whales use for communication are explored. This is a truly superb film.

Language Development

Annenberg/CPB, 1990. 30 minutes. This program, hosted by Philip Zimbardo, describes language development from its earliest babbling stages, including the genetic and environmental interaction in language development. Cross-cultural similarities in language development are also presented, as well as social communication issues.

Language

PBS Video, 1990. 30 minutes. Part of "The Mind" series, this excellent video presents the evolution of human language and the phenomenon of speech. It discusses Chomsky's theory of an innate drive for language and demonstrates that linguistic abilities exist even without speech and hearing.

You Must of Been a Bilingual Baby

Filmmakers Library, 1992. 46 minutes. This program investigates how babies become bilingual, how school children fare in immersion programs, and how adults cope with learning a foreign language. The film presents several bilingual families and takes us to a classroom where Spanish- and English-speaking children learn together while developing a sense of pride in their respective cultures.

The Human Voice: Exploring Vocal Paralanguage

U.C. Extension Center (Berkeley),1993. 30 minutes. This WPA award-winning film explores the power and importance of vocal paralanguage. Vocal paralanguage is what our voice reveals about our gender, age, geographic location, level of education, emotional state, and relationship with the person with whom we are speaking.

Intelligence

Insight Media, 1990. 30 minutes. This program shows how hard it is to define and measure intelligence. It describes what intelligence tests are designed to measure, the history of IQ testing, and some of its embarrassing failures. The arguments over whether IQ tests show achievement or aptitude and whether IQ is fixed or changeable are presented.

Testing and Intelligence

Annenberg/CPB, 1990. 30 minutes. From Zimbardo's "Discovering Psychology" series, this video provides excellent coverage of the issues surrounding what intelligence is and how it can be measured by psychologists. The history of IQ testing from Francis Galton to Alfred Binet is presented. The film describes how various tests are constructed and scored to reveal a person's abilities, behavior, and personality. The concepts of validity, reliability, and standardization procedures are discussed. This segment accurately and thoroughly introduces the complex topic of intelligence and testing.

Better Babies--Raising Intellectual Superstars

Filmmakers Library, 1991. 28 minutes. This film documents some early learning programs designed to produce "geniuses." We see parents involved in prenatal education--talking to their unborn babies in the belief that it will accelerate the babies' verbal skills. One toddler's hectic schedule is presented; his mother is teaching him art, music, computers, geography, and Japanese. This is a good discussion starter in your classroom.

Down's Syndrome

Films for the Humanities and Sciences, 28 minutes. This is a specially adapted Phil Donahue program devoted to medical and psychological breakthroughs in the treatment of children with Down's syndrome. Some children demonstrate the progress that has been made in helping children with Down's reach their potential.

Optimizing Intelligences: Thinking, Emotion, and Creativity

National Professional Resources, 1996. 45 minutes. This video presents alternative conceptions of intelligence that challenge the traditional views stemming from I.Q. and learning theory research. These perspectives include Gardner's multiple intelligences, Goleman's emotional intelligence, and the Montessori system of instruction. Implications for schools, mental health facilities, and work environments are also explored.

Race and Intelligence

Insight Media, 1994. 30 minutes. This video examines the accuracy of I.Q. tests and the degree to which cultural variables may affect scores, particularly subcultural influences on some minority groups. The debate over race and intelligence as discussed in Murray and Herrnstein's book *The Bell Curve* is presented. Questions regarding the current political climate's increasing sympathy to the ideas of eugenics and racial superiority are also addressed.

Brain Traps: Problem Solving Skills

Insight Media, 1997. 15 minutes. This video uses a series of problems to be solved to illustrate how normally efficient mental habits can sometimes lead us into "brain traps." The emphasis is on viewing problem solving itself as a skill that must be learned and practiced, and the need to be flexible in adopting new perspectives and strategies when necessary.

Language Development

Films for the Humanities and Sciences, 1996. 40 minutes. This program follows the development of language from infant cries to the relatively competent use of language by grade schoolers. First attempts at communication, the nature of grammatical errors, and the arguments concerning the role of nature versus nurture are discussed. The Whorf-Sapir hypothesis and the question of non-human primates' capacity for language are also addressed.

Growing Minds: Cognitive Development in Early Childhood

Davidson Films, 1996. 25 minutes. This video examines the work of Piaget and Vygotsky as it pertains to the development of reasoning skills, visual perception, and the use of language during the first five years of life. Children are both interviewed and observed while engaged in activities to assess the development of their intellectual capacities.

Unlocking Language

Films for the Humanities and Sciences, 1998. 29 minutes. This video presents discussion by a diverse group of experts on the origins, development, and transmission of the human capacity for language. Topics include the role of evolution, parts of the brain involved in language, the innate capacity for language expressed by infants and toddlers, and the ability of language to express abstract ideas. Also offered for examination are recent endeavors to isolate a speech gene and research regarding language disorders.

Books For Success

Epstein, Seymour with Brodsky, Archie (1993). **You're Smarter Than You Think**. Simon & Schuster. The subtitle says it all: "How to Develop Your Practical Intelligence for Success In Living."

Buzan, Tony with Buzan, Barry (1993). **The Mind Map Book**. Penguin Books USA Inc. From the creator of Mind Maps, the best book on how to use Mind Maps. Excellent illustrations show in detail how Mind Maps have been used with great success in education, and business. A complete guide to this fascinating method to maximize your concentration, memory and creativity .

Gardner, M. (1982). **Aha! Gotcha: Paradoxes to Puzzle and Delight**. Freeman. A book to stretch your thinking while having fun.

Bransford, D. John and Stein, Barry (1993). **The Ideal Problem Solver: A Guide for Improved Thinking, Learning, and Problem Solving.** W.H. Freeman & Co. This book delivers what the title promises. Recommended for students, teachers, home or business settings. It is filled with examples, strategies and exercises.

Active Learning

Active Learning Activity 7.1 - Stroop Effect

In Chapter 2 (**Activity 2.5**), we suggested using the Stroop Effect to demonstrate information processing in the left and right hemispheres of the brain. It helps to bring the transparency back to class for this chapter and repeat the demonstration. Use it in this chapter to emphasize points related to thinking and language processing. You can also point out that this same demonstration has applications to Chapter 3 (differences between sensation and perception) and Chapter 6 (how verbal processing *interferes* with visual processing). Students appreciate hearing connections between chapters. It reassures them that the work they did in earlier chapters helps them later on. As instructors we often *needlessly* worry that repeating similar demonstrations might bore the students. We forget that although we have seen the demonstration many times, our classes have had only one previous exposure. Similarly, we also repeat brief sections from important videos to show connections between chapters. To emphasize the importance of neurotransmitters in Chapter 2, for example, we talk about the role of dopamine in schizophrenia and show "Jerry"--a patient exhibiting all major symptoms, including bizarre behaviors like twirling his hair. When we fully discuss schizophrenia in Chapter 14, we show the same 10 minute video segment. Students are alert and seem pleased by the repeat showing--almost like "Jerry" is an old friend.

Active Learning Activity 7.2 - Analogies

Another way to show connections between chapters, while also demonstrating concepts for Chapter 7, is to discuss problem solving through analogies (Handout 7.1). The text discusses heuristics as a major method for problem solving, and discusses means-end analysis, working backward, and creating subgoals as the three most valuable types of *heuristics*. We like to cover analogies as an additional heuristic, and we like to discuss it right after the Stroop Effect (Activity 7.1) because items in the handout continue the theme of interchapter connections. (Activity 7.5 demonstrates "working backward" one of the text's major heuristics.)

Point out to students that analogies are a common strategy useful both for mastering new concepts and for solving problems. For example, psychology instructors often use the analogy of an iceberg to teach Freud's concept of the conscious, preconscious, and unconscious mind. To problem solve a dead end or "limbo state" relationship, there is an especially helpful analogy from the old movie *Annie Hall*. The main character, Woody Allen, tells Annie Hall "Relationships are like sharks--they have to keep moving or they die. Annie, I think we have a dead shark on our hands." Although initially surprising, many people find comfort knowing that current frustrations with dead end relationships won't last forever--the relationship will either get better or die! Ask students for examples of their favorite analogies from psychology or elsewhere.

To give students practice with analogies (while also reviewing terms from previous chapters), distribute copies of Handout 7.2, give them 5 to10 minutes, and then discuss the answers.

Handout 7.1 – Active Learning

For each question, choose the letter pair (a, b, c, or d) that is most analogous (showing the same relationship).

1. psychology : individuals ::
a. anthropology : cultures
b. sociology : observations
c. biology : physiology
d. economics : theories

2. Wundt : structuralism ::
a. James : evolution
b. Skinner : social learning
c. Freud : unconscious processes
d. Watson : behaviorism

3. correlation : experimentation ::
a. hypothesis : theory
b. ESP : perception
c. relation : causation
d. reliability : validity

4. myelin sheath : axon ::
a. nerve : ganglion
b. flour : bread
c. variable : constant
d. insulation : wire

5. sympathetic : parasympathetic ::
a. operant : classical
b. anterograde : retrograde
c. introspection : observation
d. stimulants : depressants

6. transduction : energy ::
a. sleep : dreaming
b. transmission : neurons
c. learning : memory
d. digestion : food

7. basilar membrane : audition ::
a. smell : olfaction
b. retina : vision
c. figure : ground
d. cortex : brain

8. tolerance : drugs ::
a. suggestion : hypnosis
b. forgetting : memory
c. adaptation : sensation
d. delta wave : sleep

9. algorithm : problem solving ::
a. recipe : cake
b. shoes : feet
c. inductive : deductive
d. syntax : grammar

10. divergent thinking : creativity ::
a. cortex : brain stem
b. cognition : perception
c. water : plants
d. pencil : paper

--------------------------------------*Answers to Handout 7.1*--------------------------------------

1. a	4. d	7. b	10. c
2. d	5. d	8. c	
3. c	6. d	9. a	

Active Learning Activity 7.3 - Problem Solving (Production Stage)--Class Examples

To demonstrate the production stage of problem solving, ask students for examples of ongoing problems in their lives. Ask the class to come up with possible solutions (referred to as "hypotheses" in the text). Remind the class that under normal circumstances, the larger the number of hypotheses generated, the better the chance of solving the problem. You can use this in combination with the concept of "brainstorming" and ask the students to get into groups or work as an entire class to brainstorm possible solutions.

Active Learning Activity 7.4 - Problem Solving (Production Stage--Hypotheses Through Algorithms)

The text mentions two major ways to generate hypotheses during the production stage of problem solving--algorithms and heuristics. To demonstrate **algorithms**, read the following problem:

There are 1025 tennis players participating in a single's elimination tournament. How many matches must be played before there is one winner and 1024 losers?

Allow students 3 to 5 minutes to work on this problem on their own. Remind people who quickly find the solution to give others the joy of "doing it for themselves." (This is also another example of the text and instructor's manual's focus on "hands-on" active learning.) If someone is successful, invite him or her to the front of the room to demonstrate the strategy. (This helps reinforce student interest and group work and illustrates the general teaching strategy of "sharing the stage"--discussed in the preface of the manual.) Point out how this problem and solution demonstrates the problem solving strategy the book calls "algorithms."

Answer: *2 players=1 match, 3 players=2 matches, 4 players=5 matches, and so on. The number of matches required is one less than the number of players, so it will take 1024 matches to select a winner.*

Active Learning Activity 7.5 - Problem Solving (Production Stage--Hypotheses Through Heuristics)

The text mentions two major ways to generate hypotheses during the production stage of problem solving--algorithms and heuristics. To demonstrate "working backward," a major form of **heuristics**, read the following problem to the class:

While three watchmen were guarding an orchard, a thief crept in and stole some apples. During his escape, he met the three watchmen one after the other. In exchange for his freedom, he gave each in turn one-half of the apples he had at that time, plus an extra two. After he had shared his apples with each of the three watchmen, he had one left for himself. How many apples had he stolen originally?

This problem provides an excellent demonstration of the "working backward" strategy discussed in the text. Give students a chance to solve it on their own and in groups.

Answer: (This problem can be solved with or without "resorting" to algebra.) The thief had one apple after sharing with the third watchman. After sharing with the second watchman, he had 6 apples (1/2x-2=1, x=6). After sharing with the first watchman, he had 16 (1/2x-2=6, x=16). Before sharing with the first watchman, he had 36 (1/2x-2=16, x=36). The thief stole 36 apples.

Active Learning Activity 7.6 - Barriers to Problem Solving--The Restaurant Dilemma

Read the following problem to the class:

> Three friends went to a restaurant for lunch. The bill came to $30.00, so each paid $10.00 to the waiter, who left to pay the bill. The cashier noticed that the waiter had charged full price for drinks that were at "happy hour" prices. The actual bill should have been $25.00. The waiter gave the diners their $5.00 refund. The happy friends decided they would add $2.00 to a separate tip they had left on the table and each kept one dollar. At this point, one friend noted that with the refund each had paid $9.00 for their lunch, and the waiter received $2.00 in extra tip. Three times nine=$27.00 plus $2.00=$29.00. The friend was now concerned that the waiter had kept an extra dollar. What is wrong with this friend's reasoning?

Ask students to form small groups and discuss the problem. After approximately 3 to 5 minutes, stop the exercise and ask groups to share their problem solving strategies. Tie their responses in to chapter concepts, such as functional fixedness, set, and so on.

*Answer--*There is no "other dollar." The restaurant kept $25.00, the waiter received $2.00, and the diners received $3.00. The last part of the problem suggests that 3 X $9 = $27 plus $2.00 extra tip = $29.00. A proper analysis would restate this as 3 x 9 = $27 MINUS $2.00 extra tip = $25.00--the final amount received by the restaurant.

Intriguing examples of additional problems can be found in books on problem solving, such as Thinking, Problem Solving, Cognition by Richard Mayer or Aha! Gotcha by Martin Gardner.

Active Learning Activity 7.7 - Creativity

Draw a circle on the board. Ask the class to come up with all the things this circle could represent. Using items from traditional tests of creativity, ask students to think of all the uses they can for a brick or paper clip. Ask what could be done with all the hair that is left on the floor of beauty shops and barber shops when people get haircuts? A person was fired ("downsized") from his or her job. List as many good things about this event as you can think. A therapist has a patient with a phobia about birds. Think of as many explanations as you can to account for the patient's fear.

Active Learning Activity 7.8 - Language Activities

Donna Brinton, a language specialist at the University of California, Los Angeles, authored the Handbook for Non-Native Speakers, an OUTSTANDING ancillary written to accompany the text, Psychology in Action. If you do not have a copy, contact your Wiley representative or our publisher (1-800-225-5945). In this handbook, Brinton provides excellent language related exercises for each chapter. We have used exercises from several chapters for in-class activities--they help both non-native and native speakers to master difficult concepts. In relation to the current chapter, the activities in this handbook for Chapter 7 are perfect demonstrations for language concepts.

Active Learning Activity 7.9 - Defining and Testing Intelligence

Ask students to think of the most intelligent person they have ever known. Have them write down several adjectives that describe this person. Put these adjectives on the board and use this to illustrate difficulties in defining and testing intelligence. You can repeat this same process with the term "creativity."

Active Learning Activity 7.10 - Demonstrating IQ Tests

Ask the students if they have ever taken an intelligence test. Most will not remember having taken such tests. Ask if any remember having left their home room in elementary school to take a long test with a different teacher. Some students will remember this test. If your department has copies of official intelligence tests like the Stanford-Binet or Wechsler, bring them to class and *briefly* show some of the subtests (being careful to protect the integrity of the test). After this brief exposure, more students will remember that they have taken an intelligence test. Many will want to discuss their experiences.

Active Learning Activity 7.11 - School Psychologist

Contact your local high school district and ask the school psychologist if he/she would like to come and talk about psychological testing in your class. Many school psychologists are willing to come speak to your classes. This is also a good way to establish connections between the university and high schools.

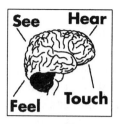

Brain-Based Learning

Brain-Based Learning Activity 7.1 - The Power of Brainstorming

For the first five minutes students sit by themselves with a sheet of paper. They have 5 minutes to write down as many different uses for a brick as they can. Have them count how many uses they proposed. If time permits score the answers not only for frequency but also for originality or diversity of applications.

For the second five minutes the class is formed into 4-5 person groups. Give a brief review of the purpose of brainstorming and the major steps of the process, emphasizing that no criticism is allowed during the initial stage. Encourage each group to come up with as many and as varied suggestions as they can. Their answers can be original - even far out. Only during the evaluation phase should they eliminate completely unworkable ideas. This time, their task is to come up with as many uses for a tire as they can. They have 5 minutes total for idea generation and idea selection. Score the answers for frequency and creativity.

Ask the students to compare the two processes. Which one did they enjoy more and why? Which process produced better answers and why? Finally, ask them where in their lives they could apply what they have learned here.

Brain-Based Learning Activity 7.2 - The Challenge of Visualization

Materials Needed: Each student should have several sheets of art paper in front of him/her.

Show them a completed Origami figure (I recommend a relatively simple form to begin with). Tell them you made it in a couple of minutes from a similar sheet of paper as is in front of them. Set your figure up high on a pedestal and challenge the students to visualize by what series of movements the sheet will be transformed into the object.

Give them a couple of minutes to think about it and then encourage them to try their solutions for the next three minutes. After the winning students are rewarded with applause, guide everyone through the process step by step using either a book or even better one of several good computer programs that display folding instructions right on the screen.

If the students are catching on, you could show them a second, slightly more advanced Origami figure. Be sure to instruct the students to not only follow the instructions, but to observe the process of their own mental processing as they attempt to fold the Origami example.

Brain-Based Learning Activity 7.3 - What is Intelligence?

Ask your students to think of the three smartest persons they have known (other than yourself) and to write down what qualities they have in common.

Then form them into 4-5 person groups and have each group together write a list of what makes a person intelligent. After a few minutes the groups compare their lists and the class can jointly compile a master list. As the blackboard slowly fills up with traits, qualities and examples announce to each student that they are in charge of constructing an IQ test, but that time and money limits in the real world force them to use ONLY THREE of the items listed on the board. Which ones would they pick? How confident do they feel of the results? Could they come up with a test that uses all of what is on the board?
This forces the students to see how difficult it is to come up with a measure that is practical and yet comprehensive.

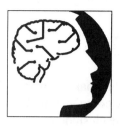

Critical Thinking

Critical Thinking Exercise 7.1 - Exploring Your Own Thinking Processes: A Test for Critical Thinkers

Throughout this text we have provided various exercises to foster critical thinking skills. In this chapter on thinking and intelligence, we felt that readers might be interested in a brief test of their overall critical thinking abilities--Handout 7.1 (adapted from Moore and Parker, 1989 and Ruggiero, 1988). The higher your score, the higher your critical thinking skills.

This exercise also appears in the text, Chapter 7. We include it here for your convenience, and you may want to discuss it in class to reinforce reading of the text.

Critical Thinking Exercise 7.2 - Using a Variety of Approaches in Problem Solving

Critical thinking includes the ability to take different approaches to problem solving. This exercise presents you with an opportunity to try a number of approaches on some everyday problems.

The major problem-solving approaches discussed in this chapter were the algorithmic approach, which involves generating possible solutions using some systematic procedure, and the heuristics approach, which involves generating possible solutions based on previous knowledge and experience.

We discussed three specific heuristics approaches: means-end analysis, working backward, and creating subgoals.

Below you will find six real-world problems, some of which you may have encountered in your own life. For each problem: (1) write down your solution to the problem; (2) identify the approach you took as algorithmic or means-end analysis, working backward, or creating subgoals; and (3) see if you can generate a different solution to the problem by using one of the other approaches.

1. Your car has broken down and is in need of major repairs. You have a final exam tomorrow morning at 8:00, so you have to get to school which unfortunately is 20 miles away. How will you get there?

2. You are having a party for 30 friends. What kind of food and drink will you serve?

3. You wake up early one morning to find a steady stream of rain water leaking through your bedroom ceiling. You must stop the leak as fast as possible. How will you do it?

4. The Internal Revenue Service has just notified you that, according to its records, you owe several

hundred dollars in back taxes and interest. You need to find your tax records from three years ago and recheck the numbers to prove that you filed an accurate return.

5. It has been weeks since you've had a good night's sleep because of your new neighbors' barking dog. You need your sleep. How are you going to ensure that you get it?

6. You want to find a gentle, considerate way to tell your girlfriend or boyfriend that the relationship is over.

This exercise also appears in the Student Study Guide, *Chapter 7. We include it here for your convenience, and you may want to discuss it in class to reinforce use of the Student Study Guide.*

Critical Thinking Exercise 7.3 -

EXERCISE I

The text describes two major ways to generate hypotheses during the production stage of problem solving—algorithms and heuristics.

To improve your algorithm strategy, try the following:

There are 1025 tennis players participating in a single's elimination tournament. How many matches must be played before there is one winner and 1024 losers?

To work on your skill in "working backwards" (a type of heuristic), try this problem:

While three watchmen were guarding an orchard, a thief crept in and stole some apples. During his escape, he met the three watchmen one after the other. In exchange for his freedom, he gave each one-half of the apples he had at the time, plus an extra two. After he had shared his apples with each of the three watchmen, he had one left for himself. How many apples had he stolen originally?

Answers can be found at the end of this study guide chapter.

Handout 7.1 - Critical Thinking

A Test For Critical Thinkers

Place a check mark next to each item that you believe is true (most of the time) of your personal thinking patterns.

_____I think for myself and am not easily manipulated by others.

_____I recognize my own values and perspectives, and I can talk insightfully about the influences on my beliefs.

_____I do not simply accept conclusions; I evaluate and critique the underlying reasons.

_____I recognize irrelevant facts and false assumptions, and I discount them.

_____I am able to consider the strengths and weaknesses of my own point of view and that of opposing positions.

_____I admit my tendency toward egocentrism and my capacity for self-deception; and I work to overcome them.

_____I am able to distinguish what I know from what I don't know; and I am not afraid when "I don't know."

_____I am willing to consider all available information when working on problems or making decisions; and I am also flexible and willing to try any good idea whether it has been done before or not.

_____When evaluating the behavior of myself and others, I am conscious of the standards I use, and I am especially concerned with the consequences of actions.

_____I am a good questioner. I like to probe deeply into issues, to dig down to root ideas, to find out what's really going on.

_____I am comfortable being questioned, and I do not become defensive, confused, or intimidated. I welcome good questions since they help to clarify my thinking.

_____I am a critical reader. I read with healthy skepticism, while reserving judgment until I fully understand the author's perspective.

EXERCISE II

Metacognition   (A Cognitive Skill)

Metacognition, also known as reflective or recursive thinking, involves a review and analysis of your own mental processes-- thinking about your own thinking. Below is a problem that involves this type of active learning. Take a few minutes and work on it.

Problem

There is a bird, Tweety, that likes to perch on the roof of Casey Jones, a locomotive that travels the 200-mile route from Cucamonga to Kalamazoo. As Casey Jones pulls out from Cucamonga, the bird takes to the air and flies to Kalamazoo, the train's destination. Because the train travels at only 50 mph whereas the bird travels at 100 mph, Tweety reaches Kalamazoo before the train and finds that it has nowhere to perch. So the bird flies back to the train and finds it still moving, whereupon Tweety flies back to Kalamazoo, then back to the train, and so on until Casey Jones finally arrives in Kalamazoo, where the bird finally rests on the locomotive's roof. How far has the bird flown?

This exercise helps apply what you've learned in your textbook about steps involved problem solving. To review these steps, fill in the name of the step, then describe the processes you used during each step in solving the above problem. Make sure you include the following terms, if applicable: algorithm   creating sub-goals   evaluation   goal   heuristics
                   hypothesis   incubation   preparation   production

Step 1: _____
Procedure: _____

_____

_____

_____

Step 2: _____
Procedure: _____

_____

_____

_____

Step 3: _____
Procedure: _____

_____

Gender and Cultural Diversity

Gender and Cultural Diversity Activity 7.1

Objective: Examining gender stereotypes and their relationship to perceptions of intelligence.

Materials: A checklist of objectives which might describe stereotypical views of male and female roles in America.

Procedures: Divide your class into small groups (4-6 members each). Ask each group to make separate lists of the top five traits of an intelligent adult, an intelligent man, and an intelligent woman. Ask two or three groups to put their results on the board. Surprisingly enough, there will be a noticeable difference between the three lists. Now pass around Handout 7.1. This is a list of traits found by Broverman et al., (1970) that clinicians reported as being associated with a "mentally healthy adult male" and a "mentally healthy adult female." Compare your class's list of traits for intelligence to this list. Place check marks next to those traits found on both lists.

Discussion: Ask students to explore the implications of their gender expectations. You'll find that they have lots to say on this matter.

Source: Broverman, I. K., Broverman, D. M., Clarkson, F. E., Rosenfrantz, P., & Vogel, S. R. (1970). Sex-role stereotypes and clinical judgments of mental health. Journal of Consulting and Clinical Psychology, 34(1), 332-332.

Handout 7.1 - Gender and Cultural Diversity

<u>Mentally Healthy Adults</u>

MEN	WOMEN
_____AGGRESSIVE	_____AGGRESSIVE
_____COMPETITIVE	_____COMPETITIVE
_____NURTURING	_____NURTURING
_____INDEPENDENT	_____INDEPENDENT
_____COMPASSIONATE	_____COMPASSIONATE
_____LOYAL	_____LOYAL
_____BRAVE	_____BRAVE
_____DEPENDENT	_____DEPENDENT
_____FEARFUL	_____FEARFUL
_____HOSTILE	_____HOSTILE
_____COMPETENT	_____COMPETENT
_____ENERGETIC	_____ENERGETIC
_____INCOMPETENT	_____INCOMPETENT

Writing Project

Writing Project - 7.1

Given the need for improved writing skills in college students and to respond to the call for "writing across the curriculum, " we offer writing projects for each chapter. In Chapter 7, we suggest a 2-3 page write up for the following activity. Recognizing the time involved in grading such writing projects, one alternative is occasionally to assign "peer grading." Collect the papers, remove student names, and assign each student a paper to grade. It helps to make their participation in peer grading a required part of the overall points for the writing project. This encourages a more thoughtful and responsible evaluation, as well as acknowledging and rewarding the additional work.

Constructing a Subculture IQ Test

Ask students to form groups of 3 to 4 . Tell them that their task is to develop a 10 to 15 item questionnaire to measure "intelligence" in their selected subculture. Ask them to think of subcultures that they currently belong to, or have experienced in the past (e.g., college student, psych major, housewife, househusband, commuter, "dormies," "surfers," "computer nerds," etc.). Have them pick one subculture and define what it means to be "intelligent" in this group. Once they have completed the task, ask them to create a questionnaire that will discriminate between highly intelligent, average, and less intelligent individuals in the selected subculture. Tell them to administer the test to 10 people who are members of the subculture and 10 members who are not.

The writing project for this activity will require a submission of the questionnaire and a 2 to 3 page response paper detailing what was learned about intelligence and intelligence testing within the selected subculture. Ask the students to tie this information into terms and concepts found in the text, and to speculate on what their IQ test might mean to groups who wanted to join the subculture.

Circle Of Quality – Chapter 7

Please give us your feedback. We thank you in advance for assisting us in improving the next edition. The contact information is listed in the preface.

What are the three most helpful teaching tools in this chapter?

1.

2.

3.

What are the three least useful teaching tools in this chapter?

1.

2.

3.

What are the three most difficult concepts to teach in this chapter?

1.

2.

3.

Additional Comments:

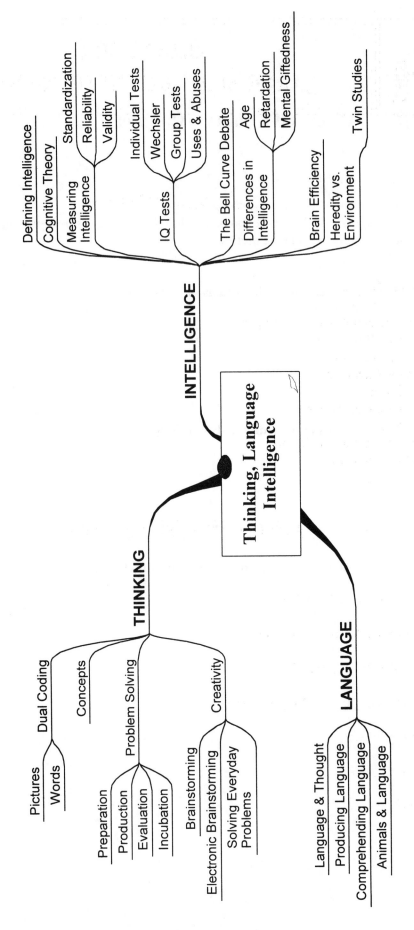

INTELLIGENCE

- Defining Intelligence
- Cognitive Theory
- Measuring Intelligence
  - Standardization
  - Reliability
  - Validity
- IQ Tests
  - Individual Tests
  - Wechsler
  - Group Tests
  - Uses & Abuses
- The Bell Curve Debate
- Differences in Intelligence
  - Age
  - Retardation
  - Mental Giftedness
- Brain Efficiency
- Heredity vs. Environment
  - Twin Studies

THINKING

- Dual Coding
  - Pictures
  - Words
- Concepts
- Problem Solving
  - Preparation
  - Production
  - Evaluation
  - Incubation
- Creativity
  - Brainstorming
  - Electronic Brainstorming
  - Solving Everyday Problems

Thinking, Language Intelligence

LANGUAGE

- Language & Thought
- Producing Language
- Comprehending Language
- Animals & Language

CHAPTER 8
LIFE SPAN DEVELOPMENT I

TEXT ENHANCEMENT

DEMONSTRATIONS, EXERCISES, PROJECTS

Outline

Studying Development

Theoretical Issues
Research Methods

Gender and Cultural Diversity
Cultural Psychology's Guidelines for
Developmental Research

Physical Development

Prenatal Development
Early Childhood Physical Development
Physical Changes in Adolescence
Physical Changes in the Adult Years

Language Development

Stages of Language Development
Think Theories of Language Development

Social-Emotional Development

Attachment in Infancy
Adult Attachment

Cognitive Development

Stages of Cognitive Development

Active Learning
Applying Your Knowledge of Piaget

Assessing Piaget's Theory
Information Processing

Research Highlight
Getting Old May Be Better
Than You Think

GOAL Learning Objectives

Upon completion of CHAPTER 8, the student will be able to:

1. Define developmental psychology, and discuss the ongoing debates in this field regarding nature versus nurture, continuity versus stages, and stability versus change (pp. 292-293).
2. Differentiate between cross-sectional and longitudinal research, and describe the major advantages and disadvantages of each method of research (pp. 293-295).
3. Discuss four ways culture has an impact on the study of human development (pp. 295-296).
4. List and describe the physical changes associated with the three stages of prenatal development (pp. 297-298).
5. Discuss the effects of maternal nutrition and exposure to teratogens on prenatal development, and describe paternal contributions to prenatal development (pp. 299-300).
6. Describe the major changes in brain, motor, and sensory/perceptual development during the early childhood years; explain how these changes have been measured in newborns and infants (pp. 300-304).
7. Define puberty and adolescence, list the major physical changes that occur during this developmental period, and explain how these changes may affect psychological adjustment (pp. 304-305).
8. Define menopause and the male climacteric, and describe other physical changes associated with middle age and later adulthood (pp. 305-306).
9. Differentiate between primary and secondary aging, and explain the programmed and damage theories for primary aging (pp. 307-308).
10. Describe the characteristics found in the pre-linguistic and linguistic stages of language development (pp. 308-309).
11. Discuss the nativist position regarding language development and contrast it with the position of the "nurturists" (pp. 309-310).
12. Define attachment, and describe the research related to both animal and human infant attachment, including Harlow's contact comfort research with monkeys (pp. 311-312).
13. Describe Ainsworth's levels of attachment, and discuss research regarding the relationship between infant attachment and adult love (pp. 312-314).
14. Discuss Piaget's approach to cognitive development, and define schemas, assimilation, and accommodation (pp. 315-316).
15. List and describe the characteristics associated with Piaget's four stages of cognitive development (pp. 316-321).
16. Briefly discuss two major criticisms of Piaget's theory, and state the ongoing contribution of his theory in psychology (pp. 321-324).
17. Compare the information processing model of cognitive development to Piaget's theory; describe the development of attention and memory using the information processing model (pp. 324-326).
18. Discuss research regarding the effects of aging on adult information processing and memory (p. 325).

Chapter Summary/Lecture Organizer

Introductory Vignette--The chapter opens with a comparison between the fictional character portrayed by Jodie Foster in the movie Nell, and the non-fictional account of the life of "Genie." The contrast between Hollywood's version of the "wild child" and true life provides insight into the limits and potential of human development.

I.   **STUDYING DEVELOPMENT** - Developmental psychology is defined as the branch of psychology that describes, explains, predicts, and sometimes aims to modify age-related behaviors from conception to death. The field emphasizes maturation, early experiences, and various stages in development.

    A. Theoretical Issues – The three most important issues in human development are: nature versus nurture, continuity versus stages, and stability versus change. This issue has been an on-going debate that dates back to the ancient Greeks.

    B. Research Methods – To study development researchers use the cross-sectional and longitudinal approaches, and each method has its own advantages and disadvantages.

        Gender and Cultural Diversity: Cultural Psychology's Guidelines for Developmental Research - Cultural psychologists have suggested that developmental researchers should be guided by four reminders: 1) culture may be the most important determinant of development; 2) human development, like most areas of psychology, cannot be studied outside its sociocultural context; 3) culture is largely invisible to its participants; and 4) each culture's ethnotheories are important determinants of behavior.

II.   **PHYSICAL DEVELOPMENT**

    A. Prenatal Development - The prenatal period of development consists of three major stages: the germinal period, the embryonic period, and the fetal period. Physical development is often affected by environmental influences. Poor prenatal nutrition is a leading cause of birth defects, and most drugs (both prescription and over-the-counter) are potentially teratogenic (capable of producing birth defects). Doctors advise pregnant women to avoid all unnecessary drugs, especially nicotine and alcohol.

    B. Early Childhood Physical Development - During the prenatal period and the first year of life, the brain and nervous system grow faster than all other parts of the body. Early motor development (crawling, standing, and walking) is largely the result of maturation. Contrary to earlier beliefs, psychologists now know that the sensory and perceptual abilities of newborns are relatively well developed.

C. Physical Changes in Adolescence - The rapid changes that occur during adolescence are discussed, including secondary sexual characteristics, physical changes, and psychological adjustments. At puberty, adolescents become capable of reproduction (the female menarche and the male spermarche). They also experience a sharp increase in height, weight, and skeletal growth as a result of the pubertal growth spurt. There are significant psychological effects due to either early or late maturation during this period.

D. Physical Changes in the Adult Years - During middle age, both men and women experience significant body changes--menopause and the male climacteric. After middle age, most physical changes are gradual and occur in the heart, arteries, brain, and sensory receptors. Although many of these changes (such as decreases in cardiac output and visual acuity) are the result of primary aging, others are the result of abuse, disuse, and disease--secondary aging. Physical aging may be genetically built-in from the moment of conception (programmed theories), or it may result from the body's inability to repair damage (wear-and-tear theories).

III. LANGUAGE DEVELOPMENT – From birth, a child has a multitude of ways, universal and innate, to communicate; both verbally and non-verbally.

A. Stages of Language Development - Children go through two major stages in their acquisition of language: prelinguistic (crying, cooing, and babbling) and linguistic (single utterances, telegraphic speech, and acquiring rules of grammar

B. Theories of Language Development - Nativists believe that language is an inborn capacity and develops primarily from maturation. Noam Chomsky suggests that humans possess a language acquisition device (LAD) that needs only minimal environmental input. Nurturists emphasize the role of the environment and suggest that language development results from rewards and punishments, and imitating models.

IV. SOCIAL-EMOTIONAL DEVELOPMENT – Along with physical and language development, developmental psychologists are interested in social-emotional development, how humans become "entire" with the help of other human beings.

A. Attachment in Infancy – Infants arrive in this world with behaviors that encourage a strong bond of attachment with primary caregivers, from the major one between mother and child to fathers, grandparents, and other caretakers. In studying attachment, researchers are often divided along that now familiar line of nature versus nurture. Ainsworth found that the following levels of attachment: securely attached, avoidant, or anxious/ambivalent affect long-term behaviors. And, although early attachment experiences may predict the future, they do not determine it.

B. Adult Attachment – Using the levels of attachment, researchers have studied the relationship between an infant's attachment to a parent figure and an adult's love for a romantic partner.

V.   **COGNITIVE DEVELOPMENT** - Jean Piaget, perhaps more than any other researcher, has demonstrated the unique cognitive processes of children. He believed that children are driven toward knowledge because of their biological need for adaptation to the environment. During adaptation, the child uses schemata (mental patterns or blueprints) to interpret the world. Sometimes new information can be assimilated into the existing schemata, but on other occasions the existing schemata must be modified, which calls for accommodation.

A.   **Stages of Cognitive Development** - The work of Jean Piaget as the primary figure in studying cognitive development is covered in some detail. Each of the four stages of cognitive development--sensorimotor (birth to 2 years), preoperational (2-7 years), concrete operational (7-11 years), and formal operational (11 and beyond)--are introduced. The sensorimotor stage is characterized by the acquisition of object permanence--the realization that objects (or people) continue to exist even when out of sight. During the preoperational stage, children are better equipped to use symbols, but their thinking is also egocentric and animistic. The concrete operational stage is characterized by the acquisition of operations and increased logic. During the formal operational stage, the adolescent is able to think abstractly and deal with hypothetical situations.

> **Active Learning/Critical Thinking: Applying Your Knowledge of Piaget** - Gives several examples of how Piaget's concepts help clarify how children react to their care takers.

B.   **Assessing Piaget's Theory** - Although Piaget has been criticized for underestimating abilities, as well as educational and cultural influences, he remains one of the most respected psychologists of modern times.

C.   **Information Processing** - Psychologists who explain cognitive development in terms of information processing have found this model especially helpful in explaining attention and memory.

> **Research Highlight: Getting Old May Be Better Than You Think** – Researchers touch on hormonal therapy, for both men and women, to offset the effects of heart disease, osteoporosis, Alzheimer's and other age related diseases. Studies on age-related changes in brain structure and function show only a modest decline in neurons count.

Teaching Resources

SECTION I - STUDYING DEVELOPMENT

Learning Objectives #'s 1, 2, 3
Lecture Lead-Ins #'s 1, 2
Discussion Questions #'s 2, 3
Active Learning Activities # 8.2
Brain-Based Activity #'s 8.1 - 8.3
Gender and Cultural Diversity Activity # 8.1
Writing Project #8.1

SECTION II - PHYSICAL DEVELOPMENT

Learning Objectives #'s 4-9
Lecture Lead-Ins #'s 2, 3, 4
Discussion Questions #'s 1,3
Active Learning Activities #'s 8.1, 8.2
Brain-Based Activity #'s 8.1, 8.3
Critical Thinking Exercise # 8.4
Gender and Cultural Diversity Activity #8.1
Writing Project # 8.1

SECTION III - LANGUAGE DEVELOPMENT

Learning Objectives #'s 10, 11
Lecture Lead-Ins #'s 1,2
Lecture Extenders #8.1
Active Learning Activities #'s 8.2, 8.3, 8.4
Brain-Based Learning #'s 8.3, 8.4
Critical Thinking Exercise # 8.2
Gender and Cultural Diversity Activity # 8.1
Writing Project # 8.1

SECTION IV - SOCIAL-EMOTIONAL DEVELOPMENT

Learning Objectives #'s 12, 13
Discussion Questions # 4
Active Learning Activities #8.2
Brain-Based Learning #'s 8.2 - 8.4

SECTION V - COGNITIVE DEVELOPMENT

Learning Objectives #'s 14 - 18
Lecture Lead-Ins #'s 1, 2, 5
Discussion Questions # 3
Active Learning Activities #'s 8.2, 8.5 - 8.9
Brain-Based Learning #8.4
Critical Thinking Exercise # 8.1
Gender and Cultural Diversity Activity # 8.1
Writing Project #8.1

Lecture Lead-Ins

1. Ask for a show of hands from students who saw the movie "Nell." Did they enjoy the depiction of the "Wild Child" and her enchanted life in the forest? Ask if the true life story of Genie (as described in the text's chapter opening) affected their feelings about Nell? Use their responses as a lead-in to the general topic of development or to specific topics such as nature versus nurture.

2. Ask students if "superstar" children should be sent to special schools away from the family in order to maximize their potential. Or are the effects of home and family more important in intellectual/cognitive development? Ask for a show of hands by the students to indicate who would volunteer to let their child be taken to a special school. Would they do it for an intellectually gifted child? What about child who is physically gifted? What about a child who is deaf? Should they be removed to special schools? What about a child who stutters? Should they be taken out of regular classes for a part of the class day to be given special training? Ask students if they were ever placed in "special" classes in elementary school. Was this a primarily good or bad experience? Use this discussion as a lead-in for your lectures on physical, language, and cognitive development.

3. Ask students what was the most important physical change that occurred during their teen years. Were they early-maturers or late-maturers? Do they agree with the text's description of the advantages and disadvantages? If you were an early or late maturer, describe your own feelings of embarrassment (e.g., tall females had to slow dance with boys whose heads were breast height, short males had fewer partners and were less often chosen for sports teams, etc.). Ask for suggestions how parents, teachers, and other adults might help an adolescent cope with such "untimely" development--either very early or very late.

4. As an introduction to adult physical development ask for examples from their own lives or their parents', regarding the changes associated with middle and old age. Ask for suggestions that might help offset the negativity generally associated with physical aging in our culture.

5. Ask the students to prepare a one-page paper for the next class meeting of the subject of aging and intelligence. Ask them to relate any personal experiences or talk about friends, parents, grandparents, or individuals in their work or schooling experiences. Most of their examples will be positive ones. Discuss our misconceptions regarding aging and the loss of cognitive functions. Be alert to any loss of function in terms of Alzheimer's disease and use this as a comparison to normal aging. This provides a nice lead-in to life-span cognitive development.

Lecture Extenders

8.1 - Learning Speech

Parents are fascinated by their children's first words and their emerging ability to speak. So are developmental psychologists. Language acquisition is one of the major concerns of researchers today, as summarized in the article, "Children's Language Acquisition" by Rice (1989).

One of the most remarkable developments that takes place in the life of an individual is the transition from a non-language-user into a language-user. Since this is an achievement that is not explicitly taught, it is incredible that almost all normal children automatically assess the elements of language. There is no disagreement on the four components of language--phonology, semantics, morphology, and syntax--although some may disagree on the relationship between them. A fifth component, not referred to as often, is the social aspect which describes knowing what to say and when to say it in a social situation. The combination of these five aspects has been referred to as "communication competence" by Hyme (cited in Rice).

There are three different theoretical models that try to explain the mechanisms within the nervous system for acquiring language. These models (transformational, case grammar, and lexical functionalist grammar) differ primarily in the relationship they postulate between syntax and semantics, that is, the degree of independence between them. The way in which children learn to avoid grammatical errors, such as "John "goed" away" while at the same time generalizing linguistic rules, is still not understood.

The decoding of the language acquisition process can only take place through observation of children who are in the emerging phase of language development. The importance of these studies can be seen in the international cooperation of countries which are participating in the Child Language Data Exchange System where video and audiotapes of verbal exchanges with children throughout the world are available.

One focus of research on language acquisition has been on the cognitive underpinnings of language. The type of words that are expressed first relate to important objects in the environment. There is also a strong tendency for the appearance of words that reflect certain events in the environment: the word "more" or some equivalent that symbolizes the desirability of a recurring event; the words "all gone" to indicate an object no longer there; and the word "no" for negation. Piaget hypothesized that language dealing with these types of relationships could only occur after a child had developed the necessary cognitive structures for this stage of thinking; for example, object permanence would have to precede the language indicating that an object has disappeared. Studies have not supported Piaget since the cognitive structures appear simultaneously with the language rather than preceding it.

One of the spectacular aspects in the development of language is the rapid gain in size of vocabulary during the preschool years. After about 18 months (and after acquiring the ability to combine two words into a sentence), children begin adding new words at the rate of about 9 per day; by the time they reach school this number will eventually total over 14,000. They do this without being coached on the meaning of new words. Children absorb words so quickly--like a "sponge"--that apparently they have maps in their brains for understanding where new words fit in and what to do with them. This rapid increase appears to be a necessary foundation for reading skills.

Language also plays an important role in developing social skills. It increases the efficiency with which one can interact with others. Parents have a strong effect upon this social aspect of language and can provide reinforcements that encourage a child to want to speak better. This developmental aspect of language is more dependent upon social learning than other aspects so one would expect different incentives and different social styles across families and cultures.

There are certain aspects of language that appear so regularly in the development of children that they are referred to as "universals." Namely, children all over the world speak at about the same age, they speak about the same types of things (significant objects), and they master meaning before they master syntax. What are the necessary conditions in the environment for a child to learn to speak? Children must hear the language, the language must make sense and, finally, they must consider language of importance. Obviously, these criteria are easily met since language acquisition is so universal.

What are some "special" conditions that surround the learning of language? Since it is the mother who spends the most time with the small child, it has been mother-child verbal interactions that have received the most attention. One well-known type of interaction is labeled "motherese." This refers to the way in which a mother modifies her language when talking to a child: here and now is emphasized; vocabulary is restricted; paraphrasing and simple sentences are used; and frequent repetitions and pauses are interjected. Another type of mother- child interaction is "semantic contingency." In this type of interaction, the mother is responding to the utterances of the child, often further clarifying a statement or giving more information. For example, if a child were pointing to a dog while saying the word dog, the mother may say, "Yes, it's a big dog." The other special socially interactive activity that actively involves language is book reading, which provides the bridge between oral language and reading skills. The only type of mother-child verbal interaction that has been shown to inhibit language development has been constant corrections of the child's language.

Children with impaired language skills are at a greater risk for educational failure. At times, impaired language skills are secondary to other problems such as deafness or mental retardation; these categories constitute about 40% of those with language problems. About 5% of all school children are referred to a speech pathologist for motor problems in language; another 3% go for "true" language disability. Since so little is known about the mechanisms involved in language disability, it is difficult to specify what is at the nature of the problem. These children do not have a general cognitive impairment, nor are they necessarily from bad environments.

Ideas about what is wrong are merely speculations. Some say there may be a problem in the mental representations of language; others say there may be a problem in the mapping of new words, something that occurs so effortlessly in other children. The general remedial approach has been to work with word meaning, especially if the words can be used as cues for syntax, to try to improve their overall competence in all areas, and to increase environmental input that will contribute to word mapping.

It still remains to be seen whether these approaches will work. It may be that Gardner's theory about multiple intelligences is correct. If so, not only will there always be some who are less linguistically able than others, there will also be some for whom linguistic ability is lower than other abilities.

Rice, M. L. (1989). Children's Language Acquisition, American Psychologist, 44, 149-156.

Key Terms

Developmental psychology (p. 292)

STUDYING DEVELOPMENT

Cohort Effects (p. 294)
Cross-Sectional Method (p. 293)
Longitudinal Method (p. 293)
Maturation (p. 292)

PHYSICAL DEVELOPMENT

Adolescence (p. 304)
Chromosomes (p. 297)
Conception (p. 297)
Embryonic Period (p. 297)
Fetal Alcohol Syndrome (p. 300)
Fetal Period (p. 297)
Genes (p. 297)
Germinal Period (p. 297)
Male Climacteric (p. 306)
Menopause (p. 305)
Myelination (p. 300)
Primary Aging (p. 307)
Puberty (p. 304)
Reflexes (p. 301)
Secondary Aging (p. 307)
Secondary Sex Characteristics (p. 304)
Teratogen (p. 299)

LANGUAGE DEVELOPMENT

Babbling (p. 308)
Language Acquisition Device (LAD) (p. 309)
Overextension (p. 309)
Overgeneralize (p. 309)
Telegraphic Speech (p. 309)

SOCIAL-EMOTIONAL DEVELOPMENT

Attachment (p. 311)
Imprinting (p. 311)

COGNITIVE DEVELOPMENT

Accommodation (p. 316)
Adolescent Egocentrism (p. 321)
Animism (p. 318)
Assimilation (p. 316)
Concrete Operational Stage (p. 318)
Conservation (p. 319)
Egocentrism (p. 317)
Formal Operational Stage (p. 319)
Information Processing Model (p. 324)
Object Permanence (p. 317)
Preoperational Stage (p. 317)
Schemata (p. 315)
Sensorimotor Stage (p. 316)

Discussion Questions

1. There are devastating consequences following the use of drugs by pregnant women. Should drug laws be stronger and more strictly enforced for pregnant women than for the general public? What about laws related to the father's drug consumption? Should tobacco or alcohol be illegal when taken by pregnant women? Is a pregnant woman who smokes or drinks guilty of child abuse? Why or why not?

2. Does childhood matter? Children are resilient and can often overcome some problems related to physical abuse, neglect, separation from parents, mentally ill parents, and inadequate parenting. When should society intervene to protect children? Should we all speak up and object when we see parents verbally abusing their children in supermarkets, restaurants, or parks? What if they are physically abusive? Why or why not?

3. Does watching TV decrease intellectual and physical development? What about language development? Does watching TV violence make children more violent? What about anxiety and fears? Do children learn too much too soon from TV? What are the global effects of television? How do you (or will you) handle television as a parent? Will you allow television in your home? Why or why not?

4. Given the importance of attachment, what could our society do to improve the chances for secure attachment? Should we invest in better day care centers? Should both parents be allowed lengthy maternity and paternity leaves? What happens to children who are raised for several months or years in foster homes or orphanages? Do they form secure attachments? What will happen to Baby Jessica (the 2 1/2-year-old) who was taken from her adoptive parents by the biological parents? Will she form a new attachment to her biological parents?

Web Sites

Infants, Babies, and Childbirth
http://www.efn.org/~djz/birth/babylist.html
This web page provides a comprehensive set of links to pages dealing with pregnancy, birthing, breastfeeding, and issues of parenting.

Classic Theories of Child Development
http://idealist.com/children/cdw.html
This site offers basic information on the major theorists of developmental psychology including Erikson, Freud, and Mahler. The site also offers a month-by-month summary of child development and a search engine for additional information on developmental psychology.

Piaget Tutorial
http://www.lincoln.ac.nz/educ/tip/30.htm
A brief tutorial with references on the work of Jean Piaget.

European Society for Developmental Psychology
http://devpsy.lboro.ac.uk/eurodev/
This page provides links to newsletters, societies, and pages on developmental psychology.

Suggested Films and Videos

The Developing Child

Annenberg/CPB, 1990. 30 minutes. This program from Zimbardo's "Discovering Psychology" series examines the impact of heredity and environment on development. The arguments of nature and nurture are discussed and supported with research. This segment is likely to promote good discussion of this controversy.

Child Development

Insight Media, 1992. 30 minutes. This program presents a historical overview of the contributions of Locke, Rousseau, Freud, Erikson, Bowlby, Watson, Gesell, and Piaget. The methods, challenges, and problems of studying development are considered.

Teenage Mind and Body

Insight Media, 1990. 30 minutes. This video explores the areas of adolescent cognitive and physical development. Highlights include Kohlberg's theory of moral development and moral reasoning, as well as Elkind's discussion of formal operations and adolescent egocentrism.

Adulthood

Insight Media, 1990. 60 minutes each. The three tapes in this series examine the psychological, biological, and social forces that contribute to adult development. Tapes are Early Adulthood, Middle Adulthood, and Late Adulthood.

Fetal Alcohol Syndrome and Other Drug Use During Pregnancy

Films for the Humanities and Sciences, 1995. 19 minutes. This program profiles an eight-year-old boy with FAS. It shows how alcohol entered his bloodstream during prenatal development. The film describes the common characteristics of FAS and the associated learning disabilities and behavioral problems. Health and developmental problems for babies born to cocaine-addicted mothers are also discussed.

Pregnancy and Substance Abuse

Films for the Humanities and Sciences, 1995. 28 minutes. This program follows several couples through pregnancy and prenatal care. Former Surgeon General C. Everett Koop talks about the risks of smoking and Michael Derris, author of The Broken Cord, discusses his life raising an adopted son with FAS.

Brandon and Rachel: Patterns of Infant Development

U.C. Media Extension Center (Berkeley), 1991. 34 minutes. Two 7-month-olds are visiting a child development class. The professor uses these infants to demonstrate principles of motor, language, and personality development. Students are asked to do a personality profile for each infant, which demonstrates stereotyped sex roles. What happens if they are wearing the wrong clothing? The surprise ending will generate lively discussion.

Maturing and Aging

Annenberg/CPB, 1990. 30 minutes. This program from Zimbardo's "Discovering Psychology" series examines the myths and realities of aging in our society. Topics include Erik Erikson's psychosocial stages and the biological and psychological changes that occur as we age. The video also presents examples of ageism and other negative stereotyping of adult behavior.

Growing Old in a New Age

Annenberg/CPB, 1993. 58 minutes each segment. This thirteen-part series explores many facets of adult development through interviews with researchers, older individuals, and health care professionals. Some individual topics include: How the Body Changes; Learning, Memory, and Speed of Processing; Intellect, Personality, and Mental Health; Social Relationships in Old Age; Work, Retirement, and Economic Status; and Dying, Death, and Bereavement.

Language Development

Annenberg/CPB, 1990. 30 minutes. This program, hosted by Philip Zimbardo, describes language development from its earliest babbling stages, including the genetic and environmental interaction in language development. Cross-cultural similarities in language development are also presented, as well as social communication issues.

Language

PBS Video, 1990. 30 minutes. Part of "The Mind" series, this excellent video presents the evolution of human language and the phenomenon of speech. It discusses Chomsky's theory of an innate drive for language and demonstrates that linguistic abilities exist even without speech and hearing.

You Must of Been a Bilingual Baby

Filmmakers Library, 1992. 46 minutes. This program investigates how babies become bilingual, how school children fare in immersion programs, and how adults cope with learning a foreign language. The film presents several bilingual families and takes us to a classroom where Spanish and English-speaking children learn together while developing a sense of pride in their respective cultures.

The Infant Mind

Insight Media, 1992. 30 minutes. This fascinating video presents traditional Piagetian perspectives of object permanence during the sensorimotor period. Then it challenges some of Piaget's assumptions to demonstrate that infants have a perception of cause and effect, number, and object permanence much earlier than formerly believed.

Better Babies--Raising Intellectual Superstars

Filmmakers Library, 1991. 28 minutes. This film documents some early learning programs designed to produce "geniuses." We see parents involved in prenatal education--talking to their unborn babies in the belief that it will accelerate the babies' verbal skills. One toddler's hectic schedule is presented; his mother is teaching him art, music, computers, geography, and Japanese. This is a good discussion starter about how fast and hard we push our children to succeed.

Language Development

Films for the Humanities and Sciences, 1996. 40 minutes. This program follows the development of language from infant cries to the relatively competent use of language by grade schoolers. First attempts at communication, the nature of grammatical errors, and the arguments concerning the role of nature versus nurture are discussed. The Whorf-Sapir hypothesis and the question of non-human primates' capacity for language are also addressed.

Growing Minds: Cognitive Development in Early Childhood

Davidson Films, 1996. 25 minutes. This video examines the work of Piaget and Vygotsky as it pertains to the development of reasoning skills, visual perception, and the use of language during the first five years of life. Children are both interviewed and observed while engaged in activities to assess the development of their intellectual capacities.

Adolescent Cognition: Thinking in a New Key

Davidson Films, 1999. 30 minutes. This video refers to the works of Piaget, Erikson, and Goffman while the changes in intellectual capacity occurring at this stage of development are examined. Although higher levels of reasoning enable adolescents to assume greater challenges and responsibilities, these changes are accompanied by new emotional and social consequences. Both interviews and observations of peer interactions during group projects are used to illustrate the thinking processes of junior high school aged children.

Aging Successfully: The Psychological Aspects of Growing Old

Davidson Films, 1997. 31 minutes. This video is prompted by the unprecedented number of people entering into old age, and offers a systematic examination of the life of the elderly. A model for adaptive change over the life span is presented, with an emphasis on old age. Methods of cognitive testing and assessing the mental abilities of the elderly are presented. The personality components leading to optimal and fulfilling lives for the elderly are discussed

Theories of Development

Insight Media, 1997. 29 minutes. The video presents an overview of the various theoretical approaches to child development. Specific theories such as cognitive, psychosexual, psychosocial, behavioral, social learning, and sociocultural development are discussed in conjunction with profiles of Piaget, Freud, Erickson, Gesell, Skinner, and Vygotsky.

Books For Success

McKay, Matthew; Fanning, Patrick (1992). **Self-Esteem (2nd Edition).** New Harbinger Publications. An interesting, easy-to-understand book on overcoming your "pathological critic" thereby improving your self-esteem.

Zimbardo, Philip G. (1997). **Shyness: What It Is What to Do About It**. Addison Wesley. A book about the hassles and restrictions of being shy - and how to deal with them.

Bolles, Richard Nelson (1990, 1995). **What Color Is Your Parachute? A Practical Manual for Job-Hunters and Career-Changers.** Ten Speed Press. The best known and ever improving resource guide to selecting careers and landing a job.

Diamond, Mary and Hopson, Janet (1999). **Magic Trees of the Mind: How to Nurture Your Child's Intelligence, Creativity and Healthy Emotions from Birth Through Adolescence.** Penguin A scientific and practical guide for parents who want to enrich their children's lives and foster the unfolding of their mental and emotional capacity. A valuable resource for once and future parents.

Active Learning

Active Learning Activity 8.1 - Conception

Invite a guest speaker from a local hospital or "prepared childbirth" class to come and speak about the problems associated with maternal drug use, local issues related to the availability of prenatal health care, or to discuss modern technology and techniques involved in childbirth. Ask speakers to bring slides or charts depicting changes in the mother's body during pregnancy and to show films of an actual childbirth. College students are fascinated by this topic and many have little or no information or experience in this area.

Active Learning Activity 8.2 - Infant and Child Observation

Arrange with a local day care (possibly your college day care if available) for your class to come visit the children. Assign times for the students to observe the children. Hold the size of the groups to 10 students. This will be a valuable chance for the students to observe the principles they have studied in this chapter at work.

Active Learning Activity 8.3 - Nonverbal Communication

To introduce the power of nonverbal communication, come to class five minutes late and nonverbally signal the students to quiet down. Using hand signals and facial gestures, rearrange students into circles, different seating patterns, and so on. Using your own imagination and acting abilities, carry this "experiment" to the point where students are obviously confused and beginning to ask you questions. This is a humorous and effective way to emphasize the importance of nonverbal communication.

Active Learning Activity 8.4 - Verbal Communication

If you approach this topic early in the course, parents with infants and young children can often collect video or audiotape samples of various stages of language development that provide a valuable demonstration. Some parents may have existing tapes that they would be willing to share and edit for classroom presentation.

Active Learning Activity 8.5 - Cognitive Development

One of the best ways to demonstrate Piaget's description of the pre-operational and concrete child is to ask parents in your class to bring their pre-operational and concrete children to class (perhaps two to four children in each stage of development). By observing these children performing conservation tasks illustrated in the text and discussed below, students are consistently surprised at the contrast between the abilities of the two groups.

Seriation:

To demonstrate the pre-operational child's lack of ability to seriate, ask six students of varying heights to stand at the front of the room and then ask the pre-operational children to take turns "arranging them from the tallest to the shortest." The children seem to enjoy moving the "big people" around and the class enjoys their creative arrangements and unusual logic. As a contrast, have the concrete operational children take their turn after the pre-operational children have finished their task.

Egocentrism:

To demonstrate the concept of egocentrism, a replica of Piaget's famous "three mountain problem" can be constructed by using cardboard cones of three sizes and colors. Seat the pre-operational child in one chair at a table and a doll or another student in a chair ninety degrees to the right. Place the cones on the table in front of the child in a predetermined arrangement. Ask the child to select the one arrangement of cones (depicted on a large poster board) that matches their own view and then to select the one that would be seen by the doll or student. Pre-operational children will select the same view in both questions, while concrete children will recognize that the doll will have a different view and will choose accordingly.

An expanded description of the three mountain problem and further details helpful for constructing the cones and posters can be found in Piaget, J., & Inhelder, B. (1956). The child's conception of space, p. 210. London: Routledge and Kegan Paul Ltd.

Active Learning Activity 8.6 - Three Beakers

Draw three beakers on the chalkboard (or use the transparency that accompanies this section). Show one beaker being half full of a clear liquid on the chalkboard or prepare an overhead transparency.

Tell students to pretend they are given three beakers of equal amounts of clear fluid. The chemical properties are unknown, but one combination of the three liquids results in a striking blue color. The task is to discover this combination. Give the students approximately ten minutes to write down a solution that might be given by a person in the concrete operational stage and another solution that might be given by someone in the formal operational stage.

Active Learning Activity 8.7 - Understanding Piaget

An understanding of Piaget's four stages of cognitive development is essential to the mastery of Chapter 8. One way to increase your students' knowledge, is to devote class time to the practice of this skill. The following test provides important practice opportunities.

Time: Approximately 20 minutes.
Instructions: Xerox copies of the "Piaget Test" and briefly review Piaget's four stages of cognitive development. Divide the class into groups of 3-4 students. Pass around copies of the "Piaget Test" (Handout 8.7) and encourage the students to answer all questions as quickly as possible. Ask someone in

each group to raise their hand as soon as the test is completed, and have the winning group come to the front of the room to read and discuss their answers.

Answers for the Piaget Test:

1. The child is in the pre-operational stage.

2. Since the child is in the pre-operational stage and lacks conservation, he believed that the spreading of his food represented an overall increase in the amount of the disliked food.

3. Janie is in the sensorimotor stage and has recently developed object permanence.

4. Tom is in the formal operational stage, and his inconsistency is explained by "adolescent egocentrism" which often results in heightened hypocrisy.

5. The older child is in the concrete stage of development, while the younger child is pre-operational. (While reading this example of the aunt giving two boys three cookies, bright and witty students will often ask "What is the aunt's stage of development?" You might want to prepare a good response or let them have the fun of "catching" you.)

Active Learning Activity 8.8 - Adults and "Lower" Stages of Development

The role of specific experiences and training in Piaget's stages can also be illustrated by asking students to describe "embarrassing" moments with learning a new skill. Adults often begin at the sensorimotor stage and work their way through pre-operational, concrete, and on to formal stages within a short period of time. Occasionally we meet with obstacles based on our lack of experience and development. One of our students once described a wonderful "concrete" example of her "friend" who was a college graduate with little experience with cooking. This friend was attempting to make meringue for a pie and since the recipe called for "6 separated eggs," she opened the eggs and put each in a separate cup. She then called the student for advice on what to do next. Ask your students for examples of their own experiences. Also ask students for stories from their childhood or their own children for Piaget's stages. They are generally happy to volunteer.

Active Learning Activity 8.9 - IQ Tests

Construct a basic vocabulary test similar to those found on the Stanford-Binet, Wechsler, or from the glossary of the text. Also construct specific spatial and pattern recognition tasks similar to those on the Stanford-Binet or Wechsler. Divide the class into medium-sized groups (six to eight students) according to those who are "over twenty-five" and "under twenty-five" years of age. Give each group fifteen minutes to answer both sections of the test. Have members of each group grade their own papers, then put the results on the board. The older group should do better on the vocabulary tests, while the younger group should do better on the spatial and pattern recognition tasks. Use this to discuss differences in cognitive development and why the "declines" associated with aging are emphasized while the advantages are typically ignored.

Handout 8.1– Active Learning

Piaget Test I

Upon meeting Mr. Rogers (host of a famous children's TV show), a young child asks, "How did you get out of the box?" What Piagetian stage does this statement represent?

A young mother is encouraging her son to try another bite of a disliked food. The child is quietly whining, but when the mother spreads the food around to cool it, the child becomes hysterical. Why did the child become so upset? Identify the cognitive stage of the child.

Last month Janie's mom could easily substitute a less offensive toy for a noisy one and Janie would continue happily playing. Now she will cry and reach for the removed toy even when it is out of sight. What cognitive changes have occurred? Identify Janie's cognitive stage of development.

Tom is deeply upset that his parents cheat on their income taxes, yet he has no difficulty justifying personally cheating on a school exam. Explain Tom's inconsistency from a Piagetian perspective, and label his stage of cognitive development.

A favorite aunt gives her two nephews three cookies and encourages them to share. The older child takes two cookies for himself and offers his brother the other cookie broken in half. Both children are happy with this arrangement. Label each child's stage of cognitive development.

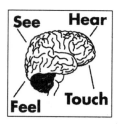

Brain-Based Learning

Brain-Based Learning Activity 8.1 - Shaped by Life

Materials Needed: Several Beanbags or Rice Balloons

Hand out beanbags to the students at the beginning of your lecture on child development. Ask the students to play with them and to pass them onto the next student when they are done. After everyone has had a turn, point out that all started with the same ingredients. However each student shaped them into a different shape by applying different pressures. Discuss how this process is similar to and how it is different from a child being reared in different environments and exposed to different influences.

Brain-Based Learning Activity 8.2 - Who is Responsible for Child Abuse?

In preparation for this activity, announce to the class that every student needs to bring a story or an article about child abuse to the next class. As the students briefly relate their story, discuss as a group whether and how this experience would impact the child's physical, cognitive, social or language development. Encourage the student to apply the concepts from the chapter to imagine how events early in a child's life can have lifelong consequences. An especially vivid example comes from prenatal drug or alcohol abuse by the mother. The point of this exercise is to make the malleability of the developing organism emotionally real to the students.

This could be followed with a discussion of who should be responsible for the protection of a child's welfare? Is it purely a parental responsibility? Should the state or community have the power to interfere "for the good of the child?"

Brain-Based Learning Activity 8.3 - Children's Books Tell A Story

In preparation for this activity, announce to the class that every student needs to bring 2 or more children's books (ranging in level from toddler through kindergarten) to the next class. Then ask the students to discover how the books for different ages reflect the developmental principles described in chapter 8. Can they see the tremendous unfolding in physical, language, cognitive, moral, and social capacities in the first few years of life? How are the books addressing the developmental challenges that face the children they are written for?

Brain-Based Learning Activity 8.4 - The Importance of Play

Give your students 5 to 6 minutes to make a list of all the ways that play is important for the growth of children. Combine all their ideas into a class master list of the many positive functions of play and write on top of the board," The importance of play." Next you add the words " for Adults" on top of the list and ask the students to eliminate functions they feel don't apply to adults. There will be a considerable list left over suggesting the value of play for adults. Why then, do so few adults spend time in play? Ask them what quality or resource adults would need before they too could rediscover the value of play?

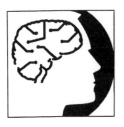

Critical Thinking

Critical Thinking Exercise 8.1 - Developing Insight Into Egocentricity: Adult versus Childhood Egocentrism

Piaget asserted that pre-operational children (ages two to seven) are egocentric. That is they are unable to take the perspective of others because of their limited cognitive development. Although Piaget believed that most adults naturally outgrow such egocentric thinking, recent research suggests that a tendency toward egocentricity may persist throughout adulthood. It is difficult to outgrow our own egocentricity because we suppress facts that are inconsistent with our conclusions and we fail to notice when our behavior contradicts our self-image.

The best antidote to egocentricity is self-awareness and critical self-analysis. To develop insight into your own egocentricity, you should use the following rating scale (Handout 8.2) to first rate the personality traits of someone you find it hard to get along with. Then using the same scale, rate your best friend and then yourself.

Handout 8.1 –Critical Thinking

Personality Rating Test

1 = never behaves in this way
2 = seldom behaves in this way
3 = occasionally behaves in this way
4 = often behaves in this way
5 = always behaves in this way

	DISLIKED PERSON	BEST FRIEND	SELF
Is aggressive and irritable with others.	_____	_____	_____
Is helpful and courteous to others.	_____	_____	_____
Offers support and encouragement to others.	_____	_____	_____
Takes advantage of others.	_____	_____	_____
Is hard working and reliable.	_____	_____	_____
Is sociable and fun to be with.	_____	_____	_____
Dominates conversations.	_____	_____	_____
Values advice from others.	_____	_____	_____
Is interested in trying new things.	_____	_____	_____
Tries to be fair and just with others.	_____	_____	_____

Now check back over the values you assigned in the first and third column. Compare the positive and negative items. Do you think the "disliked person" would agree with your evaluation? Why or why not? Can you see how your own egocentrism could explain the differences in perception?
Now compare the ratings you assigned for yourself and your best friend. If you are like most people, you will notice a strong similarity. An obvious, and somewhat egocentric, explanation for this is that similarity attracts--we like people who are like us. Further critical thinking, however, would explain this similarity as the result of sociocentricity--the extension of egocentrism to groups. The individual goes from thinking "I am right!" to "We are right!" When this egocentrism extends to ethnic groups, countries, and religions, it is sometimes referred to as ethnocentrism. The best antidote to egocentrism, sociocentrism, and ethnocentrism is to listen carefully and with an open mind to those with whom we disagree and to apply the full force of our critical thinking skills to our own behaviors.

This exercise also appears in the text, Chapter 8, We include it here for your convenience, and you may want to discuss it in class to reinforce reading of the text.

Critical Thinking Exercise 8.2 - English-Only Versus Bilingual Education

Should children who come to the United States not knowing English be offered bilingual education, with classes in both their native language and English? Or should they be instructed only in English? This topic is generating a great deal of controversy in the United States. On one side of the debate are those who believe that maintaining a child's native language, while fostering the development of English, improves self-esteem and reduces school failure and dropout. On the other side are those who suggest that time spent communicating in the child's native tongue subtracts from English language achievement, which is crucial for success in the world of school and work.

Evaluating arguments is one of the most important critical thinking skills. Rather than carelessly agreeing or disagreeing with one side or another, critical thinkers analyze the strengths and weaknesses of each position. They are especially sensitive to arguments with which they personally disagree because they recognize the natural human tendency to ignore or oversimplify opposing information. A critical thinker carefully evaluates all arguments and then develops
his or her own independent position.

To help sharpen your critical thinking skills and evaluate the English-only vs. bilingual education argument, we offer the following guidelines:

1. Discuss the issue with several people (friends, college instructors, spouse, roommate, parents, etc.). Then consult professional journal articles (e.g., Hakuta, 1988; McGroarty, 1992).

2. Now list three points and counterpoints of each argument. If a point and counterpoint is not explicitly stated, you will need to "read between the lines" to figure out exactly what is being said.

Point	Counterpoint
_____	_____
_____	_____
_____	_____

3. After clarifying the points and counterpoints, use the following analytical tools to critique each side:

a. *Recognize logical fallacies and faulty reasoning.* Several Active Learning Exercises can help you recognize faulty logic. Faulty reasoning is discussed in Chapter 3, and deceptive appeals in Chapters 11 and 13. See Appendix A for a discussion of the distorted use of statistics.

b. *Explore the implications of conclusions.* To expand your analysis of arguments, ask such questions as, "What conclusions do the proponents of each side draw?" "Are there logical alternatives?"

c. *Recognize and evaluate author bias and source credibility.* Ask yourself such questions as, "What does the author want me to think or do?" "What qualifications does the author have for writing on this subject?" You might also look back at the Active Learning Exercise in Chapter 1 on evaluating sources. Each of these steps requires time and energy, but the payoff is substantial. Not only do you refine your critical thinking skills every time you use them, but you form more educated opinions and make better decisions.

Critical Thinking Exercise 8.3 -

Chapter 8 opens with a discussion of research issues related to developmental psychology. To test your understanding of this material, try the following exercise:

Imagine yourself as a research psychologist who wants to answer the question, "Do feelings of attachment and marital happiness increase over time?" You conduct a longitudinal study of couples who've been married for 5 years, and then reexamine them when they've been married for 10 years. Your research finds couples who've been married only five years rank lowest on these measures, while the 10-year couples reports increased levels of attachment and higher marital happiness. Before submitting your paper to journals for possible publication, what factor(s) should you consider that might explain or contaminate your findings?

_____

_____

_____

_____

Possible answers appear at the end of this study guide chapter.

Critical Thinking Exercise 8.4 - <u>Evaluating Arguments: The Pro-Life/Pro-Choice Controversy</u> (A Cognitive Skill)

The evaluation of arguments is one of the most important elements of active learning and critical thinking. Rather than carelessly agreeing or disagreeing with arguments, critical thinkers analyze the relative strengths and weaknesses of each position. They are especially sensitive to the arguments with which they personally disagree because they recognize the natural human tendency to ignore or oversimplify opposing information. After carefully evaluating all arguments, the critical thinker develops his or her own independent position.

A contemporary, controversial issue involves the argument between those who support a pro-life view concerning abortion and those who support a pro-choice position. Specifically, those who support the pro-life view believe that abortion is morally and religiously wrong. They oppose abortion in almost all circumstances. On the other side, those who advocate a pro- choice position believe that the right to an abortion should not be dictated by religion or government, but is a matter of choice for the woman who is pregnant.

To help you sharpen your critical thinking skills in evaluating the pro-life/pro-choice controversy, the following guidelines are offered.

1. Begin by listing three "points" and three "counterpoints" of each argument. When all points and counterpoints are not explicitly stated, you will need to "read between the lines" and make your best guess of what each side might say.

Point   Counterpoint

_____   _____

_____   _____

_____   _____

2. After clarifying the points and counterpoints, you should attempt to use the following analytical tools to critique each side of the issue:

a. Differentiating between fact and opinion. The ability to recognize statements of fact versus statements of opinion is an important first step to successful analysis of arguments. After rereading the arguments regarding the pro-life/pro-choice issue, see if you can state at least two facts and two opinions on each side.

b. Recognizing logical fallacies and faulty reasoning. Several chapters in your textbook and their corresponding critical thinking exercises can help you recognize faulty logic. For example, the problem of "incorrect assumption of cause/effect relationships" is discussed in Chapter 1, the issue of "deceptive appeals" is presented in Chapters 11 and 13, and the "incorrect and distorted use of statistics" is discussed in Appendix A.

c. Exploring the implications of conclusions. Questions such as the following can help expand your analysis of arguments. "What are the conclusions drawn by proponents of each side of the issue?" "Are there other logical alternative conclusions?"

d. Recognizing and evaluating author bias and source credibility. Ask yourself questions such as, "What does the author want me to think or do?" "What qualifications does the author have for writing on this subject?" "Is the author a reliable source for information?"

Although each of these steps requires additional time and energy, the payoff is substantial. Such exercises not only refine your critical thinking skills, but they also help make your decisions and opinions more educated and valuable.

Gender and Cultural Diversity

Gender and Cultural Diversity Activity 8.1 -Nature vs. Nurture Activity

Materials: Chalkboard or overhead projector, transparencies.

Procedures: Using the chalkboard or overhead projector, write the words "Nature" and "Nurture" across the top portion of the board/transparency. In a column between the two terms, write the words "Physical Development," "Language Development," and "Cognitive Development." Organize the class into small groups. Instruct each group to develop their list of theorists which correspond to the categories and also develop suggestions about the apparent or stereotypical developmental differences in people (i.e., boys are stronger than girls, she was born talkative, he'll never be any good a math).

After each group has completed its list, have the group leaders write their responses on the board and whether each of these differences belong in Nature or Nurture.

NATURE   NURTURE

                        Physical Development
                            (theorist)

                        Language Development
                            (theorist)

                        Cognitive Development
                            (theorist)

Conclusion: This activity takes little time and quickly demonstrates the inter-relatedness of nature and nurture concerning all aspects of development, as well as possible gender differences.

Writing Project

Writing Project 8.1

Given the need for improved writing skills in college students and to respond to the call for "writing across the curriculum," we offer writing projects for each chapter. In Chapter 8, we suggest a 2-3 page written response to the questions on Handout 8.1 - Writing Project. Recognizing the time involved in grading such writing projects, one alternative is occasionally to assign "peer grading." Collect the papers, remove student names, and assign each student a paper to grade. It helps to make their participation in peer grading part of the overall points for the writing project. This encourages a more thoughtful and responsible evaluation, as well as acknowledging and rewarding the additional work.

Handout 8.1 –Writing Project

"Letter To My Unborn Child"

Imagine for the moment that you and your partner are pregnant. Compose a 2-3 page letter to this unborn child. If you already have a child or children, write the same type of letter but make it directed to one or all of your children. If you have decided not to have children, write a letter to a "never born" child. Imagine that the letter will be read at some future date, such as the child's eighteenth birthday, the day of the child's wedding, or at the time of your death. In composing your letter, choose the questions you find most interesting and appropriate from the following list:

1. When and why did you decide to have (or not to have) a child?

2. What qualities should a good parent possess, and why?

3. Which of your qualities do you believe will help make you a successful parent?

4. Which of your qualities may interfere with your ability to be a good parent?

5. What qualities do you want your child to possess, and why?

6. What can you do as a parent to promote your child's development in the following areas:

>   cognitive development, language development, physical development, social emotional development, personality development, gender role development, moral development, and so on?

7. What are your hopes for your child's future?

8. What bits of wisdom have you acquired that you wish to pass on to your child?

Circle Of Quality – Chapter 8

Please give us your feedback. We thank you in advance for assisting us in improving the next edition. The contact information is listed in the preface.

What are the three most helpful teaching tools in this chapter?

1.

2.

3.

What are the three least useful teaching tools in this chapter?

1.

2.

3.

What are the three most difficult concepts to teach in this chapter?

1.

2.

3.

Additional Comments:

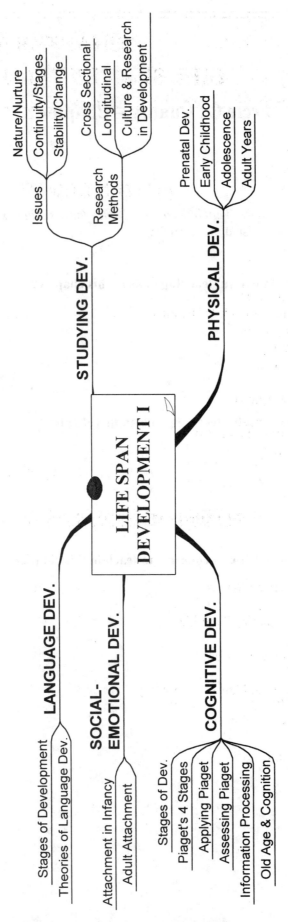

LIFE SPAN DEVELOPMENT I

STUDYING DEV.

Issues
Nature/Nurture
Continuity/Stages
Stability/Change

Research Methods
Cross Sectional
Longitudinal
Culture & Research in Development

PHYSICAL DEV.
Prenatal Dev.
Early Childhood
Adolescence
Adult Years

LANGUAGE DEV.
Stages of Development
Theories of Language Dev.

SOCIAL-EMOTIONAL DEV.
Attachment in Infancy
Adult Attachment

COGNITIVE DEV.
Stages of Dev.
Piaget's 4 Stages
Applying Piaget
Assessing Piaget
Information Processing
Old Age & Cognition

CHAPTER 9
LIFE SPAN DEVELOPMENT II

Outline

Moral Development

Kohlberg's Research

Gender and Cultural Diversity
Insights into Morality

Personality Development Over the Life Span

Thomas and Chess's Temperament Theory
Erikson's Psychosocial Theory

Research Highlight
Adolescent Rebellion, Midlife Crisis,
and the Empty Nest - Myth or Reality?

Major Influences on Personality Development

Families

Research Highlight
Children Who Survive Despite the Odds

Occupational Choices

Gender and Cultural Diversity
Cultural Differences in Ageism

Death and Dying

Attitudes Toward Death and Dying
Grief
The Death Experience
Active Learning/Critical Thinking
Dealing with Your Own Death Anxiety

GOAL

Learning Objectives

Upon completion of CHAPTER 9, the student will be able to:

1. List and describe Kohlberg's three levels of moral development, and provide an example of typical reasoning at each stage (pp. 332-335).
2. Describe the relationship between moral reasoning and moral behavior, and discuss the major criticisms of Kohlberg's theory related to political, cultural, and gender biases (pp. 335-336).
3. Describe Thomas and Chess's temperament theory of personality development, including each of their three temperamental styles and the influence of the goodness-of-fit between styles and the environment (p. 337).
4. Describe Erikson's eight stages of psychosocial development, and discuss both the criticisms and contributions of his theory (pp. 337-342).
5. Discuss the three myths of development: adolescent storm and stress, mid-life crisis, and empty nest syndrome (p. 340).
6. Describe Baumrind's three parenting styles and the subsequent criticisms of her research; discuss the impact of parental rejection and fathering on child development (pp. 342-344).
7. Discuss the causes of and treatment for family violence, the consequences of and future prevention of teen pregnancy, and the impact of divorce on social and emotional development. List nine predictors for a successful marriage (pp. 344-346).
8. Discuss research regarding factors that can increase resilience in children who are developing in "high-risk" environments (pp. 347).
9. Describe how occupational choices affect development, and discuss the activity and disengagement theories of aging (pp. 346-349).
10. Define ageism, and discuss its effects. Describe cultural, gender, and ethnic differences in the status and treatment of the elderly (p. 349).
11. Describe cultural and age variations in attitudes toward death and dying (pp. 350-351).
12. Define grief, and describe the four stages of grieving. List three strategies for coping with grief (pp. 351-353).
13. Describe Kubler-Ross's five-stage theory of death and dying, and discuss both the criticisms and contributions of her theory (p. 353).

Chapter Summary/Lecture Organizer

Introductory Vignette--The chapter opens with a comparison between four individuals of various ages (17, 20, 43, and 80) and their reactions to their respective ages. Their stories are used to illustrate age-related differences and similarities that are commonly studied by developmental psychologists..

I. **MORAL DEVELOPMENT** - The section on moral development begins with a discussion of Kohlberg's three levels of reasoning.

   A. Kohlberg's Research – Kohlberg's stages of moral development are: the pre-conventional level where morality is based on the consequences of an act (either reward or punishment); the conventional level where morality reflects the need for approval and the desire to avoid censure from authority figures; and, the post-conventional level where moral reasoning is guided by higher principles of human conduct.

   > **Gender and Cultural Diversity: Insights into Morality** - Gilligan suggests that since Kohlberg's original studies were based entirely on male responses, women naturally score lower since they have a "separate-but-equal" type of morality. The gender and cultural diversity section also discusses this from a cross-cultural perspective with a focus on nature versus nurture, and the justice and care perspectives.

II. **PERSONALITY DEVELOPMENT OVER THE LIFE SPAN** -

   A. Thomas and Chess's Temperament Theory - Thomas and Chess emphasize the genetic component of certain traits (such as sociability) and the fact that babies often exhibit differences in temperament shortly after birth.

   B. Erikson's Psychosocial Theory - Erikson expanded on Freud's ideas to develop eight psychosocial stages that cover the entire life span. The four stages that occur during childhood are trust versus mistrust, autonomy versus shame and doubt, initiative versus guilt, and industry versus inferiority. Erikson believes the major psychosocial crisis of adolescence is the search for identity versus role confusion. During young adulthood, the individual's task is to establish intimacy over isolation, and during middle adulthood, the person must deal with generativity versus stagnation. At the end of life, the older adult must establish ego integrity, which depends on the acceptance of the life that has been lived, or face overwhelming despair at the realization of lost opportunities.

Many researchers now suggest that the stage of adolescent storm and stress, the midlife crisis, and the empty nest syndrome may be exaggerated accounts of a few people's experiences and not the experience of most people.

> **Research Highlight: Adolescent Rebellion, Midlife Crisis, and the Empty Nest-Myth or Reality?** – An updated look at these three age-related beliefs.

III.   **MAJOR INFLUENCES ON PERSONALITY DEVELOPMENT** – A look at how families, parenting styles, divorce, and occupational choice may influence personality development.

A.   **Families** - Families play an important role in development. Domestic violence and child abuse, teenage pregnancies, and divorce can negatively influence all members of the family.

B.   **Parenting Styles** - Investigations of various styles of parenting found four major patterns: authoritarian, permissive-indifferent, permissive-indulgent, and authoritative. Each method had varying effects on the child's development.

> **Research Highlight: Children Who Survive Despite the Odds** – An insight into *resilient* children, and what studies have found regarding the traits and environmental circumstances surrounding them.

D.   **Occupations** - The kind of work people do and the occupational choices they make can play an important role in their lives. Before making a career decision, it is wise to research possible alternatives and take interest inventories. After retirement, there are two major theories of successful aging. The activity theory suggests people should remain active and involved throughout the entire life span, while the disengagement theory proposes that the elderly naturally and gracefully withdraw from life because they welcome the relief from roles they can no longer fulfill.

> **Gender and Cultural Diversity: Cultural Differences in Ageism** - Ageism is an important stressor for the elderly but there are some cultures where aging is revered. Within the United States, there are significant gender and ethnic differences in the status and treatment of the elderly.

IV.   **DEATH AND DYING**

A. **Attitudes Toward Death and Dying** - There is great variation across cultures and among age groups in their attitudes toward the death process. While adults generally understand the permanence, universality, and nonfunctionality of death, children often don't master these concepts until around the age of seven.

B. **Grief** - Grief is a natural and painful reaction to a loss. For most people, grief consists of four major stages--numbness, yearning, disorganization and despair, and resolution. It is important to remind students that there is no "right" way to grieve.

C. The Death Experience –In the last fifty years, Western societies have made death a medical failure rather than a natural life cycle. Elisabeth Kubler-Ross's theory of the five-stage process of dying (denial, anger, bargaining, depression, and acceptance) offers important insight and education concerning death.

> **Active Learning/Critical Thinking: Dealing With Your Own Death Anxiety -** This section provides a short self-test for students to measure their own death anxiety. It helps to take this test in class and then publicly discuss the common fears and anxieties associated with death and dying.

Teaching Resources

SECTION I - MORAL DEVELOPMENT

Learning Objectives #'s 1 - 3
Lecture Lead-Ins #'s 1, 2
Discussion Questions # 1
Writing Project p. 337

SECTION II - PERSONALITY DEVELOPMENT OVER LIFESPAN

Learning Objectives #'s 4 - 6
Lecture Lead-Ins #3
Discussion Questions # 2
Brain-Based Learning #'s 9.2, 9.3
Critical Thinking Exercise # 9.3
Writing Project p. 337

SECTION III - MAJOR INFLUENCES ON PERSONALITY DEVELOPMENT

Learning Objectives #'s 7 - 11
Lecture Lead-Ins #'s 4, 5
Lecture Extenders # 9.1
Discussion Questions #'s 2 - 5
Active Learning Activities #'s 9.1 - 9.6
Brain-Based Learning #'s 9.1, 9.3
Critical Thinking Exercise # 9.3
Gender and Cultural Diversity Activity p. 336
Writing Project p. 337

SECTION IV - DEATH AND DYING

Learning Objectives #'s 12 - 14
Lecture lead in #'s 4,5
Discussion Questions #'s 2, 6, 7
Active Learning Activities #'s 9.5, 9.6
Critical Thinking Exercise #'s 9.1 - 9.3

Lecture Lead-Ins

1. Ask students to describe a well-known, public figure with high morals. Put their descriptions on the left side of the board. Then ask them to think of one or two figures with "low morals," and put these words on the right-hand side of the board. Using the two lists, lead-in to your discussion of Kohlberg's three levels of morality.

2. Ask the question, "If you had your life to live over, would you come back as the other sex?" It works well to have the students all stand up and ask those who "strongly agree" (that they would indeed come back as the other sex) to move to one corner of the room.
    Then ask those who "agree" to move to a second corner, the "strongly disagree" to move to the third corner, and the "disagree" to move to the fourth corner. Once they have arranged themselves around the room, ask them to explain their positions. They will mention several gender-role stereotypes that you can later use to introduce the topic of gender role development. This works as a great lead-in to the topic. It gets everyone involved and their responses provide nice examples of the various theories.

3. Lead a discussion and ask the students to give examples of their own or their parents' eight stages of life (according to Erikson's model). How have the students dealt with these crises? Use this discussion as a lead-in for lectures on personality development.

4. Ask students why Americans generally have such a negative and fearful approach to aging. Is this a part of our larger fear of death and dying? How might the emotional needs of dying people be better served in your local community?

5. For a dramatic and unusual lead-in, you may want to replicate a classroom demonstration of ageism first introduced by Phillip Zimbardo (1976). In this simulation, symptoms of senility were produced in young men (eighteen to twenty two years old) within fifteen to thirty minutes. Students were first divided into groups of three, and two members of the group were told to treat the third as if he were old. The third member, unaware of this deception, reacted by rambling, presenting irrelevant discussion material, and becoming generally inattentive. Raters exposed to a tape recording of the three-member interaction also judged the third party (the "Oldster") as somewhat senile.

    As a classroom demonstration, there are numerous possibilities for variations of this technique.

    The triads can come from an actual classroom and be evaluated at once, or they can be presented visually on tapes, or even audiotapes. This simulation is an effective lead-in to discussions of several important concepts in social, clinical, and developmental psychology.

The students' behavior toward the "Oldster" can be used to discuss stereotypes of and discrimination against the elderly, while the "Oldster's" behavior can be discussed in terms of disengagement and activity theory of aging.

From a behavioral-clinical point of view, the results can be discussed in terms of learned helplessness, and from a learning theorist's viewpoint, "senile" behaviors such as repetitive story telling, rambling, and inattentiveness may simply be the results of misplaced rewards and punishments.

In following the cultural dictum of "respect for our elders," we give elders a certain amount of attention despite their inappropriate behavior, and we seldom, if ever, argue with them or present negative consequences which might weaken such behavior.

Above all, this simulation dramatically demonstrates the power of the self-fulfilling prophecy in the aging process. If fifteen to thirty minutes of being treated as if you're old can produce traditional symptoms of senility (rambling, irrelevant conversations), what happens after years of this treatment?

Students should consider the following: Why not attempt to reverse the outcome of this vicious cycle by changing society's attitude toward the elderly? For after all, if people really do become the way we treat them, ought we not treat them in the way that promotes what we want them to become?

Lecture Extenders

9.1 - The Problem of Teenage Pregnancy

This chapter, in discussing the problem of teenage pregnancy, refers to the article, "Teenage Pregnancy and Childbearing," by Furstenberg, Brooks-Gunn, and Chase-Lansdale (1989). Since this was only one issue in a wide variety of developmental topics that needed chapter coverage, the material, of necessity, was brief. As teenage pregnancy is viewed as a national social problem that will not fade away in the near future, it seems desirable to further elaborate on the material from this comprehensive article.

Although the rate of teenage pregnancy has not increased in the past few years, even declining slightly in the mid-1980s, the problem has continued to increase in visibility with various groups offering solutions for the problem. Two demographic factors appear to be important in the changing sociological scene. More teenagers are sexually active at a younger age and fewer marriages are taking place in this age group. By age 18, approximately half of white females and three fourths of African American females have become sexually active, with 19% of white females and 41% of African American females becoming pregnant. In the 1950's, the vast majority of teenage pregnancies occurred within a marriage. The reverse is true today. A trend away from marriage which began in the 1960's is occurring in all Western countries. Many reasons have been given for this shift: a higher value is placed on education; women are more likely to be involved in the labor force; premarital sex is more acceptable today and carries less risk with today's contraceptive choices; and teenage marriages are viewed as risky (and less desirable). Forty percent of all abortions in this country are performed on teenagers (these account for roughly 25% of all teenage pregnancies). At the present time, more abortions are performed on teenagers in the United States than in any other country.

How do teenagers feel about being pregnant? They do not often deliberately plan to become pregnant. It just happens. Once pregnant, the typical reaction is to become more accepting of the pregnancy as it evolves. Factors that affect the attitude are: the degree to which pregnancy is seen as interfering with educational ambitions; the perceived support of the family group; and the number of peers who are also parents. As expected, those who seek abortions are more ambitious and studious, come from a better socioeconomic background, have less intense religious feelings, and do not have friends who are having babies. Adoption has not been a popular alternative.

What happens to the relationship between the male and female who have created the "issue?" As already noted, the number who are following through with marriage is diminishing. The pregnant teenager who is most likely to marry the father of her child is the older white teenager. For the majority of pregnant teenagers, marriage is postponed indefinitely, especially for the African American woman who anticipates marriage at a later age than in earlier generations, yet is having children earlier. Some women prefer not to tell the male of the pregnancy, especially when it results from rape, a casual relationship, or some other relationship without committed involvement. Others find they have overestimated the degree of involvement on the part of the male who no longer wants to remain part of the situation. In some cases, parents actively discourage any further relationship between their pregnant teenager and the father of the child. In these cases, parents and siblings often remain sources of financial support.

Information about child support is difficult to obtain from the under-18 age group since national figures are not available. In the longitudinal Baltimore study quoted in this article, 46% of unmarried African American fathers were contributing some support at the end of one year with the number dropping to 11% by the end of 17 years.

In looking at the consequences of early parenting for teenagers, it is often difficult to assess the direction of the correlation. For example, dropping out of school may not result from having a child; having the child may in fact be a result of not caring about finishing school. However, despite these reservations, there are some general conclusions that appear to be warranted. Teenage mothers are more likely to drop out of school, even when equated for socioeconomic background and academic aptitude. Because of this educational deficit, they are less likely to find good employment. The timing of the pregnancy is of great importance; the older the teenager, the greater the chances that she will return to school and/or that she will later enter a stable marriage. The latter fact is of great importance since one third of single parent families live in poverty.

As one would expect, adolescent fathers are less likely to be adversely affected than the mother. Surprisingly, they are more likely to drop out of school after fathering a child, but this appears to have little relationship to the marital status. This finding is more robust for white and Hispanic teenagers than for African Americans.

How are the children affected? A small, but consistent difference in cognitive functioning has been found between the offspring of younger and older mothers. Differences have also been found in the psychosocial development of children of younger mothers. The impairment is manifested in increased aggressiveness, greater activity, and lack of self-control. This effect, as well as the cognitive impairment, is greater in the male offspring than in the female. Half of the African American adolescents who had a young teenage mother have failed a grade by high school and they are twice as likely to engage in school misbehaviors. Many explanations are given, including the inability of young mothers to parent effectively, less education on the part of the mothers, more family instability, and less vocalization to preschool children. One interesting finding is that the marriage of the mother or improvement in her educational status, at any time prior to her children's adolescence, will improve the performance of her offspring.

How should the problem be handled? Some speak in terms of primary prevention in which an effort is made to delay early pregnancy through education on sexuality and contraception. This approach has not been outstandingly successful. It has been difficult to prove that increased knowledge leads to more restrained behavior or more contraceptive use. Another approach is contraceptive and family planning service, an approach that is used throughout Europe. Since there is a lower teenage pregnancy rate in these countries, it is assumed that the adoption of this more open approach will reap better results. It is felt that since the media and entertainment business is constantly pushing sexual activity among teenagers, it becomes the responsibility of society to provide ways to live with heightened sexual activity without foreclosing one's future through premature childbearing.

What should be the role of society once a teenager has become pregnant? There have been a plethora of programs administered by separate agencies. The service with the best track record, that is, the highest demonstrated effectiveness, is prenatal care. Even so, large numbers of pregnant teenagers are not seeking out the medical care provided. One suggestion has been to have a single service agency that will provide all programs. At the present time, this approach has yet to be proven in terms of more pregnant females seeking out the services and their children benefiting from the intervention.

Reference: Furstenburg, F. F., Brooks-Gunn, J., & Chase-Lansdale, L. (1989). Teenage Pregnancy and Childbearing, American Psychologist, 44, 313-320.

Key Terms

MORAL DEVELOPMENT

PERSONALITY DEVELOPMENT OVER THE LIFE SPAN

MAJOR INFLUENCES ON PERSONALITY DEVELOPMENT

DEATH AND DYING

Discussion Questions

1. What would the world be like if everyone operated at Kohlberg's highest level of morality? How would this imaginary world compare to a world occupied by people who placed a higher priority on concern for others (Gilligan's "care perspective") than the rights of the individual (Gilligan's "justice perspective")? Which world would you prefer to live in?

2. If you were forced to choose a particular age to live at for the rest of your life, which age would you choose? Why? What age would be least attractive? Why?

3. If you could control the sex of your children, what gender would you choose? Why?

4. Given the importance of attachment, what could our society do to improve the chances for secure attachment? Should we invest in better day care centers? Should both parents be allowed lengthy maternity and paternity leaves? What happens to children who are raised for several months or years in foster homes or orphanages? Do they form secure attachments? What will happen to Baby Jessica (the 2 1/2-year-old) who was taken from her adoptive parents by the biological parents? Will she form a new attachment to her biological parents?

5. Day care workers are notoriously underpaid, but if their salaries were significantly improved the cost of child care would make it even more unaffordable. What should be done in this situation?

6. Do you agree with the work of Dr. Kevorkian (his assisted suicides)? Why or why not? Would you want help if you were suffering a painful and prolonged terminal illness?

7. How do cultures differ in their expression of grief? Is there a better way to grieve? How should we train our children? Ourselves? What would you consider a "perfect way to die?" What would be the worst way? Have you notified your friends and family what you want done with your body and possessions in the event of your death? If not, why not? What does your reluctance reveal about your family or culture's attitude toward death and dying?

 **Web Sites**

Marriage and Family Resources on the Web
http://www.nova.edu/ssss/FT/web.html
This resource site provides links to organizations, journals, and discussion groups relating to marriage and family issues.

Temperament
http://www.temperament.com/
This site offers a collection of links to resources on temperament.

Adult Attachment and Interpersonal Attraction
http://psychology.ucdavis.edu/shaver/h&s.html
This site provides a compilation of links to pages dealing with issues and difficulties in attachment. The site includes an FAQ on attachment.
This site provides an online assessment of adult attachment.

Attachment Home Page
http://www.attach-bond.com/
A good overview of attachment related material.

Suggested Films and Videos

Child Development

    Insight Media, 1992. 30 minutes. This program presents a historical overview of the contributions of Locke, Rousseau, Freud, Erikson, Bowlby, Watson, Gessel, and Piaget. The methods, challenges, and problems of studying development are considered.

Teenage Mind and Body

    Insight Media, 1990. 30 minutes. This video explores the areas of adolescent cognitive and physical development. Highlights include Kohlberg's theory of moral development and moral reasoning, as well as Elkind's discussion of formal operations and adolescent egocentrism.

Adulthood

    Insight Media, 1990. 60 minutes each. The three tapes in this series examine the psychological, biological, and social forces that contribute to adult development. Tapes are Early Adulthood, Middle Adulthood, and Late Adulthood.

Brandon and Rachel: Patterns of Infant Development

    U.C. Media Extension Center (Berkeley), 1991. 34 minutes. Two 7-month-olds are visiting a child development class. The professor uses these infants to demonstrate principles of motor, language, and personality development. Students are asked to do a personality profile for each infant (which follows stereotyped sex roles), but what happens if they are wearing the wrong clothing? The surprise ending will generate lively discussion.

Pulling the Punches

    Filmmakers Library, 1994. 30 minutes. This video provides an intimate view of one man's therapy to control his abusive behavior toward his wife. The patient was treated at Everyman's Center in London, where his interactions with his counselor were recorded.

Domestic Violence: Which Way Out?

    Filmmakers Library, 1994. 30 minutes. This film documents a successful treatment program in Bellevue, Washington, with a 4% repeat offense rate for those who complete the intensive therapy.

Child Sex Abusers

    Films for the Humanities and Sciences, 1995. 28 minutes. This is a specially adapted Phil Donahue show featuring mothers and their daughters who have been molested by brothers, half-brothers, and neighborhood kids. An expert who deals with abusive children (1) counsels what to look for and what to do with abusive kids, and (2) counsels kids who are being abused.

Why God, Why Me?

Filmakers Library, 1988. 27 minutes. This multi-award-winning video about childhood sexual abuse dramatizes the life of those children who grew up never feeling safe in their own homes. It is compelling, but no graphic sexual or violent scenes are presented. The program ends on a positive note, showing that survivors can establish new, loving relationships.

Where Angels Dare

National Film Board of Canada, 1993. 26 minutes. This 1994 WPA award-winning film is an intensely personal exploration of healing from childhood sexual abuse. Six men and women share their journeys and the "angels" who helped along the way.

Maturing and Aging

Annenberg/CPB, 1990. 30 minutes. This program from Zimbardo's "Discovering Psychology" series examines the myths and realities of aging in our society. Topics include Erik Erikson's psychosocial stages and biological and psychological changes that occur as we age. The video also presents examples of ageism and other negative stereotyping of adult behavior.

Growing Old in a New Age

Annenberg/CPB, 1993. 58 minutes each segment. This thirteen-part series explores many facets of adult development through interviews with researchers, older individuals, and health care professionals. Some topics include: How the Body Changes; Learning, Memory, and Speed of Processing; Intellect, Personality, and Mental Health; Social Relationships in Old Age; Work, Retirement, and Economic Status; and Dying, Death, and Bereavement.

Success

Books for Success

McKay, Matthew; Fanning, Patrick (1992). **Self-Esteem (2ⁿᵈ Edition).** New Harbinger Publications. An interesting, easy-to-understand book on overcoming your "pathological critic" thereby improving your self-esteem.

Bloomfield, Harold and Felder, Leonard (1983) **Making Peace With Your Parents** Ballantine Books A wonderful book and resource with self help exercises.

Kubler-Ross, E. (1989). **Death: The Final Stage of Growth**. Prentice-Hall. A description of the psychological aspects and experiences of seeing death as a natural phase of development.

Active Learning

Active Learning Activity 9.1 - Parenting Styles

During the discussion of social-emotional development, students often volunteer opinions about the appropriateness of the various styles of parenting discussed in the text. They also enjoy offering their own observations of "good" and "bad" parenting. If time allows, it is often helpful to allow students to form small groups and discuss four or five main suggestions for improved parenting. One member from each group can then read the list to the rest of the class and give an explanation for the group choice.

This is also an appropriate time to discuss the larger question of "Am I Parent Material?" A pamphlet of this same name with several thought-provoking, value clarifying types of questions can be obtained by writing to:

National Alliance for Optional Parenthood
2010 Massachusetts Avenue, N.W.
Washington, DC 20036

Active Learning Activity 9.2 - A Self-Test for Potential Child Abuse

As discussed in the chapter, there are various factors that increase the chances for child abuse. One of the most personally frightening, but important, realizations is that each of us has the potential for abusive behaviors. Allowing students class time to complete the following questionnaire may provide important insights and improvement in parenting skills.

Time: Approximately 15 minutes.

Advance preparation: Xerox copies of the following test.

Instructions: Review the text's discussion of the functions of the family and the factors that increase chances for child abuse. Pass around copies of the "Parenting Test" (Handout 9.2). Tell students they are free to keep the test and insist that they keep their eyes on their own paper while everyone completes the test. For students who are not parents, encourage them to answer the test as they think their mother or father would. After students have completed the test, ask students to explain why items like #1 and #2 are important to assessing abuse potential. Also discuss unusual items like #4, #9, and #12.

Handout 9.2- Active Learning

Parenting Test

Check either Yes or No.

Do you sometimes strike your child without thinking?   Yes   No

Do you feel better after you spank your child?   Yes   No

Do you sometimes spank your child with a belt or switch?   Yes   No

Are you the only person who takes care of your child?   Yes   No

Do you feel alone and frustrated by your child and without anyone?   Yes   No

Do you sometimes leave bruises or marks on your child when he's bad?   Yes   No

Does your child dirty his pants when he should be potty trained?   Yes   No

Does your husband or wife sometimes hurt the children and you're afraid to say anything?   Yes   No

Do you sometimes feel sexually attracted to your child?   Yes   No

Do you feel relieved when you yell at your child?   Yes   No

Does your child's crying and screaming make you mad?   Yes   No

When your child is bad, does it remind you of your childhood?   Yes   No

Is your child different from other children?   Yes   No

Is your child slow to potty train or not talk soon enough?   Yes   No

Do you sometimes leave your child alone when you shouldn't?   Yes   No

Is your house dirtier than it should be or not really a healthy place?   Yes   No

Were you ever abused physically or mentally as a child?   Yes   No

SCORING: According to the guidelines provided by For Kids Sake, Inc., add up your total "yes" checks and compare your results to the following:

0-1 This is a normal range for most parents.

2-3 Your answers indicate a need to reevaluate your parental role. You should discuss your parenting with a professional counselor.

4-5 You need help now. Your answers indicate a high level of frustration or hostility. Professional counseling is available free of charge (see the referrals below).

6 or more. Please seek help as soon as possible. Consider giving your child or children a vacation at Grandma's or another relative's house until you receive some counseling.

(Copyright by Kids Sake, Inc., reprinted with permission)

Referrals:

1. Call Parents Anonymous, toll free at 1-800-352-0386 to find chapters near you.

2. Your psychology instructor is also an important resource for counseling referrals.

Active Learning Activity 9.3 - Gender Bias and Parenting

Use the following exercise to demonstrate gender bias related to parenting. Give half of the class the male and the other half the female form of the following article, with its accompanying rating scale. Calculate the means for both groups and then use these data for a discussion on the differing expectations we have for males and females as parents.

---Female Form cut here---

Billings, MT--"While the cat's away, the mice will play" goes the old saying. However, for a Montana woman, the mouse got caught. It seems last month, Carl Thomas was away visiting relatives for a few days, leaving the Thomas youngsters in the care of their mother. Mrs. Thomas, however, took the opportunity to rendezvous with her secret lover Wes, leaving the two children, Rick, 4, and Jean, 3, as she had apparently done on several earlier occasions. This time, however, after many hours of neglect, fear, and hunger the Thomas children were driven to the streets in search of their mother.

The police found the children wandering the streets almost 2 miles from the Thomas home and in the process of returning the children to their mother the whole story came out. "I don't see that what I did was so terrible," Jane told an obviously upset spouse.

WOULD YOU AGREE THAT MRS. THOMAS IS A POOR PARENT? (CIRCLE ONE)

1   2   3   4   5   6   7   8

Strongly disagree   Strongly agree

(Adapted from E. Doughtie)

---Male Form cut here---

Billings, MT--"While the cat's away, the mice will play" goes the old saying. However, for a Montana man, the mouse got caught. It seems last month, Jane Thomas was away visiting relatives for a few days, leaving the Thomas youngsters in the care of their father. Mr. Thomas, however, took the opportunity to rendezvous with his secret lover, Linda, leaving the two children, Rick, 4, and Jean, 3, as he had apparently done on several earlier occasions. This time, however, after many hours of neglect, fear, and hunger, the Thomas children were driven to the streets in search of their father.

The police found the children wandering the streets almost 2 miles from the Thomas home and in the process of returning the children to their father the whole story came out. "I don't see that what I did was so terrible," Carl told an obviously upset spouse.

WOULD YOU AGREE THAT MR. THOMAS IS A POOR PARENT? (CIRCLE ONE)

1   2   3   4   5   6   7   8

Strongly disagree   Strongly agree

(Adapted from E. Doughtie)

Active Learning Activity 9.4 - Abortion, Adoption or Keeping the Child?

In view of the increasing number of teen pregnancies in America, it becomes ever more important to fully understand and appreciate the questions and conflicts a pregnant teenager must face. Should she have an abortion, give the baby up for adoption, or keep her child? Should her boyfriend or parents have a say in what she decides? This exercise is designed to improve your students' abilities to empathize. Begin by reading the following scenario.

> Anne is an average American high school student. She is a 17-year-old senior who gets top grades and has an excellent chance of obtaining several academic scholarships. In addition to school, Anne works 15 hours a week and is saving for college, which she hopes to attend the following fall. She is also pregnant.
>
> Anne's father, who is morally opposed to abortion, warned her about premarital sex. He was very upset when he found out about her pregnancy, and would never accept an abortion. He would like to see Anne keep the baby and try to get her boyfriend to marry her. Anne's mother, on the other hand, does not want anything to prevent Anne from getting a college degree, and wants her to give the baby up for adoption. Anne's boyfriend does not want to marry her or be financially responsible. He plans to enter college in the fall and wants Anne to have an abortion.
>
> Anne knows that, realistically, her pregnancy would prevent her from attending college in the fall, and that this delay would seriously jeopardize her scholarship opportunities. Without the aid of a substantial scholarship, she would need to work full-time. Anne's parents cannot afford to help her with college expenses and are unable to offer significant help with child care. Anne does not want to marry her boyfriend, nor does she assume that he will provide much support should she decide to keep the child. Anne must make a decision on her own. (Adapted from Bernards, 1988.)

Either alone or in small groups, ask students to make lists of several possible arguments from each character's perspective: Anne, her father, her mother, and her boyfriend.

Discuss which of these arguments are the most compelling for keeping the child, putting it up for adoption, and for having an abortion.

Decide which are the most persuasive arguments against each option.

Ask students, "If you, your girlfriend, or your child were pregnant and in a similar situation, how would you decide? Are your reasons different than those listed above? If so, explain why."

Active Learning Activity 9.5 - Prejudice Against the Elderly
Ask students to complete the following anonymous questionnaire (Handout 9.5). Collect their papers and discuss the most common stereotypes against the elderly. Cite examples from the text to offset these stereotypes.

Handout 9.5- Active Learning

Attitudes Toward the Elderly

Below you will find a number of statements expressing opinions. You are to indicate the degree to which you agree or disagree with each statement by writing one of the following choices in the appropriate space.

Strongly   Slightly   Slightly   Strongly
Disagree   Disagree   Disagree   Agree   Agree   Agree

Please consider each statement carefully, but do not spend too much time on any one statement. Do not skip any items. There are no "right" or "wrong" answers--the only correct responses are those that are true for you.

1. Older people generally take longer to get over an illness.

_____

2. It is foolish to claim that wisdom comes with advancing age.

_____

3. Most older people respect the privacy of others and give advice only when asked.

_____

4. It would probably be better if most old people lived in residential units that also housed younger people.

_____

5. Old people generally adapt to new ways of doing things.

_____

6. Old people very seldom lose or misplace things.

_____

7. There is something different about most old people. It's hard to figure out what makes them tick.

_____

8. Older people have a smaller vocabulary.

_____

9. Most old people are very relaxing to be with.

_____

10. You can count on finding a nice residential neighborhood when there is a sizable number of old people living in it.

_____

11. Old people have too much power in business and politics.

_____

12. Most old people are capable of new adjustments when the situation demands it.

_____

13. Most old people would prefer to quit work as soon as pensions or their children can support them.

_____

14. Most old people have little trouble concentrating and remembering things.

_____

15. Older workers have a high rate of absenteeism.

_____

16. Older employees often get occupational diseases.

_____

17. Old people are good at remembering names.

_____

Source: Adapted from Tuckman & Lorge (1953) and Kagan (1961).

Active Learning Activity 9.6 - Ageism Simulation

To informally introduce the topic of ageism, it is effective to point to an attractive middle-aged or older woman in the audience and ask the class what they think she would say if you asked her age. Once the "rudeness" of this question is established, follow up with "Would she feel complimented if I said she really looked much younger than her actual age?" Students will generally agree that this is complimentary. It is very effective at this point to turn to an attractive minority student and ask "Would you feel complimented if I said, you're really handsome or beautiful, you don't look African American (or Mexican, Chinese, etc.)?" Amidst protests that this "isn't the same thing," you can initiate a lively discussion of the overt and covert examples of ageism in our culture.

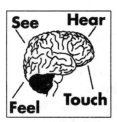

Brain-Based Learning

Brain-Based Learning Activity 9.1 - Feeling Your Age

It is often difficult for a class of mostly younger students to appreciate the different world many elderly people live in. To give the students an actual experience of what it is like to live with reduced sensory and mobility capacity the following techniques can be useful:

Vision Loss :   Have the students wear Vaseline smeared glasses or swim goggles
Hearing Loss: Put cotton balls or ear plugs into the ears
Taste Loss: Wear a nose clip and taste bland, pureed or baby food
Touch Loss: Wear mittens or extra large gloves
Mobility Loss: Wear shoes a size too small (corns!) and wrap elbow and knee joints with bandage

Allow each student to select some or all of the above artificial impairments and have him or her perform some "simple" daily tasks. Walking, talking, opening doors or pill bottles, eating, climbing stairs, reading the newspaper, looking at traffic lights etc.

During the de-briefing encourage the students to talk about what it was like to lose their taken-for-granted sensory acuity. How would they drive if they had to endure such restrictions? How would they change their life to accommodate these reduced abilities?

Brain-Based Learning Activity 9.2 - What's Your Social Clock?

Ask your students to make a list of the following numbers:

What's the best age to marry for men?
What is the best age to marry for women?
What is the best age to enter the job market?
What is the best age to select a career?
What is the time of peak earning years?
What is the best age to start having grandchildren?
What is the best age to retire?

Discuss how much agreement there is among the class in their choice of best times. If this agreement is more than "coincidence", what other factor could explain this amazing consensus?
After a discussion about the power of our society's timing norms (i.e. the social clock) have students draw a line across the paper. The left end is marked birth; the right end is marked death. After marking the line with their current position (either their age, or the year) have them look ahead into their own

future. What major milestones are they anticipating and when do they expect to reach them? Is their life plan more unique than just the social clock would predict? What major challenges or issues lie in the years just ahead? These topics could then be compared to the themes predicted by life span theorists such as Erikson.

Brain-Based Learning Activity 9.3 - Who is Old?

What is the point at which someone becomes old?
Is there a certain age beyond which most people would be considered old?
Are there other qualities (looks, health, activity patterns, mental attitude, work status, etc.) that you would look for in deciding whether a person is old?

Assuming that the course instructor is somewhat older than the majority of students, it is often useful to share how your own definition of "old" has evolved as you traveled from the early twenties to your current age.

These simple unstructured questions can elicit a great deal of evidence of "ageism" or at least the preoccupation of our culture with youth. BY FAR the best tool to introduce students to the multiple issues of aging is a video by Ken Dychtwald called, "The Age Wave". I have not listed this video in the Films & Video section since it is no longer offered commercially. It was distributed by Blue Cross of California and I urge all instructors to ask among their colleagues for a copy. The video is short and entertaining but also extremely thought provoking. It would be a perfect complement for this discussion.

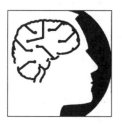

Critical Thinking

Critical Thinking Exercise 9.1 - Developing Empathy: Helping Students Deal with Grief

As discussed in the text grief is a topic of concern and difficult for all of us. We are often ill-prepared to deal with our own painful feelings or those of others. Our aversion and lack of preparation can lead us to make clumsy mistakes when dealing with others and to feel needlessly alone and isolated during our own difficult times.

This exercise is designed to directly confront the issues and pain associated with important losses (death, divorce, breakups, etc.). It will help students improve their empathy for others (an important skill of critical thinkers) and will provide specific techniques for dealing with grief.

Time: You will need a full class period to maximize the effectiveness of this exercise.

Advance preparation: Mention that you would like to have a "grief panel" and ask for student volunteers. Discuss the general problem of grief avoidance and ask for 4-5 volunteers who have had an important grief experience and would be willing to serve on the panel. Ask these students to meet with you after class or during your office hours to discuss the specifics. When talking with the volunteers, tell them that they will be asked to briefly describe their loss, their immediate feelings and reactions, their coping styles, the reactions of their friends and family, their current feelings, and what they learned by the experience. Also mention that you will encourage the class to ask questions about their experience and give specific suggestions on how other people could have helped them during their grief process. Reassure them that they are free to "pass" on any question and that you will be sitting with them to handle any awkward moments. (If you have had an important loss yourself, it is very helpful for you to also serve on the panel and to be the first volunteer.)

Instructions: During the actual class period, if you have a large class, arrange a long desk or individual stools at the front of the class for the panel. If you have a small class, arrange the chairs in a circle with the panel at one end. Thank the panel members for being brave enough to volunteer, and encourage the class to ask questions while each member is speaking. Reassure the class that the panel is prepared for questions and that they will "pass" if they prefer not to answer.

Start by asking one member of the panel to volunteer to go first, and then let each member tell his or her story for 5-6 minutes. After each panel member has spoken, encourage the class to ask general questions for all members--especially for specific suggestions on "what they should do to help." Based on actual class experience, this exercise will be extremely powerful and effective, but be prepared for some tears and awkward moments. Students often remember this as "one of the best experiences" in the entire class.

This exercise also appears in the text, Chapter 9, We include it here for your convenience, and you may want to discuss it in class to reinforce reading of the text.

Critical Thinking Exercise 9.2 - Dealing With Your Own Death Anxiety

Woody Allen once said, "It's not that I'm afraid to die. I just don't want to be there when it happens." Although some people who are very old and in poor health may welcome death, most of us have difficulty facing it. One of the most important elements of critical thinking is self-knowledge, which includes the ability to critically evaluate our deepest and most private fears.

DEATH ANXIETY QUESTIONNAIRE

To test your own level of death anxiety, indicate your response according to the following scale:

0	1	2
not at all	somewhat	very much

____1. Do you worry about dying?

____2. Does it bother you that you may die before you have done everything you wanted to do?

____3. Do you worry that you may be very ill for a long time before you die?

____4. Does it upset you to think that others may see you suffering before you die?

____5. Do you worry that dying may be very painful?

____6. Do you worry that the persons closest to you won't be with you when you are dying?

____7. Do you worry that you may be alone when you are dying?

____8. Does the thought bother you that you might lose control of your mind before death?

____9. Do you worry that expenses connected with your death will be a burden to other people?

____10. Does it worry you that your will or instructions about your belongings may not be carried out after you die?

____11. Are you afraid that you may be buried before you are really dead?

____12. Does the thought of leaving loved ones behind when you die disturb you?

____13. Do you worry that those you care about may not remember you after your death?

____14. Does the thought worry you that with death you may be gone forever?

____15. Are you worried about not knowing what to expect after death?

Source: Conte, H. R., Weiner, M. B., and Plutchik, R. (1982). Measuring death anxiety: Conceptual, psychometric, and factor-analytic aspects. Journal of Personality and Social Psychology, 43, 775-785. Reprinted with permission.

How does your total score compare to the national average of 8.5? When this same test was given to nursing-home residents, senior citizens, and college students, researchers found no significant differences, despite the fact that those tested ranged in age from 30 to 80.

This exercise also appears in the Student Study Guide, Chapter 9. We include it here for your convenience, and you may want to discuss it in class to reinforce use of the Student Study Guide.

Critical Thinking Exercise 9.3

EXERCISE I

One of the best ways for young and middle-aged people to reduce ageism is through increased exposure to the elderly. Try visiting a local senior center, retirement home, and convalescent hospital. Each of these facilities houses people with varying ages, abilities, and levels of activity. When you talk with the people in these facilities, try to really get to know them. Ask important questions about their political, spiritual, or personal beliefs about child rearing, divorce, or the value of a college education. Ask how they think things have changed since they were in their 20s, 30s, and so on. Once you've established a level of comfort, try asking about controversial topics like gun control, abortion, premarital sex, and so on. (You might also try asking similar questions with elderly relatives. Younger people sometimes complain about "having to visit" their relatives, but interest might increase if they asked interesting questions.)

Our stereotypes about aging and the elderly are generally based on lack of information. As you get to know a larger group of older people, you'll realize your previous stereotypes no longer fit. Just as African Americans or Latinos can not be categorized under a few stereotypical traits or characteristics, the same is true for the elderly.

Thinking Independently: Making Peace with Your Parents
  (An Affective Skill)

EXERCISE II

One mark of a critical thinker is the ability to think independently, which requires insight into one's own beliefs. When we feel at peace with people, we can consider their beliefs in an untroubled way and espouse them as our own or reject them freely. The following exercise will help you to clarify how psychologically independent you are from your parents by asking you to focus on your relationship with them. Many people consider independence to be merely financial. However, psychological independence is an equally significant mark of adult development. Hopefully, exploring your relationship with your parents will help you to become independent of them, as a critical thinker and as a person. In that regard, take a few moments to jot down your answers to the following:

1. Are you truly free of regrets and resentments from your childhood?

2. Are you relaxed and do you enjoy spending time with your parents? Or do you resent "having" to visit or interact with them?

3. Are you able to accept your parents, forgive them their mistakes, and give up trying to change them?

4. Do you feel loved and accepted by your parents?

5. Do you still compare yourself and compete with one of your brothers or sisters?

6. Are you still waiting to escape from your parents' rules, influence, or habits to become your own person?

7. Are you glad you had the parents you did?

8. If your parents are divorced, have you resolved your mixed feelings about this situation?

9. Do you have fears of being trapped or disappointed by a committed love relationship or marriage in your own life?

10. Have you completed your resentments and regrets toward your parent who may no longer be living? Can you accept the reality and inevitability of your own death?

Your answers to each of these questions are an important first step in actually recognizing and eventually working through these long-standing problems. These questions were adapted from the paperback book <u>Making Peace With Your Parents</u> by Harold H. Bloomfield, M.D. and Leonard Felder, Ph.D. (New York: Ballantine Books, 1983). If you desire further specific self-help information on this topic, this book is a wonderful resource. For those of you who are reading this and feeling overwhelmed by the magnitude of your problems with your parents, you may want to seek professional psychological counseling, and your instructor may be able to recommend someone in your area.

Gender and Cultural Diversity Activity

Gender and Cultural Diversity Activity 9.1 - Work and Gender

One pervasive myth in the area of gender differences regards work-related attitudes. Nieva and Gutek (1981) state that many people believe that women do not seek employment out of economic necessity, but to provide their families with money or luxuries. However, Matlin (1987) quotes U.S. Department of Labor statistics indicating that almost half of all employed women provide the only income for their families, and an additional 21 percent are in families where the two incomes together are necessary to afford the necessities. (It is surprising then that the issue of unemployment among women has received so little attention.) A second distortion is the belief that women are working only out of financial necessity and thus are less committed to their jobs than their male counterparts. Although it is economically necessary for most women to work, the majority of women, when polled, stated that they would continue to work even if there were not a financial need.

In addition to these myths, women seem to feel more role strain than men in terms of a conflict between job and family responsibilities. This may be partially due to the fact that women generally perform more household and child-care tasks than men. Paradoxically, a study by Frasher, Frasher, and Wims (1982), that asked supervisors to make decisions about a number of hypothetical personnel issues, found males who expressed family priorities over job responsibilities were more likely to be promoted than a female who expressed the same viewpoint. In addition, when a male requested leave of absence for child-care, the request was considered to be more appropriate than when the same request was made by a female.

Questions for Class Discussion

1. What are the effects of employment on the personal lives of men and women?

2. How might you explain these findings?

3. How do cultural differences in gender role ideologies affect the likelihood that one will experience role strain?

Source: Nieva, J. F. and B. A. Gutek (1981). Women and Work: a Psychological Perspective. New York: Praeger.

Writing Project

Writing Project - 9.1

Given the need for improved writing skills in college students, and to respond to the call for "writing across the curriculum," we offer writing projects for each chapter. In Chapter 9, we suggest a 2-3 page written response to the questions on Handout 9.1- Writing Project. Recognizing the time involved in grading such writing projects, one alternative is occasionally to assign "peer grading." Collect the papers, remove student names, and assign each student a paper to grade. It helps to make their participation in peer grading part of the overall points for the writing project. This encourages a more thoughtful and responsible evaluation, as well as acknowledging and rewarding the additional work.

Handout 9.1- Writing Project

Lifetime Mate

Write a personal letter to a future or current lifetime partner (husband, wife, or significant other). This letter should address most of the following questions:

1. Why did you, or will you, decide to get married or to participate in a lifetime committed relationship?

2. What qualities should a good lifetime partner possess, and why?

3. Which of your qualities do you believe will help make you a successful partner? Which of your qualities may interfere with your ability to be a good partner?

4. What specific qualities do you want your partner to possess, and why? Does your partner currently possess these traits? Are you marrying this person hoping that he or she will someday develop these traits? Would you marry this person if he or she never changes?

5. What will you do to promote your partner's growth in the following areas: cognitive development, physical development, social and emotional development, personality development, gender role development, moral development, and creativity?

6. What are your hopes for your partner's future? Your own future?

7. Do you plan to have children? Have you discussed your plans with your partner? Does he or she agree?

8. What are your deepest fears about yourself, your partner, and your relationship?

9. Do you feel that the current division of labor and responsibilities in your relationship are fair and equal? Have you discussed how this might change within a lifetime relationship or with the addition of children? Do you and your partner generally agree on how and when to spend money? If not, how do you resolve your differences?

10. What bits of wisdom from psychology and your everyday experience do you plan to apply to your relationship with your partner?

Circle of Quality – Chapter 9

Please give us your feedback. We thank you in advance for assisting us in improving the next edition. The contact information is listed in the preface.

What are the three most helpful teaching tools in this chapter?

1.

2.

3.

What are the three least useful teaching tools in this chapter?

1.

2.

3.

What are the three most difficult concepts to teach in this chapter?

1.

2.

3.

Additional Comments:

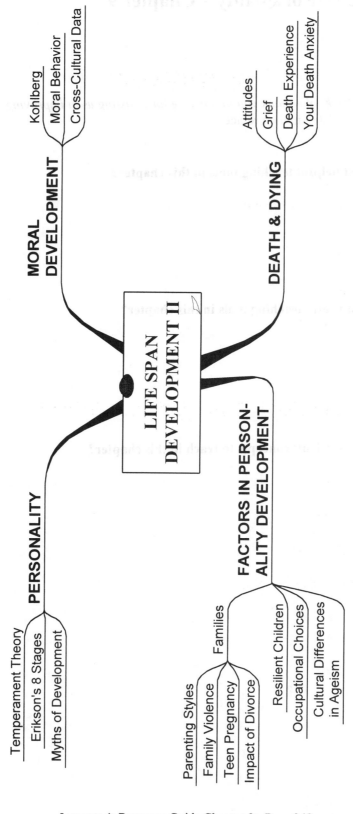

MORAL DEVELOPMENT
- Kohlberg
- Moral Behavior
- Cross-Cultural Data

DEATH & DYING
- Attitudes
- Grief
- Death Experience
- Your Death Anxiety

LIFE SPAN DEVELOPMENT II

PERSONALITY
- Temperament Theory
- Erikson's 8 Stages
- Myths of Development

FACTORS IN PERSON-ALITY DEVELOPMENT
- Parenting Styles
- Family Violence
- Teen Pregnancy
- Impact of Divorce
- Families
- Resilient Children
- Occupational Choices
- Cultural Differences in Ageism

CHAPTER 10
GENDER AND HUMAN SEXUALITY

Outline

Sex and Gender

Problems with Definition
Gender Role Development
Sex and Gender Differences

The Study of Human Sexuality

Gender and Cultural Diversity
A Cultural Look at Sexual Behaviors

Sexual Behavior

Sexual Arousal and Response

Research Highlight
Are there Evolutionary Advantages to
Female Non-monogamy?

Sexual Orientation

Sexual Problems

Sexual Dysfunction
Sexually Transmitted Diseases (STDs)

Active Learning
Rape Myths and Rape Prevention

GOAL learning Objectives

Upon completion of CHAPTER 10, the student should be able to:

1. Differentiate between sex, gender, masculinity, and femininity (p. 360).
2. Differentiate between gender identity and sexual orientation; define transsexualism, transvestitism, homosexual, and bisexual (pp. 360-362).
3. Define gender role, and describe the two major theories of gender role development: social learning theory and cognitive development theory (pp. 362-363).
4. Describe the major sex and gender differences between males and females; discuss the contributions of nature and nurture on gender differences, and the effects of gender role stereotyping (pp. 364-366).
5. Define androgyny, and discuss research on the relationship between mental health characteristics and higher scores on masculinity or androgyny (pp. 366-367).
6. Briefly discuss the contributions of Havelock Ellis, Kinsey, and Masters and Johnson to the study of human sexuality (pp. 369-370).
7. Briefly describe cultural variations in human sexual behavior, and provide an example of an ethnocentric bias related to a U.S. sexual ritual or procedure (pp. 370-373).
8. List and describe the four stages in Masters and Johnson's sexual response cycle (p. 374).
9. Discuss the two major perspectives that explain differences in sexual desire, motivation, and activity between men and women: the evolutionary perspective and the social role approach (pp. 375-376).
10. Describe the findings of naturalistic studies of human courtship rituals, including the role of the female in initiating and maintaining a flirtatious interaction (p. 367).
11. Discuss genetic/biological and psychosocial explanations for homosexuality; define homophobia and state the position of the psychological community regarding homosexuality (pp. 376-378).
12. List the major forms of sexual dysfunction and state their possible organic and/or psychological causes (pp. 378-381).
13. Discuss the impact of sexual scripts, hormones, nerve impulses, and emotions on sexual arousal, including the interaction of the sympathetic and parasympathetic nervous systems, and the role of performance anxiety (pp. 379-381).
14. Describe the four major principles of Masters and Johnson's approach to sex therapy. Describe three guidelines for improving sexual functioning (pp. 382-383).
15. List the major sexually transmitted diseases (STDs) and describe their basic symptoms and the consequences if left untreated. State age- and gender-related risk factors for contracting an STD (pp. 383-384).
16. Describe the five routes of transmission for an HIV infection, and explain the progression of the disease from initial infection to "full-blown AIDS" (pp. 384-385).
17. List six suggestions for decreasing the chances of contracting HIV/AIDS and other STDs (pp. 384-385).
18. Discuss common rape myths, and state three ways to avoid stranger rape plus three ways to prevent acquaintance rape (pp. 386, Appendix B).

Chapter Summary/Lecture Organizer

Introductory Vignette - Chapter 10 begins with the story of twins whose parents decided to raise one of them as a girl when that one was incorrectly circumcised at the age of 7 months. It tells the path that child took in regards to sexual gender as the child aged to adolescence.

I.   **SEX AND GENDER**

    A. Problems With Definition – The question of what is male and what is female can be confusing. Researchers have come to refer to "sex" as the biological meaning and "gender" as the psychological and socio-cultural meaning of maleness and femaleness. There are at least seven dimensions of sex (chromosomal sex, gonadal sex, hormonal sex, external genitals, internal accessory organs, masturbation, and intercourse) along with the two dimensions of gender (gender identity and gender role).

    B. Gender Role Development – More than any other concept, gender roles influence our lives from the moment of birth until the moment of death. There are currently two major theories of gender role development: social learning and cognitive development. Social learning theory suggests girls learn how to be feminine and boys learn how to be masculine in two major ways: by specific gender role behaviors and by the behavior of others. With cognitive development, it is believed that one's own cognitions or thought processes are responsible for gender role development.

    C. Sex and Gender Differences – Physical anatomy is the most obvious difference between malesand females. There are also functional and structural sex differences in the brains. Researchers focus on two important findings, cognitive abilities and aggression, as psychological differences. We then explore the way to minimize differences through androgyny.

        Research Highlight: The Art and Science of Flirting – Monica Moore , a scientist from the University of Missouri, has observed and recorded many scenes, of what she calls "nonverbal courtship signaling" (flirting). One of these scenes, of a man and a woman in a singles bar, is reflected here and shows what can happen with flirting behavior.

II.   **THE STUDY OF HUMAN SEXUALITY** - Although sex has always been an important part of human interest, motivation, and behavior, it received little scientific attention before the twentieth century. Havelock Ellis was among the first to study human sexuality despite the heavy repression and secrecy of nineteenth-century Victorian times. Alfred Kinsey and his colleagues were the first to conduct large-scale, systematic surveys and interviews of the sexual practices and preferences of Americans during the 1940s and 1950s. The research team of Masters and Johnson pioneered the use of actual laboratory measurement and observation of human physiological response during sexual arousal.

> **Gender and Cultural Diversity: A Cultural Look at Sexual Behaviors** - Cultural studies are also important sources of scientific information on human sexuality. Comparisons between cultures helps put sex in a broader perspective, as well as helping minimize ethnocentrism (viewing one's own ethnic group as central and "correct" or "best," and then judging the rest of the world according to this standard).

III. **SEXUAL BEHAVIOR** – *Men are from Mars and Women are from Venus* proclaims a recent book title. This section will explore this topic, as well as sexual orientation.

A. Sexual Arousal and Response – To understand differences as well as similarities in male and female behavior, it helps to begin with Masters and Johnson's four-stage sexual response cycle--the excitement phase, plateau phase, orgasm phase, and resolution phase. Male and female differences are usually the focus of most research. For example, the evolutionary perspective, which emphasizes genetic and biological forces or the social role approach, proposes that gender differences arise from different divisions of labor.

> **Research Highlight: Are There Evolutionary Advantages to Female Non-monogamy?** – While the evolutionary perspective suggests only males have a biological advantage to multiple sex partners, in at least 18 societies around the world it is female non-monogamy that offers survival value to women and children.

B. Sexual Orientation - Some theorists believe sexual orientation is determined by the environment (parental modeling, family patterns, learning through rewards and punishments), but others suggest the origin is biological (genetic or prenatal hormonal biasing).

IV. **SEXUAL PROBLEMS** – Exploring what happens when things don't go smoothly and what causes normal sexual functioning to stop for some, are two items explored in this area.

A. Sexual Dysfunction - Sexual dysfunctions are sometimes treated by sex therapists. Although defining these problems can be difficult, many people have been helped by sex therapy. Masters and Johnson emphasize the couple's relationship, an integration of physiological and psychosocial factors, cognitions, and specific behavioral techniques. Professional sex therapists offer important guidelines for everyone: Sex education should be early and positive, goal or performance orientation should be avoided, and communication should be open.

B. Sexually Transmitted Diseases (STDs) - Sexual behavior is affected by the problem of AIDS and other sexually transmitted diseases. Although AIDS is known to be transmitted only through sexual contact or exposure to infected blood, many people have irrational fears of contagion.

> **Active Learning/Critical Thinking: Rape Myths and Rape Prevention** - Students are asked to explore their own "rape myths" and then offered several both stranger and acquaintance rape.

Teaching Resources

SECTION I - SEX AND GENDER

Learning Objectives #'s 5 - 8
Lecture Lead-Ins # 4
Discussion Questions #'s 1, 3
Active Learning Activities #'s 10.1, 10.2, 10.4 - 10.7
Critical Thinking Exercise #'s 10.1 & 10.3
Gender and Cultural Diversity Activity # 10.1
Writing Project #10.1

SECTION II - THE STUDY OF HUMAN SEXUALITY

Learning Objectives #'s 1 - 4
Lecture Lead-Ins #1
Lecture Extenders #1
Discussion Questions # 2
Active Learning Activities # 10.2

SECTION III - SEXUAL BEHAVIOR

Learning Objectives #'s 8 - 11
Lecture Lead-Ins #'s 3, 4
Lecture Extenders # 10.1
Discussion Questions #'s 2, 4 ,5, & 6
Active Learning Activities #'s 10.2, 10.4, 10.5
Critical Thinking Exercise # 10.1
Gender and Cultural Diversity Activity # 10.1

SECTION IV - SEXUAL PROBLEMS

Learning Objectives #'s 12 - 18
Lecture Lead-Ins #'s 2, 5
Discussion Questions # 5
Active Learning Activities #'s 10.2 - 10.5
Critical Thinking Exercise # 10.1 & 10.2

Lecture Lead-Ins

1.   Why would psychologists want to study human sexual behavior? Isn't this more a subject matter for biology? Ask the class for some discussion on this topic. The instructor can take the opposite side to the majority of the class and argue his or her point very strongly. This will give the students a chance to relax with a subject they are all very interested in, but frequently find difficult to discuss.

2.   Pass out 3X5 cards and ask students to anonymously respond to the question, "How has AIDS changed your own thinking or behavior in regard to sexual activity?" Lead a discussion to see if this epidemic has modified student attitudes and behaviors. Use their responses as a lead-in to your discussion of sexual problems.

3.   Discuss the rights of gays and lesbians in your state and community and how they are offered no protection under current civil rights legislation. This is a very sensitive topic and care must be taken to create a classroom climate where issues can be discussed in a dignified, civil manner. This can be a productive and useful lead-in to the topic of sexual orientation and the entire chapter.

4.   Ask students to speculate on the consequences of a 16-year- old boy being introduced to sexual intercourse by a 36-year- old woman. Many will see this as a positive experience. Now reverse the roles with a 16-year-old girl and 36-year- old man. Student comments frequently reveal a strong double standard in this case. Discuss general problems associated with sexuality and double standards for male and female behavior. How does this standard affect female orgasm difficulties? What about males and performance anxiety? Use their responses as a lead-in to the sexual problems lecture.

5.   Lead a discussion of AIDS and the college student: an open discussion of sexually transmitted diseases (STD) to include AIDS. Is prevention with condoms practiced? If not, why not? Who is responsible?

Lecture Extenders

10.1 - Changing Attitudes on Masturbation

The psychiatrist, Thomas Szasz, who has been an ongoing critic of some current practices in the mental health area, has also spoken out against Masters and Johnson's approach to sexual problems. He presented these complaints in the book, Sex by Prescription (1980). The discussion below will focus on only one issue from his book: the re-labeling of a behavior once considered a disease or a cause of disease that is now thought to be so universal that an absence of this behavior is now considered a mental problem. The behavior in question is, of course, masturbation.

Masturbation was declared a hazardous activity in the 18th century, and this attitude prevailed for about 200 years. Males were believed to be the major perpetrators, and the negative reaction was based upon the belief that sperm were precious and should not be wasted. Esquirol, a French psychiatrist in the 18th century, claimed that masturbation led to insanity, stupidity, and death. Benjamin Rush, the father of American psychiatry, also took a strong anti-masturbation stand in the early 19th century. He elaborated upon a number of supposed bad outcomes: ". . . it produces seminal weakness, impotence, dysury, tabes dorsalis, pulmonary consumption, dyspepsia, dimness of sight, vertigo, epilepsy, hypochondriasis, loss of memory, managlia, fatuity, and death." (p. 17)

This was not Rush's unique opinion. Another medical voice suggested that masturbation was more deadly than the plague, war, or smallpox. Even worse, it could destroy civilization. One of the books dispensing medical advice stated that masturbation leads to spermatorrhea (seminal weakness), impotence, softening of the brain, and insanity. This particular author considered himself a specialist in the treatment of sexual disorders, mainly spermatorrhea, and he included 12 pages of testimony from satisfied patients who had been cured. Another investigator, Krafft-Ebing, said that masturbation represents coarse, animal instincts, and if practiced, weakens the desire for the opposite sex.

Freud, of course, is given credit for having opened up the whole area of sexual desire, especially in his recognition of sexual drives in children. However, he did not see sexual behavior as a valuable part of human life. As Szasz puts it, Freud felt that normal heterosexual activity leads to unwanted babies; abnormal and perverse acts lead to hysteria in women and neurasthenia in men; and sex with prostitutes leads to syphilis. Szasz interprets this to mean that Freud thought sex was more trouble than it was worth. Masturbation was a matter of special concern to psychoanalysis at the time and there were 13 meetings of the Vienna Psychoanalytic Society between 1908 and 1912 to discuss the problem of masturbation neurosis. (Neurosis was a general term for the category of anxiety disorders; more precisely, the subcategory most often implicated was neurasthenia.) Freud declared masturbation an infantile type of sexual activity and believed that it might cause organic injury (which part of the body would be injured was not designated). Freud, noted for his intuitive ability to perceive the true meaning of behavior (symbolic interpretation), noted that many other acts were symbolic behaviors for the actual act of masturbation. For example, in one case history of a young man who squeezed the pimples on his face, Freud pointed out that this behavior was a symbolic substitute for masturbation. The skin depression created by squeezing out the blackhead was equivalent to the female genitalia, thereby providing the man with the punishment (castration) for forbidden masturbation. Rituals, compulsions, and obsessions were interpreted similarly.

Karl Menninger, one of the most influential American psychiatrists of the post-Freudian era, continued to prescribe masturbation. He felt it was inevitable that guilt feelings would accompany the practice. In a more recent attack (1973) with a different twist, a psychiatrist denigrated the practice of women using running water to induce sexual excitement by declaring it a practice that results from unconscious conflicts.

Enter Masters and Johnson whose perceived role was to alert the American public to the extent and seriousness of sexual dissatisfaction. The problem was so severe according to Masters and Johnson that not only were half the marriages in America in danger, but the political stability of the country itself was threatened (p. 63). What could be done about this dangerous situation? One suggested solution for husbands and wives who were in these unfulfilling marriages was to masturbate. They especially advocated it for women during their menstrual period since it increases menstrual flow and reduces cramps, headaches, and backaches. Szasz facetiously refers to Masters and Johnson's promotion of masturbation for menstrual difficulties as better than Excedrin. As for their urging of older men to masturbate to keep in shape, Szasz refers to this bit of advice as "Use it or lose it," and equates it to "penile jogging" (p. 63).

One of the new diagnostic categories to arise during this period was masturbatory orgasmic inadequacy. This is strictly a female disorder and refers to those who have not climaxed as a result of masturbation. This term applies even if a female has found heterosexual relationships satisfactory. Since this problem should be remedied, a nine-step exercise has been developed that will overcome this deficiency.

Szasz's criticisms deal with much more than just the 180-degree change with regard to masturbation: he challenges the very concept of the "sexual expert." He is most vitriolic in his discussion of the research methods used by Masters and Johnson. Frankly, most people do not entertain a moderate position with regard to this type of research: they either agree strongly or disagree strongly with the Masters and Johnson approach. But if Szasz is right about there being no sexual experts, what's a person to do?

Reference: Szasz, T. (1980). Sex by prescription. Garden City, NJ: Anchor Press/Doubleday.

Key Terms

GENDER

Androgyny (p. 366)
Bisexual (p. 362)
Gender (p. 360)
Gender Identity (p. 360)
Gender Role (p. 363)
Homosexual (p. 362)
Sex (p. 360)
Sexual Orientation (p. 362)
Transsexualism (p. 362)
Transvestism (p. 362)

SEXUAL BEHAVIOR

Double Standard (p. 375)
Ejaculation (p. 374)
Excitement Phase (p. 374)

Homophobia (p. 377)
Orgasm Phase (p. 374)
Plateau Phase (p. 374)
Refractory Period (p. 374)
Resolution Phase (p. 374)
Sexual Response Cycle (p. 374)

SEXUAL PROBLEMS

AIDS (Acquired Immune Deficiency Syndrome) (p. 384)
Erectile Dysfunction (p. 378)
HIV Positive (p. 384)
Orgasmic Dysfunction (p. 378)
Performance Anxiety (p. 381)
Sexual Dysfunction (p. 378)
Sexual Scripts (p 379)

Discussion Questions

1. What are the major advantages and disadvantages to distinctly different male/female gender roles? Imagine that you were born as the other sex. How would your life be different? Would your career plans, hobbies, friendships, and family dynamics be different? Why is gender such a large part of our lives?

2. How did you first learn about sex? How did you feel? Was the information accurate? How would you like your own children to find out about sex? At what age should children learn about sex?

3. Birth Control: who is responsible? The onus has long been on the woman to provide for birth control or face the consequences. Has this standard changed or remained the same? How could the media and general public increase the use of birth control by both men and women?

4. U.S. rates of teen-age pregnancy and abortion are among the highest in the industrialized nations. Is this a class or race problem or a result of our society's conflicting messages about sexuality?

5. How do students feel about their sexual future? Are they afraid? What is in the future for their children? Lead a discussion of " Sex Fears in the 90's and Beyond."

6. Some politicians and famous public figures are homosexual, yet they help pass discriminatory laws or make derogatory remarks about other homosexuals. Should these individuals be "outed"-- having their sexual orientation made public by another person? Why or why not?

Web Sites

Kinsey Institute for Sex Research

http://www.indiana.edu/~kinsey/

This is one of the best research based sites on sexology. A wide variety of current and historical information and many other links are offered by this site.

Dr. Ruth Online

http://cgi.pathfinder.com/drruth/

Questions and Answers on many topics in sexuality by one of the best known sex therapist are found in this site. It is aimed at the general public. Again many links for further study.

Planned Parenthood

http://www.plannedparenthood.org/

This is a comprehensive website for contraception and other topics. It includes links to local resources grouped by zip code.

Childbirth Organization

http://www.childbirth.org

Covers all areas relating to childbirth from conception and pregnancy through childbirth. It contains personal stories as well as information and referral resources to many specialties.

Gay Community

http://www.zzapp.org/awes/egcm

A long established site called The Electronic Gay Community Magazine has an abundance of information regarding issues and interests for the gay community including lifestyle, health, political, AIDS, legal, fun and other topics.

Positive Sexuality

http://www.positive.org/cps/Home/index.html

The Coalition for Positive Sexuality addresses the topic of teenage sexuality. As the title indicates
it advocates a positive approach to sexuality based on accurate information. Topics such as safe sex, birth control, STDs, Aids, sexual lifestyle choices are discussed. The emphasis is on providing support for informed choices.

STD Mega Site

http://www.cdc.gov/nchstp/dstd/dstdp.html

The Center for Disease Control and Prevention has a special division responsible for the prevention of sexually transmitted diseases. This site contains up to date statistical and research information.

Suggested Films and Videos

The Differences Between Men and Women
Films for the Humanities and Sciences, 1995. 23 minutes. The old question "Are the differences between men and women conditioned by biology or by family and social environment?" is answered with recent research that claims that male and female brains are far from identical. The video also looks at cultural influences on gender-related behaviors.

Metamorphosis: Man into Woman
Filmmakers Library. 1990, 58 minutes. This multi-award-winning film follows Gary for three years as he goes through the difficult transition from a man into a woman. Interviews with his coworkers and family provide insight into their difficulties with Gary/Gabi.

Sex Hormones and Sexual Destiny
Insight Media. 26 minutes. A Rutgers laboratory is visited where research has demonstrated that hormones have a measurable effect on "masculine" and "feminine" behavior and that the structure of male and female brains is different. The influence of the environment on female behavior is also discussed. The film features Dr. June Rainiest, director of the Chinese Institute for Research in Sex, Gender, and Reproduction.

Gender and Relationships
Insight Media, 1990. 30 minutes. This program emphasizes that even the most respected authorities are not in agreement about what factors influence love, affection, and sexual attraction. Some questions addressed are: What is love? What makes sexual behavior "normal" or "abnormal"? Why and in what ways do men and women differ in their sexual attitudes, behaviors, and motives?

Sex Roles: Charting the Complexity of Development
Insight Media, 1991. 60 minutes. This film looks at the cultural ramifications of sex roles and the associated myths. Three theories of socialization (Freudian, social-learning, cognitive-developmental) are analyzed regarding the nature-nurture controversy. The negative impact of sex-role stereotyping is examined.

Brandon and Rachel: Patterns of Infant Development
U.C. Media Extension Center (Berkeley), 1991. 34 minutes. Two 7-month-olds are visiting a child development class. The professor uses these infants to demonstrate principles of motor, language, and personality development. Students are asked to do a personality profile for each infant (which follows stereotyped sex roles), but what happens if they are wearing the wrong clothing? The surprise ending will generate lively discussion.

Homosexuality

Films for the Humanities and Sciences. 26 minutes. This program explores the biological, genetic, psychological, and cultural roots of sexual behavior--in particular, those that influence homosexuality.

AIDS: No Nonsense Answers

Films for the Humanities and Sciences, 1995. 10 minutes. This brief, but extremely informative, video demonstrates prevention behaviors and lifestyle changes while presenting the basic facts about AIDS and HIV. Many questions that your students have will be answered in this film including, "if one in a group of children is positive, are the others at risk?"

AIDS RESEARCH: The Story So Far

Films for the Humanities and Sciences, 1995. 57 minutes. In this report from the front lines of the war on AIDS, state-of-the-art computer animation reveals the AIDS virus at work. The program explains our current knowledge about AIDS and examines current and future drugs that may control the disease.

College Students and AIDS

U.C. Extension Media Center (Berkeley), 1990. 26 minutes. This film helps students identify and overcome the social and psychological barriers that prevent them from lowering their risk of becoming infected with HIV. It features undergraduates discussing the issues related to their at-risk activities. The students include both men and women from a variety of ethnic groups.

Child Sex Abusers

Films for the Humanities and Sciences, 1995. 28 minutes. This is a specially adapted Phil Donahue show featuring mothers and their daughters who have been molested by brothers, half-brothers, and neighborhood kids. An expert who deals with abusive children counsels what to look for and what to do with abusive kids, and counsels kids who are being abused.

Why God, Why Me?

Filmakers Library, 1988. 27 minutes. This multi-award-winning video about childhood sexual abuse dramatizes the life of those children who grew up never feeling safe in their own homes. It is compelling, but no graphic sexual or violent scenes are presented. The program ends on a positive note, showing that survivors can establish new, loving relationships.

Where Angels Dare

National Film Board of Canada, 1993. 26 minutes. This 1994 WPA award-winning film is an intensely personal exploration of healing from childhood sexual abuse. Six men and women share their journeys and the "angels" who helped along the way.

Men, Women, and the Brain

Films for the Humanities and Sciences, 1998. 57 minutes. This video examines the question of whether certain differences between men and women are innate or the product of experience. Various experts from well known institutions discuss the differences between male and female brains. These differences appear to have significant affects on aging, reading ability, spatial skills, aggression, depression, schizophrenia, and sexuality.

Violence Against Women

Films for the Humanities and Sciences, 1995. 46 minutes. This program examines violent relationships, focussing on the secrecy that often surrounds cases of domestic violence. Information on how to leave an abusive partner is provided. Specific instructions for speaking out, forming a plan of action, when to leave, and where to go are provided. Additional topics including legal considerations, help for abusers, and the protection of children from abusers are also discussed.

Sexual Attraction

Insight Media, 1997. 48 minutes. This video examines human sexual attraction as a function of the complex interaction between sexual desires, biological drives, and romantic love. Real-life case studies are presented with accompanying commentary by psychologists, anthropologists, and biologists. In addition, the possible role of pheromones and the evolution of monogamy are considered.

Chemistry of Love

WETA/PBS, 1997. 60 minutes. This program presents a case for lust, love, and fidelity owing as much, if not more, to biology and evolution than to emotion and conscious thought. Panel discussion format is used to consider the roles of hormones, brain chemistry, and mental pre-dispositions in bringing about sexual arousal. These ideas are then used to challenge the traditional conceptions of sexual attraction and romantic love.

Tough Guise: Media Images and the Crisis in masculinity

Media Education Foundation, 1999. 40 minutes. This program takes a systematic look at the social construction of masculine identity and the images provided by popular culture in recent years. Role models promoting rugged individualism and violence are at odds with an ever increasing need for cooperation and interdependence. Aggressive strategies used to solve problems and settle disputes are loaded with attendant dangers to both women and men.

You, Your Body, and Your Self-Image

Films for the Humanities and Sciences, 1998. 28 minutes. This video examines the psychological and health effects on both genders as a result of the ideal body types exemplified in popular culture. The effects of eating disorders on young women fixated on being slim and those of young men using anabolic steroids to achieve muscle mass are illustrated. Alternatives to the current thin female and muscular male ideals are offered. The physical and psychological benefits to both young women and men of healthy diet, exercise, and lifestyle are presented.

Success

Books For Success

Love, Patricia with Robinson, Jo (1995). **Hot Monogamy.** Plume/Penguin.
A tremendously helpful book. The book delivers on the promise of its subtitle "Essential Steps to more passionate, intimate Lovemaking". It is filled with exercises and practical wisdom. Highly recommended.

The Boston Women's Health Book Collective (1992). **The New Our Bodies, Ourselves: A Book By and For Women.** Simon & Schuster.
A new version of the recognized compendium of factual information blended with personal experience on the topics of women's health issues and the female body.

Tannen, Deborah (1990). **You Just Don't Understand: Women and Men in Conversation**. Ballantine.
A best-selling exploration of the problems and frustrations of communication between men and women and how to work at overcoming them.

Reinisch, June M. (1990). **The Kinsey Institute New Report on Sex: What You Must Know to Be Sexually Literate.** St. Martin's Press.

Beck, Aaron T. (1988). **Love Is Never Enough.** Harper & Row.
Dr Beck (the founder of cognitive therapy) provides a great synopsis in his subtitle: "How couples can overcome misunderstandings, resolve conflicts, and solve relationship problems through cognitive therapy."

O'Connor, D. (1989. **How to Put the Love Back into Making Love**. Doubleday.
A book about overcoming intimacy problems by bringing sensuality into the relationship.

Zilbergeld, B. (1992). **The New Male Sexuality: A Guide to Sexual Fulfilllment**. Bantam.
One of the few books available providing information on male sexual functioning.

Hendrix, Harville (1990). **Getting the Love You Want - A Guide for Couples.** Harper Prennial Library.
An inspiring and challenging book on how to build mature, conscious love relationships. Filled with exercises and examples. Highly recommended.

Hendrix, Harville and Zion, Claire (1993). **Keeping the Love You Find - A Guide for Singles.** Pocket Books.
A companion volume to the couple's guide. A further application of the IMAGO approach to preparing oneself for a mature, conscious relationship. A self-help program for people who want to stop dating and start creating lasting love in their lives.

Active Learning

Active Learning Activity 10.1 - Review for Gender Dimensions

After a brief "lecturette" on the nine dimensions of gender, it helps to pass around the following handout as a quick self-test. It helps clarify the differences.

(Answers to Handout 10.1--1. biological sex or gender identity 2. gender role; sexual orientation 3. sexual orientation; is not; is not 4. gender role 5. sexual orientation; gender identity)

Active Learning Activity 10.2 - Everything You Always Wanted to Know

With an introduction to the classic book <u>Everything You Always Wanted to Know about Sex But Were Afraid to Ask,</u> pass around blank three by five inch index cards and ask students to write down anonymously at least one question concerning sexual behavior (arousal, response, or problems). Collect the cards and answer those you feel comfortable with--maybe save the more difficult ones for the sex therapist you invite to class.

Active Learning Activity 10.3 - Guest Speakers

Invite a local sex therapist or general counselor to your class to talk about sex problems and how they affect relationships. If your college has a speaker's bureau for the campus health center, invite a speaker to class for a brief discussion of the problems they treat and the services they offer (e.g., birth control, condoms, etc.).

Active Learning Activity 10.4 - Male/Female Questions

Break the class down into small (four to five members) same-sex groups Ask the members of each group to elect a spokesperson and to decide on three to five questions they would like to ask the opposite sex. After five to ten minutes of discussion, arrange the chairs in a large circle, with men on one side of the room and women on the other. Allow each group rotating turns asking one of their questions. Encourage lots of response from all students and reassure everyone that the discussion is not always about individual beliefs and practices but about what "most men or women" believe or practice. This exercise is generally great fun, and the students have often wanted a "rematch" to finish up their questions.

Handout 10.1- Active Learning

Gender Dimensions Self-Test

Using the terms gender role, biological sex, gender identity, and sexual orientation, fill in the following:

1. A transsexual has difficulty with his/her _____.

2. When someone says, "all gay men act like sissies," they are confusing _____ with _____.

3. _____ refers to a person's choice or preference in sexual partners. It is or is not (circle one) related to gender role. It is or is not related to gender identity.

4. When someone says, "all women are naturally good with babies," they are demonstrating their own _____ expectations for women.

5. The term "gay" refers to _____; whereas the term transsexual refers to _____.

Active Learning Activity 10.5 - Desirable Qualities in a Date

Break the class into small groups of four to five same-sex students. Give one-half of the female groups copies of Handout 10.5 - Form A, and the other half copies of Handout 10.5 - Form B. Do the same for the male groups. Ask each group to quietly discuss their answers, and after ten to fifteen minutes have someone from each group put their responses on the board. After all groups have entered their responses, discuss differences between the group responses. It soon becomes apparent that some groups had a different assignment: Those groups with Form A were asked to list desirable characteristics for a "casual date," while those with Form B listed characteristics desired in a "long term, committed relationship." Write the label "Form A/Casual" or "Form B/Committed" above each group's listing on the board. Ask students to discuss why all groups wanted something different in their casual versus committed relationships. Discuss any differences between male and female groups. Explore the problems with such gender differences, and the fact that long-term relations generally develop from short-term relations, which may explain some of the current dissatisfaction in dating and love relationships. This exercise provides a good "opener" for class discussion on various topics in this chapter.

Active Learning Active Learning Activity 10.6 - Dating Exercise

For the more daring instructor and smaller, more personal classes, we recommend the following "Dating Exercise." Ask males to stand and move to a line along one side of the room. Assign females to ask one male for a ten-minute out-of-class "Coke/Coffee date." Males are instructed to respond only with a yes or no to the initial invitation AND for the first five minutes of the date. Although this exercise is sometimes embarrassing to the men who are "left behind" and to the females who may face rejection, it is a powerful demonstration of the problems with gender roles for both males and females. Students have consistently found this exercise fun, stimulating, and/ or painful, but "worth it." (Adapted from Goldberg, 1976).

Active Learning Activity 10.7 - Sex Role Stereotypes

Tape excerpts from popular television programs (e.g., "Friends," "Home Improvement," "ER") which illustrate sex role stereotypes or demonstrate how some programs are working to avoid such stereotypes. After the students have viewed the tape, have them mark the perceived characteristics on Handout 10.7.

Mention to students that the first seven characteristics on both the male and the female lists are found in Broverman's list of male-valued stereotypic traits and the last seven are female-valued stereotypic traits. Discuss Broverman's research and ask students which program was MOST and which was LEAST stereotypical in their lead male/female roles. Ask students to think back to the television programs they watched as children and discuss how roles have changed in recent times and the advantages and disadvantages of these changes.

Handout 10.5- Active Learning

Desirable Qualities In A Date

Form A

Please list the five most important characteristics you would look for when selecting a partner for casual dating:

1._____

2._____

3._____

4._____

5._____

Handout 10.5- Active Learning

Desirable Qualities In A Relationship

Form B

Please list the five most important characteristics you would look for when selecting a partner for a long-term, committed relationship:

1._____

2._____

3._____

4._____

5._____

Handout 10.7 - Active Learning

Television Analysis - Male Lead Actor

	Program 1	Program 2	Program 3
Aggressive			
Independent			
Hides Emotions			
Very Objective			
Dominant			
Very Competitive			
Very Adventurous			
Very Talkative			
Very Tactful			
Passive			
Dependent			
Very Excitable in a Minor Crisis			
Very Subjective			
Has Difficulty Making a Decision			

Handout 10.7 - Active Learning

Television Analysis - Female Lead Actor

	Program 1	Program 2	Program 3
Aggressive	_____	_____	_____
Independent	_____	_____	_____
Hides Emotions	_____	_____	_____
Very Objective	_____	_____	_____
Dominant	_____	_____	_____
Very Competitive	_____	_____	_____
Very Adventurous	_____	_____	_____
Very Talkative	_____	_____	_____
Very Tactful	_____	_____	_____
Passive	_____	_____	_____
Dependent	_____	_____	_____
Very Excitable in a Minor Crisis	_____	_____	_____
Very Subjective	_____	_____	_____
Has Difficulty Making a Decision	_____	_____	_____

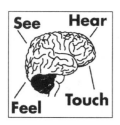

Brain-Based Learning

Brain-Based Learning Activity 10.1 - Creating an STD Prevention Program

Many studies have shown that learning more about sexuality does not necessarily translate into more health promoting sexual behavior. To encourage students to look at this disconnect in their own lives this exercise gives them the task of being in charge of creating a STD Prevention Program at the local high school. What intervention techniques do they believe will really make a difference in the actual behavior of teenagers? What factors are necessary other than the information contained in this chapter?

Divide the class into groups of 6-8 people. Each group has 15 minutes to come up with suggestions for such a program. After presenting their ideas the rest of the class discusses why such an intervention would or would not work given what they know about how teenage sexual behavior.

The point of this difficult assignment is less to create a perfect program than to explore the complexity of changing sexual behavior.

Brain-Based Learning Activity 10.2 - Helping Your Younger Brother/Sister

Hold a short discussion on where your students received most of their information about sexuality growing up and the quality or accuracy of the various sources (Parents, media, friends, magazines, books, school, Internet, videos etc.). Chances are most of them learned from their peers with a lot of mixing of fact, fiction, fibbing and ignorance.

Then give them the following task: Their younger brother/sister (10-14 years old) has come to them and asked them to tell them about sex. Their assignment is to determine what are accurate, appropriate and accessible sources of sexual information that they would feel comfortable sharing with their sibling in person or by referral.

This deceptively simple assignment can be extended into a research project where the students actually go out and locate sources locally available. Be sure to address not only the need for factually correct information but for a setting or a relationship that offers the right amount of emotional support or comfort level. Again, sexuality emerges as a complex and multilevel process.

Brain-Based Learning Activity 10.3 - Dimensions of Gender

Each student writes the answers to the following questions on a sheet of paper. Be sure to mention that their answers will remain confidential unless they choose to share them in the subsequent class discussion.

Since I am a _____ (man/woman = your own sex)

I am supposed to   1)_____ 2)_____ 3)_____
I am never to   1)_____ 2)_____ 3)_____
I can get a way with 1)_____ 2)_____ 3)_____

If I was a _____ (sex opposite of your own)

I would be expected to 1)_____ 2)_____ 3)_____
I wouldn't be allowed to 1)_____ 2)_____ 3)_____
I could get away with   1)_____ 2)_____ 3)_____

Be prepared for a lively, engaged and humorous debate as students "take sides" and discover the perspective of the other gender.

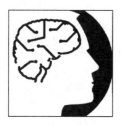

Critical Thinking

Critical Thinking Exercise 10.1 - Helping Students Evaluate their Sexual Values and Love Relationships

Chapter 10 explores important issues related to gender and human sexuality. It is interesting that these topics have a major impact on all our lives, yet they are areas where we are unlikely to employ critical thinking skills. While some people seem to distrust all emotional reactions and ignore this source of valuable information, others rely totally on emotion--"It can't be wrong, if it feels so right."

Rather than working on one particular critical thinking skill, this exercise provides a review of several elements and offers students the opportunity to practice applying critical thinking to emotional topics.

Time: Approximately 30 minutes.

Advance preparation: Make photocopies of the following pages, Handout 10.1 A - "10 Elements of Critical Thinking" and Handout 10.1 B "Critical Thinking Worksheet." Prior to this class activity, you may want to review the prologue of the text. It provides a brief description of each element of critical thinking.

Instructions: Briefly discuss the ten elements of critical thinking (ask students to take notes in the space provided). Give students approximately 5-10 minutes to individually complete the worksheet, and then form groups of 3-4 students to discuss their answers. For your own information, possible answers are included at the end of this section. You may, or may not, want to provide these answers. The purpose of this exercise is to stimulate student critical thinking, and a variety of answers may be equally valid. The fact that students will disagree with one another on the "best" answer, and with the provided answers, is in itself a good sign that critical thinking is occurring.

Handout 10.1 (A) - Critical Thinking

10 Basic Elements of Critical Thinking

1. Thinking independently_____

2. Accepting change_____

3. Tolerating ambiguity_____

4. Resisting overgeneralization _____

5. Defining problems accurately _____

6. Gathering data/asking questions _____

7. Recognizing personal biases _____

8. Welcoming divergent views _____

9. Empathizing _____

10. Delaying judgment until adequate data is available_____

Handout 10.1 (B) - Critical Thinking

Critical Thinking Worksheet

Imagine that you or a close friend has made the following statements or asked the following questions. Using the list of 10 critical thinking elements, identify at least one critical thinking skill (CTS) that could be used to improve the thought processes, and briefly explain your choice.

1. "Only gays or IV drug users get AIDS. Why should I bother with the use of a condom?"

CTS _____

Explanation_____

2. "Why do people have such trouble with their relationships?" All you really need is good communication."

CTS _____

Explanation_____

3. "My partner doesn't seem ready to get married. I wonder if I should break it off?"

CTS _____

Explanation_____

4. "Why can't women just accept that they're different from men? Why aren't they happy just being wives and mothers?"

CTS _____

Explanation_____

5. "There's no such thing as a frigid woman, only a bad lover."

CTS _____

Explanation_____

6. "For every man and woman, there is just one perfect love."

CTS _____

Explanation_____

POSSIBLE ANSWERS -- Handout 10.1B - Critical Thinking Worksheet

1. *Defining problems accurately*. The number of heterosexual AIDS victims is increasing and condoms protect users from a variety of STDs.

2. *Resisting overgeneralization*. This is an oversimplification. Communication is only one of many important factors in relationships.

3. *Tolerating ambiguity*. Although lack of commitment toward marriage might be an important sign of a troublesome relationship, it may be better to tolerate and explore this uncertainty before abandoning the relationship.

4. *Accepting change*. Changes in traditional gender roles are difficult to accept, but critical thinkers recognize that change also offers the opportunity for personal growth.

5. *Recognizing personal biases*. While some people accept the bias that men are responsible for female sexual pleasure, a critical thinker realizes there are numerous factors in sexual dysfunctions and recognizes the need for each individual to assume personal responsibility for his or her own sexuality.

6. *Gathering data*. One of the major advantages of dating and falling in love several times is the resulting recognition that people have the ability to love many people.

This exercise also appears in the text, Chapter 10. We include it here for your convenience, and you may want to discuss it in class to reinforce reading of the text.

Critical Thinking Exercise 10.2 - Rape Myths and Rape Prevention

Sexuality can be a source of vitality and bonding, but it can also be traumatizing if directed toward an unwilling partner. One of the most misunderstood forms of coercive sex is *rape*, "oral, anal, or vaginal penetration forced on an unconsenting or unwilling victim" (Denney and Quandagno, 1995, p. 593). One reason rape occurs has to do with the myths and misconceptions surrounding the whole subject. Before we go on, answer true or false to the following:

_____ 1. Women cannot be raped against their will.

_____ 2. A man cannot be raped by a woman.

_____ 3. If you are going to be raped, you might as well relax and enjoy it.

_____ 4. All women secretly want to be raped.

_____ 5. Male sexuality is biologically overpowering and beyond a man's control.

As you may have expected, all of these statements are false. Tragically, however, these myths are believed by a large number of men and women (Lonsway and Fitzgerald, 1995). Take this opportunity to examine your personal myths about rape. Examining the myths and misconceptions we hold is a requirement of critical thinking.

When we attempt to explain why these myths exist, we find three major reasons--gender role conditioning, media portrayals, and ignorance of basic information. Using your critical thinking skills, tell how each of these factors would give rise to one or more of the myths.

Gender role conditioning _____

Media portrayals _____

Ignorance of information _____

Gender role conditioning--A main part of traditional gender conditioning is the belief that women should be the "gatekeepers" for sexuality and men should be the "pursuers." This leads to the myth that male sexuality is overpowering and women are responsible for controlling the situation. People who believe the myth that women cannot be raped against their will generally overlook the fact that the female gender role encourages passivity and women are not taught how to be strong in defending themselves.

Media portrayals--Novels and films typically portray a woman resisting her attacker, and then melting into passionate responsiveness. This helps perpetuate the myth that women secretly want to be raped and the myth that she might as well "relax and enjoy it."

Ignorance of information--The myth that women cannot be raped against their will overlooks the fact that most men are much stronger and faster than most women, and a woman's clothing and shoes further hinder her ability to escape. The myth that women cannot rape men ignores the fact that many rapists (either male or female) often use foreign objects to rape their victims. The myth that all women secretly want to be raped overlooks the fact that if a woman fantasizes about being raped she remains in complete control, whereas in an actual rape she is completely powerless. Also, fantasies contain no threat of physical harm, while rape does.

We believe that by making you aware of rape myths, we can help prevent rape. In addition, we suggest the following techniques for reducing personal vulnerability to *stranger* rape (the rape of a person by an unknown assailant) and *acquaintance (or date) rape* (committed by someone who is known to the victim) (Crooks and Baur, 1996; Denny and Quadagno, 1995).

To avoid stranger rape:

1. Follow common sense advice for avoiding all forms of crime. For example, lock your car, park in lighted areas, install dead-bolt locks on your doors, don't open your door to strangers, don't hitchhike, etc.

2. Make yourself as strong as possible. Take a self-defense course, carry a loud whistle with you, and demonstrate self-confidence with your body language. Research shows that rapists tend to select women who appear passive and weak (Richards et al., 1991).

3. During an attack, run away if you can, talk to the rapist as a way to stall, and/or attempt to alert others by screaming ("Help, rape, call the police") (Shotland and Stebbings, 1980). When all else fails, women should actively resist an attack, according to current research (Fischhoff, 1992; Furby and Fischhoff, 1992). Loud shouting, fighting back, and causing a scene may deter an attack.

To prevent acquaintance rape:

1. Be careful on first dates--date in groups and in public places; avoid alcohol and other drugs (Muehlenhard and Achrag, 1991).

2. Be assertive and clear in your communication--say what you want and what you don't want. Don't say no when you mean yes. Accept a partner's refusal.

3. If sexual coercion escalates, match the assailant's behavior with your own form of escalation--begin with firm refusals, get louder, threaten to call the police, begin shouting and use strong physical resistance. *Don't be afraid to make a scene!*

This exercise also appears in the Student Study Guide for Chapter 10. We include it here for your convenience, and you may want to discuss it in class to reinforce use of the Student Study Guide.

Critical Thinking Exercise 10.3 - Personal Values Clarification: Exploring Your Own Gender Role Development (An Affective Skill)

One of the most important ingredients of active learning and critical thinking is the ability to closely examine one's own values (ideals, mores, standards, and principles that guide behavior). Are the values you currently hold a simple reflection of the values of your family or peer group? Or are they the result of careful, deliberate choice? Have you listened carefully to opposing values and compared the relative costs and benefits? Since values have such a powerful influence on thinking, you should critically evaluate each of your personal values.

To help you explore your values regarding "masculinity and femininity," we offer several critical thinking questions regarding your own gender role socialization. While reading through the questions, jot your thoughts down and try to think of specific examples from your personal history. You will find that sharing these written notes with others often leads to a fascinating discussion of "the proper roles for women and men."

1. During your early childhood, what gender messages did you receive from your favorite fairy tales, books, television shows? How were women and men portrayed? Are the roles of men and women different in the books and television programs you read and watch today?

2. Did anyone ever tell you that you were a "big boy now" or to "act like a lady?" What did they mean? How did you feel?

3. What were the power relationships like in your family? In what situations was your mother powerful? Your father? Do you remember being treated differently from your opposite-sexed brother or sister? What is the division of labor in your family today (breadwinner, housekeeper, etc.)?

4. As a child, what did you want to be when you grew up? Did that change, and if so, when? Why? What career are you now pursuing? Why?

5. What were your favorite subjects in school? Your most hated subjects? Why?

6. Have you ever wished you were born as the opposite sex? If so, why?

7. Have you ever felt competitive with friends of your same sex? If so, over what?

8. In what ways do you express your emotions (crying, slamming doors, etc.), and how is it related to your being a male or female?

9. What kinds of things do you get most rewarded for by others today (attractiveness, strength, intelligence, business success, money earned, family status, etc.)? How does this relate to your gender role?

10. Have you ever deviated from traditional expectations of you as a male or female? If so, what was your own and others' reaction to it? Have you ever felt restricted or pressured by social expectations of you as a man or woman? If so, in what way?

Gender and Cultural Diversity

Gender and Cultural Diversity Activity 10.1 - The Role of Culture and Gender on Personal Sexual Values

One of the most important ingredients of healthy sexuality is the ability to recognize and evaluate one's own values (ideals, mores, standards, and principles that guide behavior). Are the sexual values you hold a simple reflection of the values of your family or peer group? Or are they the result of careful, deliberate choice? Have you carefully examined opposing values and compared them to your own? How do your values reflect your culture and your gender role? Since values have such a powerful influence on thinking, you should critically evaluate them.

To help you explore your values regarding gender and human sexuality, we offer the following exercise. Read the four value statements. Then, in the space to the right, simply check whether you agree or disagree.

Agree

Disagree

1. Anyone who wants to prevent pregnancy should have easy access to reliable methods of contraception; it doesn't matter whether a person is married or single, young or old. _____ _____

2. Gay and lesbian couples should be allowed the same legal protections (property inheritance, shared pension plans, shared medical benefits) as heterosexual married couples. _____ _____

3. Abortion in the first four months of pregnancy should be a private decision between the woman and her doctor. _____ _____

4. Sex education belongs in the home, not in public schools. _____ _____

Each person's sexual values come from a host of sources, some internal and others external to the individual. The second part of this exercise gives you an opportunity to examine these sources. Review your agree or disagree responses to the previous four statements. Indicate the degree to which each of the sources listed in the left-hand column has influenced your beliefs by placing a check mark in the appropriate column.

VS = Very Significant Influence
SS = Somewhat Significant Influence
NS = Not a Significant Influence

Sources	Contraception			Homosexuality			Abortion			Sex Education		
	VS	SS	NS	VS	SS	NS	VS	SS	NS	VS	SS	NS
Personal experience												
Family patterns												
Peer standards												
Historical events												
Religious views												
Research findings												

Now reexamine the checks you made for each of your four sexual values and their source of influence. Do you notice any patterns in your check marks? Which source has been most influential in the development of your sexual values? Do you think this source is the most appropriate and most justifiable? Why or why not? Which source has been least influential in the development of your sexual values? How do you explain this? Do you notice any inconsistencies in your choice of sources? In what cases has personal experience played a more significant role than family patterns, peer standards, and so on? To further clarify your sexual perspective and sharpen your critical thinking skills, share your responses with a close friend, dating partner, or spouse.

Writing Project

Writing Project 10.1

Given the need for improved writing skills in college students, and to respond to the call for "writing across the curriculum," we offer writing projects for each chapter. For Chapter 10, we suggest a 2-3 page written response to one or more of the following questions. Recognizing the time involved in grading such writing projects, one alternative is occasionally to assign "peer grading." Collect the papers, remove student names, and give each student a paper to grade. It helps to make their participation in peer grading part of the overall points for the writing project. This encourages a more thoughtful and responsible evaluation, as well as acknowledging and rewarding the additional work.

1. Analyze the roles of men and women in magazine advertisements aimed at different audiences, such as those in Playboy, Cosmopolitan, Family Circle, Newsweek, Ebony. Use at least 5 different types of magazines. What are the differences? Are there any underlying similarities?

2. Analyze the roles of male and female characters in children's cartoon shows. Watch at least 5 whole shows. How many characters are of each gender? Who does what?

3. Analyze the roles of men and women in TV ads. What voice overlays are used? Who is the intended audience? What unspoken messages are conveyed? Do the messages differ according to the time of day? Watch at least 1 hour of TV from each time of day: morning, afternoon, evening.

4. Analyze rock videos on MTV for their portrayal of gender roles in both images and lyrics. Watch for 1 to 2 hours; analyze all from that time period. What messages are conveyed?

5. Analyze the Sunday comics for gender roles. Is there a difference between the older and the newer strips? Have the traditional strips also changed? If so, how?

6. Analyze the roles of male and female characters in folk tales (choose 3) from a particular culture. What can we learn about that culture's attitudes toward men and women?

7. Analyze the roles of men and women in soap operas. Watch 1/2 hour each from 3 different soap operas. Has there been an attempt to modernize the roles? Are changes significant or superficial?

8. Analyze the roles of males and females in a selection of children's books (at least 5). Who gets to do what? How are boys/girls portrayed in illustrations? What do their parents do? Are the books targeted for a specific audience? (You may want to choose books from a particular time period.)

9. Analyze newspaper photographs (choose 2 separate newspapers) and/or articles for differential treatment of men and women. Note in particular whether the focus is on faces or bodies and whether descriptions differ.

Circle of Quality – Chapter 10

Please give us your feedback. We thank you in advance for assisting us in improving the next edition. The contact information is listed in the preface.

What are the three most helpful teaching tools in this chapter?

1.

2.

3.

What are the three least useful teaching tools in this chapter?

1.

2.

3.

What are the three most difficult concepts to teach in this chapter?

1.

2.

3.

Additional Comments:

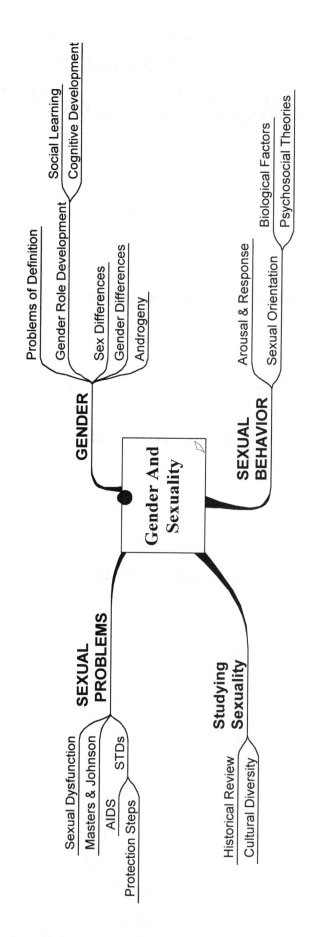

Gender And Sexuality

GENDER
- Problems of Definition
- Gender Role Development
  - Social Learning
  - Cognitive Development
- Sex Differences
- Gender Differences
- Androgeny

SEXUAL BEHAVIOR
- Arousal & Response
- Sexual Orientation
  - Biological Factors
  - Psychosocial Theories

SEXUAL PROBLEMS
- Sexual Dysfunction
- Masters & Johnson
- AIDS
- STDs
- Protection Steps

Studying Sexuality
- Historical Review
- Cultural Diversity

CHAPTER 11
MOTIVATION AND EMOTION

Outline

Understanding Motivation

Hunger and Eating
Arousal
Achievement

> **Active Learning**
> Measuring Your Own Need for
> Achievement

General Theories of Motivation

Biological Theories
Psychosocial Theories

Understanding Emotion

The Cognitive Component
The Physiological Component

The Behavioral Component
Emotional Intelligence (EQ)

General Theories of Emotion

James-Lange Theory
Cannon Bard Theory
Facial Feedback Hypothesis
Schachter's Two-Factor Theory

> **Research Highlight**
> Are Abused Children More Alert to
> Negative Emotions?

> **Gender and Cultural Diversity**
> Evolutionary, Cultural, and Gender
> Influences on Emotions

Learning Objectives

Upon completion of CHAPTER 11, the student should be able to:

1. Define motivation and emotion, and discuss how they overlap (p. 392).
2. Describe how internal factors, external factors, and the interaction between these factors trigger hunger or eating behavior (pp. 392-395).
3. State the consequences of obesity, and describe the safest, most reliable method of weight loss. Differentiate between anorexia nervosa and bulimia; state the causes and risk factors for the development of these eating disorders (pp. 396-397).
4. Describe the arousal motive and the effects of under- or over-arousal. Discuss the four factors that characterize sensation-seeking, and state the consequences to relationships in which this motive is mismatched (pp. 397-399).
5. Describe the achievement motive, possible causal factors, and the traits that characterize people with a high need for achievement. Define intrinsic and extrinsic motivation, and describe their relationship to achievement (pp. 399-403).
6. Discuss the biological theories of motivation: instinct and drive-reduction (pp. 404-405).
7. Discuss the psychosocial theories of motivation: incentive, cognitive, and Maslow's hierarchy of needs. Describe the cross-cultural research that seems to refute the sequential pursuit of Maslow's needs (pp. 405-407).
8. Describe the cognitive, physiological, and behavioral components of emotion (pp. 408-409).
9. Explain the role of the limbic system in primitive emotions and the role of the frontal lobes in monitoring and controlling emotions (pp. 409-410).
10. Describe the role of the autonomic nervous system and the neurotransmitters, epinephrine and norepinephrine, in emotional arousal (p. 410).
11. Describe the use of the polygraph in measuring sympathetic arousal; discuss the effectiveness of the polygraph in lie detection (pp. 410-412).
12. Discuss how facial expressions and body movement are used to communicate emotions; describe cross-cultural research findings regarding emotional expressions (pp. 412-413).
13. Describe how emotional intelligence combines the cognitive, physiological, and behavioral components of emotion, and discuss the controversy regarding this concept (p. 414).
14. Compare and contrast the James-Lange, Cannon-Bard, facial-feedback, and Schachter's two-factor theories of emotion; discuss the research regarding each of these theories (pp. 415-419).
15. Describe research findings on the abused child's heightened reactivity to anger, the evolutionary theory of emotional development, culturally universal emotions, culturally different display rules, and gender differences in emotional expression (pp. 419-422).

Chapter Summary/Lecture Organizer

Introductory Vignette – A moving story about Maya Angelou, one of only two poet laureate in the entire history of the United States and how she overcame the odds of extreme poverty and racism.

I. **UNDERSTANDING MOTIVATION** - Motivation is the study of the "whys" of behavior, whereas emotion is the study of feelings. Because motivated behaviors are often closely related to emotions, these two topics are frequently studied together. A wide variety of motives are discussed throughout this text. In this chapter, we focus on hunger, arousal, and achievement.

    A. Hunger and Eating - Eating is controlled by a complex interaction of both internal and external factors. The stomach, blood chemistry, and the brain are the major internal factors. Cultural conditioning is one of the external factors that play a role in hunger. A large number of people have eating disorders. Obesity seems to result from biological factors, such as the individual's genetic inheritance or from the absence of a protein called leptin, and from psychological factors. The most effective way to lose weight is a combination of exercise and diet. Anorexia nervosa (extreme weight loss due to self-imposed starvation) and bulimia (excessive consumption of food followed by vomiting or taking laxatives) are both related to an intense fear of obesity.

    B. Arousal - According to the arousal motive, people seek an optimal level of arousal that maximizes their performance. Sensory deprivation studies show that we all need a minimal amount of stimulation for our brains to function properly. There are, however, individual differences in this need. According to Zuckerman, high sensation seekers are biologically "pre-wired" to need a higher level of stimulation, whereas the reverse is true for low sensation seekers.

    C. Achievement - Achievement involves the need for success, for doing better than others, and for mastering challenging tasks. Research with intrinsic versus extrinsic motivation shows that extrinsic rewards can lower interest and achievement motivation.

        Active Learning/Critical Thinking: Measuring Your Own Need for Achievement - This exercise offers a brief self-test on achievement motivation.

II. **GENERAL THEORIES OF MOTIVATION** - There are basically two approaches to the study of motivation: biological theories (including instinct theory and drive-reduction theory) and psychosocial theories (including incentive theory and cognitive theories).

    A. Biological Theories - Instinct theories suggest there is some inborn, genetic component to motivation. Drive-reduction theory suggests that internal tensions (produced by the body's demand for homeostasis) "push" the organism toward satisfying basic needs, and that the organism learns which specific behaviors will meet this goal.

B. Psychosocial Theories - According to incentive theory, motivation results from the "pull" of external environmental stimuli. Cognitive theories emphasize the importance of thoughts, attributions, and expectations.

C. Maslow's Hierarchy of Needs - Abraham Maslow proposed a hierarchy of needs or motives that incorporates both biological and psychological theories. He believed that basic physiological and survival needs must be satisfied before a person can attempt to satisfy higher needs. The importance of sequentially working up through these steps has been questioned by critics.

III.   **UNDERSTANDING EMOTION -** There are three basic components to all emotions: the cognitive (thoughts, beliefs, and expectations); the physiological (increased heart rate, respiration rate, and so on); and the behavioral (facial expressions and bodily gestures).

A. Cognitive Component - Self-report techniques are the usual method for measuring the cognitive component of emotions.

B. Physiological Component - The polygraph measures changes in emotional arousal (increase heart rate, blood pressure, and so on). Although the polygraph is used in police work and for employment purposes, psychologists generally object to this practice because they find the polygraph is a poor predictor of guilt or innocence or of truth or lies.

Studies of the physiological component of emotion find that most emotions involve a general, nonspecific arousal of the nervous system. This arousal involves the cerebral cortex, the limbic system, and the frontal lobes of the brain. The most obvious signs of arousal (trembling, increased heart rate, sweating, and so on) result from activation of the sympathetic nervous system, a subdivision of the autonomic nervous system. The parasympathetic system restores the body to "status quo."

C. Behavioral Component - The behavioral component of emotions refers to how we express our emotions. Facial expressions and body movements are two of the major forms of nonverbal communication.

D. Emotional Intelligence - Emotional intelligence involves knowing and managing emotions, empathy, and maintaining satisfying relationships.

IV.   **GENERAL THEORIES OF EMOTION -** There are four major explanations for the activation of emotions.

A. James-Lange Theory - The James-Lange theory suggests we interpret the way we feel on the basis of physical sensations such as increased heart rate, trembling, and so on.

B. Cannon-Bard Theory - The Cannon-Bard theory suggests that feelings are created from independent and simultaneous stimulation of both the cortex and the autonomic nervous system.

C. Facial Feedback Hypothesis - The third general theory of emotion, the facial feedback hypothesis, asserts that facial movements elicit specific emotions.

D. Schachter's Two-Factor Theory - Schachters two-factor theory suggests that emotions depend on two factors--physical arousal and a cognitive labeling of the arousal. In other words, people notice what is going on around them, as well as their own bodily responses, and then label the emotion accordingly.

    Research Highlight: Are Abused Children More Alert to Negative Emotions? – Abused children's greater sensitivity to negative emotions, while adaptive in a threatening environment, causes difficulties when these children interact in normal settings.

    Gender and Cultural Diversity: Evolutionary, Cultural, and Gender Influences on Emotions - Most psychologists believe that emotions result from a complex interplay between evolution and culture. Studies have identified 7 to 10 basic emotions that are universal--experienced and expressed in similar ways across almost all cultures. Display rules differ across cultures and between men and women.

Teaching Resources

SECTION I - UNDERSTANDING MOTIVATION

Learning Objectives #'s 1 - 5
Lecture Lead-Ins # 1
Lecture Extenders # 11.1
Discussion Questions #'s 1, 2, 3, 4
Active Learning Activities #'s 11.1, 11.3, 11.5
Critical Thinking Exercise # 11.2
Gender and Cultural Diversity Activity # 11.1
Writing Project # 11.1

SECTION II - GENERAL THEORIES OF MOTIVATION

Learning Objectives #'s 6 - 10
Lecture Extenders # 11.1
Discussion Questions #'s 3, 4
Active Learning Activities #'s 11.2, 11.3, 11.4
Brain-Based Learning #'s 11.1, 11.3

SECTION III - UNDERSTANDING EMOTION

Learning Objectives #'s 8 - 11
Lecture Lead-Ins #'s 2, 3, 4
Discussion Questions # 5
Active Learning Activities #'s 11.6, 11.7, 11.9, 11.10, 11.11
Brain-Based Learning #"s 11.1 - 11.3
Critical Thinking Exercise # 11.1

SECTION IV - GENERAL THEORIES OF EMOTION

Learning Objectives #'s 12 - 15
Lecture Lead-Ins # 4
Discussion Questions # 5
Active Learning Activities #'s 11.6 - 11.11
Brain-Based Learning #11.2
Critical Thinking Exercise #11.1

Lecture Lead-Ins

1.   Read "Symptoms of Anorexia and Bulimia" from the text to the class and ask the students if they can think of a situation which would produce these symptoms. Ask if there is any reason a person would willingly subject themselves to such torture. Since you did not mention that these are symptoms of anorexia and bulimia, some students will think you are describing prisoners of war or a horrible fatal disease. Given that anorexia and bulimia are common among college students, this discussion provides a natural lead-in to motivation and emotion.

2.   Ask students what are the most important emotions, both positive and negative, in their own lives. Have them write down their answers and ask for volunteers to share their list. Are there age differences or gender differences in their responses? Discuss possible cross-cultural differences and use this as a lead-in to your lecture on emotions.

3.   Ask students if they think they could beat a polygraph. If so, what method would they use? Is polygraph testing as a requirement for employment a good idea? Why or why not?

4.   Ask students when they are attempting to interpret the feelings of another, whether they use verbal or nonverbal cues. Which verbal or nonverbal cues appear to be the most important? Ask the students if they have ever misinterpreted another person's emotions? Ask for volunteers to discuss their answers, and use their responses as a tie-in to material discussed in the text.

Lecture Extenders

11.1 - A Model of Human Motivation

Many psychotherapists have a model for human motivation that gives them a basis for deciding on patient's needs. A person can know what is wrong with his or her life, but this may not mean that the therapy is apparent. A starting place for intervention is to look at the needs or drives that propel human behavior. If these are universal, then the therapist would look at the client's behavior to satisfy these basic needs. For example, Freud, Berne, and Rogers were explicit about the propelling motivation(s) for human behavior. These needs discussed below are based upon Glasser's book, Control Theory (1984).

Glasser divides human motivations into two categories: biological and psychological. The biological drives are the needs that relate to the need to survive and reproduce. They are mandated by the old brain and some are carried out without any interference from the thinking process. An example of this is heart-beat or the reflexive withdrawal of a limb from a painful stimulus. However, some of these drives mandated by the unconscious part of the brain, are also under the control of the newer conscious brain. Hunger may originate partly as a result of the old brain (hypothalamus), but the way in which they are expressed or even felt (or repressed) is controlled by both newer and older brain functions. The new brain does not direct the typical person to deep-fry butterflies to satisfy hunger, but to go out to a fast food restaurant. One may represent hunger by diverting attentional processes to other things. Glasser does not rank the biological needs over the psychological, but it is implicit in any theory that deals with both psychological and biological needs that some degree of satisfaction for the biological needs will have to be obtained for the person to continue to exist.

The psychological needs are the ones that most psychologists view as most relevant to human happiness. Glasser lists four psychological drives in this category: belonging, power, freedom, and fun. There are some obvious similarities between his and Maslow's list, but Glasser disagrees strongly with Maslow that these psychological needs can be arranged in a hierarchical order. He feels that these psychological needs are no less important then the biological ones and that people will be dissatisfied until they have fulfilled these needs.

Glasser's first psychological need, the desire to belong, cooperate, share, and love, is also one of the needs in Maslow's theory. Human beings will strive to satisfy this need. Often, those who attempt suicide indicate that they are driven to this step because they are lonely. People often get pets because they need something to love that will love them in return. The formation of families, friendship groups, and community endeavors, are linked to this need.

The need for power is closely linked to the need for recognition from others. At one time this battle was fought mainly through physical encounters, and even today in some areas this is the route to territorial power. Some boys establish dominance or power within their peer group by physical strength. Other examples of routes to power include promotions, physical attractiveness, and favored political status.

Within smaller, more intimate groups, the need for belonging often turns into power plays to get one's way. We often judge how much another person loves us by what we can get them to do for us. For example, if you loved me, you would take out the garbage. These two needs, the need for power and love, are often in conflict. In general, when two people within a relationship are grossly mismatched with regard to power, at least one of them will be unhappy. An interesting example of this is the unequal relationship that occurs when one partner is more in love than the other one. The one who feels the less intense love will have more power, which comes from the other person trying to please him or her.

A third psychological need, the need for freedom relates to the desire to keep options open. Many people will argue against a marriage or commitment because they don't want to lose their options. When people take a job, they often barter off some freedom (loss of time), but they gain some power (money) in return. One of the reasons for the punishing effect of jail is that it interferes with a basic need--the desire for freedom.

The final psychological need, desire for fun, is not often listed by other theorists, the only exception being Berne (transactional analysis) who has an analogous concept in desire for structure. Although, higher primates appear to find humor in some of the games they play, the degree to which laughter is developed in humans is unique and largely a function of the highly developed language capacity. It is fun that provides the spice of life and one who lives constantly without fun can find life a rather boring affair. One of the benefits of power is the increased access to better ways of having fun, for example, snow skiing, golf, and gourmet dining.

As you might suspect, Glasser feels that part of the problem in satisfying psychological needs is the conflict among needs. They are not static and fixed in an individual and they vary with life stage and situation. Just when a person feels he or she has it made, a psychological need may increase in intensity and demand satisfaction, upsetting the earlier equilibrium that a person had worked out among his or her psychological drives.

Reference: Glasser, W.G. (1984). <u>Control Theory: A New Explanation of How We Control Our Lives</u>. New York: Harper & Row.

Key Terms

Discussion Questions

1. Are anorexia and bulimia caused by our society? What are the social pressures to be thin? What are the major sources of these pressures? Are there other cultures where this pressure does not exist?

2. Is competition primarily good or bad? How does it contribute to our motivation and feelings of achievement when only one person is typically considered a "winner?" What would American business and athletics be like without our intense focus on competition?

3. Should children be given grades in elementary school? How does this affect their need for achievement (nAch)? Are grades a form of extrinsic motivation? Do children stop wanting to learn once they become "graded" on their performance? What would happen to the sex motive if we were given grades?

4. If you were granted a lifetime, guaranteed income, would you continue to work? What would you change about your current life? What, if anything, does this reveal about our own need for achievement, intrinsic versus extrinsic rewards, and the arousal motive?

5. Are you more or less emotional than your friends and family members? How is your level of "emotionality" affected by your gender? How about your culture? Would you like to be more or less emotional? Why? What would be the advantages of being "emotionless?" Would you like to be more like Spock from "Star Trek" or Woody Allen? Which famous figure do you consider to have the right "balance" of emotionality?

 **Web Sites**

Official Abraham Maslow Publications Site
http://www.maslow.com/index
A detailed account of Abraham Maslow's publications is available on this site. Also available are other researchers' supportive findings for aspects of his theories of psychology and motivation.

Modeling the Evolution of Motivation
http://www.cs.ucsd.edu/~bgrundy/papers/motivate.htm
This link is essentially a paper with details describing how evolutionary accounts of motivation are necessary to understand behavior. Also describes the development of different motivation systems.

Learning: Motivation
http://users.netmatters.co.uk/pmb/LR3.html
Gives a detailed account of drive-reduction theory from Hull to current conceptualizations. Links the role of drive-reduction to learning processes.

Childhood Obesity
http://www.mayohealth.org/mayo/9705/htm/overweig.htm
From the Mayo Health Clinic, a description of how one develops the propensity to being overweight. This site also offers clear scientific explanations of the current thinking regarding individual differences in obesity.

Center for Eating Disorders
http://www.eating-disorders.com
From the Center for Eating Disorders web site, information is available on the wide array of eating disorders. Available here is information on research, treatment, and descriptions of each condition, such as Anorexia Nervosa, Bulimia Nervosa, and Binge Eating Disorder.

Suggested Films and Videos

The Will to Win

Films for the Humanities and Sciences, 1993. 28 minutes. Examines determination to succeed--in early childhood, on the playing field, in business--and ways the body responds to illness.

Motivation and Emotion

Annenberg/CPB, 1990. 30 minutes. From Zimbardo's "Discovering Psychology," this program explores why we act and feel as we do. The film compares our natural motives to seek pleasure versus society's need for restraint. Freud's, Rogers', and Maslow's beliefs about human motivation are explored, as well as Seligman's research on optimism and pessimism.

Dying to Be Thin

Films for the Humanities and Sciences, 1995. 28 minutes. Presents a young woman obsessed with the desire to be thin. Four hospitalizations and years of outpatient therapy were necessary to overcome her problem. Characteristics of anorexia and bulimia are explored, with profiles of those most likely to develop eating disorders.

Anorexia and Bulimia

Films for the Humanities and Sciences, 19 minutes. Explores the addictive nature of eating disorders, and possible effects on the cardiovascular and central nervous systems.

The Famine Within

Direct Cinema Limited, 1991. 90 minutes. This 90-minute film is well worth your class time. It is a powerful exploration of contemporary weight obsessions. The direct testimony of victims of eating disorders is combined with views of leading experts.

Motivation

Insight Media, 1990. 30 minutes. Using dramatic examples, this video examines why people think, behave, and make the choices the way they do. Motivational factors are explored including curiosity, need for achievement, and intrinsic and extrinsic rewards. Examples of PET scanning to discover the brain's role in motivation and Maslow's hierarchy of needs are also presented.

The Impossible Takes a Little Longer

National Film Board of Canada, University of Indiana, 1987. 48 minutes. This memorable video follows the everyday life of four women who are seriously disabled (paraplegic, quadriplegic, blind, and deaf). Their determination to succeed is the unifying theme. Each has developed ways to cope with common problems and an insensitive public.

 **Success**

Books For Success

Seligman, Martin E. P. (1990). **Learned Optimism: How to Change Your Mind and Your Life**. Pocket Books.
The sharing of a well-respected researcher's evolving conclusions regarding the influence of how we see life and how we live it.

Tavris, Carol (19989). **Anger: The Misunderstood Emotion**. Simon & Schuster.
The author carefully and thoroughly explores the common and frustrating emotion of anger.

Myers, David G., (1992). **The Pursuit of Happiness: Discovering the Pathway to Fulfillment, Well-being, and Enduring Personal Joy.** Avon Books.
The author explores the subject of happiness - what it is and how to bring it into your life.

Goleman, Daniel (1997). **Emotional Intelligence.** Bantam Books.
This book argues that emotional intelligence is the most important predictor of success in life. The author makes a strong case that academic measures of intelligence are too restrictive and describes the five crucial skills of emotionally intelligent people.

Csikzentmihalyi, Mihaly (1991). **Flow: The Psychology of Optimal Experience.** HarperCollins.
This research based book describes how to live a more satisfied life by entering into FLOW, a state of absorbed concentration. It is highly accessible to the layperson and offers engaging examples from brain surgeons to rock climbers.

Active Learning

Active Learning Activity 11.1 - "Motivational Genie"

Tell the class that you are the "Motivational Genie" and you are able to grant them full control of ONE of the three motives discussed in the text--hunger, arousal, and achievement. They will be able to turn on or turn off this motive at their pleasure. Now ask everyone to stand. Have those who want control of the hunger motive to move to the right of the classroom. Those who want to control arousal (stimulus-seeking) should move to the left, and those who want control of achievement should move to the back of the room. Be sure that everyone moves. Do NOT allow anyone to stay in his/her seat or in the middle of the room. Tell them this is like a multiple-choice test and they must choose. (If your class is large and doesn't allow this type of movement, you can ask them to raise left hand, right hand, or both hands.)

Once students have moved (or raised their hands), ask them to explain their choices. You'll find they have very interesting reasons for their decisions. Also, encourage them to move if they hear better reasons from other students. Remind them that one of the hallmarks of a critical thinker is the ability to remain open-minded and to change their decisions when offered new information. This exercise is a great active learning exercise that also seems to increase their interest in what can be a very dry lecture/discussion on theories of motivation.

Active Learning Activity 11.2 - Homeostasis

During your discussion of motivation, allow the students to watch while you adjust the room's thermostat. Turn it up or down depending on the season, and then continue your lecture. Wait until a student complains about the temperature. Ask them how their bodies attempted to maintain homeostasis.

Active Learning Activity 11.3 - Personal Motivation

Ask students to write down three things they do on a regular basis (excluding regular activities like sleeping, eating, going to school). Then ask them to write a short paragraph describing why they like these activities, what needs they fulfill, and whether extrinsic rewards would increase or decrease their enjoyment. Ask students to refer to this sheet while studying the various theories of motivation and the specific motives of hunger, arousal, and achievement.

Active Learning Activity 11.4 - Maslow's Hierarchy of Needs

Divide the class into five groups. Assign each group one of the five levels of Maslow's hierarchy of needs (physiological, safety, love and belonging, esteem, and self-actualization). Ask each group to identify several ways in which they typically satisfy needs at their assigned level (e.g., putting on a coat when they go outside=physiological need, putting a double lock on their home=safety needs, joining clubs=love and belonging, and so on). Discuss which level takes up most of their time and energy. Ask how this might reflect their "student status." Would their needs change if they had a high paying job, increased leisure time, or were younger or older than their present age? What does this reveal about Maslow's hierarchy of needs and differences between cultures?

Active Learning Activity 11.5 - Thick versus Thin

Divide your class into three large groups. Have one group collect several "thin" advertisements from modern magazines; have the second group collect ads for "Weight-on" from old magazines that can be found in library files; and, ask the third group to look for photos of cross-cultural variations in preferred body types (National Geographic is a good place to begin). Arrange ahead of time for these groups to make transparencies or posters of their ads. Use these photos and advertisements as a starting point for a discussion of eating disorders. Discuss how our culture contributes to eating problems such as obesity, anorexia nervosa, and bulimia. Point out how in some cultures, a degree of fatness is considered a sign of affluence and in others it is seen as a desirable hedge against starvation.

Active Learning Activity 11.6 - "Emotional Genie"

Reread the description of the "Motivational Genie" (Activity 11.1). This time inform the class that you are the "Emotional Genie," and you can offer them full control of any ONE emotion. Break the class into groups according to their preferred "emotional control" group--either joy, love, fear, sadness, or anger. Given that the text discusses male/female differences in these five basic emotions, it works well to limit their choices to these emotions. Once students are in their groups, ask them to discuss their choices and then to list their shared reasons on the board at the front of the room. While they are making their lists, take note of any gender differences in the choices. The text mentions that on four of the five emotions women report more intense and frequent reactions--anger was the one exception. Discuss why they think men "outperform" women on this one emotion. Also discuss how these gender differences might affect intimate relationships, friendships, and business interactions.

Active Learning Activity 11.7 - Startle Reaction

At the beginning of class, ask students to check and record their individual pulse rates. Begin your discussion or lecture for the day and after approximately ten minutes, have a prearranged loud noise sound (alarm clocks, loud radios, etc.). Ask students to take their pulse rate again and record it. Forewarn them that the next noise will come in five minutes. After the second noise, take another pulse rate and compare it to the first and second. This simple exercise is very effective in demonstrating the role of cognitive processes in emotional responses. Expand on this topic and discuss how these same principles apply to prepared childbirth, advance discussion before surgery, and so on.

Active Learning Activity 11.8 - Facial Feedback Hypothesis

Using the "Try This Yourself" demonstration on page 393, ask one half the class to put a pencil crosswise between their teeth with their mouth closed. Have the other half of the class hold a pencil crosswise with their mouth open and teeth showing. Continue lecturing for several minutes. Now ask the students to privately write down their primary feeling at that moment, including the words "mouth closed" or "mouth open." Collect their papers, "shuffle" them, and redistribute. Then ask for a show of hands for those with papers for "mouth open" who had emotions listed that would be described as pleasant. Put this number on the board. Now ask for a show of hands for those who had papers from the "mouth closed" group and listings of pleasant emotions. Research suggests that the mouth open should produce more pleasant emotions. Discuss your results and the implications of the facial feedback hypothesis.

Active Learning Activity 11.9 - Cultural Differences and Similarities in Emotions

The text discusses cultural differences and similarities in emotions (pp. 396-398). This is a perfect opportunity to ask students from other cultures to participate in a panel discussion. Ask them a few days ahead of time if they would be willing to participate in a brief discussion of cultural differences and similarities in emotions. Most students are willing to participate. On the day of the panel, rearrange seats with the 4-5 panel members in a group at one end of a circle. This arrangement seems to encourage more discussion and participation from the entire class. Ask the panel members to briefly explain any differences or similarities they've noted between their culture and the American culture. Encourage class members to ask questions from the panel members. This has always been a very exciting and stimulating exercise in our own classes.

Active Learning Activity 11.10 - Emotional Expressions

Ask students to practice facial expressions for joy, love, fear, sadness, and anger. Which expression is most difficult to express? Which is the easiest? Why? Now have students add the bodily posture that accompanies these five emotions, without the facial expression and then with the facial expression. If time allows, have students practice combining compatible emotions (like joy and love) and incompatible emotions (like joy and anger). Then have them mix facial expressions with a compatible but different emotion and an incompatible emotion.

Active Learning Activity 11.11 - The Language of Emotions

Divide students into five or six groups. Using Table 11.2 from the text (page 397), assign each group one of the basic emotions. Ask them to write down all possible words used to describe "how a person feels when they are in the emotional state called _____." Have each group list their responses on the board. You will typically find that sadness is the one emotion that has the most responses. Why is this? Also discuss the emotion that has least number of responses. Why is this? Is this a reflection of our culture, our literature, media, or ....?

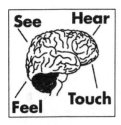

Brain-Based Learning

Brain-Based Learning Activity 11.1 - Lessons From Home

Write a list of basic human emotions on the board:

Sadness, Fear, Anger, Love, Happiness, Sexual Passion, Disgust, Hate, Joy, Curiosity, Courage etc.

Each student has a page divided in half by a line in front of him/her. The left side is labeled OK; the right half is labeled NOT OK.

As you read off each emotion you ask the students:
Was the emotion of _____ allowed/not allowed (or encouraged/not encouraged) in your home?

If it was allowed, the students write that emotion on the left half of the page; if not on the right half. If the emotion or expression of anger was allowed for some but not allowed for others in their home, then the student can choose to write the emotion on both sides of the line.

After you have finished the list, give the students a minute or two of quiet time to reflect on the pattern of emotion allowed or forbidden in their homes. Encourage them to pay attention to their inner reactions as they consider the pattern.

In the next step you ask the students to pool their data (either out loud, or via anonymous submission) on which emotions where allowed. In most all classes you will find that ALL emotions were allowed in some homes and forbidden in other homes. Copy the layout of the student's pages on the blackboard and write all emotions on both sides of the table. Then ask the students to look at the resulting pattern and ask them what conclusions can be drawn from this apparently contradictory finding. Which household is right? Could it be that all emotions are nothing but energy in motion and that it is only our personal or family judgements that weigh them down with approval/disapproval?

Brain-Based Learning Activity 11.2 - Can You Spot a Lie?

Tying into the research of Paul Ekman presented in the section on Facial Expressions, ask for a couple of volunteers. Take them aside and ask each of them to prepare 4 one-minute statements about an aspect of their personal lives they feel strongly about (someone they admire a lot, a person in the family they feel close to or angry at, something that happened in their love life, etc.) Two of these statements should be truthful. For the other two the students should describe their positions as opposite of what they really feel. The task of the class is to spot the false statements (lies) and to attempt to isolate which aspect of facial or body or voice behavior they were decoding the information from. Tabulate whether the students' truth detection ratings exceed the chance level.

Reference:
Ekman, P., O' Sullivan, M. & Frank, M. (1999, May). A Few Can Catch A Liar, Psychological Science, Vol 10 (3), pp.263-266.

Brain-Based Learning Activity 11.3 - Why Am I Here and What Can I Do About It?

Begin by asking the students to generate a list of reasons why they are at your school/class.
Sort their reasons according to Maslow's Hierarchy of needs. (survival/safety, self esteem, need for meaning or contribution, social connection, physical needs of food, sex, exercise, pleasure).

Have the students rank which three reasons give them the most amount of motivation on those difficult days when the going gets tough.

Next ask them to assess how motivated another student in this class is. What cues would they use to discern this unknown student's commitment level? Make a list. (e.g. attendance, homework done, class participation, body language, attitude, test performance etc.) Then have them apply the criteria on this list to their own behavior. Based on only these criteria how would they rank their own level of commitment to this class? Do they agree that this rating reflects how they really feel about being here? Finally, ask for ideas on what a student, who wanted to increase his/her motivation for coming to class and do the hard work of learning, could do.

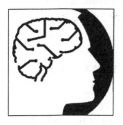

Critical Thinking

Critical Thinking Exercise 11.1 - Recognizing Emotional Appeals: Ads and Everyday Attempts to Persuade

Advertisers spend billions of dollars each year to hire highly trained professionals who understand our deepest fears and desires and how to use them to motivate us to buy a car we can't really afford or put our purchases on a bank credit card. (Our closest friends and family members can be equally adept at using emotional appeals.) Sometimes emotional appeals are made in the service of a greater good, such as public safety warnings to wear seat belts. But more often, this isn't the case and the appeal is an illegitimate exploitation of emotions. A critical thinker should be able to recognize and critically evaluate appeals to emotion as opposed to appeals to logic and good sense.

Below are a few common examples of emotional appeals used to motivate us for someone else's benefit:

A. Appeal to self-esteem - an approach that manipulates our need to feel good about ourselves ("Fine wine drinkers prefer..." or "Mothers who care...").

B. Appeal to social fears - an approach that carries an implied threat of ostracism or social rejection ("Not even your best friend will tell you...").

C. Appeal to authority or experts - quoting or using authority figures to prove a point. Although some authorities have legitimate expertise in the area in which they are advising (a qualified mechanic diagnosing a problem with a car), people often use "authorities" who are not qualified to give an expert opinion (a respected newscaster selling life insurance).

D. Appeal to pity - a person attempts to persuade you to do or buy something because he or she will be hurt if you don't agree.

E. Appeal to force - a person attempts to persuade you to do or buy something because he or she will hurt you if you don't agree.

F. Plainfolks - an approach based on the similarity principle. If you think the persuader is "like you," "just one of the guys," or "regular folk," you will be persuaded more easily.

G. Associations - using a positive symbol to endorse whatever the persuader wants you to "buy." The idea is that through classical conditioning (see Chapter 6) you will transfer the positive qualities of the endorser to the product.

The following activity will sharpen your skills in recognizing illegitimate emotional appeals. Beside each statement, mark the letter of the illegitimate appeal being used. More than one type of tactic may be applicable.

___1. A Bell telephone ad shows a small, sweet grandmother sitting patiently by the phone waiting for her loved ones to call.

___2. A teenager argues against the family's vacation plans, and the father responds by saying, "when you pay the bills, you can make the decisions."

___3. Peanut butter ads suggest that "Choosy mothers choose JIF."

___4. Scope mouthwash commercials show two people just waking up in the morning with the words "Yech! Morning breath, the worst breath of the day."

___5. A college student asks his professor to accept a late paper: "I've worked all weekend on this report. I know that it's past your deadline, but I have to work full-time while also attending college."

___6. While showing a very expensive home to a young couple, the Realtor says "You owe it to yourself and your family to buy the very best."

___7. Actor Robert Young, former star of "Father Knows Best" and "Marcus Welby, M.D.," "prescribes" Sanka coffee for people who are nervous, irritable, or in stressful situations.

___8. A political ad shows the candidate wearing a hard hat at the steel workers' company picnic and pitching horseshoes in his backyard.

___9. A Marlboro cigarette ad shows a strong, ruggedly handsome cowboy riding alone on the range.

___10. After making it clear that he values employee "loyalty," a supervisor asks for "volunteers" to help a fellow supervisor move on the weekend.

ANSWERS: 1 D; 2 E; 3 A; 4 B; 5 D; 6 A; 7 C; 8 F; 9 G; 10 E.

Although we are providing a list of *possible* answers, we encourage you to discuss your responses with your classmates. Comparing answers to each alternative helps to further your critical thinking skills.

This exercise also appears in the text, Chapter 11. We include it here for your convenience, and you may want to discuss it in class to reinforce reading of the text.

Critical Thinking Exercise 11.2 - Measuring Your Own Need For Achievement

Are you interested in measuring your own need for achievement? If so, you need approximately 20 minutes to take and score the following two tests. Before you begin, we would like to caution you about the *social desirability response* bias--people's tendency to act in ways that they believe others will approve of (Rosenberg, 1969). Given our strong cultural emphasis on independence and achievement, most people's responses to the following tests might reflect not only their appraisal of their achievement needs, but also a tendency to say good things about themselves.

Researchers are constantly on guard against social desirability biases contaminating their measurements. However, when taking and scoring your own tests, there are few safeguards against this response bias. Thus, you must rely on critical thinking skills. As you take these tests, use *meta-cognition* (thinking about your thoughts) to monitor your responses. Ask yourself, "Do I honestly feel this way, or am I just trying to look good?" Critical thinking helps us overcome our personal biases and self-deceptive reasoning. Using meta-cognition will result in a more accurate measurement of your need for achievement. Complete both tests before you begin to score your answers.

TEST 1

Based on how you feel in MOST situations, answer the following questions honestly with a "yes" or "no."

_____ 1. If offered a choice of tasks, would you pick one that is moderately difficult rather than one that is very difficult or easy?

_____ 2. Do you enjoy tasks more if you have competed against others?

_____ 3. Do you prefer tasks that have clear, definable goals and measurable outcomes?

_____ 4. Do you like receiving feedback about how well you are doing when you are working on a project?

_____ 5. Would you rather receive criticism from a harsh but competent evaluator than from one who is friendlier but less competent?

_____ 6. Do you prefer tasks where you are personally responsible for the outcome?

_____ 7. When working on a difficult task, do you persist even when you encounter roadblocks?

_____ 8. Do you typically receive high performance evaluations (e.g., receiving top honors or special recognition in sports, clubs, and other activities)?

TEST 2

The Thematic Apperception Test (TAT) consists of a series of ambiguous pictures such as the one shown in Figure 11.5 (page 377 in the text). The TAT is one of the most common methods for measuring achievement motivation. Look closely at the two women in Figure 11.5, and write a short story answering the following questions:

1. What is happening in this picture, and what led up to it?
2. Who are the people in this picture, and how do they feel?
3. What is going to happen in the next few moments, and in a few weeks?

SCORING

Test 1 These eight questions are based on the characteristics of achievers discussed in the text. People with a higher number of "yes" answers tend to be high in achievement motivation.

Test 2 Give yourself one point each time any of the following is mentioned: (1) defining a problem, (2) solving a problem, (3) obstructions to solving a problem, (4) techniques that can help overcome the problem, (5) anticipation of success or resolution of the problem. The higher your score on this test, the higher your overall need for achievement.

INTERPRETATION

How did you do? Some students in our classes have found that they score high on one test and low on the other. This may be because self-report measures (such as Test 1) are more reflective of attitudes, while fantasy measures (such as Test 2) are more predictive of action (Koestner and McClelland, 1990; McClelland et al., 1989). Some researchers believe fantasy measures are better predictors because they reflect a more basic level of motivational functioning. In a meta-analysis of 105 research studies on achievement, Spangle (1992) found the TAT (a fantasy measure) a reliable measure of achievement motivation. As you will discover in Chapter 13, however, fantasy (or projective) tests have their critics. In addition, it is important to remember that self-interpretation is limited. Extensive education and training are required to adequately interpret psychological tests.

This exercise also appears in the Student Study Guide, Chapter 11. We include it here for your convenience, and you may want to discuss it in class to reinforce use of the Student Study Guide.

Critical Thinking Exercise 11.3 - <u>Charting</u> <u>Your</u> <u>Moods</u> <u>and</u> <u>Emotions</u> (An Affective Skill)

The *recite* step in the SQ4R method requires you to be an ACTIVE learner. By completing the following exercises, you will test and improve your mastery of the chapter material, which will also improve your performance on quizzes and exams.

EXERCISE I

Self-understanding requires the ability to recognize and analyze your own emotions and to recognize the external factors that affect your emotions. From this place of self-understanding, you will, hopefully, be able to be more in control of your own moods and needs, gain insight into the moods and needs of others, and improve your relationships.

One of the best ways to understand the three basic components of emotions and to understand your own daily or monthly "mood swings" is to chart your emotions for at least one week. Each morning when you first wake up or each night before retiring, complete your daily mood evaluation chart. Describe your primary mood at the time of your writing, how your body physiologically registers that emotion or mood, the thoughts, expectations, or beliefs surrounding that mood, and give a number or word to rank or evaluate the pleasure or intensity of that emotion. Charting your moods or emotions helps you to recognize your own fluctuations and helps you to explain yourself to others.

	Primary Mood	Physiological Description	Cognitive (Thoughts)	Behavioral Description	Subjective Evaluation
Day					
(1)					
(2)					
(3)					
(4)					
(5)					
(6)					
(7)					

EXERCISE II

Having practiced identifying your emotional states in the previous active learning exercise, now we can explore a related topic, that of *subjective well being*. Researchers in this area often ask participants to evaluate either their overall life satisfaction or their feelings of happiness (sometimes defined as a high ratio of positive to negative feelings). Stop for a moment and write down your own life satisfaction and happiness scores (on a scale from one to 100 with one as the lowest) in the space provided. Life Satisfaction score _____ Happiness score _____

Now circle true or false to the following items:

1. Among all age groups, America's senior citizens are the least happy and most dissatisfied with their life. True or False?
2. People who have complete quadriplegia (with both arms and both legs paralyzed) report their lives are below average in happiness. True or False?
3. Having children is life's greatest joy; thus, parents report more overall happiness than those who do not have children. True or False?
4. Most people would be happier if they had more money. True or False?
5. People with a college education are happier and report more life satisfaction than people with only a high school diploma. True or False?

The answers to this exercise can be found at the end of this study guide chapter—and they may surprise you!

Gender and Cultural Diversity

Gender and Cultural Diversity Activity 11.1 - Motivation

The most widely researched motivation theory is that of McClelland (1961). McClelland's theory of motivation is based upon achievement and power motives. McClelland's achievement motive corresponds to that of the masculine risk taker. It is not surprising that this theory is so popular in the United States. McClelland's theory has been tested in other cultures with mixed results. It may be most useful as a way of self-describing motivation.

Hofstede (1980/1984) proposes a model that is based on cultural values. He draws out similarities between motivational patterns of persons from cultures with similar values, and cultural groups with similar motivational patterns. (This work is based on extensive international research and proposes no judgment regarding which motivational pattern is "best.") His strong attention to culture and its influence on motivation is controversial, and Hofstede recognizes this. He contends that a recognition of culture is powerful and attempting to understand it is not the same as building, which is based on the construct of racial groups. A summary of his very complex "motivational map" is presented in a four-quadrant model as follows:

1. United States, Great Britain, and their former dominions and colonies:

    Motivation by personal, individual success in the form of wealth, recognition, and "self-actualization." This is the classic McClelland-Maslow-Herzberg pattern.

2. Japan, German-speaking countries, some Latin countries, and Greece:

    Motivation by personal, individual security. This can be found in wealth, and especially in hard work. Second-quadrant countries have grown fastest economically in the 1960 to 1970 period (contrary to McClelland's theory).

3. France, Spain, Portugal, Chile, and other Latin and Spanish countries:

    Motivation by security and belonging. Individual wealth is less important than group solidarity.

4. North European countries, plus the Netherlands:

    Motivation by success and belonging. In this quadrant, success will be measured partly as collective success and in the quality of human relationships and the living environment (Hofstede, 1984).

Activity: In small groups, students could reflect upon their ethnic, cultural backgrounds and the culture with which they most identify and discuss their motivation and work values as they connect to cultural values.

Questions for Class Discussion

1. Can students imagine how to understand motivation and work values as connected to culture without embarking on another version of stereotyping?

2. What represents power in the dominant American culture? In the African-American culture? In the Asian-American culture? In the Hispanic-American culture?

3. How do women contribute to the world's work force?

4. Create a model that represents your motivations according to your cultural heritage (review the four quadrant models if you need help).

Source: Hofstede, G. H. (1980/1984). <u>Culture's Consequences: International Differences in Work-Related Values</u> (Abridged Edition). Newbury Park: CA: Sage Publications.

Writing Project

Writing Project 11.1

Given the need for improved writing skills in college students, and to respond to the call for "writing across the curriculum," we offer writing projects for each chapter. In Chapter 11, we suggest a 2-3 page written response to the food attitude questionnaire found on Handout 11.4. Recognizing the time involved in grading such writing projects, one alternative is occasionally assign "peer grading." Collect the papers, remove student names, and give each student a paper to grade. It helps to make their participation in peer grading part of the overall points for the writing project. This encourages a more thoughtful and responsible evaluation, as well as acknowledging and rewarding the additional work.

The topic of hunger and eating disorders is especially relevant to college-age women and increasingly, men. This exercise is an interesting way to introduce these topics, along with doing a quick writing project. After students have completed the following questionnaire, ask them to compare their responses to 2-3 friends or family members. Their food attitude write up should include personal reactions and specific tie-ins to the text.

Handout 11.1- Writing Project

Food Attitude Questionnaire

Use a 1-7 scale to answer these 26 questions. (1=the statement almost always applies to you, 4=sometimes applies, and 7=almost never applies).

_____1. I feel great after eating a meal.

_____2. I have trouble controlling myself at all-you-can-eat restaurants.

_____3. I genuinely love the taste of foods.

_____4. My family has pleasant conversations during meals.

_____5. My family argues during the evening meal.

_____6. When I go to a party, I like to sample novel foods.

_____7. I eat while watching television or when I am bored.

_____8. Mom hated to cook our meals, and we frequently had to prepare our own.

_____9. I go out of my way to try new foods.

_____10. Our entire family is usually present at evening meals.

_____11. My parents punished me by making me skip a meal or by withholding dessert.

_____12. At home, our meals are friendly and relaxed.

_____13. My mother takes a lot of pride in her cooking.

_____14. At school, I care about what I eat; I try to stick with healthy food.

_____15. My parents forced me to eat foods that I didn't like.

_____16. It makes a difference if food looks attractive.

_____17. My father enjoyed cooking.

_____18. I snack mindlessly while I study.

_____19. I skip meals.

_____20. I always avoid eating foods that might be unhealthy.

_____21. Cooking a meal is usually more trouble than it is worth.

_____22. I believe the important thing about food is that it is cheap and fast.

_____23. I would be happy eating hamburgers and pizza every day.

_____24. Things are quite relaxed when my family sits down to a dinner.

_____25. My mother was obsessively worried that our food was not spoiled.

_____26. My weight stays pretty constant.

Scoring:

Add your scores for items: 1, 3, 4, 6, 9, 10, 12, 13, 14, 16, 17, 24, and 26. Low scores on these items indicate a positive orientation to food.

Add your scores for items: 2, 5, 7, 8, 11, 15, 18, 19, 20, 21, 22, 23, and 25. Low scores on these items indicate a negative orientation to food.

*C*ircle of *Q*uality – Chapter 11

Please give us your feedback. We thank you in advance for assisting us in improving the next edition. The contact information is listed in the preface.

What are the three most helpful teaching tools in this chapter?

1.

2.

3.

What are the three least useful teaching tools in this chapter?

1.

2.

3.

What are the three most difficult concepts to teach in this chapter?

1.

2.

3.

Additional Comments:

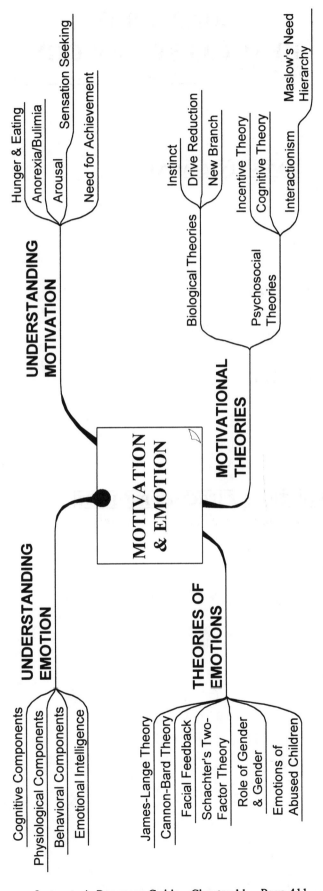

MOTIVATION & EMOTION

UNDERSTANDING MOTIVATION

- Hunger & Eating
- Anorexia/Bulimia
- Arousal
- Sensation Seeking
- Need for Achievement

MOTIVATIONAL THEORIES

- Biological Theories
  - Instinct
  - Drive Reduction
  - New Branch
- Psychosocial Theories
  - Incentive Theory
  - Cognitive Theory
  - Interactionism
  - Maslow's Need Hierarchy

UNDERSTANDING EMOTION

- Cognitive Components
- Physiological Components
- Behavioral Components
- Emotional Intelligence

THEORIES OF EMOTIONS

- James-Lange Theory
- Cannon-Bard Theory
- Facial Feedback
- Schachter's Two-Factor Theory
- Role of Gender & Gender
- Emotions of Abused Children

CHAPTER 12
HEALTH PSYCHOLOGY

Outline

Health Psychology in Action

What Health Psychology   Chronic Pain
Smoking
Binge Drinking

Stress and Its Role In Health
Causes of Stress

Research Highlight
Procrastination, Performance, and
Health

Results of Stress

Stress and Serious Illness

Cancer
Cardiovascular Disorders

Gender and Cultural Diversity
The Effects of Lifestyle on Health

Coping with Stress

Emotion-Focused Forms of Coping
Problem-Focused Forms of Coping

Active Learning
Testing Your Understanding

Resources for Effective Coping
Specific Coping Strategies

GOAL

Learning Objectives

Upon completion of CHAPTER 12, the student should be able to:

1. Define health psychology, and identify occupational options for health psychologists (pp. 428-429).

2. Define chronic pain and state its prevalence; describe the use of operant conditioning, biofeedback, and relaxation in the treatment of chronic pain (pp. 429-431).

3. Describe consequences of cigarette smoking; explain psychological, social, and biological factors that lead to smoking; and describe methods for prevention and quitting (pp. 432-435).

4. Discuss binge drinking on college campuses; describe how to reduce the social reinforcers that contribute to this problem (pp. 436-437).

5. Differentiate between stress and stressors, eustress and distress (p. 438).

6. Describe the relationship between stress and life changes; explain how appraisal is related to stress (pp. 438-440).

7. Describe research findings related to chronic stressors, daily hassles, frustrations, and conflict; differentiate the three basic conflicts (pp. 441-443).

8. Describe the physiological effects of stress, including the general adaptation syndrome, the suppression of the immune system, and the development of physical disorders (pp. 444-446).

9. Describe how stress-related behavior contributes to the development and progression of cancer (pp. 447-448).

10. Explain the relationship between stress and essential hypertension; describe the negative consequences of this disorder (pp. 448-449).

11. Explain the relationship between stress and heart disease, focusing on the autonomic nervous system, fatty deposits in the arteries, and cholesterol ratios (p. 449).

12. Differentiate between Type A and Type B personalities; describe the research related to Type A personality and heart disease; compare the shotgun and target behavior approaches to behavior modification (pp. 450-451).

13. Discuss cross-cultural research regarding the effects of lifestyle on health (pp. 451-452).

14. Compare and contrast emotion-focused and problem-focused forms of coping with stress, and provide an example of each (pp. 453-454).

15. Describe how each of the following resources improve coping: health and energy, positive beliefs, an internal locus of control, social skills, social support, and material resources (pp. 454-456).

16. Explain how relaxation, exercise, and self-care can reduce stress (pp. 456-458).

Chapter Summary/Lecture Organizer

I. **THE NATURE OF HEALTH PSYCHOLOGY** - Health psychology is the study of the relationship between psychological behavior and physical health and illness, with an emphasis on "wellness" and the prevention of illness. Health psychologists work with patients who are about to undergo complex surgical procedures by teaching them what to anticipate during and after the operation and by giving them and their families suggestions for dealing with psychological problems that may develop following surgery.

A. Chronic Pain - Health psychologists help chronic pain patients by teaching them to cope with their pain through operant conditioning, biofeedback, and relaxation techniques.

B. Smoking - Because smoking is the single most preventable cause of death and disease in the United States, prevention and cessation of smoking are of primary importance to all health practitioners, including health psychologists. Smoking prevention programs involve educating the public about short and long-term consequences of smoking, trying to make smoking less socially acceptable, and helping nonsmokers resist social pressures to smoke. Approaches to help people quit smoking include cognitive and behavioral techniques to aid smokers in their withdrawal from nicotine; and techniques for dealing with social pressures.

C. Binge Drinking - Since binge drinking is fairly common, especially among college aged individuals, and a potentially dangerous habit it is also a target of prevention programs. The focus of these programs is to reduce or remove the social reinforcers that encourage binge drinking.

II. **STRESS AND ITS ROLE IN HEALTH** - Stress is the body's nonspecific response to any demand made on it. Any stimulus that causes stress is called a stressor. There are both beneficial and non-beneficial types of stress.

A. Causes of Stress - The major causes of stress are life changes, hassles, frustration, and conflicts. Frustrations have to do with blocked goals. In recent years constantly changing technology has increased the hassles and frustrations of day to day living. Conflicts may be of three types: approach-approach, avoidance-avoidance, and approach-avoidance.

B. Results of Stress - When stressed, the body undergoes physiological changes. The sympathetic part of the autonomic nervous system is activated, increasing heart rate and blood pressure. This sympathetic activation is beneficial if people need to fight or flee, but it can have negative consequences if they do not. Hans Selye described a generalized physiological reaction to severe stressors, which he called the general adaptation syndrome. The general adaptation syndrome has three phases: the alarm reaction, the resistance phase, and the exhaustion phase.

Prolonged stress can suppress the immune system and render the body susceptible to many diseases, from colds and flu to cancer and heart disease.

III. STRESS AND SERIOUS ILLNESS

A. Cancer - Cancer can be caused by environmental factors, such as cigarette smoke or asbestos, or by changes in body chemistry that affect how certain cells within the body replicate. During times of stress, the body may be less able to check cancerous cell changes because the immune system is suppressed.

B. Cardiovascular Disorders - The leading cause of death in the United States is cardiovascular disease. The two major cardiovascular diseases are essential hypertension and heart disease. Essential hypertension is an increase in blood pressure that does not have a medical cause. Hypertension causes the heart to work harder, making the individual more prone to stroke and heart attack. Heart disease includes all illnesses that affect the heart muscle and lead to heart failure. Risk factors in heart disease include smoking, stress, obesity, a high-fat diet, lack of exercise, and Type A personality traits. The two main approaches to modifying Type A behavior are the shotgun approach and the target behavior approach.

> **Gender and Cultural Diversity** - The Ni-Hon-San study and the Adventist Health Study point out the significant role of the Western lifestyle in coronary heart disease and cancer. In the Ni-Hon-San study, Japanese men maintaining a traditional Japanese lifestyle have had lower rates of coronary heart disease than those who migrated and adopted a Western lifestyle. Similarly, Seventh-day Adventists, who follow the same healthful lifestyle no matter where they live, are less likely than others living in the same country to develop coronary heart disease, stroke, or cancer.

IV. COPING WITH STRESS - The two major forms of coping with stress are emotion-focused and problem-focused.

A. Emotion-Focused Forms of Coping - Emotion-focused forms of coping change how we view stressful situations.

B. Problem-Focused Forms of Coping - This approach to coping with stress deals directly with the situation or causative factors so as to decrease or eliminate the problems.

C. Resources for Effective Coping - The ability to cope with a stressor also depends on the resources available to a person. Resources include health and energy, positive beliefs, an internal locus of control, social skills, social support, and material resources.

D. Specific Coping Strategies - Relaxation, exercise, and self-care strategies are active methods people can use to cope with stress.

Teaching Resources

SECTION I - THE NATURE OF HEALTH PSYCHOLOGY

Learning Objectives #'s 1 - 4
Discussion Questions # 1
Active Learning Activities # 12.3

SECTION II - STRESS AND ITS ROLE IN HEALTH

Learning Objectives #'s 5, 6, 7
Lecture Lead-In's #'s 1, 2
Discussion Questions #'s 2, 5
Active Learning Activities #'s 12.1, 12.2
Brain-Based Learning #'s 12.1, 12.2
Critical Thinking Exercise #'s 12.1, 12.2

SECTION III - STRESS AND SERIOUS ILLNESS

Learning Objectives #'s 9 - 13
Lecture Extender p. 418
Discussion Questions # 4
Active Learning Activities # 12.4
Gender and Cultural Diversity Activity p. 435

SECTION IV - COPING WITH STRESS

Learning Objectives #'s 14 - 16
Lecture Lead-Ins # 1
Discussion Questions #'s 2, 3
Active Learning Activities #'s 12.3, 12.5
Brain-Based Learning #'s 12.1 - 12.3
Critical Thinking Exercise # 12.3
Writing Project p. 436

Lecture Lead-Ins

1.   In Billings, Montana, at 3:30 a.m., a man walks into an all night casino, pulls out a gun, and shoots the manager and two customers to death. He then turns and walks out to where police are waiting; he points the gun at the officers and they shoot him dead. What has caused this tragedy? When interviewed by the local radio station, the man's mother said that her son had been a loner and recluse since returning from Saudi Arabia and had "never been quite the same." Ask the students what has happened to this individual. There will be many different answers but someone should discover the Saudi Arabia connection. Explain that this incident could be explained in terms of stress from the war experience. This illness is called posttraumatic stress syndrome. Ask students if they believe this disorder is real or just an attempt by psychologists to explain behaviors they cannot otherwise explain. Ask them if they know any individuals who might have this problem. Ask for students to volunteer their experiences in stressful war situations; you are likely to have a Vietnam or Gulf War veteran in your class. This can be an excellent start to your lectures on stress.

2.   Ask why anyone would willingly undergo dangerous, stressful situations? The stress can be at a maximum and yet individuals do this for recreation. Very good examples are mountain biking, skiing, hang gliding, and white water sports. They all are stress-inducing behaviors. Ask individual volunteers why they do these sports. Can this type of behavior be stress-reducing? Use this discussion for a lead-in for your stress lectures.

Lecture Extenders

12.1 - Hypertension

A common disorder that has been suspected of having psychological roots is hypertension. The logic for relating stress and hypertension is the known relationship between a "threat" to the person, either physical or psychological, and the arousal of the sympathetic nervous system. The sympathetic nervous system plays an important role in the constriction of the blood vessels which has an immediate effect upon blood pressure. Since many cases of hypertension occur without any known etiologic factor, investigators have hypothesized that chronic tension and repressed anger are the villains. Within the last few years the medical profession has become aware of the differential rates in hypertension between African Americans and white Americans with the former group suffering the most from this disorder. The issue of psychological versus physiological factors in the demographics of the disorder was summarized by Daniel Goleman in The New York Times (April 24, 1990). The discussion below is based upon this material.

Hypertension is twice as common among African American as white Americans, amounting to what some refer to as an epidemic among African Americans and contributing to a higher rate of death from heart problems, kidney disease, and stroke. Seeking to explain this differential, investigators have focused on two explanations: repressed anger and rage which is accentuated through racial prejudice, and racial genetic differences which make the African American person more susceptible to hypertension. Dr. Elijah Saunders, a cardiologist at the University of Maryland Medical School and co-author of a leading textbook, Hypertension in African Americans, contends that the rage which comes from the prevailing racism in American society is the important factor that sets up the African American for more hypertension. He does not dispute that there may be some genetic differences, but he feels it is the additional stress that creates such a disparity between the two groups. Support for this position has come mainly from anecdotal accounts from physicians and psychotherapists who have had an opportunity to talk with African Americans and to observe their reactions to racial injustice. Presumably, one of the important factors in this rage reaction is that the African American person feels he or she has to repress the felt rage because of fear of retaliation.

In general, it has been difficult to obtain empirical data for this type of approach; however, a recently published study in Health Psychology provides some empirical data in support of the position. Twenty-seven African American college students were shown scenes from movies portraying three different types of scenes: a neutral one, an anger provoking scene, and a racial incident scene. Measures of blood pressure indicated that the racially disturbing scene led to a rise of three points in diastolic pressure while the other emotional scene was followed by a rise of only one point. Advocates of the stress position say that even though this is a small increment, it can accumulate, and over the years, push a person into hypertension.

Other well-known risk factors include high salt intake, alcohol consumption, and obesity. These factors may also be distributed differentially in the two populations. For example, it is known that African American women are more prone to be overweight than white women.

The major empirical relationships that have been found in the last few years include: people who repress their anger, regardless of their race, tend to have higher blood pressure; African Americans do appear to have a greater genetic susceptibility to hypertension; 25% of all African Americans retain sodium while under emotional stress which leads to an increase in blood pressure; and racism is an especially potent trigger of high blood pressure in African Americans.

Many see this as a complex issue without any easy resolution of the relative weights of the factors that contribute to hypertension. Undoubtedly, it would be desirable to eliminate racial prejudice; however it has not yet been demonstrated that this would be sufficient to eliminate the disparity in hypertension rates between the two groups.

Source: Goleman, D. (1990, April 24). Anger over racism is seen as a cause of blacks' high blood pressure. The New York Times, p. C3.

Key Terms

HEALTH PSYCHOLOGY IN ACTION

Binge Drinking (p. 436)
Chronic Pain (p. 429)
Electromyograph (EMG) (p. 430)
Endorphins (p. 430)
Health Psychology (p. 428)
Internal Locus of Control (p. 430)
Relaxation Techniques (p. 431)

STRESS AND ITS ROLE IN HEALTH

Approach-Approach Conflict (p. 443)
Approach-Avoidance Conflict (p. 443)
Avoidance-Avoidance Conflict (p. 443)
Conflict (p. 443)
Distress (p. 438)
Eustress (p. 438)
Frustration (p. 442)
General Adaptation Syndrome (p. 445)
Hassles (p. 441)

Stress (p. 438)
Stressor (p. 438)

STRESS AND SERIOUS ILLNESS

Essential Hypertension (p. 448)
Heart Disease (p. 449)
Hypertension (p. 448)
Shotgun Approach (p. 450)
Target Behavior Approach (p. 450)
Type A Personality (p. 450)
Type B Personality (p. 450)

COPING WITH STRESS

Coping (p. 453)
Emotion-Focused Forms of Coping (p. 453)
Problem-Focused Forms of Coping (p. 453)

Discussion Questions

1. Would you like the work of a health psychologist? Do you think this career will increase in importance in the future? If we move toward a nationalized health care system where everyone will have access to medical care, how will this affect the field of health psychology?

2. What are the most important sources of stress in our society? What could be done to combat these stressors on a societal level? As an individual? What were the most important stressors for your parents when they were your age? Do you have more or less stress in your life compared to your parents? What about your resources for coping with stress, are they better than your parents? Why or why not?

3. What are the advantages and disadvantages of relying on emotion-focused styles of coping? Problem-focused forms of coping? What about the use of defense mechanisms? Do you overuse some defense mechanisms? Is this preventing you from finding better ways to combat your stress and conflict? Do you think it is possible to live free of defense mechanisms? Why or why not?

4. Are you a Type A or a Type B person? What are the advantages and disadvantages to each? If you could change to the opposite style, would you?

5. When people from other countries visit America, they often report feeling stressed by the large number of choices in everyday life (e.g., the number of career choices, channels on television, and even the number and variety of shampoos). Does this have a similar effect on your own level of stress? Is this an example of approach-approach conflict, approach-avoidance, or avoidance-avoidance?

 **Web Sites**

ATP Site
http://www.atp.cygnet.co.uk/ATPart.html
This site summarizes most of the major aspects of Freudian theory, up to and including therapy.

The Five-Factor Model in Personality: A Critical Appraisal
http://www.psych.nwu.edu/~pizzurro/mcadams.html
This article offers six limitations to the Five-Factor Model. A list of references is included.

Taxonomy of Personality with the Five-Factor Theory
http://galton.psych.nwu.edu/greatideas/papers/popkins.html
Offers a detailed account of how personality may be classified according to the Five-Factor model.

The PEN (Psychoticism-Extroversion-Neuroticism) model
http://galton.psych.nwu.edu/greatideas/papers/jang.html
This site provides elaborate information on the Eysenck model of personality, with relevant findings from the research literature. Most notable is the research on psychophysiological responses associated with different personality attributes

Psychology Links: Humanistic Psychology
http://www.tamiu.edu/coah/psy/person.htm
Gives a detailed account of humanistic theories of personality and therapy including Rogers and Maslow.

Suggested Films and Videos

Can't Slow Down
Films for the Humanities and Sciences, 1995. 28 minutes. This video explores how we are spending our time and how the constant rush is affecting everything about our relationships and health.

Running Out of Time: Time Pressure, Overtime and Overwork
Films for the Humanities and Sciences, 1995. 52 minutes. Explores the impact of time pressure and overwork on American society. The program contrasts expectations about saving time with the reality that there are more time savers and less time to use them. Interesting comparisons are made to conditions in other countries and other times.

Stress
Films for the Humanities and Sciences, 1995. 23 minutes. Explains that stress is a biological response of an organism to its environment and is necessary to survival. However, when stress becomes chronic it can lead to sickness and even death.

Health, Mind and Behavior
Annenberg/CPB, 1990. 30 minutes. This program from Zimbardo's "Discovering Psychology" series examines how the new biopsychosocial model of medicine is replacing the traditional biomedical approach. Highlights include a discussion of the use of traditional Native American medical techniques in modern medicine, the use of biofeedback in stress management, and a review of psychological and medical research on AIDS.

Healing and the Mind
Insight Media, 1993. About 60 minutes each. In this five-part series, Bill Moyers discusses a number of issues in health psychology and behavioral medicine. Highlights include a discussion and demonstration of biofeedback, acupuncture, and massage, Eastern approaches to medicine (including meditation), and changes in U.S. traditional medical practices as a result of incorporation of psychological insights in medicine.

Health, Stress and Coping
Insight Media, 1990. 30 minutes. This program explores a range of stressors including daily stress, loss of a love relationship, and posttraumatic stress disorder. Selye's GAS, the relationship between stress and physical illness, and strategies for coping with stress are also discussed.

Books For Success

Myers, David G. (1992). **The Pursuit of Happiness: Who Is Happy - And Why**. Morrow.
This book explores the concept of happiness and how personal happiness can be enhanced through modifying the "subjective assessment" of one's life.

Greenberg, Jerrold S. (1990, 1992). **Comprehensive Stress Management**. William C. Brown.
A practical presentation of the nature and causes of stress including stress in particular populations, and various techniques for stress management.

Keys, Ralph (1991). **TIMELOCK: How Life Got So Hectic and What You Can Do About It**.
HarperCollins.
A presentation of analyses and case studies to fulfill the subtitle's message.

Elliot, Robert S. and Breo, Dennis L. (1984). **Is It Worth Dying For?** Bantam Books.
A very readable book which explains a connection between stress and risk of heart attack. Also, suggests lifestyle changes to diminish this risk.

(Edited by) Goleman, Daniel and Gurin, Joel (1993). **Mind/Body Medicine: How to Use Your Mind for Better Health.** Consumer Reports Books.
A compilation of 25 chapters on health psychology written by recognized experts in the topics discussed.

Covey, Stephen; Merrill, Roger; Merrill Rebecca (1996).**First Things First: To Live, to Love, to Learn, to Leave a Legacy.** Fireside
This highly recommended book is a practical guide that helps you determine the most important things in your life and that motivates you to live a life that truly empowers you to put first things first. It offers a new paradigm that shift from old style time management organized around a clock to a balanced life approach organized around the compass. It is designed to help people move out of stress and into fullfillment.

Active Learning

Active Learning Activity 12.1 - The Social Readjustment Rating Scale

Have students rate themselves on the original Social Readjustment Rating Scale (Table 12.1, p. 412). Then ask the students who score high on the scale if they have had any recent illness. Do the same for those scoring in the moderate and low ranges. In this way, you can test the validity of the scale for your class. You might also want to discuss why each of the events listed on the scale would be a cause of stress.

Active Learning Activity 12.2 - Group Exercise for Social Readjustment Rating Scale

Another classroom exercise is to break the class into groups and have each group assign new ratings to the life events listed in Table 12.1 (p. 412). They should rank each event with a score between 1 and 100 with "Marriage" being assigned "50." You can examine the differences between your class rankings and the original rankings of Holmes and Rahe which are shown in the text. This could lead to a discussion of social changes over the past two decades.

Active Learning Activity 12.3 - Bad Habits

Have the students list on a piece of paper the two bad health habits they would like to change (e.g., smoking, drinking too much, eating too much/not enough, not exercising enough). After the students have made these lists, have each student try to figure out a behavior modification program to change these behaviors (describe a positive reinforcer and a schedule to produce the change). Have them break down into small groups (5-6 individuals) and discuss the modification programs. Have the students try to help each other with their programs. Reassemble and ask for volunteers to share their programs with the class.

Active Learning Activity 12.4 - Type A Behavior

Make photocopies of Handout 12.4 and an overhead transparency. Have students identify whether their personalities best fit the Type-A or Type-B profile. Lead a discussion of the merits of both types of personality profile. Ask the students to identify situations when it might be desirable to modify the behavior of people with Type-A behavior. Put the overhead on again but this time, have them list behaviors for each characteristic that might help a Type-A behave more like a Type-B. For example, Type-A's might try to slow down their speech and soften their voice, they might wait in the longest line at the bookstore, or they might drive a longer way home from school.

Handout 12.4 – Active Learning

Increase Your Self Awareness: Are You A Type A?

Circle the number on the scale below that best characterizes your behavior for each trait.

1. Casual about appointments	1 2 3 4 5 6 7 8	Never late
2. Not competitive	1 2 3 4 5 6 7 8	Very competitive
3. Never feel rushed	1 2 3 4 5 6 7 8	Always rushed
4. Take things one at a time	1 2 3 4 5 6 7 8	Try to do many things at once
5. Slow doing things	1 2 3 4 5 6 7 8	Fast (eating, walking, etc.)
6. Express feelings	1 2 3 4 5 6 7 8	Sit" on feelings
7. Many interests	1 2 3 4 5 6 7 8	Few interests outside work

Source: Adapted from R.W. Bortner, (1969, June). Short Rating Scale as a Potential Measure of Pattern A Behavior, Journal of Chronic Diseases, pp. 87-91. Used with permission.

Scoring Key:
Total your score on the seven questions. Now multiply it by 3. A total of 120 or more indicates you're a hard-core Type A. Scores below 90 indicate you're a hard-core Type B. The following gives you more specifics:

Points	*Personality Type*
120 or more	A+
106-119	A
100-105	A-
90-99	B+
Less than 90	B

Active Learning Activity 12.5 - Coping with Stress

After discussing emotion-focused and problem-focused forms of coping, pages 426-427 of the text, describe a few stress-producing situations and have the class suggest both an emotion-focused and a problem-focused coping strategy. Then ask for a show of hands on which type of coping strategy--emotion-focused, problem-focused, or a combination of the two--would be best for each situation. Use the following examples or your own class generated examples.

Examples of Stressful Situations

1. You are terrible at making introductions, you walk into your first day of fraternity rush and are asked to go around the room and introduce everyone.

2. It is the first day of classes and you are an entering freshman. About five minutes into your first class you realize you are in classroom 242 not room 424. This is a physics class not a psychology class.

3. Your department chairman has just told you that in three hours you are to make your first major presentation to the faculty to ask for continued funding for your department.

4. Your significant other has just told you that he/she is in love with someone else, is moving out tonight and is getting married next August, but wants to still be friends.

5. Your car has stalled on a deserted country road; before you can get out of your car to check under the hood, two large dogs run up to your door and start barking and growling at you.

6. Your car insurance has just been cancelled because of a mistake in your driving record.

7. You are the owner of a professional Hockey team that has just lost eight games in a row.

8. You have just finished entering a twenty-page paper into your word processor which is due in one hour. Before you have a chance to print out the report, the electrical power in your room fails and you lose the entire paper.

9. The fantastic-looking person sitting next to you says hello and invites you to go out for a drink after class.

10. You come into your history class perfectly prepared to take notes only to find that this is the day of the first examination.

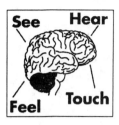

Brain-Based Learning

Brain-Based Learning Activity 12.1 - Road Rage

One of the most stressful aspects of everyday life in most urban areas is driving. The news media have popularized the term "Road Rage" as an explosion of uncontrolled emotion under stress. It is a term most of your students are familiar with and a good gateway to a discussion on monitoring and expressing emotions.

Begin by asking students to think of frustrating driving situations, such as being stuck behind a slow driver, or finding a parking space on campus. Once students have two or three specific examples in mind ask them to write down for each of those situations:

What did you feel?
What did you say?
What did you do?

Discuss how the coping techniques suggested in the textbook chapters could be applied to the examples given by the students. Which techniques do they think would work, which not?

For an extra credit assignment, have students tape themselves in their cars for one week. Every time they get frustrated they record themselves and say out loud what they feel on the inside.

Brain-Based Learning Activity 12.2 - Finding the Stress in Life

Ask the students to make a list of the ten most stressful situations or issues in their life. Ask them to rank the top three. Then hold a discussion of what they can do about these. The student counseling office may have a handout on where to go locally for sources of help.

A companion exercise is to ask students to describe the two people they personally know who live the most balanced lives (work, play, family, food, exercise, recreation etc.). What characteristics do they have in common? How can the students incorporate these skills into their lives?

Brain-Based Learning Activity 12.3 - Meditation Tape

For five minutes play a relaxation or meditation music tape. If feasible, have the students close their eyes sit quietly breathing long and deep. During debriefing ask the students how it felt to slow down and ease up. Did they like it? Did it make them uneasy? How much time do they give to this type of experience during the typical week?

For extra credit, students could select a relaxation exercise to practice each day for two weeks and to write up their observations and reactions.

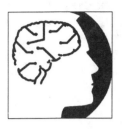

Critical Thinking

Critical Thinking Exercise 12.1 - Employing Precise Terms and Developing Self-Understanding: Improving Critical Thinking Regarding Conflict

The ability to identify terms in a clear and concise way is a hallmark of critical thinkers. This exercise was developed to help students master the terms and concepts associated with the text's discussion of conflict. This activity will also help students to clarify their own beliefs and values--another important component of critical thinking. **Time:** Approximately 30 minutes.

Instructions: After discussing the three major types of conflict (Approach-Approach, Avoidance-Avoidance, and Approach-Avoidance), ask students to stand up and move to the center of the room. Tell them you are going to give them a series of "forced choices," and that they must make a quick decision and move to the side of the room which best reflects their choice. For example, if you ask them if they prefer to play tennis or racquetball, the people who prefer tennis should move to the right and those who prefer racquetball should move to the left.

The first 2-3 choices should be "approach-approach" type examples: going to the movies versus going to a play, buying a new book versus buying a new compact disk, having a first date which involves a picnic and a walk on the beach versus an expensive dinner and movie. The second round of choices should be "avoidance- avoidance" examples: having a relationship that is quiet (and boring) versus one that is exciting (and dangerous), enduring a painful toothache versus going to the dentist for an extraction, staying in a bad relationship because you or your partner is unhappily pregnant versus breaking up and giving the baby up for adoption.

After several rounds, ask students to return to their seats while you list the three types of conflict on the chalkboard. Explain that you did not have them move around on the "approach-avoidance" conflicts because they essentially involve only one goal with both attractive and unattractive features. Offer examples such as: getting married, quitting school, or buying an expensive car. Of the examples you gave, ask students which were the easiest, hardest, and most stressful to resolve. During the discussion, mention that vacillation, indecision, and "leaving the field" are common behaviors associated with difficult conflicts. Ask them for elaboration on why some women wait until the last minute for an abortion, why some people seem reluctant to commit to relationships, or why some students feel like dropping out of school during finals week.

If time allows, the student's self-understanding is enhanced by having them complete the following sentences on half sheets of paper: "I learned that...;" "I was surprised that...;" and "I was pleased that..." Do NOT have them put their name on the paper. Collect the papers and redistribute them and then go around the room having students read from the most interesting responses.

This exercise also appears in the text, Chapter 12. We include it here for your convenience, and you may want to discuss it in class to reinforce reading of the text.

Critical Thinking Exercise 12.2 - Making Sound Decisions: Recognizing the Role of Personal Values in Conflict Resolution

Most of us can readily supply examples of approach-approach, avoidance-avoidance and approach-avoidance conflicts in our lives and tell how we resolved the problem. In some cases, when faced with a conflict, we turned to others for advice. Although others' opinions are valuable, critical thinkers recognize that ultimately, any decision must be guided by the decision maker's own personal values and goals. Good decision makers take full responsibility for their own future. They realize that they are the only ones who can truly evaluate the merits of each alternative. A critical thinker also recognizes that decisions are often stressful, but that they cannot be avoided. Avoiding a decision is, in fact, making one without the benefit of a careful analysis of the problem.

To improve your decision-making skills, we offer the following chart that may help to clarify some of your current conflicts (adapted from Seech, 1987).

1. At the top of the chart, identify your specific conflict as approach-approach, avoidance-avoidance, and approach-avoidance.

2. On the lines in the left-hand column, list all possible alternatives or possible courses of action. Although the wording of the "approach-approach" discussion may imply only two choices, most conflicts involve several options or alternatives. Identifying all your options will require a good deal of homework. Read up on your problem. Talk to as many people as you can.

3. Now list the logical outcome or consequence of each alternative, regardless of whether the consequence is significant or insignificant and regardless of whether it is a certain or a possible outcome.

4. Next assess both the probability and significance of each outcome. Using a 0 to 5 rating scale (0 = won't occur and 5 = certain to occur), assign a numerical rating for the likelihood that each consequence will actually occur. Using a similar 0 to 5 rating scale (0 = no significance and 5 = high significance), assess the importance you place on each consequence.

5. Now review the chart. In some cases, you may find it helpful to multiply your probability and significance ratings and then compare your results for the various alternatives. In other cases, you will find it difficult to assign numerical values to complex issues and feelings. Even in the most difficult decisions, however, the thinking and evaluation elicited by this chart may provide useful insights to your conflict. Also note the feelings you associate with each alternative. Careful decision making tries to integrate feelings and cognitions.

6. After you've reviewed each alternative, ask yourself which choice is most in line with your overall goals and values. Some alternatives may look more-or less appealing when weighed against long-term relationship plans, career goals, and personal belief systems. You may want to discuss your chart with a trusted friend before you make a final decision.

Handout 12.2 - Critical Thinking

Making Sound Decisions

Type of Conflict_____

	Alternatives	Logical Outcome	Probability	Significance
1.				
2.				
3.				

Once you make your decision, commit yourself and give it all you've got. Throw away your expectations. Many decisions don't turn out the way we imagine, and if we focus on the way it is supposed to be we miss enjoying the way it is. If the decision doesn't work out, don't stubbornly hang on for dear life. Change or correct your course.

This exercise also appears in the Student Study Guide for Chapter 12. We include it here for your convenience, and you may want to discuss it in class to reinforce use of the Student Study Guide.

Critical Thinking Exercise 12.3

After reading pages 453-454 of the text, try identifying both an emotion-focused and a problem-focused coping strategy for each of the following situations:

1. It is the first day of classes for a new semester and about five minutes into your first class you realize you are in classroom 242 not room 424. This is a physics class not a psychology class.

2. Your significant other has just told you that he/she is in love with someone else and is getting married next August.

3. Your car has stalled on a deserted country road. As you start to get out to check the problem, two large dogs run up to your door and start barking and growling at you.

4. Your car insurance has just been cancelled because of a mistake in your driving record.

5. You come to your history class expecting a normal lecture class, but you discover this is the day of the first major examination.

Gender and Cultural Diversity

Gender and Cultural Diversity Activity 12.1 - Modifying Type-A Behavior

Begin the demonstration by asking students to look at the transparency you made from handout 12.1. Does their personality qualify as a Type-A or Type-B?

Ask the Class

1. What are the advantages of a Type-A personality for a white male/female, African-American male/female, Hispanic male/female?

2. What are the disadvantages of a Type-A personality for a white male/female, African-American male/female, Hispanic male/female?

3. What effect does socioeconomic status have on Type-A's or Type-B's?

Explain that often it is desirable to modify the behaviors of people with Type-A patterns because of their susceptibility to heart disease. (Remind students that hostility seems to be the critical factor in heart disease with Type-A individuals.) Have the students look at table again, this time have them list behaviors for each characteristic that might help any of the Type-A's behave more like Type-B's.

For example, Type-A's might try to slow down their speech and soften their voice (as opposed to barking out rapid orders), they might wait in the longest line at the supermarket (while intentionally practicing progressive relaxation techniques rather than fuming at their wait), or they might take a longer way home from school (listening to a favorite disc or tape and enjoying the new view).

Writing Project

Writing Project 12.1

Given the need for improved writing skills in college students, and to respond to the call for "writing across the curriculum," we offer writing projects for each chapter. In Chapter 12, we suggest a 2-3 page written response to the following activity. Recognizing the time involved in grading such writing projects, one alternative is occasionally to assign "peer grading." Collect the papers, remove student names, and give each student a paper to grade. It helps to make their participation in peer grading part of the overall points for the writing project. This encourages a more thoughtful and responsible evaluation, as well as acknowledging and rewarding the additional work.

Using information on pages 426-427 of the text, describe a few stress-producing situations from your current life and describe one or two emotion-focused and one or two problem-focused forms of coping. Which form of coping do you generally use? Discuss advantages and disadvantages of each style.

Circle of Quality – Chapter 12

Please give us your feedback. We thank you in advance for assisting us in improving the next edition. The contact information is listed in the preface.

What are the three most helpful teaching tools in this chapter?

1.

2.

3.

What are the three least useful teaching tools in this chapter?

1.

2.

3.

What are the three most difficult concepts to teach in this chapter?

1.

2.

3.

Additional Comments:

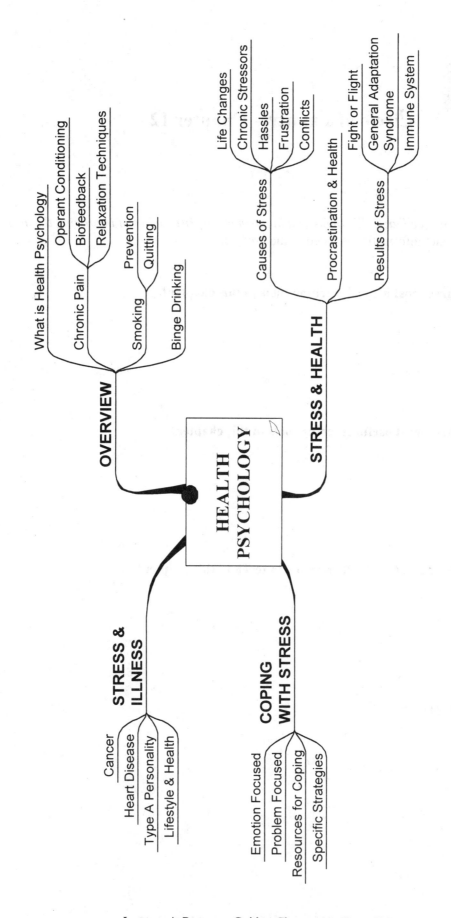

HEALTH PSYCHOLOGY

OVERVIEW
- What is Health Psychology
- Chronic Pain
  - Operant Conditioning
  - Biofeedback
  - Relaxation Techniques
- Smoking
  - Prevention
  - Quitting
- Binge Drinking

STRESS & HEALTH
- Causes of Stress
  - Life Changes
  - Chronic Stressors
  - Hassles
  - Frustration
  - Conflicts
- Procrastination & Health
- Results of Stress
  - Fight or Flight
  - General Adaptation Syndrome
  - Immune System

STRESS & ILLNESS
- Cancer
- Heart Disease
- Type A Personality
- Lifestyle & Health

COPING WITH STRESS
- Emotion Focused
- Problem Focused
- Resources for Coping
- Specific Strategies

CHAPTER 13
PERSONALITY

Outline

GOAL

Learning Objectives

Upon completion of CHAPTER 13, the student should be able to:

1. Define personality and explain the scientific standards that allow today's psychologists to more accurately measure personality than they did in the past (p. 464).
2. Briefly describe how interviews and observations are used to assess personality (p. 465).
3. List four multi-trait objective tests; briefly describe the characteristics of the MMPI/MMPI-2; differentiate between vocational interest, aptitude, and achievement tests (pp. 465-467).
4. Briefly describe the characteristics of a Rorschach inkblot test and the Thematic Apperception Test (pp. 467-469).
5. Discuss three logical fallacies that explain the widespread acceptance of "pseudo" personality tests (p. 468).
6. Discuss the relative strengths and weaknesses of the four major methods of personality assessment (p. 469).
7. Describe the evolution of the trait theories of personality from Allport to Cattell to Eysenck, ending with the five-factor (Big Five) model (pp. 470-472).
8. Discuss the research findings regarding the five-factor model of personality and the three major criticisms regarding trait theories, in general (pp. 473-474).
9. Describe how trait theories differ from the psychoanalytic theory of personality; differentiate among Freud's three levels of consciousness: conscious, preconscious, and unconscious (pp. 475-477).
10. Discuss current research regarding terror management theory and evidence for the existence of unconscious information processing (p. 479).
11. Define id, ego, and superego, and discuss how the pleasure principle, reality principle, and morality principle correspond to each of these personality structures. Define and explain the role of defense mechanisms employed by the ego (pp. 477-478, 480).
12. Discuss Freud's five stages of psychosexual development and the effects of successful or unsuccessful completion at each stage (pp. 480-482).
13. Compare Freud's original theories to the approaches of the Neo-Freudians: Adler, Jung, and Horney (pp. 482-485).
14. Discuss the five major criticisms of psychoanalytic theories (pp. 485-486).
15. Discuss humanistic theories of personality, comparing the approaches of Rogers and Maslow (pp. 487-490).
16. Discuss three of the major criticisms of humanistic theories (p. 490).
17. Discuss social-cognitive theories of personality, comparing the approaches of Bandura and Rotter; state two strengths and two weaknesses of these theories (pp. 491-493).
18. Describe the role of brain structures, neurochemistry, and genetics advanced in biological theories of personality (pp. 493-494).
19. Describe how the interactionist approach to personality is blending views based on research findings (p. 494).
20. Describe how cultural variations in the concepts of the "self" affect the study of personality (pp. 494-496).

Chapter Summary/Lecture Organizer

Introductory Vignette--Chapter 13 begins with a brief "bogus" personality description designed to apply (and appeal) to the general public, much as horoscopes do. Problems with this type of "pseudo" personality test are used to introduce the topic of personality and difficulties with its definition and assessment.

Personality is defined as an individual's relatively stable and enduring pattern of thoughts, emotions, and actions. Psychologists describe and explain personality differences according to different theoretical orientations.

I.   **HOW WE MEASURE PERSONALITY: FOUR MAJOR METHODS** - Psychologists use several methods to measure or assess personality, including interviews, observations, self-report inventories, and projective techniques. Reliability and validity are the two major criteria for assessing personality assessment techniques.

   A. Interviews - Interviews may be either structured (specific questions and a set procedure) or unstructured (informal and random questions).

   B. Observational Methods - During observations, psychologists look for specific behaviors and follow a set of evaluation guidelines.

   C. Objective Tests - Personality is most commonly measured through objective tests (such as the MMPI-2), which ask test-takers to respond to paper-and-pencil questionnaires or inventories. These tests provide objective standardized information about a large number of personality traits. But they have been criticized for the possibility of deliberate deception and social desirability bias, diagnostic difficulties, and inappropriate use.

   D. Projective Tests - Projective tests are the second major category of personality assessment. They ask test-takers to respond to ambiguous stimuli (such as the Rorschach "inkblot" or the TAT pictures). These tests are said to provide insight into unconscious elements of personality. Critics, however, contend that these tests have unacceptably low levels of reliability and validity.

   E. Are Personality Measurements Accurate? Evaluating The Methods - Interviews and observations provide invaluable information, but are very time consuming both in terms of professional training and the actual implementation. Objective tests (such as the MMPI) provide specific, objective information in a short period of time, but they have been criticized for deliberate deception and social desirability bias, diagnostic difficulties, and inappropriate use. Projective tests are believed to offer unique opportunities for accessing the unconscious, but, critics object to the expense and time required to administer and interpret them, and the relatively low reliability and validity.

II. **TRAIT THEORIES** - Trait theorists believe personality consists of relatively stable and consistent characteristics.

A. **Early Trait Theorists** - The focus of early theorists was identifying the actual traits people possess, and the degree to which they pervade the overall personality.

Allport's Trait Theory: - Allport focuses on cardinal, central, and secondary traits. Cardinal traits are relatively uncommon, while central traits are highly characteristic of someone and easy to infer. Secondary traits influence few situations or behaviors.

Cattell's Trait Theory: - Cattell emphasizes the importance of source traits (basic personality traits shared by most individuals).

Eysenck's Trait Theory: - Eysenck believes personality can be described along three dimensions (introversion-extroversion, stability-instability, and psychotism).

B. **The "Big 5" Model** - Recent research has found five major traits, the "Big 5" (openness to experience, conscientiousness, extroversion, agreeableness, and neuroticism), that can be used to describe most individuals. This may reflect a biologically based set of universal human personality characteristics.

III. **PSYCHOANALYTIC THEORIES**

A. **Freud's Psychoanalytic Theory** - The psychoanalytic approach to personality was founded by Freud. Freud emphasized the power of the unconscious and believed that the mind (or psyche) functioned on three levels, the conscious, the preconscious, and the unconscious. In Freud's theory, personality has three distinct parts, the id, ego, and superego. The ego struggles to meet the demands of the id and superego, and when these demands are in conflict the ego may resort to defense mechanisms to relieve the resultant anxiety. According to Freud, all human beings pass through five psychosexual stages: oral, anal, phallic, latency, and genital. How the conflicts at each of these stages are resolved is important to personality development. Anxieties arising from these early experiences reveal themselves as negative personality traits in adulthood.

B. **Neo-Freudian Theories** - Followers of Freud, who later revised his theory, are known as neo-Freudians. Three of the most influential were Adler, Jung, and Horney. While they generally agreed with many of Freud's theories, they broke away because they emphasized different issues. Adler emphasized the "inferiority complex" and the compensating "will-to-power." Jung introduced the "collective unconscious" and "archetypes." Horney stressed the importance of "basic anxiety" and refuted Freud's idea of "penis envy," replacing it with "power envy."

C. **Evaluating Psychoanalytic Theories** - Critics of the psychoanalytic approach, especially Freud's theories, argue that it is difficult to test, overemphasizes biology and unconscious forces, has inadequate empirical support, is sexist, and lacks cross-cultural support. Despite these criticisms, Freud remains a notable pioneer in psychology.

IV. **HUMANISTIC THEORIES** - Humanistic theories emphasize internal experiences, thoughts, and feelings that create the individual's self-concept; sometimes known as the phenomenological perspective.

A. Carl Rogers - Carl Rogers emphasized the concepts of self-esteem and unconditional positive regard. People with low self-esteem generally have poor congruence between their self-concept and life experiences.

B. Abraham Maslow - Maslow emphasized the basic goodness of human nature and a natural tendency toward self-actualization (an innate tendency toward growth that motivates all human behavior).

C. Evaluating Humanistic Theories - Critics of the humanistic approach argue that these theories are based on naive assumptions, and have poor scientific testability and inadequate empirical evidence. In addition, their focus on description, rather than explanation, makes them narrow.

V. SOCIAL/COGNITIVE PERSPECTIVE

A. Bandura's and Rotter's Approaches - Bandura's social-cognitive approach focuses on self-efficacy and reciprocal determinism, while Rotter's locus of control theory emphasizes a person's internal or external focus as a major determinant of personality.

B. Evaluating Social/Cognitive Theory - The social/cognitive theories emphasizes the interaction between the environment and the individual, and meet the standards for scientific research by offering testable and objective hypotheses as well as operationally defined terms. Critics argue that social/cognitive theories ignore unconscious and emotional components of personality and overlook developmental aspects.

VI. BIOLOGICAL THEORIES

- Biological theories emphasize the physical and chemical substrates and the inherited genetic components of personality. Research on specific traits such as sensation seeking and extroversion strongly support the biological approach.

A. The Brain and Neurochemistry - Research suggests that certain brain areas involved in emotional responses may account for some personality traits. Along these same lines, certain neurotransmitters that affect the level of arousal may be the source of some personality traits.

B. Genetics - Studies show a strong influence of hereditary factors on personality, but further research is needed before we have a cohesive biological theory of personality.

C. Interactionism - The interactionist approach suggests that the major theories overlap and each contributes to our understanding of personality.

> **Gender and Cultural Diversity** - Most theories of personality are biased toward Western individualistic cultures and their perception of the "self." Recognizing and understanding this bias helps keep our study of personality in perspective.

Teaching Resources

SECTION I - PERSONALITY ASSESSMENT

Learning Objectives #'s 1 - 6
Lecture Lead-Ins #' 1, 2
Active Learning Activities #'s 13.1- 13.5
Brain-Based Learning #'s 13.1 - 13.3
Critical Thinking Exercise p. 461, 463
Gender and Cultural Diversity Activity p. 466

SECTION II - TRAIT THEORIES

Learning Objectives #'s 7, 8
Lecture Lead-Ins #'s 1, 2
Lecture Extenders p. 446
Discussion Questions # 1
Active Learning Activities # 13.1
Brain-Based Learning #'s 13.1, 13.3
Critical Thinking Exercise p. 460, 463
Gender and Cultural Diversity Activity p. 466

SECTION III - PSYCHOANALYTIC THEORIES

Learning Objectives #'s 9 - 14
Discussion Questions #'s 2, 3, 4
Active Learning Activities #'s 13.2, 13.3
Brain-Based Learning #'s 13.1, 13.2
Critical Thinking Exercise #s 13.1, 13.4

SECTION IV - HUMANISTIC THEORIES

Learning Objectives #'s 15, 16
Active Learning Activities # 13.4
Brain-Based Learning # 13.1
Critical Thinking Exercise p. 460
Writing Project p. 467

SECTION V - SOCIAL/COGNITIVE PERSPECTIVE

Learning Objectives # 17
Lecture Extenders p. 446
Discussion Questions # 4
Active Learning Activities # 13.4
Brain-Based Learning #'s 13.1, 13.2

SECTION VI - BIOLOGIAL THEORIES

Learning Objectives # 18
Lecture Extenders p. 446
Discussion Questions # 4
Critical Thinking Exercise p. 460

SECTION VI - INTERACTIONISM

Learning Objectives #'s 19, 20

Lecture Lead-Ins

1.　　Use an overhead of Sheldon's body types, and present this to the class with a short lecture on the proposed types and personality variables. Ask the students if there is any validity to this concept of personality. Some will say yes and use an example of a friend or relative. Explain the problems with this research and with trying to explain personality in terms of personal observations and common experiences. Use this discussion as a springboard for lectures on personality theory.

2.　　Have the students write on a piece of paper their "best" and "worst" personality characteristic. Be sure the students do not write their names on their papers and instruct any individual who does not want the information to be made public to so indicate. Have the papers passed in and discuss the best as a lead-in for your lectures in personality theory.

Lecture Extenders

13.1 - Does Body Build Matter?

Much of the theorizing about biological determinants of personality have fallen upon bad times in American psychology, especially those related to body types. However, in recent years the findings in abnormal psychology, especially in the area of schizophrenia and affective disorders, have re-oriented American psychology to the possibility of biology playing more than a trivial role in human behaviors. Other evidence for biological contributions in the area of "normal" personality is emerging in the twin studies referred to in the next chapter. This increasing interest in biology should lead to exploration of other areas, including body types since this concept also relates to constitutional factors that influence behavior. Two researchers, Wilson and Herrstein, who are interested in the factors that contribute to criminal behavior have examined Sheldon's material and feel there is some merit to it. The discussion below is based upon the data presented in their book, Crime and Human Nature (1985).

Wilson and Herrstein define constitutional factors as those aspects that are present at birth or soon after birth and may later have behavioral consequences in terms of increasing or decreasing the probability of criminal behavior. They state emphatically that they do not believe there is such a thing as a criminal gene, only correlating factors, and they are not looking for causes. (This strong statement is necessary since so many "environmentalists" refer to these researchers as believing heredity causes crime.)

One constitutional factor that emerges in the literature on criminal behavior is body type as defined in Sheldon's typology into mesomorphy, ectomorphy, and endomorphy. Applying his body typing to a group of 200 young men with problem behaviors who had been assigned to a residential facility near Boston, Sheldon found a high preponderance of mesomorphic body builds and a low number of ectomorphic configurations. Thirty years later, in a comparison of those who went on to a criminal career versus those whose behaviors improved, the former group proved to be more mesomorphic relative to the average for the facility. Other investigators have found the same bodybuild in delinquent populations, both males and females, in England.

Sheldon and Eleanor Glueck have conducted what is probably the classic study on juvenile delinquency. This study began in the 1930's when the subjects were approximately 14 years of age and continued into adulthood. The study began with 500 delinquents matched with non-delinquents on a variety of important variables such as age, IQ, ethnic background, and socioeconomic level (including actual neighborhood). Body typing was done by researchers who were not aware of group membership. The delinquents were significantly more mesomorphic than the non-delinquent group.

It should be pointed out again that no reputable researcher is saying that body build causes crime: the relationship is correlational, not causal. Why does this correlation occur? Sheldon hypothesized that the mesomorphic personality tends to be more extroverted, domineering, and impulsive than the other body types. The Glueck study found different clusters of personality traits in the delinquents and non-delinquents. For example, some of the personality traits that appeared more strongly in the delinquent group were social assertion, self-assertiveness, impulsiveness, and extroversion. Are these correlations the product of learning? For example, do muscular children learn they can get their way more often because they are stronger, thus, learning to be aggressive? Wilson and Herrstein report some pertinent data from adoption studies in Denmark. This data, based on the largest systematic adoption study of criminality ever undertaken, represented over 13,000 adoptees along with their biological and adoptive parents. Data form conviction records were used for evidence of criminality. The greatest chance of a conviction in an offspring occurred if both the biological and adoptive parents had a criminal record--24.5%. What if only the adoptive or biological parents had a record? The chances were greater that the offspring would be involved in criminal behavior if the criminal record was in the biological parents' record--20.0% versus 14.7%. Even when the adoptive parents had a clear record, chances were increased from 13.5% (no record for the biological parents) to 20.0% (biological parents have a record).

So what are these biological factors that increase the chances of criminal behavior? It is possible that what others refer to as temperament or desire for a higher level of stimulation relate in some way to body build. Again, since so many factors interact to produce the final behaviors, desirable or undesirable, it would be very difficult to determine the amount of blame that should be assigned to bodybuild.

Source: Wilson, J. Q. & Herrstein, R. J. (1985). Crime and Human Nature. New York: Simon & Schuster.

Key Terms

PERSONALITY ASSESSMENT

Personality (p. 464)
Projective Tests (p. 467)
Rorschach Inkblot Test (p. 467)
Thematic Apperception Test (TAT) (p. 467)

TRAIT THEORIES

Factor Analysis (p. 471)
Five-Factor Theory (p. 472)
Trait (p. 470)

PSYCHOANALTIC THEORIES

Anal Stage (p. 481)
Archetypes (p. 484)
Basic Anxiety (p. 485)
Collective Unconscious (p. 484)
Conscious (p. 476
Defense Mechanism (p. 478)
Ego (p. 478)
Genital Stage (p. 482)
Id (p. 477)
Inferiority Complex (p. 482)
Latency Stage (p. 482)
Oedipus Complex (p. 482)
Oral Stage (p. 481)

Phallic Stage (p. 482)
Pleasure Principle (p. 477)
Preconscious (p. 476)
Psychosexual Stage (p. 480)
Reality Principle (p. 478)
Repression (p. 478)
Superego (p. 478)
Unconscious (p 476)

HUMANISTIC THEORIES

Phenomenological Perspective (p. 487)
Self-Actualization (p. 489)
Self-Concept (p. 488)
Self-Esteem (p. 488)
Unconditional Positive Regard (p. 489)

SOCIAL/COGNITIVE PERSPECTIVE

Locus of Control (p. 492)
Reciprocal Determinism (p. 491)
Self-Efficacy (p. 491)

BIOLOGICAL THEORIES

Behavioral Genetics (p. 494)
Interactionism (p. 495)

Discussion Questions

1. How might trait theorists explain the influence of genetic and environmental factors on personality?

2. What impact could the Victorian culture in Vienna have had on Freud's theories? Would Freud maintain the same emphasis on sexuality if he were alive today? Have the students think about this question and be prepared to discuss the answers at the next class meeting.

3. Freud's personality theories have been criticized for lacking testability, being based on little scientific evidence and being sexist. With this very strong criticism, why has this approach to personality endured for so long? Are these applied theories useful? Compare humanistic theories with Freud's theory using applied criteria of effectiveness and therapeutic value.

4. Do the behavioral and biological schools of personality explain the data any better than the Freudian and humanistic approaches? Which do you prefer? Why?

 **Web Sites**

ATP Site
http://www.atp.cygnet.co.uk/ATPart.html
This site summarizes most of the major aspects of Freudian theory, up to and including therapy.

The Five-Factor Model in Personality: A Critical Appraisal
http://www.psych.nwu.edu/~pizzurro/mcadams.html
This article offers six limitations to the Five-Factor Model. A list of references is included.

Taxonomy of Personality with the Five-Factor Theory
http://galton.psych.nwu.edu/greatideas/papers/popkins.html
Offers a detailed account of how personality may be classified according to the Five-Factor model.

The PEN (Psychoticism-Extroversion-Neuroticism) model
http://galton.psych.nwu.edu/greatideas/papers/jang.html
This site provides elaborate information on the Eysenck model of personality, with relevant findings from the research literature. Most notable is the research on psychophysiological responses associated with different personality attributes

Psychology Links: Humanistic Psychology
http://www.tamiu.edu/coah/psy/person.htm
Gives a detailed account of humanistic theories of personality and therapy including Rogers and Maslow.

Suggested Films and Videos

The Self

Annenberg/CPB, 1990. 30 minutes. This program from Zimbardo's "Discovering Psychology" series examines the inner mind, including James' early concepts of the mind, Freud's id, ego, superego, Rogers' humanistic perspective, and Bandura's social learning approach. The video also includes practical applications of the self and self-image through interpersonal communication.

Personality

Insight Media, 1990. 30 minutes. This program looks at various theories of personality including psychoanalytic, humanistic, social learning, and behaviorist. It also investigates the five-factor trait model of personality and uses PET scans to examine the biological component of personality.

Freud Under Analysis

PBS Video (a NOVA production), 1987. 58 minutes. This is an excellent investigation into the development of Freud's major ideas with actual footage of him at work in his office. It explores his ideas of id, ego, and superego, psychoanalytic techniques, and the importance of early childhood experiences. Questions the scientific nature of Freud's theories.

The World Within

Insight Media, 1990. 60 minutes. Using extensive interviews and home movies, this program provides a glimpse of the philosophy and life of Carl Jung, with discussions of his work on dreams, memory, and the collective unconscious.

Being Abraham Maslow

Filmmakers Library, 1972. 30 minutes each. This is an older film that features a wonderful interview with Abraham Maslow discussing his life and humanistic theory. He also explains why he rejected Freud's theory and the behaviorist position.

Carl Rogers

Insight Media, 1969. 50 minutes each segment. In this two-part series, Rogers compares his theory of personality with other theories. Part I discusses motivation, perception, learning and the self, while Part II discusses Rogers' views on education.

Albert Bandura

Insight Media, 1988. 28 minutes each. Social learning theorist Albert Bandura compares his approach to the study of personality with other major theories. Part I includes Bandura discussing major influences on his theories and cognitive and social behavior modification, social learning, modeling, and aggression. In Part II he discusses his classic Bobo doll experiment, as well as morality and moral disengagement, and the effects of aggression and violence in the media.

Success

Books For Success

Nye, Robert D. (1992) **Three Psychologies: Perspectives from Freud, Skinner, and Rogers**. Brooks/Cole.
A concise, readable introduction to the ideas of three highly influential 20th century theorists.

Freeman A. and DeWolf, R. (1992). **The Ten Dumbest Mistakes Smart People Make and How to Avoid Them.** HarperCollins.
An informative book on the cognitive view of personality, including self-help techniques in modifying thinking.

Goleman, Daniel (1997). **Emotional Intelligence.** Bantam Books.
This book argues that emotional intelligence is the most important predictor of success in life. The author makes a strong case that academic measures of intelligence are too restrictive and describes the five crucial skills of emotionally intelligent people.

Csikzentmihalyi, Mihaly (1991). **Flow: The Psychology of Optimal Experience.**
Harper Collins.
This research based book describes how to live a more satisfied life by entering into FLOW, a state of absorbed concentration. It is highly accessible to the layperson and offers engaging examples from brain surgeons to rock climbers.

Active Learning

Active Learning Activity 13.1 - Measuring Personality Traits

The best way to introduce students to personality traits and the personality tests employed to study these traits is to let the students "have at them." In addition to the *Internal-External Locus of Control Scale (I-E Scale)* included in the text, page 466, the two described below are particularly useful.

Sensation-Seeking Scale (SS Scale)
Zuckerman contends that this test measures an innate biological "set-point" for our need for novelty and sensory stimulation. In our classes, we have found similar average scores for males and females (about .5 apart), despite the cultural difference in encouragement for males to engage in more sensation-seeking activities. See what data you obtain and discuss the implications.

This scale can be found in both a long form (34 items) and a short form (13 items). The long form is found in:

Zuckerman, M., Kolin, E. A., Price, L., and Zoob, I. (1964). Development of a Sensation-Seeking Scale. Journal of Consulting Psychology, 28, 477-482.

The short form is found in: Zuckerman, M. (1978, February). The Search for High Sensation. Psychology Today, pp. 38-39.

There is also a short version found in the text, Chapter 11--page 374.

The Kiersey Temperament Sorter
This seventy-item test measures four pairs of preferences and can be used to develop sixteen personality profiles. The pairs (based on Jung's dimensions) are:

> extraversion-introversion
>
> intuition-sensation
>
> thinking-feeling
>
> judging-perceiving

Use all of the items or select one pair such as extroversion-introversion to illustrate the concept of a continuum of bipolar dimensions.

The scale is found in: Kiersey, D., and Bates, M. (1984). Please Understand Me: Character and Temperament Types. Del Mar, California: Prometheus Nemesis Book Company

Active Learning Activity 13.2 - Identifying Defense Mechanisms

This exercise can be done individually or in small groups. After discussing Freud's defense mechanisms, distribute Handout 13.2 and allow students to complete the examples. Review the answers in class, and ask students to add examples from their own lives.

Answers to Handout 13.2: Identifying Defense Mechanisms
1. c, 2. a, 3. e, 4. g, 5. b, 6. d, 7. e, 8. d, 9. c, 10. b, 11. a, 12. f, 13. g

Active Learning Activity 13.3 - Dream Diary

As an extension to your discussion of psychoanalysis, invite your students to keep a dream diary for a week or two. Suggest keeping a pad and pencil next to their beds to record details of their dreams. In addition, ask them to complete Handout 13.2 for each dream. Encourage them to look for patterns (e.g., How much of the dream tied into events that are occurring in everyday life?). Invite them to share their experiences as part of class discussion or as a structured writing project.

Active Learning Activity 13.4 - Adaptive and Maladaptive Self Talk

Have students make suggestions for both adaptive and maladaptive self-talk for each of the following circumstances:

1. You desperately need an "A" on the exam you are taking.

2. You are preparing to make a speech in front of the entire student body.

3. You are attempting a free-throw in a basketball game.

4. You are being introduced to a particularly attractive member of the opposite sex.

5. You are late for a job interview.

Active Learning Activity 13.5 - Constructing an Empirically Developed Test

In order to help students understand what is involved in developing an empirically developed test such as the MMPI, have your students make up a test to clearly differentiate a typical male personality from a typical female personality. To do this, have students suggest items that would clearly be answered differently by members of each group. After you have a significant number of items, present the "test" to a naive group; then, as a class, analyze the items to determine which ones should be retained for a final version of the test. In my experience, we have found few items that are answered in strongly opposite ways and clearly differentiate males from females.

Handout 13.2 - Active Learning

Identifying Defense Mechanisms

Label each statement with the correct defense mechanism from this list:

A. Repression   B. Denial   C. Reaction Formation
D. Rationalization   E. Displacement   F. Sublimation
G. Projection

___1. Sarah is heavily involved with an anti-pornography campaign and fights her own erotic interest in it. She hopes her campaign will convince others of her purity.

___2. A woman who was assaulted and raped a number of years ago in a terrifying attack has forgotten the incident.

___3. Your boss yelled at you, you yelled at your co-worker, your co-worker yelled at his wife, his wife spanked the kid, and the kid kicked the dog.

___4. "Stop asking me! I don't want any ice cream. I think YOU want more ice cream!"

___5. Eduardo reads an article about skin cancer. He goes home and examines the marks on his leg. He then comments to his friend on the tendency for his family to have very dark moles with irregular borders.

___6. Joshua had a bad semester and was put on academic probation. Instead of returning to college, he quits to "pursue something worthwhile."

___7. Mia is usually an angry, hostile person. But since she's been playing on the volleyball team her mood has improved.

___8. You got fired and couldn't make your car insurance payments, so you're riding your bike. You tell friends, "I really prefer to ride my bike. I need the exercise."

___9. A young woman who finds herself attracted to other women proclaims that she hates lesbians and joins a vicious anti-gay group.

___10. The parents of Jim say that "Everyone goes through a drinking stage; it's not a problem" even though Jim just received his third DUI.

___11. Soldiers exposed to traumatic experiences in concentration camps sometimes had amnesia and were unable to recall any of their ordeal.

___12. A priest converts his sexual energy into running a busy soup kitchen to feed the poor.

___13. A woman with a strong sexual drive constantly criticizes her female co-workers for dressing seductively and flirting.

Handout 13.3 - Active Learning

Dream Diary Score Sheet

Use the following scale for each of your dreams:

1	2	3	4	5	6	7	8	9
None		Some		Moderate		A lot		Exclusively

___1. How much of the dream tied into events that are occurring in your life?

___2. How much of the dream involved violence or aggression?

___3. How much of the dream involved academics or school?

___4. How much of the dream involved your being happy?

___5. How much of the dream involved romance?

___6. How much of the dream involved danger?

___7. How much of the dream involved sex?

___8. How much of the dream involved your family?

___9. How much of the dream involved complete strangers?

___10.How much of the dream have you had before?

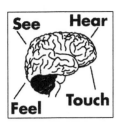
See Hear
Feel Touch

Brain-Based Learning

Brain-Based Learning Activity 13.1 - My Most Important Self

Your students' personal doctor has told them that they have a terminal brain disease. There is a new method of brain surgery that has a very high rate of total success BUT in a few cases there has been a side effect of major amnesia. After the operation the patient can't remember much about who they are. Give the students five minutes to write a secret letter to their future, post-operative self about who they really are, what the most important part of their identity is, what makes them "them" and not someone else. Be sure to tell them this letter will not be read by anyone else and that they should try as best as possible to describe who they are.

After time is up ask how people described themselves. By their actions, by their possessions, by their likes or dislikes, by their motivations, by their family or relationships, by their work etc.?

Ask students if this was an easy or difficult exercise. Most of the time they will find it quite difficult. This provides the perfect introduction to understanding the goal and the complexity of personality theories.

Brain-Based Learning Activity 13.2 - Life is a Projective Experience

Hold up one TAT card or use the Figure 13.2 from the textbook.
Ask the students to write down briefly what they think is going on there. What is happening in the scene? What comes next? What came before? Who are the people? Etc.

Once everyone has had a chance to write down their own interpretation go around the class and sample as many different perspectives as time allows. You may want to write down the major categories that your students' responses could be sorted by, such as anger, praise, jealousy, family argument, lover's sorrow, success story, failure story etc.. Ask the students how they would explain the tremendous diversity of answers and perspectives.

Then ask, "How is Life like a Projective Test"? Be sure to emphasize the ambiguity of many situations, the critical importance of cognitive mindsets (e.g. Martin Seligman's work on Learned Optimism).

Finally, ask each student to select one or two experiences from their life today that illustrate how their reaction or behavior was patterned more by what they attributed to the situation rather then by "just the facts". Can they remember an experience where they saw a situation (such as a dance or a date) one way while their friend(s) had a totally different take on what happened? If time permits, you could group the students in teams of 5 or 6 and ask one or two students to describe a challenging situation in their lives and how they make sense of it. Then have the other members of the group describe how they would interpret such a situation and their possible response. The point here is not to give advice, but for the students to look at one or two real life situations with different sets of glasses.

What are the implications if the life they experience is based less on the world as it is and more on the filter they bring to it? On the other hand, if our interpretation of life is based on our personality, can taking a "Positive Mental Attitude" really work?

Brain-Based Learning Activity 13.3 - Personality: Water or Stone?

One of the paradoxes inherent in personality theory is the concept of stability over time.

Ask your students to think of someone they have known for a long time, preferably someone they know personally, rather than a public figure. A good example would be a grandparent or a relative. Ask them how that person has changed over the last 10 (20, 30) years and how they have stayed the same. Ask them to imagine meeting that person ten years in the future. What will have remained the same? What will have changed?

After the class has discussed their answers for a while, ask them if the person that has lived through the time span is till the same person? Has their personality changed or is it just their behavior? What would have to happen before they could conclude that the person has changed so much, they really are no longer the personality that you knew?

Finally, have them go forward in time to their own thirty-year high school reunion. Will they still be the same person they are today? Will their friends think they are still the same person?

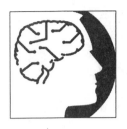

Critical Thinking

Critical Thinking Exercise 13.1 - Tolerating Ambiguity: Exploring Five Theories of Personality

One difficulty students have with Chapter 13 is the focus on competing theories of personality. They often ask which is the "best" or most correct explanation. Given this predisposition, Chapter 13 offers a good opportunity for practice with the critical thinking skill of tolerating ambiguity.

Time: One full 50-minute class.

Advance preparation: Ask for 10 class volunteers to serve on a "personality panel." Divide the group into pairs, and provide each pair of students with a written summary of the five major theories of personality (psychoanalytic, humanistic, behavioristic, cognitive, and biological). Include a brief biographical sketch of the major figure associated with each perspective. Ask each pair of students to play the role of either Sigmund Freud, Carl Rogers, B. F. Skinner, Albert Ellis, or "Dr. Generic." (Since there is no one specific figure commonly associated with the biological perspective, just call this person "Dr. Generic.") (The use of pairs of students helps to reduce their anxiety and also compensates for predictable absences on the day of the panel.) Inform panel members that they should be prepared to answer questions from the audience, to defend their perspective, and to debate amongst themselves. Encourage students to dress up with beards, glasses, old-fashioned suits, etc. Provide each panel member with large name tags (Freud, Skinner, etc.) that can be read by students at the back of the room.

Instructions: Spend at least one full class period prior to the panel discussing the five major theories of personality. At the end of your lecture, distribute 3" x 5" index cards and ask students to write at least one question that they want to ask "Dr. Freud," "Dr. Skinner," etc. Stand at the door and collect the cards as the students leave the room.

On the day of the presentation, arrange a table at the front of the room and encourage class members to rearrange their chairs so they can easily see every member of the panel. Start the discussion by asking each pair of students to take turns briefly describing their various perspectives. Allow 3-5 minutes for each pair. Ask for questions from the audience. If the discussion "lags," redistribute the 3" x 5" cards from the previous class meeting and call on the quieter students to read from the cards in front of them. End the class discussion by asking panel members to discuss the major similarities and differences between the five theories. Mention that most modern-day psychologists believe there are strong points to each theory and that an eclectic perspective is preferred. Close the class period by emphasizing the importance of competing theories to scientific advancement and that the student's acceptance of this type of conflict improves an important critical thinking skill--tolerance for ambiguity.

Consult a text on personality for the biographical sketches and theory summaries, or contact Karen Huffman, Palomar College, San Marcos, CA 92069.

This exercise also appears in the text, Chapter 13. We include it here for your convenience, and you may want to discuss it in class to reinforce reading of the text.

Critical Thinking Exercise 13.2 - Why Are "Pseudo" Personality Tests So Popular?

Sagittarius (Nov. 22-Dec. 21): You're a free-wheeling, adventuresome spirit. When others try to bring the Archer down to earth with facts and responsibilities, you strongly resist. People who get in your way may suffer your piercing insults or "looks that can kill." While you may be quick to release these barbed arrows from your Archer's quiver, your quick-witted responses and charming nature often come to your rescue.
Cancer (June 22-July 22): Your strength and persistence are admired by all, and your careful nature will help you gain great financial rewards. Like your fellow Crabs, you love the cozy safety of your shell. Your idea of a romantic evening is a bottle of wine, a soft blanket, and your partner lying in front of a warm fire--in your own home behind locked doors! While your partner may appreciate this same scene and your protective nature, be alert that your prudent way with money isn't overdone. Invest in a good bottle of wine--the kind with a cork.

If you are an "Archer" or a "Crab," do you think these horoscopes fit? While we risk offending those who honestly believe in astrology, we believe that it's very important to point out the logical fallacies in horoscopes and the "pseudo" personality tests mentioned in the chapter opening. Most people were shocked by the news that Nancy Reagan consulted an astrologer and passed along advice to the President, but some of these same people also read their own newspaper horoscopes "for entertainment" without realizing that even such casual reading can create problems. Given that over time we forget the source of our memories (see Chapter 7), reading unreliable sources may have subtle, but important, ramifications.

Throughout this test we have emphasized the value of critical thinking, which requires that we *recognize our personal biases* and *analyze data for value and content.* By carefully evaluating the evidence and credibility of the source, critical thinkers recognize appeals to emotions and faulty logic. In the case at hand, there are at least four different logical fallacies: the Barnum effect, the fallacy of positive instances, the self-serving bias, and the ad hoc explanations.

THE BARNUM EFFECT

The first reason we often accept horoscopes and "pseudo" personality descriptions is that we think they are accurate, when they are actually just ambiguous, broad statements that fit just about anyone. The fact that we are so readily disposed to accept such generalizations is known as the *Barnum Effect* after P.T. Barnum, the legendary circus promoter who said, "Always have a little something for everyone" and "There's a sucker born every minute." Read the horoscopes here and the personality profile at the beginning of the chapter, noting the general and ambiguous statements.

THE FALLACY OF POSITIVE INSTANCES

Now count the number of times both sides of a personality trait are given ("You have a strong need for other people to like you...You pride yourself on being an independent thinker.") According to the *fallacy of positive instances*, we tend to notice and remember events that confirm our expectations, and ignore those that are non-confirming. If we see ourselves as independent thinkers, for example, we ignore the "needing to be liked by others" part. Similarly, horoscope readers easily find "Sagittarius" characteristics in a Sagittarius horoscope, but fail to notice times when Sagittarius predictions miss or when the same traits appear for Scorpios or Leos.

THE SELF-SERVING BIAS

Evaluate the horoscopes and introductory personality profile for their overall tone. Are the descriptions primarily flattering or negative in spirit? The self-serving bias refers to our tendency to prefer information that maintains a positive self-image (Brown, 1991). As noted at the beginning of this chapter, most nonscientific personality tests are composed of flattering or neutral characteristics. In fact, research shows that the more favorable a personality description, the more people believe it, and the more likely they are to believe it is unique to themselves (Guastello et al., 1989). (The self-serving bias might also explain why people prefer "pseudo" personality tests over bona fide tests--they're generally more flattering).

AD HOC EXPLANATIONS

Think back to your reactions when you read the personality profile at the beginning of the chapter. Did you make excuses for parts of the description that did not fit you? *Ad hoc* is Latin for "special purpose." Thus, when a horoscope or personality description doesn't exactly fit, it's easy to give an ad hoc explanation--an improvised explanation for the situation at hand. Suppose you go to an astrologer and are told you have a strong need for other people to like and admire you. When you object, a "talented" astrologer might offer this ad hoc explanation: "Given your exceptional abilities and people skills, you automatically receive liking and admiration from others. Therefore, you don't recognize how much you need approval because you get it all the time." Ad hoc explanations make it impossible to logically refute astrological claims because even when they're wrong, they're right!

Taken together, you can see how these four logical fallacies help perpetuate a belief in horoscopes and "pop psych" personality tests. They offer "something for everyone" (the Barnum effect); we pay attention only to what confirms our expectations (the fallacy of positive instances); we like flattering descriptions (the self-serving bias); and any inconsistencies can be readily explained away (ad hoc explanations). Be alert to these deceptive appeals, and remember that the best antidote to any form of nonscientific personality assessment is applying critical thinking skills.

This exercise also appears in the Student Study Guide for Chapter 13. We include it here for your convenience, and you may want to discuss it in class to reinforce use of the Student Study Guide.

Critical Thinking Exercise 13.3 -

One way to understand personality and its assessment is to practice testing your friends and family members. In Chapter 13, you were given the following "Try This Yourself" exercise:

Before going on, answer "true" or "false" to the following:

1. People get ahead in this world primarily by luck and connections rather than their own hard work and perseverance.

2. When someone doesn't like you there is little you can do about it.

3. No matter how hard I study; I can't get high grades in most classes.

4. I sometimes keep a rabbit's foot or other special objects as good-luck charms.

5. I sometimes refuse to vote because little can be done to control what politicians do in office.

Using these same five statements, ask at least 10 women and 10 men from your family and friends to complete this test. Be sure NOT to introduce it as an "internal versus external" scale, which could bias their responses. Once you collect their answers and analyze the data, you will probably find that the female scores are slightly more *external* than males (i.e., they are more likely to answer true to each of the five statements). Can you explain this? Do you think the responses would be different when given to different ethnic groups? Why or why not? If you would like to see the original full-length version of Rotter's internal external scale, check out the following reference:

Rotter, J. B. (1966). Generalized expectancies for internal versus external control of reinforcement. Psychological Monographs, 80, 1-28.

Critical Thinking Exercise 13.4 - <u>Employing</u> <u>Precise</u> <u>Terms</u>: <u>Defense</u> <u>Mechanisms</u> (A Behavioral Skill)

A critical thinker is capable of reading a description of an event and determining if this event matches a given situation or individual. Often events are not easily described, but a critical thinker can analyze a situation and often determine which of a number of events best describes it. Thus, if presented with a number of behavioral descriptions of an individual, such as defense mechanisms, the critical thinker should be able to determine which mechanism best applies in a given situation.

By Freud's definition, defense mechanisms operate at the unconscious level; therefore, according to Freud, we are not aware when we are using them. If, however, we can easily observe the use of defense mechanisms in others from their excessive or inappropriate behaviors, we may be able to identify when we ourselves use them. By doing this, we are in a better position of being able to replace inappropriate behaviors with more beneficial problem-solving approaches.

Apply your behavioral, critical thinking skill and try to identify the type of defense mechanisms being used by the people described in the following examples (answers are at the back of this chapter), and see if you can identify when you or others in the real world use defense mechanisms.

1. A woman who was assaulted and raped several years ago in a terrifying attack has forgotten the incident. _____

2. John told his fiancée Susan about his ongoing sexual involvement with other women, but Susan refuses to believe it even when she's seen him kissing other women. _____

3. Laleh has just read several articles describing danger signals for skin cancer. She carefully examines a dangerous looking mole on her own neck, and then with her doctor she calmly and academically discusses the pros and cons of various treatment strategies and the fact that her mother died skin cancer. _____

4. Matt received a notice that he has been put on academic probation. Since he will not be able to play football during the coming semester while on probation, he decides to drop out and tells everyone he wants to spend his time doing something "worthwhile." _____

5. The President of Parents Against Pornography was extremely active in campaigning against the "filth" our children are exposed to on the Internet. He was later arrested and convicted of 40 counts of soliciting minors on the Internet. _____

Answers are found at the end of this study guide chapter.

Gender and Cultural Diversity

Gender and Cultural Diversity Activity 13.1 - Measuring Personality Traits

The best way to introduce students to gender and cultural problems with personality tests is to distribute a typical test and allow students time in class to take the test and discuss their results..

Materials: Internal-External Locus of Control Scale (I-E Scale).

Procedure: When introducing this scale, refer to it as "the I-E Scale," to avoid giving away the name of the trait being measured (within the scale, filler items have been included to disguise the trait). The scale can be found in:

Rotter, J. B. (1966). Generalized Expectancies for Internal Versus External Control of Reinforcement. Psychological Monographs, 80 (1, entire no. 609), 1-28.

A sample of 10 items, which can provide you with examples of external and internal locus of control, can be found in:

Rotter, J. B. (1971, June). External Control and Internal Control. Psychology Today, 37-59.

An abbreviated version can be found in the text on page 466.

Discussion: If you collect the scales and tabulate the data, you will probably find that the female scores will average about two points higher than male scores (based on data obtained in my class), with a disproportionate number of very high scores (external locus of control) for females. If you don't tabulate the data, discuss students' predictions for a male/female difference in locus of control and discuss the variables that influence this dimension.

Questions for Class Discussion:

1. The scale was introduced in 1966. What changes have occurred in the dominant American culture that might affect the results?

2. What are three possible causes for the differences in the male and female scores?

3. Would the results of this scale be considered reliable when given to a multicultural group? Why or why not?

Writing Project

Writing Project 13.1

Given the need for improved writing skills in our college students, and to respond to the call for "writing across the curriculum," we offer writing projects for each chapter. In Chapter Thirteen, we suggest a 2-3 page written response to the following activity. Recognizing the time involved in grading such writing projects, one alternative is occasionally to assign "peer grading." Collect the papers, remove student names, and assign each student a paper to grade. It helps to make their participation in peer grading part of the overall points for the writing project. This encourages a more thoughtful and responsible evaluation, as well as acknowledging and rewarding the additional work.

To augment your presentation on Maslow, discuss "peak experiences" and then ask students to respond to the assignment on Handout 13.1 - Writing Project. The wording is taken from Maslow's questionnaire which he used to collect similar written accounts from college students (Maslow, 1962). Students generally enjoy this writing assignment. It allows them to reminisce about the happiest times of their life.

Handout 13.1 - Writing Project

Peak Experiences

Think of the most wonderful experience of your life; the happiest moments, ecstatic moments, moments of rapture, perhaps from being in love, or from listening to music or suddenly "being hit" by a book or painting, or from some creative moment. Describe this time in careful detail, and discuss how you might increase your opportunities for more "peak experiences." Your paper should be approximately two to three typewritten pages in length.

Circle of Quality – Chapter 13

Please give us your feedback. We thank you in advance for assisting us in improving the next edition. The contact information is listed in the preface.

What are the three most helpful teaching tools in this chapter?

1.

2.

3.

What are the three least useful teaching tools in this chapter?

1.

2.

3.

What are the three most difficult concepts to teach in this chapter?

1.

2.

3.

Additional Comments

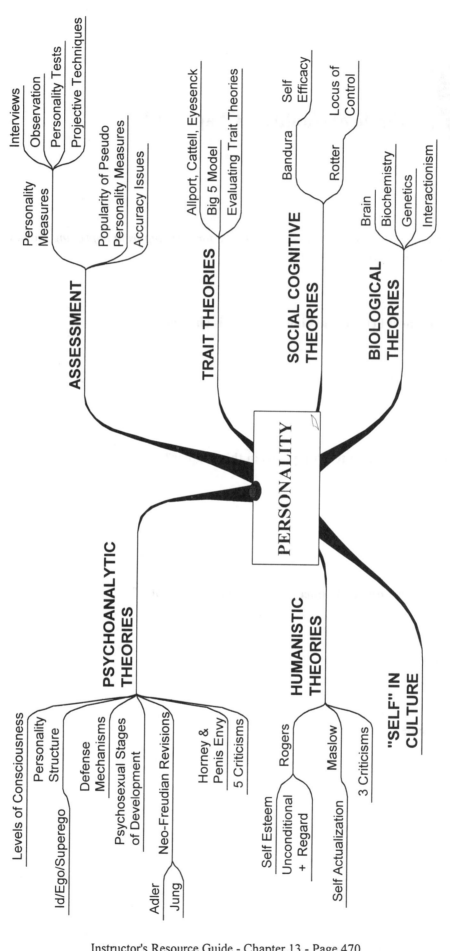

CHAPTER 14
PSYCHOLOGICAL DISORDERS

TEXT ENHANCEMENT

DEMONSTRATIONS, EXERCISES, PROJECTS

Outline

Studying Psychological Disorders

Identifying Abnormal Behavior

Gender and Cultural Diversity
A Cultural Look at Disorders

Explaining Abnormality
Classifying Abnormal Behaviors

Research Highlights
"Being Insane in Insane Places"

Anxiety Disorders

Unreasonable Anxiety
Causes of Anxiety Disorders

Mood Disorders
Understanding Mood Disorders
Causes of Mood Disorders

Schizophrenia

Symptoms of Schizophrenia
Types of Schizophrenia
Causes of Schizophrenia

Gender and Cultural Diversity
Culture and Schizophrenia

Other Disorders

Dissociative Disorders
Personality Disorders
Substance-Related Disorders

Active Learning
Testing Your Knowledge of Abnormal
Behavior

Gender and Cultural Diversity
Gender, Culture, and Depression

Suicide

Learning Objectives

Upon completion of CHAPTER 14, the student should be able to:

1. Define the medical student's disease, and describe five common myths regarding mental health and illness (pp. 502-503).
2. Define abnormal behavior, and describe the four basic standards for identifying such behavior and the limitations for each approach: statistical infrequency, disability or dysfunction, personal distress, and violation of norms (pp. 503-504).
3. Differentiate between culture-general symptoms and culture-bound disorders. State at least five culture-general symptoms, and explain the use of the Langer index. Describe at least one culture-bound disorder (pp. 504-506).
4. Summarize the historical progression in the definition of abnormality from the demonological to the medical model; describe Szasz's criticism of the medical model of mental illness (pp. 506-507).
5. Describe the development of the Diagnostic and Statistical Manual (DSM), including the DSM-IV's classification system, purpose, and limitations. Differentiate between neurosis, psychosis, and insanity (pp. 507-511).
6. Briefly describe and explain the importance of Rosenhan's classic experiment regarding the consequences of being labeled and treated for mental illness (pp. 511).
7. Describe five major anxiety disorders and their possible causes (pp. 512-517).
8. Describe two major mood disorders and their possible biological and psychosocial causes (pp. 518-520).
9. Describe similarities and differences in depression across cultures and between genders (p. 520).
10. Discuss eight common myths regarding suicide, and describe what steps to take if someone is suicidal (pp. 520-522).
11. Define schizophrenia, and describe its five characteristic symptoms; differentiate between positive and negative symptoms (pp. 523-526).
12. Discuss biological and psychosocial theories that attempt to explain schizophrenia; state the major criticisms for each theory (pp. 526-529).
13. Describe similarities and differences in symptoms of schizophrenia across cultures (pp. 529-530).
14. Identify the common characteristic for all dissociative disorders; differentiate between dissociative amnesia, dissociative fugue, and dissociative identity disorder (pp. 531-532).
15. Describe the essential characteristics for all personality disorders; describe the four hallmark symptoms for an antisocial personality disorder and discuss its biological, environmental, and psychological causes (pp. 532-534).
16. Differentiate between substance abuse and substance dependence; state the most common problems associated with alcohol related disorders and describe current biological and learning theories regarding its causes (pp. 534-535).

Chapter Summary/Lecture Organizer

Introductory Vignette--Chapter 14 begins with three case studies of individuals, one with an anxiety disorder, one who suffers from schizophrenia, and one who would be diagnosed as an antisocial personality. The preview focuses student attention on influences involved in creating and defining abnormal behaviors; this provides a context for examining the complex causes of deviant behaviors. Additionally, throughout the chapter, there will be examples of cross-cultural differences in definitions of abnormality.

I. **STUDYING PSYCHOLOGICAL DISORDERS**

A. Identifying Abnormal Behavior - Abnormal behavior is identified as patterns of emotion, thought, and action considered pathological for one or more of these reasons: statistical infrequency, disability or dysfunction, personal distress, or violation of norms.

> **Gender and Cultural Diversity** - Culture-bound disorders (such as "windigo psychosis") are unique and found only in specific cultures. This section compares several culture-bound disorders to culturally universal and culturally relative disorders.

B. Explaining Abnormality - The belief that demons cause abnormal behavior was common in ancient times. The medical model, which emphasizes disease and illness, replaced this demonological model. During the Middle Ages, demonology returned and exorcisms were used to treat abnormal behavior. Asylums began to appear toward the close of the Middle Ages.

Critics of the medical model often use psychological perspectives, which emphasize unconscious conflicts, inappropriate learning, faulty cognitive processes, and negative self-concepts in the development of abnormal behavior. Modern biological theories emphasize physiological causes for problem behaviors.

C. Classifying Abnormal Behaviors - The *Diagnostic and Statistical Manual of Mental Disorders* (DSM-IV) categorizes disorders and provides detailed descriptions useful for communication among professionals. Although an adequate diagnosis is needed for proper treatment, labels can also become self-fulfilling.

II. ANXIETY DISORDER

A. Unreasonable Anxiety - People with anxiety disorders have persistent feelings of threat in facing everyday problems. In generalized anxiety disorders, there is a persistent free-floating anxiety. In panic disorder, anxiety is concentrated into brief or lengthy episodes of panic attacks. Phobias are exaggerated fears of specific objects or situations, such as agoraphobia, a fear of being in open spaces. In obsessive-compulsive disorder, persistent anxiety-arousing thoughts (obsessions) are relieved by ritualistic actions (compulsions) such as hand-washing.

In posttraumatic stress disorder (PTSD), a person who has experienced an overwhelming trauma, such as rape, has recurrent maladaptive emotional reactions, such as exaggerated startle responses, sleep disturbances, and flashbacks.

B. Causes of Anxiety Disorders - Research on the causes of anxiety disorders have focussed on learning, biology, and cognitive processes. Learning theorists suggest anxiety disorders result from classical and operant conditioning, as well as modeling and imitation. The biological perspective suggests that genetic pre-dispositions, disrupted biochemistry, or unusual brain activity influence the development of anxiety disorders. The cognitive approach emphasizes distorted thinking that magnifies ordinary threats and failures, resulting in anxiety disorders.

III. SCHIZOPHRENIA - Schizophrenia is a serious psychotic mental disorder that afflicts approximately one out of every 100 people.

A. Symptoms of Schizophrenia - The major symptoms are disturbances in perception (impaired filtering and selection, and hallucinations); language and thought disturbances (impaired logic, word salads, neologisms, and delusions); emotional disturbances (either exaggerated or blunted emotions); and behavioral disturbances (social withdrawal, bizarre mannerisms, catalepsy, waxy flexibility).

B. Types of Schizophrenia - In reaction to problems with previous categorization of schizophrenia (paranoid, catatonic, disorganized, and undifferentiated), an alternative classification system has been proposed. Schizophrenic symptoms involving distorted or excessive mental activity (e.g., delusions and hallucinations) would be classified as *positive symptoms*, whereas symptoms involving behavioral deficits (e.g., toneless voice, flattened emotions) would be classified as *negative symptoms*.

C. Causes of Schizophrenia - Biological theories of the causes of schizophrenia emphasize genetics (people inherit a predisposition), disruptions in neurotransmitters (primarily dopamine), and abnormalities in brain structure or function (such as enlarged ventricles or low levels of activity in the frontal and temporal lobes).

Psychosocial theories of schizophrenia focus on stress as a trigger for initial episodes and for relapse. Family communication deviance also has been suggested. Studies of family environments suggest that high expressed emotionality may be linked to a worsening and relapse of schizophrenic symptoms.

Explanations for schizophrenia get mixed research support. Biological theories cannot necessarily determine the direction of cause and effect relationships. Psychosocial theories have been unable to exactly determine how and why certain life events trigger schizophrenic episodes in some cases, but not in others. Overall, schizophrenia is probably a combination of interacting (known and unknown) factors.

Gender and Cultural Diversity - Schizophrenia is the most culturally universal mental disorder in the world. There are numerous culturally general symptoms (such as delusions), but also four major differences across cultures: prevalence, form, onset, and prognosis.

IV. MOOD DISORDERS

A. Understanding Mood Disorders - Mood disorders are characterized by extreme disturbances of emotional states. The hallmark of major depressive disorder is a pervasive feeling of deep sadness. Bipolar disorder is characterized by episodes similar to major depressive disorder alternating with episodes of mania in which speech and thinking are rapid, and the person may experience delusions of grandeur and engage in impulsive behaviors.

B. Causes of Mood Disorders - Biological theories of mood disorders emphasize disruptions in neurotransmitters (especially dopamine and serotonin). Antidepressants are often effective in relieving major depression. Bipolar disorders are generally treated with lithium carbonate. Recent research has also implicated certain brain areas that may trigger episodes of mood disorder. There is also evidence for a genetic predisposition for both major depression and bipolar disorder.

Psychological theories of mood disorders emphasize disturbed interpersonal relationships, faulty thinking, poor self-concept, and maladaptive learning. Learned helplessness theory suggests that depression results from repeated failures at attempted escape from the source of stress.

Depression also has been shown to be related to seasons of the year. Most seasonal affective disorder (SAD) sufferers report problems with depression in the winter. Studies with controlled periods of light have been effective in relieving this type of depression.

Gender and Cultural Diversity - Depression seems to involve several culture-general symptoms (such as sad affect and loss of enjoyment). Women are more likely than men to suffer depressive symptoms in many countries. Some researchers explain this in terms of hormonal differences, but a large-scale study found cultural factors (such as poverty and discrimination) were strong predictors. Other researchers suggest women are socialized toward certain behaviors (such as passivity and dependence) that predispose them toward depression.

Active Learning - This section provides a short self-test that students take to determine if their attributional style makes them more at risk of depression.

C. Suicide - Suicide is a serious problem associated with depression. By becoming involved and showing concern, we can help reduce the risk of suicide.

V. OTHER DISORDERS

A. Dissociative Disorders - In dissociative disorders, critical elements of personality split apart. This split is manifested in failing to recall or identify past experiences (dissociative amnesia), by leaving home and wandering off (dissociative fugue), or by developing completely separate personalities (dissociative identity disorder [DID] or multiple personality disorder).

B. Somatoform Disorders - In somatoform disorders, there are physical symptoms without physical causes. In the somatoform disorder called conversion disorder, the person converts an emotional conflict into a physical symptom such as blindness or paralysis. In hypochondriasis, another somatoform disorder, a person is preoccupied with an extreme fear of illness and disease.

> **Gender and Cultural Diversity** - Conversion disorders were once known as hysteria or hysterical neurosis. In ancient times hysteria was believed to be caused by a female's "wandering uterus" and the longing for procreation. Freud thought sufferers of hysteria were converting their sexual urges into bodily complaints.

C. Personality Disorders - Personality disorders involve inflexible, maladaptive personality traits. The best known type is the antisocial personality, characterized by egocentrism, lack of guilt, impulsivity, and superficial charm. Some research has suggested this disorder may be related to defect in brain waves and arousal patterns, genetic inheritance, and disturbed family relationships.

D. Substance-Related Disorder - Substance-related disorder is diagnosed when use of a psychoactive drug interferes with social or occupational functioning and drug tolerance or withdrawal symptoms occur. Learning theories point to maladaptive reinforcement in substance-related disorder. Genetic inheritance patterns occur for abuse of alcohol. Another factor is comorbidity, wherein those suffering from other types of disorders begin to abuse psychoactive drugs, particularly alcohol.

Teaching Resources

SECTION I - STUDYING PSYCHOLOGICAL DISORDERS

Learning Objectives #'s 1 - 6
Lecture Lead-Ins #'s 1 - 3
Lecture Extenders # 14.1
Discussion Questions #'s 1, 2, 4
Active Learning Activities #'s 14.1 - 14.6
Brain-Based Learning #'s 14.1, 14.3
Critical Thinking Exercise #'s 14.1, 14.3
Gender and Cultural Diversity Activity
Writing Project

SECTION II - ANXIETY DISORDERS

Learning Objectives (#7)
Active Learning Activities # 's 14.4, 14.5
Critical Thinking Exercise # 14.3

SECTION III - MOOD DISORDERS

Learning Objectives #'s 8 - 10
Critical Thinking Exercise #'s 14.2, 14.3

Active Learning Activities # 14.4
Brain-based Learning #'s 14.2, 14.3
Critical Thinking Exercise #'s 14.2, 14.3

SECTION IV - SCHIZOPHRENIA

Learning Objectives #'s 11 - 13
Lecture Lead-Ins # 3
Active Learning Activities #'s 14.4, 14.5
Critical Thinking Exercise # 14.3

SECTION V - OTHER DISORDERS

Learning Objectives #'s 14 - 16
Discussion Questions # 3
Active Learning Activities # 14.4 - 14.6
Critical Thinking Exercise #14.3

Lecture Lead-Ins

1. Ask students to define abnormal behavior. Most of the students will have biases which can be discussed in class. Use this discussion as a reference point for your lectures and refer back to specific examples as you lecture on the specific major disorders.

2. Bring the DSM-IV to class and read descriptions of several disorders. Ask students if this description "fits" anyone they know. Many students will admit that this description fits a "friend." Ask each student to prepare a one-page description of their "friend's" symptoms and to prepare to discuss their description at the next class meeting. At this next meeting, after discussing the student papers, describe the "medical student's syndrome" and point out that students in psychology classes often fear they have the same symptoms described in the DSM. Reassure them that this is usually an unjustified fear, and if not, there are professionals who can help with almost any problem. Use their responses and questions as lead-ins to the chapter topics.

3. Review the lecture extender for this chapter which presents detailed information regarding Rosenhan's classic study with pseudopatients, and/or read the original article (Rosenhan, D.L. (1973). On Being Sane In Insane Places, Science, 173, 250-258). Point out that eight "normal" people presented only one complaint--hearing voices saying "Empty, hollow, and thud." No one distorted any other information about themselves, yet all were admitted to the hospital as patients; seven of them were diagnosed as schizophrenic. After being admitted the "pseudopatients" acted normally. The staff never knew these people had faked their symptoms; the patients, on the other hand, quickly recognized the deception. The hospital stays lasted several days and when the seven pseudopatients were released, they were released as "schizophrenic in remission." Ask the students if they think the mental health system is really this sloppy in their diagnoses. How could this happen? What are the effects of psychiatric labels on the judged "normality" of behavior? Use their responses as a lead-in to the chapter.

Lecture Extenders

14.1 The Myth of Mental Illness

Thomas Szasz, whose thoughts on sexual behaviors were discussed in an earlier extender section, has many strong feelings about the profession of psychiatry. Most of his antipsychiatry feelings have been directed at involuntary hospitalization and the myth of mental illness. He decries the expansion of the mental health system, the use of a diagnostic system that is fobbed off on the public as a scientific document whereas it is actually a means of detecting "psychiatric sin." The following material discusses his beliefs about similarities between witchcraft and psychiatry and are based on his book, The Manufacture of Madness (1970).

Szasz states that all societies have to provide certain functions: they must acknowledge events, devise an explanation for what happens, and then institute social control. He compares the social function of the psychiatrist and all others who practice in the mental health field to that of the witchpricker of the middle ages--they both provide explanations for and social control of events or undesirable behaviors that bother us. Both professions were designed to uplift and protect society from what most people would call deviant behaviors (Szasz deliberately refuses to use this word since he says it implies an inferior position). Szasz's special target is institutional psychiatry. Here, he is referring to those who serve as the gatekeepers of the mental institutions, where most patients are involuntarily admitted.

There are several similarities he cites between the practice of witchcraft and modern day psychiatry. First, just as one had to determine who was a witch during the middle ages, the psychiatrist has to know the people in need of treatment. How was this knowledge obtained for witches? The best way was believed to be through confessions, many of which came after days of torture; nevertheless, the public felt this was a fair procedure. The equivalent of confession in the mental patient is the admission that one may have problems, feel anxious, and so forth. These statements, which presumably will make things better for the person, may be used as evidence of one's incompetence or mental disorder. What if the person refuses to admit to an emotional problem? The same "heads I win, tails you lose" game is played: the "sickest" patients are those who refuse to admit they are sick just as the worst sinners were the witches who refused to admit to the practice. It is the expert who knows best--it is always the person suspected of either witchcraft or mental disorder that can do no right. Szasz is indignant that the institutional psychiatrist who is portrayed as a friend of the patient, urging him or her to confide innermost secrets, can use this information to destroy the credibility of the patient. Furthermore, records are kept in the accuser's possession. Neither the patient nor the witch has access to records and so neither generally knows the contents. Szasz points out that the records are in the "language" of the keeper; this means that the terms are put in psychological jargon that the patient neither understands nor is able to challenge. The psychiatrist is not an agent for the patient, but for society who pays for the service, just as witchprickers were working for the local government or church and not for the person they were pricking.

A second similarity between the two groups is in the use of special tests for diagnosing the problem. One of the beliefs during the witchcraft period was that the devil made a pact with the individual before he entered the body. This was supposed to be evidenced by a skin blemish with the general shape of a claw; however, there was no difficulty in most cases in finding moles, birthmarks, and other lesions that were similar enough to warrant a diagnosis. As time went by, the effort to find these marks intensified, so people were shaved to facilitate the procedure. Finally, it was decided that since the devil was a cunning creature, he might rely upon invisible marks on the skin that could be identified by a lack of sensitivity. Thus, the art of witch pricking began in which "workers for the movement," armed with the newest diagnostic procedure, stuck people with pins. Another procedure was the water test. An accused witch would be tied up and tossed in deep water: if she floated, she was guilty; sinking was a sign of innocence--in which case she was dead right after all.

Szasz points out that the modern day equivalent of this is the use of personality tests for detecting emotional problems. He especially incriminates projective testing such as the Rorschach and Thematic Apperception Tests (perhaps, because they are more subjective than personality inventories) by saying there is no such thing as a normal testing response on these tests. He claims that it was easier for an accused witch to survive dunking than for an accused mental patient to survive testing.

Other similarities include the profit that accrues to those who hold these jobs. During the witchhunting era, witchhunters were paid per head, so the more people they diagnosed the greater their financial security. There is a similar trend in the area of mental health. The public is constantly bombarded with surveys as to the number of people who are mentally ill and told of dire consequences if there treatment needs are not met. State legislatures then appropriate money for clinics and for professionals in these clinics. The longer a person stays in treatment (the worse their condition), the easier it is for the therapist. Another way to get more patients is to increase the number of categories of mental disorder. Each editing of the Diagnostic and Statistical Manual has become larger and includes more categories. Szasz, giving examples of all "suspect" childhood behaviors (which include everything a child does), compares this over-classification with the standard psychiatric joke of the anxious patient who comes early, the hostile patient who comes late, and the obsessive-compulsive who comes on time. You can't win.

What actually stopped the practice of witchcraft? Szasz does not credit this to the emergence of altruistic motivations. He says it ceased when the practice of witchpricking became so common that it was a nuisance to society. Are we approaching that point with seeing mental disorder in all behaviors? Do we really need psychiatry for infants or psychotherapy for unhappy dogs and cats?

Source: Szasz, T. S. (1970). The Manufacture of Madness. New York: Dell Publishing Co.

Key Terms

STUDYING PSYCHOLOGICAL DISORDERS

Abnormal behavior (p. 503)
Diagnostic and Statistical Manual of
Mental Disorders (DSM-IV) (p.508)
Insanity (p. 508)
Medical Model (p. 506)
Neurosis (p. 508)
Psychiatry (p. 506)
Psychosis (p. 508)

ANXIETY DISORDERS

Anxiety Disorders (p. 512)
Generalized Anxiety Disorder (p. 513)
Obsessive-Compulsive Disorder (OCD) (p. 514)
Panic Disorder (p. 513)
Phobia (p. 513)
Posttraumatic Stress Disorder (PTSD) (p. 515)

MOOD DISORDERS

Bipolar Disorder (p. 519)
Learned Helplessness (p. 520)
Major Depressive Disorder (p. 518)

SCHIZOPHRENIA

Delusions (p. 525)
Dopamine Hypothesis (p. 527)
Hallucinations (p. 524)
Schizophrenia (p. 523)

OTHER DISORDERS

Anti-social Personality (p. 533)
Comorbidity (p. 535)
Dissociative Disorder (p. 531)
Dissociative Identity Disorder (DID) (p. 531)
Personality Disorders (p. 532)
Substance-Related Disorders (p. 534)

Discussion Questions

1. Who should have the power to define abnormality: societies, political groups, governmental or legal agencies, or mental health professionals? What might be the advantages and disadvantages to allowing one or all of these groups have the final say?

2. How do you feel about someone who has been hospitalized for a mental disorder? Would you date someone if you knew they had been hospitalized? What if they had been in the hospital for a strictly physical illness? Is there a difference in your feelings? Why? Does this affect your willingness to seek therapy for your own problems, or for those of your friends and family? Why is our society so frightened by psychological disorders?

3. With the increased use of drugs by our society there is a corresponding increase in substance related disorders. What can we as a society do, to decrease both the drug use and the substance related disorders? Why is it so difficult? What is our best hope for a reduction?

4. Use of drugs to "cure" psychological disorders is on the increase. Is it ethical to change someone's behavior with drugs because they don't conform to societal standards? Prozac is helping many so-called "normal" people improve their overall enjoyment of life. Is it ethical to use drugs in this way? If not, why not? Do we have the right to control others' behaviors with drugs if they refuse? Do we have the right to refuse drugs to people who want them for minor "personality improvement" or small mood elevation? Why or why not?

 **Web Sites**

Diagnosis and Classification Section of the American Psychiatric Association
http://www.appi.org/diagnosi.html
This portion of the APA website details research on the current diagnostic manual, the DSM-IV, and offers links to examine other diagnostic models and the attempts that the APA has made to be compatible with these systems (such as the International Classification of Diseases, ICD-10).

Anxiety Disorders Association of America
http://www.adaa.org
This site offers a comprehensive guide to resources on anxiety disorders, as well as their relation to other conditions. Consumer and professional resources available here.

Schizophrenia Home Page
http://www.schizophrenia.com
Information on schizophrenia, family-support, and general information for researchers, clinicians and general public is available here.

Depression.com
http://www.depression.com
This site discusses research and treatment into depression and related disorders.

Eating Disorders Links
http://www.perigee.net/~mgross/eatlink.htm
Links to other sites relative to eating disorders.

Diagnosis and Classification Section of the American Psychiatric Association
http://www.appi.org/diagnosi.html
This portion of the APA website details research on the current diagnostic manual, the DSM-IV, and offers links to examine other diagnostic models and the attempts that the APA has made to be compatible with these systems (such as the International Classification of Diseases, ICD-10).

Anxiety Disorders Association of America
http://www.adaa.org
This site offers a comprehensive guide to resources on anxiety disorders, as well as their relation to other conditions. Consumer and professional resources available here.

Schizophrenia Home Page

http://www.schizophrenia.com

Information on schizophrenia, family-support, and general information for researchers, clinicians and general public is available here.

Depression.com

http://www.depression.com

This site discusses research and treatment into depression and related disorders.

Eating Disorders Links

http://www.perigee.net/~mgross/eatlink.htm

Links to other sites relative to eating disorders.

Suggested Films and Videos

Through Madness

Filmmakers Library, 1993. 38 minutes. This award-winning documentary demystifies mental illnesses and humanizes those who suffer from them. We learn about three disorders from the perspectives of those who experience them: a schizophrenic, a paranoid schizophrenic, and a bipolar patient. A sensitive presentation.

Mistreating the Mentally Ill

Films for the Humanities and Sciences, 1995. 56 minutes. This program takes a cross-cultural look at the treatment of the mentally ill. The United States, Japan, India, and Egypt are examined as to how each culture views mental illness and treats less accepted members of society. It concludes that the problem is not a lack of funding, but indifference of societies to the mentally ill.

Madness

Brook Productions, 1992. 23 minutes. Produced for BBC and KCET/Los Angeles, this is a 5-part series: (1) *To Define True Madness* explores past and present myths about mental illness; (2) *Out of Sight* looks at the history of institutionalization of mental patients; (3) *Brain Waves* discusses the history of medical discovery regarding structure and function of the brain; (4) *The Talking Cure* looks at Freud and modern variations of his work; (5) *In Two Minds* discusses schizophrenia.

Psychopathology

Annenberg/CPB, 1990. 30 minutes. This program from Zimbardo's "Discovering Psychology" series is excellent because it amplifies the text in several ways and presents abnormal behavior from a historical and a contemporary perspective. Symptoms and causes are the specific content areas covered. A cultural case study shows the impact of our society on the Native American population.

What Is Normal

Insight Media, 1990. 30 minutes. This video distinguishes normal from abnormal behavior, and experts identify when people need help, describe treatment strategies, and show how professionals classify disorders using DSM-III-R. Includes a discussion of classification controversies concerning the DSM.

The Mind of a Serial Killer

Films for the Humanities and Sciences, 1995. 60 minutes. Originally produced for NOVA, this fascinating video goes behind the scenes to give the real story behind the special investigative unit of the FBI portrayed in the film *Silence of the Lambs*. Using a detailed psychological profile, this unit helped catch a notorious serial killer who targeted prostitutes.

The World of Abnormal Psychology

Toby Levine Communications, 1992. 60 minutes each segment. This 13-part series contains footage of actual case histories as well as interpretive commentary. This is one of the newest and most complete sources available on the subject of abnormal behavior. The programs include: (1) Looking at Abnormal Behavior, (2) The Nature of Stress, (3) The Anxiety Disorders, (4) Psychological Factors and Physical Illness, (5) Personality Disorders, (6) Substance Abuse Disorders, (7) Sexual Disorders, (8) Mood Disorders, (9) The Schizophrenias, (10) Organic Mental Disorders, (11) Behavior Disorders of Children, (12) Psychotherapy, (13) An Ounce of Prevention.

The Compulsive Mind

Films for the Humanities and Sciences, 1995. 28 minutes. This video focuses on one woman with OCD with a fear of contamination who washes her hands 200 times a day. A psychiatrist defines OCD and discusses the role of the neurotransmitter serotonin. Both drug treatment and behavioral treatments are presented.

The Touching Tree

Awareness Films, 1993. 38 minutes. This short, touching drama depicts a young boy with obsessive-compulsive disorder. We watch him face his fears and begin the process of recovery.

Leslie: A Portrait of Schizophrenia

Filmmakers Library, 1990. 57 minutes. This award-winning video presents a young black man suffering from paranoid schizophrenia who heard voices and hallucinated as a child, was abandoned by his parents, and jumped from a fifth-floor apartment at the command of his voices. What makes this an especially compelling video is the fact that Leslie conceived and developed the outline for the program, including the artwork and graphics, and composed the original music.

Psychotic Disorders: Schizophrenia

Insight Media, 1990. 30 minutes. This video examines symptoms of schizophrenia, discusses current theories on causation, and presents a multifaceted treatment approach.

Depression: Beyond the Darkness

Insight Media, 1991. 50 minutes. Explores several possible causes of depression, including cognitive and biological factors, and various therapies, including cognitive therapy, antidepressant drugs, and ECT.

Understanding and Communicating with an Individual Who Is Experiencing Mania

NuSeminars Inc., 1990. 60 minutes. Focusing on mania, this program describes its signs and symptoms, alterations in brain function, lithium treatments, and communication techniques to deal with the interpersonal difficulties.

The Many Faces of Marsha

Insight Media, 1991. 48 minutes. This *48-Hours* program illuminates the mysteries of multiple personality disorder through the case of one woman with more than 200 personalities. Demonstrates how the personalities interact with each other and documents how Marsha's therapists worked with her many personalities to try to cure her illness.

Books For Success

Torrey, E. Fuller (1995). **Surviving Schizophrenia: A Family Manual.** HarperCollins.
A clarification of schizophrenic disorders: their development, treatment, and implications for the patient's family.

Arieti , Silvano (1995). **Understanding & Helping the Schizophrenic - A Guide for Families and Friends.** Jaron Aronson.
A compassionate and informative book by this highly respected psychologist. Offers resources and advice for those who live with or care for a person with schizophrenia.

Goleman, Daniel (1996). **Vital Lies simple Truth : The Psychology of Self-Deception.** Touchstone Books.
An excellent book on the systems the human body uses to deal with pain. It draws parallels between the processing of physical pain and psychological pain. A highly readable discussion on how our mind is wired to "defend" us from pain through self-deception and how to guard against it.

Active Learning

Active Learning Activity 14.1 - Identifying Abnormal Behavior

To demonstrate the difficulties in identifying abnormal behavior, use the 30-item questionnaire (Handout 14.1) that requires students to judge which sexual behaviors are normal. After they complete the questionnaire, assign them to groups and ask them to write a definition of NORMAL and ABNORMAL sexual behavior. Students will have considerable difficulty reaching a group decision. Class discussion can focus on the implications for defining or identifying general abnormal behavior.

Active Learning Activity 14.2 - Prejudice and Abnormal Behavior

Instruct students to form small groups. Inform them that you will offer some reward (extra credit points, active learning points, quiz points, etc.) for the one group with the largest number of words or phrases for abnormal behavior. Mention that you are interested in discussing the problems of prejudice and stereotypes regarding mental illness, and reassure them that they can include slang terms such as "crazy" or "loony." Give them approximately 5 minutes for their brainstorming session. Ask for the total number of words from each group and award your points. Ask volunteers from several groups with high numbers of words to come to the front of the room and write their words on the board. This takes approximately 10 additional minutes, but it is definitely worth the class time. You will be amazed at the enormous variety and number of terms. In our classes we have had up to 60 or 70 different terms. There will be some official terms like schizophrenia or antisocial, but there will be a dominance of derogatory terms. This provides a wonderful demonstration of prejudice and helps explain historical and modern day problems with identifying, defining, and classifying abnormal behavior. This activity could also be used to introduce or tie in with the therapy chapter (Chapter 15) since it provides a dramatic demonstration of why people are so often reluctant to seek therapy.

Active Learning Activity 14.3 - Class Project: Examples of Disorders Presented in the Media

The purpose of this exercise is to show students how textbook descriptions of disorders relate to the real world. Have students collect examples from newspapers, magazines, books, television and radio reports of behavior that appears to be caused by psychological disorders. For each example, have students:

1. Note the symptoms identified.

2. Check whether an official diagnosis is reported.

3. Discuss what impression of abnormal behavior is created by the report.

As a way of summarizing the various types of disorders, or during coverage of each disorder, have students present these popularized examples and discuss the points listed above.

Handout 14.1 – Active Learning

Evaluation of Normal Sexual Behavior

Please rate whether or not each of the following activities represents normal sexual behavior by placing either a Y (yes) or N (no) in the blank.

___1. Watching X-rated movies several times a week.
___2. Having sex with more than one person at the same time.
___3. Preferring oral sex over intercourse.
___4. Having intercourse with a member of the same sex.
___5. Fantasizing about having sex with a member of the same sex.
___6. Fantasizing about a person other than one's partner during sexual intercourse.
___7. Masturbating in front of a partner.
___8. Having sex somewhere other than a bed (e.g., floor, shower, kitchen, outdoors).
___9. Never engaging in masturbation.
___10. Becoming excited by exposing oneself in public.
___11. Being celibate.
___12. Being unable to achieve orgasm.
___13. Enjoying being physically restrained during sex (e.g., bondage).
___14. Becoming aroused by voyeurism (e.g., Peeping Toms).
___15. Playing with food (e.g., fruit and whipped cream) during sex.
___16. Dressing in the clothing of the other sex.
___17. Preferring that one's partner initiates sex.
___18. Inflicting pain during sex.
___19. Receiving pain during sex.
___20. Using sex toys (e.g., a vibrator) during sex.
___21. Having rape fantasies.
___22. Masturbating after marriage.
___23. Not being aroused by a nude member of the other sex.
___24. Being aroused by receiving an obscene phone call.
___25. Being aroused by making an obscene phone call.
___26. Engaging in sex with animals.
___27. Deriving sexual pleasure from seeing or touching dead bodies.
___28. Becoming aroused by being urinated on.
___29. Becoming aroused by soiling the clothing of the other sex.
___30. Becoming aroused by viewing or touching feces.

Source: Kite, M. E. (1990). Defining Normal Sexual Behavior: A Classroom Exercise. Teaching of Psychology, 17, p. 119. Copyright 1990 by Lawrence Erlbaum Associates, Inc. Reprinted by permission

Active Learning Activity 14.4

As a follow-up to Activity 14.3, or as a separate activity, ask students to rent videos of favorite movies related to abnormal behavior (Sybil, I Never Promised You a Rose Garden, Sea of Love, Vertigo, Primal Fear, etc.) and then cue up a favorite scene that lasts approximately 1-2 minutes. Have them play the video segment for the class and lead a discussion regarding possible diagnoses, symptoms displayed, and so on. You might ask a group to make a "collage" of all these video segments for your future classes.

Active Learning Activity 14.5 - Role Playing

Have students act out the roles of people with various types of psychological disorders. These can be students who have been carefully screened from your own classes or students from the drama department. Whichever the case, be sure the students understand that this role playing is not to be taken lightly, and that they will be expected to spend a specified amount of time outside of class to practice. You will need to set up times for these practice sessions and will need to spend time of your own in coaching them on appropriate abnormal behaviors. You might consider playing some of the roles of client and/or therapist yourself. It helps show students that you're willing to take a chance and helps model appropriate behaviors.

Active Learning Activity 14.6 - A "Norm" Violation

After you lecture on defining normality, ask the students to devise a plan to display deviant behavior (e.g., talking to themselves or an inanimate object, dressing in bizarre clothes, using bizarre hand or facial gestures). Emphasize that the behavior cannot be illegal, dangerous or against any college rules. Have the students form small groups of at least three students, with one student being the abnormal person and the others the observer/recorders. The observer recorder's task is to observe and record how it feels to be perceived as different. How do people react? Do they ask if you are all right, or simply avoid you? Have each group present their experiences to the class during the next class meeting. Use these discussions as examples throughout your lectures on abnormal behavior.

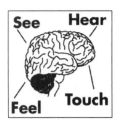

Brain-Based Learning

Brain-Based Learning Activity 14.1 - What's Your Clue?

You have heard through the grapevine that one of the students in your class is mentally disordered but don't know who it is. What clues or behaviors would signal you that you have identified the right person? Give the students 3-5 minutes to generate a list.

Write the answers on the board and note how much agreement/disagreement there is amongst the students. Select several of the most frequently mentioned behaviors and assign each of these to a group of students. They have 3-5 minutes to come up with situations that would explain the selected behavior as harmless or normal. How important is a person's age, sex, social status, previous history or state of inebriation in broadening the students' willingness to define such behavior as acceptable?

Would it be easier or harder to detect signs of mental abnormality in a person you know really well, such as a close family member?

Brain-Based Learning Activity 14.2 - How Low Is your Depression?

We all have good days and bad days. Think back over the last five years of your life to the lowest, bluest days during that timeframe. Looking back from today, would you describe your then-self as depressed? If yes, how which of the DSM-IV criteria did you meet? If no, what else would you have to do/say/feel before such a diagnosis would apply to you?

Imagine you met with a friend during that period of your life and your friend asked how you are doing.
Make a list of what advantages there are in telling your friend:" I am depressed."
Make a list of what disadvantages there are in telling your friend: "I am depressed."
Are you better off admitting you have a "problem" or would such a label just encourage you to play "victim"?

Encourage the class discussion on these questions to show the complexity of this issue. If time allows, you could bring in the arguments over including mental health coverage as part of health insurance.

Brain-Based Learning Activity 14.3 - The Sadness of Aging

How would your students feel if they lost most of their friends and relatives to death, could no longer participate in any sports, had trouble getting around the home or taking a shower, suffered the pain of arthritis in several joints, and they knew that they had only a short time left to live? How would they feel if their frailness would force them into a nursing home or a residence for the aged?

Quite often students will answer: I would feel sad, or depressed. I might no longer want to live.
Then ask them: Is being sad or depressed a normal part of aging? Should you accept it if your grandmother or grandfather spends long hours sad about the loss of loved ones?

Younger students often have difficulty imagining how they could not be depressed under such circumstances. For extra credit you could have them visit a senior center or home for the aged and ask seniors how they react to the changes and losses that growing old has brought? If time allows they could report back to the class the wide variety of personal reactions and coping styles with which today's senior citizens react to the challenge of living longer.

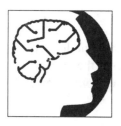

Critical Thinking

Critical Thinking Exercise 14.1 - Recognizing Personal Biases: Exploring Student Misperceptions

The text discusses the hazards of diagnostic labeling, and the text's critical thinking exercise teaches students to critically evaluate arguments "for" and "against" these labels. As a prologue to this topic and as a general introduction to the chapter, conduct the following demonstration. It exposes student misperceptions and helps them to recognize their personal biases about abnormal behavior.

Time: Approximately 50 minutes.

Advance preparation: Arrange for a guest speaker from a local mental hospital or community mental health center. Ask them to spend the first 10 minutes of their presentation pretending to be a former mental patient and then to leave the room for 10 minutes. Arrange with them to later return to the class, and to spend the remaining time discussing the problems with labels, their experiences working in the field, and answering student questions.

Instruction: At the class meeting before the scheduled guest speaker, inform students that an individual who was diagnosed as _____ (choose your own diagnosis) is coming to speak. Ask them to write down at least one question they have about the disorder, problems they have living in our society, etc. Collect their questions as they leave the room for the day.

On the day of the guest speaker, introduce your guest and encourage class questions. After 10 minutes thank your speaker and allow him or her to leave the room. Ask students to share their reactions. Do they think this person will have difficulty finding a job? Did they notice any lingering side effects to the medication? When students have finished describing their observations, inform them of your deception and invite the speaker to return to the room. (Prearrange for the speaker to remain waiting outside the classroom. You may want to give him or her the student questions from the previous class meeting to peruse while they are waiting.)

Thank the students for their cooperation with your demonstration and discuss the obvious problems with diagnostic labels (and with deception in research). Allow the remaining class time for interactions with the guest speaker.

This exercise also appears in the text, Chapter 14. We include it here for your convenience, and you may want to discuss it in class to reinforce reading of the text.

Critical Thinking Exercise 14.2 - How Your Thoughts Can Make You Depressed

Try to vividly imagine yourself in the two situations described below. Then answer the questions by circling the number that most closely describes how you feel. Events have many causes, but if these situations really happened to you, what do you think would be the most likely cause?

SITUATION 1

You are introduced to a new person at a party and are left alone to talk. After a few minutes, the person appears bored.

1. Is this outcome caused by you? Or is it something about the other person or the circumstances?

   1   2   3   4   5   6   7
   Other person or   Me
   circumstances

2. Will the cause of this outcome also be present in the future?

   1   2   3   4   5   6   7
   No   Yes

3. Is the cause of this outcome unique to this situation, or does it also affect other areas of your life?

   1   2   3   4   5   6   7
   Affects just this   Affects all situations
   situation   in my life

SITUATION 2

You receive an award for a project that is highly praised.

4. Is this outcome cause by you or something about the circumstances?

   1   2   3   4   5   6   7
   Circumstances   Me

5. Will the cause of this outcome also be present in the future?

   1   2   3   4   5   6   7
   No   Yes

6. Is the cause of this outcome unique to this situation, or does it also affect other areas of your life?

   1   2   3   4   5   6   7
   Affect just this   Affects all situations
   situation   in my life

You have just completed a modified version of the *Attributional Style Questionnaire*. This test measures people's explanations for the causes of good and bad events. People with a depressive explanatory style tend to explain *bad* events--Situation 1--in terms of internal factors ("It's my fault"), a stable cause ("it will always be this way"), and a global cause ("It's this way in many situations"). In contrast, people with an optimistic explanatory style tend to make external ("It's someone else's fault"), unstable ("It won't happen again"), and specific ("It's just in this one area") explanations. However, when *good* things happen the opposite occurs. People with a depressive explanatory style tend to make external, unstable, specific explanations, while people with an optimistic style tend to make internal, stable, global explanations.

	Depressive Explanatory Style	Optimistic Explanatory Style
Bad Events	Internal, stable, global	External, unstable, specific
Good Events	External, unstable, specific	Internal, stable, global

If you had mostly high scores (5-7) on questions 1, 2, and 3 and low scores (1-3) on questions 4, 5, and 6, you probably have a depressive explanatory style. If the reverse is true (low scores on the first three questions and high scores on the last three), you tend to have an optimistic explanatory style.

What difference does your explanatory style make? There is good evidence that people who attribute bad outcomes to themselves and good outcomes to external factors are more prone to depression than people who do the opposite (Abramson, Seligman, and Teasdale, 1978; Seligman, 1991, 1994). Obviously, if you have a bad experience and then blame it on your personal (internal) inadequacies, interpret it as unchangeable (stable), and draw far-reaching (global) conclusions, you are more likely to feel depressed. This self-blaming, pessimistic, and over-generalizing explanatory style results in a sense of hopelessness (Abramson, Metalsky, and Alloy, 1989; Metalsky et al., 1993).

As expected, the idea that depression can be caused by attributional style has its critics. The principal problem lies in separating cause from effect (Barnett and Gotlib, 1988). Does a depressive explanatory style cause depression, or does depression cause a depressive explanatory style? Or could both be caused by another variable, such as neurotransmitters or some other biological factor? Actually, evidence suggests that all three possibilities may interact and influence depression. Although biological explanations undoubtedly play an important role in major depressive disorders and professional help is needed, you may find that changing your explanatory style can help dispel mild or moderate depression.

This exercise also appears in the Student Study Guide for Chapter 14. We include it here for your convenience, and you may want to discuss it in class to reinforce use of the Student Study Guide.

Critical Thinking 14.3 - Distinguishing Fact From Opinion (A Behavioral Skill)

When thinking critically about controversial issues, it is helpful to make a distinction between statements of *fact* and statements of *opinion*. (A fact is a statement that can be proven true. An opinion is a statement that expresses how a person feels about an issue or what someone thinks is true.) Although it is also important to later determine whether the facts are true or false, in this exercise simply mark "O" for opinion and "F" for fact. After you have responded to each of the items, you may wish to discuss your answers with your friends and classmates.

_____ 1. The mentally ill are more dangerous than the general public.

_____ 2. The insanity plea allows criminals back on the street too soon.

_____ 3. Individuals who are diagnosed as having a "split personality" are also known as schizophrenics.

_____ 4. People who talk to themselves are probably schizophrenics.

_____ 5. Everyone has a behavioral disorder of one type or another.

_____ 6. Delusions and hallucinations are basically one in the same.

_____ 7. Individuals who are compulsive about keeping their rooms clean probably suffer from an obsessive compulsive disorder.

_____ 8. Any form of depression is considered abnormal and likely requires professional treatment.

_____ 9. Post-traumatic stress as a disorder is the invention of psychologists and psychiatrists and probably does not really exist.

_____ 10. If not properly treated, neurosis can turn into psychosis.

Gender and Cultural Diversity

Gender and Cultural Activity 14.1 - Evaluating Arguments: Do Diagnostic Labels of Mental Disorders Help or Hinder Effective Treatment?

Some researchers, including David Rosenhan, argue that diagnostic labels create a dangerous self-fulfilling prophecy, but others believe that diagnostic classification is necessary and valuable. As a reader, what do you think about this debate? Which argument do you believe is strongest?

Evaluating arguments is one of the most important critical thinking skills. Critical thinkers do not simply endorse the popular position, or choose any side just to avoid saying "I don't know." Critical thinkers analyze the relative strengths and weaknesses of each position in an argument. They are especially sensitive to arguments with which they personally disagree because they recognize the natural human tendency to ignore or oversimplify opposing information. The critical thinker keeps an open mind, objectively evaluates the reasons both sides give, and then develops his or her own independent position.

To sharpen your skills in critically evaluating arguments, we offer the following guidelines.

Begin by listing the points and counterpoints of each argument. When all points and counterpoints are not explicitly stated, you will need to read between the lines and make your best guess of what each side might say. Here is an example of this process using the Rosenhan labeling debate:

POINT   COUNTERPOINT

Diagnostic labels are sometimes   Errors are a natural part of
incorrectly applied.   all human endeavors.

Labels can become a self-fulfilling   This can be minimized by
prophecy for the doctor.   careful attention.

Here are samples to explore your gender biases.

POINT   COUNTERPOINT

Women are more emotional than men.   Men are trained not to show emotions.

Men are naturally aggressive.   Women are trained not to be aggressive.

Women are naturally good parents.   Men are not reinforced for nurture.

Can you add your own additional points and counterpoints?

_____   _____

_____   _____

_____   _____

After clarifying the points and counterpoints, you should attempt to use the following analytical tools:

a. Differentiating between fact and opinion. As discussed in the previous critical thinking exercise (14.3), the ability to recognize statements of fact versus statements of opinion is an important first step to successful analyses of arguments. After rereading the arguments regarding diagnostic labels, see if you can label at least two facts and two opinions on each side.

b. Recognizing logical fallacies and faulty reasoning. Several chapters in this text and their corresponding critical thinking exercises can help you recognize faulty logic. For example, the incorrect assumption of cause/effect relationships is discussed in Chapter 1, the issue of deceptive appeals are presented in Chapters 11 and 13 and incorrect or distorted use of statistics is discussed in Appendix A.

c. Exploring the implications of conclusions. Questions such as the following can help expand your analysis of arguments. "What are the conclusions drawn by proponents of each side of the issue?" "Are there other logical alternative conclusions?"

d. Recognizing and evaluating author bias and source credibility. Ask yourself questions such as, "What does the author want me to think or do?" "What qualifications does the author have for writing on this subject?" "Is the author a reliable source for information?"

Writing Project

Writing Project 14.1

Given the need for improved writing skills in our college students, and to respond to the call for "writing across the curriculum," we offer writing projects for each chapter. For Chapter Fourteen, we suggest a 2-3 page paper as discussed below. Recognizing the time involved in grading such writing projects, one alternative is occasionally to assign peer grading. Collect the papers, remove student names, and assign each student one paper to grade. It helps to make their participation in peer grading part of the overall points for the writing project. This encourages a more thoughtful and responsible evaluation, as well as acknowledging and rewarding the additional work.

Have students perform a "norm violation" (Activity 14.5) alone, and write a 2-3 page paper detailing what they did, how they felt, how others responded, and what they learned about abnormal behavior.

*C*ircle of *Q*uality – Chapter 14

Please give us your feedback. We thank you in advance for assisting us in improving the next edition. The contact information is listed in the preface.

What are the three most helpful teaching tools in this chapter?

1.

2.

3.

What are the three least useful teaching tools in this chapter?

1.

2.

3.

What are the three most difficult concepts to teach in this chapter?

1.

2.

3.

Additional Comments:

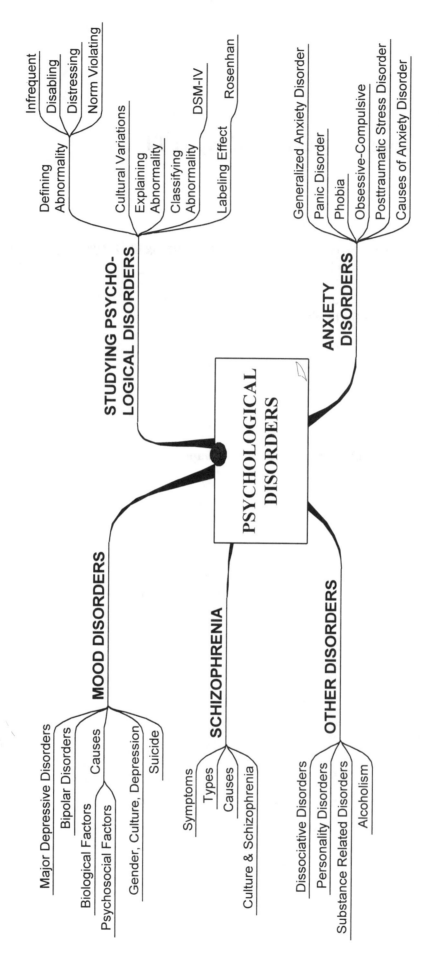

CHAPTER 15
PSYCHOTHERAPY

Outline

Essentials of Psychotherapy

Psychoanalysis

Goals and Methods of
Freudian Psychoanalysis
Evaluating Psychoanalysis

Cognitive Therapies

Rational-Emotive Therapy
Cognitive-Behavior Therapy
Evaluating Cognitive Therapy

Humanistic Therapies

Client-Centered Therapy
Gestalt Therapy
Evaluating Humanistic Therapy

Behavior Therapies

Classical Conditioning Techniques
Operant Conditioning Techniques
Modeling
Evaluating Behavior Therapy

Group and Family Therapies

Benefits of Group Therapy
Family Therapies

Biomedical Therapies

Drug Therapy
Electroconvulsive Therapy
Psychosurgery

  Active Learning
  Synthesizing Multiple Forms of
  Psychotherapy

Issues in Therapy

Institutionalization
Seeking Therapy

  Research Highlight
  A Scientific Look at Therapeutic Touch

  Gender and Cultural Diversity
  Cultural Variations and the Special
  Needs of Women in Therapy

GOAL

Learning Objectives

Upon completion of CHAPTER 15, the student should be able to:

1. Define psychotherapy and eclectic therapy, discuss the five goals of psychotherapy, and describe differences in emphasis for the various approaches to therapy (pp. 542-543).
2. Differentiate between the five types of therapists (psychologists, psychiatrists, psychoanalysts, social workers, and counselors); describe four common misconceptions about psychotherapy and therapists (pp. 543-544).
3. Define psychoanalysis, and describe its major goals and methods of practice: free association, interpretation, dream analysis, resistance, transference, and interpretation (pp. 545-547).
4. Discuss the two major criticisms of psychoanalysis; differentiate between psychoanalysis of the past and modern psychodynamic therapy (pp. 547-548).
5. Define cognitive therapy, and describe its emphasis on changing self-talk via cognitive restructuring (p. 550).
6. Compare and contrast Ellis' rational-emotive therapy with Beck's cognitive-behavior therapy (pp. 550-551).
7. Describe the successes reported for cognitive therapies, and discuss the major criticisms of this method (pp. 551-553).
8. Identify a common emphasis in cognitive and humanistic therapies, and state the basic assumptions underlying the humanistic therapies (pp. 553-554).
9. Discuss Rogers' client-centered therapy and the four qualities of client-therapist communication he advocated; elaborate on the similarities and differences between client-centered therapy and Gestalt therapy as practiced by Perls (pp. 554-556).
10. Discuss the research regarding the effectiveness of humanistic therapies (p. 556).
11. Define behavior therapy, and describe its major area of focus. Describe how classical conditioning, operant conditioning, and observational learning are applied to increase adaptive behaviors and decrease maladaptive ones (pp. 557-562).
12. Describe the successes reported for behavioral therapy, and discuss the three major criticisms of this method (p. 562).
13. Discuss three advantages of group therapy, and differentiate between self-help groups and family therapy (pp. 563-565).
14. Define biomedical therapy, and describe the advantages and limitations of drug therapy, electroconvulsive therapy, and psychosurgery (pp. 565-571).
15. Discuss the controversies regarding de-institutionalization and involuntary commitment; discuss community mental health centers as an alternative to institutionalization (pp. 572-573).
16. Describe the results of controlled research regarding the effectiveness of therapy, and recent research on therapeutic touch; state several strategies for finding an appropriate therapist (pp. 573-575).
17. Describe the six culturally universal characteristics of therapy; describe differences in therapy found in individualist versus collectivist cultures; and discuss the five major areas of concern for women in therapy (pp. 576-577).

Chapter Summary/Lecture Organizer

Introductory Vignette--The chapter preview of Frances Farmer highlights the issue of evaluating the effectiveness of therapeutic interventions. It is intended to provide students with a context for exploring present-day issues such as de-institutionalization and the choice of a particular therapy.

I. **ESSENTIALS OF PSYCHOTHERAPY** - Psychotherapy is a general term for the various methods designed to improve psychological functioning and promote adjustment to life. There are numerous forms of psychotherapy, but they all focus treatment on five basic areas of disturbance -- thoughts, emotions, behaviors, interpersonal and life situations, and biomedical.

II. **PSYCHOANALYSIS** - The psychoanalytic method of therapy was developed by Sigmund Freud to uncover unconscious conflicts, which usually date back to childhood experiences, and bring them into conscious awareness.

   A. Goals and Methods of Freudian Psychoanalysis - The five major techniques of psychoanalysis are free association, dream analysis, identifying resistance, working through transference, and interpretation. In free association, the patient says whatever comes to mind, regardless of how painful, embarrassing, or irrelevant it may seem. Dream analysis is similar to free association, the content of dreams is examined on a superficial level (manifest content) and a deeper level (latent content) that is presumed to reveal the true hidden meaning. Resistance is a stage in psychoanalysis where the patient avoids (resists) the analyst's attempts to bring unconscious material to conscious awareness. Transference is the process whereby the patient displaces (or transfers) onto his or her relationship with the therapist emotions experienced in the past--especially relationships with the mother or father or other important figures. Interpretation is the psychoanalyst's explanation of the significance of a patient's free associations, dreams, resistance, and transference. The therapist attempts to tie what has been learned by these methods to problem patterns of behavior.

   B. Evaluating Psychoanalysis - Like psychoanalytic theories of personality, psychoanalysis has been the subject of great debate. There are two major areas of criticism. It has limited availability because it is time-consuming, expensive, and so is restricted to a small group of people. It has also been criticized for a lack of scientific credibility, particularly the inability to prove or disprove its theories. Modern psychodynamic therapies are designed to overcome some of these limitations.

III. **COGNITIVE THERAPIES** - Cognitive therapy emphasizes the importance of faulty thought processes and beliefs in the creation of problem behaviors.

A. Rational-Emotive Therapy - Ellis' rational-emotive therapy (RET) performs a type of cognitive restructuring by examining the belief system intervening between an activating experience and a consequence. RET assumes that misconceptions within the belief system can be consciously evaluated and replaced with more effective ways of thinking.

> **Active Learning** - Students are given an opportunity to apply Elllis' approach of rational-emotive therapy to their own faulty reasoning.

B. Cognitive-Behavior Therapy - Beck, a cognitive-behavior therapist, takes a more active approach with clients--emphasizing changes in thought processes along with changes in behavior. Beck has identified faulty thinking patterns that lead to depression, among the most important are selective perception, overgeneralization, magnification, and all-or-nothing thinking.

C. Evaluating Cognitive Therapy - Evaluations of cognitive therapies find Beck's procedures particularly effective for relieving depression; Ellis has had success with a wide variety of disorders. Both Beck and Ellis, however, have been criticized for ignoring the importance of unconscious processes and the client's history. Some critics suggest that when cognitive therapies are successful it is because they have also changed behavior.

IV. **HUMANISTIC THERAPIES** - Humanistic therapies are based on the premise that problems result when an individual's normal growth potential is blocked.

A. Client-Centered Therapy - In Rogers' client-centered approach, the therapist offers empathy, unconditional positive regard, genuineness, and active listening as a means of facilitating personal growth.

B. Gestalt Therapy - Perls' Gestalt therapy emphasizes awareness and personal responsibility to help the client integrate present experiences into a "whole" or gestalt.

C. Evaluating Humanistic Therapy - Humanistic therapies are difficult to evaluate scientifically, and research on specific therapeutic techniques has had mixed results. Nevertheless, the therapy seems to help, particularly the newer form known as experiential.

V. **BEHAVIOR THERAPIES** - Behavior therapies use learning principles to change maladaptive behaviors.

A. Classical Conditioning Techniques - Behavior therapists use classical conditioning principles to change associations. In systematic desensitization, the client replaces anxiety with relaxation, and in aversion therapy, an aversive stimulus is paired with maladaptive behaviors.

B. Operant Conditioning Techniques - Shaping, reinforcement, punishment, and extinction are used based on principles of contingency between behaviors and consequences.

C. Modeling - Modeling principles are employed by having clients watch and imitate positive role models.

D. Evaluating Behavior Therapy - Behavior therapies have been successful with a number of psychological disorders. But they have also been criticized for lack of generalizability, the chance of symptom substitution, and the questionable ethics of controlling behavior.

VI.   GROUP AND FAMILY THERAPIES - Group and family therapies treat multiple individuals simultaneously, often applying psychoanalytic, cognitive, humanistic, and/or behavioral techniques.

A. Benefits of Group Therapy - The members of the group often provide mutual support and counseling as they work together toward therapeutic goals. They also provide each other with information from shared insights. Another advantage is the opportunity to engage in behavioral rehearsal in which group members role-play the significant individuals in each others lives to allow members to practice new social skills.
A variation on group therapy is the self-help group in which a professional does not guide the group. Groups of people sharing a common problem meet to give and receive support.

B. Family Therapies - In family therapy the members of the family are brought together in order to change maladaptive interactions and so improve interpersonal relationships.

VII.   BIOMEDICAL THERAPIES - Biomedical therapies use biological techniques to relieve psychological disorders. Three major forms of biomedical therapy are drug therapy, electroconvulsive therapy (ECT), and psychosurgery.

A. Drug Therapy - Drug therapy is the most common form of biomedical therapy. Anti-anxiety drugs, such as Valium, have been used in the treatment of anxiety disorders; anti-psychotic drugs, such as Thorazine, are used to relieve the symptoms of schizophrenia; antidepressants, such as Elavil, are used to treat depression; and mood stabilizers, such as lithium, are used to stabilize bipolar disorders. While drug therapy has been responsible for major improvements in many disorders, there are also problems with overuse, dosage levels, side effects, and patient cooperation.

B. Electroconvulsive Therapy - Electroconvulsive therapy (ECT) is used as a last resort because it produces brain seizures, can cause memory loss, and because no one really knows how it works. Today it is used primarily to relieve serious depression, for which other methods have been ineffective.

C. Psychosurgery - Psychosurgeries, such as lobotomies, have been successful in treating certain disorders, but they are highly risky. Modern techniques seek to alter very circumscribed areas believed to be responsible for specific disorders.

VIII. ISSUES IN THERAPY

A. Institutionalization - People believed to be mentally ill and dangerous to themselves or others can be involuntarily committed to mental hospitals for diagnosis and treatment. Due to abuses of involuntary commitments and other problems associated with state mental hospitals, many states practice a policy of de-institutionalization--discharging as many patients as possible and discouraging admissions. In place of institutionalization, community services such as Community Mental Health (CMH) centers have been recommended.

B. Seeking Therapy - Research on the effectiveness of psychotherapy has found that 40 to 80 percent of those who receive treatment are better off than those who do not receive treatment.

Gender and Cultural Diversity - Studies of cultural variations in therapy have found six major features that are culturally universal: naming a problem, qualities of the therapist, establishing credibility, placing the problems in a familiar framework, applying techniques to bring relief, and a special time and place.

There are also important cultural differences in therapies. While therapies in individualistic cultures emphasize the "self" and control over one's life, collectivist cultures therapies emphasize interdependence. Japan's Naikan therapy is a good example of a collectivist culture's therapy.

There are five areas of special concern therapists need to take into account when treating women clients: higher rate of diagnosis and treatment of mental disorders, stresses of poverty, stresses of multiple roles, stresses of aging, and violence against women.

Teaching Resources

SECTION I - ESSENTIALS OF PSYCHOTHERAPY

Learning Objectives #'s 1 - 2
Lecture Lead Ins #'s 1 - 3
Lecture Extender # 15.1
Discussion Questions #'s 1 - 5
Active Learning Activities #'s 15.1-15.4, 15.8
Critical Thinking Exercise # 15.1
Gender and Cultural Diversity Activity # 15.1

SECTION II -PSYCHOANALYSIS

Learning Objectives #'s 3 - 4
Discussion Questions # 1
Active Learning Activities #'s 15.4, 15.8
Critical Thinking Exercise # 15.1

SECTION III - COGNITIVE THERAPIES

Learning Objectives #'s 5 - 7
Discussion Questions # 1
Active Learning Activities #'s 15.4, 15.8, 15.9
Critical Thinking Exercise #'s 15.1 - 15.2
Writing Project # 15.1

SECTION IV - HUMANISTIC THERAPIES

Learning Objectives #'s 8 - 10
Discussion Questions # 1
Active Learning Activities #'s 15.4, 15.8
Brain-Based Learning # 15.3
Critical Thinking Exercise #'s 15.1, 15.3

SECTION V - BEHAVIOR THERAPIES

Learning Objectives #'s 11 - 12
Discussion Questions # 1
Active Learning Activities #'s 15.4, 15.8
Brain-Based Learning # 15.2
Critical Thinking Exercise # 15.1

SECTION VI - GROUP & FAMILYTHERAPIES

Learning Objectives # 13
Discussion Questions # 1
Active Learning Activities # 15.4, 15.8
Critical Thinking Exercise # 15.1

SECTION VII - BIOMEDICAL THERAPIES

Learning Objectives # 14
Discussion Questions # 1
Active Learning Activities #'s 15.4, 15.6 - 15.8
Critical Thinking Exercise # 15.1

SECTION VIII - ISSUES IN THERAPY

Learning Objectives #'s 15 - 17
Lecture Lead Ins #'s 1 - 3
Lecture Extender # 15.1
Discussion Questions #'s 1 - 5
Active Learning Activities #'s 15.1-15.3, 15.5, 15.8, 15.10
Brain-Based Learning # 15.1
Critical Thinking Exercise # 15.1
Gender and Cultural Diversity Activity # 15.1

Lecture Lead-Ins

1. Ask students if they have seen any homeless people on the streets of their community. Even in the smallest, isolated community, most will have had at least some interactions with the homeless. Point out that many homeless individuals were former mental patients and have been displaced from the hospitals for both political and monetary reasons. Estimates from Goleman (1986) indicate that one third of New York City's 75,000 homeless are suffering from some mental disorder. Ask the students how this could happen. Would they support tax increases to help these homeless people? What other measures should be taken? Use this as an introduction for your lectures on therapy and institutionalization.

2. Ask students how many of them would be interested in a field trip to a local mental hospital. A show of hands will indicate the interest level. If the level is sufficient, arrange for a trip to a state mental hospital or private facility. Many students think this is one of the most valuable experiences they have in college. It will also provide a wonderful source of lead-ins for several topics in this chapter.

3. Ask students if they are aware of the psychological services that are available in your area? Do they know how to find or make use of them? You may want to assign one or more groups to investigate this issue and report back to the class. Use their knowledge (or lack of knowledge) of available resources as a lead-in to your lectures on general therapy or problems with therapy.

Lecture Extenders

15.1 - Witchdoctors and Psychiatrists

E. Fuller Torrey and Thomas Szasz are probably the two most prolific psychiatrists writing for the general public today. Szasz tends to speak out against psychiatry while Torrey is more supportive of the "establishment." Although Torrey is not interested in flaming a revolution, he has keen insights into the practice of psychotherapy and is able to dissemble its elements so that the myths are stripped away. The material below is based upon his book, Witchdoctors and Psychiatrists: The Common Roots of Psychotherapy and its Future (1986).

Torrey refers to psychotherapy as the second oldest profession in the world. Psychotherapy is a large enterprise in the U.S., employing over 150,000 psychotherapists who dispense 250 different brands of psychotherapy. The cost in 1980 was 1.7 billion per year, much of which is paid by medical insurance. Why do people go in for psychotherapy? The problems cited by psychiatrists most often are marital and family problems, job-related problems, and physical complaints related to stress and anxiety. These problems are often referred to as intrapersonal and interpersonal problems in living. One of the recent changes in patient populations has been that people are increasingly coming in for "life enhancement" rather than problems; the complaint is that life has no meaning and is boring.

Psychotherapy is not just an American phenomenon--it exists worldwide. We like to think our psychotherapy is superior to that in less-developed countries but, according to Torrey, psychotherapists in all countries utilize the same principles, the only exception being the prescription of medication. If all psychotherapy that was not based on scientific principles were eliminated, there would be virtually nothing left. There is no evidence that patients who see a witchdoctor in a grass hut are any less satisfied than those who see a psychotherapist in a high-rise in New York City.

There are four principles that are basic to psychotherapy in every part of the world. One is the principle of "Rumplestiltskin." This refers to the ability to name a problem. When we see a physician for a physical pain, we are relieved when he or she has a name for the disorder. This implies to us that the doctor understands what caused the problem and knows what to do about it. The same is true when there is a psychological pain. The psychotherapist's ability to name the cause relieves part of the anxiety. However, with psychological pain the cause is more subjective. In psychotherapy, the explanations have to agree with the cultural norms for "why." For example, to tell an American with psychological pain that a hex caused the anxiety will probably lead to the patient seeking out another psychotherapist. If one were to tell an African that the cause of his or her problem was a repressed love for the mother would probably lead to the same result. All cultures give three explanations for why things happen in the mental world: biological, experiential, and metaphysical. By far, the most common explanation worldwide is metaphysical and psychotherapists in most of the world utilize this in their explanations. Torrey says that in postindustrial societies, people tend to forget that the roots of psychotherapy are tied in to the same type of practices as religion and that psychotherapists, to some extent, fulfill many religious functions.

The second important aspect of psychotherapy is that it remains, the world over, a relationship between two people. Clients or patients want psychotherapists to whom they can relate. Numerous studies have indicated the importance of empathy, genuineness, and warmth on the part of the therapist. The knowledge skills that a therapist brings to therapy are far less important than his or her personality traits. Patients want to like the people they go to for help with their problems and they want to feel that they are liked in return.

The third important aspect of psychotherapy is what Torrey calls the "Edifice Complex." This is equivalent to the placebo effect, (i.e. belief alone can cure). There are several ways in which a psychotherapist communicates competence; the therapist's belief that the patient can be cured, the number of diplomas on the wall, the furnishings within the office, the professional affiliations, and so forth. For example, when one travels to the Menninger Clinic one expects to be treated with a high level of expertise. The greater the "trappings" surrounding the psychotherapist, the more the patient "believes" in him or her, therefore, expecting to get better.

The last aspect of psychotherapy is the feeling that knowledge has been gained that now equips one to get along better in life. Torrey refers to this as the "superman effect." Quite often, one hears former patients say that they have more self-insight or self-understanding. However, they are often saying this as they are entering therapy again, so apparently the beneficial effects of additional insight are short-lived.

Whatever the objective merits of psychotherapy, it does seem to fill a human need that is universal. People may be deceiving themselves with regard to objective benefits, but as long as psychotherapy makes people feel better, psychotherapy will continue to attract people who need someone to talk with and to reassure them that things can be better.

Torrey, E. F. (1986). Witchdoctors and psychiatrists: The Common Roots of Psychotherapy and its Future. New York: Harper & Row.

Key Terms

Psychotherapy (p. 542)

ESSENTIALS OF PSYCHOTHERAPY

Eclectic Approach (p. 543)

PSYCHOANALYSIS

Catharsis (p. 546)
Free Association (p. 546)
Interpretation (p. 547)
Psychoanalysis (p. 546)
Resistance (p. 547)
Transference (p. 547)

COGNITIVE THERAPIES

Cognitive-Behavior Therapy (p. 552)
Cognitive Restructuring (p. 550)
Cognitive Therapy (p. 550)
Rational-Emotive Therapy (RET) (p. 550)
Self-Talk (p. 550)

HUMANISTIC THERAPIES

Active Listening (p. 555)
Client-Centered Therapy (p. 554)
Empathy (p. 554)
Genuineness (p. 555)
Gestalt Therapy (p. 555)
Humanistic Therapy (p. 553)

Unconditional Positive Regard (p. 554)

BEHAVIOR THEERAPIES

Aversion Therapy (p. 559)
Behavior Therapy (p. 557)
Extinction (p. 561)
Modeling Therapy (p. 561)
Systematic Desensitization (p. 558)

GROUP AND FAMILY THERAPIES

Family Therapy (p. 564)
Group Therapy (p. 563)
Self-Help Group (p. 563)

BIOMEDICAL THERPIES

Anti-anxiety Drugs (p. 566)
Anti-depressant Drugs (p.568)
Anti-psychotic Drugs (p. 567)
Biomedical Therapy (p. 565)
Drug Therapy (p. 566)
Electroconvulsive Therapy (ECT) (p. 568)
Lobotomy (p. 570)
Psychosurgery (p. 570)
Tardive Dyskinesia (p. 567)

ISSUES IN THERAPY

De-institutionalization (p. 572)

Discussion Questions

1. Based on the therapies and techniques described in this chapter, which type of therapist would you consult if you were suffering from childhood sexual abuse? What if you were drug-dependent? What if you had a severe fear of flying? If you were so depressed that you were considering suicide, what type of therapist would you consult? Would you consent to electroshock therapy for your depression if you had tried everything else? Why or why not?

2. If you were planning to become a therapist, which type of therapy do you think you would be most interested in practicing? Is there a type of client/patient that you would prefer to treat? Is there anyone or any type that you would refuse to treat?

3. Radio call-in programs for psychological advice are becoming very popular. In your opinion, is this type of therapy effective? What are the advantages and disadvantages to this "telephone therapy?"

4. Has your opinion about psychotherapy changed after reading this chapter? Are you more or less inclined to seek therapy for yourself, friends or family members? Why or why not?

5. What are the ethics of forced mandatory treatment for psychological disorders? What are the patient's rights to refuse treatment? When is it society's right to control an individual and force treatment or involuntary commitment? If a person is threatening suicide, should he or she be forced into treatment? Would it be right for a therapist to allow a person to make suicide a matter of personal choice, an expression of "free will?"

 **Web Sites**

Association for Advancement of Behavior Therapy
http://server.psych.vt.edu/aabt
The official web site of the official organization dedicated to theory and research in behavior therapy.

Clinical Psychology Links
http://www.psych.westminster.edu/mjs/clinlinks.htm
Provides links to many other clinical psychology web sites.

American Academy of Psychoanalysis Home Page
http://www.aapsa.org
This site offers contemporary thought on psychoanalysis and information describing the origins of this treatment technique

American Psychoanalytic Association
http://www.apsa.org
A broad based site devoted to psychoanalytic (and psychodynamic) theory and research.

Society for a Science of Clinical Psychology
http://www.sscp.psych.ndsu.no.nodak
The society is section III of Division 12 of the American Psychological Association.

Association for Advancement of Behavior Therapy
http://server.psych.vt.edu/aabt
The official web site of the official organization dedicated to theory and research in behavior therapy.

Clinical Psychology Links
http://www.psych.westminster.edu/mjs/clinlinks.htm
Provides links to many other clinical psychology web sites.

American Academy of Psychoanalysis Home Page
http://www.aapsa.org
This site offers contemporary thought on psychoanalysis and information describing the origins of this treatment technique

American Psychoanalytic Association
> http://www.apsa.org
> A broad based site devoted to psychoanalytic (and psychodynamic) theory and research.

Society for a Science of Clinical Psychology
> http://www.sscp.psych.ndsu.no.nodak
> The society is section III of Division 12 of the American Psychological Association.

Suggested Films and Videos

Mistreating the Mentally Ill

Films for the Humanities and Sciences, 1995. 56 minutes. This program takes a cross-cultural look at the treatment of the mentally ill. The United States, Japan, India, and Egypt are examined as to how each culture views mental illness and treats less accepted members of society. It concludes that the problem is not a lack of funding, but indifference of societies to the mentally ill.

Health, Mind and Behavior

Annenberg/CPB, 1990. 30 minutes. This program from Zimbardo's "Discovering Psychology" series discusses the new biopsychosocial model of treating the mentally ill. The history of treatments for the mentally ill is presented along with a model that integrates traditional biomedical and psychological approaches with a new social awareness that our relationships with others can affect our health.

Psychotherapy

Annenberg/CPB, 1990. 30 minutes. This program from Zimbardo's "Discovering Psychology" series discusses how theory, research, and practice are integrated in the treatment of the mentally ill. Social attitudes toward the mentally ill are discussed. This is an excellent video that will be an asset to your presentation of psychotherapy.

Approaches to Therapy

Insight Media, 1990. 30 minutes. One client is seen in three one-on-one sessions demonstrating psychodynamic, humanistic, and cognitive-behavioral approaches to therapy. Experts discuss how the three approaches differ and explain the value of an eclectic approach. They also offer strategies for finding a good therapist.

The Talking Cure: A Portrait of Psychoanalysis

Insight Media, 1988. 56 minutes. A rare audio recording of Freud opens this program. Experienced therapists explain and describe what happens in traditional psychoanalysis and reveal how patients commonly respond to the process. Images of the daily lives of the patients are integrated with their personal reflections to present the experience from the patient's perspective.

The Royal Road: Psychoanalytic Approaches to the Dream

Insight Media, 1988. 33 minutes. This video examines a single dream showing how dream imagery relates to the patient's associations, the analyst's interpretations, and the supervising analyst's commentary.

Anxiety: Cognitive Therapy with Dr. Aaron T. Beck

Psychological and Educational Films, 1989. 43 minutes. In this excellent video, Dr. Beck discusses his theory of cognitive therapy and presents an assessment outline for the treatment of anxiety. He demonstrates his theory and techniques on a young man whose problems with procrastination are seated in his fears of how others view him.

Books For Success

Ehrenberg, Otto and Ehrenberg, Miriam (1986). **The Psychotherapy Maze.** Aronson.
A readable presentation of practical information and issues of being involved with psychotherapy.

Engler, Jack and Goleman, Daniel (1992). **The Consumer's Guide to Psychotherapy.** Simon & Schuster.
A thorough handbook of facts and advice on making informed decisions regarding psychotherapy.

Seligman, P. Martin & Seligman, E.P. Seligman (1995). **What You Can Change ... and What You Can't: The Complete Guide to Successful Self-Improvement: Learning to Accept Who You Are.** Fawcett Books.
Avoiding the excesses of the "you can change anything you want" self-help misinformation gurus as well as the psychological determinism that insists we are forever branded by the wounds of our childhood this highly readable book, based on the best available research evidence, looks at common conditions like anxiety, phobias, depression, sexual problems, weight problems, alcoholism, and post traumatic stress. It describes what we know of these conditions, what treatment options there are and how successful they have been at producing permanent change.
Highly Recommended.

Active Learning

Active Learning Activity 15.1 - Prejudice and Psychotherapy

(This activity and several others replicate and extend some of the same activities found in Chapter 14. Even if you chose some of the same activities, they are all worth repeating and it helps integrate the two chapters.)

Instruct students to form small groups. Inform them that you will offer some reward (extra credit points, active learning points, quiz points, etc.) for the one group with the largest number of words or phrases for "therapist" (in Activity 14.2 the class came up with words for "abnormal behavior"). Mention that you are interested in discussing the problems of prejudice and stereotypes regarding therapy, and reassure them that they can include slang terms such as "shrink" or "head doctor." Give them approximately 5 minutes for their brainstorming session. Ask for the total number of words from each group and award your points. Ask a volunteer from several groups with a high number of words to come to the front of the room and write their words on the board. This takes approximately 10 additional minutes, but it is definitely worth the class time. You will be amazed at the enormous variety and number of terms. In our classes we have had up to 20 or 30 different terms (about half the number of terms typically generated for "abnormal behavior"). There will be some official terms like psychiatrist or clinical psychologist, but there will be a dominance of derogatory terms. This provides a wonderful demonstration of prejudice and helps explain historical and modern day problems with treating abnormal behavior. This activity could also be used as a tie-in with the chapter on abnormal behavior (Chapter 14) since it provides a dramatic demonstration of why people are so often reluctant to be labeled "abnormal."

Active Learning Activity 15.2 - Class Project: Examples of Therapy Presented in the Media

The purpose of this exercise is to show students how textbook descriptions of therapy relate to the real world. Have students collect examples from newspapers, magazines, books, television and radio reports of therapy sessions. For each example, have students:

1. Note the type of therapy being conducted (psychoanalysis, behavior, biomedical, etc.).

2. Discuss what impression of therapy is created by the report.

As a way of summarizing the various types of therapy or during coverage of each therapy, have students present these popularized examples and discuss the points listed above.

Active Learning Activity 15.3

As a follow-up to Activity 15.2, or as a separate activity, ask students to rent videos of favorite movies related to therapy (Ordinary People, Prince of Tides, Sybil, I Never Promised You a Rose Garden, Sea of Love, Vertigo, Primal Fear, etc.), and then cue up a favorite scene that lasts approximately 1-2 minutes. Have them play the video segment for the class and lead a discussion regarding possible diagnoses, symptoms displayed, form of therapy, and so on. You might ask a group to make a "collage" of all these video segments for your future classes.

Active Learning Activity 15.4 - Role Playing

Have students act out the roles of people with various types of psychological disorders, while another student role plays various types of therapists. These can be students who have been carefully screened from your own classes or students from the drama department. Whichever the case, be sure the students understand that this role playing is not to be taken lightly, and that they will be expected to spend a specified amount of time outside of class to practice. You will need to set up times for these practice sessions and will need to spend time of your own in coaching them on appropriate abnormal behaviors. You might consider playing some of the roles of client and/or therapist yourself. It helps show students that you're willing to take a chance and helps model appropriate behaviors.

Active Learning Activity 15.5 - Visit A Mental Hospital

Arrange for a visit to a local state mental hospital or local private facility. Many students will consider this one of the most important experiences they have in college. Explain the need for confidentiality of patient identities as some students could know someone in the hospital. Tell the students that this is a totally voluntary trip and does not affect any course credit.

Active Learning Activity 15.6 - Systematic Desensitization

Step 1: Relaxation

Illustrate a thorough relaxation process by starting with the feet and going through the body parts in order or use a tape-recording with suggestions for relaxation.

Step 2: Constructing a Hierarchy

Divide the students into small groups and have each group construct a visualization hierarchy for a specific type of phobia. Have them write specific items that can be placed on the board to share with other class members.

Step 3: Combine relaxation technique with hierarchy.

Active Learning Activity 15.7 - Extinguishing Problem Behaviors

Discuss the behavior of speeding (driving a car in excess of the speed limit.) Describe the ways this behavior is punished and the reasons the current system of controlling the speed limit is not effective. Design a more effective system of extinguishing this behavior.

Reference: Martin, G., and Pear, J. (1992). Behavior Modification. Englewood Cliffs: Prentice-Hall.

Active Learning Activity 15.8 - Guest Speakers

Most students have little familiarity with local resources for counseling and therapy. Invite a professional from your local community or from your college or university student counseling facility to come to class and discuss options and fees. In addition, you may want to invite therapists who specialize in particular areas. For example, contact a local therapist who uses biofeedback in his/her therapy. Ask the individual if he/she would like to give a short demonstration of his/her techniques. Schedule this demonstration for the day after you lecture on behavior therapies.

Active Learning Activity 15.9 - RET

Describe the A-B-C steps in Ellis' rational-emotive therapy--activating event, belief, consequence. Read the following aloud to the class and have volunteers identify the activating event and consequences. Then have the student attempt to identify the belief that intervenes in each case. Lead a discussion in a search for alternatives to any self-defeating or irrational beliefs.

1. My professor makes me so angry when he will not call on me in class when I have the correct answer.

2. I don't like being around Linda, she makes me very depressed.

3. I had a tee time for 2:52 but my playing companion never made the time.

4. I get so depressed thinking about the final in my psychology class.

5. I scored 20 on my ACT; I will get into a good university.

Active Learning Activity 15.10 - Debate

After your last lecture on therapies, lead a debate concerning the most effective method. By this point in the course, students generally have a good understanding of psychological principles and therapy techniques. If time allows, encourage your students to conduct a formal debate with pros and cons on several issues related to therapy. If you arrange ahead of time, most colleges and universities have debate teams that are often interested in practicing their skills. You can ask at the beginning of the term for the debate team to come to your introductory course and present a formal debate related to therapy.

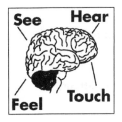

Brain-Based Learning

Brain-Based Learning Activity 15.1 - How To Choose A Therapist

Survey all the advertising (yellow pages, newspapers), professional organizational membership listings and web-sites of therapists in your area. Have each student or group of students take responsibility for surveying a certain section of these listings (i.e. clinical psychologists, MFCCs, Counselors, Psychiatrists).

If your students or one of their friends needed therapy how would they select the "right" person from such an abundance of choices? Have the class generate their ideas on how to choose a therapist before you offer your own guidelines or handouts on locally recommended sources of help.

Brain-Based Learning Activity 15.2 - Systematic Desensitization Experience

Ask each student to think of an experience in their life that scared them a good bit, but be sure to spell out that you don't want them to select an experience of deep personal trauma. Once the student has thought of a specific experience have them select something about that experience that they saw or felt or heard, something that could serve as a trigger or representation of the painful experience.

Explain to them that they will get a first hand experience of systematic desensitization and encourage them to observe their own internal reactions even as they complete the exercise. Be sure to caution the students that this is a demonstration of the process not a full blown therapeutic technique.

Begin by having each student sit comfortably in their chair and breathe long and deep in a quiet steady rhythm. Guide them to feel alert and relaxed in the safety of their chair. Then tell them to slowly increase the memory of the trigger. If it is a sight be sure to start with it far away, if a sound, start it at a low volume, if a feeling start it at a barely detectable level. Guide the students to maintain their awareness of the breath and their own body relaxation. Anytime their body reaction gets too strong have them decrease the strength of the triggering stimulus, until once again they feel balanced and steady after which they can again increase the signal strength in a series of small steps. Over the course of 5 minutes each student progresses at their own rate increasing the strength of the trigger, as long as they are able to do so while maintaining their positive inner state. If any student feels the memory of the scary experience becomes too strong have them open their eyes and just breathe quietly until the five minutes are up.

During debriefing ask students what it was like to have an emotional experience while simultaneously monitoring their own reactions. Do they believe such a technique would be helpful to patients with a phobic condition?

Brain-Based Learning Activity 15.3 - The Importance of Being Heard

Have the students pair up with a partner. Partner A begins by relating something that happened to them during past few weeks that was upsetting to them. Partner B's main task is to listen with empathy to what is being said. From time to time they reflect back to their partner what they heard and ask: Did I understand that right? And tell me more about it. The key is to give your partner your full attention, genuine interest and positive regard.

After a few minutes Partner A is then asked to describe what it was like. Did they feel heard? Did they feel understood or appreciated? Was there something in this experience which is better and different from their normal, day to day interactions? How hard was it for Partner B to give full attention and support? Would this be a stance they could maintain in an ongoing love or family relationship? Explore with the class how the Rogerian tools of a client centered approach are useful not only for the therapy setting but also for our own personal life and relationships.

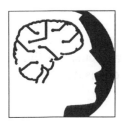

Critical Thinking

Critical Thinking Exercise 15.1 - Synthesizing: Helping Students Appreciate Commonalities of Different Psychotherapies

When students are introduced to the various forms of psychotherapy, they often fail to fully appreciate the mutual values and complementary interests of each of the major therapies. Their inability to see the interrelationships may be a reflection of their need for improvement in the critical thinking skill known as synthesizing. The following exercise will provide an opportunity for practice with this skill, while also helping students to master the major principles underlying the various therapeutic approaches.

Time: Approximately 30 minutes.

Advance preparation: Make five large posters with the following words in large letters: PSYCHOANALYTIC, BEHAVIORISTIC, HUMANISTIC, COGNITIVE, BIOLOGICAL. Post the signs at five locations on the classroom walls.

Instructions: Assign the reading of Chapter 15 and on the day of this demonstration briefly review the five major approaches to psychotherapy--psychoanalytic, behavioristic, humanistic, cognitive, and biological. Ask students to stand up and go to the center of the room. When they are gathered in the middle, read the first of the following "case histories." Then ask them to move and stand beneath the sign that they feel would be the best type of therapy for this particular problem. Once they are grouped under the various signs, call on specific individuals to explain their choice. Encourage students to move and stand under a different sign if they hear arguments or explanations from their colleagues that make them reconsider their initial decision. Spend about 5-7 minutes on the first case history and then have them return to the center of the room. Repeat the same "read, move, and discuss" procedure with the second, third, and fourth case histories.

At the end of the class period, ask students to return to their chairs and briefly discuss their reactions to the exercise. Students often report increased understanding of the various therapies and a greater appreciation for the similarities.

CASE HISTORIES

Joe is 18 years of age and is deeply concerned over the thought that he might be schizophrenic. Both his parents were schizophrenic, and his college friends have complained about his extreme sensitivity to criticism and his paranoia.

Ann is 42 years of age and is very depressed. She has planned all her life to have a large family, yet the men she dates never seem to be the right type for marriage or proper "father material."

Tim is 35 and dissatisfied with his work situation. His co-workers seem to avoid him and have complained to his superiors about his abusive personality. Tim believes these people are just weak individuals who envy his strength and greater intelligence.

Sue is 27 years of age and is feeling frustrated with her current employment situation. She thinks about quitting and starting her own business, but she worries about her finances and the possibility of failure.

This exercise also appears in the text, Chapter 15. We include it here for your convenience, and you may want to discuss it in class to reinforce reading of the text.

Critical Thinking Exercise 15.2 - Confronting Your Own Faulty Reasoning

Albert Ellis' approach to psychotherapy is based on his belief that illogical thinking is the basis for most human suffering. To improve your logical, critical thinking skills, we will briefly discuss the two basic tests for sound reasoning, and then give you a chance to apply these principles to your own irrational beliefs.

Part I

Consider the following syllogism:

Premise 1:   *All dogs are animals.*
Premise 2:   *All animals are blue.*
Conclusion: *Therefore, all dogs are blue.*

Is this sound and logical reasoning? To determine whether an argument is sound and whether the conclusions should be accepted, critical thinkers ask two major questions: "Is the argument valid?" and "Are all premises true?" An argument is considered valid *if* the conclusion logically follows from the premises. The previous syllogism, for example, would be considered valid because *if* all dogs are animals, and all animals are blue, then *logically* all dogs *must* be blue.

The second step in evaluating the soundness of arguments does require an examination of the content of argument. For an argument to be sound, each premise must also be true. This is where the previous syllogism falls apart. All dogs are obviously not blue.

Part II

The same faulty reasoning that underlies the blue-dog syllogism underlies the irrational beliefs that Ellis' form of cognitive therapy seeks to dispel. See if you can identify the problems with the following misconception.

Premise 1:   *I must have love or approval from all the people I find significant*
                         (in order to be happy).
Premise 2:   *I don't have approval from my mother, whom I consider significant.*
Conclusion: *Therefore, I am unhappy.*

Is this argument valid? If not, why not?

Are the premises of this argument true? If not, which ones are false and why?

Think carefully now about your own personal irrational misconception (e.g., "I must make everyone happy," "Life must be fair," etc.). In the following spaces, analyze your "self-talk" about this misconception and try to put it in syllogism form by identifying your two basic premises and your conclusion.

Premise 1: _____

Premise 2: _____

Conclusion: _____

Now answer the following questions:

Is my argument valid? If not, why not?

_____

Are the premises of my argument true? If not, which one is false and why?

_____

To further practice on your reasoning skills, you may want to follow this same procedure and logically examine each of your irrational misconceptions. By actively applying your logical skills to your own thought processes, you will not only improve your basic critical thinking skills, but, according to Ellis you will also be in a better position to subsequently change these self-destructive thought patterns which will, in turn, lead to changes in behavior.

This exercise also appears in the Student Study Guide for Chapter 15. We include it here for your convenience, and you may want to discuss it in class to reinforce use of the Student Study Guide.

Critical Thinking Exercise 15.3 - Expressing Empathy - <u>Expressing Empathy</u>   (An Affective Skill)

According to Dr. Thomas Gordon, people who wish to express empathy must avoid asking questions or giving advice when it is more appropriate to explore the other person's emotional state. Instead, the technique of "active listening" he recommends uses open-ended statements that enable your partner to express feelings. Three active listening techniques are:

   a. repeat what was said as a statement rather than a question

   b. slightly reword (or paraphrase) the statement

   c. state the feeling you assumed was being expressed

Use either of the last two possibilities for each of the following (the first example has been completed for you so that you will get the idea):

1. "I had the worst day of my life today at work."

<u>"Do you mean that everything you did at work</u>
<u>today seemed to go wrong?"</u>

2. "I feel like a nobody--no one ever pays attention to me or seems to care about me."

_____

_____

3. "You always seem to hurt my feelings."

_____

_____

Gender and Cultural Diversity

Gender and Cultural Activity 15.1 - Traits Associated with Mental Health

Materials: Blank 3x5 cards.

Procedure: Divide the class into small groups of same-sex students. Give the male groups a 3x5 card on which this question is posed:

"What are the traits of a mentally healthy woman?"

Give the female groups a 3x5 card with this question:

"What are the traits of a mentally healthy man?"

Allow approximately 10 minutes to develop a minimum of 10 traits. Collect the cards from each group, keeping the "male" and "female" cards separate. Now ask the class to describe their group's findings.

Writing Project

Writing Project 15.1

Given the need for improved writing skills in our college students, and to respond to the call for "writing across the curriculum," we offer writing projects for each chapter. In Chapter Fifteen, we suggest a 2-3 page written response to the following questions. Recognizing the time involved in grading such writing projects, one alternative is occasionally to assign "peer grading." Collect their papers, remove student names, and assign one paper to each student to grade. It helps to make their participation in peer grading part of the overall points for the writing project. This encourages a more thoughtful and responsible evaluation, as well as acknowledging and rewarding the additional work.

As a way to gain experience with cognitive restructuring (and personal self-help), complete the following:

1. Choose three friends or family members and interview them regarding their negative thoughts involving school, work, or personal relationships (e.g., "I am a poor test taker," "I hate my job," or "I just can't ask someone out on a date.") List at least five negative thoughts for each of the three people.

2. Help each person develop alternative positive thoughts for the same situations and include these positive thoughts in your paper.

3. Ask these three people to practice the positive thoughts for one week. Interview them once again at the end of the week and explore whether the positive thoughts had any effect on their thoughts, feelings, or behaviors. Include their responses in your paper.

4. Give your personal evaluation of cognitive restructuring as a tool for psychotherapy. Does it work? Why or why not? Can it be used only in a professional setting, or is it a useful self-help technique? Can you use it it your own life? Why or why not?

Circle of Quality – Chapter 15

Please give us your feedback. We thank you in advance for assisting us in improving the next edition. The contact information is listed in the preface.

What are the three most helpful teaching tools in this chapter?

1.

2.

3.

What are the three least useful teaching tools in this chapter?

1.

2.

3.

What are the three most difficult concepts to teach in this chapter?

1.

2.

3.

Additional Comments:

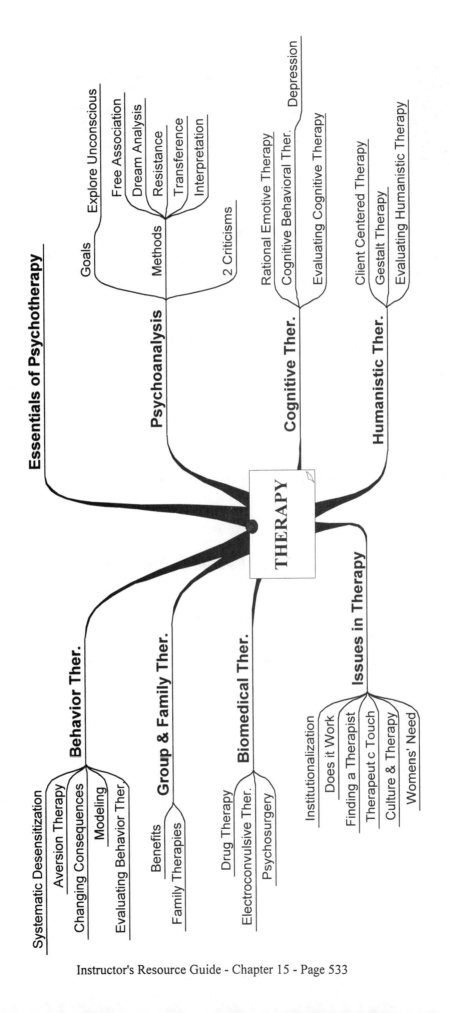

Essentials of Psychotherapy

Psychoanalysis

Goals — Explore Unconscious

Methods
- Free Association
- Dream Analysis
- Resistance
- Transference
- Interpretation

2 Criticisms

Cognitive Ther.
- Rational Emotive Therapy
- Cognitive Behavioral Ther.
- Evaluating Cognitive Therapy
- Depression

Humanistic Ther.
- Client Centered Therapy
- Gestalt Therapy
- Evaluating Humanistic Therapy

THERAPY

Behavior Ther.
- Systematic Desensitization
- Aversion Therapy
- Changing Consequences
- Modeling
- Evaluating Behavior Ther.

Group & Family Ther.
- Benefits
- Family Therapies

Biomedical Ther.
- Drug Therapy
- Electroconvulsive Ther.
- Psychosurgery

Issues in Therapy
- Institutionalization
- Does it Work
- Finding a Therapist
- Therapeut c Touch
- Culture & Therapy
- Womens' Need

CHAPTER 16
SOCIAL PSYCHOLOGY

Outline

Our Thoughts About Others

Attribution
Attitudes

Our Feelings About Others

Prejudice and Discrimination
Interpersonal Attraction

Gender and Cultural Diversity
Physical Attractiveness Across Cultures

Our Actions Toward Others

Social Influence

Active Learning
Would You Have Obeyed Milgram's Experimenters?

Group Processes
Aggression

Research Highlight
Juvenile Aggression and Mass Murder in Jonesboro

Altruism

GOAL

Learning Objectives

Upon completion of CHAPTER 16, the student should be able to:

1. Define social psychology, and describe the results of research on several commonsense statements regarding social interactions; briefly describe Milgram's classic obedience study (pp. 583-585).
2. Define attribution, and explain how choosing between dispositional and situational attributions results in two critical misjudgments: the fundamental attribution error and the self-serving bias (pp. 585-587).
3. Define attitude, and describe its three basic components (pp. 587-588).
4. Describe cognitive dissonance theory, the impact of dissonance on attitudes and behavior, and how culture impacts cognitive dissonance (pp. 588-590).
5. Using the three components of an attitude, differentiate between a stereotype, prejudice, and discrimination. Describe the four major sources of prejudice and discrimination: learning, cognitive processes, economic and political competition, and displaced aggression (pp. 591-593).
6. Explain how cooperation, superordinate goals, and increased contact can reduce prejudice and discrimination (pp. 593-594).
7. Describe the three key factors in interpersonal attraction: physical attractiveness, proximity, and similarity. Discuss cross-cultural and historical similarities and differences in physical attractiveness (pp. 594-597).
8. Describe the three components that distinguish liking from loving in Rubin's research: caring, attachment, and intimacy (p. 597).
9. Compare and contrast romantic and companionate love; discuss problems associated with romantic love (pp. 597-600).
10. Define conformity, and explain the three factors that contribute to this behavior: normative social influence, informational social influence, and the role of reference groups (pp. 600-602).
11. Define obedience, and describe how authority, responsibility, graduations in requests, and disobedient models affect this behavior (pp. 603-604).
12. Define a group; define roles; describe the effect of roles on the behavior of "prisoners" and "guards" in Zimbardo's classic prison study (pp. 605-606).
13. Discuss how group polarization and group-think affect group decision making (pp. 606-608).
14. Define aggression, and explain the factors that contribute to its expression: instinct, genes, the brain and nervous system, substance abuse and other mental disorders, hormones and neurotransmitters, frustration, and cultural learning (pp. 609-610).
15. Describe three approaches to controlling or eliminating aggression. Identify five misconceptions and controversies regarding juvenile aggression (pp. 610-612).
16. Define altruism, and describe its evolutionary benefit. Compare and contrast the egoistic model and the empathy-altruism hypothesis explanations of this behavior (pp. 612-613).
17. Describe Latane and Darley's decision-making model for helping behavior, and discuss how it can be used to increase the likelihood of helping (pp. 613-614).

Chapter Summary/Lecture Organizer

Introductory Vignette--Chapter 16 begins with Stanley Milgram's obedience experiment, which is used throughout the chapter to illustrate various principles in social psychology.

I.   **OUR THOUGHTS ABOUT OTHERS**

A. Attribution - Attributions are statements that are designed to explain why people behave as they do. The basic question is whether their actions are due to internal dispositions (derived from their own traits and motives) or external situations (derived from the environment or situation).

Attribution is subject to several forms of error and bias. The fundamental attribution error reflects our tendency to overestimate internal, personality influences and underestimate external influences when judging the behavior of others. The self-serving bias occurs when we attempt to find reasons for our own behavior, as we tend to take undue credit for positive outcomes and attribute negative outcomes to external causes.

> **Gender and Cultural Diversity** - The self-serving bias may be partially an artifact of western society due to the strong emphasis on the self and individuality. More collectivist cultures (such as Asian and certain Native American societies) do not define themselves as much in terms of individual traits and accomplishments.

B. Attitudes - Attitudes are learned pre-dispositions to respond cognitively, effectively, and behaviorally to a particular object. The three components of all attitudes are the cognitive response (thoughts and beliefs), affective response (feelings), and behavioral tendencies (pre-dispositions to actions).

We sometimes change our attitudes because of cognitive dissonance, which is the state of tension or anxiety we feel when there is a difference between two or more attitudes or when our attitudes do not match our behaviors. This mismatch and tension motivate us to change our attitude to restore balance. Self-perception theory, which suggests that people infer their attitudes from watching their behavior, developed in response to cognitive dissonance theory.

> **Gender and Cultural Diversity** - Cognitive dissonance may reflect a particular way of evaluating the self that is distinctively western. Bad decisions have strong negative effects on individual self-esteem and so motivate attitude change. Collectivist cultures (such as Asians) are not as threatened by losses to individual self-esteem, so this may not be as strong a motivator for attitude change.

II.   OUR FEELINGS ABOUT OTHERS

A. Prejudice and Discrimination - Prejudice is a generally negative attitude directed toward people solely on the basis of their membership in a specific group. It contains all three components of attitudes (cognitive, affective, and behavioral elements). Discrimination is not the same as prejudice. It refers to the actual negative behavior directed at members of a group. People do not always act on their prejudices.

The major sources of prejudice are learning (classical and operant conditioning and social learning), cognitive processes (in-group favoritism, out-group negativity, out-group homogeneity effect, and blaming-the-victim), economic and political competition, and displaced aggression (scape goating).

Cooperation, superordinate goals, and increased contact are three major methods for reducing prejudice and discrimination.

B. Interpersonal Attraction - The degree of positive or negative feelings we have toward each other account for a variety of social experiences including admiration, liking, friendship, intimacy, lust, and love. There are three factors that influence interpersonal attraction; physical attractiveness, proximity, and similarity.

Physical attractiveness is very important to initial attraction. Physically attractive people are often perceived as more intelligent, sociable, and interesting than less attractive people.

> **Gender and Cultural Diversity** - Standards for physical attractiveness vary across cultures and historically. Physical attractiveness is generally more important to men than to women. Physical proximity increases one's attractiveness. The nearer you live to or work with someone, the more likely it is you will like that person. Although people commonly believe that "opposites attract," research shows that similarity is a much more important factor in attraction.

Proximity is also very important to initial attraction. People who are in the same place at the same time are more likely to become friends just due to mere exposure.

Similarity is the most important factor in holding together long-term relationships over time. There are two ways in which this factor acts. One is need compatibility, we need others who are like us to share interests, attitudes, and so on. Another is by need complementarily, we also need others who have very different qualities, and so each provides important resources for the other.

Loving others is more of a mystery. Often love relationships develop from initial feelings of liking, and it is not always clear when one gives way to the other. Rubin's research on liking and loving found that love can be defined in terms of caring, attachment, and intimacy. Romantic love is highly valued in our society, but because it is based on mystery and fantasy, it is hard to sustain in long-term relationships. Companionate love relies on mutual trust, respect, and friendship and seems to grow stronger with time.

III. OUR ACTIONS TOWARD OTHERS

A. Social Influence - Through the process of social influence, we are taught important cultural values and behaviors that are essential to successful social living. Two of the most important forms of social influence are conformity and obedience.

Conformity refers to changes in behavior in response to real or imagined pressure from others. Asch's classic study of conformity demonstrated that people will often conform to group opinion even when the group is clearly wrong. People conform for approval and acceptance (normative social influence), out of a need for more information (informational social influence), and to match the behavior of those they admire and feel similar to (their reference group). People also conform because it is often adaptive to do so.

Obedience involves giving in to a command from another. Milgram's experiment with obedience to authority demonstrated that a large number of people will follow orders even when another human being is physically threatened. Assignment of responsibility and the presence of disobedient models are the two most important factors in reducing destructive forms of obedience.

> **Active Learning** - This exercise offers students an opportunity to explore various forms of social influence, and to develop critical thinking skills that might reduce being manipulated by unethical authority figures.

B. Group Processes - Groups differ from mere collections of people if members share a mutually recognized relationship with one another.

Group membership is the basic relationship members of a group immediately recognize and share. As a member of a group we then play various roles. The importance of these roles in determining and controlling behavior was dramatically demonstrated in Philip Zimbardo's Stanford Prison Study. College students who were assigned to play the role of either a prisoner or guard in a simulated prison became so completely and dangerously immersed in acting out their roles that the experiment was prematurely ended.

Group decision making is influenced by how group discussions affect individual opinions (group polarization) and how group membership affects access to information (group-think). Groups are often trusted with decisions because we believe their response will be more conservative and "middle of the road" than the potentially extreme decisions of individuals. Research shows, however, that groups are actually more extreme in their decisions. Sharing ideas with "like-minded" others often reinforces the group's preexisting and dominant tendencies, resulting in group polarization. Group-think is a dangerous type of thinking that occurs when the group's desire for agreement overrules its tendency to critically evaluate information. The Challenger explosion is often given as an example of the consequences of group-think.

C. Aggression - Aggression is any deliberate attempt to harm another living being who is motivated to avoid such treatment. Research points to both internal and external factors leading to aggression.

In the search for internal factors leading to aggression, some researchers have focused on inborn instinctual factors and the role of genetic pre-dispositions toward aggression. Others have done research on the brain (primarily on the hypothalamus and other parts of the limbic system). Substance and mental disorders are also recognized as sources of aggression. Biological investigations have also explored the role of hormones (elevated levels of testosterone) and neurotransmitters (lowered levels of serotonin and GABA).

External factors also play a role in aggression. Frustration (and displaced aggression), social learning (observation of models who are rewarded for aggression), and group influence (role behaviors and de-individuation) are the most important external factors.

Releasing aggressive feelings through violent acts or watching violence has not been shown to be an effective way to reduce aggression. More effective ways are to produce incompatible responses (such as humor), and to improve social and communication skills.

D. Altruism - Altruism refers to actions designed to help others with no obvious benefit to oneself.

Why do we help? Evolutionary theorists believe altruism is innate and has survival value. Psychological explanations for altruism emphasize the egoistic model, which suggests that helping is motivated by anticipated gain, or the empathy-altruism hypothesis, which proposes that helping is activated when the helper feels empathy for the victim.

Why don't we help? Whether or not someone helps depends on a series of interconnected events, starting with noticing the problem and ending with a decision to help. Altruism is inhibited by the fact that many emergency situations are ambiguous and the potential respondent is unsure of what to do. Inhibition also comes from not taking personal responsibility and assuming someone else will respond (the diffusion of responsibility phenomenon).

To increase the chances of altruism, we should increase the rewards and decrease the costs. We can also reduce ambiguity by giving clear directions to those who may be watching.

Teaching Resources

SECTION I - OUR THOUGHTS ABOUT OTHERS

Learning Objectives #'s 1 - 5
Lecture Lead-Ins #'s 2 & 4
Discussion Questions #'s 4
Active Learning Activities #'s 16.4 - 16.7
Brain-Based Learning #'s 16.1 - 16.3
Critical Thinking Exercise # 16.1
Gender and Cultural Diversity Activity # 16.1
Writing Project # 16.1

SECTION II - OUR FEELINGS ABOUT OTHERS

Learning Objectives #'s 6 - 9
Lecture Lead-Ins #'s 2 & 4
Lecture Extenders # 16.1

Discussion Questions #'s 2 & 4
Active Learning Activities #'s 16.4, 16.5, 16.8 & 16.12
Brain-Based Learning #'s 16.1 & 16.2
Critical Thinking Exercise #'S 16.2 & 16.3
Gender and Cultural Diversity Activity # 16.1
Writing Project# 16.1

SECTION III - OUR ACTIONS TOWARDS OTHERS

Learning Objectives #'s 10 - 17
Lecture Lead-Ins #'s 1 - 4
Lecture Extenders # 16.1
Discussion Questions #'s 1 - 4
Active Learning Activities #'s 16.1 - 16.6, 16.10 & 16.11
Brain-Based Learning #'s16.1 & 16.2
Critical Thinking Exercise # 16.2
Gender and Cultural Diversity Activity # 16.1

Lecture Lead-Ins

1. Ask students to take out a blank piece of paper and to write a ten minute paper on a very unusual, esoteric topic (e.g., the role of structuralism in modern cognitive neuroscience.) Remind them to use their very best grammar and to be sure to include their name and social security number on their papers. The students will grumble about your sudden shift from your syllabus but most will comply with the assignment. Allow about 5 minutes and note how many students try to complete the assignment and how many simply give up. Stop and ask the students why they complied with an obviously irrational demand. Most will say because you (authority figure) told them to. Use their behavior as a lead-in for your lectures on obedience and Milgram's study.

2. Ask students to discuss crowding and behavior from a personal viewpoint. Students often live in a relatively small amount of square footage per person. Some will have children and spouses, some still live at home or with several roommates, while others will live in the dorms. Discuss how crowded conditions affect their behaviors, both positively and negatively. Would more space improve their lives? Use this as a lead-in to the general field of social psychology and how the presence of others affects our individual behavior.

3. Janis (1972) has extensively discussed the role of group-think in business and governmental organizations. Ask the students to prepare a one-page paper on any personal experiences they might have in group problem solving. Have the students be prepared to discuss their examples at the next class meeting. Most will have examples of group-think in action. Use these examples as a lead-in for your lectures on group processes.

4. Ask for a show of hands of those who are prejudiced toward a minority group (hopefully no one will raise a hand). Discuss the overt and covert nature of prejudice. Then ask minority students in your class which they would prefer. Most will answer overt. Discuss the difficulties of studying and reducing prejudice in nations that pride themselves on democratic principles. Use this as a lead-in to prejudice.

5. Ask students to imagine a situation where they would be in desperate need of help. This could be modified to suit your location, for example, in a big city, a mugging; a small town, a heart attack. Have students write down the optimal number of bystanders they think would be necessary to elicit the most help. Now ask for a show of hands for various numbers (10 and above, 5-9, 3-4, 1-2). Most students will vote for the highest numbers. Use their responses as a lead-in for your lectures on altruism.

Lecture Extenders

16.1 - A Community of Individuals

This chapter, in dealing with the individual in society, looks at the processes of conformity and obedience. These have been the aspects most emphasized since the 1960's when individualism became a high priority in this country. Others have looked at the interaction between society and the individual and have seen it as an equal-exchange situation: the individual gives up something, but gets back something in return. Surprisingly, one of the best known "philosophers" on this subject, Dr. Sigmund Freud, was the one who voiced this opinion. The material below deals with Freud's ideas on the nature of this "deal" and is based upon his book, Civilization and its Discontents (1930/1961).

Freud has often been called "anti-society" since he viewed society as responsible for individuals' neuroses; however, he was quite the opposite. While he did agree that neuroses were experienced by some who could not tolerate instinctual frustrations (aggressive and sexual), he felt that there was no alternative. Civilization, by its very nature, has to put restrictions on the ways in which instincts can be satisfied. Freud said all civilizations have to satisfy two basic functions: to protect man from nature and to regulate the relationships among individuals within society.

The history of humankind, according to Freud, has centered on the increasing control of nature. The ability to create fire at will and to use tools were two of the greatest achievements that enhanced the way in which man could deal with nature. Today, we have buildings that protect us from the elements, clothing that allows us to go out into the elements, modern medicine that inoculates us against many diseases, and so forth. Other types of technological advances allow us to improve upon both our sensory and motor equipment. Through a telephone we can hear sounds a continent away and automobiles provide the power for faster movement than any group of muscles. However, Freud points out that technological advances do not automatically make humankind happier. For example, people marvel at the ability to hear, via telephone, a beloved's voice from many miles away; however, if technology had not provided the means of transport, one would have the loved one next door.

The other primary aim of society is to regulate the relationships among individuals within a society. Before the dawn of civilization, relationships among people were regulated by who was the strongest one. And, always, there was another person out there who would be able to topple the earlier winner. Society replaces rule by physical force with the rule of law--the mandates for how one behaves supersede the will of an individual, no matter how strong that individual may be. The power of the group has now become stronger than that of the individual. Justice becomes the equal application of these laws to everyone.

The person, by choosing to be a member of the society, gives up the unlimited right to express all possible behaviors. Freud agrees that there was more freedom before societies formed; however, this freedom was a short-lived affair until someone bigger came along. Freud, assuming that humans are motivated by the two basic instincts of aggression and sex, points out that the greatest degree of happiness comes from the satisfaction of "wild impulses." However, in society these aspects of human nature have to be curbed, along with the intense happiness that might accrue from indulging uninhibited appetites. Many of the political struggles have centered on the resolution between the needs of the individual and of the society. For example, the upheaval in Eastern Europe centers on how much freedom an individual may have in regulating his or her own life.

Society uses several techniques for controlling instincts. The socialization of the sexual instinct is one that begins very early when children learn that only some forms of sexual expression are acceptable. In general, in Western society, this has meant heterosexual genital sex between married partners.

The other instinct that Freud refers to as a troublesome one for society to regulate is aggression. If people are going to work together in community units, there has to be a way for them to relate to one another emotionally. One way to do this is through "aim-inhibited" sexual ties: attachments are stripped of their sexual basis and become friendships, and so forth. Generally, this alone is insufficient. Another tactic is to indoctrinate people into the idea that they should love one another--a tenet that is found in major religious writings in all societies.

Are these control techniques sufficient for ridding one of aggression? Freud says not always. Another method is to find someone outside the group (such as another country with envied resources) and direct the aggression outward. One can also turn aggression inward, producing guilt which further controls one's feeling that aggression is bad. Some countries, namely the socialist countries, have tried to control aggression by getting rid of private property which can serve as a source of conflict between people. Freud says there is no way to equalize people since nature itself imposes inequality through unequal abilities, physical attractiveness, and so forth, and this leads to a feeling that life is unfair. In addition, competition for sexual objects further reduces "good will" among individuals. In other words, aggressiveness cannot be totally eliminated.

Freud seems to feel that we have a good bargain: "give a little--take a little." Besides, there is nothing better out there as an alternative. For those who think so, they should try it--they will return.

Source: Freud, S. (1961). Civilization and its discontents (J. Strachey, Trans.) New York: W. W. Norton & Co. (Original work published 1930).

16.2 - Biological Aggression

Explanations for aggression have occupied psychological journals and textbooks for years. Until the 1980's, the explanations found most often were related to learning theory: aggressive behavior was a product of a faulty nurturing environment. However, recently, more attention has been directed back to the products of nature: neurotransmitters, hormonal factors, or neural systems in the brain. The majority of the data on biological factors has come from animal studies in which one has more ethical freedom to invade the brain or alter the prenatal hormonal balance. The first data on humans which correlated testosterone levels with behaviors was collected on special populations such as prison inmates. Although few psychologists contested the positive correlations that were found, many felt that this type of data only related to socially deviant behaviors. Now, new data is emerging which suggests that testosterone plays a role in a wider variety of social behaviors. The discussion below is based upon Goleman's (1990) summary of these studies.

Many researchers argue that the level of testosterone in the body is an inconsequential factor in determining the level of aggression. These investigators agree that testosterone level varies among individuals, but they believe that the more important influences upon aggression are social factors. They also note that females who, on the average, have one-tenth the level of testosterone of males, vary in their aggressive behaviors. Another complaint (noted above) has been that studies on testosterone level did not apply to the population at large.

Now, several new studies have extended these findings into the general population. One of the strongest supporting studies comes from a study on aging in the Boston area. The subjects, 1,706 men, ages 39 to 70, were interviewed in their homes and given personality tests and blood tests. Dr. John B. McKinlay, one of the psychologists who directed the research in this study, reports that a relationship was found between dominance and level of testosterone. Men who had the higher levels of testosterone expressed opinions more readily, anger more freely, and tended to dominate social interaction.

In another study, reported by Dr. James Dabbs, Jr., data was collected on 4,462 Vietnam veterans. Started in 1985, this study was designed to measure the long-term effects of military service. Data was collected relative to income and educational level; this information was used for assignment to either an upper or lower socioeconomic level. Differences in adjustment related to level of testosterone: those with higher levels contributed a greater share of delinquent behaviors such as drug abuse, friction with teachers, and going AWOL while in service. They also reported a greater number of sexual partners. However, testosterone was not the only factor that mattered. The effect of testosterone depended upon the socioeconomic level. Those who were from the lower socioeconomic level were more likely to be involved in anti-social activity.

McKinlay feels that Dabbs' findings support his own results. He says that the outlet one chooses to express more aggression depends upon social class. One can steal a car (if one is poor) or one can race with a motor boat (if one has the money). A person can choose to become dominant in the corporate world or to beat up people on the street. Obviously, having money increases the choices available. However, with very high testosterone levels, one may find it difficult to fit into society at any level because of sheer need for physical activity or a low threshold for frustration which prevents one from cooperating with others or conforming sufficiently to move upwards in the corporate world. One interesting factor from the study by Dabbs is his finding that men with high testosterone levels are two and a half times more likely to be in the lower socioeconomic group.

Does testosterone level influence a person's occupational choice? If testosterone does increase need for physical activity and dominance, then one would expect that those high in this hormone would naturally seek out occupations and professions that allow expression of this need. Dabbs has measured the amount of testosterone in various professions ranging from ministers, physicians, college professors, football players, firemen, and actors. As expected, those who seek out football have the highest testosterone levels. Surprisingly, actors also share this high hormonal level. Dabbs points out that this agrees with the Vietnam data in which he found that individuals involved in entertainment also had high levels. He says that actors tend to shrug off traditional roles; this is correlated with a certain amount of social aggressiveness.

Alan Mazur, a sociologist at the University of Syracuse, adds a qualifying note regarding the direction of the correlations: competitive activity raises the hormonal level. It has been demonstrated that winning a game leads to a rise in testosterone. It has also been shown that those who are the most psyched up about a game and feel ready to "win for the team" have a higher level of testosterone. Similar changes have been shown with other achievements such as being awarded a medical degree.

Despite the difficulty of untangling these various factors, this area will remain an area of intense research. Meanwhile, in looking at the future, is it possible that guidance and careers counselors will be using blood tests to assist in decision making?

Source: Goleman, D. (1990, July 17). Aggression in men: Hormone levels are a key. The New York Times, pp., C1, C6.

Key Terms

Social Psychology (p. 585)

OUR THOUGHTS ABOUT OTHERS

Attitude (p. 587)
Attribution (p.585)
Cognitive Dissonance Theory (p. 588)
Fundamental Attribution error (p. 586)
Saliency Bias (p. 586)
Self-Serving Bias (p. 586)

OUR FEELINGS ABOUT OTHERS

Companionate Love (p. 599)
Discrimination (p. 591)
In-group Favoritism (p. 592)
Interpersonal Attraction (p. 594)
Need Compatibility (p. 597)
Need Complementarity (p. 597)
Out-group Homogeneity Effect (p. 592)
Physical Attractiveness (p. 594)
Prejudice (p. 591)
Proximity (p. 595)
Romantic Love (p. 597)
Similarity (p. 596)

Stereotype (591)
Superordinate Goal (p. 593)

OUR ACTIONS TOWARD OTHERS

Aggression (p. 609)
Altruism (p. 612)
Conformity (p. 601)
Diffusion of Responsibility (p. 614)
Egoistic Model (p. 613)
Empathy - Altruism Hypothesis (p. 613)
Foot-in-the-Door Technique (p. 603)
Frustration - Aggression Hypothesis (p. 610)
Group (p. 605)
Group Polarization (p. 607)
Groupthink (p. 607)
Informational Social Influence (p. 602)
Norm (p. 601)
Normative Social Influence (p. 601)
Obedience (p. 603)
Personal Space (p. 601)
Reference Groups (p. 602)
Role (p. 605)

Discussion Questions

1.   What are the ethical considerations of using human subjects in the Milgram (1965) experiments? Should individuals be subjected to the pressure of this experiment? Was the data worth the consequences to the subjects? Ask the students to write a one-page paper and be prepared to discuss their answers at the next class meeting.

2.   What is the value of Zimbardo's prison study? Can we really learn anything from role playing or is the real prison situation too different from a group of college students being paid to role play? Is role playing a valid method for collecting social data?

3.   Based on your own behaviors, do you agree or disagree with the frustration-aggression hypothesis? What do you think about biological theories such as the role of testosterone? Should violent prisoners be allowed to be castrated? Should this increase their chances for parole? Would this help reduce violence? Why or why not?

4.   Are humans innately aggressive or are these behaviors learned? To the extent they are learned, what can parents and society do to decrease violence? Should we reduce the amount of aggression on TV? Would our society be better off without TV? Could this ever happen? Have the students prepare a one-page paper and be prepared to discuss their answers at the beginning of the next class.

 **Web Sites**

National Self-Esteem Society
http://www.self-esteem-nase.org
This site offers comprehensive information on self-esteem, definitions, and resources for improving self-image.

TIP: Theories
http://www.gwu.edu/~tip
This site is primarily concerned with covering different theories within psychology, such as social psychology.

Cognitive Dissonance Theory
http://spot.colorodo.edu/~craigr/Dissonance.html
An offering of details on cognitive dissonance theory, as well as recent research findings.

Institute of Cognitive and Decision Sciences
http://hebb.oregon.edu
This institute is concerned principally with cognitive science, and social cognition.

Adult Attachment and Interpersonal Attraction
http://psychology.ucdavis.edu/shaver/h&s.html
This site provides an online assessment of adult attachment.

Links to Social Psychology Topics
http://www.wesleyan.edu/spn/social.htm
A comprehensive reference site that provides links to a variety of topics in social psychology including group behavior, interpersonal relations, social influence, prejudice, gender, and pro-social behavior.

The Shyness Home Page
http://www.shyness.com/
This site contains links to web pages relating to the topic of social shyness.

Stanford Prison Experiment
http://www.ed.ac.uk/~mlc/marble/psycho/prison/
Dr. Zimbardo has created an on-line slide show detailing scenes from the famous Stanford Prison study.

Obedience to Authority

http://caps.otago.ac.nz:801/grant/PSYC/OBEDIANCE.HTML
This site provides a clear and concise description of the obedience studies carried out by Dr. Stanley Milgram. The site presentation is enhanced by the inclusion of photos that depict scenes of the original research project.

Web Links on Violence

http://www.mincava.umn.edu/global.asp
A set of links on issues in the study of violence. The site provides a comprehensive listing of topics ranging from guns to sexual violence to the impact of television on violence.

Suggested Films and Videos

Constructing Social Reality

Annenberg/CPB, 1990. 30 minutes. This program from Zimbardo's "Discovering Psychology" series profiles group behavior and the effects of the social environment. It begins with the Jonestown mass suicide and explores Jane Elliot's famous brown-eyes and blue-eyes demonstration.

The Power of the Situation

Annenberg/CPB, 1990. 30 minutes. Another program from Zimbardo's "Discovering Psychology" series that blends well with the text material. It reviews the major social psychological research, including Lewin's leadership styles, Asch's work on conformity, Milgram's obedience studies, and Zimbardo's prison study.

Social Psychology

Insight Media, 1990. 30 minutes. Explores how social psychology attempts to understand the social forces that influence behavior, including stereotyping and prejudice, attribution theory, the power of social roles, and in-group/out-group studies.

Conformity, Obedience and Dissent

Insight Media, 1990. 30 minutes. Explores when and why people conform, obey, and dissent in social situations, including Milgram's obedience studies, Asch's conformity studies, research on styles of dissent and styles of leadership, and the phenomenon of group-think.

The Wave

Insight Media, 1984. 46 minutes. This Emmy award-winning program dramatically recreates the classroom experiment where a high-school teacher formed his own "Reich" to explain how the German people could so willingly embrace Nazism. Very powerful.

Group Decision Making and Leadership

Insight Media, 1989. 30 minutes. This video shows strategies for effective group work in a variety of situations, providing suggestions for boosting group efficiency and productivity. It explores interpersonal relationships among group decision makers and discusses the functions of leadership.

Face Value: Perceptions of Beauty

Films for the Humanities and Sciences, 1995. 26 minutes. Examines the belief that perceptions of attractiveness may be universal and biologically programmed, and that certain features of the face have an instinctive appeal, such as large eyes, high cheekbones, smooth skin texture, and a narrow jaw. Presents experts who support these theories and those who strongly disagree, maintaining that beauty reflects time and fashion. Guaranteed to spark interesting discussion.

Eye of the Storm

Insight Media, 1970. 29 minutes. This classic film documents the original experiment by Jane Elliot, a third-grade teacher in Iowa, who separated her class into eye color groups, with one color having superior status over the other. It is amazing to watch and a "must see" for intro students.

A Class Divided

PBS for Frontline, 1985. 54 minutes. This program updates the original experiment by Jane Elliot (see above listing). Original footage from "Eye of the Storm" is included, as well as interviews with the original students and their reactions to the experiment.

Understanding Prejudice

Thinking Allowed Productions, 1992. 86 minutes. In this two-part video, Jeffrey Mishlove interviews Price Cobbs, who describes principles of ethnotherapy, which facilitates a deep examination of the ways we think about other groups.

Human Aggression

Insight Media, 1975. 24 minutes. This classic video features Stanley Milgram and real-life incidents of aggression, the Bobo doll studies, the psychological training of police, and Milgram's studies of the influence of groups on aggression.

Pulling the Punches

Filmmakers Library, 1994. 30 minutes. This video provides an intimate view of one man's therapy to control his abusive behavior toward his wife. The patient was treated at Everyman's Center in London, where his interactions with his counselor were recorded.

Domestic Violence: Which Way Out?

Filmmakers Library, 1994. 30 minutes. This film documents a successful treatment program in Bellevue, Washington, with a 4% repeat offense rate for those who complete the intensive therapy.

When Will People Help? The Social Psychology of Bystander Intervention

Harcourt Brace Jovanovich, 1976. 25 minutes. This program is hosted by Daryl Bem and explores the public murder of Kitty Genovese and investigates bystander intervention. Why do people ignore emergency situations? What makes people help in a crisis? Experiments are used in attempts to answer these and other questions.

Books For Success

McKay, Matthew; Fanning, Patrick (1992). **Self-Esteem (2nd Edition).** New Harbinger Publications. An interesting, easy-to-understand book on overcoming your "pathological critic", thereby improving your self-esteem.

Beck, Aaron T. (1988). **Love Is Never Enough.** Harper & Row.
Dr. Beck (the founder of cognitive therapy) provides a great synopsis in his subtitle:
"How couples can overcome misunderstandings, resolve conflicts, and solve relationship problems through cognitive therapy."

Pratkanis, A. R. and Aronson, E (1992). **Age of Propaganda: The Everyday Use and Abuse of Persuasion.** Freeman.
This book shows how propaganda is based on the principles of social psychology of persuasion.

Cialdini, Robert (1993). **Influence: The Psychology of Persuasion.** Quill.
In a book both scholarly and practical Cialdini describes the six major strategies on how to change a customer's mind. With many examples from the world of sales and business the author shows how powerful and pervasive are the forces of social influence and what we can do to guard ourselves against them. Recommended for all consumers and students of the human condition.

Active Learning

Active Learning Activity 16.1 - Being Different: Norm Violations

Ask students to wear clothing that is very different for them (but within the standards of the school) to the first class meeting that discusses conformity. Have the students be as creative as they can; you could even award extra credit for the best efforts. Devise a formal norm violation assignment by asking students to deliberately break a norm outside of class. Rules: You must be alone, the behavior must be legal and non-threatening to others, and you should debrief your participants. Have the students discuss their norm violations in class.

Active Learning Activity 16.2 - Seat Reassignment

Enter class with a copy of your most recent class roll sheet and begin to call out students by name, asking them to move to another chair in the room. You will probably get through the entire list without any complaints--total conformity. For the daring instructor, you can have fun with this one by also asking students to sit on your desk, to stand in the hall, to stand on one foot, and so forth. If someone refuses, you can even ask another student to gently assist the recalcitrant student, or you can say "You have no other choice" and demand that he/she move. This exercise is fun and assuming you have good rapport with your students, they will accept the joke and appreciate the unique lesson in conformity and possibly obedience. (Some social psychologists make a distinction between conformity, compliance, and obedience--conformity referring to "going along with the crowd," compliance as "going along with a request," and obedience as "going along with a demand." For a general introductory course it may not be necessary to go into this level of detail.)

Active Learning Activity 16.3 - Peer Pressure

Have the students form small informal groups of several friends and assign the task of using peer pressure on one of their friends not in your class. Have the group try to force conformity of the non-psychology student with the will of the group. This can be something as simple as eating food the subject does not like, going to a event, or meeting people the subject does not like. Ask the students to be creative but to stay within the bounds of good taste. Ask for volunteers to discuss the results at the next class meeting.

Active Learning Activity 16.4 - Rumor Transmission

Cut a brief "back page" news report from your local newspaper and make copies for everyone or use an overhead transparency. Ask for five volunteers to step outside while you explain the three major factors in rumor transmission:

Leveling--the stories become shorter and certain details are omitted.
Sharpening--certain details are highlighted and elaborated.
Assimilation--details of the story are distorted in line with the listener's expectancies, habits, and prejudices.

Ask your students to listen for examples of each of these factors as you demonstrate rumor transmission. Start by bringing one of the five volunteers to the front of the room and ask him/her to listen as you read the brief newspaper report. Then bring in the second student and ask the first to retell the story with as much accuracy as possible. Repeat this until all five students have heard the story and have the last student repeat it to the class at large. Mention that group membership does provide us with invaluable information, but they should be forewarned concerning the dangers of rumor transmission.

Active Learning Activity 16.5 - Space Invasion

On the first day of lecture in social psychology ask students to get acquainted with the students around them. After five minutes, interrupt the students and ask them to notice how far apart they are currently standing--an average of two to four feet is normal. Now ask the students to continue talking but increase the distance to four to twelve feet. After a minute or two, interrupt once again and ask them to move within twelve inches of one another. Having their toes touch is about twelve inches. After the laughter has subsided, discuss how they felt at each of the three distances. Ask students who have traveled to or lived in foreign countries to describe their feelings concerning people of other nationalities who have a much smaller personal space. Tell the students to form groups and discuss the problems with communication between two groups with large differences in personal space. Have each group report to the class on their findings. This activity is similar to the "Try This Yourself" section on page 568 of the text

Active Learning Activity 16.6 - Understanding Cults

Start by describing the horrifying account of the mass suicide/massacre in Waco, Texas and/or Jonestown, Guyana. Given that college students are often prime targets of cult recruiters, it is important to discuss the identifying characteristics of cults and to explore their differences from mainstream religions. The following class activity encourages this understanding while also encouraging your students' ability to welcome divergent views. Critical thinkers recognize the importance of exploring controversial and contradictory values and beliefs--especially when they conflict with their own personal perspectives.

Time: Approximately 40-50 minutes.

Advance preparation: Arrange for a 5-6 member guest panel representing various mainstream religions and one or two "cults," (e.g., Orthodox Jews, Roman Catholics, Fundamentalists, Protestants, Mormons, Hare Krishna, Moonies, etc.). You can usually obtain referrals for these speakers from your college's "Religious Studies" Department. Inform each guest that they will be asked to briefly describe the basic tenets of their own religion, to discuss how their faith differs from that of "cults", and to describe how their group recruits (or encourages) new members. Ask each guest to allow time for student questions.

Instructions: Introduce each of your panel members. Explain the purpose of the panel and encourage class members to ask questions as the discussion progresses. During the presentation, it will become clear that each member does not consider his or her religion to be a "cult" and will present conflicting definitions. They will also present interesting comparisons regarding recruitment of new members. If the discussion "lags," you may want to ask one or more of the following questions:

1. From your religious perspective or personal opinions, how would you explain the Jonestown and Waco suicides?

2. What are the most dangerous elements of cults?

3. Why are college students the primary targets of cults?

4. Do you believe that strong religious beliefs are contradictory to critical thinking?

5. What suggestions do you have for a group of young adults to decrease their chance of being victimized by cults?

Although this panel sometimes causes discomfort among highly religious students, they consistently report strong appreciation for the opportunity to hear the divergent views. Generally class members report an increased understanding of the meaning of cults and of the various religions. From a purely academic perspective, this presentation can be useful in later class discussions of conformity and obedience, and the effects of group membership.

Active Learning Activity 16.7 - Fundamental Attributional Error

Have one of your assistants arrive late to class with a projector and an old film (one that is no longer used). During the first few minutes of your lecture have the assistant start to set up the film in the back of the room. When the assistant opens the film can he should drop the film and roll it toward the front of the class. After the film has been unrolled the assistant should hurriedly try to pick up the film and leave the class, the more embarrassed the better. Ask the students to write a short paragraph on what caused this incident. After collecting the papers read several that emphasize internal factors and then lead a discussion of the fundamental attributional error.

Active Learning Activity 16.8 - I Find You Attractive

Have the students walk around campus before class and try to find and describe the characteristics of the most attractive male and female on campus. Small groups of 3-4 students works best. Have each group choose a leader and have this leader present the characteristics of the most attractive male/female. Most groups will have similar characteristics, usually physical beauty. Use this discussion as a lead-in for your lectures on attraction

Active Learning Activity 16.9 - Newsletter

For a reliable source of good teaching ideas for social psychology, we recommend subscribing to the Society for the Advancement of Social Psychology (SASP) Newsletter. The cost is very low, and forms can be obtained by writing to:

Frank Dane
Department of Psychology
Clemson University
Clemson, SC 29631

Active Learning Activity 16.10 - Aggression and the Media

Videotape about fifteen minutes of a recent evening news program, and play it for the students. Ask students to look for examples of internal as well as external factors in aggression and look for any insights as to ways to reduce aggression. Does the evening news cause an overestimation of danger? How does this affect other aspects of life?

Active Learning Activity 16.11 - Help Me

During the first few minutes of your lecture on altruism have an assistant (or student confederate) who is sitting in the front row of the class fake a serious illness (fall to the floor and moan loudly). Note the reactions of the students. In many cases there will be a classic reaction of no help being given. In other cases someone with emergency training will come to the aid of the "victim". Either way you will have a very graphic demonstration of altruism.

Active Learning Activity 16.12 - Age Discrimination

As a "safer" and less divisive way to discuss prejudice, focus on the topic of age discrimination-- a commonplace occurrence in our own lives. Distribute the following questionnaire and then form groups of five or six to discuss student responses.

Handout 16.1 - Active Learning

PERSONAL SURVEY

If you could choose any age to "return to," what age would it be? Why? Would you do anything different to change the current course of your life?

If you could choose any age to "advance to," what age would it be? Why?

What is the best and worst thing about your current age? Are you discriminated against because of your age (increased automobile insurance cost, lack of jobs, etc.)?

Describe the physical, cognitive, and psychosocial changes you expect within the next 10, 20, 30, ...years. Given our society's current level of prejudice and discrimination against the elderly, how will you deal with your own inevitable changes? What will be the best and worst part of growing older? Can you think of ways to reduce ageism?

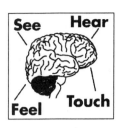

Brain-Based Learning

Brain-Based Learning Activity 16.1 - How Do I Compare?

We live in a sea of social interconnectedness that we normally accept as given and ignore.

Write a few of the major categories of social comparison on the blackboard such as attractiveness, intelligence, athletic ability, social status, and challenge the students to come up with their own suggestions of how people compare themselves.

Next ask students to pick two specific social situations one in which they feel comfortable comparing themselves to others (i.e. they are making a favorable self rating) and one in which they feel less comfortable. Give each student a few minutes to write down aspects of each of these two situations.

Ask for a few volunteers to share their two situations: What is the setting? What are they paying attention to? How long does the comparison take? How much of the interaction is based on words? Where and how did they learn the standards by which they are being judged or judging themselves? What are the feelings that result from the judgements? How do the judgements influence their own subsequent actions?

The idea here is to penetrate the illusion that we are all independent actors and for them to experience the power of social comparison as an ongoing, often background process that molds our reactions and behaviors.

Brain-Based Learning Activity 16.2 - The Power Of Social Constraints

A second way of illustrating the power of social constraints is to have your students consider the following scenario:

If you found a ring with the power to make you invisible to all human eyes (including video cameras and surveillance gear) what ten things would you do (or try out) that you wouldn't do as long as people could see you?

First, have the students write down their list of ten. It is very important to tell them that this list is for their eyes only and to be really honest in their responses. Once everyone has written their list, ask students how they would feel if someone found their list and its content became known to their family or friends? Ask them to observe their own reaction as they imagine this private information being uncovered. What are their feelings? What are their thoughts? Who are they reacting to? Then ask for a count of how many of the 10 items would they feel comfortable sharing with the class?

Without going into details, make a list of which norms or values their items would violate (For instance, sexual voyeurism, property theft, espionage, violating others privacy, violence etc.) Another way of getting this information is to have the students give you anonymous copies of their list and then sorting it for common attributes.

Once some of the major social norms are listed (private property, sexual privacy, respect for the rights of others) have students examine how the constraining power of these social standards are operating in their lives, how they are like invisible fences that most members of the group respond to.

Brain-Based Learning Activity 16.3 - Exposing the Fundamental Attribution Error

Line up six chairs one behind the next all facing forward. Ask for volunteers to come to each chair bringing a pen and an empty notepad to write on. Once the students sit down they can only see their own pad and the back of the person sitting in front of them

To the student in the first seat only you give or show a simple but multi angled design. An example would be the outline of a six-pointed star or a simple spider web or a cloverleaf freeway exchange. Don't use just a simple circle or rectangle, that would be too easy.

Be very firm with these instructions: The student must instruct the rest of the volunteers on how to move their pens so they re-create the figure s/he is viewing. The student cannot use the name of the design but may only say move the pen left, right, up, down, in a curve or a straight line.

It will usually take only a few minutes for the leader to finish their instructions. Encourage the rest of the class that has observed this demonstration to come up to look at the model and then at the various drawings made by the other volunteers. Usually most of them look quite different from the "original".

Then ask the class why the performance was so unimpressive. Many explanations will be offered. Even if you have just discussed the Fundamental Attribution Error in class, very few of the explanations will focus on the power of the situation that did not allow for: face to face contact, anyone to see each other's work; and, the leader to refer to well known drawing symbols by name.

After you point out this pattern have the students look back on their comments and consider what prevented them from noticing this "obvious" factor?

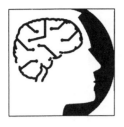

Critical Thinking

Critical Thinking Exercise 16.1 - Developing Self-Understanding: Exploring the Processes of Attitude Formation

Critical thinking requires self-understanding and an awareness that our most important attitudes are developed from specific learning experiences and the influence of important people in our lives. Critical thinkers know what their attitudes are and how and why they acquired them. Understanding one's self is the first step toward self-control and self-improvement.

To help your student's clarify their own attitudes, we offer the following exercise and Handout 16.1 - Critical Thinking.

This exercise also appears in the text, Chapter 16.   We include it here for your convenience, and you may want to discuss it in class to reinforce reading of the text.

Critical Thinking Exercise 16.2 - Fostering Independent Thinking: Would You Have Obeyed Milgram's Experimenters?

Have you always considered yourself an independent thinker? Perhaps even a bit of a nonconformist? But does the fact that 65 percent of Milgram's participants administered the maximum shock make you wonder just how well you know yourself? Experts in the field of critical thinking believe some destructive behavior results from not knowing how social forces influence behavior and from lack of practice in confronting authority figures (see Chaffee, 1992).

To encourage your own independent thinking and increase your resistance to unethical manipulation by others, we have developed the following exercise.

Handout 16.1 - Critical Thinking

ATTITUDE FORMATION

In the space next to each issue, place a number (1 to 5) that indicates your CURRENT attitude and your PAST attitude (five to ten years ago).

1 = Strongly support

2 = Mildly support

3 = Neutral

4 = Mildly oppose

5 = Strongly oppose

	CURRENT	PAST
Drinking and driving	_____	_____
Gun control	_____	_____
Abortion	_____	_____
Smoking in public places	_____	_____
Divorce	_____	_____

1. Circle the top three issues you currently feel most strongly about. Briefly state your attitudes toward each of these issues. How did these attitudes develop (classical conditioning, operant conditioning, social learning, self-perception, cognitive dissonance, etc.)? What important experiences or significant individuals influenced these attitudes? Can you identify the three components of each of your three attitudes (cognitive, affective, and behavioral)?

2. Now compare your CURRENT attitudes to those of your PAST. Which attitudes were the most subject to change? Why? On what issues were you most resistant to change? How would you explain this?

3. How might you use the persuasion principles discussed in this chapter to change another's attitude? (Consider the characteristics of the communicator, the message, and the audience.) Can you apply the same principles to changing your own attitudes?

4...Cognitive dissonance theory asserts that "changing behavior changes attitudes." Using this theory, how would you design a program to change an undesirable attitude (in yourself and others)?

Part I

Rank order the following three situations by placing a 1 next to the situation you believe is the most unacceptable form of social influence and a 3 by the least objectionable.

_____Jane is 19 and wants very much to become a commercial artist. She has been offered a scholarship to a good art school, but her parents strongly object to her choice of career. After considerable pressure, she enrolls at the same engineering school that her father attended.

_____Bill is 21 and is having serious doubts about his decision to marry Sue. After discussing his concerns with Sue, he realizes how brokenhearted she would be if he cancelled the wedding. He decides to marry her.

_____Mary is 20 and a senior in college. She desperately wants to get into a graduate program at a very prestigious school, but she is failing an important class. The instructor has made it clear that she could have an A in his course if she would sexually "cooperate." She agrees.

Part II

To overcome destructive obedience, John Sabini and Maury Silver (1993) believe that individuals should actively practice confronting authority, they should be taught about the social forces that operate on them, and they should eliminate intellectual illusions that foster nonintellectual obedience. These three suggestions can be usefully applied to the three situations you just rank ordered.

1. Mentally review the situation you ranked as most unethical and carefully rehearse how you could effectively combat a similar form of coercion. What would you say? What could you do?

2. This chapter's discussion on social influence should help to educate you about why people conform, comply, and obey, as well as how to resist such manipulation. For example, can you see how normative social influence, reference groups, and guilt induction played a role in the three situations described above? Can you use the text material to help develop an effective defense?

3. One of the most common intellectual illusions that hinders critical thinking is the belief that "only evil people do evil things" or that "evil announces itself." In Milgram's research the experimenter who ordered the subjects to continue looked and acted like a reasonable person who was simply carrying out a research project. Because he was not seen as personally corrupt and evil, the subject's normal moral "guards" were not alerted. But if we are to think critically about destructive obedience, we must avoid looking at personality and focus instead on the morality of our own and others' acts. In each of the three situations, can you identify the "evil" acts without looking at individual personalities?

Now that you have analyzed Jane, Bill, and Mary's situations, think of a current or past situation in your own life where you were unethically persuaded. Applying Sabini and Silver's three suggestions to your own situation can further develop your own autonomous thinking and help you to resist future manipulation.

Critical Thinking Exercise 16.3 - Prejudice On Our Campus

Applying Knowledge To New Situations   (A Behavioral Skill)

A critical thinker is often able to take an existing situation and apply the knowledge acquired to new or future situations. This type of analysis leads the critical thinker to interpret events or situations in new, important ways. By being a critical thinker, you will be able to apply the information learned about prejudice in Chapter 16 to future events.

To increase your own awareness of the prejudices on your college campus, ask a member of the opposite sex to be your partner in the following exercise:

Visit both the male and female bathrooms (use your opposite sex partner for the appropriate bathroom) of three separate buildings on your college campus (e.g., the art department, the business department, the psychology department). Record your observations after each question.

1. Did you notice any graffiti directed at certain minority groups?

   _____

   _____

2. Was there a difference between the male and female prejudices (as expressed by the graffiti)?

   _____

   _____

3. Did you notice a difference in "graffiti prejudice" in the three buildings?

   _____

   _____

4. What does this say about the causes of and treatment for prejudice?

   _____

   _____

Gender and Cultural Diversity

Gender and Cultural Diversity Activity 16.1 - Why Are We Attracted to Each Other?

Materials: List of determinants of attractiveness in varying cultures. You may want to use the traits found by Buss and his colleagues (Table 13.2 p. 446), or you could use differing socioeconomic levels.

Procedures: Instruct student groups to determine which characteristics of attractiveness apply to the dominant American culture. Have the groups design a "perfect" male and female who display the most desired traits. Have a representative of each group list the preferred traits on the board.

Conclusion: This activity encourages students to analyze the possibly arbitrary nature of the stereotyped values of attractiveness and desirability in the dominant American culture. This activity also invites recognition of varying standards of attractiveness in other cultures. Students may also develop a better understanding of social factors controlling perceptions of attractiveness.

Writing Project

Given the need for improved writing skills in college students, and to respond to the call for "writing across the curriculum," we offer writing projects for each chapter. For Chapter 16, we suggest a 2-3 page written response to the following questions. Recognizing the time involved in grading such writing projects, one alternative is occasionally to assign "peer grading." Collect their papers, remove student names, and give one paper to each student to grade. It helps to make their participation in peer grading part of the overall points for the writing project. This encourages a more thoughtful and responsible evaluation, as well as acknowledging and rewarding the additional work.

1. Rank order the top five characteristics you consider most important in a platonic (non-sexual) friend. Now rank order the top five characteristics for a boyfriend or girlfriend. Finally, rank order the top five characteristics you want in a serious long-term relationship (e.g., husband or wife).

2. Discuss differences between the three lists. How do your choices compare to the variables that scientists find are important--similarity, proximity, and physical attractiveness?

3. Using the three lists from Step 1, go back and identify items you consider "NON-negotiable" (you could not live without) and those you consider ""negotiable" (you want them but you COULD live without them). Briefly explain your choices.

You might want to make extra copies of this paper for your own records. Students from previous classes have found these papers make interesting keepsakes.

Circle of Quality – Chapter 16

Please give us your feedback. We thank you in advance for assisting us in improving the next edition. The contact information is listed in the preface.

What are the three most helpful teaching tools in this chapter?

1.

2.

3.

What are the three least useful teaching tools in this chapter?

1.

2.

3.

What are the three most difficult concepts to teach in this chapter?

1.

2.

3.

Additional Comments:

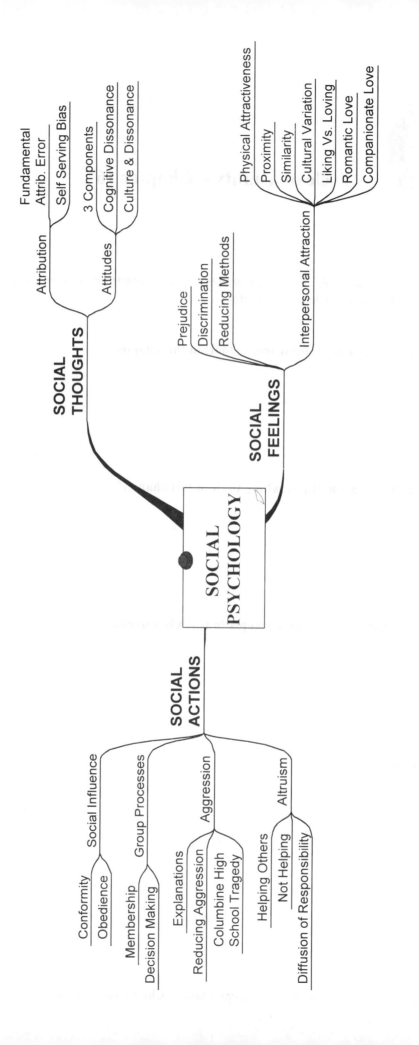

SOCIAL PSYCHOLOGY

SOCIAL THOUGHTS

Attribution
- Fundamental Attrib. Error
- Self Serving Bias

Attitudes
- 3 Components
- Cognitive Dissonance
- Culture & Dissonance

SOCIAL FEELINGS

Prejudice
Discrimination
Reducing Methods

Interpersonal Attraction
- Physical Attractiveness
- Proximity
- Similarity
- Cultural Variation
- Liking Vs. Loving
- Romantic Love
- Companionate Love

SOCIAL ACTIONS

Social Influence
- Conformity
- Obedience

Group Processes
- Membership
- Decision Making

Aggression
- Explanations
- Reducing Aggression
- Columbine High School Tragedy

Altruism
- Helping Others
- Not Helping
- Diffusion of Responsibility

CHAPTER 17
INDUSTRIAL/ORGANIZATIONAL PSYCHOLOGY

Outline

The Development of I/O Psychology

The Beginnings
Modern Times

Human Factors Psychology

The Human-Machine System
Displays
Controls

Personnel Psychology

Recruitment and Selection
Employee Training

Gender and Cultural Diversity
What Happens to Business
When Cultures Clash?

Evaluating Workers
Problems with Sexual Harassment

Organizational Psychology

Managerial Style
Worker Motivation
Job Satisfaction

Research Highlight
Job Satisfaction and Psychotherapy

Active Learning
Are You in the Right Job?

Learning Objectives

Upon completion of CHAPTER 17, the student should be able to:

1. Define industrial/organizational (I/O) psychology, and identify its three areas of focus (p. 620).
2. Summarize the historical origins of I/O psychology in the workplace, and the contributions of Scott, Taylor, and Munsterberg (p. 621).
3. Describe the importance of the following world events in the progression of I/O psychology: World War I, the General Electric Hawthorne study, World War II, and the Civil Rights movement (pp. 622-625).
4. Define human factors psychology; describe the major components of a human-machine system, and provide an example of such a system (pp. 626-628).
5. Describe how a machine "talks" to people via displays, and how people "talk" to machines via controls; explain how human senses and motor responses are related to the human-machine system (pp. 628-630).
6. Define personnel psychology, and identify its three areas of focus (p. 631).
7. Describe the process of recruitment and selection, including job analysis and the selection of a field of candidates (p. 631).
8. Differentiate between structured and unstructured interviews, and describe the kinds of information an employer wants to know. Describe the advantages of interviews to applicants and interviewers, and list the characteristics of a successful candidate (pp. 631-632).
9. Define organizational culture, and describe how an employee orientation can provide clues to this culture; differentiate between skills training, general training, and diversity training (p. 633).
10. Describe the effects of cultural clashes in business, and discuss three ways to minimize such misunderstandings (pp. 633-635).
11. Define performance evaluations, and describe how they are used and what makes them most effective; differentiate between objective and subjective evaluation measures, including the benefits and limitations of each, and the halo effect (pp. 635-637).
12. Define sexual harassment, and discuss common misconceptions about its occurrence; describe five steps an organization can take to limit legal liability for harassment, and four steps an employee (or student) can take to prevent or deal with sexual harassment (pp. 637-639).
13. Define organizational psychology, and identify its three areas of focus (p. 639).
14. Compare and contrast Theory X and Theory Y with respect to managerial styles, including a description of participative decision making and quality circles (pp. 640-641).
15. Describe three worker motivation theories: goal setting, equity, and expectancy (pp. 641-643).
16. Discuss the benefits to management and employees of worker job satisfaction; discuss the factors that contribute to job satisfaction (pp. 643-645).
17. Describe the research findings regarding job satisfaction for psychotherapists (p. 645).

Chapter Summary/Lecture Organizer

Introductory Vignette--Chapter 17 begins with a description of a driver error involving unintended acceleration at a time when braking was desired. This incident is used to introduce the work and interests of industrial/organizational psychologists.

I. **THE DEVELOPMENT OF I/O PSYCHOLOGY** - Industrial/organizational (I/O) psychology is the study of how individual behavior affects and is affected by the physical environment and the organizational structure of the workplace.

   A. The Beginnings - I/O psychology was founded at the beginning of the twentieth century. Walter Dill Scott, Fredrick W. Taylor, and Hugo Munsterberg provided the insight and the drive for applying psychology to the workplace. The personnel needs of World War I occasioned psychologists, headed by Robert Yerkes, to develop the first group IQ test, the Army Alpha.

   Between World War I and World War II many companies added human resource departments for the first time, and psychologists conducted research to determine how people behaved in the workplace. Foremost among these workplace research projects were the studies at the Western Electric Hawthorne Works. Among the important findings was a phenomenon termed the Hawthorne effect. The Hawthorne effect occurs whenever people change their behavior because of the novelty of a research situation or because they know that they are being observed.

   B. Modern Times - World War II led to the expansion of scientifically designed worker training programs to improve productivity for the war effort. It also led to the expansion of human factors psychology, as the workplace and the role of the soldier and pilot became more complicated.

   After World War II, many I/O psychologists turned their attention from the manufacturing floor to the executive management offices, thereby creating organizational psychology. The Civil Rights Act of 1964 required I/O psychology to create employment tests, training programs, and recruitment programs that were fair to all job applicants regardless of ethnicity, religion, age, or gender.

II. **HUMAN FACTORS PSYCHOLOGY** - Human factors psychology is a branch of I/O psychology that studies ways to improve the design and function of machines and the work environment to better meet the needs of human users.

   A. The Human-Machine System - Researchers consider humans and the machines they use as a human-machine system. A human-machine system is an arrangement of people and machines, tools, and other devices that produce a product or service.

B. Displays - As the machine part of the human-machine system, devices such as gauges and video monitors (referred to as displays) form the machine output.

C. Controls - Controls (such as wheels, levers, knobs, and pedals) function as input for the machine from the human in the human-machine system.

III. **PERSONNEL PSYCHOLOGY**

A. Recruitment and Selection - Personnel recruitment and selection begins with a job analysis, followed by selection of the best candidate. Of all the possible selection methods, interviews remain the most popular. Structured interviews are better predictors of future job performance that unstructured interviews. The three best ways to prepare for an interview are research, role playing, and emphasis on desirable personality traits.

B. Employee Training - Employee training typically begins with an orientation program. One of the major unstated goals of orientation is the transmission of organizational culture--the group's shared pattern of thought and action. Training thereafter can focus on developing or improving specific, technical skills and interpersonal skills, including diversity training.

> **Gender and Cultural Diversity** - Using examples from real-life cases, students are exposed to possible culture clashes and their effect on business transactions.

C. Evaluation of Workers - Performance evaluation is the formal procedure an organization uses to assess the job performance of employees. Evaluations can be objective (such as the number of sales) or subjective (such as a supervisor's rating). The subjective method is the most popular, but the halo effect (the tendency to rate individuals too high or too low based on one outstanding trait) can create a major problem. To overcome the halo effect, some organizations use multiple evaluations from supervisors, peers, subordinates, and even customers. Special rating scales are also used by many organizations as a means of obtaining more objective information.

D. Problems with Sexual Harassment - Sexual harassment involves sexual advances, requests for sexual favors, and other unwelcome verbal or physical conduct of a sexual nature. Most sexual harassment is an assertion or abuse of power, not an expression of sexual desire. Victims of sexual harassment often suffer financial losses and psychological difficulties. There are several steps that employers can take to reduce sexual harassment, and there are tips to help the victim.

IV. **ORGANIZATIONAL PSYCHOLOGY** - Organization psychologists are interested in how interpersonal relations affect productivity.

A. Managerial Style - Studies of managerial styles show that Theory X managers take a basically negative approach to employees, believing they need close supervision and extrinsic rewards for motivation. Theory Y managers are basically positive and believe employees are self-motivated. Theory Y managers often use participative decision making, involving employees in the decisions they will be responsible for implementing. Quality circles, involving regular meetings of supervisors and employees, are a form of participative decision making.

B. Worker Motivation - Goal-setting is one of three major forms of worker motivation. Research shows that setting specific and difficult goals improves performance. Equity theory, the second major form of worker motivation, suggests that workers strive for balance between their input and outcomes in the work setting. Expectancy theory, on the other hand, maintains that employees are motivated to work according to their expectancy of outcomes, the desirability of those outcomes, and the effort needed to achieve them.

C. Job Satisfaction - Job satisfaction is important to both employer and employee. Employers gain because they save money (lower absenteeism and fewer resignations) and increase productivity. Employees gain because they are under less stress, enjoy better physical health, and have an improved overall quality and length of life. According to personality-fit theory, job satisfaction results from a match between personality and occupation.

> **Active Learning** - After taking a short quiz, students discover whether their current job is "right" for them. Supportive colleagues, supportive working conditions, mentally challenging work, and equitable rewards are discussed as important factors in finding the right job.

Teaching Resources

SECTION I - THE DEVELOPMENT OF I/O PSYCHOLOGY

Learning Objectives #'s 1 - 3
Lecture Extender # 17.1
Discussion Questions # 1
Active Learning Activities #'s 17.1 & 17.2

SECTION II - HUMAN FACTORS PSYCHOLOGY

Learning Objectives #'s 4 & 5
Lecture Extender # 17.1
Discussion Questions #'s 1 & 2
Active Learning Activities #'s 17.1 & 17.2
Brain-Based Learning #"s 17.1 & 17.3

SECTION III - PERSONNEL PSYCHOLOGY

Learning Objectives #'s 6 - 12
Lecture Lead Ins #'s 1 - 3
Lecture Extender # 17.1
Discussion Questions #'s 1 & 5
Active Learning Activities #'s 17.1, 17.2 & 17.4
Brain-Based Learning #' 17.2
Critical Thinking Exercise #'s 17.1 & 17.2
Gender and Cultural Diversity Activity # 17.1
Writing Project # 17.1

SECTION IV - ORGANIZATIONAL PSYCHOLOGY

Learning Objectives #'s 13 - 17
Lecture Lead Ins #'s 1 & 3
Lecture Extender # 17.1
Discussion Questions #'s 1, 3 & 4
Active Learning Activities #'s 17.1 - 17.4
Critical Thinking Exercise # 17.1
Gender and Cultural Diversity Activity # 17.1
Writing Project # 17.1

Lecture Lead-Ins

1. Jobs predominantly held by women are paid less than jobs predominantly held by men. Ask students why an organization would be motivated to change this situation since it would negatively affect profits. If this disparity were suddenly eliminated, what effects would this have on our nation's productivity? Use student responses as a lead-in.

2. Ask students if they (or a friend) has suffered from sexual harassment on the job or as a student. What happened? What should organizations do to minimize sexual harassment and to protect their students and employees? Is this problem getting worse, or is it just getting more media attention? Use student responses as a lead-in to the topic.

3. The use of autonomous work groups increases job satisfaction, does not hurt productivity, and allows organizations to use fewer employees because these groups take over supervisory jobs previously belonging to others. Ask students why most organizations continue using traditional structures? If the business did switch to autonomous work groups, should they return some of the cost savings to the work groups to compensate them for their additional responsibilities? Use their responses as lead-ins to the chapter topics.

Lecture Extenders

17.1 - At the beginning of the 20th century, less than two percent of high school graduates in the United States went on to college, while in the 1990's approximately 60 percent go on. College for our grandparents (and great-grandparents) was an elitist experience reserved for children of the upper class, while today, in much of the world, higher education has become a product for the masses.

Ironically, higher educational institutions now serve a dramatically different group of students, yet the structure and basic curricula have not changed much since the turn of the century. Why, in times when almost every business firm is having to completely overhaul its traditional practices to survive, do most colleges and universities continue to operate as they always have? The typical undergraduate experience--four years of course work, broken down into 8 or 12 terms, with students taking 3 to 6 courses per term, taught mostly by instructors who lecture to their class--may not be the most efficient or effective way to educate today's diverse student body. Critics have challenged the notion that knowledge should be compartmentalized into narrow departmental specialties or broken into three-unit segments. They also question the continued reliance on the lecture method. While this technique might have been appropriate a century ago, today's students have ready access to libraries and on-line databases--a much more direct means for transferring information. From a business angle, critics also challenge the practice of building large, expensive campuses with dormitories and other facilities for resident students when, in fact, most students commute. Why should taxpayers subsidize an increasingly expensive, unresponsive system?

What would a college or university be like if it were reengineered using current, business models? National University in San Diego breaks its curriculum into monthly courses that are offered all-year round and taught almost entirely by working practitioners rather than full-time faculty. Other colleges are experimenting with team-teaching classes with faculty linking courses from diverse disciplines. Critics suggest these changes are minor. True progress requires starting from scratch, creating an entire new structure and method for educating today's student.

Source: Robbins, S. (1996). Reengineering the college experience. <u>Organizational behavior</u> (627-628). Englewood Cliffs, NJ: Prentice Hall.

Key Terms

THE DEVELOPMENT OF I/O PSYCHOLOGY

Hawthorne Effect (p. 623)
Industrial/Organizational (I/O) Psychology
 (p. 620)

HUMAN FACTORS PSYCHOLOGY

Controls (p. 626)
Displays (p. 626)
Human Factors Psychology (626)
Human-Machine System (626)

PERSONNEL PSYCHOLOGY

Halo Effect (p. 636)

Job Analysis (p. 631)
Organizational Culture (p. 633)
Performance Evaluation (p. 635)
Personnel Psychology (p. 631)
Sexual Harassment (p. 637)

ORGANIZATIONAL PSYCHOLOGY

Equity Theory (p. 642)
Expectancy Theory (p. 642)
Goal-setting Theory (p. 641)
Organizational Psychology (p. 639)
Participative Decision Making (p. 640)
Personality-Job Fit Theory (p. 644)
Quality Circles (p. 640)
Theory X (p. 640)
Theory Y (p. 640)

Discussion Questions

1. I/O psychologists are frequently employed by business and industry to do research that solves problems or increases efficiency. Management generally expects all relevant employees to participate. Should employees have the right to refuse? What if an I/O psychologist finds ways to increase productivity but at the expense of increased hazard to workers (e.g., repetitive motion injuries)? What are the ethical implications for the psychologist? How might he or she avoid these ethical problems? What new problems might be created?

2. What do you like or dislike about the way the controls are set up in most automobiles? Do you prefer analog or digital speedometers? The addition of high-mounted brake lights had dramatically decreased accidents. Can you think of other useful changes? For example, can you design something that would encourage more drivers to use their turn signals when making a turn?

3. If a job evaluation reveals that people in Job X ought to be paid $30,000 per year, but a salary survey reveals that other companies pay such employees $40,000, what are the advantages and disadvantages of paying your employee $30,000? $40,000?

4. Many people believe it is inappropriate to use rewards to regulate behavior (which is the essence of operant conditioning--Chapter 5 of the text). Do you agree with this criticism? Why or why not? Parents and teachers control behavior through rewards and punishments, why would it be inappropriate to use these same methods in the workplace?

5. What is the distinction between flirting and sexual harassment? Should faculty or employers be allowed to date their students or employees? Why or why not? If an accusation of sexual harassment is raised in the workplace, how should management respond? If an employee is found guilty, what penalty should he or she suffer?

 **Web Sites**

I/O Do it Yourself Exercise
Bad Human Factors Designs
> http://www.baddesigns.com/
> This page has nearly 20 examples of bad human factors designs, from airports
> to can openers. You can view photographs of good and bad designs with
> explanations of why some are bad and why some are good designs. See if you can
> figure out why some of the designs are good or bad.

Organizations
Human Factors and Ergonomics Society
> http://hfes.org/
> The Human Factors and Ergonomics Society is the largest human factors
> organization in the United States. You can access the tables of contents of
> its several journals from this page.

The Society for Industrial Organizational Psychology
> http://siop.org/
> Internet resources, journals, and other information about I/O psychology.

I/O Sites with Extensive WWW Links
ErgoWeb
> http://www.ergoweb.com/Pub/ewhome.shtml
> ErgoWeb offers lots of useful ergonomics information.

UConn Industrial/Organizational Psychology Links
> http://gopher.uconn.edu/~wwwiopsy/links.html
> Links to several I/O related sites.

Internet Survival Guide of Industrial/Organizational Psychology
> http://allserv.rug.ac.be/~flievens/guide.htm
> Many links to Internet sites that are valuable to those interested in I/O
> psychology.

Bureau of Labor Statistics

The Bureau of Labor Statistics Home Page

http://stats.bls.gov/blshome.htm

The Bureau of Labor Statistics, an agency within the U. S. Department of Labor, has lots of information on jobs and the economy.

Occupational Outlook Handbook: BLS

http://stats.bls.gov/ocohome.htm

The Occupational Outlook Handbook contains information on the outlook for jobs in all sectors in the American labor market. It also includes future trends, career information, and suggestions on how to find a job and how to evaluate a job offer.

Suggested Films and Videos

American Workers Trying to Survive in the '90s

Nightline (September 6, 1993). About 50 minutes. This video describes how American workers see themselves as overworked, underpaid, and underappreciated by modern employers. Pressures for higher productivity and threats of massive layoffs--on a magnitude not seen since the Great Depression of the 1930's--increase worker stress. Employers replace laid off workers with part-time workers, and those who survive layoffs must work longer hours and for less pay. The new workplace is highly threatening and undermines employee loyalty.

The Fairer Sex

Prime Time (October 7, 1993). About 50 minutes. This program follows two ABC employees (Julie and Chris) as they attempt to purchase a new car, get a comparable set of clothes dry cleaned, obtain a tee time for golf, and apply for a managerial position. In each case, Julie (the woman) suffers great discrimination and stereotyping. Provides a good lead-in for discussions of what senior management can do to eliminate sexism in the workplace.

Their Excellencies

Prime Time (September 16, 1993). About 50 minutes. Describes outlandish perks enjoyed by public officials, including lavish vacations, expensive housing, and large personal staff-- all at taxpayers expense. This video could be helpful in explaining how non-financial rewards affect expectancy, equity, and goal-setting theories of motivation.

Employers Spying on Employees

World News Tonight (March 28, 1994). About 15 minutes. When discussing organizational culture or managerial styles, this video would spark great class participation. Secret videotaping of employees at Kmart and Sheraton Hotels brings into question the line between corporate control and personal freedom. One government estimate indicates over 6 million American workers are spied on each year. Management argues that videotaping protects assets and helps monitor premises for illegal activities.

Assembly Line Teams are Better Trained and More Efficient

World News Tonight (February, 24, 1993). About 15 minutes. This video provides a nice example of self-managed teams and their effect on production. Square D, a manufacturer of electrical equipment in Lexington, Kentucky, converted from a system where workers did narrow, specialized tasks and never saw the finished product to small self-managed teams. These "little factories within a factory" greatly improved quality, speed in filling orders, and overall productivity.

Negotiation and Persuasion

Insight Media, 1989. 30 minutes. This program demonstrates techniques used to influence attitudes and behaviors, focusing on such elements of nonverbal communication as body language, facial expression, and touch. It discusses persuasive techniques, including ingratiation, supplication, intimidation, foot-in-the-door techniques, door-in-the-face techniques, and the that's-not-all technique.

Group Decision Making and Leadership

Insight Media, 1989. 30 minutes. This video shows strategies for effective group work in a variety of situations, providing suggestions for boosting group efficiency and productivity. It explores interpersonal relationships among group decisions makers and discusses the functions of leadership.

Optimizing Intelligences: Thinking, Emotion, and Creativity

National Professional Resources, 1996. 45 minutes. This video presents alternative conceptions of intelligence that challenge the traditional views stemming from I.Q. and learning theory research. These perspectives include Gardner's multiple intelligences, Goleman's emotional intelligence, and the Montessori system of instruction. Implications for schools, mental health facilities, and work environments are also explored.

The Impaired Employee

The Haight-Ashbury Training Tapes, 1992. 57 minutes. Part 1 of Volume III: "Drugs in the Workplace" series, this video presents information on methods of supervisor intervention in cases of employee drug and alcohol abuse. Details are provided on identification and documentation of problems, action to be taken, referral services, and long term follow-up.

Books for Success

Norman, Donald (1988). **The Psychology of Everyday Things.** Harper Collins.
Perhaps the best introduction to human factors engineering or industrial psychology ever. Very accessible to the layperson it is extremely informative with many examples of badly designed "everyday things" and how they could be, no should be, improved.

Norman, Donald (1994). **Things That make Us smart : Defending Human Attributes in the Age of the Machine.** Perseus Press.
Describes how technology can enhance human intelligence, if it is well designed, or constrict it, if it is improperly designed. The book persuasively argues that technology should be designed to fit human beings not force human beings to conform to a mis-design. A book with many examples and a good sense of humor.

Covey, Stephen (1992). **Principle Centered Leadership.** Fireside.
One of the best books on how to create organizations that encourage human beings to activate all of their potential in a culture built on trust, trustworthiness and contribution to mission. A new paradigm of leadership based on character, competence and principles encompasses a tremendously thought out approach on how to build organizational cultures that maximize job satisfaction and the fulfillment of stakeholder needs. A brilliant book!

Active Learning

Active Learning Activity 17.1 - Guest Speakers

If you are at a university or college with a graduate program in industrial psychology invite a faculty member or graduate student to class to speak about the current state of the field. You might consider inviting a combination of several faculty and students to create a panel. Try to get as wide a variety of backgrounds and interests as possible to reflect the diversity in the field.

Active Learning Activity 17.2 - Community Business Leaders

A second type of panel is to invite a group of community business leaders. Look for people from several areas of interest and specialization. Have students prepare questions ahead of time so that the class time will be spent in a productive manner. Encourage students to ask questions related to the chapter (e.g., "What managerial style do you practice--Theory X or Theory Y?" "What do you think are the most important factors in job satisfaction for your employees?")

Active Learning Activity 17.3 - Conflict in the Workplace

David Johnson and Frank Johnson described five ways in which people generally manage conflicts (turtles, sharks, teddy bears, foxes, and owls). Pass around copies of Handout 17.3(A) and ask each student to identify which style most closely matches their own. Pass out copies of Handout 17.3(B) and ask students to respond individually or in groups. Follow up with discussions and tie-ins to chapter material on managerial styles and employee relations.

Active Learning Activity 17.4 - Testing Your International-Culture IQ

Make photocopies of Handout 17.4.

Answers: 1. b, 2. a, 3. d, 4. b, 5. b

Scores of 4 or more indicate a high level of cultural awareness. Scores of 2 or less suggest need for improvement.

Handout 17.3(A) – Active Learning

How Do You Handle Conflict?

1. *Turtles withdraw into their shells to avoid conflicts.* They give up personal goals and relationships and avoid controversy. Turtles believe it is hopeless to try to resolve conflicts. They feel helpless. They believe it is easier to withdraw (physically and psychologically) from a conflict than to face it.

2. *Sharks try to overpower opponents.* Their goals are highly important to them, and relationships are of minor importance. They seek to achieve their goals at all costs and are not concerned with the needs of others. Sharks assume that conflicts are settled by one person winning and overpowering, overwhelming, and intimidating others.

3. *Teddy bears seek to maintain harmony.* To teddy bears the relationship is of great importance while their own goals are of little consequence. Teddy bears want to be accepted and liked by others. They think that conflict should be avoided in favor of harmony and that people cannot discuss conflicts without damaging relationships. Teddy bears try to smooth over the conflict out of fear of harming the relationship.

4. *Foxes seek compromise.* They are moderately concerned with their own goals and their relationships with others. Foxes give up parts of their goals and persuade the other person toward a solution where both sides gain and lose something--the middle ground between two extreme positions.

5. *Owls seek solutions.* They view conflicts as problems to be solved and seek a solution that achieves both their own goals and the goals of the other person. Owls see conflict as a way to improve relationships by reducing tension between two persons. Owls are not satisfied until a solution is found that achieves their own goals and the other person's goals.

Handout 17.3(B) – Active Learning

Workplace Conflicts

Below are some examples of conflicts-in-action. Can you label the style being used by the person in each example?

1. Ricardo has an appointment with his dentist that accommodates his vacation plans but conflicts with an important assignment from his boss. Ricardo resolves his conflict by cancelling his vacation plans and rescheduling his dental appointment.

   _____

2. Veronica asks her coworker Katie for a small loan until payday at which time repayment will be made. Although Katie is short of funds herself and will probably have to skip buying the new party dress she has been considering, she decides to loan Veronica the money in exchange for borrowing one of her dresses.

   _____

3. Sally is a young executive in a construction company. Since being employed by this business, she has always felt that Bill, one of her managers, was undermining her power and decisions. In fact, she was certain that Bill wanted her job and would do anything to get it. With such an unworkable situation , she decides to fire Bill.

   _____

Handout 17.4 – Active Learning

Testing Your International Culture IQ

1. **In Japan it is important to**

a. Present your business card only after you have developed a relationship with your Japanese host.
b. Present your business card with both hands.
c. Put your company name on the card, but never your position or title.
d. all of the above
e. none of the above

2. **For an American businessperson, touching a foreign businessperson would be least acceptable in which one of the following countries?**

a. Japan
b. Italy
c. Slovenia
d. Venezuela
e. France

3. **Which would be an appropriate gift?**

a. A clock in China
b. A bottle of liquor in Egypt
c. A set of knives in Argentina
d. A banquet in China
e. None of the above

4. **On first meeting your prospective Korean business partner, Lo Kim Chee, it would be best to address him as:**

a. Mr. Kim
b. Mr. Lo
c. Mr. Chee
d. Bud
e. Any of the above

5. **Traditional western banking is difficult in which of the following countries because their law forbids both the giving and taking of interest payments?**

a. Brazil
b. Saudi Arabia
c. Mongolia
d. India
e. Greece

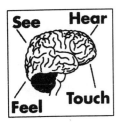

Brain-Based Learning

Brain-Based Learning Activity 17.1 - Designing A Better Classroom

To apply the concepts of this chapter to a situation they are quite familiar with ask the students:
What was the worst classroom you have ever been in?
What was the best classroom you have ever been in?

Divide the class into groups of 4-5 and have each group design their ideal classroom as far as lighting, furniture, technology, sound, temperature regulation, handicapped access, ease of maintenance etc. are concerned. . Be sure to tell them that they must include realistic financial constraints or you will wind up with the specs for the Taj Mahal.

See which group can present the best scenario.

This can be a short group exercise or it can be an elaborate term project. For instance to make it even more realistic the students could present the winning proposal to the campus facility planner and get their reaction to the proposal. The group could talk to a sample of students, or review research summaries from user surveys.

Brain-Based Learning Activity 17.2 - Rating the Job Interview

Ask the students:
What is the worst job interview you ever endured?
What is the best job interview you took part in?

Divide the class into groups of 4-5 and have each group design an ideal job interview situation (If they feel different types of interviews are needed for different types of positions have them pick one type of job category and create a favorable interview design. Be sure to point out that the interview structure they suggest must be appropriate not only for the applicant but also for the employer.

Have each group present their scenario and discuss which features are best. Again, such a proposal could be presented to the campus human resource professional for their feedback and comments.

Brain-Based Learning Activity 17.3 - Human Factors Engineering In <u>Your</u> Life

What man-made object in <u>your</u> life causes you the most hassles?
Which man-made object in <u>your</u> life causes you the most satisfaction?

Each student writes down for him/herself what aspects of the product make the one so easy to deal with and the other so frustrating. You may want to exclude computers (especially software) from this discussion to keep the discussion simple. Examples of man-made objects include common household items, their homes or cars, a school or library, furniture, tools, clothing etc.)

If several of the students complain about the same frustrating object challenge the class how they would improve the design.

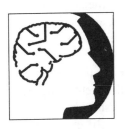

Critical Thinking

Critical Thinking Exercise 17.1 - Empathy: Appreciating Another's Thoughts, Feelings and Behaviors

Empathy is an important asset in all our interpersonal relationships, business endeavors, and as a basic foundation for critical thinking. Being an empathic person means really listening to what another person is saying while fully engaging one's critical thinking faculties. The following exercise demonstrates the need for empathy and good communication skills, and will serve as an effective introduction to major terms and concepts associated with industrial/organizational psychology.

Time: Approximately 20 minutes.

Advance preparation: You will need 7 small lunch bags and an assortment of flat wooden blocks cut into various geometric shapes. Each shape is of a different color. These forms are readily available at educational supply stores. (They are used by many elementary school teachers to teach math and number concepts.) In each bag, place 4 squares, 5 triangles, 6 circles, 4 rectangles, 4 parallelograms, 3 hexagons, and 3 octagons. Divide the assortment of blocks evenly between the 7 bags.

Instructions: Ask for 7 volunteers and arrange 7 student desks in a row ("train style") at the front of the classroom. Each student should be looking at the back of the student in front of him or her. Ask the rest of the class to stand so they can see the desk of each student volunteer. Appoint the first student in the line of desks as the "boss" and the other six students as "employees." Distribute the bags of blocks and have students open the bags onto their desk tops. Ask the boss to build something with his or her blocks and encourage the other volunteers to follow along as closely as possible. Remind the leader to use his or her best communication skills, but not to mention the color of the blocks. Remind the other volunteers to use their best listening skills and to carefully follow directions.

As the building begins, encourage the rest of the class to crowd around the line of desks and watch the progress. Restrict onlookers from adding comments or giving suggestions. When the "boss" completes his or her project, have all volunteers stand up and carefully move away from their desks. This exercise never fails to elicit a great deal of laughter. In spite of careful instructions by the leader on a very simple task, the volunteers find the verbal instructions extremely hard to understand and follow. They always create a wide arrangement of blocks.

Collect the bags of blocks and have all students return to their original chairs. Ask the six volunteer "employees" to explain why their block pattern didn't match that of the "boss." These students will talk about the fact that they couldn't see what the boss was doing, they couldn't see his or her face, and they couldn't ask questions. (Although you did NOT restrict them from asking question, they almost never ask. Even when they do ask, the leader typically repeats the same or similar instructions and the errors continue.) After you have listed their problems on the board, discuss how each of these issues are important reminders of the essentials of good communication: paying close attention to the speaker and audience, careful monitoring of body language and facial expressions, asking questions, and performing perception checks ("Am I hearing you correctly?" "Am I doing this right?" "Did you mean...?").

Ask everyone to describe what happened with these "communication blocks" and to relate this exercise to similar problems in the workplace. Students often mention how things often look different from the boss's viewpoint versus that of the workers, how hard it is to be in the position of leadership or a follower, and general managerial problems. Students who did not actively participate in the exercise generally have numerous suggestions for the volunteers, which they think would have improved the situation. If you have time it is useful to repeat the exercise with a new set of volunteers. The same thing will happen again, and it provides further proof of the difficulties in good communication and the need for empathy for both employees and employers.

This exercise also appears in the text, Chapter 17. We include it here for your convenience, and you may want to discuss it in class to reinforce reading of the text.

Critical Thinking Exercise 17.2 - Are You in the Right Job?

Like many students, you may be working part-time or full-time while attending college. Our students generally complain that their jobs are unfulfilling and pay poorly. At the same time, they feel overwhelmed by the idea of finding a job that they might want to do for the rest of their lives. With a seemingly unlimited number of career choices, they often wish someone would wave a magic wand and set them down the path to the job that's just right for them.

An important component of critical thinking is the ability to *define problems accurately.* By carefully identifying the nature of the problem in clear and concrete terms, critical thinkers prevent confusion and lay the foundation for gathering relevant information. Therefore, in solving the problem of career choice, the critical first step is to identify what you like and don't like about your current (and past) jobs. What you are actually doing is identifying the factors you find most important for job satisfaction. With this information in hand, you are prepared to research jobs that will suit your interests, needs, and abilities.

Answer "Yes" or "No" to these questions:

1. Is there a sufficient amount of laughter and sociability in your workplace?

2. Does your boss notice and appreciate your work?

3. Is your boss understanding and friendly?

4. Are you embarrassed by the physical conditions of your workplace?

5. Do you feel safe and comfortable in your place of work?

6. Do you like the location of your job?

7. If you won the lottery and were guaranteed a lifetime income, would you feel truly sad if you also had to quit your job?

8. Do you watch the clock, daydream, take long lunches, and leave work as soon as possible?

9. Do you frequently feel stressed and overwhelmed by the demands of your job?
10. Compared to others with your qualifications, are you being paid what you are worth?

11. Are promotions made in a fair and just manner?

12. Given the demands of your job, are you fairly compensated for your work?

Now score your answers. Give yourself one point for each answer that matches the following: 1. No; 2. No; 3. No; 4. Yes; 5. No; 6. No; 7. No; 8. Yes; 9. Yes; 10. No; 11. No; 12. No.

The questions you just answered are based on four factors that research shows are conducive to job satisfaction: supportive colleagues, supportive working conditions, mentally challenging work, and equitable rewards (Robbins, 1996). Your total score reveals your overall level of dissatisfaction, while a look at specific questions can help identify which of these four factors is most important to your job satisfaction--and most lacking in your current job.

Supportive Colleagues (Items 1, 2, 3). For most employees, work fills important social needs. Therefore, having friendly and supportive colleagues and superiors leads to increased satisfaction.

Supportive Working Conditions (Items 4, 5, 6). Not surprisingly, studies find that most employees prefer working in safe, clean, and relatively modern facilities. They also prefer jobs that are close to home.

Mentally Challenging Work (Items 7, 8, 9). Jobs that have too little challenge create boredom and apathy, while too much challenge creates frustration and feelings of failure.

Equitable Rewards (Items 10, 11, 12). Employees want pay and promotions that are based on job demands, individual skill levels, and community pay standards.

This exercise also appears in the Student Study Guide for Chapter 17. We include it here for your convenience, and you may want to discuss it in class to reinforce use of the Student Study Guide.

Critical Thinking Exercise 17.3 - <u>Applying</u> <u>Knowledge</u> <u>To</u> <u>New</u> <u>Situations</u> (A Behavioral Skill)

A critical thinker is often able to take an existing situation and apply the knowledge acquired to new or future situations. This type of analysis leads the critical thinker to interpret events or situations in new, important ways. By being a critical thinker, you will be able to apply the information learned about prejudice in Chapter 16 to future events.

To increase your own awareness of the prejudices on your college campus, ask a member of the opposite sex to be your partner in the following exercise:

Visit both the male and female bathrooms (use your opposite sex partner for the appropriate bathroom) of three separate buildings on your college campus (e.g., the art department, the business department, the psychology department). Record your observations after each question.

1. Did you notice any graffiti directed at certain minority groups?

_____

_____

2. Was there a difference between the male and female prejudices (as expressed by the graffiti)?

_____

_____

3. Did you notice a difference in "graffiti prejudice" in the three buildings?

_____

_____

4. What does this say about the causes of and treatment for prejudice?

_____

Gender and Cultural Diversity

Gender and Cultural Diversity Activity 17.1 - Communication Problems

The following exercise is extremely effective when you discuss organizational culture, cultural differences, communication difficulties, and so on. Make photocopies of the following "partner instructions" (Handout 17.1 - Gender and Cultural Diversity), and cut each page in half. At the beginning of class, divide students into pairs and let each pair decide who is Partner A or Partner B. Pass around the half-sheets to the appropriate partners, while reminding each to keep his/her sheet private. Allow partners to interact for approximately 5 to 10 minutes. Before you discuss the different instructions given to each partner, ask Partner A's how they felt during the interaction, and write their comments on one-half of the blackboard. On the other half of the blackboard, add Partner B's responses to the same question. Use differences between the lists to discuss gender and cultural differences and common problems in communication.

If the class is very large, the exercise could be modified to include a group of observers who would simply watch the exchange of partners A and B. These observers should take notes to help remember what happened.

Handout 17.1 - Gender and Cultural Diversity

Partner A and Partner B Communication

---CUT HERE--

PARTNER A

Important instructions:

1. Make your partner feel "at home." Achieve eye contact, smile, nod and stay physically close to your partner. (You may touch him/her if he/she seems to feel comfortable with it.)

2. Create an atmosphere of warmth and trust. You may need to talk about yourself as a way of encouraging your partner to open up about himself/herself. Be friendly. Get to know your partner.

3. Your goal is to find out as much as you can about your partner. What are his/her interests, abilities, talents, problems? What about his/her family, etc.? FIND OUT ALL YOU CAN.

---(CUT HERE)--

PARTNER B

Important instructions:

1. Your partner is an authority figure. Be SURE that your behavior towards your partner is respectful. Do NOT insult your partner, or act as if you are friends or equals.

2. In your culture, the way to act respectful is to:
   a. Answer questions politely.
   b. Avoid eye contact. (It is rude to look directly into an authority figure's eyes. Look down!
   c. Maintain an appropriate distance. Be sure not to move in too close to him/her.
   d. If you are insulted, don't get angry.
   e. Avoid asking "nosy" personal questions.

3. Your goal is to show respect to the authority figure, and to get through this interview without acting insulted. It is very important to KEEP YOUR PRIVATE AFFAIRS TO YOURSELF! (Private information may be used against you in the future.)

Writing Project

Writing Project 17.1

Given the need for improved writing skills in college students, and to respond to the call for "writing across the curriculum," we offer writing projects for each chapter. In Chapter 17, we suggest a 2-3 page written response to one of the issues found on Handout 17.1 - Writing Project. Recognizing the time involved in grading such writing projects, one alternative is occasionally to assign "peer grading." Collect their papers, remove student names, and give one paper to each student to grade. It helps to make their participation in peer grading part of the overall points for the writing project. This encourages a more thoughtful and responsible evaluation, as well as acknowledging and rewarding the additional work.

Handout 17.1 – Writing Project

Choose one of the following articles, find the original, read it carefully, and write a brief 2-3 page summary and response.

Article 1

Schwartz, F. N. (January/February 1989). *Management women and the new facts of life*. Harvard Business Review, 65-677.

Schwartz advocates two career tracks for working women--the "career-primary" track where women are treated like male employees, and the "career and family" track (since referred to as the "Mommy Track") in which there would be more flexibility and a slower career progression.

In your paper discuss implications from Schwartz's article regarding (1) the parenting role of men, (2) the supposed "deviance" of women who attempt to integrate career and family, and (3) how this type of thinking may be related to the under-representation of women in positions of power.

Article 2

Lips, H. M. (1991). Women, men and power. Mountain View, CA: Mayfield.

According to Lips (1991), women are stereotyped as:

1. *Less competent* Women are less likely to be given opportunities to demonstrate their competence and when they do succeed, their success is likely to be attributed to luck, effort, or other non-ability factors.

2. *Inadequate as leaders* Women are placed in a double bind where they are rejected as leaders if they display traditionally feminine behaviors, and condemned as unfeminine if they comply to the male criteria for leaders.

3. *Weak and frail* This stereotype has been used to bar women from a variety of positions; in some cases (e.g., the military) these barred positions are key to advancement. Reproductive safety laws are a controversial topic for discussion. Do these laws protect women, or (since evidence increasingly suggests reproductive hazards exist for males as well) are they an aid to discrimination?

In your paper discuss how these stereotypes affect women in the general workplace, as well as how they affect women as employees and employers.

Circle of Quality – Chapter 17

Please give us your feedback. We thank you in advance for assisting us in improving the next edition. The contact information is listed in the preface.

What are the three most helpful teaching tools in this chapter?

1.

2.

3.

What are the three least useful teaching tools in this chapter?

1.

2.

3.

What are the three most difficult concepts to teach in this chapter?

1.

2.

3.

Additional Comments:

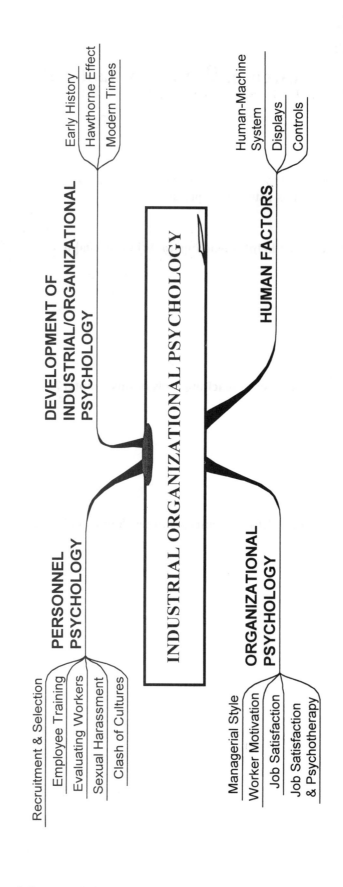

INDUSTRIAL ORGANIZATIONAL PSYCHOLOGY

DEVELOPMENT OF INDUSTRIAL/ORGANIZATIONAL PSYCHOLOGY
- Early History
- Hawthorne Effect
- Modern Times

HUMAN FACTORS
- Human-Machine System
  - Displays
  - Controls

PERSONNEL PSYCHOLOGY
- Recruitment & Selection
- Employee Training
- Evaluating Workers
- Sexual Harassment
- Clash of Cultures

ORGANIZATIONAL PSYCHOLOGY
- Managerial Style
- Worker Motivation
- Job Satisfaction
- Job Satisfaction & Psychotherapy

TEACHER RESOURCES

FILMS AND VIDEO SOURCES

ABC-TV--American Broadcasting Co. 1330 Avenue of the Americas New York, NY 10019

Access Network 295 Midpark Way SE Calgary, Alberta, CANADA T2X 2AS

Aims Media, Inc. 6901 Woodley Ave. Van Nuys, CA 91406

Ambrose Video Publishing Exclusive Distributors of Time Life Video 381 Park Ave. S. Suite 1601 New York, NY 10016

American Association for Counseling and Development 5999 Stevenson Ave. Alexandria, VA 22304

Barr Films 12801 Schabarum Ave. P.O. Box 7878 Irwindale, CA 91107

Carousel Films 260 Fifth Ave. Room 705 New York, NY 10001

Cinema Guild 1697 Broadway New York, NY 10019

Cinema 16 Film Library 196 W. Houston St. New York, NY 10014

Coast District Telecourses 11460 Warner Ave. Fountain Valley, CA 92708

Coronet Films and Video 108 Wilmot Rd. Deerfield, IL 60015

CRM McGraw-Hill P. O. Box 641 Del Mar, CA 92014-9988

CTV Television Network Ltd. 42 Charles St. East Toronto, Ontario, CANADA M4Y 1T4

Educational Dimensions Group P.O. Box 126 Stamford, CT 06904

Encyclopedia Britannica Educational Corp. 310 So. Michigan Ave. Chicago, IL 60604

Extension Media Center University of California 2176 Shattuck Ave. Berkeley, CA 94704

Federal Mogul Service P.O. Box 1966 Detroit, MI 48235

Filmakers Library, Inc. 124 E. 40th St. New York, NY 10016

Films for the Humanities P.O. Box 2053 Princeton, NJ 08540-2053

Films Incorporated 5547 N. Ravenswood Chicago, IL 60640-1199

Harcourt Brace Jovanovich, Inc. 1250 Sixth Ave. San Diego, CA 92101

HarperCollins 10 E. 53rd St. New York, NY 10022

Houghton Mifflin Co. One Beacon St. Boston, MA 02108

Indiana University Media and Teaching Resources Center Bloomington, IN 47405-5901

Institute For Rational Emotive Therapy (See Pennsylvania State University)

International Film Bureau 332 S. Michigan Ave. Chicago, IL 60604

John Wiley and Sons, Inc. Educational Services Department 605 Third Ave. New York, NY 10158

Karol Media 350 N. Pennsylvania Ave. Wilkes Barre, PA 18773-7600

McGraw-Hill Films 674 Via DE La Valle P.O. Box 641 Del Mar, CA 92014

Motivational Media 12001 Ventura Place #202 Studio City, CA 91604

New York University Film Library 26 Washington Place New York, NY 10003

Pennsylvania State University Psychological Cinema Register Audio-Visual Services University Park, PA 16803

Phoenix/Bfa Films and Video, Inc. 468 Park Ave. South New York, NY 10016

Psychological Cinema Register (see Pennsylvania State University)

Psychological Films Distribution Center 110 N. Wheeler Orange, CA 92669

Pyramid Film & Video Cornell University Audio-Visual Resource Center 8 Research Park Ithaca, NY 14850

Research Press Box 3170 Champaign, IL 61826

San Diego State University 5402 College Ave. San Diego, CA 92115

Time Life Films (see Ambrose Video Publishing)

University of Illinois Film and Video Center 1325 S. Oak St. Champaign, IL 61820

University of Minnesota University Film and Video 1313 Fifth St. SE, Suite 108. Minneapolis, MN 55414

RESOURCES

GENERAL TEACHING TEXTS

Angelo, T., & Cross, K. P. (1993). <u>Classroom assessment techniques: A handbook for college teachers</u> (2nd ed.). San Francisco, CA: Jossey-Bass.

Bonwell, C. C., & Eison, J. A. (1991). <u>Active learning: Creating excitement in the classroom</u>. ASHE-ERIC Higher Education Report No. 1. Washington, DC: The George Washington University, School of Education and Human Development.

Brislin, R. W., et al. (1983). <u>Intercultural interactions: A practical guide</u>. Newbury Park, CA: Sage.

Cross, K. P. (1981). <u>Adults as learners</u>. San Francisco, CA: Jossey-Bass.

Davis, B. C. (1993). <u>Tools for teaching</u>. San Francisco, CA: Jossey-Bass.

Renner, P. F. (1989). <u>The instructor's survival kit: A handbook for teachers of adults</u>. Vancouver, B.C: Training Associates LTD.

TEACHING MANUALS

The following publications may be ordered directly from the American Psychological Association, 1200 Seventeenth Street, N. W., Washington, DC 20036.

<u>Activities handbook for the teaching of psychology</u>.

<u>Directory of teaching innovations in psychology</u>.

READERS

Atkinson, R. C. (Ed.). <u>Psychology in progress: Readings from Scientific American</u>. San Francisco: Freeman.

Cohen, I. S. (Ed.). <u>Perspectives on psychology: Introductory readings</u>. New York: Praeger.

CRM Books. <u>Readings in Psychology Today</u>. Del Mar, CA: CRM.

Doyle, K. O. (Ed.). <u>Interaction: Readings in human psychology</u>. Lexington, MA: Heath.

Dushkin Publishing Group. <u>Annual edition readings in psychology</u>. Guilford, CN: Dushkin.

Janis, I. L. (Ed.). <u>Current trends in psychology: Readings from American Scientist</u>. Los Altos, CA: William Kaufmann.

Rubinstein, J. & Slife, B. D. (Eds.). <u>Taking Sides: Clashing Views on Controversial Psychological Issues</u>. Guilford,CN: Dushkin.

SIMULATIONS

Copies of the simulation game *STARPOWER* can be obtained by writing to: Western Behavioral Science Institute, 1150 Silverado, La Jolla, CA 92037